Ernest
HEMINGWAY

A Literary Reference

EDITED BY

ROBERT W. TROGDON

CARROLL & GRAF PUBLISHERS
NEW YORK

To MICHAEL S. REYNOLDS, for his work in Hemingway studies

ERNEST HEMINGWAY
A Literary Reference

Carroll & Graf Publishers
An Imprint of Avalon Publishing Group Incorporated
161 William Street, 16th Floor
New York, NY 10038

Library of Congress Cataloging-in-Publication Data is available.

ISBN: 0-7867-0975-8

Printed in the United States of America
Distributed by Publishers Group West

Contents

Acknowledgments

This book was produced by Bruccoli Clark Layman, Inc. Karen L. Rood is senior editor. Denis Thomas was the in-house editor.

Production manager is Philip B. Dematteis.

Administrative support was provided by Ann M. Cheschi, Tenesha S. Lee, and Joann Whittaker.

Accountant is Sayra Frances Cox. Assistant accountant is Angi Pleasant.

Copyediting supervisor is Phyllis A. Avant. Senior copyeditor is Thom Harman. The copyediting staff includes Ronald D. Aiken II, Brenda Carol Blanton, Worthy B. Evans, Melissa D. Hinton, and William Tobias Mathes. Freelance copyeditors are Brenda Cabra, Rebecca Mayo, Nicole M. Nichols, Raegan E. Quinn, and Jennie Williamson.

Editorial trainee is Carol A. Fairman.

Indexing specialist is Alex Snead.

Layout and graphics supervisor is Janet E. Hill. Graphics staff includes Zoe R. Cook.

Office manager is Kathy Lawler Merlette.

Photography editors are Margo Dowling, Charles Mims, Scott Nemzek, Alison Smith, and Paul Talbot. Digital photographic copy work was performed by Joseph M. Bruccoli.

SGML supervisor is Cory McNair. The SGML staff includes Tim Bedford, Linda Drake, Frank Graham, and Alex Snead.

Systems manager is Marie L. Parker.

Database manager is Javed Nurani. Kimberly Kelly performed data entry.

Typesetting supervisor is Kathleen M. Flanagan. The typesetting staff includes Karla Corley Brown, Mark J. McEwan, Patricia Flanagan Salisbury, and Kathy F. Wooldridge. Freelance typesetter is Delores Plastow.

Walter W. Ross and Steven Gross did library research. They were assisted by the following librarians at the Thomas Cooper Library of the University of South Carolina: Linda Holderfield and the interlibrary-loan staff; reference-department head Virginia Weathers; reference librarians Marilee Birchfield, Stefanie Buck, Stefanie DuBose, Rebecca Feind, Karen Joseph, Donna Lehman, Charlene Loope, Anthony McKissick, Jean Rhyne, and Kwamine Simpson; circulation-department head Caroline Taylor; and acquisitions-searching supervisor David Haggard.

The editor warmly thanks the following curators and librarians for their assistance in preparing this volume: Stephen Plotkin, the Ernest Hemingway Collection of the John F. Kennedy Library, Boston, Massachusetts; Saundra Taylor, The Lilly Library, Indiana University; Don C. Skemer and John Delaney, Department of Rare Books and Special Collections, Princeton University; Patrick Scott, Special Collections, Thomas Cooper Library, University of South Carolina; and Jean Somers and Nancy Birk, Special Collections, Kent State University Library. Special thanks also go to Michael Katakis, representative of the Hemingway Estate, and to Allen Josephs, president of the Hemingway Foundation. Helpful information was provided by Judy Baughman and Park Bucker of the Department of English, University of South Carolina. The editor enjoyed the assistance of the following members of the Institute for Bibliography and Editing at Kent State University: S. W. Reid, Gale Graham, Xavier Brice, and student assistants Brian Malia and Bridget Wilmot. The editor also wishes to thank the Kent State University Library Inter-Library Loan, Periodical and Information Services, and Circulation staffs, especially Tom Warren.

Permissions

Permissions

"Faulkner and Hemingway" from *Sherwood Anderson's Memoirs: A Critical Edition,* edited by Ray Lewis White, excerpted with permission of Harold Ober Associates, Inc. Copyright © 1969 by the Estate of Sherwood Anderson.

Letter from Sherwood Anderson to Ernest Hemingway from *Sherwood Anderson: Selected Letters,* edited by Charles E. Modlin, excerpted with permission of Harold Ober Associates, Inc. Copyright ©1984 by the Estate of Sherwood Anderson.

"Bull in the Afternoon" and "Hemingway in Madrid" reprinted with permission of *The New Republic.*

"Glorious Dirt" from *Newsweek,* 18 October 1937. Copyright © 1937 Newsweek, Inc. All rights reserved. Reprinted by permission.

"Oscar Bait" from *Newsweek,* 18 March 1940. Copyright © 1940 Newsweek, Inc. All rights reserved. Reprinted by permission.

Selection from *The Autobiography of Alice B. Toklas* by Gertrude Stein. Copyright © 1933 by Gertrude Stein. Copyright renewed © 1961 by Alice B. Toklas. Reprinted by permission of Random House.

Review of *Winner Take Nothing* from *The Times Literary Supplement,* 8 February 1934. Reprinted with permission of *The Times Literary Supplement.*

Review of *Green Hills of Africa* from *The Times Literary Supplement,* 4 April 1936. Reprinted with permission of *The Times Literary Supplement.*

Letter from Archibald MacLeish excerpted from *The Letters of Archibald MacLeish: 1907–1982,* edited by R. H. Winnick. Copyright © 1983 by The Estate of Archibald MacLeish and by R. H. Winnick. Reprinted by permission of Houghton Mifflin Company. All rights reserved.

Selections from *Papa: A Personal Memoir.* Copyright © 1976 by Gregory H. Hemingway. Reprinted by permission of Houghton Mifflin. All rights reserved.

"The Ghost of a Writer." Copyright © 1931 by the *Kansas City Star.* Reprinted by permission.

"An Essay in Criticism." Copyright © 1927 by The New York Times, Inc. Reprinted by permission.

"Ernest Hemingway Singing in Africa." Copyright © 1935 by The New York Times, Inc. Reprinted by permission.

"Hemingway Curses, Kisses, Reads at Sylvia Beach Literary Session." Copyright © 1937 by The New York Times, Inc. Reprinted by permission.

"Hemingway Slaps Eastman in Face." Copyright © 1937 by The New York Times, Inc. Reprinted by permission.

"The Author's Name is Hemingway." Copyright © 1950 by The New York Times, Inc. Reprinted by permission.

"Mrs. Hemingway Is Cautious on Publication of Manuscripts." Copyright © 1961 by The New York Times, Inc. Reprinted by permission.

Review of *A Moveable Feast* by Lewis Galantiére. Copyright © 1964 by The New York Times, Inc. Reprinted by permission.

"Braver Than We Thought." Copyright © 1986 by The New York Times, Inc. Reprinted by permission.

"A New Book by Hemingway." Copyright © 1998 by The New York Times, Inc.. Reprinted by permission. "The Last Olé," reprinted by permission of William Kennedy. Copyright © 1985 by William Kennedy.

"The Case of Mr. Hemingway," by Evelyn Waugh. Copyright © 1950 Commonweal Foundation. Reprinted with permission.

"His Mirror Was Danger" by Archibald MacLeish, reprinted from *A Continuing Journey.* Copyright © 1967 by Archibald MacLeish. Reprinted by permission of Houghton Mifflin.

"The Way It Was" by Morley Callaghan. Copyright © 1964 by *The Spectator.* Reprinted with permission.

"Hemingway Out of the Jungle; Arm Hurt, He Says Luck Holds," reprinted with permission of United Press International. Copyright © 1954 by UPI.

"Papa's Sad Testament," excerpted from *The New Statesman.* Copyright © 1970 by *The New Statesman.* Reprinted with permission.

"A Book of Great Short Stories" and "Mr. Hemingway's Finest Story Yet," reprinted with permission of Dorothy Parker Permissions, National Association for the Advancement of Colored People.

World Within World by Stephen Sepnder, excerpted with the permission of Harcourt, Brace. Copyright © 1951 by Stephen Spender.

Chapter One: 1899–1925

1899

21 July   Ernest Miller Hemingway is born in Oak Park, Illinois. He is the eldest son of Dr. Clarence and Mrs. Grace Hall Hemingway.

1905

September   Hemingway enters the first grade.

1914

28 July   Austria-Hungary declares war on Serbia as World War I begins.

1915

September   Hemingway begins writing for the Oak Park High School newspaper, *The Trapeze*.

1916

February   Hemingway publishes his first short story, "The Judgement of Manitou." in *The Tabula*, the literary magazine of his high school.

1917

6 April   The United States declares war on Germany.

June   Hemingway graduates from high school.

October   Hemingway starts work as a cub reporter for the *Kansas City Star*.

1918

Spring   Barred from service in the U.S. Army because of his poor eyesight, Hemingway enlists in the American Red Cross as an ambulance driver.

Chapter One: 1899–1925

23 May	Hemingway sails from New York for service in Italy.
4 June	Hemingway arrives in Italy. He is stationed at Schio.
8 July	While visiting the front to pass out chocolate and cigarettes to Italian troops, Hemingway is wounded by an Austrian trench mortar shell.
Summer/Fall	Recuperating at the Red Cross Hospital in Milan, Hemingway falls in love with his nurse, Agnes Von Kurowsky. He also meets British officer E. E. "Chink" Dorman-Smith.
11 November	Armistice is declared, and World War I ends.

1919

4 January	Hemingway is discharged from the Red Cross and leaves for New York.

1920

8 January	After spending a year at home, Hemingway begins writing freelance articles for the *Toronto Star*.
October	Hemingway moves to Chicago. He meets Sherwood Anderson, author of *Winesburg, Ohio,* and Hadley Richardson, a St. Louis woman with whom he falls in love.
December	Hemingway begins editing and writing for the *Cooperative Commonwealth*.

1921

3 September	Ernest and Hadley are married at his family's summer cottage at Horton Bay, Michigan.
8 December	With letters of introduction from Sherwood Anderson to Gertrude Stein and Ezra Pound, Ernest and Hadley Hemingway leave for France. He plans to supplement the income from Hadley's trust fund with freelance assignments for the *Toronto Star*.

1922

4 January	Hemingway meets Sylvia Beach, owner of Shakespeare & Company.
2 February	James Joyce's *Ulysses* is published by Shakespeare & Company.
Late February	Hemingway meets Pound.
8 March	The Hemingways go to tea at Gertrude Stein and Alice B. Toklas's home.
6–27 April	Hemingway covers the Genoa Economic Conference for the *Toronto Star*. He meets Lincoln Steffens and William Bird, owner of Three Mountains Press.
Summer	In proposing that Bird's Three Mountain Press publish a series of six books as "an inquest into the state of contemporary English prose," Pound asks Hemingway to contribute a volume to it.
29 September–18 October	Hemingway is in Constantinople to report the Greco-Turkish War.
21 November	Hemingway goes to Switzerland to cover the Lausanne Peace Conference.
2 December	Taking Hemingway's works-in-progress with her, Hadley Hemingway leaves for Lausanne. In the Paris train station someone steals the suitcase containing these manuscripts.

1923

January	*Poetry* publishes six of Hemingway's poems.
7–10 February	The Hemingways visit Pound in Rapallo, where they meet painter Henry "Mike" Strater, editor Edward O'Brien, and poet and publisher Robert McAlmon. O'Brien decides to include Hemingway's "My Old Man" in his *Best Short Stories of 1923*; McAlmon agrees to publish a collection of Hemingway's fiction and poetry.
Spring	*The Little Review* publishes six of Hemingway's vignettes later collected in his *in our time*.
ca. 1 June	Accompanied by McAlmon and Bird, Hemingway makes his first trip to Spain for the bullfights.
6 July	The Hemingways attend the Fiesta of San Fermin in Pamplona, Spain.
13 August	McAlmon's Contact Editions publishes Hemingway's *Three Stories and Ten Poems*.
4 September	Landing in Montreal, the Hemingways return to Toronto for the birth of their first child. Hemingway plans to work at the *Toronto Star* for a year before returning to Europe.
10 October	John Hadley Nicanor Hemingway, nicknamed "Bumby," is born.
ca. 30 December	Hemingway resigns from the *Toronto Star*.

1924

30 January	The Hemingways return to France.
February	Hemingway begins working as associate editor of *The Transatlantic Review*, the magazine edited by British novelist Ford Madox Ford.
16 March	John Hemingway is baptized; Dorman-Smith, Stein, and Toklas are the godparents.
April	Bird's Three Mountains Press publishes *in our time*, Hemingway's collection of prose vignettes and the last volume of Pound's Inquest series.
26 June–13 July	The Hemingways go to Pamplona with novelist John Dos Passos and humorist Donald Ogden Stewart.
14 September	With fourteen stories ready to publish in a book, Hemingway begins circulating the manuscript among New York publishers.

1925

21 February	On the advice of F. Scott Fitzgerald, Maxwell Perkins, editor at Charles Scribner's Sons, writes to Hemingway, but the letter does not reach him.
6 March	Hemingway accepts Boni & Liveright's offer to publish his story collection, *In Our Time*.
14 March	Hemingway assists Ernest Walsh in preparing the first number of *This Quarter*.
ca. March	Hemingway meets Pauline Pfeiffer, writer for *Vogue*.
10 April	Fitzgerald's *The Great Gatsby* is published by Scribners.
Late April	Hemingway meets Fitzgerald at the Dingo Bar in Paris.
25 June–13 July	The Hemingways travel to Spain with Bill Smith, Stewart, Harold Loeb, Duff Twysden, and Pat Gutherie. Hemingway uses some incidents of this trip in his first novel, *The Sun Also Rises*, which he begins writing on 21 July.

9 or 15 September	Hemingway finishes the first draft of *The Sun Also Rises*.
5 October	*In Our Time* is published in New York.
23 November– 2 December	Hemingway writes *The Torrents of Spring*, a satire of *Dark Laughter* by Sherwood Anderson, Hemingway's former mentor and Boni & Liveright's best-selling author.
30 December	Horace Liveright rejects *The Torrents of Spring*, a decision that frees Hemingway from his contract with the firm.

Ernest Hemingway, the second child and first son of Dr. Clarence and Mrs. Grace Hall Hemingway, was born on 21 July 1899 in Oak Park, Illinois, a suburb of Chicago. While his parents were fairly strict with their children (Dr. Hemingway did not allow his children even to have their own library cards), Ernest seems to have enjoyed a happy childhood. His father instilled in him a love of outdoor activities such as hunting and fishing during the family's annual vacations in Michigan. Hemingway's mother was a talented musician and painter who encouraged her son's interest in the arts.

Hemingway began his literary apprenticeship when he wrote for the Oak Park and River Forest Township High School weekly newspaper, *The Trapeze*, and its literary magazine, *The Tabula*. His early articles and stories, many of which are imitations of those of Ring Lardner, lack originality, but they show Hemingway's early interest in writing about sports and in exploring the subject of violence.

After graduation in 1917 Hemingway moved to Kansas City, Missouri, and began working as a cub reporter for the *Kansas City Star*. He later claimed that in becoming a writer this was the best training he received, because it taught him to be concise and accurate. He left this job in January 1918, when he enlisted as an ambulance driver in the American Red Cross.

His service during World War I was brief. He arrived in Italy in early June 1918 and in July took over operation of a Red Cross canteen near Fossalta on the Piave River. On 8 July while he was distributing choco-

Clarence and Grace Hemingway with their children: Ursula, Ernest, and Marcelline (October 1903)

Hemingway at Horton Creek, near Horton Bay, Michigan, July 1904

late and cigarettes at an Italian listening post, he suffered wounds from Austrian trench-mortar and machine-gun fire, and more than two hundred pieces of shrapnel had to be removed from his legs. Hemingway never returned to the front. After being sent to the Red Cross hospital in Milan, he there met and fell in love with Agnes Von Kurowsky, an American nurse whom he wanted to marry. After he returned to America in 1919 and began writing short stories, however, she broke off their relationship. He later incorporated these wartime experiences in *A Farewell to Arms* (1929).

He received a hero's welcome when he returned to Oak Park in early 1919, and, although he wrote some stories, he was unable to interest any magazine in publishing them. He spent much of that summer fishing and camping in Michigan. In 1920 he joined the staff of the *Toronto Star* and contributed to *The Cooperative Commonwealth,* a publication of the Cooperative Society of America, but he was still unable to sell any of his fiction. While in Chicago that same year Hemingway met Hadley Richardson of St. Louis. After carrying on a courtship mainly though letters, Hemingway proposed in 1921; on 3 September the two married and moved to Chicago.

That same year Hemingway had also met author Sherwood Anderson, who encouraged him to continue writing and advised him to go to Paris to work. Planning to supplement the income from his wife's trust fund by selling articles to the *Toronto Star*

while he worked on his fiction, Hemingway and his wife left for Paris in December. Settling there in January, the couple found the city to be the center for a large community of American and British expatriates who had been drawn to the city by the low cost of living, the favorable currency exchange rate, and the congenial atmosphere it provided for writers and artists living there. Hemingway soon became friends with the two leading American writers in Paris, Ezra Pound and Gertrude Stein. They read and criticized his works in progress, and through them Hemingway met other writers and the editors and owners of some of the little magazines and publishing firms based in Paris.

Traveling extensively in 1922 and 1923, the Hemingways went to Austria, Germany, Italy, and Spain—where Hemingway saw his first bullfights. He also published his first book, *Three Stories and Ten Poems,* through Robert McAlmon's Contact Editions in 1923. The couple moved to Toronto that year for the birth of their son, John, but they missed Paris and, after Hemingway quit his job with the *Star,* the family returned to Europe at the end of the year.

In 1924 Hemingway began to get his works published frequently in the little magazines based in Europe—*The Little Review, Transatlantic Review,* and *This Quarter*—and his second book, *in our time,* was published. That year he wrote some of his best stories, such as "Indian Camp," "Soldiers Home," and "Big Two-Hearted River." He began looking for an American publisher for his short stories, and, through the influence of his friends Harold Loeb and Sherwood Anderson, he signed a contract with Boni & Liveright (Anderson's publisher) in March 1925.

The agreement stated that the firm had an option to publish Hemingway's next two books, but if it rejected his next book the contract would be void. In May 1925 he met F. Scott Fitzgerald, author of *The Great Gatsby*. The two writers became friends, and Fitzgerald tried to advance Hemingway's career.

In July, Hemingway began writing a novel based on his recent visit to Pamplona, Spain, with a group of other friends from Paris. He completed the first draft of it in six weeks, but Hemingway was reluctant to submit it to Horace Liveright, his publisher, because he was disappointed with the way in which Boni & Liveright had promoted *In Our Time,* his short-story collection. In December he wrote *The Torrents of Spring* (1926), a parody of Anderson's novel *Dark Laughter* (1925), which had been a best-seller for Boni & Liveright. When the firm rejected this parody, its decision freed Hemingway from his contract with them.

In addition to reporting in his high-school newspaper, Hemingway wrote humor columns in the manner of sportswriter and short-story writer Ring Lardner. The following column appeared in the 24 November 1916 issue of The Trapeze.

A "RING LARDNER" ON THE BLOOMINGTON GAME

Right half Smearcase of Bloomington kicked off to Cole who returned the ball to his own one-yard line. Wilcoxen signalled for the hit and run play but Gordon was caught at second by a perfect throw from the catcher. Hemingway went over for the first touchdown by way of the Lake Street "L." Colville missed goal, the ball hitting the bar and causing havoc with the free lunch.

Score, Oak Park 6, Bloomington 0.

Wilkins replaced Cole. Blum kicked off to fullback Roquefort of Bloomington, who was nailed in his tracks. Baldwin of Oak Park wielded the hammer. On the first ball pitched Limburger cracked one to Moore, who stepped on the bag and shot to Wilcoxen at first, doubling the runner.

Savage tried a drop kick from the 90-yard line but it went foul by three inches. Timme then smashed through center for 110 yards for Oak Park's touchdown. Thistlewaite kicked goal.

Score, Oak Park 13, Bloomington 0.

Time was called but refused to answer.

Second Quarter

Lofberg went in at Worthington's tackle. Kendall kicked off to Eycleshymer's front porch. Ball was run back by Quarterback Cambrian to Oak Park's line of demarcation. Thistlewaite on incomplete returns claimed three precincts out of 1,396. Hemingway made a tackle. Miss Biggs fainted. Thistlewaite was carried unconscious from the field. Time was called while Fat Tod sent out for a package of **censored*** Maker's name furnished **on request**.

Dunning kicked out of Danger and Lofberg shot a basket from the middle of the field.

Score, Oak Park 15, Bloomington 0.

The captains matched pennies to see who would kick off. Shepherd lost and Bloomington kicked to Phelps, who knocked a clean threebagger, scoring Bell, George and Golder. Hill popped to the pitcher.

Score, Oak Park 18, Bloomington 0.

Wilcoxen went color blind and tackled the water boy. Canode went in at Fullback. The lightning fast Hemingway scored Oak Park's third touchdown, crossing the goal line by way of the Chicago avenue car line, transferring at Harlem and Lake.

Thexton missed goal, the ball striking the bar and falling to the brass rail.

Score, Oak Park 24, Bloomington 0.

Overstreet kicked the ball outside the field and was penalized twenty-seven yards for unnecessary roughness. Wilcoxen again went color blind and tackled a goal post. He was penalzed thirty-eight yards for holding.

"Dope" MacNamara replaced the slight Wilkins, who was injured by a kick in the middle of the line of scrimmage.

The game broke up in a riot when the student Cops refused to keep the crowd off the field unless they were given Major Monograms as a farther incentive.

Final score:

Oak Park 24, Bloomington 0.

Late Bulletin

Hemingway is reported as convalescing, but the Doctors Fear his mind is irreparably Lost.

LATER

A large and enthusiastic crowd attended Hemingway's Funeral. A pleasant Time was had By all.

Hemingway's childhood home, 600 North Kenilworth Avenue, Oak Park, Illinois

The Hemingways' summer cottage, Windemer, on Walloon Lake, Michigan. The handwritten caption is by Hemingway's mother.

THE TRAPEZE

VOL. V. NO. 7   OAK PARK, ILL., THURSDAY, FEBRUARY 10, 1916   PRICE 2 CENTS

MIDGETS WIN FIVE STRAIGHT

Trim Deerfield and Lewis by Good Scores—Oak Park Lands in Second Division

BASKETBALL SCHEDULE OUT

Heavyweight

Team	W.	L.	Pct.
Oak Park	2	1	.667
Thornton	2	1	.667
Bloom	2	1	.667
Morton	0	3	.000

Lightweight

	W.	L.	Pct.
Oak Park	2	1	.667
Morton	2	1	.667
Deerfield	1	2	.333
Bloom	1	2	.333

Basket Ball Schedule

Feb. 11—Bloom at Oak Park. Both teams.

Feb. 19—Oak Park at Thornton. Heavyweight.

Feb. 19—Oak Park at Deerfield. Lightweight.

Feb. 25—Oak Park at Morton. Both teams.

Oak Park's flying lightweights trimmed Lewis 26 to 5 last Tuesday, making it five straight. Holden, a former Oak Parker, scored Lewis first point with a free throw. Stanley came back for Oak Park with a basket, and Uteritz and Fox made two more. Then Lewis ceased to threaten. The half ended 12-3.

Lewis braced and held Oak Park scoreless for five minutes. Then Radcliffe took the ball down the floor and made a basket. Stanley threw the ball in on the next play. Fox scored and then Lewis made another. In a mix-up that occurred, Fox was thrown to the floor and had to be carried out of the game. Cole was injected into the fray and the scoring went on.

The line-up:

Oak Park (26)

	B.	T.	F.
Uteritz, lf	5	0	1
Stanley, lf	4	0	1
Fox, c	3	0	0
Beli, rg	0	0	0
Radcliffe, lg	1	0	0
Cole, c	0	0	0

Lewis (5)

	B.	T.	F.
Holden	0	1	0
McEldowney	1	0	0
Jellenech	1	0	0
McCracken	0	0	0
Ward	0	0	0

Showing championship form, the rejuvenated lightweights beat Deerfield 17 to 8. The battered and crippled heavies lost their game, and as a result went into a triple tie for first place in the second division.

The lightweights had an easy time of it, as Deerfield was unable to break up their plays. Oak Park's passing was remarkably accurate and all the team was able to shoot well. Most of Oak Park's score was made in the first half; the team being too willing to take chances with long shots in the second period.

The heavies were fighting to land in the first division, but superior team work on the part of Deerfield and the poor shooting of Oak Park, coupled with the absence of Steele, spelled defeat. Oak Park was 3 points behind at the half, and fought desperately in the second half to even the count. A flock of Deerfield bas-

(Continued on page 3)

A REHEARSAL

WHEN A CLASS PLAY IS'NT A CLASS PLAY

WASHINGTON'S BIRTH-DAY INFORMAL DANCE

General Good Time For All Students Planned by Parents-Teachers' Social Committee

By Susan Lowrey

Here's good news, everybody! The Social committee of the Parents and Teachers' association has planned a big party, for everybody in school, which will take place in the boys' gym, Monday, February 21, after school. It will be a school affair, which means that the Freshmen and Sophs, as well as Juniors and Seniors, will need only to don their tennis shoes, bring a lot of "pep" and come for a good time.

The main entertainment will be dancing, not a formal parade with programs filled out a week ahead, but "robber's dances," and general mix-ups, where one may see a blushing Freshie whirling around with some tall, no-longer-dignified Senior. The music will be voluntary, so, please, all you piano-players don't wait for an invitation! We know Kohler will be there and we all know what good music that means.

At Austin High, dances like this are every-week affairs and tickets are issued for the purpose. Each student receives a ticket and goes to dance, not to sit around and watch—a gallery is provided for those who wish to do that. For the rule is: "He or she who refuses to dance even one dance must forfeit his ticket for the next week." So if there aren't enough fellows to "go around," Sarah Maud dances with Cornelia.

At U. High, also, the gym is open every Friday afternoon for a social dance. How would you like Oak Park added to the list? The honorable committee says our dances may be frequent if a big crowd comes out, joins in with spirit and has such a good time that they want more. This is an experimental party, so **everybody out!** No, you won't be out even a penny—it's free. Also, there is no school the next day, Washington's birthday, so there will be no lessons to get. Now there aren't any excuses, so come on out, everybody, and show 'em what a lot of fun you can have!

PERSONAL

Gladys Ball, '15, has been made a member of the Deltho club of the University of Chicago.

Howard Hales, ex-'16, saved the lives of four children at the Charlton Nursery fire of last Thursday night. James Adams is very ill with blood poisoning. Harry Redfearn is substituting for him in the class play, in case he is not able to take his part.

Esther McLean, '14, has been chosen as a member of the Quadrangle club at the University of Chicago.

PRACTICAL EDUCATION VS. THEORETICAL

Hanna Club, With Largest Attendance in Its History, Enthuse Over This Question

By Ernest Hemingway

The Hanna club held the liveliest meeting of its career, Friday night. It was snappy and full of hot discussions from start to finish, and over half of the fellows took part.

After the usual good supper, a few jokes were told, Trafton starring with his story of the "nostril" of the gun. The discussion then began. The question before the club was: "Which is the better, a practical or theoretical education in college?"

Stewart Hawes upheld the theoretical side in a masterful manner. He spoke against specialization and said that a fellow should try and obtain a general education so that he would be thus fitted to take up some special branch of work. He also spoke of the broadening influence of a classical education and the essential culture that it imparts to every man.

Clyde Reading spoke as strongly for the practical side and said that a fellow should specialize so that he would be able to do one thing well and not be a "jack of all trades" and master of none.

After the two leaders made their speeches the hot arguments started. At times four and five fellows would be on their feet at a time and the trend of argument seemed to be in favor of the practical side. The theoretical side, however, was ably supported by Worthington, Priebe and Shorney. Chappell, Darnall, Henderson, Rogers, Trafton and Pringle spoke for the practical or specializing side. Harold Sampson and Henry Pringle also became embroiled in an argument over the manual department of the high school. During the discussion many new phases and sidelights on the question were brought out by the many speakers, and the fellows were sorry to see the hands of the clock reach 7:30, the time limit for the meeting. Tickets for the next meeting are 25 cents and should be purchased by Thursday night. The subject will be announced later.

Richard Steele, '16, was taken to the hospital last Monday with a serious illness, which will prevent his taking part in the Senior class play. He has had hard luck all year, having broken his leg during the early part of the football season, which kept him out the rest of the fall. He was captain of the basketball team, but could play in but few games before this illness came on, which will keep him out of all athletics the rest of the year.

GOOD MUSIC AND CUP AWARD

Interesting Assembly With A Popular Musical Program and Scholarship Mixed

FRANCIS LANGWORTHY WINNER

By Frances Coates

The assembly program of last Friday morning proved the most interesting and enjoyable one this year. Mr. Erickson's musical numbers met with immediate success and each number was applauded with appreciative enthusiasm. "The Only Girl" selection, while it was played with spirit, showed evidence of the careful workmanship that marks all of Mr. Erickson's productions. "Shadowland," the catchy fox trot, with its clever "raggy" effects made it agony to be compelled to sit quietly in our seats. The "Aloloe Oe Waltz," was rendered all the more beautiful by Nelson Brabrook's solo. The last number, "Semper Fidelis" proved exceedingly popular, calling fourth two encores. The cornet obligatos were played by Moffat Elton, Nelson Brabrook, William Burbank, Chester Radke, and Raymond Thompson.

Honor Seniors Called to Stage

Principal McDaniel then read the names of the Seniors who have attained the grade of 90 in all their subjects for the three and one-half years of their high school course, and called them to the platform, amidst the cheers of the whole student body. The following filed to their appointed seats:

Frances Langworthy, Helen Golder, Esther Hebert, Jean Davies, Eleanor Atkins, Margaret Scarritt, Kathryn Tenney, Clara Hoover, Charlotte Dakin, Stewart Hawes, Sibyl de Joannis, Josephine Taylor, Joseph Townsend, Franklin Pearce, Selma Bransbach, Jean Plummer and Evelyn Rogovsky.

Mary Carney and Jean Pickett have the average of 90, but they have not been in this school the required three and a half years.

Leroy Grosser Makes Speech

Principal McDaniel then introduced Leroy Grosser, who represented the class of 1915 in the presentation of the scholarship cup. In a very able speech it was awarded to Frences Langworthy, who stands at the head of her class with the splendid average of 95 per cent. He said in part:

"It seems like returning home, after an extended absence, to be here among you this morning. One never appreciates what he has until it is taken from him. When I left this school last June, diploma in hand, I little realized that I would ever miss the school or its surroundings. But I have missed it mightily during the past few months.

"I am more than glad to be here, as the representative of the class of 1915 in presenting to its winner the 1915 scholarship cup.

"This cup was presented to the school by last year's senior class to perpetuate its memory and to promote a high standard of scholarship.

"It affords me great pleasure to present this token to Miss Frances Langworthy, the senior, who has obtained the highest average during the past three and a half years.

"Miss Langworthy, yours is the honor of being the first to have your name inscribed upon this trophy.

"Accept it with the congratulations of the school and the class of 1915."

Front page of Hemingway's high-school newspaper

The following article appeared in the 21 April 1918 Kansas City Star, p. 1. Although unsigned, the article is attributed to Hemingway by Charles Fenton in The Apprenticeship of Ernest Hemingway *(New York: Farrar, Strauss & Young, 1954). It is the last piece Hemingway wrote for the paper. The article anticipates his mature style in its use of implicit contrast and avoidance of sentimentality.*

MIX WAR, ART AND DANCING

Outside a woman walked along the wet street-lamp lit sidewalk through the sleet and snow.

Inside in the Fine Arts Institute on the sixth floor of the Y.W.C.A. Building, 1020 McGee Street, a merry crowd of soldiers from Camp Funston and Fort Leavenworth fox trotted and one-stepped with girls from the Fine Arts School while a sober faced young man pounded out the latest jazz music as he watched the moving figures. In a corner a private in the signal corps was discussing Whistler with a black haired girl who heartily agreed with him. The private had been a member of the art colony at Chicago before the war was declared.

Three men from Funston were wandering arm in arm along the wall looking at the exhibition of paintings by Kansas City artists. The piano player stopped. The dancers clapped and cheered and he swung into "The Long, Long Trail Awinding." An infantry corporal, dancing with a swift moving girl in a red dress, bent his head close to hers and confided something about a girl in Chautauqua, Kas. In the corridor a group of girls surrounded a tow-headed young artilleryman and applauded his imitation of his pal Bill challenging the colonel, who had forgotten the password. The music stopped again and the solemn pianist rose from his stool and walked out into the hall for a drink.

A crowd of men rushed up to the girl in the red dress to plead for the next dance. Outside the woman walked along the wet lamp lit sidewalk.

It was the first dance for soldiers to be given under the auspices of the War Camp Community Service. Forty girls of the art school, chaperoned by Miss Winifred Sexton, secretary of the school and Mrs. J. F. Binnie were the hostesses. The idea was formulated by J. P. Robertson of the War Camp Community Service, and announcements were sent to the commandants at Camp Funston and Fort Leavenworth inviting all soldiers on leave. Posters made by the girl students were put up at Leavenworth and on the interurban trains.

The first dance will be followed by others at various clubs and schools throughout the city according to Mr. Robertson.

The pianist took his seat again and the soldiers made a dash for partners. In the intermission the soldiers drank to the girls in fruit punch. The girl in red, surrounded by a crowd of men in olive drab, seated herself at the piano, the men and the girls gathered around and sang until midnight. The elevator had stopped running and so the jolly crowd bunched down the six flights of stairs and rushed waiting motor cars. After the last car had gone, the woman walked along the wet sidewalk through the sleet and looked up at the dark windows of the sixth floor.

Hemingway was wounded on 8 July 1918 near Fossalta while passing out cigarettes and chocolate to Italian soldiers. In his letter home he exaggerates his bravery before his family. From Selected Letters, *pp. 13–16.*

18 August 1918

Dear Folks:

That includes grandma and grandpa and Aunt Grace. Thanks very much for the 40 lire! It was appreciated very much. Gee, Family, but there certainly has been a lot of burbles about my getting shot up! The Oak Leaves and the opposition came today and I have begun to think, Family, that maybe you didn't appreciate me when I used to reside in the bosom. It's the next best thing to getting killed and reading your own obituary.

You know they say there isn't anything funny about this war. And there isn't. I wouldn't say it was hell, because that's been a bit overworked since Gen. Sherman's time, but there have been about 8 times when I would have welcomed Hell. Just on a chance that it couldn't come up to the phase of war I was experiencing. F'r example. In the trenches during an attack when a shell makes a direct hit in a group where you're standing. Shells aren't bad except direct hits. You must take chances on the fragments of the bursts. But when there is a direct hit your pals get spattered all over you. Spattered is literal. During the six days I was up in the Front line trenches, only 50 yds from the Austrians, I got the rep. of having a charmed life. The rep of having one doesn't mean much but having one does! I hope I have one. That knocking sound is my knuckles striking the wooden bed tray.

Hemingway (bottom row, second from right) with the staff of The Trapeze, *the Oak Park High School newspaper, 1916*

It's too hard to write on two sides of the paper so I'll skip.

Well I can now hold up my hand and say I've been shelled by high explosive, shrapnel and gas. Shot at by trench mortars, snipers and machine guns, and as an added attraction an aeroplane machine gunning the lines. I've never had a hand grenade thrown at me, but a rifle grenade struck rather close. Maybe I'll get a hand grenade later. Now out of all that mess to only be struck by a trench mortar and a machine gun bullet while advancing toward the rear, as the Irish say, was fairly lucky. What, Family?

The 227 wounds I got from the trench mortar didn't hurt a bit at the time, only my feet felt like I had rubber boots full of water on. Hot water. And my knee cap was acting queer. The machine gun bullet just felt like a sharp smack on my leg with an icy snow ball. However it spilled me. But I got up again and got my wounded into the dug out. I kind of collapsed at the dug out. The Italian I had with me had bled all over my coat and my pants looked like somebody had made current jelly in them and then punched holes to let the pulp out. Well the Captain who was a great pal of mine, It was his dug out said "Poor Hem he'll be R.I.P. soon." Rest In Peace, that is. You see they thought I was shot through the chest on account of my bloody coat. But I made them take my coat and shirt off. I wasn't wearing any undershirt, and the old torso was intact. Then they said I'd probably live. That cheered me up any amount. I told him in Italian that I wanted to see my legs, though I was afraid to look at them. So we took off my trousers and the old limbs were still there but gee they were a mess. They couldn't figure out how I had walked 150 yards with a load with both knees shot through and my right shoe punctured two big places. Also over 200 flesh wounds. "Oh," says I, "My Captain, it is of nothing. In America they all do it! It is thought well not to allow the enemy to perceive that they have captured our goats!"

The goat speech required some masterful lingual ability but I got it across and then went to sleep for a couple of minutes. After I came to they carried me on a stretcher three kilometers to a dressing station. The stretcher bearers had to go over lots because the road was having the "entrails" shelled out of it. Whenever a big one would come, Whee-whoosh-Boom-they'd lay me down and get flat. My wounds were now hurting like 227 little devils were driving nails into the raw. The dressing station had been evacuated during the attack so I lay for two hours in a stable, with the roof shot off, waiting for an ambulance. When it came I ordered it down the road to get the soldiers that had been wounded first. It came back with a load and then they lifted me in. The shelling was still pretty thick and our batteries were going off all the time way back of us and the big 250's and 350's going over head for Austria with a noise like a railway train. Then we'd hear the bursts back of the lines. Then there would come a big Austrian shell and then the crash of the burst. But we were giving them more and bigger stuff than they sent. Then a battery of field guns would go off, just back of the shed—boom, boom, boom, boom, and the Seventy-Fives or 149's would go whipping over to the Austrian lines, and the star shells going up all the time and the machines going like rivetters, tat-a-tat, tat-a-tat.

After a ride of a couple of kilometers in an Italian ambulance, they unloaded me at the dressing station where I had a lot of pals among the medical officers. They gave me a shot of morphine and an anti-tetanus injection and shaved my legs and took out about Twenty 8 shell fragments varying from [drawing of fragment] to about [drawing of fragment] in size out of my legs. They did a fine job of bandaging and all shook hands with me and would have kissed me but I kidded them along. Then I stayed 5 days in a field hospital and was then evacuated to the base Hospital here.

I sent you that cable so you wouldn't worry. I've been in the Hospital a month and 12 days and hope to be out in another month. The Italian Surgeon did a peach of a job on my right knee joint and right foot. Took 28 stitches and assures me that I will be able to walk as well as ever. The wounds all healed up clean and there was no infection. He has my right leg in a plaster splint now so that the joint will be all right. I have some snappy souvenirs that he took out at the last operation.

I wouldn't really be comfortable now unless I had some pain. The Surgeon is going to cut the plaster off in a week now and will allow me on crutches in 10 days.

I'll have to learn to walk again.

You ask about Art Newburn. He was in our section but has been transferred to II. Brummy is in our section now. Don't weep if I tell you that back in my youth I learned to play poker. Art Newburn held some delusions that he was a poker player. I won't go into the sad details but I convinced him otherwise. Without holding anything I stood pat. Doubled his

The cover of Hemingway's high-school literary magazine

openers and bluffed him out of a 50 lire pot. He held three aces and was afraid to call. Tell that to somebody that knows the game Pop. I think Art said in a letter home to the Oak Parkers that he was going to take care of me. Now Pop as man to man was that taking care of me? Nay not so. So you see that while war isn't funny a lot of funny things happen in war. But Art won the championship of Italy pitching horse shoes.

This is the longest letter I've ever written to anybody and it says the least. Give my love to everybody that asked about me and as Ma Pettingill says, "Leave us keep the home fires burning!"

Good night and love to all.

Ernie

P.S. I got a letter today from the Helmles addressed Private Ernest H—what I am is S. Ten, or Soto Tenenente Ernest Hemingway. That is my rank in the Italian Army and it means 2nd Lieut. I hope to be a Tenenente or 1st Lieut. soon.

Sepi Jingan

By ERNEST HEMINGWAY, '17

"'VELVET'S' like red hot pepper; 'P. A.' like cornsilk. Give me a package of 'Peerless'."

Billy Tabeshaw, long, lean, copper-colored, hamfaced and Ojibway, spun a Canadian quarter onto the counter of the little north-woods country store and stood waiting for the clerk to get his change from the till under the notion counter.

"Hey, you robber!" yelled the clerk. "Come back here!"

We all had a glimpse of a big, wolfish-looking, husky dog vanishing through the door with a string of frankfurter sausages bobbing, snake-like, behind him.

"Darn that blasted cur! Them sausages are on you, Bill."

"Don't cuss the dog. I'll stand for the meat. What's it set me back?"

"Just twenty-nine cents, Bill. There was three pounds of 'em at ten cents, but I et one of 'em myself."

"Here's thirty cents. Go buy yourself a picture post-card."

Bill's dusky face cracked across in a white-toothed grin. He put his package of tobacco under his arm and slouched out of the store. At the door he crooked a finger at me and I followed him out into the cool twilight of the summer evening.

At the far end of the wide porch three pipes glowed in the dusk.

"Ish," said Bill, "they're smoking 'Stag!' It smells like dried apricots. Me for 'Peerless.'"

Bill is not the redskin of the popular magazine. He never says "ugh." I have yet to hear him grunt or speak of the Great White Father at Washington. His chief interests are the various brands of tobacco and his big dog, "Sepi Jingan."

We strolled off down the road. A little way ahead, through the gathering darkness, we could see a blurred figure. A whiff of smoke reached Bill's nostrils. "Gol, that guy is smoking 'Giant'! No, it's 'Honest Scrap'! Just like burnt rubber hose. Me for 'Peerless.'"

The edge of the full moon showed above the hill to the east. To our right was a grassy bank. "Let's sit down," Bill said. "Did I ever tell you about Sepi Jingan?"

"Like to hear it," I replied.

"You remember Paul Black Bird?"

"The new fellow who got drunk last fourth of July and went to sleep on the Pere Marquette tracks?"

"Yes. He was a bad Indian. Up on the upper peninsula he couldn't get drunk. He used to drink all day—everything. But he couldn't get drunk. Then he would go crazy; but he wasn't drunk. He was crazy because he couldn't get drunk.

"Paul was Jack-fishing [spearing fish illegally] over on Witch Lake up on the upper, and John Brandar, who was game warden, went over to pinch him. John always did a job like that alone; so next day, when he didn't show up, his wife sent me over to look for him. I found him, all right. He was lying at the end of the portage, all spread out, face down and a pike-pole stuck through his back.

"They raised a big fuss and the sheriff hunted all over for Paul; but there never was a white man yet could catch an Indian in the Indian's own country.

"But with me, it was quite different. You see, John Brandar was my cousin.

"I took Sepi, who was just a pup then, and we trailed him (that was two years ago). We trailed him to the Soo, lost the trail, picked it up at Garden River, in Ontario; followed him along the

This story of death in the north country was published in the November 1916 issue of the Tabula

Reporters' assignment sheet for the Kansas City Star, *8 January 1918 (Monroe County Public Library, Key West, Florida). Hemingway's assignments were routine for cub reporters, and the short-stop run—covering the railroad terminal, hospital, and police station—exposed him to violence and death and later provided material for two vignettes in* in our time *and his story "God Rest You Merry Gentlemen."*

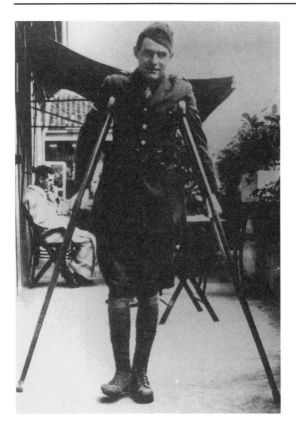

Hemingway in Milan, about two months after he had been wounded by a trench-mortar shell in July 1918 (Hemingway Collection, John F. Kennedy Library)

trian shrapnel, about as thick as a .22 calibre bullet and an inch long, like small cuts from a length of wire, smote him. Some of these bits have been extracted after a dozen or more operations and young Hemingway hopes finally to get them all out, but he still retains a hundred or more.

Hemingway joined the Red Cross in France and was transferred to the Italian front last July. He was distributing cigarettes in the Piave district in the front line trenches when a shell from a trench mortar burst over his head. He said the slugs from the shell felt like the stings of wasps as they bore into him. He crumpled up and two Italian stretcher bearers started over the parapet with him, knowing that he needed swift attention. Austrian machine gunners spotted the party and before they could get over he and the stretcher bearers went down under a storm of machine gun bullets, one of which got Hemingway in the shoulder and another in the right leg. Two of his stretcher men took the tall American through the communication trenches in the rear, where he received first aid.

Hemingway was in the Red Cross Hospital at Milan three months and the surgeons extracted thirty-two fragments from his head and body, telling him he was in for a series of operations that might last a year or more. He is preparing for such an ordeal, which he hopes will relieve some of his lameness. After that he believes he will be qualified to take a job on any New York newspaper that wants a man that is not afraid of work and wounds.

He did not give up war work when he got rid of those thirty-two slugs. Weary of doing nothing, he obtained permission to go to the front again in October, staying there until the armistice.

The following interview shows Hemingway's tendency to exaggerate his war experience: he did not return to the front in October. From the New York Sun, *22 January 1919, p. 8.*

Has 227 Wounds, but Is Looking for Job

The first wounded American from the Italian front arrived yesterday by the steamship Giuseppe Verdi of the Transatlantica Italiano line with probably more scars than any other man in or out of uniform, who defied the shrapnel of the Central Powers.

His wounds might have been much less if he had not been constructed by nature on generous proportions, being more than six feet tall and of ample beam.

He is Ernest M. Hemingway, before the war a reporter for the *Kansas City Star,* and hailing from Oak Park, Ill. The surgical chart of his battered person shows 227 marks, indicating where bits of a peculiar kind of Aus-

Hemingway contributed freelance articles to the paper before going to Paris in 1921. This article displays the depth of his reading as well as his skill as a humorist. From the Toronto Star Weekly, *20 August 1920.*

Condensing the Classics

They have nearly finished with their job of condensing the classics. They are a little group of earnest condensers, said to be endowed by Andrew Carnegie, who have been laboring for the last five years at reducing the literature of the world into palatable morsels for the tired businessman's consumption.

Les Miserables has been cut to ten pages. *Don Quixote* is said to run to about a column and a half. Shakespeare's plays would be cut to eight hundred words each. The *Iliad* and the *Odyssey* might reduce to about a stick and a half apiece.

It is a splendid thing to bring the classics within range of the tired or retired businessman, even though it casts a stigma on the attempt of the colleges and universities to bring the businessman within range of the classics. But there is a quicker way to present the matter to those who must run while reading: reduce all literature to newspaper headlines, with a short news dispatch following, to give the gist of the matter.

Take *Don Quixote* for example:

CRAZED KNIGHT IN WEIRD TILT

Madrid, Spain (By Classic News Service) (Special).– War hysteria is blamed for the queer actions of "Don" Quixote, a local knight who was arrested early yesterday morning when engaged in the act of "tilting" with a windmill. Quixote could give no explanation of his actions.

William Blake would reduce well.

BIG CAT IN FLAMES
Heat-maddened brute terrorizes jungle

Rajputana, India, June 15 (By Classic News Service) (Special).– William Blake, widely known English poet, arrived here today in a state of nervous collapse after a series of nerve-racking adventures in the Rajputana jungle. Blake was lost without food or clothing for eleven days.

Blake, still delirious, cries, "Tiger, tiger, burning bright in the forest of the night."

Local hunters have gone out in search of the beast. The "forest of the night" is believed to refer to the Nite River, a stream near Rajputana.

Then there is Coleridge:

ALBATROSS-SLAYER FLAYS PROHIBITION
"Ancient" Mariner in bitter assault on bone-dry enforcement

Cardiff, Wales, June 21 (By Classic News Service) (Delayed).– "Water, water everywhere and not a drop to drink" is the way John J. (Ancient) Mariner characterized the present Prohibition regime in an address before the United Preparatory Schools here yesterday. Mariner was mobbed at the end of his address by a committee from the Ornithological Aid Society.

Operas are much too long–there's *Pagliacci*–it doesn't even merit a large headline.

RIOT IN SICILY, 2 DEAD, 12 WOUNDED

Palermo, Sicily, June 25 (By Classic News Service).– Two are dead and half a score wounded as the result of a brawl started in the local opera house here last night. Giuseppe Canio, a ringleader of the rioters, committed suicide.

Shakespeare was obviously verbose and his plots are too sensational. Here's the gist of *Othello*:

SLAYS HIS WHITE BRIDE
Society girl, wed to African war hero, found strangled in bed.

Jealousy, fanned into fury by primitive jungle rage, is believed by the police to have caused the death of Mrs. Desdemona Othello of 2345 Ogden Avenue.

It was just a little over two years ago that Captain Frank Othello stepped off the transport at Hoboken. On his breast glittered the decorations bestowed by an admiring sovereign. His dark face gleamed with pleasure as he saw the lithe figure.

There would be more–much more–perhaps. Shakespeare wasn't so verbose after all. The Othello case would fill almost as much space in the newspapers as the Stillman case. Special articles, psychoanalysts' reports, discussions of intermarriage by women feature writers would flood the papers. Perhaps Shakespeare is pretty well condensed as he is.

The Hemingways arrived in Paris in December 1921 with letters of introduction that Sherwood Anderson—best-known as the author of Winesburg, Ohio *(1919)—wrote to Ezra Pound and Gertrude Stein. After meeting these writers, Hemingway sent Anderson this account of his new life in Paris. From* Selected Letters, *pp. 62–63.*

9 March 1922

Dear Sherwood:

You sound like a man well beloved of Jesus. Lots of things happen here. Gertrude Stein and me are just like brothers and we see a lot of her. Read the preface you wrote for her new book and like it very much. It made a big hit with Gertrude. Hash says to tell you, quotes, that things have come to a pretty pass between her and Lewy–close quotes. My operatives keep a pretty close eye on the pair of them.

Joyce has a most god-damn wonderful book. It'll probably reach you in time. Meantime the report is that he and all his family are starving but you can find the whole celtic crew of them every night in Michaud's where Binney and I can only afford to go about once a week.

Gertrude Stein says Joyce reminds her of an old woman out in San Francisco. The woman's son struck it rich as hell in the Klondyke and the old woman went around wringing her hands and saying, "Oh my poor Joey! My poor Joey! He's got so much money!" The damned Irish, they have to moan about something or other, but you never heard of an Irishman starving.

Pound took six of my poems and sent them wit a letter to Thayer, Scofield, that is, you've heard of him maybe. Pound thinks I'm a swell poet. He also took a story for the Little Review.

I've been teaching Pound to box wit little success. He habitually leads wit his chin and has the general grace of the crayfish or crawfish. He's willing but short winded. Going over there this afternoon for another session but there aint much job in it as I have to shadow box between rounds to get up a sweat. Pound sweats well, though, I'll say that for him. Besides it's pretty sporting of him to risk his dignity and his critical reputation at something that he don't know nothing about. He's really a good guy, Pound, wit a fine bitter tongue onto him. He's written a good review of Ulysses for April Dial.

I don't know whether he has much drag with Thayer so I don't know whether Thayer will take the poems or not—but I wish to hell he would.

Bones is called Binney now. We both call each other Binney. I'm the male Binney and she is the female Binney. We have a saying—The Male Binney protects the Female—but the Female bears the young.

We've met and liked Le Verrier—he's done a review of the Egg for a french magazine here. I'll get it and send it to you if he hasn't done so already.

Your book sounds swell. Paid you to go to New Orleans—huh? I wish I could work like that. This goddam newspaper stuff is gradually ruining me—but I'm going to cut it all loose pretty soon and work for about three months.

When you've seen Benny Leonard you've seen them all. Hope he was having a good night when you viewed him. I've seen this Pete Herman. He's blind in one eye you know and sometimes blood or sweat gets into the other and they cuff him all over the place— but he must have been seeing well the night you lamped him. He's a fine little wop and can hit to beat hell.

Well this is getting too damned voluminous. Write us again will you? It puts a big kick into the day we get your letter.

Oh Yes. Griffin Barry is still in Vienna and living, they say, with Edna St. Vincent etc. The Rotonde is cluttered with the various young things, female, she's led astray. Like Lady Lil, she piles her victims up in heaps.

Well, bye-bye and any amount of love to Tennessee and yourself from us—

Ernest

I wrote some pretty good poems lately in Rhyme. We love Gertrude Stein.

―――――――――

In the following section of Gertrude Stein's The Autobiography of Alice B. Toklas *(New York: Harcourt, Brace, 1933), pp. 260–265 (told from the point of view of her companion), she recounts her meeting of Hemingway and their early years of friendship.*

The first thing that happened when we were back in Paris was Hemingway with a letter of introduction from Sherwood Anderson.

I remember very well the impression I had of Hemingway that first afternoon. He was an extraordinarily good-looking young man, twenty-three years old. It was not long after that that everybody was twenty-six. It became the period of being twenty-six. During the next two or three years all the young men were twenty-six years old. It was the right age apparently for that time and place. There were one or two under twenty, for example George Lynes but they did not count as Gertrude Stein carefully explained to them. If they were young men they were twenty-six. Later on, much later on they were twenty-one and twenty-two.

So Hemingway was twenty-three, rather foreign looking, with passionately interested, rather than interesting eyes. He sat in front of Gertrude Stein and listened and looked.

They talked then, and more and more, a great deal together. He asked her to come and spend an evening in their apartment and look at his work. Hemingway had then and has always a very good instinct for finding apartments in strange but pleasing localities and good femmes de ménage and good food. This his first apartment was just off the place du Tertre. We spent the evening there and he and Gertrude Stein went over all the writing he had done up to that time. He had begun the novel that it was inevitable he would begin and there were the little poems afterwards printed by McAlmon in the Contact Edition. Gertrude Stein rather liked the poems, they were direct, Kiplingesque, but the novel she found want-

Invitation for Hemingway's first wedding (McKeldin Library, University of Maryland). Ernest and Hadley decided to marry in Horton Bay, with fewer guests attending than might otherwise have been expected.

Ernest and Hadley on their wedding day, with Hemingway's sisters (left)—Carol and Ursula—and his mother, brother Leicester, and father (photograph by Alice Hunt Sokoloff)

La Closerie des Lilas, 171 Boulevard du Montparnasse, at Avenue de l'Observatorie, was one of Hemingway's favorite cafés. "The Closerie des Lilas was the nearest good café when we lived in the flat over the sawmill at 113 rue Notre-Dame-des-Champs, and it was one of the best cafés in Paris" (Hemingway, A Moveable Feast *[New York: Scribners, 1964]).*

ing. There is a great deal of description in this, she said, and not particularly good description. Begin over again and concentrate, she said.

Hemingway was at this time Paris correspondent for a canadian newspaper. He was obliged there to express what he called the canadian viewpoint.

He and Gertrude Stein used to walk together and talk together a great deal. One day she said to him, look here, you say you and your wife have a little money between you. Is it enough to live on if you live quietly. Yes, he said. Well, she said, then do it. If you keep on doing newspaper work you will never see things, you will only see words and that will not do, that is of course if you intend to be a writer. Hemingway said he undoubtedly intended to be a writer. He and his wife went away on a trip and shortly after Hemingway turned up alone. He came to the house about ten o'clock in the morning and he stayed, he stayed for lunch, he stayed all afternoon, he stayed for dinner and he stayed until about ten o'clock at night and then all of a sudden he announced that his wife was enceinte and then with great bitterness, and I, I am too young to be a father. We consoled him as best we could and sent him on his way.

When they came back Hemingway said that he had made up his mind. They would go back to America and he would work hard for a year and with what he would earn and what they had they would settle down and he would give up newspaper work and make himself a writer. They went away and well within the prescribed year they came back with a new born baby. Newspaper work was over.

The first thing to do when they came back was as they thought to get the baby baptised. They wanted Gertrude Stein and myself to be god-mothers and an english war comrade of Hemingway was to be god-father. We were all born of different religions and most of us were not practising any, so it was rather difficult to know in what church the baby could be baptised. We spent a great deal of time that winter, all of us, discussing the matter. Finally it was decided that it should be baptised episcopalian and episcopalian it was. Just how it was managed with the assortment of god-parents I am sure I do not know, but it was baptised in the episcopalian chapel.

Writer or painter god-parents are notoriously unreliable. That is, there is certain before long to be a cooling of friendship. I know several cases of this, poor Paulot Picasso's god-parents have wandered out of sight and just as naturally it is a long time since any of us have seen or heard of our Hemingway god-child.

However in the beginning we were active god-parents, I particularly. I embroidered a little chair and I knitted a gay coloured garment for the god-child. In the meantime the god-child's father was very earnestly at work making himself a writer.

Gertrude Stein never corrects any detail of anybody's writing, she sticks strictly to general principles, the way of seeing what the writer chooses to see, and the relation between that vision and the way it gets down. When the vision is not complete the words are flat, it is very simple, there can be no mistake about it, so she insists. It was at this time that Hemingway began the short things that afterwards were printed in a volume called In Our Time.

One day Hemingway came in very excited about Ford Madox Ford and the Transatlantic. Ford Madox Ford had started the Transatlantic some months before. A good many years before, indeed before the war, we had met Ford Madox Ford who was at that time Ford Madox Hueffer. He was married to Violet Hunt and Violet Hunt and Gertrude Stein were next to each other at the tea table and talked a great deal together. I was next to Ford Madox Hueffer and I liked him very much and I liked his stories of Mistral and Tarascon and I liked his having been followed about in that land of the french royalist, on account of his resemblance to the Bourbon claimant. I had never seen the Bourbon claimant but Ford at that time undoubtedly might have been a Bourbon.

We had heard that Ford was in Paris, but we had not happened to meet. Gertrude Stein had however seen copies of the Transatlantic and found it interesting but had thought nothing further about it.

Hemingway came in then very excited and said that Ford wanted something of Gertrude Stein's for the next number and he, Hemingway, wanted The Making of Americans to be run in it as a serial and he had to have the first fifty pages at once. Gertrude

Ezra Pound at Shakespeare and Company (Sylvia Beach Collection, Princeton University Library)

Stein was of course quite overcome with her excitement at this idea, but there was no copy of the manuscript except the one that we had had bound. That makes no difference, said Hemingway, I will copy it. And he and I between us did copy it and it was printed in the next number of the Transatlantic. So for the first time a piece of the monumental work which was the beginning, really the beginning of modern writing, was printed, and we were very happy. Later on when things were difficult between Gertrude Stein and Hemingway, she always remembered with gratitude that after all it was Hemingway who first caused to be printed a piece of The Making of Americans. She always says, yes sure I have a weakness for Hemingway. After all he was the first of the young men to knock at my door and he did make Ford print the first piece of The Making of Americans.

I myself have not so much confidence that Hemingway did do this. I have never known what the story is but I have always been certain that there was some other story behind it all. That is the way I feel about it.

Alice B. Toklas and Gertrude Stein in Stein's Model T Ford, circa 1926 (Gertrude Stein Collection, Beinecke Library, Yale University)

Hemingway's account of the controversy over René Maran's novel displays the importance he placed on a writer's ability to make a reader experience what is being described, a point he also makes in Green Hills of Africa *(New York: Scribners, 1935). From the* Toronto Star Weekly, *25 March 1922, p. 3.*

Black Novel a Storm Center

Paris.– "Batouala," the novel by René Maran, a Negro, winner of the Goncourt Academy Prize of 5,000 francs for the best novel of the year by a young writer, is still the center of a swirl of condemnation, indignation and praise.

Maran, who was born in Martinique and educated in France, was bitterly attacked in the Chamber of Deputies the other day as a defamer of France, and biter of the hand that fed him. He has been much censured by certain Frenchmen for his indictment of French imperialism in its effects on the natives of the French colonies. Others have rallied to him and asked the politicians to take the novel as a work of art, except for the preface, which is the only bit of propaganda in the book.

Meanwhile, René Maran, black as Sam Langford, is ignorant of the storm his book has caused. He is in the French government service in Central Africa, two days' march from Lake Tchad, and seventy days' travel from Paris. There are no telegraphs or cables at his post, and he does not even know his book has won the famous Goncourt Prize.

The preface of the novel describes how peaceful communities of 10,000 blacks in the heart of Africa have been reduced to 1,000 inhabitants under the French rule. It is not pleasant and it gives the facts by a man who has seen them, in a plain, unimpassioned statement.

Launched into the novel itself, the reader gets a picture of a native village seen by the big-whited eyes, felt by the pink palms, and the broad, flat, naked feet of the African native himself. You smell the smells of the village, you eat its food, you see the white man as the black man sees him, and after you have lived in the village you die there. That is all there is to the story, but when you have read it, you have seen Batouala, and that makes it a great novel.

It opens with Batouala, the chief of the village, waking up in his hut, roused by the cold of the early morning and the crumbling of the ground under his body where the ants are tunneling. He blows his dead fire into life and sits, hunched over, warming his chilled body and wondering whether he will go back to sleep or get up.

It closes with Batouala, old and with the stiffened joints of his age, cruelly torn by the leopard that his spear-thrust missed, lying on the earth floor of his hut. The village sorcerer has left him alone, there is a younger chief in the village, and Batouala lies there feverish and thirsty, dying, while his mangy dog licks at his wounds. And while he lies there, you feel the thirst and the fever and the rough, moist tongue of the dog.

There will probably be an English translation shortly. To be translated properly, however, there should be another Negro who has lived a life in the country two days' march from Lake Tchad and who knows English as René Maran knows French.

Gertrude Stein with her godson, John "Bumby" Hemingway (Ernest Hemingway Collection, John F. Kennedy Library)

This account of McAlmon's first meeting with Hemingway, from McAlmon's memoir Being Geniuses Together: An Autobiography *(London: Secker & Warburg, 1938), pp. 155–159, was written after his break with Hemingway.*

Intending to return to Paris, I stopped en route at Rapallo, having proofs of books I was publishing to read (Carnevali's *A Hurried Man* and Mina Loy's *Lunar Baedecker*). It was the town Ezra Pound had chosen for permanent residence, but he was not there at the time. Ernest Hemingway, whom I had not met, but had heard was a Canadian newspaper man, and Mike (Henry) Strater were there with their wives and I met them naturally, there being few restaurants in the town. Henry Strater, a painter, later did illustrations for the Three Mountains Press edition of Ezra's first sixteen *Cantos*.

Hemingway was a type not easy to size up. At times he was deliberately hard-boiled and case-hardened; again he appeared deliberately innocent, sentimental, the hurt, soft, but fairly sensitive boy trying to conceal hurt, wanting to be brave, not bitter or cynical but being somewhat both, and somehow on the defensive, suspicions lurking in his peering analytic glances at a person with whom he was talking. He approached a café with a small-boy, tough-guy swagger, and before strangers of whom he was doubtful a potential snarl of scorn played on his large-lipped, rather loose mouth. Mike Strater was a far more simple and direct, clear-cut young American, unpretending and actually modest.

We all worked those days. There was a French painter about with an American wife who was a stage designer and interior decorator, and one of the other wives was inclined to think she was designing in other ways. Nevertheless we worked, Strater painted portraits of his wife and infant son, the Frenchman painted, Hemingway and I wrote, and at nights we all drank, moderately. Rapallo is situated in a bay which I find emprisoning, although along the coast are hotels beautifully situated. They, however, are generally occupied by elderly English people, and although the Sitwell trio seemed happy in the environment, Rapallo after the sun goes down struck me as dismal and depressing.

Hemingway was suffering a minor tragedy. His wife had lost a briefcase of his containing the script of writing which he had done for nearly a year's period. However, he had three short stories and a few poems on hand; he knew Sherwood Anderson and Ezra Pound and perhaps Ford then, and talked of Ring Lardner's work. I was publishing books in Paris and decided to do his three stories and ten poems. One story, *My Old Man,* was distinctly in the tone of Sher-

Hemingway's borrowing record from Shakespeare and Company's lending library, which documents his admiration for the works of Russian and French authors (Sylvia Beach Papers, Princeton University Library)

wood Anderson's *I'm a Fool,* and some other race-track story of Anderson, but the other two stories, or rather sketches, were fresh and without derivation so far as I detected.

It is difficult to say who started the attitude in writing which occurs in *My Old Man* and much present American work. It is not so much a style or an approach as an emotional attitude; that of an older person who insists upon trying to think and write as a child, and children in my experience are much colder and more ruthless in their observations than the child characters, be they of child age or old men, in this type of writing.

Ring Lardner wrote about boob baseball players for boobs to read, but he knew it, and therefore his work took on a satirical value amusing to adults. Anita Loos, a sophisticated woman, did the same thing in *Gentlemen Prefer Blondes.* Whether these two took the manner from Sherwood Anderson and added adult wit, or whether Sherwood Anderson took their ironic attitude seriously and became childishly soulful about this

naive outlook, one cannot judge. Since, however, Hemingway and a number of others have written in that, to me, falsely naive manner. They may write of gangsters, prize-fighters, bullfighters, or children, but the hurt-child-being-brave tone is there, and all conversation is reduced to lone words or staccato phrases. Possibly I forget my childhood. Some day I'll write to the new air director of the United States, Eugene Vidal, and ask him to check back in his memory. I have a theory that quite a gang of us in South Dakota—a wild and dreary plains state—talked whole sentences and paragraphs, and calculated and often outwitted our elders as very astute intriguers. During those days I was growing up with football and baseball players and track stars, and roughnecks from the roundhouse gang. Several of us used to hop freight cars and bum about doing the harvest seasons and mingle with the hoboes in the jungle. My sceptical nature tells me that in war books, and in this false-naive type of writing, there is altogether too much attitudinized insistence upon the starry-eyed innocence and idealism and sentimentality of not only the child but of the "sensitive roughneck." Possibly South Dakota's hot summers and freezing winters and its pioneer qualities of that not-so-far-back period made us different, however. As it is I read with an incredulous eye when reviewers comment much about this or that writer's ability to capture the "inflection" and "intonation" of American types and the American language. . . .

Dos Passos manages to suggest horror enough without picking complete mental deficients, prize-fighters, gangsters, or hurt children of whatever age. Possibly the old Spanish writers of the picaresque novels got their tough lads better. Certainly now in Barcelona, in Berlin and Paris, it is possible to talk to virtual children of the streets, and find no hurt-baby wail in their conversation. They're tough and they're knowing. I may be wrong, but it appears that there is a new-preciousness in one stream of contemporary American writing, and that is the fake child-mentality quality. It was not there in Hawthorne, or Henry James, or O. Henry, or Dreiser; it is not there in a quantity of present writers, but reviewers seem to adjudge it as the true American, and surely America produces many adults and types who are as alertly aware and sophisticated as any in the world.

One night in Rapallo the lot of us were talking of birth control, and spoke of the cruelty of the law which did not allow young unmarried women to avoid having an unwanted child. Recalling an incident of college days I told a story of a girl who had managed to have herself taken care of. Her attitude was very casual. "Oh, it was nothing. The doctor just let the air in and a few hours later it was over."

Two years later there appeared in some magazine a story by Hemingway called "Hills Like White Elephants." A young couple are arguing about whether the girl should or should not do something. It isn't immediately clear. After several beers she retires and when she returns she says sadly, "Well, it's done." I didn't see the point of the story and reread it and encountered the phrase "Let the air in." Later Hemingway informed me that my remark suggested the story.

Yes, Hemingway was a new type for me. He must be actually young and naive, for he, in telling me, still seemed to believe that young ladies could help themselves out of difficulties while at the same time many undesired children are being born. Later, a protesting flapper who had read his story and was made hopeful, one gathers, commented bitterly that the tale was all lies, like white elephants.

Hadley and Ernest Hemingway at Chamby, Switzerland, 1922

Robert McAlmon recounts Hemingway's first visit to Spain in 1923 in Being Geniuses Together *(pp. 159–163).*

Later the lot of us were in Paris at the same time and after a trip to London I talked of going to Spain. Hemingway, who knew Gertrude Stein—I didn't then—wanted much to see a bullfight. I had missed seeing one in Mexico, at Juarez, mercifully, as they are generally bad shows: small bulls and poor matadors. After a week or so of talking about it we headed towards Spain. Hemingway and his then wife had a fondness for pet names, which they called each other, their baby, and their puppy. Beery-poppa (Hemingway) said a loving good-bye to Feather-kitty (Mrs. Hemingway), Bumby (baby), and waxen-puppy, and he and I well lubricated with whisky got into the train.

The next day, on the way to Madrid, our train stopped at a wayside station for a time. On the track beside us was a flat car, upon which lay the maggot-eaten corpse of a dog. I, feeling none too hale

IN OUR TIME

EVERYBODY was drunk. The whole battery was drunk along the road in the dark. We were going to the Champagne. The lieutenant kept riding his horse out into the fields and saying to him, "I'm drunk I tell you, mon vieux. Oh I am so soused." We went along the road all night in the dark and the adjutant kept riding up alongside my kitchen and saying, "You must put it out. It is dangerous. It will be observed." We were fifty kilometers from the front but the adjutant worried about the fire in my kitchen. It was funny going along that road. That was when I was a kitchen corporal.

*　*　*

The first matador got the horn through his sword hand and the crowd hooted him on his way to the infirmary. The second matador slipped and the bull caught him through the belly and he hung onto the horn with one hand and held the other tight against the place, and the bull rammed him wham against the barrera and the horn came and he lay in the sand; and then got up like crazy drunk and tried to slug the men carrying him away and yelled for a new sword, but he fainted. The kid came out and had to kill five bulls because you can't have more than three matadors and the last bull he was so tired he couldn't get the sword in. He couldn't hardly lift his arm. He tried eight times and the crowd was quiet because it was a good bull and it looked like him or the bull and then he finally made it. He sat down in the sand and puked and they held a cape over him while the crowd come down the barrera into the bull ring.

*　*　*

3

First page for the series of six vignettes published in The Little Review, *9 (Spring 1923). These and twelve other vignettes were collected in* in our time *(1924).*

and hearty, looked away, but Hemingway gave a dissertation on facing reality. It seems that he had seen the stacked corpses of men maggot-eaten in the war in a similar way. He advised a detached and scientific attitude towards the corpse of the dog. He tenderly explained that we of our generation must inure ourselves to the sight of pain and grim reality. I recalled that Ezra Pound had talked once of Hemingway's "self-hardening process." At last he said, "Hell, Mac, you write like a realist. Are you going to be a romantic on us?"

I spurted forth some oath and went to the dining car to order whisky. Not only was the sight of the dog before my eyes, its stench was in my nostrils, and I have seen many dead dogs, cats, and corpses borne in on the tide of New York harbor when working on a lumber barge. That dog had no distinction or novelty as a corpse. Several years later Paul Rosenfeld informed me that Hemingway had told this story to prove his assertion that I was a romanticist. He was realist enough himself to join me in the dining car and have a whisky, however, but he surely had duly analyzed all of his sensations "on seeing the maggot-eaten corpse of a dog on a flat car in Spain while wondering what it is that makes a guy who has seen so much of life as McAlmon shudder."

The day that we were to see our first bullfight we agreed that the horse part of it might repel us, so we had a few drinks before taking our seats. We would doubtless have had them anyway. We had a bottle of whisky with us, with the understanding that if shocked we would gulp down a quantity to calm ourselves. My reactions to the bullfight were not at all what one had anticipated. At first it seemed unreal, like something happening on the screen.

The first bull charged into the ring with tremendous violence, and did not refuse a charge. When the horses were brought in the bull charged head-on and lifted the horse over its head. The horns did not penetrate.

Instead of a shock of disgust I rose in my seat and let out a yell. Things were happening too quickly for my mind to think of the horse's suffering. Later, however, when one of the horses was galloping in hysteria about the ring, treading on its own entrails, I decidedly didn't like it and looked away. Since, I discover that many a hardened Spanish "aficionado," even the brother of a bullfighter, does likewise.

Hemingway at once became an "aficionado," that is, a passionate bullfight fan or enthusiast intent upon learning all about the art. If I suspect that his need to love the art of the bullfight came from Gertrude Stein's praise of them, as well as from his belief in the value of self-hardening, it is only because his bullfight book takes a belligerent attitude defending his right to love bullfighting. There are quantities of English and Ameri-

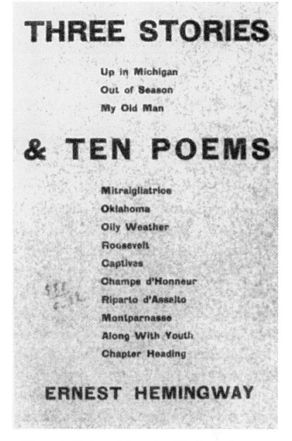

Title page for Hemingway's first book, published in an edition of 300 copies by Robert McAlmon's Contact Editions (Paris, 1923)

can people who have been bullfight enthusiasts for years before that summer of 1924, when Hemingway and I each saw our first.

By the end of that day my temper about all connected with the bullfight was much what it is now. I resented the crowd's brutality, and the way they would throw mats and articles into the ring at moments dangerous to the matadors. The crowd was taking no chances. The bull was—when he was—a magnificent animal, a snorting engine of black velocity and force. The matadors moved beautifully and did their dance well, and played seriously with death. The horses I decided to overlook as a Spanish brutality no worse than many a French and Anglo-Saxon cruelty. It has always been the Portuguese bullfight which I prefer, for the bull is properly killed from on horseback, and the horse is a magnificent Arabian mare or stallion, and beautifully trained and never injured by the bull without disgrace to the "rejoneador" or rider. In this there is breathless speed and terrifying beauty of power and velocity. It is

Hemingway's inscription recounting the publication history of Three Stories and Ten Poems, *in the copy belonging to Dr. Carlos Guffey, Pauline Hemingway's obstetrician (Sotheby Parke Bernet, Goodwin Sale, Item 398, 25 October 1977)*

not so intricate or so daring an art as Spanish bullfighting, but it has more throbbing and breathtaking excitement, for me, generally. The wonderful matadors and their fights are rare and I recall too many degrading exhibitions.

William Bird, who was then associated with me in the publishing of books, joined Hemingway and myself in Madrid and we did a tour, seeing Granada, Seville, Ronda, and more bullfights. Bird also liked bullfights, and neither he nor I were putting ourselves through a "hardening process." After the first bullfight we each took them as matter-of-factly as if we'd been seeing them all our lives, and our criticism of the matador without art was as ruthless as any Spaniard's.

Before leaving Paris Hemingway had been much of a shadow-boxer. As he approached a café he would prance about, sparring at shadows, his lips moving to call his imaginary opponents bluff. Upon returning from Spain he substituted shadow-bullfighting for shadow-boxing. The amount of imaginary cape-work and sword thrusts which he made in those days was formidable. Later he went to Key West and went in for barracuda fishing and I wonder if he took then to shadow-barracuda-fighting, or if in Africa he will shadow-lion-hunt. He has a boy's need to be a tough guy, a swell boxer, a strong man.

In summer 1923 Hemingway made his first trip to Spain and saw the bullfights for the first time. Culminating in the publication of Death in the Afternoon *(New York: Scribners, 1932), the subject became one of lifelong study for him. The following, from the* Toronto Star Weekly, *20 October 1923, p. 23, is his first article on the subject.*

Bullfighting a Tragedy

It was spring in Paris and everything looked just a little too beautiful. Mike and I decided to go to Spain. Strater drew us a fine map of Spain on the back of a menu of the Strix restaurant. On the same menu he wrote the name of a restaurant in Madrid where the specialty is young suckling pig roasted, the name of the pensione on the Via San Jerónimo where the bullfighters live, and sketched a plan showing where the Grecos are hung in the Prado.

Fully equipped with this menu and our old clothes, we started for Spain. Our objective—to see bullfights.

We left Paris one morning and got off the train at Madrid the next noon. We saw our first bullfight

Hemingway and Robert McAlmon in Spain, July 1923

at 4:30 that afternoon. It took about two hours to get tickets. We finally got them from scalpers for twenty-five pesetas apiece. The bullring was entirely sold out. We had barrera seats. These, the scalper explained in Spanish and broken French, were the first row of the ringside, directly under the royal box, and immediately opposite where the bulls would come out.

We asked him if he didn't have any less distinguished seats for somewhere around twelve pesetas, but he was sold out. So we paid the fifty pesetas for the two tickets, and with the tickets in our pockets sat out on the sidewalk in front of a big café near the Puerta del Sol. It was very exciting, sitting out in front of a café your first day in Spain with a ticket in your pocket that meant that rain or shine you were going to see a bullfight in an hour and a half. In fact, it was so exciting that we started out for the bullring on the outskirts of the city in about half an hour.

The bullring or Plaza de Toros was a big, tawny brick amphitheater standing at the end of a street in an open field. The yellow and red Spanish flag was floating over it. Carriages were driving up and people getting out of buses. There was a great crowd of beggars around the entrance. Men were selling water out of big terra-cotta water bottles. Kids sold fans, canes, roasted salted almonds in paper spills, fruit and slabs of ice cream. The crowd was gay and cheerful but all intent on pushing toward the entrance. Mounted civil guards with patent-leather cocked hats and carbines slung over their back sat their horses like statues, and the crowd flowed through.

Inside they all stood around in the bullring, talking and looking up in the grandstand at the girls in the boxes. Some of the men had field glasses in order to look better. We found our seats and the crowd began to leave the ring and get into the rows of concrete seats. The ring was circular—that sounds foolish, but a boxing ring is square—with a sand floor. Around it was a red board fence—just high enough for a man to be able to vault over it. Between the board fence, which is called the barrera, and the first row of seats ran a narrow alleyway. Then came the seats which were just like a football stadium except that around the top ran a double circle of boxes.

Every seat in the amphitheater was full. The arena was cleared. Then on the far side of the arena out of the crowd, four heralds in medieval costume stood up and blew a blast on their trumpets. The band crashed out, and from the entrance on the far side of the ring four horsemen in black velvet with ruffs around their necks rode out into the white glare of the arena. The people on the sunny side were baking in the heat and fanning themselves. The whole sol side was a flicker of fans.

Behind the four horsemen came the procession of the bullfighters. They had been all formed in ranks in the entranceway ready to march out, and as the music started they came. In the front rank walked the three espadas, or toreros, who would have charge of the killing of the six bulls of the afternoon.

They came walking out in heavily brocaded yellow and black costumes, the familiar "toreador" suit, heavy with gold embroidery, cape, jacket, shirt and collar, knee breeches, pink stockings, and low pumps. Always at bullfights, afterward the incongruity of those pink stockings used to strike me. Just behind the three principals—and after your first bullfight you do not look at their costumes but their faces—marched the teams, or cuadrillas. They are dressed in the same way but not as gorgeously as the matadors.

Back of the teams ride the picadors. Big, heavy, brown-faced men in wide flat hats, carrying lances like long window poles. They are astride horses that make Spark Plug look as trim and sleek as a King's Plate winner. Back of the pics come the gaily harnessed mule teams and the red-shirted monos, or bullring servants.

The bullfighters march in across the sand to the president's box. They march with easy professional stride, swinging along, not in the least theatrical except for their clothes. They all have the easy grace and slight slouch of the professional athlete. From their faces they might be major league ball players. They salute the president's box and then spread out along the barrera, exchanging their heavy brocaded capes for the fighting capes that have been laid along the red fence by the attendants.

We leaned forward over the barrera. Just below us the three matadors of the afternoon were leaning against the fence talking. One lighted a cigarette. He was a short, clear-skinned gypsy, Gitanillo, in a wonderful gold brocaded jacket, his short pigtail sticking out under his black cocked hat.

"He's not very fancy," a young man in a straw hat, with obviously American shoes, who sat on my left, said.

"But he sure knows bulls, that boy. He's a great killer."

"You're an American, aren't you?" asked Mike.

"Sure," the boy grinned. "But I know this gang. That's Gitanillo. You want to watch him. The kid with the chubby face is Chicuelo. They say he doesn't really like bullfighting, but the town's crazy about him. The one next to him is Villalta. He's the great one."

I had noticed Villalta. He was straight as a lance and walked like a young wolf. He was talking and smiling at a friend who leaned over the barrera. Upon his tanned cheekbone was a big patch of gauze held on with adhesive tape.

"He got gored last week at Málaga," said the American.

The American, whom later we were to learn to know and love as the Gin Bottle King, because of a great feat of arms performed at an early hour of the morning with a container of Mr. Gordon's celebrated product as his sole weapon in one of the four most dangerous situations I have ever seen, said: "The show's going to begin."

Out in the arena the picadors had galloped their decrepit horses around the ring, sitting straight and stiff in their rocking-chair saddles. Now all but three had ridden out of the ring. These three were huddled against the red painted fence of the barrera. Their horses backed against the fence, one eye bandaged, their lances at rest.

In rode two of the marshals in the velvet jackets and white ruffs. They galloped up to the president's box, swerved and saluted, doffing their hats and bowing low. From the box an object came hurtling down. One of the marshals caught it in his plumed hat.

"The key to the bullpen," said the Gin Bottle King.

The two horsemen whirled and rode across the arena. One of them tossed the key to a man in torero costume, they both saluted with a wave of their plumed hats, and had gone from the ring. The big gate was shut and bolted. There was no more entrance. The ring was complete.

The crowd had been shouting and yelling. Now it was dead silent. The man with the key stepped toward an iron-barred, low, red door and unlocked the great sliding bar. The door swung open. The man hid behind it. Inside it was dark.

Then, ducking his head as he came up out of the dark pen, a bull came into the arena. He came out all in a rush, big, black and white, weighing over a ton, and moving with a soft gallop. Just as he came out the sun seemed to dazzle him for an instant. He stood as though he were frozen, his great crest of muscle up, firmly planted, his eyes looking around, his horns pointed forward, black and white and sharp as porcupine quills. Then he charged. And as he charged, I suddenly saw what bullfighting is all about.

For the bull was absolutely unbelievable. He seemed like some great prehistoric animal, absolutely deadly and absolutely vicious. And he was silent. He charged silently and with a soft, galloping rush. When he turned he turned on his four feet like a cat. When he charged the first thing that caught his eye was the picador on one of the wretched horses. The picador dug his spurs into the horse and they galloped away. The bull came on in his rush, refused to be shaken off, and in full gallop crashed into the animal from the side, ignored the horse, drove one of his horns high into the thigh of the picador, and tore him, saddle and all, off the horse's back.

The bull went on without pausing to worry the picador lying on the ground. The next picador was sitting on his horse braced to receive the shock of the charge, his lance ready. The bull hit him sideways on, and horse and rider went high up in the air in a kicking mass and fell across the bull's back. As they came down the bull charged into them. The dough-faced kid, Chicuelo, vaulted over the fence, ran toward the bull and flapped his cape into the bull's face. The bull charged the cape and Chicuelo dodged backward and had the bull clear in the arena.

Without an instant's hesitation, the bull charged Chicuelo. The kid stood his ground, simply swung back on his heels and floated his cape like a ballet dancer's skirt into the bull's face as he passed.

"Olé!"–pronounced Oh-Lay!–roared the crowd.

The bull whirled and charged again. Without moving, Chicuelo repeated the performance. His legs rigid, just withdrawing his body from the rush of the bull's horns and floating the cape out with that beautiful swing.

Again the crowd roared. The Kid did this seven times. Each time the bull missed him by inches. Each time he gave the bull a free shot at him. Each time the crowd roared. Then he flopped the cape once at the bull at the finish of a pass, swung it around behind him and walked away from the bull to the barrera.

"He's the boy with the cape all right," said the Gin Bottle King. "That swing he did with the cape's called a veronica."

The chubby-faced Kid who did not like bullfighting and had just done the seven wonderful veronicas was standing against the fence just below us. His face glistened with sweat in the sun but was almost expressionless. His eyes were looking out across the arena where the bull was standing making up his mind to charge a picador. He was studying the bull because a few minutes later it would be his duty to kill him, and once he went out with his thin, red-hilted sword and his piece of red cloth to kill the bull in the final set it would be him or the bull. There are no drawn battles in bullfighting.

I am not going to describe the rest of that afternoon in detail. It was the first bullfight I ever saw, but it was not the best. The best was in the little town of Pamplona high up in the hills of Navarre, and came weeks later. Up in Pamplona, where they have held six days of bullfighting each year since A.D. 1126, and where the bulls race through the streets of the town each morning at six o'clock with half the town running ahead of them. Pamplona, where every man and boy in town is an amateur bullfighter and where there is an amateur fight each morning that is attended by 20,000 people in which the amateur fighters are all unarmed and there is a casualty list at least equal to a Dublin election. But Pamplona, with the best bullfight and the wild tale of the amateur fights, comes in the second chapter.

I am not going to apologize for bullfighting. It is a survival of the days of the Roman Colosseum. But it does need some explanation. Bullfighting is not a sport. It was never supposed to be. It is a tragedy. A very great tragedy. The tragedy is the death of the bull. It is played in three definite acts.

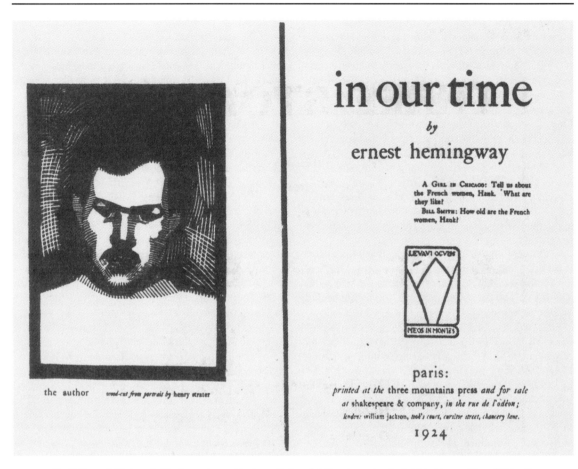

the author   wood-cut from portrait by henry strater

in our time

by

ernest hemingway

A Girl in Chicago: Tell us about the French women, Hank. What are they like?

Bill Smith: How old are the French women, Hank?

LEVAVI OCVEN

MEOS IN MONTES

paris:

printed at the three mountains press *and for sale at* shakespeare & company, *in the rue de l'odéon;*

london: william jackson, *took's court, cursitor street, chancery lane.*

1924

Frontispiece and title page for Hemingway's second book, a collection of eighteen prose vignettes published in an edition of 170 copies

The Gin Bottle King—who, by the way, does not drink gin—told us a lot of this that first night as we sat in the upstairs room of the little restaurant that made a specialty of roast young suckling pig, roasted on an oak plank and served with a mushroom tortilla and vino rojo. The rest we learned later at the bullfighters' pensione in the Via San Jerónimo, where one of the bullfighters had eyes exactly like a rattlesnake.

Much of it we learned in the sixteen fights we saw in different parts of Spain from San Sebastian to Granada.

At any rate bullfighting is not a sport. It is a tragedy, and it symbolizes the struggle between man and the beasts. There are usually six bulls to a fight. A fight is called a corrida de toros. Fighting bulls are bred like racehorses, some of the oldest breeding establishments being several hundred years old. A good bull is worth about $2,000. They are bred for speed, strength and viciousness. In other words a good fighting bull is an absolutely incorrigible bad bull.

Bullfighting is an exceedingly dangerous occupation. In the sixteen fights I saw there were only two in which there was no one badly hurt. On the other hand it is very remunerative. A popular espada gets $5,000 for his afternoon's work. An unpopular espada though may not get $500. Both run the same risks. It is a good deal like Grand Opera for the really great matadors except they run the chance of being killed every time they cannot hit high C.

No one at any time in the fight can approach the bull except directly from the front. That is where the danger comes. There are also all sorts of complicated passes that must be done with the cape, each requiring as much technique as a champion billiard player. And underneath it all is the necessity for playing the old tragedy in the absolutely custom-bound, law-laid-down way. It must all be done gracefully, seemingly effortlessly and always with dignity. The worst criticism the Spaniards ever make of a bullfighter is that his work is "vulgar."

The three absolute acts of the tragedy are first the entry of the bull when the picadors receive the shock of his attacks and attempt to protect their horses with their lances. Then the horses go out and the second act is the planting of the banderillos. This is one of the most interesting and difficult parts but among the easiest for a new bullfight fan to appreciate in technique. The banderillos are three-foot, gaily colored darts with a small fishhook prong in the end. The man who is going to plant them walks out into the arena alone with the bull. He lifts the banderillos at arm's length and points them toward the bull. Then he calls "Toro! Toro!" The bull charges and the banderillero rises to his toes, bends in a curve forward and, just as the bull is about to hit him, drops the darts into the bull's hump just back of his horns.

They must go in evenly, one on each side. They must not be shoved, or thrown or stuck in from the side. This is the first time the bull has been completely baffled, there is the prick of the darts that he cannot escape and there are no horses for him to charge into. But he charges the man again and again and each time he gets a pair of the long banderillos that hang from his hump by their tiny barbs and flush like porcupine quills.

Last is the death of the bull, which is in the hands of the matador who has had charge of the bull since his first attack. Each matador has two bulls in the afternoon. The death of the bull is most formal and can only be brought about in one way, directly from the front by the matador, who must receive the bull in full charge and kill him with a sword thrust between the shoulders just back of the neck and between the horns. Before killing the bull he must first do a series of passes with the muleta, a piece of red cloth about the size of a large napkin. With the muleta, the torero must show his complete mastery of the bull, must make the bull miss him again and again by inches, before he is allowed to kill him. It is in this phase that most of the fatal accidents occur.

The word "toreador" is obsolete Spanish and is never used. The torero is usually called an espada, or swordsman. He must be proficient in all three acts of the fight. In the first he uses the cape and does veronicas and protects the picadors by taking the bull out and away from them when they are spilled to the ground. In the second act he plants the banderillos. In the third act he masters the bull with the muleta and kills him.

Few toreros excel in all three departments. Some, like young Chicuelo, are unapproachable in their capework. Others like the late Joselito are wonderful banderilleros. Only a few are great killers. Most of the greatest killers are gypsies.

Poet Claude McKay, one of the writers associated with the Harlem Renaissance, lived in Paris during the 1920s. In the following selection from his memoir, A Long Way from Home *(New York: Furman, 1937), pp. 249–252, McKay recalls his reaction to Hemingway's* in our time *and evaluates Hemingway's career after that book was published.*

Ernest Hemingway was the most talked-about of young American writers when I arrived in Paris. He was the white hope of the ultra-sophisticates. In the motley atmosphere of Montparnasse, there was no place for the cult of little hero worship. James Joyce was worshipped, but he had won out with a work that took men's eyes like a planet. But in Montparnasse generally writers and artists plunged daggers into one another. That atmosphere in its special way was like a good tonic, if you didn't take too much of it. Good for young creative artists who have a tendency to megalomania. And many of them do. And also it was an antidote for the older ones who have already arrived and are a little haughty, expecting too much homage from the young.

It was therefore exciting that Ernest Hemingway had won the regard and respect of the younger creative artists and even of the older. I remember Nina Hamnett pointing him out to me at the Dôme and remarking ecstatically that Hemingway was a very handsome American and that he had a lovely son. But it was long after that before I met him for a moment through Max Eastman.

In Our Time, that thin rare book of miniature short stories, was published, and it was the literary event among the young expatriates. I cherish an unforgettable memory of it and of Montparnasse at that time. A cultivated and distinguished American, liberal of attitude and pocket to unpopular causes, was sitting at the Dôme, reading a copy of *In Our Time.* He invited me to his table and offered a drink. He read aloud Chapter III, and wondered whether there was a *double entendre* in that last sentence: "It rained all through the evacuation." I said I did not know and did not think it mattered, and I asked the *garçon* to bring me a double cognac. My friend and host said: "They are talking in a big way about this Hemingway, but I just can't get him. I like the young radical crowd and what they are aiming to do. But this thing here"–he pointed to *In Our Time*–"I don't like it. It is too brutal and bloody."

"But so is life," I ventured to say, and not too aggressively, because I was expecting my host to come across with a gift of money.

William Bird, publisher of Hemingway's in our time. *Bird inscribed this photograph for Sylvia Beach (Sylvia Beach Collection, Princeton University Library).*

"The only thing I admire about this book is the cover," he said. "That sure is in our time all right. If you like it you can have it." My hand trembled to take it. The book was worth something between thirty and fifty francs, which was more than I could afford. I have it still. It became so valuable that I once consigned it for a loan. But I redeemed it and, excepting my typewriter, I hardly ever trouble to redeem the things I pawn.

Yet I would be lying if I should say here that when I read *In Our Time* in 1924 I thought the author soon would be one of the famous American writers. I liked the style of the book, but I thought more of it as a literary rarity, and that the author would remain one of the best of the little coterie writers.

I must confess to a vast admiration for Ernest Hemingway the writer. Some of my critics thought that I was imitating him. But I also am a critic of myself. And I fail to find any relationship between my loose manner and subjective feeling in writing and Hemingway's objective and carefully stylized form. Any critic who considers it important enough to take the trouble can trace in my stuff a clearly consistent emotional-realist thread, from the time I published my book of dialect verse (*Songs of Jamaica*) in 1912, through the period of my verse and prose in *The Liberator,* until the publication of *Home to Harlem.*

But indeed, yes, I was excited by the meteor apparition of Ernest Hemingway. I cannot imagine any ambitious young writer of that time who was not fascinated in the beginning. In Paris and in the Midi, I met a few fellows of the extreme left school, and also a few of the moderate liberal school and even some of the ancient fossil school—and all mentioned Hemingway with admiration. Many of them felt that they could never go on writing as before after Hemingway.

The irritating pseudo-romantic style of writing about contemporary life–often employed by modernists and futurists, with their punctuation-and-phraseology tricks, as well as by the dead traditionalists–that style so admirably parodied in *Ulysses*; had reached its conventional climax in Michael Arlen's *The Green Hat.* When Hemingway wrote, *The Sun Also Rises,* he shot a fist in the face of the false romantic-realists and said: "You can't fake about life like that."

Apparently Hemingway today is mainly admired by a hard-boiled and unsophisticated public whose mentality in a curious way is rather akin to that of the American who contemptuously gave away Hemingway's first book to me. I don't think that that is any of Hemingway's fault. And what excites and tickles me to disgust is the attitude of the precious coteries toward Hemingway. One is not certain whether they hate Hemingway because of his success or because of his rough handling of some precious idols. The elect of the coteries could not possibly object to the Hemingway style and material. For the Hemingway of *In Our Time* is the same Hemingway of *The Sun Also Rises, A Farewell to Arms,* and the masterpiece of *Death in the Afternoon.* The only difference I see is that whereas Hemingway is a little cryptic in the earlier work, he is clear, unequivocal and forthright in his full-sized books. *In Our Time* contains the frame, the background, and the substance of all of Hemingway's later work. The hard-boilism–the booze, blood and brutality are all there. The key to *A Farewell to Arms* may be found in *In Our Time.* The critics whose sensibilities were so shocked over *Death in the Afternoon* will find its foundation in the six miniature classics of the bull ring in *In Our Time,* developed and enlarged with riper experience in the big book.

I find in Hemingway's works an artistic illumination of a certain quality of American civilization that is not to be found in any other distinguished American writer. And that quality is the hard-boiled contempt for and disgust with sissyness expressed among all classes of Americans. Now this quality is distinctly and definitely American–a conventionalized rough attitude which is altogether un-European. It stands out conspicuously, like the difference between American burlesque shows and European music-hall shows. Mr. Hemingway has taken this characteristic of American life from the streets, the barrooms, the ringsides and lifted it into the realm of real literature. In accomplishing this he did revolutionary work with four-letter Anglo-Saxon words. That to me is a superb achievement. I do not know what Mr. Hemingway's personal attitude may be to the material that he has used, and I care less. All I can say is that in literature he has most excellently quickened and enlarged my experience of social life.

Edmund Wilson's review of Three Stories and Ten Poems *and* in our time, *published in* The Dial, *77 (October 1924), pp. 340–341, was the first notice of Hemingway's work in an American periodical.*

MR HEMINGWAY'S DRY-POINTS

Mr Hemingway's poems are not particularly important, but his prose is of the finest distinction. He must be counted as the only American writer but one– Mr Sherwood Anderson–who has felt the genius of Gertrude Stein's Three Lives and has been evidently influenced by it. Indeed, Miss Stein, Mr Anderson, and Mr Hemingway may now be said to form a school by themselves. The characteristic of this school is a naïveté of language often passing into the colloquialism of the character dealt with which serves actually to convey profound emotions and complex states of mind. It is a distinctively American development in prose–as opposed to more or less successful American achievements in the traditional style of English prose–which has artistically justified itself at its best as a limpid shaft into deep waters.

Not, however, that Mr Hemingway is imitative. On the contrary, he is rather strikingly original, and in the dry compressed little vignettes of In Our Time has almost invented a form of his own:

"They shot the six cabinet ministers at half-past six in the morning against the wall of the hospital. There were pools of water in the courtyard. There were dead leaves on the paving of the courtyard. It rained hard. All the shutters of the hospital were nailed shut. One of the ministers was sick with typhoid. Two soldiers carried him downstairs and out into the rain. They tried to hold him up against the wall but he sat down in a puddle of water. The other five stood very quietly against the wall. Finally the officer told the soldiers it was no good trying to make him stand up. When they fired the first volley he was sitting down in the water with his head on his knees."

Mr Hemingway is remarkably successful in suggesting moral values by a series of simple statements of this sort. His more important book is called In Our Time, and below its cool objective manner really constitutes a harrowing record of barbarities: you have not only political executions, but criminal hangings, bull-fights, assassinations by the police, and all the cruelties and enormities of the war. Mr Hemingway is wholly unperturbed as he tells about these things: he is not a propagandist even for humanity. His bull-fight sketches have the dry sharpness

The letter sent by Hemingway's father to Ezra Pound, to order copies of the untitled book published as in our time *(Pound Collection, Lilly Library, Indiana University)*

and elegance of the bull-fight lithographs of Goya. And, like Goya, he is concerned first of all with making a fine picture. He is showing you what life is, too proud an artist to simplify. And I am inclined to think that his little book has more artistic dignity than any other that has been written by an American about the period of the war.

Not perhaps the most vivid book, but the soundest. Mr Hemingway, who can make you feel the poignancy of the Italian soldier deciding in his death agony that he will "make a separate peace," has no anti-militaristic *parti pris* which will lead him to suppress from his record the exhilaration of the men who had "jammed an absolutely perfect barricade across the bridge" and who were "frightfully put out when we heard the flank had gone, and we had to fall back." It is only in the paleness, the thinness of some of his effects that Mr Hemingway sometimes fails. I am thinking especially of the story called Up In Michigan, which

should have been a masterpiece, but has the curious effect of dealing with rude and primitive people yet leaving them shadowy.

In Our Time has a pretty and very amusing cover designed from scrambled newspaper clippings. The only objection I have to its appearance is that the titles are throughout printed without capitals—thus: "in our time by ernest hemingway—paris." This device, which used to be rather effective when the modernists first used to use it to call attention to the fact that they had something new to offer, has now grown common and a bore. The American advertisers have taken it over as one of their stock tricks. And it is so unsightly in itself that it is rather a pity to see it become—in the case of Mr Hemingway's book and Mr Hueffer's "transatlantic review"—a sort of badge of everything that is freshest and most interesting in modern writing.

In 1925 Hemingway returned to Spain with a group of friends for his second fiesta in Pamplona. Parts of this trip provided material for The Sun Also Rises *(New York: Scribners, 1926). The following account was written by Robert McAlmon (*Being Geniuses Together, *pp. 212–216). The "English captain" McAlmon mentions is E. E. "Chink" Dorman-Smith.*

Hemingway had become much of a bullfight enthusiast since his 1924 trip to Spain. In one of his earlier short stories one character says, "It's no fun if you can't skee any more," and the other character responds, "No, it's no fun if you can't skee any more." He now carried this manner of perfect dialogue and the intonation of the American language over to bullfighting and bullfight stories. It was all muscular and athletic prose, but for this period in the spirit of "it's no fun if you can't see bullfights any more."

He talked a great deal about bullfights as the great art, the beautiful dance involving death, and withal one summer, quite a number of people decided to do the July fiesta week in Pampeluna, Spain. Having done a quick trip to Egypt, and back via Athens and Constantinople, I also hied myself to Pampeluna, and there before me were Donald Ogden Stewart, Dos Passos, William and Sally Bird, young George O'Neill, Hadley and Ernest Hemingway, and an English captain from Sandhurst, who had known Hemingway in Milan after the war.

The days and the nights were hot with a heat that sweated through one's flesh and bones. However, the fiesta spirit was rampant, and everybody was willing to drink plenty of pernod and forget the heat. The town, the first two days before the bullfights came on, was quiet till noon, when the café terraces were crowded. After lunch the streets were empty again, but at six o'clock the fiesta gaieties began. Innumerable throngs of peasants from the mountains filled the town, their necks encircled with necklaces of garlic, and various shaped goatskins bags of wine thrown over their shoulders. Some were made into the form of ships, or of dolls or animals. To drink one held the goatskin high, squeezed, and a small stream of goaty-tasting wine poured into one's open lips. This took learning, but the natives were adept. Continually little crowds of natives came and went, blowing whistles or playing more or less primitive musical instruments. Groups formed and danced solos in circles. Donald Ogden Stewart proved himself a born comedian with an inherent clowning instinct, for after his first solo dance he was the friend of the peasants from all the surrounding countryside. He knew how to utilize his yankee professor's appearance.

Eric Edward "Chink" Dorman-Smith, in Paris, 1924. Hemingway had met Dorman-Smith, a British captain in World War I, while serving on the Italian front in 1918.

With the Americans he had the advantage of having his "crazy-fool" cracks and witticisms understood, but he managed to troupe his comedy across to the Spaniards without a common language.

All of the American-English gathering proceeded to lose each other generally the first two nights. Each one tagged on to or got picked up by some wandering group of musicians and boys from the mountains, and the dancing and drinking continued till early morning. The town slept till well past noon.

We all went to inspect the bulls which were to be used in the corridas. The third morning, the day of the first bullfight, everyone was up by six o'clock, and in the boarded street down which the bulls for the day were to be driven. Hundreds of boys and young men, natives, stood along the sides of the street and ran ahead as the bulls dashed towards the bull ring. A few got butted or knocked against the walls by an excited and bewildered bull, but no one was badly injured or killed, as does happen sometimes. Later, when the fierce bulls had been driven into their corrals to wait for the afternoon corridas, the amateur fun began. A heifer, light-bodied steer, or yearling bull—but seldom—would be released into the ring. Hundreds of aspiring bullfighters were in the ring, and the bewildered heifer, steer, or young bull would dash here and there, sometimes charging, but as often merely looking for means of escape.

Hemingway had been talking a great deal about courage, and how a man needs to test himself to prove to himself that he can take it. I am doubtful. If one takes it too much one may begin to get nervy, or shellshocked, or plainly fed up. Hemingway, however, had persuaded himself that he must prove himself. With his coat he tried to attract the charge and the repeated charge of a steer, but the two hundred odd others in the ring were all trying to capture that mystified animal's attention also. Finally, Hemingway took a charge straight on face, and then catching the steer's horns, attempted to throw it. He did break its strength and got cheered by the crowd. When the steer was released it ran away bellowing a bewildered moo, its tail wagging pathetically, and an expression on its face indicating that it was having no fun at all.

Bill Bird and Dos Passos were either the bravest or just plain quitters. Anyway, they didn't get into the ring to play with them calves. George O'Neill, then about seventeen, Don Stewart, Hemingway, and myself, however, were all there. The first day only Hemingway proved himself. My idea was to evade getting butted, and the others ran out of the path of a charge also. Later, however, Hemingway talked about bravery to Donald Ogden Stewart. Stewart confessed to me that maybe one might as well save one's courage to use when an actual crisis occurs, if it is there to use. You cannot judge one's reaction to one type of danger by his bravado.

I was drinking altogether too much pernod and goat-skin tasting red wine, and eating heavy Spanish food. The idea of having a calf, steer, or young bull, charge into my breadbasket did not appeal to me. I never did anything but dodge out of the way of those cattle, and if they appeared to pursue I jumped the fence.

All members of the party liked aspects of the bullfights by the skilled matadors, but no one ever became the fervid enthusiast which Hemingway elected to become. Bullfights that are truly great are too rare, and one must see many to see fine ones. For the rest, nothing is more vulgar and disgusting than a bad bullfight, and clumsy killings of the bull are more horrible than the horse part of the fight. The lost, baby-calf look of wondering stupidity on a bull's face is heartbreaking, particularly when it is a brave bull, but does not want to fight or to charge horses. It is complete nonsense that all bulls are naturally attacking and fighting animals. Even goaded by torture some of them remain brave but fight only to be let alone.

The fiesta week over at Pampeluna, Bill and Sally Bird and I boarded a bus and went to Burguette, a Spanish town near the French border. It was tiny and quiet, with one bare peasant inn, and but a few cottages. Herds of sheep and goats flocked in the surrounding hills, and muleteers drove their donkeys down the road, bearing cordwood or wine bags. Some miles up in the mountains was an old mine shaft and a stream where trout-fishing was good. After a few days Hemingway and his wife joined us, and we took walks to the fishing falls, and it was here that Hemingway fished one day while thinking out his story *Great Two-Hearted River*. He was so intent thinking about what it was that a man who was fishing would be thinking about, and what Bird and I would be thinking about, that he didn't catch many trout, but he jotted down notes for the story. Some declare it great. I find it a stunt and artificial, and do not believe his mind works that way at all. I think he is a very good business man, a publicist, who looks ahead and calculates, and uses rather than wonders about people.

For a few days things were restful and pastoral at Burguette, and the country about was beautiful with innumerable walks to be taken. Later Chink Smith, Dos Passos, and George O'Neill arrived, and the next day these three and I started to take a walk in the Pyrenees, intending to spend about a fortnight with the little republic of Andorra as our goal. Hemingway accompanied us for about five kilometres and then dutifully returned to his wife.

Inscription in Dorman-Smith's copy of in our time, *the book Hemingway dedicated to him, William Bird, and Robert McAlmon. "Popplethwaite" was Dorman-Smith's nickname for Hemingway.*

Ford Madox Ford, editor of Transatlantic Review *and a former associate and collaborator with Joseph Conrad, asked Hemingway to contribute an essay for a memorial number of the magazine. For the October 1924 issue Hemingway provided the following essay, "Conrad, Optimist and Moralist" (pp. 341–342), which is infamous because of his statements about T. S. Eliot.*

What is there you can write about him now that he is dead?

The critics will dive into their vocabularies and come up with articles on the death of Conrad. They are diving now, like prairie dogs.

It will not be hard for the editorial writers; Death of John L. Sullivan, Death of Roosevelt, Death of Major Whittlesey, Death of President Coolidge's Son, Death of Honored Citizen, Passing of Pioneer, Death of President Wilson, Great Novelist Passes, it is all the same.

CONRAD, OPTIMIST AND MORALIST

Admirers of Joseph Conrad, whose sudden death is an occasion for general regret, usually think of him as an artist of the first rank, as a remarkable story teller and as a stylist. But Mr. Conrad was also a deep thinker and serene philosopher. In his novels, as in his essays etc.

It will run like that. All over the country.

And what is there that you can say about him now that he is dead?

It is fashionable among my friends to disparage him. It is even necessary. Living in a world of literary politics where one wrong opinion often proves fatal, one writes carefully. I remember how I was made to feel how easily one might be dropped from the party, and the short period of Coventry that followed my remarking when speaking of George Antheil that I preferred my Stravinsky straight. I have been more careful since.

It is agreed by most of the people I know that Conrad is a bad writer, just as it is agreed that T. S. Eliot is a good writer. If I knew that by grinding Mr. Eliot into a fine dry powder and sprinkling that powder over Mr. Conrad's grave Mr. Conrad would shortly appear, looking very annoyed at the forced return, and commence writing I would leave for London early tomorrow morning with a sausage grinder.

One should not be funny over the death of a great man but you cannot couple T. S. Eliot and Joseph Conrad in a sentence seriously any more than you could see, say, André Germain and Manuel Garcia (Maera) walking down the street together and not laugh.

The second book of Conrad's that I read was *Lord Jim*. I was unable to finish it. It is, therefore, all I have left of him. For I cannot re-read them. That

Hemingway's inscription in Dr. Carlos Guffey's copy of in our time, *recounting the publication of the book (Parke Bernet Galleries, Library of Dr. Carlos Guffey, Item 152, 14 October 1958)*

may be what my friends mean by saying he is a bad writer. But from nothing else that I have ever read have I gotten what every book of Conrad has given me.

Knowing I could not re-read them I saved up four that I would not read until I needed them badly, when the disgust with writing, writers and everything written of and to write would be too much. Two months in Toronto used up the four books. One after another I borrowed them from a girl who had all of his books on a shelf, bound in blue leather and had never read any of them. Let us be exact. She had read *The Arrow of Gold* and *Victory*.

In Sudbury, Ontario, I bought three back numbers of the Pictorial Review and read *The Rover,* sitting up in bed in the Nickle Range Hotel. When morning came I had used up all my Conrad like a drunkard, I had hoped it would last me the trip, and felt like a young man who has blown his patrimony. But, I thought, he will write more stories. He has lots of time.

When I read the reviews they all agreed *The Rover* was a bad story.

And now he is dead and I wish to God they would have taken some great, acknowledged technician of a literary figure and left him to write his bad stories.

The first issue of This Quarter *(Spring 1925), edited by poet Ernest Walsh and painter Ethel Moorhead, was dedicated to Ezra Pound. Hemingway's essay (pp. 221–225) shows his appreciation for Pound as well as his contempt for the other writers Pound had assisted.*

HOMAGE TO EZRA

An editor has written asking me to write an appreciation of Ezra Pound, to be written as though Pound were dead. One does not write appreciations of dead men but only of their work. Dead men themselves are most uncomfortable to have around and sooner or later one buries them or walks behind them to where others bury them or reads about their funeral in the newspaper and perhaps sends telegrams in which it is impossible to avoid clichés. And if one tries to write about dead men who were one's friends one fails for one reason or another and it is no good.

Stylists can do it because they have a way of wrapping things around in their style like *emballeurs* or the men who wrapped mummies in Egypt. Even stylists though do it only to their own satisfaction. No one else is very pleased.

So thank God Pound isn't dead and we don't have to write about him as though he were.

Ezra Pound devotes perhaps one fifth of his working time to writing poetry and in this twenty per cent of effort writes a large and distinguished share of the really great poetry that has been written by any American living or dead—or any Englishman living or dead or any Irishman who ever wrote English. I do not mention other nationalities because I do not know the poetry of other countries nor do I know Gaelic. There is only one living poet who ranks with Pound and that is William Butler Yeats. Some of Pound's later manner is done better by T. S. Eliot. But Eliot is, after all, a minor poet. Just as Marianne Moore is a minor poet and Wallace Stevens is a minor poet. Fine poetry is written by minor poets.

Pound happens to be a major poet just as Yeats is and Browning and Shelley and Keats were. What is the difference? It seems hardly necessary to point it out but it is easier to do through the case of Eliot. All of Eliot's poems are perfect and there are very few of them. He has a very fine talent and he is very careful of it. He never takes chances with it and it is doing very well thank you. Whitman, on the other hand, if a poet, is a major poet.

The most perfect poem to me in the *Oxford Book of English verse* was written by Anonymous. Yet I have to consider Anonymous a minor poet because if he were a major poet there would have been a name to him. That may sound like Dr. Frank Crane. But take A. E. Houseman. There is the perfect case of the minor poet. He did it once and did it perfectly with the *Shropshire Lad* but when he tried to do again it wouldn't come off and the trick of mind all showed through and it imperilled the poems in the first book. One more book would have killed off all the poems. They proved to be unimportant.

Minor poets do not fail because they do not attempt the major thing. They have nothing of major importance to say. They do a minor thing with perfection and the perfection is admirable. Ezra has written great poetry.

This is an appreciation rather than a critical article. If it were the latter I would have to stop here and go up to Paris to verify quotations. There ought to be quotations if this were to prove anything. Fortunately an appreciation does not have to prove anything.

So then, so far, we have Pound the major poet devoting, say, one fifth of his time to poetry. With the rest of his time he tries to advance the fortunes, both material and artistic, of his friends. He defends them when they are attacked, he gets them into magazines and out of jail. He loans them money. He sells their pictures. He arranges

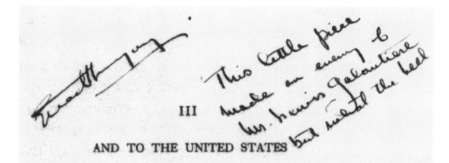

III

AND TO THE UNITED STATES

The Quarter. Early Spring.

An American citizen, not yet thirty five years old, of French-German-Jewish parentage, writing in the Paris Sunday Literary Supplement of the World's Greatest Newspaper under the name of Louis Gay says:

"Remember that less than twenty years ago the reading matter to be found in the home of the average American of means—the American who sent his boys to college—was composed almost entirely of the New England Poets, the *Christian Register* and the *Youth's Companion...*"

As Mr. Gay is frequently denunciatory, rarely unpersonal, and always insistent on the lack of a cultural background of almost everyone of whom he writes, the above selection from his article will have a certain biographical significance in the critical study of American Criticism which should be written to carry to its end the present phenomenon on American letters.

For every writer produced in America there are produced eleven critics. Now that the *Dial* prize has gone to a critic the ratio may be expected to increase to 1/55 or over. As I have always regarded critics as the eunuchs of literature... But there is no use finishing that sentence. If this letter is accepted that means one hundred and fifty francs which relieves one of that responsibility to follow through which is imposed in golf and creative writing. Did you, however, ever see a bull which has withstood the bad sticking of the matador, led off to the corrals by three thin steers? And did you ever see a bull who had earned the president's reprieve to the corrals, and after, of course to the abattoir, dully refuse to follow the steers and insist on being killed in the ring? And then did you watch the terror of the trained steers and their angular attempts to jump out of the ring over the barriers?

As for America, Henry Strater has just gone there. New York gets a good painter and the newly opened *Boxing Montparnasse* in the rue de la Gaieté loses a needed supporter. The *Boxing Montparnasse* is not, as yet fashionable; the ringside

355

Hemingway contributed these short, satirical news items to the Transatlantic Review *(May–June 1924). The first item has Hemingway's note about critic and translator Lewis Galantiére (Clifton Waller Barrett Library, University of Virginia).*

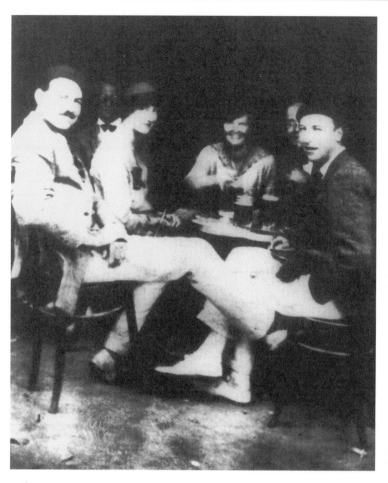

Ernest Hemingway, Duff Twysden, Hadley Hemingway, Donald Ogden Stewart, and Pat Gutherie during the July 1925 visit to Pamplona that inspired The Sun Also Rises *(Ernest Hemingway Collection, John F. Kennedy Library)*

concerts for them. He writes articles about them. He introduces them to wealthy women. He gets publishers to take their books. He sits up all night with them when they claim to be dying and he witnesses their wills. He advances them hospital expenses and dissuades them from suicide. And in the end a few of them refrain from knifing him at the first opportunity.

Personally he is tall, has a patchy red beard, fine eyes, strange haircuts and is very shy. But he has the temperament of a *toro di lidia* from the breeding establishments of Don Eduardo Miura. No one ever presents a cape, or shakes a muleta at him without getting a charge. Like Don Eduardo's product too he sometimes ignores the picador's horse to pick off the man and no one goes into the ring with him in safety. And though they can always be sure of drawing his charge yet he gets his quota of bull-baiters each year.

Many people hate him and he plays a fine game of tennis. He would live much longer if he did not eat so fast. Young men in the years after the war coming over from America where Pound was a legendary person to Paris where they found him with a patchy red beard, very accessible, fond of tennis and occasionally playing the bassoon, decided there could not be anything in the Pound legend and that he was probably not a great poet after all. As the army rhyme used to say: hence criticism in America.

Like all men who become famous very young he suffers from not being read. It is so much easier to talk about a classic than to read it. There is another generation, though, in America that is replacing the generation that decided Ezra could not be a great poet because he was actually alive and kicking, and this generation is reading him. They

Bill Smith, a childhood friend of Hemingway and a partial model for Bill Gorton in The Sun Also Rises, *being tossed by a bull in Pamplona, July 1925*

come to Paris now and want to meet him. But he has gone to Italy.

As he takes no interest in Italian politics and does not mind Italian cookery he may stay there sometime. It is good for him to be there because his friends cannot get at him so easily and energy is thus released for production. Pound is among other things a composer and has done a splendid opera on Villon. It is a first rate opera. A very fine opera.

But I feel about Ezra and music something like about M. Constantin Brancusi and cooking. M. Brancusi is a famous sculptor who is also a very famous cook. Cooking is, of course, an art but it would be lamentable if M. Brancusi would give up sculpture for it or even devote the major part of his time to cookery.

Still Ezra is not a minor poet. He has never been troubled by lack of energy. If he wants to write more operas he will write them and there will be plenty of force left over.

As this is an appreciation there is one thing to be emphasized about Ezra. He has never been a piti-ful figure. He has fought his fights with a very gay grimness and his wounds heal quickly. He does not believe that he came into the world to suffer. He is no masochist and that is one more reason why he is not a minor poet.

Hemingway's review of Sherwood Anderson's A Story-Teller's Story, *which was published in* Ex Libris, *2 (March 1925), pp. 176–177, was paired with a review of the book by Gertrude Stein. Written before Hemingway had read* Dark Laughter, *this review shows his uncertainty over Anderson's discipline and modifies the theory that Hemingway's* The Torrents of Spring *(New York: Scribners, 1926) was written mainly to break his contract with Boni & Liveright.*

The reviewers have all compared this book with the "Education of Henry Adams" and it was not hard for them to do so, for Sherwood Anderson twice refers to the

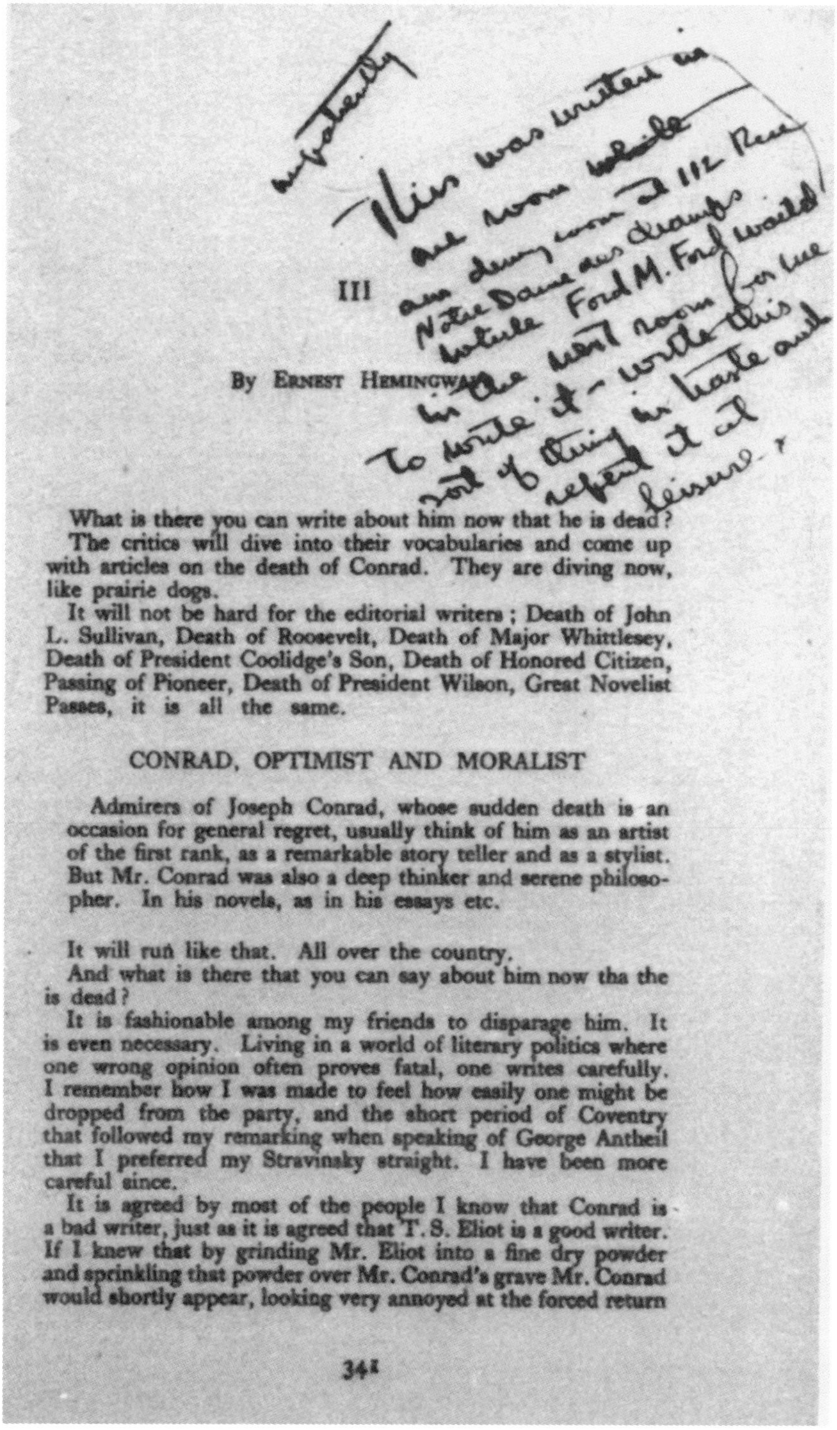

III

By Ernest Hemingway

[handwritten annotation:] This was written in one room while waiting in the next room for the toilet to be free. To write it—write this sort of thing in haste and repeat it at leisure.

[handwritten annotation:] evidently

[handwritten annotation:] our downstairs, 112 Rue Notre Dame des Champs when Ford M. Ford would.

What is there you can write about him now that he is dead?

The critics will dive into their vocabularies and come up with articles on the death of Conrad. They are diving now, like prairie dogs.

It will not be hard for the editorial writers ; Death of John L. Sullivan, Death of Roosevelt, Death of Major Whittlesey, Death of President Coolidge's Son, Death of Honored Citizen, Passing of Pioneer, Death of President Wilson, Great Novelist Passes, it is all the same.

CONRAD, OPTIMIST AND MORALIST

Admirers of Joseph Conrad, whose sudden death is an occasion for general regret, usually think of him as an artist of the first rank, as a remarkable story teller and as a stylist. But Mr. Conrad was also a deep thinker and serene philosopher. In his novels, as in his essays etc.

It will run like that. All over the country.

And what is there that you can say about him now tha the is dead?

It is fashionable among my friends to disparage him. It is even necessary. Living in a world of literary politics where one wrong opinion often proves fatal, one writes carefully. I remember how I was made to feel how easily one might be dropped from the party, and the short period of Coventry that followed my remarking when speaking of George Antheil that I preferred my Stravinsky straight. I have been more careful since.

It is agreed by most of the people I know that Conrad is a bad writer, just as it is agreed that T. S. Eliot is a good writer. If I knew that by grinding Mr. Eliot into a fine dry powder and sprinkling that powder over Mr. Conrad's grave Mr. Conrad would shortly appear, looking very annoyed at the forced return

341

Hemingway's annotation on the first page of his tribute to Joseph Conrad, published in the Transatlantic Review, *October 1924 (Clifton Waller Barrett Library, University of Virginia)*

Hemingway in Gstaad, Switzerland (1927)

the warehouse where he worked, you get at the same time, a very definite sharp picture of the baseball player, drunk, sullen and amazed, knocking him down as soon and as often as he got up while the two teamsters watched and wondered why this fellow named Anderson had picked a fight when he couldn't fight.

There are very beautiful places in the book, as good writing as Sherwood Anderson has done and that means considerably better than any other American writer has done. It is a great mystery and an even greater tribute to Sherwood that so many people writing today think he cannot write. They believe that he has very strange and sometimes beautiful ideas and visions and that he expresses them very clumsily and unsuccessfully. While in reality he often takes a very banal idea of things and presents it with such craftsmanship that the person reading believes it beautiful and does not see the craftsmanship at all. When he calls himself "a poor scribbler" don't believe him.

He is not a poor scribbler even though he calls himself that or worse, again and again. He is a very great writer and if he has, at times, in other books been unsuccessful, it has been for two reasons. His talent and his development of it has been toward the short story or tale and not toward that highly artificial form the novel. The second reason is that he has been what the French say of all honest politicians *mal entouré*.

In "A Story Teller's Story", which is highly successful as a piece of work because it is written in his own particular form, a series of short tales jointed up sometimes and sometimes quite disconnected, he pays homage to his New York friends who have helped him. They nearly all took something from him, and tried to give him various things in return that he needed as much as a boxer needs diamond studded teeth. And because he gave them all something he is, after the manner of all great men, very grateful to them. They called him a "phallic Chekov" and other meaningless things and watched for the sparkle of his diamond studded teeth and Sherwood got a little worried and uncertain and wrote a poor book called "Many Marriages". Then all the people who hated him because he was an American who could write and did write and had been given a prize and was starting to have some success jumped on him with loud cries that he never had written and never would be able to write and if you didn't believe it read "Many Marriages". Now Sherwood has written a fine book and they are all busy comparing him to Henry Adams.

Anyway you ought to read "A Story Teller's Story". It is a wonderful comeback after "Many Marriages".

Adams book and there is plenty in the "Story Teller's Story" about the cathedral at Chartres. Evidently the Education book made a deep impression on Sherwood for he quotes part of it. He also has a couple of other learned quotations in Latin and I can imagine him copying them on the typewriter verifying them carefully to get the spelling right. For Sherwood Anderson, unlike the English, does not quote you Latin in casual conversation.

As far as I know the Latin is correct although English reviewers may find flaws in it, and all of my friends own and speak of "The Education of Henry Adams" with such solemnity that I have been unable ever to read it. "A Story Teller's Story" is a good book. It is such a good book that it doesn't need to be coupled in the reviewing with Henry Adams or anybody else.

This is the Life and Times of Sherwood Anderson and a great part of it runs along in a mildly kidding way as though Sherwood were afraid people would think he took himself and his life too seriously. But there is no joking about the way he writes of horses and women and bartenders and Judge Turner and the elder Berners and the half allegorical figure of the poor devil of a magazine writer who comes in at the end of the book. And if Sherwood jokes about the base-ball player beating him up at

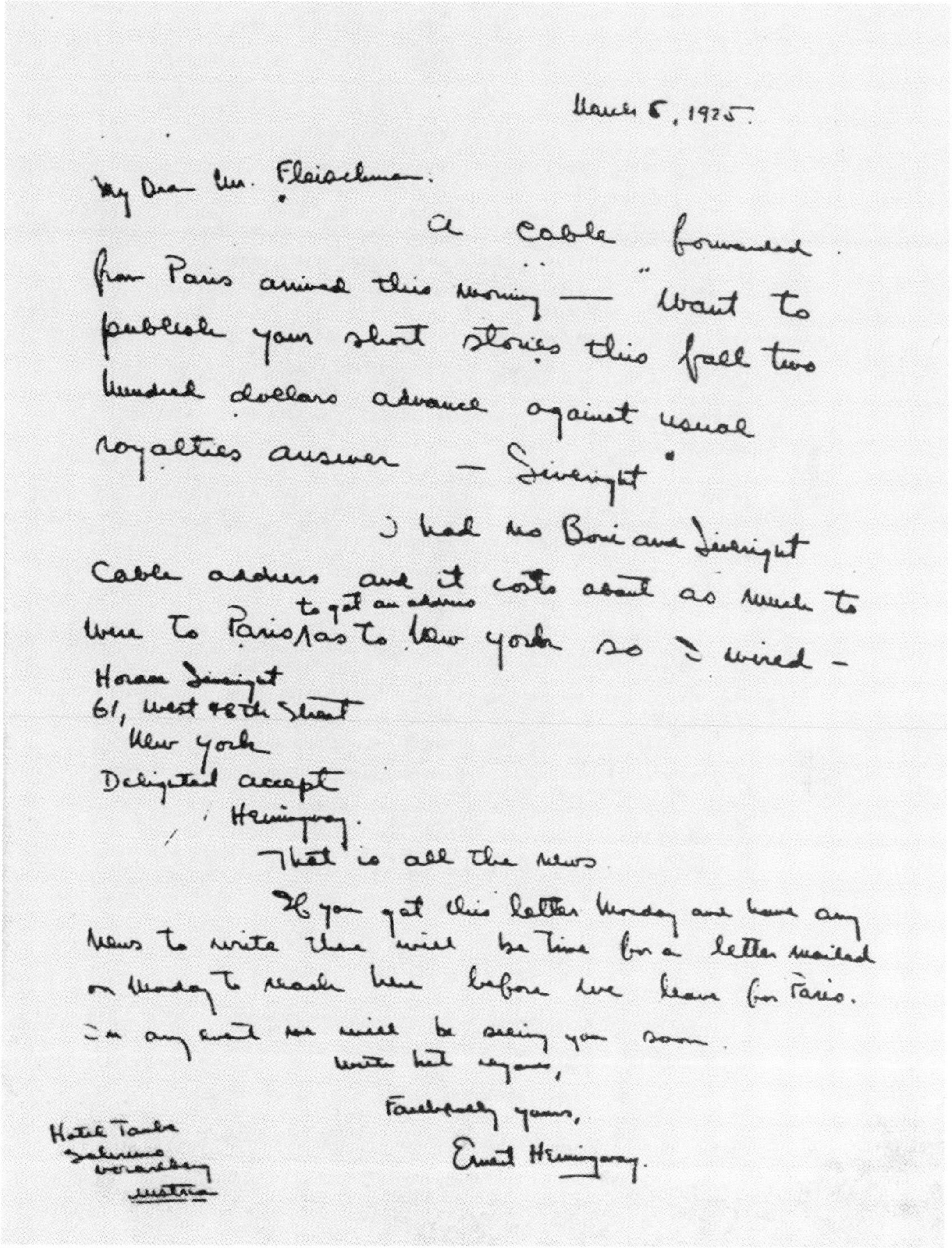

March 5, 1925.

My Dear Mr. Fleischman:

A cable forwarded from Paris arrived this morning — "Want to publish your short stories this fall two hundred dollars advance against usual royalties answer — Liveright"

I had no Boni and Liveright Cable address and it costs about as much to wire to Paris to get an address as to New York so I wired —

Horace Liveright
61, West 48th Street
New York
Delighted accept
Hemingway.

That is all the news.

If you get this letter Monday and have any news to write there will be time for a letter mailed on Monday to reach here before we leave for Paris. In any event we will be seeing you soon.

Write but again,

Faithfully yours,
Ernest Hemingway.

Hotel Taube
Schruns
Vorarlberg
Austria

Hemingway's letter accepting Boni & Liveright's offer to publish In Our Time. *Leon Fleischman was Horace Liveright's literary scout in Europe (Louis Henry Cohn Collection, University of Delaware).*

113 Rue Notre Dame des Champs ,
Paris VI France.
May 22,1925.

Dear Mr. Liveright :

I am mailing the galley proofs back
teday marked for the Mauretania sailing tomorrow se
with this letter they ought to reach you in a few
days .

The type the stories are set in is
splendid and I am delighted with the way they leek and with
the few sheets of page proof . I have already written
Mr. Keareff about the tee black caps in the italics the
chapters are set in . They give an entirely false
emphasis and jerk that is not intended every time the
upper case is used .

As you will see I have revised the
Mr. and Mrs. Elliet story and entirely eliminated the
obscene image . As the whole story hung again and
again en the repetition of the words"they tried very hard
to have a baby ;" I have inserted some stuff about the
beat and Paris to pick up the old rhythm and keep it
funny . It has to have the repetions te hold it
together .

It is a shame it had to be changed but as you say
it would
be a a very silly play to get an entire first
beek suppressed fer the sake of a few funny cracks in one
story . New that ~~Ashens~~ you have out it and I have
smoothed it ever again will you make quite sure from
various epinions that it is not suppressable ? Fer it
would be an even werse business to be suppressed fer a
story after it has had the dynamite cut out .

Jane Heap ran it in its original form and did
not get inte any trouble . It is just as funny new ,to anyone
that did net read the original ,and not dangereus . But
remember that new that I have agreed to your cuts and
made them even milder it's up to you . To me it is net a
serieus story and I was glad to change it for you .

Whoever did the editing on the whole beek
was very intelligent and most ef the changes ef punctuation
I agree with . Those I den't I have changed te their original
form . My attitude toward punctuation is that it ought to
be as conventional as possible . The game of golf would
lese a good deal if croquet mallets and billard cues were
allowed on the putting green . You ought to be able te
shew that you can de it a good deal better than anyone else
with the regular tools before you have an license te bring

in your own ~~agenitsehinsem~~ improvements . But don't
let this inspire whoever went over it fer punctuation
te any further action because it is all right new
It leeks very good .

Reading it over it is even a better beek than
I remember . That isn't egetistical because every time
I read a story after a long time I wonder hewthe hell
did I ever write suchm a swell story ?

I will be anxious te get the page proofs as soon
as possible .

With best regards ,

Very sincerely ,

Ernest H. Hemingway .

Hemingway's letter to Liveright about the editing of In Our Time *(Louis Henry Cohn Collection, University of Delaware)*

March 17th, 1925.

Mr. Ernest Hemingway,
113 Rue Notre Dame des Champs,
Paris, France.

Dear Mr. Hemingway:

We hereby agree to publish at our own expense in the fall of 1925 your volume of short stories.

We agree to pay you the following royalties on all copies sold in the United States of America; 10% on the first 2500 copies sold, 12½% on the next 2500 copies and 15% thereafter. Upon your signing of this agreement, we shall send you our check for $200.00 as an advance against royalties. Royalty statements shall be submitted in February and August of each year, and royalty payments made not later than sixty days thereafter. Royalties in Canada shall be one-half of the above.

We agree to use our best efforts to sell the second serial rights to this book and it is understood and agreed that we are to share equally in any sums received from such sale. We are also to act as your agents for the disposition of the motion picture and dramatic rights to this book and in case of such sale, we shall be entitled to one-third (1/3) of any moneys received by us for these rights.

In consideration of our publishing this book at our own expense, it is agreed that we are to have the option to publish your next three books, one of which shall be a full length novel, on the same terms as outlined in this agreement with the following exceptions : On your second book you are to receive from us on our acceptance an amount equal to the sum earned in royalties by your first book up to date of publication, and on the third book you are to receive as an advance against royalties on our acceptance of the manuscript an amount equal to the sum earned in royalties by your second book up to date of publication. It is agreed on our part that unless we exercise our option to publish your books within 60 days of our receipt of the manuscripts, our option shall lapse, and that unless we publish your second book, we relinquish our option to the third book.

It is understood and agreed by you that we shall be permitted to make such excisions as we deem necessary and we shall eliminate the story which we now believe to be censorable.

BONI AND LIVERIGHT, Inc.

2.

All terms not specifically covered in this agreement shall be interpreted, if occasion arises, according to the standard contract of The Authors' League of America.

Faithfully,

BONI AND LIVERIGHT, Inc.

Horace B. Liveright

P R E S I D E N T

THESE TERMS ARE ACCEPTABLE TO ME

Ernest Hemingway

HBL:IG

Contract for In Our Time *(Louis Henry Cohn Collection, University of Delaware)*

Horace Liveright, the first publisher of Hemingway's books in the United States

Liveright accepted In Our Time *because of the efforts of Harold Loeb and Sherwood Anderson. In this, his first letter to his new publisher, Hemingway shows his willingness to compromise in order to get his book published. From* Selected Letters, *pp. 154–155.*

31 March 1925

Dear Mr. Liveright:

Enclosed is the signed contract and a new story to replace the one you are eliminating as censorable.

As the contract only mentions excisions it is understood of course that no alterations of words shall be made without my approval. This protects you as much as it does me as the stories are written so tight and so hard that the alteration of a word can throw an entire story out of key. I am sure you and Mr. T. R. Smith understand this.

There is nothing in the book that has not a definite place in its organization and if I at any time seem to repeat myself I have a good reason for doing so.

As for obscenities you and Mr. Smith being on the spot know what is and what is not unpublishably obscene much better than I do. I under-

stand that it is no longer necessary to eliminate the fine old word son of a bitch. This is indeed good news.

As for the book selling or not selling, I don't look on it in any way as a lost cause. I think, looking at it quite dispassionately, that it has a good gambling chance to sell.

The classic example of a really fine book that could not sell was E. E. Cumming's Enormous Room. But Cumming's book was written in a style that no one who had not read a good deal of "modern" writing could read. That was hard luck for selling purposes. My book will be praised by highbrows and can be read by lowbrows. There is no writing in it that anybody with a high-school education cannot read.

That is why I say it has a good 3/1 chance. And I never bet on Jeffries at Reno nor Carpentier nor other sentimental causes.

If cuts are made outside of possible necessary elimination of obscenities, if there are any, it will be shot to pieces as an organism and nobody will praise it and nobody want to read it. The reason I mention this is that there was a report over here that certain things were to be eliminated because they did not seem to have anything to do with the story. Probably it was without foundation.

The new story makes the book a good deal better. It's about the best I've ever written and gives additional unity to the book as a whole.

You are eliminating the second story–Up In Michigan. The next three stories move up one place each and this new story–The Battler–takes the place at present occupied by–The Three Day Blow.

I do not need to tell you how pleased I am to be published by Boni and Liveright and I hope I *will* become a property. That's up to both of us.

I would like to have the proofs as soon as possible.

> With best regards,
> Sincerely
> Ernest Hemingway

Enclosures Signed Agreement
   New Index showing place of new story
   Story entitled
   The Battler
   ~~The Great Little Fighting Machine~~

In October 1924 Maxwell Perkins, editor at Charles Scribner's Sons, had been advised by F. Scott Fitzgerald to attempt to sign Hemingway for the firm. Perkins's initial letter to Hemingway was not sent until February 1925—and then to the wrong address. Perkins had to wait another year to add Hemingway to his stable of writers. Hemingway's letter—from The Only Thing That Counts: The Ernest Hemingway–Maxwell Perkins Correspondence, 1925–1947, *edited by Matthew J. Bruccoli (New York: Scribners, 1996), pp. 156–157—mentions for the first time his wish to write a treatise on bullfighting, published in 1932 as* Death in the Afternoon *(New York: Scribners).*

113 Rue Notre Dame des Champs,
Paris VI, France
April 15, 1925

Dear Mr. Perkins:

On returning from Austria I received your letter of February 26 inclosing a copy of a previous letter which unfortunately never reached me. About ten days before your letter came I had a cabled offer from Boni and Liveright to bring out a book of my short stories in the fall. They asked me to reply by cable and I accepted.

I was very excited at getting your letter but did not see what I could do until I had seen the contract from Boni and Liveright. According to its terms they are to have an option on my next three books, they agreeing that unless they exercise this option to publish the second book within 60 days of the receipt of the manuscript their option shall lapse, and if they do not publish the second book they relinquish their option on the third book.

So that is how matters stand. I cannot tell you how pleased I was by your letter and you must know how gladly I would have sent Charles Scribner's Sons the manuscript of the book that is to come out this fall. It makes it seem almost worth while to get into Who's Who in order to have a known address.

I do want you to know how much I appreciated your letter and if I am ever in a position to send you anything to consider I shall certainly do so.

I hope some day to have a sort of Daughty's Arabia Deserta of the Bull Ring, a very big book with some wonderful pictures. But one has to save all winter to be able to bum in Spain in the summer and writing classics, I've always heard, takes some time. Somehow I don't care about writing a novel and I like to write short stories and I like to work at the bull fight book so I guess I'm a bad prospect for a publisher anyway. Somehow the novel seems to me to be an awfully artificial and worked out form but as some of the short stories now are stretching out to 8,000 to 12,000 words may be I'll get there yet.

The In Our Time is out of print and I've been trying to buy one to have myself now I hear it is valuable, so that probably explains your difficulty in getting it. I'm

Maxwell Perkins, Hemingway's editor at Charles Scribner's Sons from 1926 to 1947. Perkins was also the editor for Fitzgerald, Lardner, and Thomas Wolfe.

awfully glad you liked it and thank you again for writing me about a book.

Very Sincerely,
Ernest Hemingway

113 Rue Notre Dame des Champs is a permanent address

From Cahiers d'Art, *9, no. 1–4 (1934), pp. 28–29. In this article Hemingway describes his purchase of Joan Miró's painting* The Farm *in September 1925. Evan Shipman, a friend, was a minor poet and a horse-racing enthusiast. Hemingway never sold the painting.*

"THE FARM"

When I first knew Miró he had very little money and very little to eat and he worked all day every day for nine months painting a very large and wonderful picture called "The Farm." He did not want to sell this

"The Farm" by Spanish painter Joan Miró. Hemingway purchased it for 5,000 francs ($240) in 1925 (National Gallery of Art, Washington, D.C.)

picture nor even to have it away from him. No one could look at it and not know it had been painted by a great painter and when you are painting things that people must take on trust it is good to have something around that has taken as long to make as it takes a woman to make a child (a woman who isn't a woman can usually write her autobiography in a third of that time) and that shows even fools that you are a great painter in terms that they understand.

After Miró had painted "The Farm" and after James Joyce had written *Ulysses* they had a right to expect people to trust the further things they did even when the people did not understand them and they have both kept on working very hard.

If you have painted "The Farm" or if you have written *Ulysses,* and then keep on working very hard afterwards, you do not need an Alice B. Toklas.

Finally everyone had to sell everything and if Miró was to have a dealer he had to let "The Farm" go with the other pictures. But Shipman, who found him the dealer, made the dealer put a price on it and agree to sell it to him. This was probably the only good business move that Shipman ever did in his life. But doing a good business move must have made him uncomfortable because he came to me the same day and said, "Hem, you should have *The Farm.* I do not love anything as much as you care for that picture and you ought to have it."

I argued against this explaining to him that it was not only how much I cared about it. There was the value to consider.

"It is going to be worth much more than we will ever have, Evan. You have no idea what it will be worth," I told him.

"I don't care about that," he said. "If it's money I'll shoot you dice for it. Let the dice decide about the money. You'll never sell it anyway."

"I have no right to shoot. You're shooting against yourself."

"Let the dice decide the money," Shipman insisted. "If I lose it will be mine. Let the dice show."

So we rolled dice and I won and made the first payment. We agreed to pay five thousand francs for *The Farm* and that was four thousand two hundred and fifty francs more than I had ever paid for a picture. The picture naturally stayed with the dealer.

When it was time to make the last payment the dealer came around and was very pleased because there was no money in the house or in the bank. If we did not pay the money that day he kept the picture. Dos Passos, Shipman and I finally borrowed the money around various bars and restaurants, got the picture and brought it home in a taxi. The dealer felt very bad because he had already been offered four times what we were paying. But we explained to him as it is so often explained to you in France, that business is business.

In the open taxi the wind caught the big canvas as though it were a sail and we made the taxi driver crawl along. At home we hung it and everyone looked at it and was very happy. I would not trade it for any picture in the world. Miró came in and looked at it and said, "I am very content that you have *The Farm*."

When I see him now he says, "I am always content, *tu sais*, that you have *The Farm*."

It has in it all that you feel about Spain when you are there and all that you feel when you are away and cannot go there. No one else has been able to paint these two very opposing things. Although Juan Gris painted it how it is when you know that you will never go there. Picasso is very different. Picasso is a business man. So were some of the greatest painters that ever lived. But this is too long now and the thing to do is look at the picture: not write about it.

F. Scott Fitzgerald at the time of his first meeting with Hemingway in Paris

---

F. Scott Fitzgerald, author of The Great Gatsby *(1925), met Hemingway in the Dingo Bar in April 1925 and attempted to promote his new friend's career through this review, one of the few written for Hemingway's first American book. From Fitzgerald, "'How to Waste Material—A Note on My Generation': Essay and Review of Ernest Hemingway's* In Our Time," The Bookman, *63 (May 1926), pp. 262–265.*

"In Our Time" consists of fourteen stories, short and long, with fifteen vivid miniatures interpolated between them. When I try to think of any contemporary American short stories as good as "Big Two-Hearted River", the last one in the book, only Gertrude Stein's "Melanctha", Anderson's "The Egg", and Lardner's "Golden Honeymoon" come to mind. It is the account of a boy on a fishing trip—he hikes, pitches his tent, cooks dinner, sleeps, and next morning casts for trout. Nothing more—but I read it with the most breathless unwilling interest I have experienced since Conrad first bent my reluctant eyes upon the sea.

The hero, Nick, runs through nearly all the stories, until the book takes on almost an autobiographical tint—in fact "My Old Man", one of the two in which this element seems entirely absent, is the least successful of all. Some of the stories show influences but they are invariably absorbed and transmuted, while in "My Old Man" there is an echo of Anderson's way of thinking in those sentimental "horse stories", which inaugurated his respectability and also his decline four years ago.

But with "The Doctor and the Doctor's Wife", "The End of Something", "The Three Day Blow", "Mr. and Mrs. Elliot", and "Soldier's Home" you are immediately aware of something temperamentally new. In the first of these a man is backed down by a half breed

Exterior and interior of the Dingo, 10 rue Delambre, where Hemingway first met F. Scott Fitzgerald in May 1925

Indian after committing himself to a fight. The quality of humiliation in the story is so intense that it immediately calls up every such incident in the reader's past. Without the aid of a comment or a pointing finger one knows exactly the sharp emotion of young Nick who watches the scene.

The next two stories describe an experience at the last edge of adolescence. You are constantly aware of the continual snapping of ties that is going on around Nick. In the half stewed, immature conversation before the fire you watch the awakening of that vast unrest that descends upon the emotional type at about eighteen. Again there is not a single recourse to exposition. As in "Big Two-Hearted River", a picture–sharp, nostalgic, tense–develops before your eyes. When the picture is complete a light seems to snap out, the story is over. There is no tail, no sudden change of pace at the end to throw into relief what has gone before.

Nick leaves home penniless; you have a glimpse of him lying wounded in the street of a battered Italian town, and later of a love affair with a nurse on a hospital roof in Milan. Then in one of the best of the stories he is home again. The last glimpse of him is when his mother asks him, with all the bitter world in his heart, to kneel down beside her in the dining room in Puritan prayer.

Anyone who first looks through the short interpolated sketches will hardly fail to read the stories themselves. "The Garden at Mons" and "The Barricade" are profound essays upon the English officer, written on a postage stamp. "The King of Greece's Tea Party", "The Shooting of the Cabinet Ministers", and "The Cigar-store Robbery" particularly fascinated me, as they did when Edmund Wilson first showed them to me in an earlier pamphlet, over two years ago.

Disregard the rather ill considered blurbs upon the cover. It is sufficient that here is no raw food served up by the railroad restaurants of California and Wisconsin. In the best of these dishes there is not a bit to spare. And many of us who have grown weary of admonitions to "watch this man or that" have felt a sort of renewal of excitement at these stories wherein Ernest Hemingway turns a corner into the street.

D. H. Lawrence, best known as the author of Lady Chatterley's Lover *(1928), wrote the following review of the English edition of* In Our Time *(London: Cape, 1926) for* The Calendar of Modern Literature, *4 (April 1927), pp. 72–73.*

In Our Time is the last of the four American books, and Mr. Hemingway has accepted the goal.

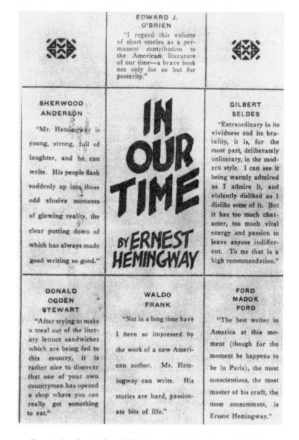

Dust jacket for the first of Hemingway's books to be published in America. He disliked the design, told Liveright that massing these blurbs "put the reader on the defensive," and later cited this jacket as one of his reasons for abandoning Boni & Liveright as his publisher.

He keeps on making flights, but he has no illusion about landing anywhere. He knows it will be nowhere every time.

In Our Time calls itself a book of stories, but it isn't that. It is a series of successive sketches from a man's life, and makes a fragmentary novel. The first scenes, by one of the big lakes in America–probably Superior–are the best; when Nick is a boy. Then come fragments of war–on the Italian front. Then a soldier back home, very late, in the little town way west in Oklahoma. Then a young American and wife in post-war Europe; a long sketch about an American jockey in Milan and Paris; then Nick is back again in the Lake Superior region, getting off the train at a burnt-out town, and tramping across the empty country to camp by a trout-stream. Trout is the one passion life has left him–and this won't last long.

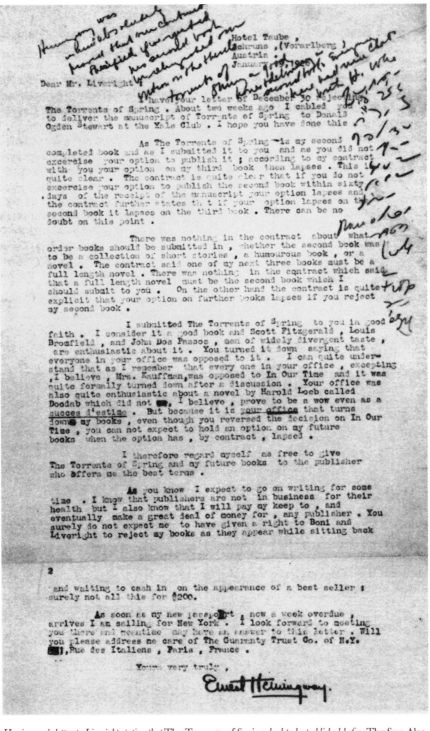

Hemingway's letter to Liveright stating that The Torrents of Spring *had to be published before* The Sun Also Rises, *with Liveright's notes from his meeting with Hemingway on 10 February 1926 (Louis Henry Cohn Collection, University of Delaware)*

It is a short book: and it does not pretend to be about one man. But it is. It is as much as we need know of the man's life. The sketches are short, sharp, vivid, and most of them excellent. (The "mottoes" in front seem a little affected.) And these few sketches are enough to create the man and all his history: we need know no more.

Nick is a type one meets in the more wild and woolly regions of the United States. He is the remains of the lone trapper and cowboy. Nowadays he is educated, and through with everything. It is a state of *conscious,* accepted indifference to everything except freedom from work and the moment's interest. Mr. Hemingway does it extremely well. Nothing matters. Everything happens. One wants to keep oneself loose. Avoid one thing only: getting connected up. Don't get connected up. If you get held by anything, break it. Don't be held. Break it, and get away. Don't get away with the idea of getting somewhere else. Just get away, for the sake of getting away. Beat it! "Well, boy, I guess I'll beat it." Ah, the pleasure in saying that!

Mr. Hemingway's sketches, for this reason, are excellent: so short, like striking a match, lighting a brief sensational cigarette, and it's over. His young love-affair ends as one throws a cigarette-end away. "It isn't fun any more."–"Everything's gone to hell inside me."

It is really honest. And it explains a great deal of sentimentality. When a thing has gone to hell inside you, your sentimentalism tries to pretend it hasn't. But Mr. Hemingway is through with the sentimentalism. "It isn't fun any more. I guess I'll beat it."

And he beats it, to somewhere else. In the end he'll be a sort of tramp, endlessly moving on for the sake of moving away from where he is. This is a negative goal, and Mr. Hemingway is really good, because he's perfectly straight about it. He is like Krebs, in that devastating Oklahoma sketch: he doesn't love anybody, and it nauseates him to have to pretend he does. He doesn't even *want* to love anybody; he doesn't want to go anywhere, he doesn't want to do anything. He wants just to lounge around and maintain a healthy state of nothingness inside himself, and an attitude of negation to everything outside himself. And why shouldn't he, since that is exactly and sincerely what he feels? If he really *doesn't* care, then why should he care? Anyhow, he doesn't.

Hemingway reacted to an unlocated assessment that Fitzgerald wrote of the stories in In Our Time. *His signature in the following letter is a joke: "Yogi" is a character in* The Torrents of Spring, *and "Liveright" refers to Hemingway's publisher, Horace Liveright. From* Selected Letters, *pp. 180–183.*

c. 24 December 1925

Dear Scott: . . .

Your rating of I.O.T. stories very interesting. The way I like them as it seems now, without re-reading is Grade I (Big 2 Hearted. Indian Camp. 1st ¶ and last ¶ of Out of Season. Soldier's Home) Hell I cant group them. Why did you leave out My Old Man? That's a good story, always seemed to me, though not the thing I'm shooting for. It belongs to another categorie along with the bull fight story and the 50 Grand. The kind that are easy for me to write.

Cat in the Rain wasnt about Hadley. I know that you and Zelda always thought it was. When I wrote that we were at Rapallo but Hadley was 4 months pregnant with Bumby. The Inn Keeper was the one at Cortina D'Ampezzo and the man and the girl were a harvard kid and his wife that I'd met at Genoa. Hadley never made a speech in her life about wanting a baby because she had been told various things by her doctor and I'd–no use going into all that.

The only story in which Hadley figures is Out of Season which was an almost literal transcription of what happened. Your ear is always more acute when you have been upset by a row of any sort, mine I mean, and when I came in from the unproductive fishing trip I wrote that story right off on the typewriter without punctuation. I meant it to be a tragic about the drunk of a guide because I reported him to the hotel owner–the one who appears in Cat in the Rain–and he fired him and as that was the last job he had in town and he was quite drunk and very desperate, hanged himself in the stable. At that time I was writing the In Our Time chapters and I wanted to write a tragic story *without* violence. So I didnt put in the hanging. Maybe that sounds silly. I didn't think the story needed it. . . .

The ear that gets pushed is (Referring Battler) the stump.

McAlmon is a son of a bitch with a mind like an ingrowing toe nail. I'm through defending that one. I still feel sorry for him but damned little. After I called him on you he went around for two nights talking on the subject of what a swine I was, how *he* had done everything for me, started me off etc. (i.e. sold out an edition each of that lousy little book and In Our Time at 15 francs and 40 francs a copy. I not receiving a sou. The only books he ever sold of all the books he's published) and that all I did was exploit people emotionally.

I've defended the lousy little toe nail paring for 3 years against everybody because I knew his horribly unhappy English arrangement etc. But am through now. Am going to write a Mr. and Mrs. Elliot on him. Might as well give his emotional exploitation story some foundation.

Seem to be in a mood of Christ like bitterness this A.M. Have swell piano in her room for Hadley and she's practicing. Played poker last night and drank too much beer. 7 bottles. Won 158,000 Kronen. Makes about $2.35.

No fairies in Vorarlberg anyway.

Will report in full on Dostoevsky.

I think MacLeishes and Murphys are swell. Also Fitzgeralds. . . .

Review of In Our Type from Chicago Post says all of it obviously not fiction but simply descriptive of passages in life of new Chicago author. God what a life I must have led.

Am reading Peter Simple by Capt. Marryat. Havent read it since I was a kid. Great book. He wrote 4 great books. Frank Mildmay or the Naval Officer. Midshipman Easy. Peter Simple and Snarleyow or the Dog Fiend. He wrote a lot of kids books in later life and people get them mixed up. You ought to read Peter Simple.

If you want to read about war read any of those 1st 3. . . .

Original ending of story had dose of clapp (referring to Very Short Story) instead of gonorreaha but I didn't know whether clap had two ps or one, so changed it to gonoccoci. The hell I did. Try and get it.

(This is a piece of slang I invented down here). Hope you have a swell Christmas.

Yrs. always
Yogi Liveright.

Ernest Walsh was a minor American poet and co-editor (with Ethel Moorhead) of This Quarter. *Hemingway had served as an unpaid advisor and literary scout for the little magazine, and he published two short stories in it—"Big Two-Hearted River" and "The Undefeated." Walsh's poem about Hemingway was published in the second number of the magazine (Autumn-Winter 1925–1926), p. 67.*

ERNEST HEMINGWAY

Papa soldier pugilist bullfighter
Writer gourmet lionhead aesthete
He's a big guy from near Chicago
Where they make the shoes bigger and
It's a good thing that because he aint
Got french feet Napoleon and him
Wouldn't have said much together
He'd have pulled Buonaparte's nose
And absolutely ruined french history
In Solomon's winy days he'd abeen in court
A few times and the King of Israel would have
Said *This kid knows a few things* and given him
Two plump dancing jewesses to lean on
While he ordered up a fat roasted calf
For in those days Kings preferred art to business

Chapter Two: 1926–1929

1926

9 February	Hemingway arrives in New York. After meeting with Liveright to break formally with that publisher, Hemingway consults Scribners' Maxwell Perkins on 11 February.
17 February	Hemingway signs a contract to publish *The Torrents of Spring* and *The Sun Also Rises* with Scribners.
20 February	Hemingway sails on the *Roosevelt* for France. Robert Benchley and Dorothy Parker are also on board.
12 April	Hemingway accepts Jonathan Cape's offer to publish *In Our Time* in England. Cape remains Hemingway's British publisher thereafter.
28 May	*The Torrents of Spring* is published in New York. Hemingway comes from Spain to join Hadley and Bumby at Antibes. Fitzgerald reads the typescript of *The Sun Also Rises* and sends Hemingway a ten-page critique.
ca. 12 August	Following Hemingway's affair with Pauline Pfeiffer, he and Hadley set up separate residences.
22 October	*The Sun Also Rises* is published.
18 November	Hemingway promises to give Hadley all royalties from *The Sun Also Rises* and asks her to begin divorce proceedings.

1927

14 April	The Hemingways' divorce becomes final.
10 May	Ernest and Pauline are married in Paris.
July	*The Atlantic Monthly* publishes "Fifty Grand," the first Hemingway story to appear in a major American magazine.
14 October	Scribners publishes Hemingway's second short-story collection, *Men Without Women*.

1928

March	Hemingway begins writing a novel about World War I.
April	The Hemingways vacation in Key West, Florida.
28 June	Pauline gives birth to the couple's first child, Patrick, in Kansas City.
30 July	Hemingway arrives in Wyoming for a hunting trip; it is his first visit to the American West.
20–22 August	Hemingway finishes the first draft of *A Farewell to Arms*.

17 November	The Hemingways and the Fitzgeralds attend the Princeton-Yale game.
December	Hemingway meets Ring Lardner in Perkins's office.
6 December	Dr. Clarence Hemingway commits suicide.

1929

25 January–February	Perkins travels to Key West to fish with Hemingway and to read the typescript of the author's new novel.
13 February	*Scribner's Magazine* offers $16,000 for the serial rights to *A Farewell to Arms*.
5 April	The Hemingways sail for France.
June	Hemingway is knocked down by Morley Callaghan while the two are boxing. In serving as timekeeper, Fitzgerald apparently let the round go too long, and Hemingway is livid.
29 June	The June issue of *Scribner's Magazine* is banned in Boston, because the second installment of *A Farewell to Arms* is judged to be obscene.
27 September	*A Farewell to Arms* is published in New York. It becomes a best-seller.
29 October	The market for stocks on the New York Stock Exchange crashes.
20–31 December	The Hemingways, the Fitzgeralds, John and Katy Dos Passos, Donald Ogden Stewart, and Dorothy Parker visit Gerald and Sara Murphy in Montana-Vernala, Switzerland.

In February 1926 Hemingway traveled to New York to end his short relationship with the publishing firm of Boni & Liveright. Fitzgerald had shared encouraging words about his publisher, Charles Scribner's Sons, with Hemingway, and during this trip Hemingway signed a new contract with Scribners to publish his parody, *The Torrents of Spring,* and his novel, *The Sun Also Rises.* With this contract Hemingway began a twenty-one-year association with Scribners editor Maxwell Perkins.

Following his return to France, Hemingway continued to revise *The Sun Also Rises* and work on new stories. In May, Scribners published *The Torrents of Spring,* and, although critics gave the book little attention and the number of copies sold was small, its publication marked the end of Hemingway's friendship with Anderson and the beginning of a new friendship with Gertrude Stein.

Since January Hemingway had also been having an affair with Pauline Pfeiffer, a wealthy American who worked for the Paris edition of *Vogue.* In July he and Hadley agreed to establish separate residences, and soon afterward she began divorce proceedings against Hemingway. As part of their divorce settlement Hemingway assigned to Hadley and their son the royalties from his forthcoming *The Sun Also Rises.* On 10 May 1927 Hemingway and Pauline were married.

The Sun Also Rises was published on 22 October 1926 and received generally favorable reviews. Most critics pointed out Hemingway's style—his "lean, athletic prose"—for special notice, and the novel created a sensation in Paris, where readers amused themselves by identifying the people who had been the models for Hemingway's characters. Through 1927 an increasing number of copies were sold, and writers of newspaper articles reported about undergraduates who were reading the novel for guidance in how to behave.

With the success of this novel American magazines began asking Hemingway to contribute stories. In 1927 *Atlantic Monthly* published "Fifty Grand," and *Scribner's Magazine* published "The Killers," "In Another Country," and "A Canary for One." On 14 October that year Scribners published *Men Without Women,* Hemingway's second short-story collection, which included those four stories as well as "Hills Like White Elephants," "Ten Indians," and "The Undefeated." Most reviews of this book were favorable, and, partly because of the publicity that *The Sun Also Rises* had generated, Scribners sold 16,835 copies in 1927, a good total for a short-story collection.

Hemingway began working on a novel about a revolutionary and his son in July 1927, but he abandoned this project in March 1928 to work on another novel based on his experiences during

World War I. In April the Hemingways sailed for the United States and spent six weeks in Key West, Florida, before traveling to Kansas City. On 27 June that year Pauline gave birth to Hemingway's second son, Patrick. After leaving his wife and newborn son at her parents' home in Piggott, Arkansas, on 25 July, Hemingway traveled to Sheridan, Wyoming, to fish, hunt, and finish his World War I novel. He completed the first draft by the end of August, and he and his wife decided to return to Key West, where he revised the novel.

On 6 December 1928 Hemingway's father, who was suffering from depression, high blood pressure, and insomnia, committed suicide. Thrust into the role of providing for his mother and siblings, Hemingway established a trust fund for them with the $16,000 that *Scribner's Magazine* paid him for serial rights to his novel. Publications of installments began in the May issue and attracted many readers, but Hemingway was upset when the June issue was banned in Boston because of his graphic presentation of Frederic Henry and Catherine Barkley's relationship.

In April the Hemingways returned to Paris, where he revised galley proofs for the book. There he also boxed with Canadian novelist and fellow Scribners author Morley Callaghan. In one of their matches Callaghan knocked Hemingway down–apparently when Fitzgerald, who was serving as timekeeper, let the round continue too long. Newspaper reports of the incident were published in December, and when Hemingway accused Callaghan of spreading the story, their friendship ended.

On 27 September 1929 *A Farewell to Arms* was published, and it became Hemingway's first bestseller, with more than 60,000 copies sold by the end of the year. Reviewers were nearly unanimous in praising Hemingway's narrative of the love story and his skill in presenting the war, especially the retreat from Caporetto.

After reading The Torrents of Spring, *Anderson wrote the following letter to Hemingway. From* Sherwood Anderson: Selected Letters, *ed. Charles E. Modlin (Knoxville: University of Tennessee Press, 1984), pp. 78–80.*

[14 June 1926]

Dear Ernest Hemingway,

I bought a farm at Troutdale, Va–had just written you a note suggesting that you and Hadley stop here on your way to Arkansas. Thought you might be going this summer.

However I hadn't your address. All my letters files still packed. If you weren't coming over soon, I wanted to send a young fellow–friend of mine from California–to see you. I'm giving him a note to you. His name is Church.

About the book–your letter–all your letters to me these last two or three years–it's like this. Damn it, man, you are so final–so patronizing. You always do speak to me like a master to a pupil. It must be Paris–the literary life. You didn't seem like that when I knew you.

You speak so regretfully, tenderly, of giving me a punch. You sound like Uncle Ezra. Come out of it, man. I pack a little wallop myself. I've been middleweight champion. You seem to forget that.

Honestly, man, you sound like a chap I met once in Cleveland. He also had been drinking and talking with literary guys. He went home and wrote an article. The whole gang worked on the Cleveland *Plain Dealer*. Then he came down to my hotel, still drunk, and cried on my shoulder.

"I tore the article up," he said. "Great Christ, it was good. After I wrote it I sat down and read it. I knew, if I published it, you would never write another word and no one would read you any more."

About the little plug I put in for you with Liveright. I'm sorry I even mentioned it. I've done the same for men I hated and I like you. The only reason I even spoke of it was to let you know I liked your work.

Tell the truth, I think the Scribner book will help me and hurt you. Spite of all you say, it's got the smarty tinge. You know it. Fitz & Dos must have baited you.

But in your turn now, man, don't get sore at me. If you are going to wallop, you've got to take yours. You started it. I didn't.

We are trying to build a house on our farm–in the Blue Ridge. If we have any money left in the fall, plan to come to Paris. Anyway when you start–for Arkansas–find out if we're here and if we are stop and see us. It's on the way to Arkansas all right–will prepare you some.

Sherwood Anderson

D'you ever hear of Kid McAllister–the nonpareil–that was me.

AUTHOR'S PREFACE.

Many critics commenting on a book of stories written by myself and published last fall remarked on how much whatever excellencies they detected in these stories resembled the excellencies of Mr. Sherwood Anderson. Having just read a novel by Mr. Anderson which was called, I believe, Dark Laughter and which is, I believe, generally acknowledged to be a masterpiece and being exceedingly impressed by what these critics had written I resolved to write henceforth exclusively in the manner of Mr. Anderson. The careful reader will see that in my attempt to write as Mr. Anderson writes I have failed most signally. It is therefore to his indulgence that I commend myself most diffidently.

Typescript of Hemingway's rejected preface and inscription for The Torrents of Spring. *Hemingway gave the typescript to the Fitzgeralds (F. Scott Fitzgerald Collection, Princeton University Library)*

Allen Tate, a member of the Fugitive group at Vanderbilt University, wrote the following review of The Torrents of Spring *for* The Nation, *123 (28 July 1926), pp. 89–90. Hemingway and Tate eventually met in Paris in 1928.*

The Spirituality of Roughnecks

Ernest Hemingway says he wrote this novel in ten days, and there is no reason for believing that Mr. Hemingway, besides being the best contemporary writer of eighteenth-century prose, is also a liar. The novel is short. But it would have done him or anybody else much credit had its author labored with its perfect style (perfect within honorable limitations) for ten months. "The Torrents of Spring" differs in important features from Mr. Hemingway's first American volume, published last autumn; its differences from "In Our Time" spring from a basically different intention.

"In Our Time" is naturalistic fiction done for purely creative ends. "The Torrents of Spring" grew out of a motive a little this side of that; its motive is satire and, if one may produce an undemonstrable but wholly convincing bit of internal evidence, its object is Sherwood Anderson's "Dark Laughter."

"Pamela" is still worth reading; "Joseph Andrews" is better worth reading. "Dark Laughter" is a good novel, but, like "Pamela," it contains emotion in excess of the facts, and "The Torrents of Spring" is better worth reading. Lacking, as Fielding did in "Joseph Andrews," a motive originally creative, Mr. Hemingway has nevertheless written a novel which is on its own account, irrespective of momentary aim, a small masterpiece of American fiction.

Mr. Hemingway's consistently limited performance is not generally due to missed intention. He knows what he wishes to do; he usually does it. His

```
THE TORRENTS OF SPRING


A Romantic Novel In Honor of The Passing Of

A Great Race.



By ERNEST HEMINGWAY.
```

To Scott and Zelda with love from Ernest.

```
And perhaps there is one reason why a
comic writer should of all others be
the least excused for deviating from
nature, since it may not be always
so easy for a serious poet to meet with
the great and the admirable; but life
everywhere furnishes an accurate observ-
er with the ridiculous.

                    Henry Fielding.
```

intention is fundamentally opposed to any other naturalism of the age. He gets his effects not by complete documentation but by the avoidance of explanatory statement; he keeps his explicit knowledge of the characters exactly equal to the reader's knowledge. Neither do the characters ever rationalize or generalize their successive predicaments. His naturalism is a modified naturalism, and its principles have become more and more unfamiliar since the influence of Zola caught up with the more difficult method of "Bouvard et Pecuchet" and obscured it; while Zola has actually instructed the American novel since Frank Norris, Flaubert has been simply admired. Mr. Hemingway, apparently careless about the choice of material, exercises the greatest zeal in isolating its significant aspects; his selective naturalism achieves its effects through indirect irony, the irony of suppressed comment. Few of his characters are fools; all

of them are Bouvards and Pecuchets in that their conduct is so arranged as to rouse the reader's sense of value to the appropriate judgement of it, while they are themselves immersed in a "pure present" and lack the power of generalizing it at all. "In Our Time" proved Hemingway to be a master of this irony. It is an irony preeminently fitted for sustained satire of the sort conspicuous in Defoe and Swift; and Hemingway's success with it in "The Torrents of Spring" is a triumph, but not a surprise.

The material of the story is slight and insignificant in outline; a summary would be impertinent here. But Scripps O'Neil, Mrs. Scripps, Yogi Johnson, the big Indian and the little Indian, "Brown's Beanery the Best by Test," the drinking club of the educated Indians whence Yogi hears the "dark Negro laughter" of the ebony bartender after he is kicked out for being not an Indian but a Swede—these characters and places focus

THE TORRENTS
OF SPRING

A ROMANTIC NOVEL
IN HONOR OF THE PASSING
OF A GREAT RACE

ERNEST HEMINGWAY
AUTHOR OF "IN OUR TIME"

Dust jacket for Hemingway's parody of Sherwood Anderson's Dark
Laughter. *The book was the first Hemingway published
with Scribners.*

the best genial satire of the "spirituality" of roughnecks,
the most deftly tempered ribaldry, and the most economically realized humor of disproportion that this
reviewer has read in American prose.

*The following is Anderson's account of his last meeting with
Hemingway. From* Sherwood Anderson's Memoirs: A
Critical Edition, *ed. Ray Lewis White (Chapel Hill: Univer-
sity of North Carolina Press, 1969), pp. 462–465.*

Faulkner and Hemingway

I was in a southern town, sitting with him, one
evening, before the cathedral, in New Orleans, while he
contended, with entire seriousness, that the cross
between the white man and the negro woman always
resulted, after the first crossing, in sterility. He spoke of
the cross between the jack and the mare that produced

the mule and said that, as between the white man and
the negro woman, it was like that.

However there was never any doubt in my mind
about Faulkner. He was, from the first, a real writer. He
had the touch and there was always in him something
finer and certainly more generous than, for example, in
Hemingway.

I speak of the two men together because it happened that I knew both men before either had published and it was through my efforts that both first got
published.

It was a thing Hemingway couldn't stand. When
he began to write he began with the short story and I
had already published my *Winesburg, Ohio.* I had published also my *Horses and Men* and my *Triumph of the Egg,*
and I dare say more than one critic, in speaking of his
work, attributed his impulse to me. They had even perhaps intimated that I was his master.

It is a thing that happens to every writer when he
begins. My own impulse had been attributed to Dreiser,
to the Russians, whom I had, at that time, never read.
Anyway it is sure that, if others had said that I had
shown Hemingway the way, I had not said so. I
thought, as I did in the case of Faulkner, that he had his
own gift that had nothing particularly to do with me.
What man doesn't look to others? I am sure I constantly do.

In the case of Hemingway there may have been
something else. Having a very great talent, there are
men who say that he is incapable of friendship.

At any rate I had taken it for granted that we
were friends when he went off to Paris and later, I am
told, he attributed what happened to the influence of
Scott Fitzgerald, and there is even a story, born in the
brain of Hemy, that, wanting to leave the firm of Boni
and Liveright, and that, figuring that they would not
stand for an attack upon me, I being a special little pet
of that firm, etc., he wrote the book to break his connection with the firm.

If I had ever been a special pet of the Liveright
firm I wish someone had let me know of it. I might
have got more money from them.

I got a letter from Hemy. This after he had written and published the book called *The Torrents of Spring,*
and I thought it the most completely patronizing letter I
had ever received.

In the letter he spoke of what had happened as
something fatal to me. He had, he said, written the
book on an impulse, having only six weeks to do it. It
was intended to bring to an end, once and for all, the
notion that there was any worth in my own work. This,
he said, was a thing he had hated doing, because of his
personal regard for me, etc., but that he had done it in

the interest of literature. Literature, I was to understand, was bigger than both of us.

There was something in the letter that was gigantic. It was a kind of funeral oration delivered over my grave. It was so raw, so pretentious, so patronizing, that it was amusing but I was filled with wonder. Just what I said to him, in return, I don't remember. It was something to the effect that I thought it foolish that, while there was so much to be done in writing, we writers should devote our time to the attempt to kill each other off. In the letter he had used a prize fighting term, speaking of the knockout blow he had given me, and in my answer I think I did say that I had always thought of myself as a pretty good middle weight and that I doubted his ever being able to make the heavy weight class.

However I can't be sure. I kept no copy of my letter. I find that I am often inclined to think of what I consider rather clever replies I make long after the event.

I did not see Hemingway for a long time after the above incident. When he had gone to Paris I had given him a note to my friend Gertrude Stein, with whom he was also, for several years, friends. Later she told me, in regard to the above incident, that Hemingway's difficulty was that I had written two stories, "I'm a Fool" and "I Want to Know Why," and that he could not bear the thought of my having written them. She suggested that he had, in his own mind, staked out the whole field of sports for himself. He could not bear, she said, having anyone else write of sports.

When he had gone to Paris I had given Hemingway several letters to friends there and among others one to Mr. Ralph Church, who was, at that time, a student at Oxford (he was specializing in philosophy), who ran over to Paris and, for a year or two, he and Hemingway were much together.

And then, after several years, I came to Paris and there was Church and there was also Hemingway and Church was amused. He used to go to Hemingway saying, "Sherwood is in town. Why don't you go to see him?" and, when he had said it, he told me that Hemingway always declared his real friendship for me.

"I am going to see him today," he said, each time when the matter was brought up, but he did not come.

It came to my last day in Paris and I was sitting in my room, having packed. Church had told him of my plan to depart and there was a sudden knock on the door of my hotel room and there he was.

He stood in the doorway.

"How about a drink?" he asked and I followed him down a stairway and across a street.

We went into a small bar.

"What will you have?"

"Beer."

Sherwood Anderson

"And you?"

"Beer."

"Well, here's how."

"Here's how."

He turned and walked rapidly away. It was the sum of what happened between us after our having known each other well in Chicago, after what I had thought of as an old friendship, and, in fancy, I can still see the man, after the "here's how" and after the beer had been gulped, as he hurried away.

Hemingway cut the first fifteen pages of the typescript of The Sun Also Rises *per Fitzgerald's suggestion. Perkins was not convinced by Hemingway's arguments about the reference to Henry James, for whom the novel uses only the name "Henry." From* The Only Thing That Counts, *pp. 40–41.*

Dear Mr. Perkins=. . .

I believe that, in the proofs, I will start the book at what is now page 16 in the Mss. There is nothing in those first sixteen pages that does not come out, or is explained, or re-stated in the rest of the book—or is unnecessary to state. I think it will move much faster

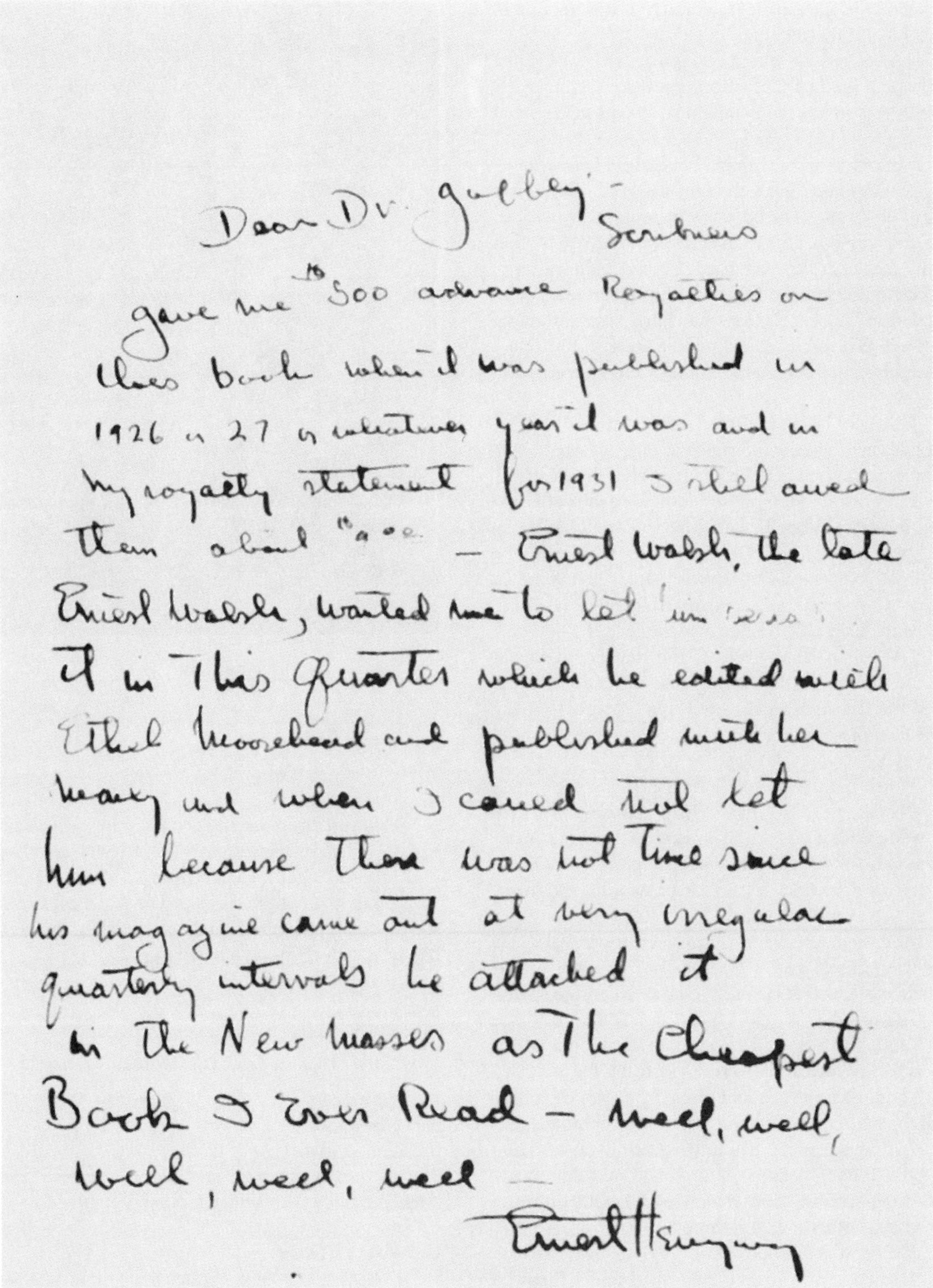

Dear Dr. Guffey –

Scribners gave me $500 advance Royalties on this book when it was published in 1926 or 27 or whatever year it was and in my royalty statement for 1931 I still owed them about $ .00 — Ernest Walsh, the late Ernest Walsh, wanted me to let him serialize it in This Quarter which he edited with Ethel Moorehead and published with her money and when I could not let him because there was not time since his magazine came out at very irregular quarterly intervals he attacked it in The New Masses as The Cheapest Book I Ever Read — well, well, well, well, well —

Ernest Hemingway

Inscription in Dr. Carlos Guffey's copy of The Torrents of Spring, *with Hemingway's comments about poet Ernest Walsh, who edited* This Quarter *(Sotheby Parke Bernet, Goodwin Collection, Item 133, 29 March 1989)*

Hadley, John ("Bumby"), and Ernest Hemingway in Schruns, Austria, 1926

from the start that way. Scott agrees with me. He suggested various things in it to cut out—in those first chapters—which I have never liked—but I think it is better to just lop that off and he agrees. He will probably write you what he thinks about it—the book in general. He said he was very excited by it.

As for the Henry James thing—I haven't the second part of the Ms. here—it is over at Scott's—so I can't recall the wording. But I believe that it is a reference to some accident that is generally known to have happened to Henry James in his youth. To me Henry James is as historical a name as Byron, Keats, or any other great writer about whose life, personal and literary, books have been written. I do not believe that the reference is sneering, or if it is, it is not the writer who is sneering as the writer does not appear in this book. Henry James is dead and left no descendants to be hurt, nor any wife, and therefore I feel that he is as dead as he will ever be. I wish I had the ms. here to see exactly what it said. If Henry James never had an accident of that sort I should think it would be libelous to say he had no matter how long he were dead. But if he did I do not see how it can affect him—now he is dead. As I

recall Gorton and Barnes are talking humourously around the subject of Barnes' mutilation and to them Henry James is not a man to be insulted or protected from insult but simply an historical example. I remember there was something about an airplane and a bicycle—but that had nothing to do with James and was simply a non-sequitor. Scott said he saw nothing off-color about it.

Until the proofs come I do not want to think about the book as I am trying to write some stories and I want to see the proofs, when they come, from as new and removed a viewpoint as possible.

Up till now I have heard nothing about a story called—An Alpine Idyll—that I mailed to you sometime the first week in May. Did you ever receive it? I have another copy which I will send if you did not. In Madrid I wrote three stories ranging from 1400 to 3,000 words. I haven't had them re-typed and sent on as I was waiting word about The Alpine Idyll.

What is the news about Torrents? Have any copies been mailed to me as yet?

Could you send me a check for $200. in a registered letter to the Guaranty Trust Co. address? It was very pleasant to get your letter and learn that you liked the book.

Yours very sincerely
Ernest Hemingway

Villa Paquita
Juan les Pins
(A.M.)
June 5. 1926

The following review of The Sun Also Rises *was written by Ernest Boyd for* The Independent, *117 (20 November 1926), p. 594.*

Readers and Writers

Last June, when "The Torrents of Spring" was published, it was my pleasure to confess that the author, Ernest Hemingway, had enabled me to distinguish him from the surrounding Americans in Paris who contribute to esoteric Franco-American magazines, and now and then publish a volume in France which would not pass the vigilant scrutiny of American or English printers. The fact that one very great book, to wit, James Joyce's "Ulysses," was published in that manner had never converted me to the notion that any book printed in English in France must necessarily be

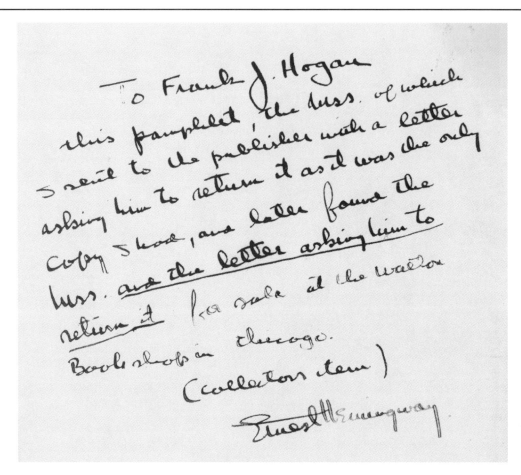

Inscription in book collector Frank J. Hogan's copy of Today Is Friday *(Englewood, N.J.: As Stable, 1926)*

the masterpiece of an expatriate and misunderstood genius. When Mr. Hemingway brought out his first volume of short stories, "In Our Times" (Liveright), I felt that anything he had to say might well be said over the imprint of an American publisher, and that he ought on no account to become the victim of that spurious fame attaching to books published in France and barred from this country.

With remarkable foresight Mr. Hemingway made the supreme sacrifice for an American of his generation; he left Paris for a few weeks and rested his feet upon the barren soil of his native land. He rested them long enough to interest one of the oldest and most dignified publishing houses in America in two manuscripts, of which the second, "The Sun Also Rises" (Scribner's), has just appeared in direct and apostolic succession to "The Torrents of Spring." The latter, I may say, was regarded coldly by those who take their Sherwood Anderson straight, and it was even said that the author was that creature who is sharper than a serpent's tooth, namely, a thankless child. Mr. Hemingway, it seems, was an admirer, nay, a disciple, of Mr. Anderson, and in parodying him, he was biting the literary hand that had been outstretched to feed him at the outset of a great career. It was my impartial opinion that this base ingratitude was a hopeful sign of conversion.

"The Sun Also Rises" is a first offering from the convert, for which I return thanks unto the gods who thus touch the hearts of wayward men. The aura of æstheticism no longer lingers about Mr. Hemingway. Innocent of his past, one would never guess that he once toyed with synthetic heresies and bowed down to æsthetic idols of wood and stone. What one felt as a potential quality of certain stories in "In Our Times" is here realized with masterly cunning. It all looks so simple! He hasn't even a story to tell. There are no witty

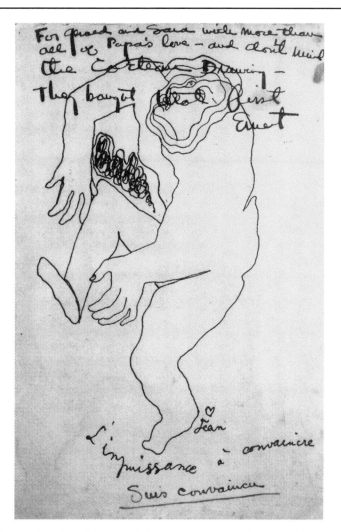

Hemingway's inscription in Gerald and Sara Murphy's copy of Today Is Friday. *The Murphys were wealthy American expatriates and friends of Hemingway, John Dos Passos, and F. Scott Fitzgerald (Maurice Neville Collection,)*

and no purple patches. Yet, when the book is finished, the reader has heard a story, his mind has been titillated by something which must obviously have been the author's sense of humor, and flashes of scenes remain in the memory despite his refusal to do more than hint at what he sees.

In the first place, Ernest Hemingway writes dialogue so effectively that he has merely to allow one to hear the sound of a character's voice in order to plant him vividly before the reader. Those familiar with the particular world of Paris which is the axis of the narrative will further note with amusement how Mr. Hemingway has managed to introduce several easily identified people, of minor importance intrinsically, but of deep importance as typical phenomena. Robert

Cohn, who learned boxing "painfully and thoroughly to counteract the feeling of inferiority and shyness he had felt on being treated as a Jew at Princeton," is something more than an impression of a certain American editor in exile. His portrait becomes at Mr. Hemingway's hands an amazing character study.

Another figure who lives intensely in these pages, although her activities consist mainly of having drinks, lovers, and passionate moments of sincerity with the author's *alter ego,* is Lady Ashley, a perfect product of that postwar world of which Mr. Hemingway is the brilliant chronicler. After all that we have suffered from novelists intent on describing hard-boiled flappers, Ernest Hemingway comes along with his modern version of *la femme de trente ans,* and we know more about the eternal

Duff Twysden, the model for Lady Brett Ashley in The Sun Also Rises

drinks and dishes consumed in the course of that hectic week. All these matters are equal in the sight of Mr. Hemingway, and with the utmost gravity, certain in managing his effects, he carefully records exactly what each person drinks or does.

The technique of this book is fascinating. When one is not swept along by astonishing dialogue, subtle, obvious, profound, and commonplace,–but always alive,–one is listening to careful enumeration of little facts whose cumulative effect is to give them the importance of remarkable incidents. The description of Pamplona during the festival week is reporting of the most laconic type. We are told what preparations are made, we see the bulls being unloaded from the train, the peasants swarming in from the countryside, and we are plunged into tavern brawls and carouses. At no time does the author attempt to "write up" his scenes, but in the end one has the feeling of having spent the week there.

In the midst of all this Mr. Hemingway never loses sight of his psychological *déracinés,* who so strongly merge their highly complicated modern selves in the stream of elementary consciousness. Remote as they seem from the setting, they are a part of it. Fishing in Spain or drinking at Zelli's, these American men express themselves, the curious syncopated rhythm of their lives, just as Frances, the American girl, endures in a nagging scene outside a café, and Brett, the English-woman, bares her soul in fierce

feminine, model 1926, than ever before. If there are people who wonder why six cocktails grow where one grew before, this book will tell them. The consumption of liquor to the square inch in "The Sun Also Rises" reaches maximum pressure, and just as these characters would not exist without their frequent and generous libations, so, I think, Mr. Hemingway's story could not be told within the limits of what is so preposterously known in this country as "Law Enforcement"–meaning usually the illegal imposition of one measure.

Mr. Hemingway is not merely a student of expatriate alcoholism, he is a bullfighting connoisseur, and when his group of tragic comedians arrive in Pamplona for the *fiesta,* he dwells with an expert's affection upon every aspect of the affair without once giving the impression that he is determined to show how much he knows. He enters into the technicalities and leaves the picturesque to emerge as best it can, and it does emerge more truly and impressively than from any bravura passage. The reason being that the technical details of a bullfight are no more and no less to the author than the details of the innumerable

American humorist Donald Ogden Stewart, the partial model for Bill Gorton in The Sun Also Rises

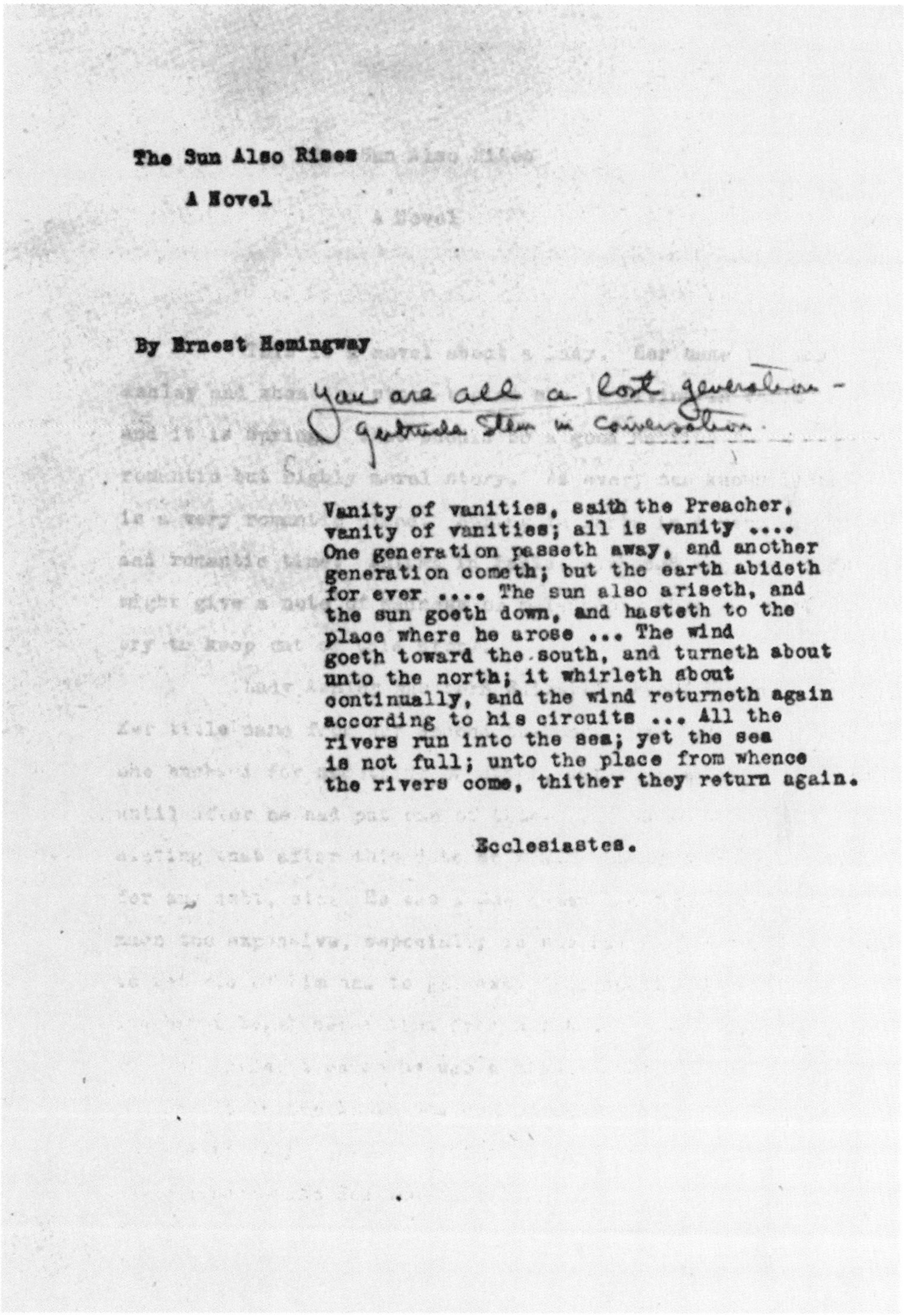

The Sun Also Rises

A Novel

By Ernest Hemingway

You are all a lost generation –
Gertrude Stein in conversation.

Vanity of vanities, saith the Preacher,
vanity of vanities; all is vanity ....
One generation passeth away, and another
generation cometh; but the earth abideth
for ever .... The sun also ariseth, and
the sun goeth down, and hasteth to the
place where he arose ... The wind
goeth toward the south, and turneth about
unto the north; it whirleth about
continually, and the wind returneth again
according to his circuits ... All the
rivers run into the sea; yet the sea
is not full; unto the place from whence
the rivers come, thither they return again.

Ecclesiastes.

Typescript for the title page for Hemingway's first novel (Hemingway Collection, John F. Kennedy Library). The epigraph from Stein provided a phrase to identify the writers of Hemingway's generation. See his "Une Génération Perdu" in A Moveable Feast *(New York: Scribners, 1964).*

Cayetano Ordoñez
"Niño de la Palma"

FIESTA

I saw him for the first time in his room at the Hotel Quintana in Pamplona. ~~Quintana~~ We met Quintana on the stairs as Bill and I were coming up to the room to get the wine bag to take to the bull fight ~~comida~~. "Come on," said Quintana. "Would you like to meet Niño de la Palma?" He was in room number eight, I knew what it was like inside, a gloomy room with the two beds separated by monastic partitions. Bill had lived in ~~there room~~ and gotten out to take a single room when the fiesta started. Quintana knocked and opened the door. ~~He introduced us.~~ The boy stood very straight and unsmiling in his white shirt and good pants he was dressed all except his coat and his hair had just been wound. He nodded seeming far away ~~unsmiling~~ and dignified when we shook hands. Quintana made a little speech about what great aficionados we were and how we wanted to wish him luck. Niño turned to me. He was the best looking kid I have ever seen. "You go to see the bull fight," he said in English

First and last pages of the manuscript for The Sun Also Rises *(Hemingway Collection, John F. Kennedy Library)*

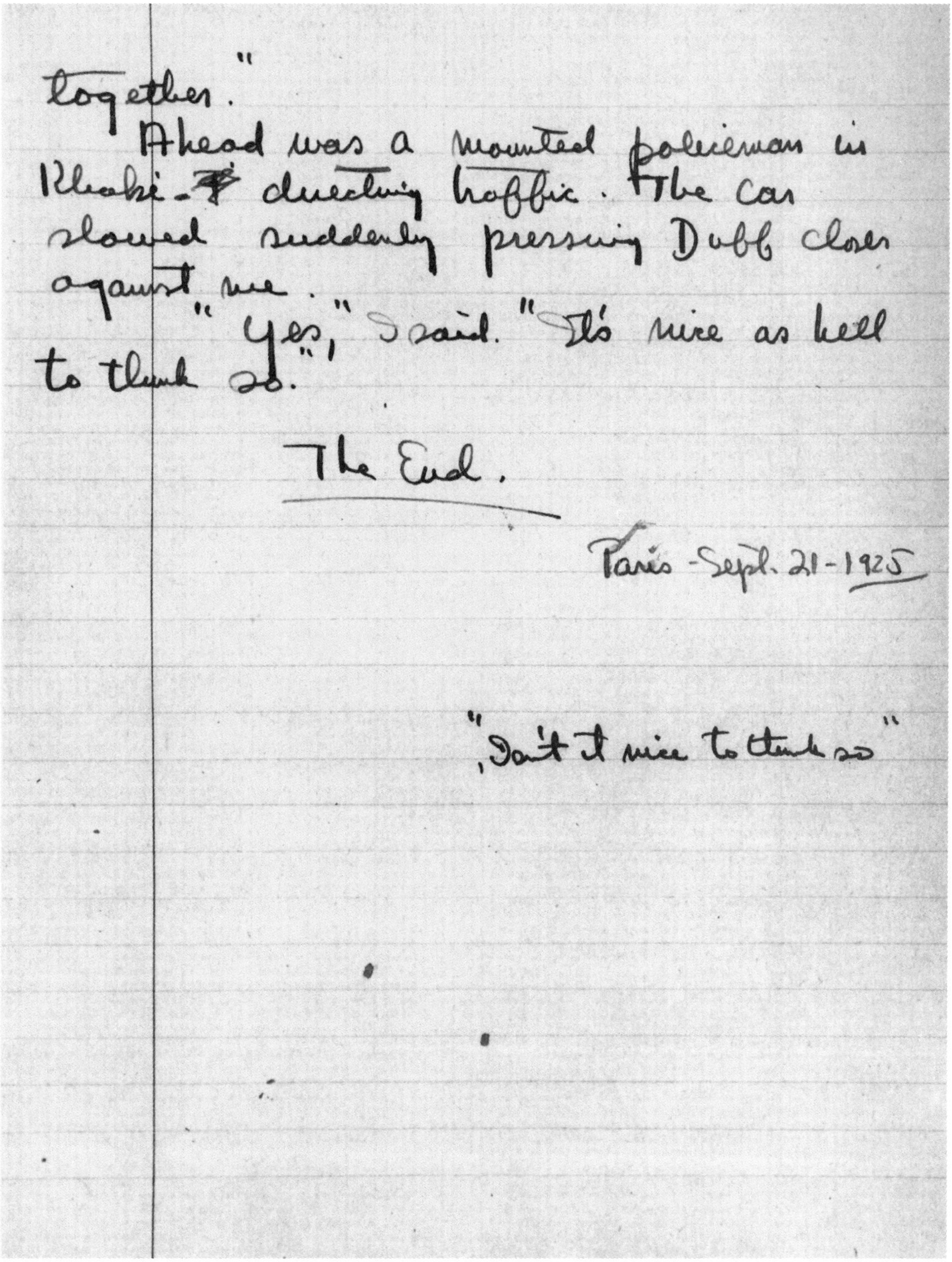

together."

Ahead was a mounted policeman in Khaki — directing traffic. The car slowed suddenly pressing Dubb closer against me.

"Yes," I said. "It's nice as hell to think so."

The End.

Paris - Sept. 21 - 1925

"Isn't it nice to think so"

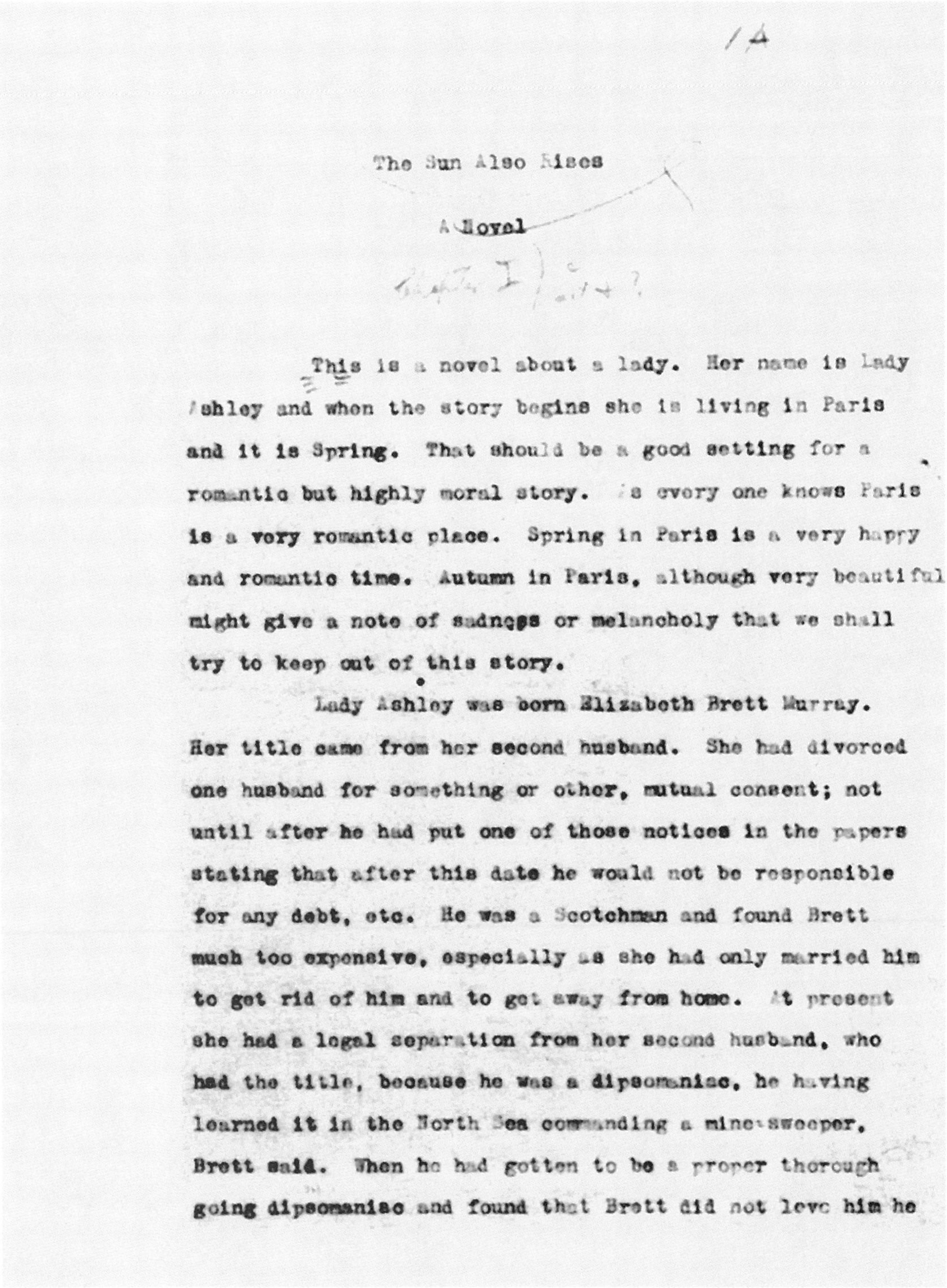

1 A

The Sun Also Rises

A Novel

This is a novel about a lady. Her name is Lady
Ashley and when the story begins she is living in Paris
and it is Spring. That should be a good setting for a
romantic but highly moral story. As every one knows Paris
is a very romantic place. Spring in Paris is a very happy
and romantic time. Autumn in Paris, although very beautiful
might give a note of sadness or melancholy that we shall
try to keep out of this story.

Lady Ashley was born Elizabeth Brett Murray.
Her title came from her second husband. She had divorced
one husband for something or other, mutual consent; not
until after he had put one of those notices in the papers
stating that after this date he would not be responsible
for any debt, etc. He was a Scotchman and found Brett
much too expensive, especially as she had only married him
to get rid of him and to get away from home. At present
she had a legal separation from her second husband, who
had the title, because he was a dipsomaniac, he having
learned it in the North Sea commanding a minesweeper,
Brett said. When he had gotten to be a proper thorough
going dipsomaniac and found that Brett did not love him he

Typescript of the original opening for The Sun Also Rises *(Clifton Waller Barrett Library, University of Virginia). Acting on Fitzgerald's
advice, Hemingway cut the first fifteen pages of the typescript before the novel was published.*

moments of tortured feeling. Ernest Hemingway has so completely realized his types and mastered his medium that he triumphantly adds a new chapter to the story which Scott Fitzgerald began in "This Side of Paradise."

Hemingway and John Dos Passos, author of Three Soldiers *(1921) and* Manhattan Transfer *(1925), believed that they had met during the war, but it is more probable that their first meeting occurred in the early 1920s in Paris. Dos Passos was an early supporter of Hemingway's career, as this review of* The Sun Also Rises *he wrote for the Communist magazine* The New Masses, *2 (December 1926), p. 26 reveals. The two remained close until they disagreed over events of the Spanish Civil War.*

A Lost Generation

It's a dangerous thing to quote the Bible in the beginning of a book. It raises the readers' hopes as to the meatiness of the matters to be served up by the author, and sets up a standard of skill in word and phrase, not unbeatable, but pretty much unbeaten. This book starts out with Gertrude Stein saying, presumably to the author and his contemporaries, "You are all a lost generation," and with a passage from Ecclesiastes: "the passing of generations, the rising and going down of the sun, the whirling of the wind, the flowing of rivers into the sea."

Instead of these things of deep importance you find yourself reading about the tangled love affairs and bellyaches of a gloomy young literatizing Jew, of an English lady of title who's a good sport, and of a young man working in the Paris office of an American newspaper, the "I" who tells the story.

Backgrounds; Montparnasse, American Paris, the Dome, Rotonde, Zelli's and the Select, then Pamplona during the fiesta of San Firmin.

It's an extraordinarily wellwritten book, so wellwritten that while I was reading it I kept telling myself I must be growing dough-headed as a critic for not getting it. Paris is a damned interesting place even at its most Bohemian; the fiesta at Pamplona is the finest in Spain and that means something! The people are so vividly put down you could recognize their faces on a passport photo. What the devil am I grumbling about anyway?

I suppose I want the generations, the sun also rising, the declamation of "Vanity of vanities, saith the preacher," the rivers running into the sea and the sea not yet full. I have a right to expect it too. Hemingway's short stories have that.

I don't think that there is anything in the division that critics are always making between a subject and the way it is treated; a subject can be treated any way. A novel is an indissoluble entity made up of as many layers as an onion. The style of an onion is its layers. By the time you've peeled off all the layers there's no onion left. Then why am I saying the book is well written? I mean that anywhere I open it and read a few sentences they seem very good; it's only after reading a page that the bottom begins to drop out. Maybe the trouble was sitting down to write a novel; maybe if it had been packed into a short unbroken story it would have given that feeling of meaning a lot to somebody, to everybody and to nobody that good work has got to have. As it is, instead of being the epic of the sun also rising on a lost generation—there's an epic in that theme all right—a badly needed epic—this novel strikes me as being a cock and bull story about a lot of summer tourists getting drunk and making fools of themselves at a picturesque Iberian folk-festival—write now to Thomas Cook for special rate and full descriptive leaflet. It's heartbreaking. If the generation of young intellectuals is not going to lose itself for God's sake let it show more fight; if it is, let's find a good up-to-date lethal chamber that's never been used before.

There's a conversation between "I" and a certain Bill that gives you a feeling that maybe the author was worried about these things. Like most Americans when they are saying what they mean, he has inverted it all into wisecracks.

Bill says to "I":

"Say something pitiful."
"Robert Cohn."
"Not so bad. That's better. Now, why is Cohn pitiful? Be ironic."
He took a big gulp of coffee.
"Aw hell," I said. "It's too early in the morning."
"There you go. And you claim you want to be a writer too. You're only a newspaper man. You ought to be ironical the minute you get out of bed. You ought to wake up with your mouth full of pity."
"Go on," I said. "Who did you get this stuff from?"
"Everybody. Don't you read? Don't you ever see anybody? Don't you know what you are? You're an expatriate . . .
"You're an expatriate. You've lost touch with the soil. You get precious. Fake European standards have ruined you. You drink yourself to death. You become obsessed by sex. You spend all your time talking, not working. You are an expatriate see? You hang around cafes."

There's a lot in it. This is a novel of Montparnassia for Montparnassians; if it weren't so darn well written I'd say by a Montparnassian. There's a lot of truth in the old saying that Paris is where good Americans go

Hemingway, Maria Glaser, John Dos Passos, and Gerald Murphy in Schruns, Austria, March 1926. In A Moveable Feast *(1964) Hemingway refers to Dos Passos as "the pilot fish" who led "the rich" (the Murphys) to Schruns.*

when they die. When a superbly written description of the fiesta of San Firmin in Pamplona, one of the grandest events in the civilized uncivilized world, reminds you of a travelbook by the Williamsons, it's time to call an inquest.

What's the matter with American writing anyway? Is it all just the Williamsons in different yearly models? If it is, the few unsad young men of this lost generation will have to look for another way of finding themselves than the one indicated here.

Following publication of The Sun Also Rises, *Hemingway wrote to Perkins, his Scribners editor, about an attempt he was making to trap Samuel Roth, a New York publisher who was pirating the work of James Joyce; the attempt failed. Hemingway's account of his trip with Fitzgerald is given in "Scott Fitzgerald,"* A Moveable Feast *(New York: Scribners,*

1964), pp. 147–176. Duff Twysden, the model for Lady Brett Ashley in Hemingway's The Sun Also Rises, *was also the model for Iris March in Michael Arlen's* The Green Hat *(1924). From* The Only Thing That Counts, *pp. 54–55.*

December 7, 1926

Dear Mr. Perkins;

Today your letter of Nov. 26 came. I dont think the book could have been better made nor finer looking.

One thing I would like—four copies only were sent me—and I would like a few more as I had to buy it here at 70 francs a copy to send over to Curtis Brown for his negotiations with Heinemann etc. I have set a trap for Roth by letting a local N.J. printer get out a few hundred copies of a thing of mine called Today Is Friday—which Roth will be very liable to lift for one of his publications. This I have had copyrighted and have just received the certificate of copyright registration from Washington. We may be able to bag him with that.

About the drawing—it really makes no difference. At the time I hated to have my family think that I really

looked like that. They feel, I understand, very humili-
ated because of "the way I write." A copy of The Literary Digest Book Review Magazine from my father has
underlined in blue and red pencil the following–The
Penn Publishing Company, of Philadelphia, which
reports a <u>constantly increasing sale</u> for the books of
Temple Bailey, wrote in part–"Our feeling is that there
is a strong reaction against the sex <u>novel</u>, and even the
highbrow realistic—novel and that (later on) the clean,
romantic, or stirring adventure tale will always <u>com-
mand the wider public</u>." But the drawing may have
pleased them. And it seems to reproduce very well.

What you say about The Green Hat is quite true.
My contact with Arlen was through Scott's talking
about him and his stuff when we once drove Scott's car
from Lyons to Paris. I remember telling Scott who the
people were that had taken Arlen up–and even getting
quite irritated about Arlen–Don Stewart talked about
him too. I took it for granted that the Green Hat must
be a cheap book when I heard that the heroine killed
herself–because the one very essential fact about all
those people that Arlen knew was that none of them
had the guts to kill themselves. So I guess it was really
protesting about that sort of twaddle that I made Brett
so damned accurate that practically nobody seemed to
believe in her. Maybe they do now though. Anyway it
was very funny.

There really is, to me anyway, very great glam-
our in life–and places and all sorts of things and I
would like sometime to get it into stuff. People aren't all
as bad as Ring Lardner finds them–or as hollowed out
and exhausted emotionally as some of The Sun generation. Ive known some very wonderful people who even
though they were going directly toward the grave
(which is what makes any story a tragedy if carried out
until the end) managed to put up a very fine performance enroute. Impotence is a pretty dull subject compared with war or love or the old lucha por la vida. I do
hope though that The Sun will sell a tremendous lot
because while the subject is dull the book isn't. Then
maybe sometime, and with that impetus to go on, we'll
have a novel where the subject won't be dull and try
and keep the good qualities of this one. Only, of course,
you don't have subjects–Louis Bromfield has subjects–
but just write them and if God is good to you they
come out well. But it would always be much better to
write than to talk about writing.

My son looks forward very much to the Christmas book and told his mother very excitedly–Max Perkins va me dormer un joli cadeau! When she asked him
what it was he said it was a very beautiful big book not
written by papa.

Yours always
Ernest Hemingway

Dust jacket for Hemingway's novel of expatriate life

Hemingway's letter to his parents following publication of The
Sun Also Rises *defends his writing style and justifies his choice
of material. From* Selected Letters, *pp. 243–244.*

5 February 1927

Dear Mother:

Thank you very much for sending me the cata-
logue of the Marshal Field exhibit with the reproduc-
tion of your painting of the Blacksmith Shop in it. It
looks very lovely and I should have liked to see the
original.

I did not answer when you wrote about the Sun
etc. book as I could not help being angry and it is very
foolish to write angry letters; and more than foolish to
do so to one's mother. It is quite natural for you not to
like the book and I regret your reading any book that
causes you pain or disgust.

77

On the other hand I am in no way ashamed of the book, except in as I may have failed in accurately portraying the people I wrote of, or in making them really come alive to the reader. I am sure the book is unpleasant. But it is not *all* unpleasant and I am sure is no more unpleasant than the real inner lives of some of our best Oak Park families. You must remember that in such a book all the worst of the people's lives is displayed while at home there is a very lovely side for the public and the sort of thing of which I have had some experience in observing behind closed doors. Besides you, as an artist, know that a writer should not be forced to defend his choice of a subject but should be criticized on how he has treated that subject. The people I wrote of were certainly burned out, hollow and smashed—and that is the way I have attempted to show them. I am only ashamed of the book in whatever way it fails to really give the people I wished to present. I have a long life to write other books and the subjects will not always be the same—except as they will all, I hope, be human beings.

And if the good ladies of the book study club under the guidance of Miss Butcher, who is *not* an intelligent reviewer—I would have felt very silly had she praised the book—agree unanimously that I am prostituting a great talent etc. for the lowest ends—why the good ladies are talking about something of which they know nothing and saying very foolish things.

As for Hadley, Bumby and myself—altho Hadley and I have not been living in the same house for some time (we have lived apart since last Sept. and by now Hadley may have divorced me) we are the very best of friends. She and Bumby are both well, healthy and happy and all the profits and royalties of The Sun Also Rises, by my order, are being paid directly to Hadley, both from America and England. The book has gone into, by the last ads I saw in January, 5 printings (15,000) copies, and is still going strongly. It is published in England in the Spring under the title of Fiesta. Hadley is coming to America in the Spring so you can see Bumby on the profits of Sun Also Rises. I am not taking one cent of the royalties, which are already running into several thousand dollars, have been drinking nothing but my usual wine or beer with meals, have been leading a very monastic life and trying to write as well as I am able. We have different ideas about what constitutes good writing—that is simply a fundamental disagreement—but you really are deceiving yourself if you allow any Fanny Butchers to tell you that I am pandering to sensationalism etc. etc. I get letters from Vanity Fair, Cosmopolitan etc. asking me for stories, articles, and serials, but am publishing nothing for six months or a year (a few stories sold to Scribner's the end of last year and one funny article out) because I know that now is a very crucial time and that it is much more important for me to write in tranquility, trying to write as well as I can, with no eye on any market, nor any thought of what the stuff will bring, or even if it can ever be published—than to fall into the money making trap which handles American writers like the corn-husking machine handled my noted relative's thumb.

I'm sending this letter to both of you because I know you have been worried about me and I am always sorry to cause you worry. But you must not do that—because, although my life may smash up in different ways I will always do all that I can for the people I love (I don't write home a lot because I haven't time and because, writing, I find it very hard to write letters and have to restrict correspondence to the letters I have to write—and my real friends know that I am just as fond of them whether I write or not) that I have never been a drunk nor even a steady drinker (You will hear legends that I am—they are tacked on everyone that ever wrote about people who drink) and that all I want is tranquility and a chance to write. You may never like any thing I write—and then suddenly you might like something very much. But you must believe that I am sincere in what I write. Dad has been very loyal and while you, mother, have not been loyal at all I absolutely understand that it is because you believed you owed it to yourself to correct me in a path which seemed to you disastrous.

So maybe we can drop that all. I am sure that, in the course of my life, you will find much cause to feel that I have disgraced you if you believe everything you hear. On the other hand with a little shot of loyalty as anaesthetic you may be able to get through all my obvious disreputability and find, in the end, that I have not disgraced you at all.

Anyhow, best love to you both,

Ernie

In Henry Goodman's Creating the Short Story: A Symposium-Anthology *(New York: Harcourt, Brace, 1929), p. 121, Hemingway recounts how he wrote some of the stories in* Men Without Women *(1927).*

WHO KNOWS HOW?

For the guidance of your classes, the way in which I wrote a story called "The Undefeated" was as follows:

I got the idea of writing it while on an AE bus in Paris just as it was passing the Bon Marché (a large

First page of Hemingway's letter to his father, in which the writer announces the end of his first marriage (Sotheby Parke Bernet, Goodwin Collection, Item 151, 29 October 1977)

Ernest and Pauline Hemingway en route to the United States, 1928

department store on the Boulevard Raspail). I was standing on the back platform of the bus and was in a great hurry to get home to start writing before I would lose it. I wrote all during lunch and until I was tired. Each succeeding day I went out of the house to a café in the morning and wrote on the story. It took several days to finish it. I do not remember the names of the cafés.

I wrote a story called "The Killers," in Madrid. I started it when I woke up after lunch and worked on it until supper. At supper I was very tired and drank a bottle of wine and read *La Voz, El Heraldo, Informaciones, El Debate* so as not to think about the story. After supper I went out for a walk. I saw no one I knew and went back to bed. The next morning I wrote a story called "Today Is Friday." I forget what we had for lunch. That afternoon it snowed.

My other stories have mostly been written in bed in the morning. If the above is not practical for the pupils perhaps they could substitute Fifth Avenue bus for AE bus; Saks for the Bon Marché; drug store for café–I believe there would be little difference except that they might not be permitted to write in a drug store.

<hr>

Virginia Woolf's review of Men Without Women *was published in the* New York Herald Tribune Books *on 9 October 1927, pp. 1, 8.*

An Essay in Criticism

Human credulity is indeed wonderful. There may be good reasons for believing in a King or a Judge or a Lord Mayor. When we see them go sweeping by

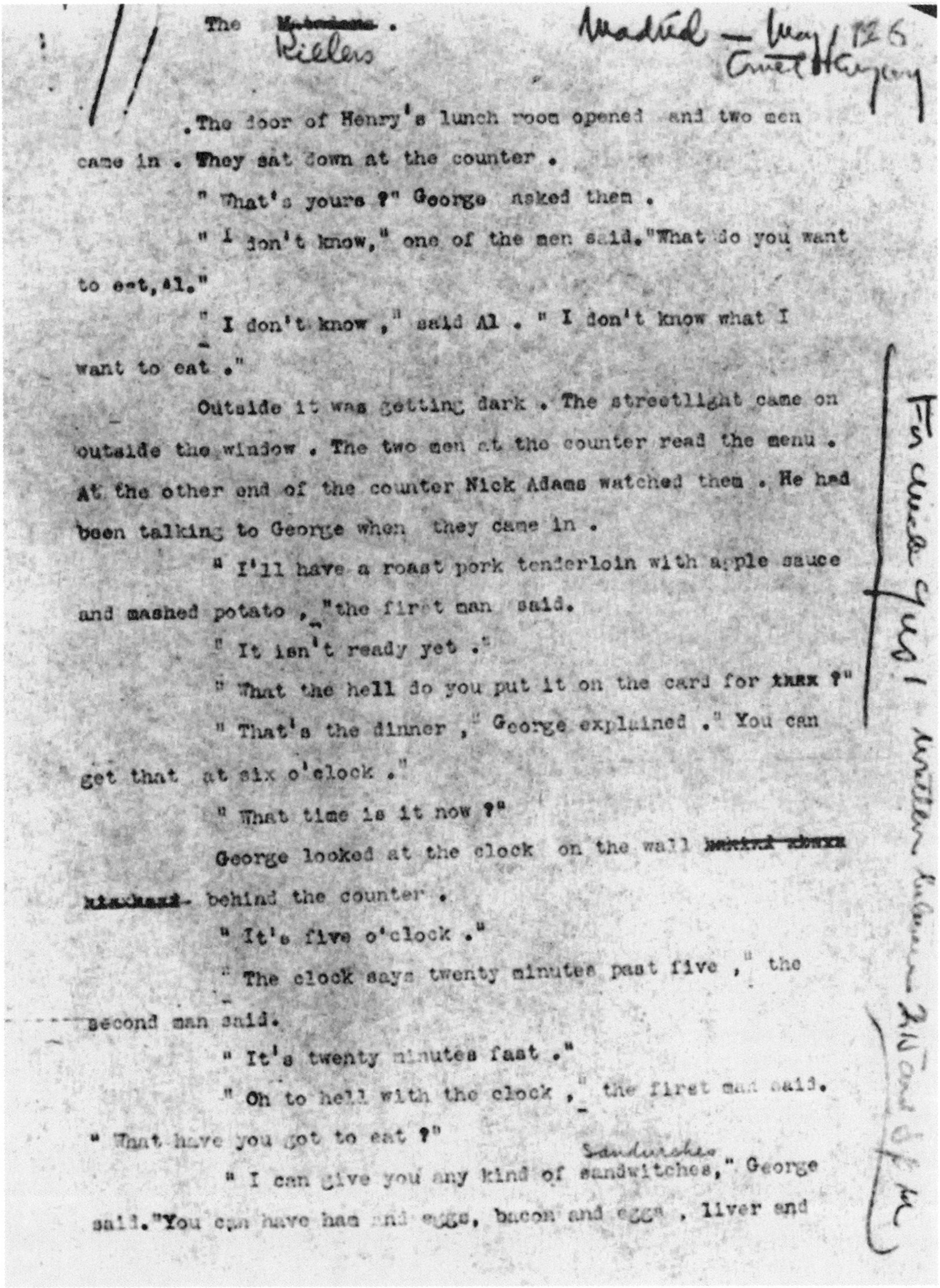

The ~~Matadors~~ Killers

Madrid — May 1926
Ernest Hemingway

.The door of Henry's lunch room opened and two men came in . They sat down at the counter .

" What's yours ?" George asked them .

" I don't know," one of the men said."What do you want to eat,Al."

" I don't know ," said Al . " I don't know what I want to eat ."

Outside it was getting dark . The streetlight came on outside the window . The two men at the counter read the menu . At the other end of the counter Nick Adams watched them . He had been talking to George when they came in .

" I'll have a roast pork tenderloin with apple sauce and mashed potato ,"the first man said.

" It isn't ready yet ."

" What the hell do you put it on the card for ~~that~~ ?"

" That's the dinner ," George explained ." You can get that at six o'clock ."

" What time is it now ?"

George looked at the clock on the wall ~~behind the~~ ~~blackboard~~ behind the counter .

" It's five o'clock ."

" The clock says twenty minutes past five ," the second man said.

" It's twenty minutes fast ."

" Oh to hell with the clock ," the first man said.

" What have you got to eat ?"

" I can give you any kind of ~~sandwiches~~ sandwitches," George said."You can have ham and eggs, bacon and eggs , liver and

First page of the typescript for "The Killers," originally titled "The Matadors" (Hemingway Collection, John F. Kennedy Library). The inscription is to Gustavus Pfeiffer, Pauline Hemingway's uncle, in appreciation for his generosity toward the couple.

in their robes and their wigs, with their heralds and their outriders, our knees begin to shake and our looks to falter. But what reason there is for believing in critics it is impossible to say. They have neither wigs nor outriders. They differ in no way from other people if one sees them in the flesh. Yet these insignificant fellow creatures have only to shut themselves up in a room, dip a pen in the ink, and call themselves "we", for the rest of us to believe that they are somehow exalted, inspired, infallible. Wigs grow on their heads. Robes cover their limbs. No greater miracle was ever performed by the power of human credulity. And, like most miracles, this one, too, has had a weakening effect upon the mind of the believer. He begins to think that critics, because they call themselves so, must be right. He begins to suppose that something actually happens to a book when it has been praised or denounced in print. He begins to doubt and conceal his own sensitive, hesitating apprehensions when they conflict with the critics' decrees.

And yet, barring the learned (and learning is chiefly useful in judging the work of the dead), the critic is rather more fallible than the rest of us. He has to give us his opinion of a book that has been published two days, perhaps, with the shell still sticking to its head. He has to get outside that cloud of fertile, but unrealized, sensation which hangs about a reader, to solidify it, to sum it up. The chances are that he does this before the time is ripe; he does it too rapidly and too definitely. He says that it is a great book or a bad book. Yet, as he knows, when he is content to read only, it is neither. He is driven by force of circumstances and some human vanity to hide those hesitations which beset him as he reads, to smooth out all traces of that crab-like and crooked path by which he has reached what he chooses to call "a conclusion". So the crude trumpet blasts of critical opinion blow loud and shrill, and we, humble readers that we are, bow our submissive heads.

But let us see whether we can do away with these pretences for a season and pull down the imposing curtain which hides the critical process until it is complete. Let us give the mind a new book, as one drops a lump of fish into a cage of fringed and eager sea anemones, and watch it pausing, pondering, considering its attack. Let us see what prejudices affect it; what influences tell upon it. And if the conclusion becomes in the process a little less conclusive, it may, for that very reason, approach nearer to the truth. The first thing that the mind desires is some foothold of fact upon which it can lodge before it takes flight upon its speculative career. Vague rumours attach themselves to people's names. Of Mr. Hemingway, we know that he is an American living in France, an "advanced" writer, we suspect, connected with what is called a movement, though which

of the many we own that we do not know. It will be well to make a little more certain of these matters by reading first Mr. Hemingway's earlier book, *The Sun Also Rises,* and it soon becomes clear from this that, if Mr. Hemingway is "advanced", it is not in the way that is to us most interesting. A prejudice of which the reader would do well to take account is here exposed; the critic is a modernist. Yes, the excuse would be because the moderns make us aware of what we feel subconsciously; they are truer to our own experience; they even anticipate it, and this gives us a particular excitement. But nothing new is revealed about any of the characters in *The Sun Also Rises.* They come before us shaped, proportioned, weighed, exactly as the characters of Maupassant are shaped and proportioned. They are seen from the old angle; the old reticences, the old relations between author and character are observed.

But the critic has the grace to reflect that this demand for new aspects and new perspectives may well be overdone. It may become whimsical. It may become foolish. For why should not art be traditional as well as original? Are we not attaching too much importance to an excitement which, though agreeable, may not be valuable in itself, so that we are led to make the fatal mistake of overriding the writer's gift?

At any rate, Mr. Hemingway is not modern in the sense given; and it would appear from his first novel that this rumour of modernity must have sprung from his subject matter and from his treatment of it rather than from any fundamental novelty in his conception of the art of fiction. It is a bare, abrupt, outspoken book. Life as people live it in Paris in 1927 or even in 1928 is described as we of this age do describe life (it is here that we steal a march upon the Victorians) openly, frankly, without prudery, but also without surprise. The immoralities and moralities of Paris are described as we are apt to hear them spoken of in private life. Such candour is modern and it is admirable. Then, for qualities grow together in art as in life, we find attached to this admirable frankness an equal bareness of style. Nobody speaks for more than a line or two. Half a line is mostly sufficient. If a hill or a town is described (and there is always some reason for its description) there it is, exactly and literally built up of little facts, literal enough, but chosen, as the final sharpness of the outline proves, with the utmost care. Therefore, a few words like these: "The grain was just beginning to ripen and the fields were full of poppies. The pasture land was green and there were fine trees, and sometimes big rivers and chateaux off in the trees"—which have a curious force. Each word pulls its weight in the sentence. And the prevailing atmosphere is fine and sharp, like that of winter days when the boughs are bare against the sky.

Fifty Grand.

(A Story)

~~Ixxxyxxxx~~ *over the*

Up at the Garden one time somebody says to

Jack , "Say Jack how did you happen to beat Leonard anyway ?"
see
and Jack says , "Well , ~~he says~~, "you/Benny's an awful smart

boxer . All the time he's in there he's thinking and all the

time he's thinking I was hitting him ."

That got a big laugh and somebody ,Soldier
lett
Bartfield I think , says , "You're quite a kidder aint you

Jack?"

"Yes, says Jack."I'm quite a kidder ."

" How did you beat Kid Lewis ?" Asked Soldier .

" That kike ," Jack says .

" Benny's a kike too ," Soldier says .

" No he's not ," Jack said ."Benny s no kike .Beny's

a Jewish boy . ~~He's a d amm fine fighter .~~"

"He's an actor now ," somebody said .

" Corbett got to be an actor too ," somebody else said .

There was a laugh in that too if you could find it .

"Benny's not that way ,"Harry Collins said .

" Well " says Jack ."I'm not an actor anyway ."

" No you're just a big hearted kidder ," Soldier

says .

"You make a lot of funny cracks ," Jack says .

"It's just my happy nature ," Soldier says ."When
When
I'm/ around with a lot of you big hearted spenders. ~~I just~~

~~have to talk~~

" All right ," Jack says ," Come one . I'll buy

you the drink ."

Typescript of Hemingway's original opening for "Fifty Grand," with his holograph comment on F. Scott Fitzgerald's editorial advice: "1st 3 pages of story [mutilated] by Scott Fitzgerald with his [   ]" (Hemingway Collection, John F. Kennedy Library).

2383 – mj

i0063

NOTE. This sketch has been prepared with a view to its inclusion in the next edition of WHO'S WHO IN AMERICA. If any important fact (conformatory to the plan of the book) has been omitted, it should be supplied. All blank spaces should be properly filled. Christian names should be given in full. Every sketch must receive approval of the editor to insure inclusion. Please revise and return immediately.

Return to THE A. N. MARQUIS COMPANY, 670 Cass Street, Chicago, Ill.

HEMINGWAY, Ernest, author; b. Oak Park, Ill., July 21, 1898; s. Clarence Edmonds and Grace (Hall) H.; ed. pub. schs.; unmarried. Author: Three Stories and Ten Poems, 1923; In our Time, 1924; The Torrents of Spring, 1926; The Sun Also Rises, 1926; Men Without Women, 1927. Contbr. to Scribner's, Atlantic Monthly, New Republic, etc. Home: 1 rue des Italiens, Paris, France. Address: care Guaranty Trust Co., 140 Broadway, New York, N.Y.

No Home

Charles Scribner's Sons, 5th ave. and 48th Street New York, N.Y.

JAN 13 1928

Leading essentials of every sketch are: Full Name, Place and Date of Birth, Full Names of Parents, Education, College Degrees (including dates) and Marriage (including full name and date).

Please furnish here both home and business address, if not correctly given above.

Home Address ..... *none*

Business Address ..... *Charles Scribner's Sons, Fifth ave. and 48th Street, New York City*

Returned [Date] ....19...... by ....

472-9

Printed in U.S.A.

Biographical data that Hemingway provided for his first mention in Who's Who in America

(But if we had to choose one sentence with which to describe what Mr. Hemingway attempts and sometimes achieves, we should quote a passage from a description of a bullfight: "Romero never made any contortions, always it was straight and pure and natural in line. The others twisted themselves like corkscrews, their elbows raised and leaned against the flanks of the bull after his horns had passed, to give a faked look of danger. Afterwards, all that was faked turned bad and gave an unpleasant feeling. Romero's bullfighting gave real emotion, because he kept the absolute purity of line in his movements and always quietly and calmly let the horns pass him close each time.") Mr. Hemingway's writing, one might paraphrase, gives us now and then a real emotion, because he keeps absolute purity of line in his movements and lets the horns (which are truth, fact, reality) pass him close each time. But there is something faked, too, which turns bad and gives an unpleasant feeling–that also we must face in course of time.

And here, indeed, we may conveniently pause and sum up what point we have reached in our critical progress. Mr. Hemingway is not an advanced writer in the sense that he is looking at life from a new angle. What he sees is a tolerably familiar sight. Common objects like beer bottles and journalists figure largely in the foreground. But he is a skilled and conscientious writer. He has an aim and makes for it without fear or circumlocution. We have, therefore, to take his measure against somebody of substance, and not merely line him, for form's sake, beside the indistinct bulk of some ephemeral shape largely stuffed with straw. Reluctantly we reach this decision, for this process of measurement is one of the most difficult of a critic's tasks. He has to decide which are the most salient points of the book he has just read; to distinguish accurately to what kind they belong, and then, holding them against whatever model is chosen for comparison, to bring out their deficiency or their adequacy.

Recalling *The Sun Also Rises,* certain scenes rise in memory: the bullfight, the character of the Englishman, Harris; here a little landscape which seems to grow behind the people naturally; here a long, lean phrase which goes curling round a situation like the lash of a whip. Now and again this phrase evokes a character brilliantly, more often a scene. Of character, there is little that remains firmly and solidly elucidated. Something indeed seems wrong with the people. If we place them (the comparison is bad) against Tchekov's people, they are flat as cardboard. If we place them (the comparison is better) against Maupassant's people they are crude as a photograph. If we place them (the comparison may

Dust jacket for the British edition of Hemingway's second collection of short stories (London: Cape, 1928)

be illegitimate) against real people, the people we liken them to are of an unreal type. They are people one may have seen showing off at some café; talking a rapid, high-pitched slang, because slang is the speech of the herd, seemingly much at their ease, and yet if we look at them a little from the shadow not at their ease at all, and, indeed, terribly afraid of being themselves, or they would say things simply in their natural voices. So it would seem that the thing that is faked is character; Mr. Hemingway leans against the flanks of that particular bull after the horns have passed.

After this preliminary study of Mr. Hemingway's first book, we come to the new book, *Men Without Women,* possessed of certain views or prejudices. His talent plainly may develop along different lines. It may broaden and fill out; it may take a little more time and go into things–human beings in particular–rather more deeply. And even if this meant the sacrifice of some energy and point, the exchange would be to our private liking. On the other hand, his is a talent which may contract and harden still further, it may come to depend more and more upon the emphatic moment; make more and more use of dialogue, and cast narrative and description overboard as an encumbrance.

The fact that *Men Without Women* consists of short stories, makes it probable that Mr. Hemingway has taken the second line. But, before we explore the new book, a word should be said which is generally left unsaid, about the implications of the title. As the publisher puts it . . . "the softening feminine influence is absent—either through training, discipline, death, or situation". Whether we are to understand by this that women are incapable of training, discipline, death, or situation, we do not know. But it is undoubtedly true, if we are going to persevere in our attempt to reveal the processes of the critic's mind, that any emphasis laid upon sex is dangerous. Tell a man that this is a woman's book, or a woman that this is a man's, and you have brought into play sympathies and antipathies which have nothing to do with art. The greatest writers lay no stress upon sex one way or the other. The critic is not reminded as he reads them that he belongs to the masculine or the feminine gender. But in our time, thanks to our sexual perturbations, sex consciousness is strong, and shows itself in literature by an exaggeration, a protest of sexual characteristics which in either case is disagreeable. Thus Mr. Lawrence, Mr. Douglas, and Mr. Joyce partly spoil their books for women readers by their display of self-conscious virility; and Mr. Hemingway, but much less violently, follows suit. All we can do, whether we are men or women, is to admit the influence, look the fact in the face, and so hope to stare it out of countenance.

To proceed then—*Men Without Women* consists of short stories in the French rather than in the Russian manner. The great French masters, Mérimée and Maupassant, made their stories as self-conscious and compact as possible. There is never a thread left hanging; indeed, so contracted are they that when the last sentence of the last page flares up, as it so often does, we see by its light the whole circumference and significance of the story revealed. The Tchekov method is, of course, the very opposite of this. Everything is cloudy and vague, loosely trailing rather than tightly furled. The stories move slowly out of sight like clouds in the summer air, leaving a wake of meaning in our minds which gradually fades away. Of the two methods, who shall say which is the better? At any rate, Mr. Hemingway, enlisting under the French masters, carries out their teaching up to a point with considerable success.

There are in *Men Without Women* many stories which, if life were longer, one would wish to read again. Most of them indeed are so competent, so efficient, and so bare of superfluity that one wonders why they do not make a deeper dent in the mind than they do. Take the pathetic story of the Major whose wife died—"In Another Country"; or the sardonic story of a conversation in a railway carriage—"A Canary for One"; or stories like "The Undefeated" and "Fifty Grand" which are full of the sordidness and heroism of bull-fighting and boxing—all of these are good trenchant stories, quick, terse, and strong. If one had not summoned the ghosts of Tchekov, Mérimée and Maupassant, no doubt one would be enthusiastic. As it is, one looks about for something, fails to find something, and so is brought again to the old familiar business of ringing impressions on the counter, and asking what is wrong?

For some reason the book of short stories does not seem to us to go as deep or to promise as much as the novel. Perhaps it is the excessive use of dialogue, for Mr. Hemingway's use of it is surely excessive. A writer will always be chary of dialogue because dialogue puts the most violent pressure upon the reader's attention. He has to hear, to see, to supply the right tone, and to fill in the background from what the characters say without any help from the author. Therefore, when fictitious people are allowed to speak it must be because they have something so important to say that it stimulates the reader to do rather more than his share of the work of creation. But, although Mr. Hemingway keeps us under the fire of dialogue constantly, his people, half the time, are saying what the author could say much more economically for them. At last we are inclined to cry out with the little girl in "Hills Like White Elephants": "Would you please please please please please please stop talking?"

And probably it is this superfluity of dialogue which leads to that other fault which is always lying in wait for the writer of short stories: the lack of proportion. A paragraph in excess will make these little craft lopsided and will bring about that blurred effect which, when one is out for clarity and point, so baffles the reader. And both these faults, the tendency to flood the page with unnecessary dialogue and the lack of sharp, unmistakable points by which we can take hold of the story, come from the more fundamental fact that, though Mr. Hemingway is brilliantly and enormously skilful, he lets his dexterity, like the bullfighter's cloak, get between him and the fact. For in truth story-writing has much in common with bullfighting. One may twist one's self like a corkscrew and go through every sort of contortion so that the public thinks one is running every risk and displaying superb gallantry. But the true writer stands close up to the bull and lets the horns–call them life, truth, reality, whatever you like–pass him close each time.

Mr. Hemingway, then, is courageous; he is candid; he is highly skilled; he plants words precisely where he wishes; he has moments of bare and nervous beauty; he is modern in manner but not in vision; he is self-consciously virile; his talent has contracted rather than expanded; compared with his novel his stories are a little dry and sterile. So we sum him up. So we reveal some of the prejudices, the instincts and the fallacies out of which what it pleases us to call criticism is made.

American humorist and short-story writer Dorothy Parker wrote the following review of Hemingway's Men Without Women *as part of her "Constant Reader" column for* The New Yorker, 3 *(29 October 1927), pp. 92–94. Parker and Hemingway had met in 1926.*

A Book of Great Short Stories

Ernest Hemingway wrote a novel called *The Sun Also Rises.* Promptly upon its publication, Ernest Hemingway was discovered, the Stars and Stripes were reverentially raised over him, eight hundred and forty-seven book reviewers formed themselves into the word "welcome," and the band played "Hail to the Chief" in three concurrent keys. All of which, I should think, might have made Ernest Hemingway pretty reasonably sick.

For, a year or so before *The Sun Also Rises,* he had published *In Our Time,* a collection of short pieces. The book caused about as much stir in literary circles as an incompleted dogfight on upper Riverside Drive. True, there were a few that went about quick and stirred with admiration for this clean, exciting prose, but most of the reviewers dismissed the volume with a tolerant smile and the word "stark." It was Mr. Mencken who slapped it down with "sketches in the bold, bad manner of the Café du Dôme," and the smaller boys, in their manner, took similar pokes at it. Well, you see, Ernest Hemingway was a young American living on the left bank of the Seine in Paris, France; he had been seen at the Dôme and the Rotonde and the Select and the Closerie des Lilas. He knew Pound, Joyce, and Gertrude Stein. There is something a little––well, a little

you-know––in all of those things. You wouldn't catch Bruce Barton or Mary Roberts Rinehart doing them. No, sir.

And besides, *In Our Time* was a book of short stories. That's no way to start off. People don't like that; they feel cheated. Any bookseller will be glad to tell you, in his interesting *argot*, that "short stories don't go." People take up a book of short stories and say, "Oh, what's this? Just a lot of those short things?" and put it right down again. Only yesterday afternoon, at four o'clock sharp, I saw and heard a woman do that to Ernest Hemingway's new book, *Men Without Women.* She had been one of those most excited about his novel.

Literature, it appears, is here measured by a yard-stick. As soon as *The Sun Also Rises* came out, Ernest Hemingway was the white-haired boy. He was praised, adored, analyzed, best-sold, argued about, and banned in Boston; all the trimmings were accorded him. People got into feuds about whether or not his story was worth the telling. (You see this silver scar left by a bullet, right up here under my hair? I got that the night I said that any well-told story was worth the telling. An eighth of an inch nearer the temple, and I wouldn't be sitting here doing this sort of tripe.) They affirmed, and passionately, that the dissolute expatriates in this novel of "a lost generation" were not worth bothering about; and then they devoted most of their time to discussing them. There was a time, and it went on for weeks, when you could go nowhere without hearing of *The Sun Also Rises.* Some thought it without excuse; and some, they of the cool, tall foreheads, called it the greatest American novel, tossing *Huckleberry Finn* and *The Scarlet Letter* lightly out the window. They hated it or they revered it. I may say, with due respect to Mr. Hemingway, that I was never so sick of a book in my life.

Now *The Sun Also Rises* was as "starkly" written as Mr. Hemingway's short stories; it dealt with subjects as "unpleasant." Why it should have been taken to the slightly damp bosom of the public while the (as it seems to me) superb *In Our Time* should have been disregarded will always be a puzzle to me. As I see it–I knew this conversation would get back to me sooner or later, preferably sooner–Mr. Hemingway's style, this prose stripped to its firm young bones, is far more effective, far more moving, in the short story than in the novel. He is, to me, the greatest living writer of short stories; he is, also to me, not the greatest living novelist.

After all the high screaming about *The Sun Also Rises,* I feared for Mr. Hemingway's next book. You know how it is–as soon as they all start acclaiming a writer, that writer is just about to slip downward. The littler critics circle like literary buzzards above only the sick lions.

So it is a warm gratification to find the new Hemingway book, *Men Without Women,* a truly magnificent work. It is composed of thirteen short stories, most of which have been published before. They are sad and terrible stories; the author's enormous appetite for life seems to have been somehow appeased. You find here little of that peaceful ecstasy that marked the camping trip in *The Sun Also Rises* and the lone fisherman's days in "Big Two-Hearted River" in *In Our Time.* The stories include "The Killers," which seems to me one of the four great American short stories. (All you have to do is drop the nearest hat, and I'll tell you what I think the others are. They are Wilbur Da'm a Fool," and Ring Lardner's "Some Like Them Cold," that story which seems to me as shrewd a picture of every woman at some time as is Chekhov's "The Darling." Now what do *you* like best?) The book also includes "Fifty Grand," "In Another Country," and the delicate and tragic "Hills Like White Elephants." I do not know where a greater collection of stories can be found.

Ford Madox Ford has said of this author, "Hemingway writes like an angel." I take issue (there is nothing better for that morning headache than taking a little issue). Hemingway writes like a human being. I think it is impossible for him to write of any event at which he has not been present; his is, then, a reportorial talent, just as Sinclair Lewis's is. But, or so I think, Lewis remains a reporter and Hemingway stands a genius because Hemingway has an unerring sense of selection. He discards details with a magnificent lavishness; he keeps his words to their short path. His is, as any reader knows, a dangerous influence. The simple thing he does looks so easy to do. But look at the boys who try to do it.

Hemingway probably wrote the following letter to F. Scott Fitzgerald in October 1927, but he never finished and did not send this record of his violent reaction to the reviews of Men Without Women. *Burton Rascoe's review had been published in* The Bookman *(New York) in September 1927. The "poor fish" is Perry Hutchinson, whose review in* The New York Times *(16 October 1927) had been laudatory. "F. Adamski" is a reference to columnist Franklin P. Adams (F.P.A.). From Matthew J. Bruccoli,* Fitzgerald and Hemingway: A Dangerous Friendship *(New York: Carroll & Graf, 1995), pp. 241–242.*

Dear Scott,

Yes I read that fucking Rascoe who hadn't read a damn thing in the book but knew it contained 50 G. and so reviewed it on that alone and dismissed the unread stories with a few well placed kisses of Miss Westcott's sphincter muscle. Also read Virginia Woolf also read a poor fish in the Times who missed that lovely little wanton Lady Ashley—that's all have read so far and hope to God I read no more. These goddam reviews are sent to me by "friends" any review saying the stuff is a pile of shit I get at least 2,000 copies of. After I'd stopped Scribner's sending them because when one single damn one comes it throws me all off to hell when all I want is to be let alone to write. Glad to see F. Adamski has found it is easy to do and that anybody and especially he, Adamski, can do it much better.

Have about 50,000 words done on a novel and due to these bloody damned reviews coming in and the piles and one thing and another have been knocked to hell on working all this week—going to Berlin tonight for a week and forget about the whole bloody business. Got a wire from Max Perkins yesterday that the book had sold 7,000 plus and as I only drew down $750 advance that means after paying off what I still owe on the Torrents that I'll have a thousand bucks maybe as Pauline and I are going for a week and see the Six Days, Flechtheim, Rowahlt my German publisher and drink a little beer. I suppose it may sell a thousand or so more though Imagine that the 7,000 was largely advance sale on acct. of The Sun and probably the last advance sale I'll ever get. Am thinking of quitting publishing my stuff for the next 10 or 15 years as soon as I get my debts paid up. To hell with the whole goddam business. I'm writing Max to send you a check for 100 bucks, I'm sorry as hell you've been nervous—it is a hell of a business but imagine that laying off liquor and smoking these coughless carloads will fix you up/Do you sleep all right? I've been sleeping fine ever since last spring and working better than ever but I'm in a hell of a temper today after reading that shit ass Adamski talking about my swashbuckling affectations of style—that sonofabitch when—oh shit no use talking about a turd like that falls for a book like Dusty Answer.

What do you think about quitting either writing or publishing? The only reason I publish the damn stuff is because that is the only way to get rid of it and not think it is any good. There is certainly no other way to show up that shit to yourself. I didn't care anything about that 10 Indians story either and ouldn't have published it except they wanted enough for a book aid like White Elephants and In Another Country—I suppose that last is a swashbuckling affectation too.

Dear Mr. Curtin:

c/o Guaranty Trust Co. of N.Y.
1, rue des Italiens
Paris
Nov. 1, 1927

If your stationery hadn't said Frank A. Curtin, lawyer, at the top I would have had to send back the check for 5 dollars. But as this is the first time I have ever received money from a lawyer I'd better keep it.

The autographs aren't worth a damn thing and I'm awfully happy to write them for you. In fact for 5 dollars I'd be glad to rewrite any parts of the books you'd mention — or put in what the reviewers all seem to want — more female characters.

About the Torrents — I never could figure out what happened to it — I was very fond of it — but Nobody else seemed to like it except yourself.

I don't think Scribner's have anything against it except the fact that it only sold 1200 copies + which is 200 more than In our Time sold.

First page of Hemingway's letter to Frank Curtin, a reader who had requested autographs (Sotheby's New York, Sale 6925, Item 100, 4 December 1996)

Hemingway with painter Waldo Pierce at Key West, Florida,
February 1928

Guy Hickok, a friend of Hemingway, was a European corre-
spondent for The Brooklyn Daily Eagle. *He accompanied*
Hemingway on a March 1927 trip to Italy that Hemingway
recounted in "Che Ti Dice La Patria?" This article was pub-
lished in the 4 March 1928 issue of Hickok's newspaper.

PARIS WON'T LET HEMINGWAY LIVE A PRIVATE LIFE

Novelist Who Insists on Seclusion Is Subject of Fantastic Rumors

Paris, Feb. 25–They won't let anybody have a private life any more. If you do not make your own private life public, they will do it for you–look at poor Helen of Troy.

Yes, and look at Ernest Hemingway, who wrote "The Sun Also Rises" and "Men Without Women."

Nobody tries harder to live a private life than Hemingway in Paris. He buries himself away in an old, narrow street near the Church of St. Sulpice, runs away to Germany to escape being a guest of honor at literary dinners, hunts out hard-to-get-at places in Spain (Pampluna having turned tourist resort after the success of "The Sun Also Rises"), and goes off to small Swiss villages when the snow gets deep enough to ski.

Deaf to Publicity Appeals.

He denies his publishers the intimate details that they need for modern publicity. He answers few letters and accords no interviews.

The result is that he has a whole series of wilder private lives than he could possibly live.

Clipping services bring them back to him. It seems from the clippings that anybody who has spent any time in the Paris Latin Quarter is expected to know Hemingway, and all about him. And the visitors who like to shine in the reflected glory of wild notables they have met love to please.

"Hemingway is a tall, sad, pale bald-headed young man who goes about alone bareheaded, always with his finger in a book," said one of them. "He is always thinking. He never talks to anybody. He just walks about Paris in golf pants with his finger in a book."

Good Word Picture of Somebody.

It is a good description of somebody.

As a matter of fact there is a bald-headed young man who walks about Paris in golf pants, with his finger in a book; and he was probably pointed out to some visitor as Hemingway. But Hemingway himself has no golf pants; and he is not pale; and he does not go about bareheaded; and he is not bald; and he does not keep one finger always in a book; and he is not at all sad. And the man who answers the description is suspected of being something of a nut.

Another Wild Story.

Another story has it that Hemingway lives up in Montmartre, which he never has done, and that he is always drunk. He is supposed to be kept up in Montmartre, drunk, in some back room where he writes priceless pages that fall on the floor and are taken out and sold by the people who keep him drunk. There is supposed to be a sort of syndicate of unscrupulous men who keep Hemingway intoxicated and a prisoner, and who pick up the pages he writes and throws on the floor. Hemingway himself is not supposed to get any of the money for these pages, except in the form of drink to keep him drunk and make him write more pages.

That, too, is a case of mistaken identity. Hemingway has probably been drunk in his life, but not too often, and not for long. And he gets up early at home and writes while he is sober while his wife tells callers that he is out.

Montmartre Man Drunken Artist.

The man in Montmartre was a painter known as Utrillo, though that was not exactly his name; and he was kept in a back room, not by people who kept him drunk, but by people who tried to keep him sober and couldn't. Utrillo insisted on being drunk; and when they wouldn't let him he broke up the furniture and jumped out the window.

Then there was another story. The heroine of "The Sun Also Rises," called Lady Brett Ashley in the novel, is supposed to have come back to Paris from some awful junket swearing that she was going to take Hemingway away from his wife.

She was going to take Hemingway away from his wife, and all England and America was going to know about it. There was a lot of embroidery with that story, too, the only trouble being that the original of Lady Brett Ashley straightway went and married a young man named——

But while we are at it why not let Lady Brett Ashley that was have a private life, even if Hemingway cannot have one?

And as for anybody taking Hemingway away from his wife, the bets are that they won't.

In the following letter Hemingway announces that he has begun A Farewell to Arms. *He did not resume work on his abandoned novel, which had the working titles of "Jimmy Breen" and "A New Slain Knight" and was about a boy and his father. From* The Only Thing That Counts, *pp. 68–70.*

March 17

Dear Mr. Perkins—

Guy Hickock showed me a cable today from Scribners asking about my good health and I hope you werent worried I was tired of recounting accidents so was not going to mention it. However it was the sky light in the toilet—a friend had pulled the cord that raised it instead of pulling the chain of the toilet—and cracked the glass so that when I tried to hook up the cord (going into the bathroom at 2 a m. and seeing it dangling) the whole thing fell. We stopped the hemmorage with 30 thicknesses of toilet paper (a magnificent absorbent which I've now used twice for that purpose in pretty much emergencies) and a tourniquet of kitchen towel and a stick of kindling wood. The first two tourniquets wouldnt stop it due to being too short—(face towels) and I was rather worried as we had no telephone. The chance of getting a doctor at 2 a.m. and there were two little arteries cut. But the third held it very well and we went out to Neuilly to Am. Hospital where they fixed it up, tying the arteries, putting in three stitches underneath and six to close it. No after effects but a damned nusiance. . . .

I asked a (Mrs.) Emily Holmes Coleman to send you her novel about an insane asylum. (She was in one for a while as a patient and, I think, can write) I have never read it, but she was going to send it to Boni and Liveright (who published a book on psychology by her husband) and I prefferred if it should chance to be good that you see it.

I would like to have finished the novel—but (1) I have been laid up and out a good deal.

doesnt go after I get to America I will drop it and put it away and go on with the other one I am writing since two weeks that I thought was only a story but that goes on and goes <u>wonderfully</u>.

The first one was supposed to be a sort of Modern Tom Jones. (Never mention that because I do not write comparison but only to name the sort of book) But there is a <u>very very</u> good chance that I dont know enough to write that yet and whatever success I have had has been through writing what I know about—

I know very well that Scott for his own good should have had his novel out a year or two years ago I dont want you to think that I am falling into that thing or alibi-ing to myself. But this next book <u>has</u> to be good. The thing for me to do is write but it may be better not to publish until I get the right one.

I should have gone to America two years ago when I planned. I was through with Europe and needed to go to America before I could write the book that happened there. But I didnt go—but now have, suddenly, a great kick out of the war and all the things and places and it has been going very well.

My wife says that she will see that I'm bled just as often as I cant write—judging by the way it's been going this last week. Hope to be able to work on the boat. If I find I've any readers in America will change my name. . . . I am glad you are publishing Morley. I was never off of him but only a poor correspondent—

Yours always,
Ernest <u>Hemingway</u> . . . .

Sylvia Beach and Hemingway in front of her Paris bookstore, Shakespeare and Company, after he was injured by a falling skylight in 1928 (Sylvia Beach Collection, Princeton University Library)

(2) It took me 5 years to write all the stories in In Our Time.

(3) It took 5 years to write the ones in Men Without Women.

(4) I wrote Sun Also Rises in 6 weeks but then did not look at it for 3 months—and then rewrote it for another three months. How much time I wasted in drinking around before I wrote it and how badly I busted up my life in one way or another I cant fit exactly in time.

(5) I work <u>all</u> the time. But I dont think I can make even an irregular schedule and keep up the quality. I know very well I could turn books out when they should come out And you have been very damned decent about not even asking me to or putting any pressure on me but we only want good ones—Both of us. You see my whole life and head and everything had a hell of a time for a while and you come back slowly (and must never let anyone know even that you were away or let the pack know you were wounded) But I would like to write a really damned good novel—and if the one I have 22 chaps and 45,000 words of done

Malcolm Cowley, an influential critic and editor of modern American writers, wrote much on Hemingway, including The Portable Hemingway *(New York: Viking, 1944). The following was the first article that Cowley wrote on Hemingway; it appeared in* Brentano's Book Chat, *a publication of Brentano's Bookstore, 7 (September-October 1928), pp. 25–29.*

THE HEMINGWAY LEGEND

This is the first real pen-picture of Ernest Hemingway that has ever appeared in print. Mr. Hemingway does not give interviews. He does not talk for the press, and he is about the hardest man to get hold of in all of Europe.

I was paying a rather formal visit to Ezra Pound, in Paris during the summer of 1922, when Ernest Hemingway knocked and came striding through the door. It was the first time I had seen him. I noticed that he was tall, broad and handsome, with a good chin, a dark moustache, nice eyes, and rather short hair that just

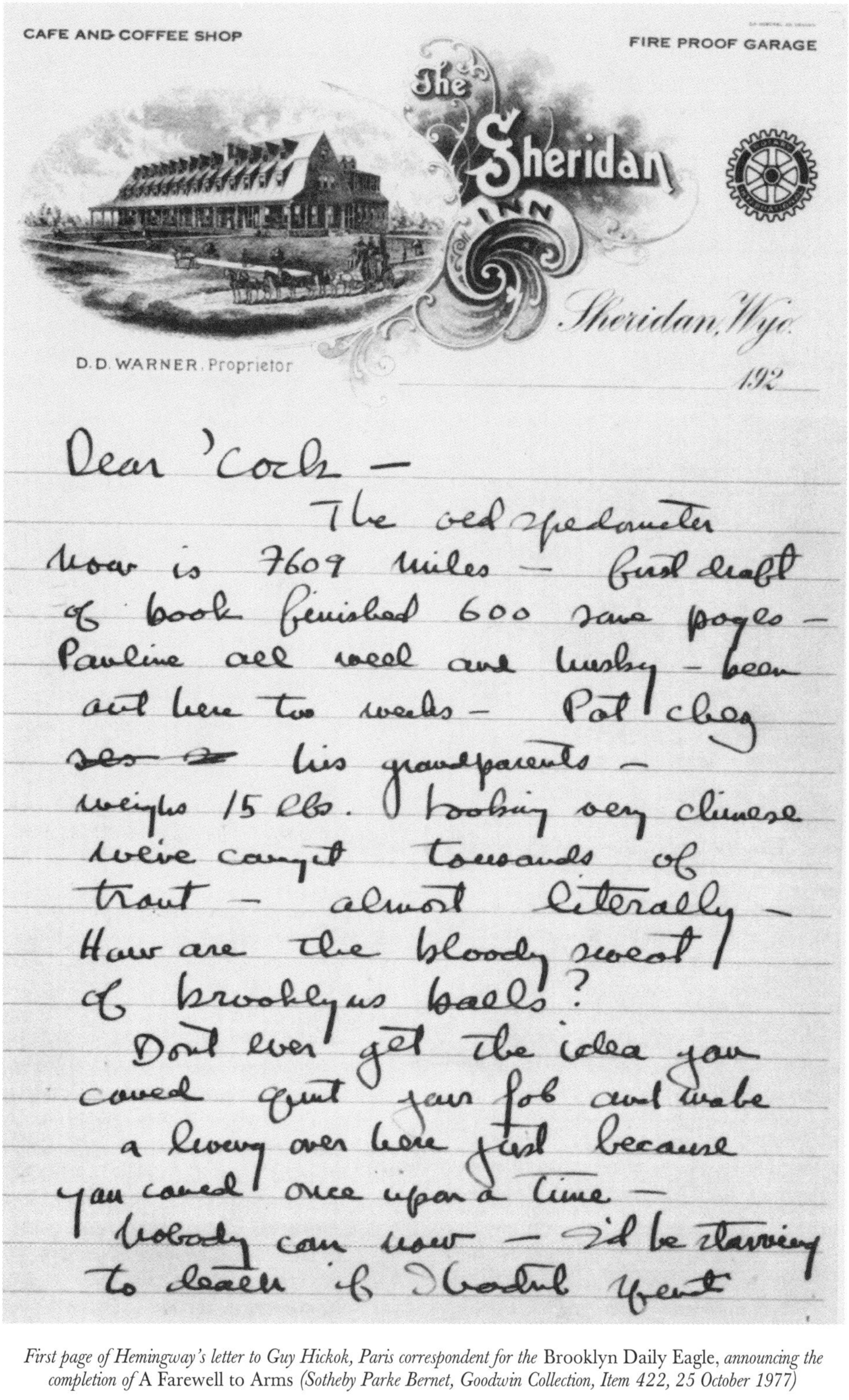

CAFE AND COFFEE SHOP

FIRE PROOF GARAGE

The Sheridan INN

Sheridan, Wyo.

192

D. D. WARNER, Proprietor

Dear 'Cock —

The old speedometer now is 7609 miles — first draft of book finished 600 some pages — Pauline all well and husky — been out here two weeks — Pat chez ses — his grandparents — weighs 15 lbs. Looking very chinese we've caught tousands of trout — almost literally — How are the bloody sweat of Brooklyns balls?

Don't ever get the idea you could quit your job and make a living over here just because you could once upon a time — Nobody can now — I'd be starving to death if I hadn't your

First page of Hemingway's letter to Guy Hickok, Paris correspondent for the Brooklyn Daily Eagle, *announcing the completion of* A Farewell to Arms *(Sotheby Parke Bernet, Goodwin Collection, Item 422, 25 October 1977)*

Hemingway's letter to Fitzgerald, ca. 9 December 1928 (Fitzgerald Collection, Princeton University Library). Hemingway had been traveling from New York to Key West when he received news of his father's suicide. He went to Oak Park after Fitzgerald met him in Philadelphia.

failed to be curly. He carried himself with an arrogant and not unpleasant slouch. He looked like some former stroke of a Yale crew, one that had entered Wall Street after his graduation, and was making good. He looked, I decided, like a hero out of the *Saturday Evening Post*.

His career for the six preceding years had been that of such a hero. He had come to France before we entered the war, as a volunteer in the American ambulance service. Later he had gone to Italy, had enlisted in the Arditi, had been seriously wounded, and had received two medals: the *Medaglia d'argento al valore militare* and the *Croce di guerra*. After returning to the States, he had married and gone to work for a newspaper. In Toronto the following year he had become the star reporter for the Star–a sort of double luminary. He had finally been made its European correspondent. Having reported a few battles in the Near East and a couple of Greek revolutions, he was now in Paris–working, I believe, for William Randolph Hearst. At twenty-five

he had achieved a position which many older journalists would have envied. He was settled and the father of a family. He was a success.

That he also desired success as a man of letters was known only to his more intimate friends. His interest in sports was better advertised. He played tennis almost daily and spent his vacation in long bicycle tours. He was a rabid fisherman. He liked to talk of bull-fighting in Spain. He was said to be a dangerous boxer, and had been the amateur champion of what or where I never learned. One would hardly have suspected that he carried silver plates in places where several of his bones should have been. Nor, would one have believed that he found time to write in the midst of his thousand activities.

Yet Paris at the time was full of young American writers. They contributed to *Broom, Secession, Gargoyle,* the *Little Review;* they spoke of founding new magazines in which their work should also appear. Hemingway, so far, had published nothing. The young American exiles were convinced that one or more of their number would shortly become famous. They were not sure whether it would be Smith or Brown or Estlin Cummings. I doubt that any of them would have chosen Hemingway.

Meanwhile, in Mr. Pound's high-ceilinged room, the conversation dragged on. We spoke of Joyce, the Elizabethan drama, the danger of revolution in Austria, and the poems of Mr. Ezra Pound. Occasionally Hemingway let fall a sentence. I learned for the first time that he was writing stories. He impressed me as being what he himself would call a swell guy, but Paris at the time was crowded with swell guys. Paris was crowded with young writers.

Two years later, in New York, I learned that Hemingway was becoming a legendary figure.

In the hidden saloons which are patronized by the returning exiles, by the repatriated expatriates; in the little noisy bars which take the place of the Dome and the Jockey, I began to hear his name. I would meet an acquaintance lately returned from Paris. "Hello Dick," I would say, "How's Montparnasse?"

"Swell. You can bet I was sorry to leave. . . . And say, did you hear what Hemingway did last?"

He launched into a story which I repeat without any pretense of its accuracy. It seems that Hemingway had attended one of the boxing matches in the Salle Wagram. Being a reporter, he managed to get a ringside seat. The feature of the evening was a bout between the middleweight champion of France and a promising kid from the provinces. Their managers had agreed that the challenger was to let himself be knocked out in the third round. But the kid had other plans for himself. In the second round he really began to fight, hoping to beat the champion as Siki had beaten Carpentier. He was a clever kid, but he hadn't a chance in the world. The champion lost his temper, knocked him down, kicked him in the groin, and began to dance on his body, while the crowd howled its pleasure as French crowds sometimes do. People rose from their seats; there was a general confusion.

In the midst of it all, Hemingway climbed into the ring. He was boiling with anger against the victorious boxer. He came forward on his toes, crouching; he jabbed once or twice, and handicapped by the silver plate in his shoulder, but aided by forty pounds advantage in weight, he knocked out the middleweight champion of France.

"He's a swell guy, Hemingway," my acquaintance added.

Shortly before this time, his stories had begun to appear in the little magazines of the day: in Mr. Ford's *Transatlantic Review* and in Ernest Walsh's *This*

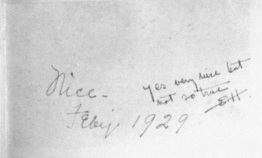

Advertisement proof for A Farewell to Arms. *Hemingway's holograph comment is his response to Maxwell Perkins's "Nice. Feby 1929"* (McKelding Library, University of Maryland).

Quarter. Each of his contributions won him new disciples. I began to notice that a whole battalion of young men were copying his candid drawl, his interest in dangerous sports, and his manner of walking with his elbows crooked and his arms swinging from the shoulder, like a boxer. A few were copying his prose style, although it is certain that Hemingway's literary influence has been discovered in quarters where it never existed.

In 1923 and 1924 he had published two slim volumes in Paris, both of which are valuable today as collectors' items. It was not until 1925 that his first work appeared in New York. "In Our Time," a volume consisting of 14 stories and 16 admirable sketches, was vigorously praised by a few critics with a gift for prophecy. The public showed very little interest in prophets. The total sale of the book, during the first year, was something like four hundred copies.

A FAREWELL TO ARMS 209

looked up. She looked perhaps a year younger. Aymo put his hand on the elder girl's thigh and she pushed it away. He laughed at her.

"Good man," he pointed at himself. "Good man," he pointed at me. "Don't you worry." The girl looked at him fiercely. The pair of them were like two wild birds.

"What does she ride with me for if she doesn't like me?" Aymo asked. "They got right up in the car the minute I motioned to them." He turned to the girl. "Don't worry," he said. "No danger of _____," using the vulgar word. "No place for _____." I could see she understood the word and that was all. Her eyes looked at him very scared. She pulled the shawl tight. "Car all full," Aymo said. "No danger of _____. No place for _____." Every time he said the word the girl stiffened a little. Then sitting stiffly and looking at him she began to cry. I saw her lips working and then tears came down her plump cheeks. Her sister, not looking up, took her hand and they sat there together. The older one, who had been so fierce, began to sob.

"I guess I scared her," Aymo said. "I didn't mean to scare her."

Bartolomeo brought out his knapsack and cut off two pieces of cheese. "Here," he said. "Stop crying."

The older girl shook her head and still cried, but the younger girl took the cheese and commenced to eat. After a while the younger girl gave her sister the second piece of cheese and they both ate. The older sister still sobbed a little.

"She'll be all right after a while," Aymo said.

An idea came to him. "Virgin?" he asked the girl next to him. She nodded her head vigorously. "Virgin too?" he pointed to the sister. Both the girls nod-

Maurice Coindreau's copy of Hemingway's novel, with the blanks filled in by Hemingway (Memorial Library, State University of New York at Buffalo)

However, it had increased the number of Hemingway's admirers. During the spring of 1926 they were repeating another of the stories which cling to his name. "Did you hear," they said, "that Hem and a bunch of guys went to Pamplona, in Spain, for the bull-fights? They went into the arena and some of them nearly got killed. They had a swell time. But they took an English girl along with them—Lady Somebody, I forget her name—and she had them all fighting before the trip ended."

This expedition to Pamplona was of course the basis of "The Sun Also Rises." It was a strange experience for me to read a book in which I could recognize almost all the characters, knew that they were described exactly, and yet sometimes could see a bitter prejudice that distorted the value of all the incidents. Perhaps the readers of that curious novel would be interested in hearing the later adventures of the characters. Robert Cohn is still in France; he has married again, and is writing a third book. Frances, having separated from him definitely, is living with a French poet of talent. Brett, who holds a curious position in modern literature—she was the heroine of "The Green Hat" as well as of "The Sun Also Rises"—has lately been reported as landing in New York. She has married an American millionaire. Hemingway himself was last seen in Florida. His younger admirers are no longer quite so enthusiastic; it is hard for them to idolize a writer who is also the idol of the public. They say lugubriously that he is getting fat.

Out of his career it would be easy to extract a formula for literary success, an infallible recipe to be followed by the struggling author. First of all, he must live at least three thousand miles from the quarrels, the cliques, and the easily satisfied curiosity of literary New York. He must next be handsome, so that women say of him, "Did you see So-and-so when you were abroad? Yes, really? Tell me, is he as good-looking as everybody claims?" Among the men he knows, he must have the gift of arousing loyalty. He must do interesting things on impulse, and thus become a legend.

Having fulfilled these not impossible conditions, he can begin to write. His first stories should appear in the little magazines whose readers think they hold the key to the future. When collected, they should be published in a small edition of interest to bibliophiles, and should meet with a purely critical success. In his second book he had better attack some writer of established fame; there is no better method for arousing the sort of hostility that melts into admiration. And now the time has come for him to publish a novel. It will inevitably be widely sold,

Advertisement for serialization of Hemingway's second novel
(Publishers' Weekly, 20 April 1929)

widely attacked, wildly defended, if only the directions have been carefully followed. Of course it is also desirable that our writer should possess a certain amount of literary talent, but this is by no means essential to his success.

Hemingway, however, is possessed of such talent. One can even say that he has the sort of talent which ought to be unquestioned. One can go still further. One can say that Hemingway, at the age of thirty-one, has shown more talent than any other American writer of his generation, with the probable exceptions of Estlin Cummings and Hart Crane. One can say that he has expressed his generation better than any other writer whatsoever.

This generation, as it happens, has been very widely discussed. It has been thundered against from the pulpit; it has been praised or deplored in controversial essays; it has been psycho-analyzed in very serious novels. As a result, and in spite of many wild statements, its leading characteristics have been pretty clearly recognized. We have agreed that the

Chapter Two: 1926–1929

Canadian writer Morley Callaghan, Hemingway's sparring partner in Paris

post-war generation has shown itself to be more practical–"hard-boiled" is the fashionable term–more energetic in the attainment of its limited ends, more candid in the pursuit of pleasure, and at the same time, in its own way, perhaps more fundamentally religious.

One might add that it is a very simple generation, after all. Its elders by ten years felt that they were living in a complex age and at a time when civilization was beginning to decay. They wrote in a knowing and discouraged fashion about the problems with which they were faced, chief among which was the relationship of man to the machine. For writers like Hemingway, this relationship is no longer a problem; they have mastered the machine; they sit unheedingly at the wheel of a high-powered automobile or the joy-stick of an airplane; they have become the primitives of a new age. They have learned, some of them at least, the sort of deliberate innocence which is the goal of sophistication.

Being simple, they like to write of simple themes. Consider, for example, the subjects of Hemingway's stories. One of them deals with the failure of two hired assassins. One deals with a boy who deserts the girl to whom he is engaged. One describes the pleasures of

fishing. One treats the endless dilemma of a man who has given more than life for a country that was not his own. One tells of six cabinet ministers led out to be shot at half-past six in the morning, when pools of water stood in the courtyard and the paving of the courtyard was covered with wet dead leaves. Essentially, these are themes which might have interested Villon or Catullus, Pushkin or Li T'ai Po. They differ remarkably from the subjects chosen by Hemingway's immediate predecessors, who were so obsessed with the complexity of their age and so bitterly determined to be original that most of their stories were written, as it were, on the very margins of experience. Hemingway is convinced of his originality; he does not need to prove it by being finical or obscure. Having found a new manner of writing, he dares to attack the ancient themes of love and death.

This new manner of writing, being part of the Hemingway legend, has been discussed in a vague and legendary way. Critics have endeavored to explain, to find the "secret," of his literary power. And, as a rule, they have sought this secret in his "pungently colloquial style" or in his "lean athletic prose."

Personally I find that his prose as such explains very little. It has several admirable qualities–ease, simplicity, the rhythm of familiar speech–but it also has defects that would ruin a less gifted writer. Hemingway's secret, if secret he has, is to be sought less in the qualities of his style than in the qualities of his mind. Here again Remy de Gourmont's judgment applies– that a man who thinks, feels, and sees well, writes well inevitably.

One cannot be certain that Hemingway thinks well. In his stories he has always avoided the discussion of ideas. One can be sure, however, of his emotions and perceptions. He feels well; he feels, that is, with an intensity and a delicacy that enable him to convey very difficult emotional states. He sees well: he sees the nuances of action that are missed by other eyes. Where an ordinary observer would merely see a bridge, a kingfisher, and a number of shadowy fish, Hemingway records a whole series of actions:

> As the shadow of the kingfisher moved up the stream, a big trout shot upstream in a long angle, only his shadow marking the angle, then lost his shadow as he came through the surface of the water, caught the sun, and then, as he went back into the stream under the surface, his shadow seemed to float down the stream with the current, unresisting, to his post under the bridge where he tightened, facing up into the current.

His other senses are as keenly developed as his sight. He hears the rhythms of conversation as very few writer have done. He remarks in one story that his tongue is very sensitive, and proves the statement by his

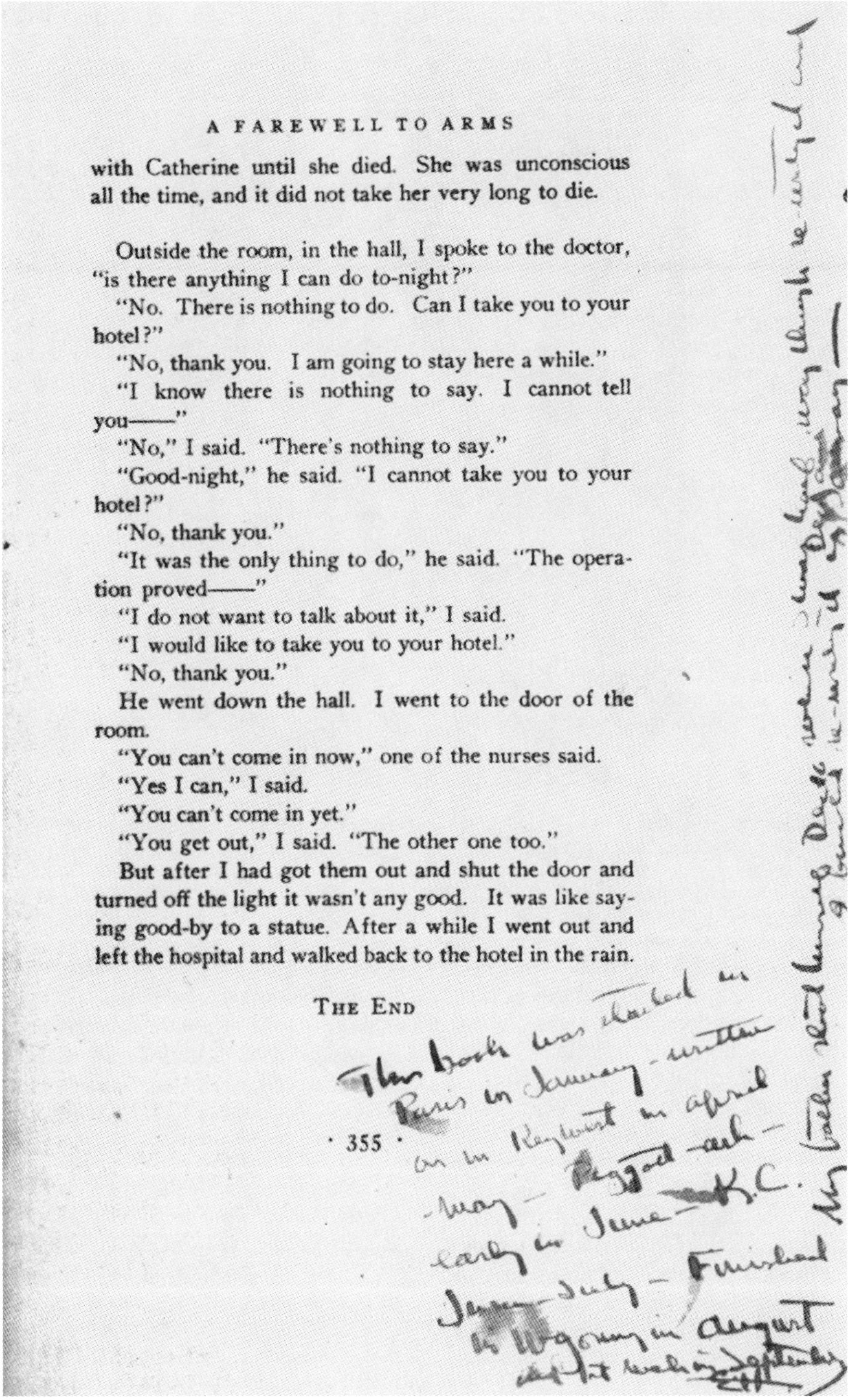

A FAREWELL TO ARMS

with Catherine until she died. She was unconscious all the time, and it did not take her very long to die.

Outside the room, in the hall, I spoke to the doctor, "is there anything I can do to-night?"

"No. There is nothing to do. Can I take you to your hotel?"

"No, thank you. I am going to stay here a while."

"I know there is nothing to say. I cannot tell you——"

"No," I said. "There's nothing to say."

"Good-night," he said. "I cannot take you to your hotel?"

"No, thank you."

"It was the only thing to do," he said. "The operation proved——"

"I do not want to talk about it," I said.

"I would like to take you to your hotel."

"No, thank you."

He went down the hall. I went to the door of the room.

"You can't come in now," one of the nurses said.

"Yes I can," I said.

"You can't come in yet."

"You get out," I said. "The other one too."

But after I had got them out and shut the door and turned off the light it wasn't any good. It was like saying good-by to a statue. After a while I went out and left the hospital and walked back to the hotel in the rain.

THE END

· 355 ·

Hemingway's annotation on the last page of Dr. Carlos Guffey's copy of A Farewell to Arms *outlines a chronology of events before the book was published (Sotheby Parke Bernet, Item 214, 21 January 1975).*

Poet Archibald MacLeish, who met Hemingway in Paris during summer 1924. Although their close friendship did not last through the 1930s, Hemingway dedicated Winner Take Nothing *(New York: Scribners, 1933) to him.*

description of things to eat. He devotes paragraphs at a time to the sense of touch. He makes his readers smell the good smell of dry canvas, the dry smell of pine needles, the pungency of sweet-fern crushed between the fingers. And certainly it is from the keenness of these sensory perceptions that his stories derive most of their richness and a good share of their emotional power.

Curiously enough, the qualities which distinguish his work—its appeal to the senses, its emotional intensity, its lack of general ideas, its absolute freshness—are not the qualities one ordinarily assigns to a novelist. They are, on the other hand, the qualities of a good lyric poem. And the more I reflect, the more I am convinced that this hard-boiled athlete, this husky voice of our own generation, this author of a legendary novel, is really not a novelist at all. Is he not rather a lyric poet by instinct—a poet who has stumbled into the less thorny paths of prose?

In the following letter to his editor, Hemingway discusses his need to have A Farewell to Arms *published as he wrote it. Perkins eventually concluded that Scribners could not publish the words* shit, fuck, cocksucker, *and* balls. *The first three were replaced by dashes; the last was changed to* scrotum. *From* The Only Thing That Counts, *pp. 101–104.*

7 June 1929

Dear Max:

I got the proofs—two days ago—They were held up at the Customs because the notation "Proofs for Correction"—was made in such small type—without capitals—on the label that the Customs People did not notice it—I cleared them at the Customs and was on them all day yesterday and today—

I am sorry to have made you so much trouble having the corrections made on the original galleys copied.

I find many more suggested—some of them very good. Others bad. When it makes no difference I am glad always to make it conventional as to punctuation.

About the words—I have made a notation at the side about the bed pan—Originally I had about 2,000 words of that aspect of hospital life—It really <u>dominates</u> it—I cut it all out with the exception of the one reference to the bed pan.

It is the same with other words.

You say they have not been in print before—one may not have—but the others are all in Shakespeare—

But more recently you will find them in a book called All Quiet on the Western Front which Scott gave me and which has sold in the 100s of thousand copies in Germany and is around 50,000 copies in England with the word shit, fart etc. Never dragged in for coloring but only used a few times for the thousands of times they are omitted. Please read the statement on page 15 of that book.

The trouble is Max that before my book will be out there will be this All Quiet on The Western Front book and possibly at the same time the Second volume of the man who wrote Sergeant Grischa—who knows his eggs also—and I hate to kill the value of mine by emasculating it when I looked up in the Quiet on W.F. book to find the words to show you I had a very hard time finding them. They don't stand out. But you should not go backwards. If a word can be printed and is needed in the text it is a <u>weakening</u> to omit it. If <u>cannot</u> be printed without the book being suppressed all right.

There has always been first rate writing and then American writing—(genteel writing)

No one that has read the Mss. has been shocked by <u>words</u> The words do not stand out unless you put a ring around them.

There is no good my pleading the case in a letter. You know my view point on it. What would have happened if they had cut the Sun also? It would have flopped as a book and I would have written no more for you.

The first place you say you think a word must go is in Galley 13—

I can consider you leaving that a blank—but in galley 51 where the same word is used by Piani if that is cut out it is pretty ruinous—I don't consent and it's done over my head.

On galley 57 a word is used that is used again at the top of galley 60.

If you think this word will cause the suppression of the book make it C—S—R.

You see I have kept out all the words that are the constant vocabulary—but have given the sense of them by using once, twice or three times the real words. Using then only the most classic words.

You know what General Cambronne said at the battle of Waterloo instead of "The Old Guard Dies but Never Surrenders! He said <u>Merde</u> when they called on him to surrender.

In a purely conversational way in a latin language in an argument one man says to another "Cogar su madre!"

You see there is Nothing Wrong with any of the words I have used except the last—the one on Galley 57—which is used as an expression of Supreme insult and contempt—The others are common enough and I dare say will all be in print in U.S.A. before the year is out.

It's unsatisfactory to write this and I hope you don't think I'm getting snooty about it. I wish we could talk and you could tell me just how far you <u>can</u> go and what the danger is. I do not want trouble—But want everything that can be had without trouble—I thought you said that if I accepted certain blanks etc for the serialization the book would be published as it was. I see in the 2nd installment cuts made without my knowledge but am of course in their hands.

Anyway am working all the time on this proof and will get it back to you as soon as possible—By a boat the first of the week.

I hope you got the signed sheets O.K. I mailed them about a week ago Am enclosing the contract.

Yours always
Ernest <u>Hemingway</u>

P.S.

I found the place in galley 38 where F.H. is talking to the hospital matron—I don't know what to do—It is supposed to be the deliberate insult and routing of a person through the use of direct language that she expected by her sex and position never to be exposed to—The final forced conflict between someone from the front and someone of the genteel base. Is the word so impossible of printing?

If it is, the incident is killed. It was the one word I remember we omitted from The Sun. Maybe if it had been printed then we'd know now if it was printable.

If you decide that it is unprintable how about

<u>b—ls</u>

I think that's the only solution.
I suppose on galley 57
C—S—RS and C—KS—R will do for the other too.

galley 60
Certainly those letters cannot corrupt anyone who has not heard or does not know the word. There's no proof it isnt cocksure

Memorandum of Agreement, *made this* — twenty-fifth — *day of* September 1929

between ERNEST HEMINGWAY

of Paris, France, — - — - — *hereinafter called "the* AUTHOR*,"*
and CHARLES SCRIBNER'S SONS, *of New York City, N. Y., hereinafter called "the*
PUBLISHERS*." Said* — Ernest Hemingway — — *being the* AUTHOR
and PROPRIETOR *of a work entitled:*

A FAREWELL TO ARMS

in consideration of the covenants and stipulations hereinafter contained, and agreed to be performed by the PUBLISHERS, *grants and guarantees to said* PUBLISHERS *and their successors the exclusive right to publish the said work in all forms during the terms of copyright and renewals thereof, hereby covenanting with said* PUBLISHERS *that he is the sole* AUTHOR *and* PROPRIETOR *of said work.*

Said AUTHOR *hereby authorizes said* PUBLISHERS *to take out the copyright on said work, and further guarantees to said* PUBLISHERS *that the said work is in no way whatever a violation of any copyright belonging to any other party, and that it contains nothing of a scandalous or libelous character; and that he and his legal representatives shall and will hold harmless the said* PUBLISHERS *from all suits, and all manner of claims and proceedings which may be taken on the ground that said work is such violation or contains anything scandalous or libelous; and he further hereby authorizes said* PUBLISHERS *to defend at law any and all suits and proceedings which may be taken or had against them for infringement of any other copyright or for libel, scandal, or any other injurious or hurtful matter or thing contained in or alleged or claimed to be contained in or caused by said work, and pay to said* PUBLISHERS *such reasonable costs, disbursements, expenses, and counsel fees as they may incur in such defense.*

Said PUBLISHERS, *in consideration of the right herein granted and of the guarantees aforesaid, agree to publish said work at their own expense, in such style and manner as they shall deem most expedient, and to pay said* AUTHOR, *or - his - legal representatives,*
FIFTEEN (15) ------------------- *per cent. on their Trade-List (retail) price, cloth style, for* the first Twenty-five Thousand (25,000) copies *of said work sold by them in the United* States and TWENTY (20) per cent. for all copies sold thereafter.
Provided, nevertheless, that one-half the above named royalty shall be paid on all copies sold outside the United States; and provided that no percentage whatever shall be paid on any copies destroyed by fire or water, or sold at or below cost, or given away for the purpose of aiding the sale of said work.

It is further agreed that the profits arising from any publication of said work, during the period covered by this agreement, in other than book form shall be divided equally between said PUBLISHERS *and said* AUTHOR.

Hemingway's contract for his second novel, with his increased royalty rate (Charles Scribner's Sons Archive, Princeton University Library). By the end of 1929 sixty thousand copies of the book, at $2.50 each, had been sold, and Hemingway earned $26,875 from these sales.

Expenses incurred for alterations in type or plates, exceeding twenty per cent. of the cost of composition and electrotyping said work, are to be charged to the AUTHOR's account.

The first statement shall not be rendered until six months after date of publication; and thereafter statements shall be rendered semi-annually, on the AUTHOR's application therefor, in the months of February and August; settlements to be made in cash, four months after date of statement.

If, on the expiration of   five   years from date of publication, or at any time thereafter, the demand for said work should not, in the opinion of said PUBLISHERS, be sufficient to render its publication profitable, then, upon written notice by said PUBLISHERS to said AUTHOR, this contract shall cease and determine; and thereupon said AUTHOR shall have the right, at his option, to take from said PUBLISHERS, at cost, whatever copies of said work they may then have on hand; or, failing to take said copies at cost, then said PUBLISHERS shall have the right to dispose of the copies on hand as they may see fit, free from any percentage or royalty, and to cancel this contract.

Provided, also, that if, at any time during the continuance of this agreement, said work shall become unsalable in the ordinary channels of trade, said PUBLISHERS shall have the right to dispose of any copies on hand paying to said AUTHOR - fifteen (15) - per cent. of the net amount received therefor, in lieu of the percentage hereinbefore prescribed.

It is further understood and agreed that the first Twenty Thousand Dollars ($20,000) of said royalties shall be paid to The City Bank Farmers Trust Company as Trustee.

In consideration of the mutuality of this contract, the aforesaid parties agree to all its provisions, and in testimony thereof affix their signatures and seals.

Witness to signature of
Ernest Hemingway

Henry H. Strater

Witness to signature of
Charles Scribner's Sons

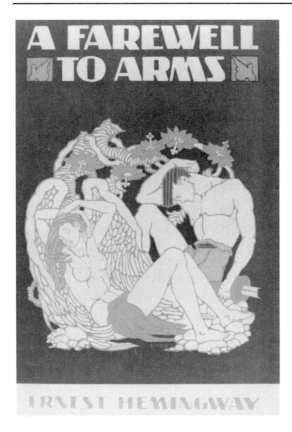

Dust jacket for Hemingway's World War I novel. Hemingway disliked the artwork by Cleonike Damianakes and wrote to Maxwell Perkins that "if the book is banned anywhere I think it will be on account of that girl on the cover."

In Being Geniuses Together *(pp. 163–164) McAlmon gives this account of the boxing match between Callaghan and Hemingway in Paris in June 1929. Callaghan, who had worked with Hemingway at the* Toronto Star *and was one of Maxwell Perkins's authors at Scribners, gave his own account of the fight in* That Summer in Paris: Memories of Tangled Friendships with Hemingway, Fitzgerald, and Some Others *(New York: Coward-McCann, 1963).*

All of this shadow-boxing [by Hemingway] was to keep himself fit, naturally, and a couple of years later when Morley Callaghan, also a bit of a boxer, arrived in Paris, he and Hemingway staged bouts. Before, Hemingway had a bout with a young French writer, Jean Prévost, but it seems that it was a draw, a sparring match with no referee.

The Callaghan-Hemingway bout, however, was apparently not a draw, and it was reported to me several ways, by Hemingway, Callaghan, and from Scott Fitzgerald. Callaghan's report was that Scott was to referee and they were to have three or four two-minute rounds. Scott got very interested in the boxing match. Hemingway was the taller and heavier man. Callaghan was short, inclined to a look of flabbiness and rotundity. Scott was sure that Hemingway would need to play with Callaghan and let him down easily without showing him up in a mortifying way. The first round did not come out that way and Scott forgot to tell time, Callaghan had Hemingway backing away, and getting winded; but the fight went on and on. Neither of the boxers would suggest that the round-time was up, but after some minutes Scott called time. Callaghan was sure that Hemingway thought Scott forgot to call time purposely.

Hemingway's story was that he had been drinking the night before and was boxing on three pick-me-up whiskies so that his wind gave out. The decision results were, however, that neither Hemingway nor Callaghan could decide what the bout proved. Was one a better boxer but not so good a writer as the other, or was the other a better writer and boxer, or had Scott framed one or the other of them?

At this time Hemingway felt that Callaghan was imitating his style, and it is true that Callaghan was writing about prize-fighters, gangsters, and inarticulate roughnecks, but there was Ring Lardner who had done a bit of this before either of them. Gertrude Stein was the repeating child, and Sherwood Anderson had injected highfalutin' sensibility into the hearts of childish boobs. Possibly then their writing bout was a draw. The final bell has not rung. Callaghan, admittedly a pedestrian writer and perhaps dull—but it is the fashion in some quarters to court the dull—seems interested in wider and more normal phases of life. At least much less of his writing is a defence and explanation of himself and of the reactions and emotions which he feels he ought to have. Hemingway is always protesting and explaining his emotions so much that one is able to wonder if he has not invented some convention for himself as to how one should feel in each particular circumstance. To be brave, professionally here, tough there, gentle and inarticulate with tenderness there, the rough man, reticent but full of sensibility.

Hemingway in Key West, 1929

Poet Archibald MacLeish wrote Hemingway with the following reaction to A Farewell to Arms. From Letters of Archibald MacLeish, 1907 to 1982, *edited by R. H. Winnick (Boston: Houghton Mifflin, 1983), p. 230.*

1 September

Dear Pappy:

I have just finished the Sept. instal.. I haven't anything to say. It is beautiful–beautiful beyond words. The seriousness & precision & candor of your writing makes you feel the way you feel after tears when everything is suddenly simple & profoundly clear & perfectly tender. I cannot think about Catherine without love for her nor of you without emotions which are simply not to be spoken. You see it is merely silly for me to attempt to talk of it. And yet I go on–there are two moments equal in tenor to the crisis of *The Killers*. And there is something you have never reached before–a deep & true pity with no irony & no self-consciousness. I was terribly moved by the lad under the canvas on the car. By Ferguson. By Catherine. By that night.

What has happened is that you have mastered the self-imposed problems of your technique. There was a time when I wondered whether the restrained & tense understatement of your prose would not limit you to a certain kind of material. Now no one can wonder that. The world of this book is a complete world, a world of emotion as well as of feeling. To subject the whole experience of a man's soul to the pure & perfect art of your prose is a great, a very great, achievement. I send you my complete praise & my profound respect. You become in one book the great novelist of our time. It is not for me to supply you with accolades & titles. But I *know*. And I am glad with all my heart. I think now you can forgive me my stupidity in Saragossa, for it was this achievement that I then wished for you. And do always wish. And, because I feel as I do about you, with no envy but with pride.

Cover for sheet music published in 1933. The first line is "Farewell to arms, arms that have held me" (Ernest Hemingway Collection, John F. Kennedy Library)

When can we meet? We shall be here in the spring—winter in Chicago. This house is yours.

Give my love to Pauline & forgive my literary-isms about the book. I know no other way to write. I hear praise of you on all sides from all kinds of people. You should be completely happy. Of course you won't be. You have planned so long a journey for yourself. But, for the rest of us, it is accomplished in this book.

A.

Hemingway liked the following review in the Sunday supplement to the Richmond Times-Dispatch *(6 October 1929, p. 3) so much that he suggested to Maxwell Perkins that it be used in advertisements for the novel: "In spite of having written the bloody book and having worked over it so much that I am completely unable to read it when I read this review I wanted to go right out and buy one–" (17 November 1929,* The Only Thing That Counts, *p. 125).*

Critic Lavishes Praise On New Hemingway Novel By James Aswell

I have finished "A Farewell to Arms," and am still a little breathless, as people often are after a major event in their lives. If before I die I have three more literary experiences as sharp and exciting and terrible as the one I have just been through, I shall know it has been a good world.

That, I am aware, is extravagant praise. Perhaps I should have begun more cautiously. Because I do not know whether "A Farewell to Arms" is a "great" book or not, or whether it will "live." I do not know and I do not give a damn: those are considerations for The New York Times and the sages in the great institution ninety miles to Richmond's northwest. I only know that there are many people who will be deeply stirred by this tender, brutal, devastatingly simple love story; stirred as they have never been by Dreiser's clumsy magnificence, or Anderson's naively cynical rusticism, or Cabell's anagrams. These people may well stand before some imposing fifty-foot shelf and wonder, frightened, "Where is there another to go, candidly, by his side? Where can I match that hot, four-dimensional life or that prose stripped of a thousand years of prolixities? With all the great names it's unnerving that I should have to think at all!"

"A Farewell to Arms" is not a war story primarily, despite the publisher's blurbs and the assumptions of the two or three reviews I have read. The war is always there, a background, "in the mountains," but it can no more be considered the theme than hospitals can be considered the theme because the last few thousand words have their setting in one. What Hemingway wants to do, and does do, is to tell the story of Frederick Henry and Catherine Barkley. It is the story of two young people and what they said to each other and the loving they had together. And secondarily it is a story of the sentient natural world enjoyed not through the head but through the senses properly, of cold mornings and rain and good food; of wine and pain and fear and deep sleep; of the rank, healthy talk of men together and fine, blasphemous laughter.

More than any other writer I know Hemingway has eliminated the odor of the lamp from his prose. Years ago in Paris he told Sisley Huddleston that he wanted to divorce language "from its superfluities." No wonder poor, old, grandiloquent Sisley didn't like him at all! I cannot imagine Hemingway in his first literary company, under the pale, effete, pseudo-cerebral auspices of This Quarter and The Dial and The Little Review. But it is certain he could not have gotten his stuff into print anywhere else, and I suppose they saw only that he was "different," without recognizing his, to them, treacherous masculinity.

An unconscious compliment to Hemingway's simplicity is Harry Hansen's remark that he writes "the most mannered prose now being written in English." It means that he has thrown overboard so much of the affectation of Aldous Huxley's dessicated company that his directness seems to be a trick!

But verbal health is only a part of the man, albeit an essential one. Other writers have achieved a simplicity that is ingratiating but without the emotional tenseness, the boiling interior life of "A Farewell to Arms." They have not found Hemingway's faculty of contemporaneousness. There is in the book a pervading atmosphere of tight, unfolding events. The story is happening as we read. It is not told in the past tense, emotionally.

Lieutenant Henry is an American with the Italian army. Catherine Barkley is an English nurse. He wants her first because he is weary of bought love and "the officer's hours." Then he becomes tender and possessive after the ancient sequence: he is in love. When he is wounded and she brightens his nights in the hospital he realizes he is much in love. Later he deserts from the army–"It's not deserting from the army," she says. "It's only the Italian army"–and they escape to Switzerland, where she is to have a baby. A Caesarian is performed and she dies. The baby dies too. This is the end of the book.

Yet "A Farewell to Arms" is not a gloomy book. Frederick and Catherine are brave and healthy; they have a splendid time before the end. If there are tears for you at last–and I suspect there will be–you will not know whether you are choken because of the tragedy that occurs or because of the rich, passionate beauty of the happiness they have had. There are descriptive passages growing out of their sojourn in Switzerland that will probably cause uneasy sleep in authorial flats down the years:

> There was an inn in the trees at Bains de L'Alliaz, where the woodcutters stopped to drink, and we sat inside warmed by the stove and drank hot read wine with spices and lemon in it. . . . The inn was dark and smoky inside and afterward when you went out the cold air came sharply into your lungs and numbed the edge of your nose as you inhaled. We looked back at the inn with the light coming from the windows and the wood cutters' horses stamping and jerking their heads outside to keep warm. There was frost on the hairs of their muzzle and their breathing made plumes of frost in the air. Going up the road toward home the road was smooth and slippery for a while and the ice orange from the horses until the wood hauling truck turned off. Then the road was clean-packed snow and

led through the woods, and twice coming home in the evening, we saw foxes.

Perhaps the thing that sets Hemingway head and shoulders above the "sophisticates" with whom he has often been libelously grouped, is his not being afraid of tenderness. But the tenderness is always removed a little, in space, as it were, from the passage. He seeks no euphemisms; he is never whimsical in the revolting Milne-Barrie sense. But he is sensitive to sorrowful beauty without feeling pity about it. He seems to say, "These people are headed for a bad time, but it is good that they are living fully now." Once Catherine asks Frederick whether they shoot larks in America. "Not especially," he replies. It may be that I am sinking into obscurantism, but I believe that interchange conveys the sort of tenderness, humorous, warm, that Hemingway has. Its absence is what frequently betrays imitators of the Hemingway manner such as Morley Callaghan.

"A Farewell to Arms" is a rhythmic, plethoric, bitterly lovely story. If anything better has been produced by a native of the New World I do not know what it is. And as for me, I have never gotten a greater kick out of any book.

The following review of Hemingway's World War I novel was written by John Dos Passos and published in The New Masses, *5 (1 December 1929), p. 16.*

A Farewell to Arms

Hemingway's *A Farewell to Arms* is the best written book that has seen the light in America for many a long day. By well-written I don't mean the tasty college composition course sort of thing that our critics seem to consider good writing. I mean writing that is terse and economical, in which each sentence and each phrase bears its maximum load of meaning, sense impressions, emotion. The book is a firstrate piece of craftsmanship by a man who knows his job. It gives you the sort of pleasure line by line that you get from handling a piece of wellfinished carpenter's work. Read the first chapter, the talk at the officers' mess in Gorizia, the scene in the dressingstation when the narrator is wounded, the paragraph describing the ride to Milan in the hospital train, the talk with the British major about how everybody's cooked in the war, the whole description of the disaster at Caporetto to the end of the chapter where the battlepolice are shooting the officers as they cross the bridge, the caesarian operation in which the girl dies. The stuff will match up as narrative prose with anything that's been written since there was any English language.

It's a darn good document too. It describes with reserve and exactness the complex of events back of the Italian front in the winter of 1916 and the summer and fall of 1917 when people had more or less settled down to the thought of war as the natural form of human existence when every individual in the armies was struggling for survival with bitter hopelessness. In the absolute degradation of the average soldier's life in the Italian army there were two hopes, that the revolution would end the war or that Meester Weelson would end the war on the terms of the Seventeen Points. In Italy the revolution lost its nerve at the moment of its victory and Meester Weelson's points paved the way for D'Annunzio's bloody farce at Fiume and the tyranny of Mussolini and the banks. If a man wanted to learn the history of that period in that sector of the European War I don't know where he'd find a better account than in the first half of *A Farewell to Arms*.

This is a big time for the book business in America. The writing, publishing and marketing of books is getting to be a major industry along with beautyshoppes and advertising. Ten years ago it was generally thought that all writers were either drunks or fairies. Now they have a halo of possible money around them and are respected on a par with brokers or realtors. The American people seems to be genuinely hungry for books. Even good books sell.

It's not surprising that *A Farewell to Arms*, that accidentally combines the selling points of having a lovestory and being about the war, should be going like hot-cakes. It would be difficult to dope out just why there should be such a tremendous vogue for books about the war just now. Maybe it's that the boys and girls who were too young to know anything about the last war are just reaching a bookbuying age. Maybe it's the result of the intense military propaganda going on in schools and colleges. Anyhow if they read things like *A Farewell to Arms* and *All Quiet on the Western Front*, they are certainly getting the dope straight and it's hard to see how the militarist could profit much. Certainly a writer can't help but feel good about the success of such an honest and competent piece of work as *A Farewell to Arms*.

After all craftsmanship is a damn fine thing, one of the few human functions a man can unstintedly admire. The drift of the Fordized world seems all against it. Rationalization and subdivision of labor in industry tend more and more to wipe it out. It's getting to be almost unthinkable that you should take pleasure in your work, that a man should enjoy doing a piece of work for the sake of doing it as well as he damn well can. What we still have is the mechanic's or motorman's pleasure in a smoothrunning machine. As the operator gets more mechanized even that disappears; what you get is a division of life into drudgery and leisure instead of into work and play. As industrial society evolves and the workers get control of the machines a new type of craftsmanship may work out. For the present you only get opportunity for craftsmanship, which ought to be the privilege of any workman, in novelwriting and the painting of easelpictures and in a few of the machinebuilding trades that are hangovers from the period of individual manufacture that is just closing. Most of the attempts to salvage craftsmanship in industry have been faddy movements like East Aurora and Morris furniture and have come to nothing. *A Farewell to Arms* is no worse a novel because it was written with a typewriter. But it's a magnificent novel because the writer felt every minute the satisfaction of working ably with his material and his tools and continually pushing the work to the limit of effort.

Chapter Three: 1930–1935

1930

1 November   Hemingway breaks his right arm in an auto accident near Billings, Montana. He undergoes three operations to set the break and is confined until 21 December in St. Vincent's Hospital in Billings. He later uses his hospital experiences in writing "The Gambler, The Nun, and The Radio."

1931

April   Pauline's uncle, Gus Pfeiffer, supplies money for the Hemingways to buy the house they have been renting at 907 Whitehead Street, Key West.

June–
September   Gathering material for his book on bullfighting, *Death in the Afternoon,* Hemingway spends the summer in Spain.

12 November   Pauline gives birth to Ernest's third child, Gregory.

December   Hemingway finishes the first draft of *Death in the Afternoon.*

1932

April–June   Hemingway spends two months in Havana, fishing and revising the proof of *Death in the Afternoon.*

23 September   Scribners publishes *Death in the Afternoon.*

6 December   While staying at the home of Pauline's parents in Piggott, Arkansas, Hemingway refuses to see the movie premiere of *A Farewell to Arms.*

1933

ca. 7 January   Hemingway meets Thomas Wolfe in Perkins's office.

20 January   In Captain Louis Henry Cohn's House of Books, New York City, Hemingway meets Arnold Gingrich, a magazine editor preparing to launch *Esquire.*

March   *Scribner's Magazine* publishes "A Clean, Well-Lighted Place."

3 April   Hemingway agrees to contribute a series of letters to *Esquire.* He eventually publishes twenty-five articles and six stories in the magazine.

27 October   Scribners publishes *Winner Take Nothing,* Hemingway's third short-story collection.

22 November   The Hemingways and Charles Thompson, a friend from Key West, sail from Marseilles for Africa.

20 December– 20 February	Philip Percival leads the Hemingways and Thompson on safari, and Hemingway uses his experiences during this trip to write three *Esquire* essays, *Green Hills of Africa,* and two short stories: "The Short Happy Life of Francis Macomber" and "The Snows of Kilimanjaro."

1934

27 March	The Hemingways leave France for New York aboard the *Ile de France,* on which they meet actress Marlene Dietrich.
4 April	Hemingway sees Gerald Murphy, Waldo Pierce, and F. Scott Fitzgerald in New York. He orders his own fishing boat from Wheeler Shipyard in Brooklyn.
11 May	Hemingway sails his new boat, the *Pilar,* from Miami to Key West.
Late May	Hemingway begins writing an account of his safari.
16 November	Hemingway completes the first draft of *Green Hills of Africa.*

1935

May	*Scribner's Magazine* begins serializing *Green Hills of Africa.*
2–3 September	A hurricane hits Matecumbe Key, killing 458 war veterans who were working in a Civilian Conservation Corps camp. Hemingway assists in cleaning up the site and disposing of the bodies.
17 September	*The New Masses,* a hard-line leftist periodical, publishes Hemingway's "Who Murdered the Vets?"
25 October	*Green Hills of Africa* is published in New York.

During the first half of the 1930s, Hemingway wrote two works of nonfiction and published a new collection of short stories. After completing *A Farewell to Arms,* he began writing *Death in the Afternoon,* a history of and guide to bullfighting that also included his opinions on art and writing.

After spending the first part of 1930 in Key West, where he worked on the bullfight treatise and fished, Hemingway and his wife traveled to Lawrence Nordquist's L Bar T Ranch near Cooke City, Montana, where he could fish for trout, hunt, and not be distracted by visitors and tourists. Work on his new book was suspended on 1 November 1930, when Hemingway broke his right arm in a car accident near Billings, Montana. He spent seven weeks in St. Vincent's Hospital and then returned to Key West in January 1931, but he could not resume writing until April.

That spring the Hemingways moved into their new home (a gift from Pauline's uncle, Gustavas Adolphus Pfeiffer) at 907 Whitehead Street. Hemingway spent the summer in Spain where he followed the bullfights and gathered photos for his book. He and Pauline returned to Kansas City for the birth of their second child, Gregory, on 12 November 1931. After Pauline's recovery the couple returned to Key West, where Hemingway completed his book in January 1932.

He revised galley proofs for *Death in the Afternoon,* wrote new stories in the first half of the year, and spent much of May and June in Havana, where he lived and worked at the Ambos Mundos Hotel. In July he returned to Wyoming and remained there through October.

Published on 23 September 1932, *Death in the Afternoon* received mixed reviews. While most critics praised Hemingway's style and depth of knowledge, some reviewers complained that he tried too hard to prove that he was tough and needlessly attacked other writers such as Waldo Frank, William Faulkner, and T. S. Eliot. The number of copies sold did not match the number that had been sold of *A Farewell to Arms,* in part because the retail price of *Death in the Afternoon* ($3.50) was higher and because the latter was nonfiction.

After his return to Key West in October 1932, Hemingway began preparing his next short-story collection. *Winner Take Nothing* was published on 27 Octo-

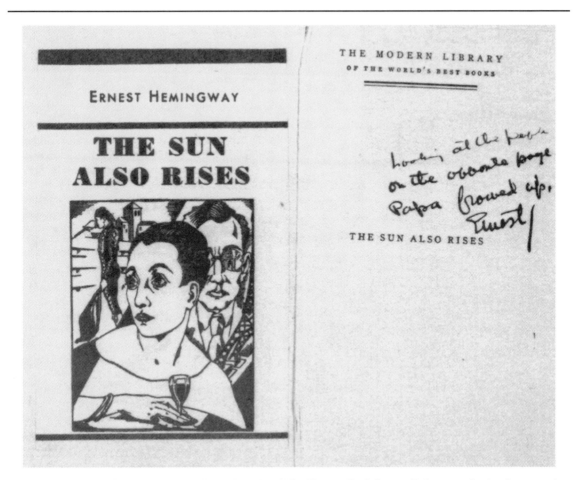

THE MODERN LIBRARY
OF THE WORLD'S BEST BOOKS

THE SUN ALSO RISES

Hemingway's inscription in Dorothy Parker's copy alludes to her review of The House at Pooh Corner. *Parker was an American short-story writer, poet, and celebrated wit (Clifton Waller Barrett Library, University of Virginia).*

ber 1933, and while it includes some of Hemingway's best stories—"A Clean, Well-Lighted Place," "The Light of the World," and "Fathers and Sons"—the collection as a whole is Hemingway's weakest. Reviews again were mixed, with some critics complaining that the stories were too similar in style and substance to Hemingway's previous works. Scribners ordered only one printing of 20,300 copies—2,000 of which were remaindered.

In 1933 Hemingway also met Arnold Gingrich, an editor who was preparing to launch a new magazine, *Esquire,* and who asked Hemingway to become a contributor. Hemingway agreed, as long as he were allowed to write about any subject that interested him. While many of the essays published in his "Letters" column were about hunting and fishing, he also used this forum to publish articles on writing and politics during the three years he contributed to the magazine.

In November 1933 Ernest, Pauline, and Charles Thompson (a friend from Key West) traveled to Africa

for a three-month safari, a trip financed by Pauline's Uncle Gus. Hemingway was fascinated by the animals, natives, and landscape, and when he returned to Key West in April 1934 he began writing an account of the last month of the safari. As he had done with *Death in the Afternoon,* he incorporated his thinking about writing and writers into this work.

The first draft of *Green Hills of Africa* was completed in November 1934. *Scribner's Magazine* purchased serial rights and began publishing the book in May 1935. Hemingway revised proofs for both the serial and the book during the summer, much of which he spent on the island of Bimini. *Green Hills of Africa* was published as a book on 25 October 1935, and reviews again were mixed. While some critics such as Charles Poore of *The New York Times Book Review* and Edward Weeks of the *Atlantic Monthly* found the book to be interesting and well written, others such as Edmund Wilson of the *New Republic* and Bernard DeVoto of the *Saturday*

Review of Literature thought it was Hemingway's weakest. Most of the dissatisfied reviewers thought that Hemingway should write about something more important than hunting. The number of books sold–less than twelve thousand copies between October 1935 and October 1937–was disappointing.

Hemingway contributed this piece to Modern Writers at Work, *edited by Josephine K. Piercy (New York: Macmillan, 1930), pp. 488, 490.*

ERNEST HEMINGWAY
Novelist, story-writer

Mr. Hemingway has been catalogued as one of the "newer writers." His style is succinct and vivid. He tells what he sees of life, mostly of men and women who want of life what they have not or squander what they have. Certainly he is realistic; sometimes he is naturalistic. His stories are plain tales, plainly and therefore strikingly told.

"Everyone writes prose badly to start but by continuing some get to write it well. Stop or go on is the only advice I know.

"As for the practical side; I believe the typewriter is a curse of modern writing. It makes it too easy and the writing is solidified in type and is hard to change when it might still be kept plastic and be worked over and brought nearer to what it should be before it is cast in type. This all sounds very high flown but you must remember that you are asking some one engaged in a craft which he is constantly studying, practicing and trying to learn more about.

"I should think it might take a lifetime to learn to write prose well; your own prose that is; for if it is not your own it is of no value. Then if you had spent your life doing it perhaps you would have nothing to write about.

"The ideal way would be to live and then write or live and write at the same time. But it is very hard to serve two masters and a writer is very lucky if he has only two.

"At any rate what we should avoid is developing a lot of completely articulate young professional novelists just out of the university who write one interesting novel; well written in anyone else's way of writing; fresh because it has youth; and successful for any of the above reasons–then to be followed by other novels, demanded by the success of the first and because the author is a professional writer, and all the time the author is never living any life or learning anything or seeing anything because he, or even more possibly she, is so busy writing novels.

"You can study how this works out in England."

In 1930 Scribners acquired the rights to In Our Time *from Boni & Liveright. Maxwell Perkins suggested that Hemingway write an introduction for the Scribner republication, but Hemingway, claiming that he was too busy working on* Death in the Afternoon, *submitted only a new story, "Introduction by the Author," which was retitled "On the Quai at Smyrna" in subsequent collections. He did suggest that Edmund Wilson write an introduction to* In Our Time, *and the piece Wilson wrote was published only in this edition (pp. ix–xv).*

"In Our Time" is Ernest Hemingway's first book, and it has the appearance of a miscellany. It consists of sketches and short stories, among which we are able to recognize, as we reread them, early experiments with almost all the themes which he has since treated more elaborately. There are bull-fight scenes; drinking conversations; Gertrude Stein comedy; memories of the Italian front. And one piece, "A Very Short Story," is a sort of scenario for "A Farewell to Arms," with an ending perhaps more convincing that the rather romanticized idyll of the novel.

Yet "In Our Time" is complete and satisfactory in itself: it has the whole of Hemingway in it already. And its very mixed and fragmentary character enables us to understand this whole, to identify its various elements, better than any of his subsequent books has done. "In Our Time" is made up of two alternating series: a set of short stories dealing chiefly with the growing-up of a boy in the American Northwest; and sandwiched in with these, a set of brief and brutal sketches of happenings mostly connected with the War. The sensitiveness and candor of the boy strike a sharp discord with the cold-bloodedness and barbarity of the executions, the police shootings and the battles; but though the boy appears in one of the intermediary sketches as a wounded soldier, hit in the spine and ready to "make a separate peace," it does not require this to establish a relation between the two series. They both represent the same world, and the contrast which at first disconcerts us is at the centre of Hemingways's point of view. It is the source of the peculiar emotional effects which his later books have been able to produce so powerfully.

Candor and cold-bloodedness both belong to the same humanity. Has the the young man who gets wounded in the War, who watches the cabinet ministers shot and who pots the enemy as they are trying to get

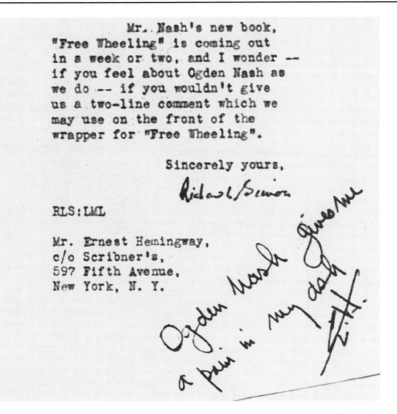

Mr. Nash's new book,
"Free Wheeling" is coming out
in a week or two, and I wonder —
if you feel about Ogden Nash as
we do — if you wouldn't give
us a two-line comment which we
may use on the front of the
wrapper for "Free Wheeling".

Sincerely yours,

Richard Simon

RLS:LML

Mr. Ernest Hemingway,
c/o Scribner's,
597 Fifth Avenue,
New York, N. Y.

Ogden Nash gives me
a pain in my dash.
Hty.

Hemingway's response to Richard Simon, poet Ogden Nash's publisher, when Simon asked him to provide a blurb (Swann Galleries, Sale 1681, 2 February 1995, Item 106)

over a simply priceless barricade, really come such a long way from the boy who went fishing at Big Two-Hearted River? Was not life back in Michigan woods equally destructive and cruel? In an Indian shanty, a squaw had once had to have a Caesarian operation with a jack-knife and without anaesthetic, and the Indian hadn't been able to bear it and had cut his throat in his bunk; Nick's father, who is a doctor, had saved the life of another squaw, and the Indian had insolently picked a quarrel with him rather than pay him with work; Nick himself had sent his girl about her business when he found out how terrible her mother was. Life is fine: the woods are enjoyable; fishing is enjoyable; being with one's friends is enjoyable; even the War is enjoyable. But the brutality of life is always there, and it is somehow bound up with the enjoyment. Bull-fights are especially enjoyable. Even Nick's fishing-trip, when he is away by himself happy and free in the woods, has aspects which must make it unique among the fishing-trips of literature—for through all Nick's tranquil exhilaration we are made conscious in a curious way of the cruelty involved for the fish—and not only this, but

even of the martyrdom of the grasshoppers used for bait. The condition of life is still pain—and every calm or contented surface still vibrates with its pangs. The resolution of that discord in art makes the beauty of Hemingway's stories.

"In Our Time" thus provides a sort of key to Hemingway's late and more ambitious books. Suffering and making suffer, and their relation to the sensual enjoyment of life, are the subject of them all—though the evenness, the prose perfection, of the surface in these books seems sometimes to have concealed from their readers the conflicts which it covers but which it has been stretched so taut precisely to convey. "A Farewell to Arms," which probably contains Hemingway's best narrative and most moving scenes, seems to me in some ways less characteristic and less interesting in this respect than "The Sun Also Rises" and his short stories; because in "A Farewell to Arms" the making suffer is all blamed on things in general, and the hero and heroine are represented as perfectly innocent victims with no relation to the forces that torment them: their story lacks the conflict of impulses which makes the real drama in Hemingway, and when they emerge from the stream of action, when they escape together after the Caporetto retreat, we cease to believe in them as human personalities. "The Sun Also Rises," on the other hand, has a profound unity and a disquieting reality because there is an intimate relation established between the fiesta in the little Spanish town, with its processions, its bull-fighting and its hilarity, and the atrocious behavior of the group of Americans and English who have come down from Paris to enjoy it. In the heartlessness of these people toward each other we recognize the same principle at work as in the pagan orgy of the festival. The persecution of Cohn is as much a natural casualty of a barbarous world as the unexpected fate of the man who gets accidentally gored by the bull on the way to the bull-ring. Hemingway's most remarkable effects in this book are those, as in the fishing-trip, where we are made to feel behind the gusto of the appetite for the physical world the falsity or the tragedy of a moral situation. This undruggable consciousness of something wrong seems never to arouse Hemingway to passionate violence; but it poisons him and makes him sick, and this invests with a singular sinister quality—a quality I suppose new in fiction—the sunlight and the green summer landscapes of "The Sun Also Rises."

The interest of "The Sun Also Rises" arises from the attempts of the hero and heroine to disengage themselves from such a world, or rather to find some way of living in it honorably. Life, which we devour so voraciously for the very things about it which destroy us, is always in the long run a losing game; but it is a game and at least allows of the the kind of virtues proper to a game. We must stick to the code of the sportsman and lose in a sportsmanlike way. And so the bull-fight itself, with which Hemingway has always been so much preoccupied, becomes a symbol of life: you stab or you get gored—and in the meantime many unoffending horses are casually being disembowelled; the highest aim is to kill the bull, or if the time has come to die, to die game—like the old bullfighter in "The Undefeated." This conceiving of life as a game—even though Hemingway's favorite sport is bull-fighting—is peculiarly Anglo-Saxon. How Anglo-Saxon it is we realize when we think of Maupassant or Dostoevsky, both occupied like Hemingway with the problem of suffering and making suffer, and when we see how completely different are the terms in which this problem presents itself to them. And Hemingway can hardly yet be compared to Dostoevsky, he is certainly, I should say, a more interesting writer that Maupassant. When we put them together, we recognize how much is conventional and mechanical in Maupassant's French pessimism, and we feel, on the other hand, that Hemingway has invested the

Anglo-Saxon idea of sport with a seriousness which not even Kipling had previously been able to give it.

At any rate, Hemingway's artistic personality has already come of age in "In Our Time." It is the book, not of an amateur, but of an artist who has already found his vocation—who, though he is still trying out with small subjects, displays already a mastery of his craft. The naïve colloquial accent—partly learned from Sherwood Anderson and Gertrude Stein—is already a limpid shaft in deep waters. The bull-fight sketches have the dry sharpness and elegance of Goy's lithographs. Yet Hemingway should perhaps more than any one else be allowed to escape the common literary fate of being derived from other people. He is one of the most original of contemporary writers. There have been few first-rate writers in the United States, but these, if they have been often peculiarly isolated, have been also likely to be peculiarly original. They have created for themselves directly new and personal ways of writing for personal ways of seeing and feeling. And with the descriptions in "In Our Time" of American wood and water Hemingway has brought into literature a new pair of eyes for landscape, as in his sketches of the War, where the steady cheerful tone of everyday wakes such strange qualms of insecurity and anguish, he catches as they have never yet been caught the blind excited emotions of the American of 1917 and thereafter.

Caresse Crosby, wife of poet and publisher Harry Crosby, included this portrait of Hemingway in her memoir, The Passionate Years *(London: Redman, 1955), pp. 293–300. Her publishing house, Crosby Continental Editions, specialized in reprinting American and British books. The firm republished Hemingway's* The Torrents of Spring *in 1931.*

Midsummer. Jacques and I motored back to Paris from Cannes via Biarritz—to do this, one passed along the coast as far as Sete, then Carcassonne and on across the foothills of the Pyrennes through remote little Basque villages. We had friends at Biarritz and it was while visiting them that we decided to go across the Spanish border into St. Sebastian to see the American bullfighter, Franklin, make his début in that arena. Ernest Hemingway had told us that he would be there too; he was writing a book on bullfighting and we arranged to meet at an appointed rendezvous near the bullring—a corner café frequented by toreadors, and one where Hemingway must have found much of his local colour.

Hemingway, Pauline and his eldest son, a boy of about six, were there already. The child Bumbi was being given lessons in the handling of the cape by one of the elderly fighters, already retired. When we arrived at the bistro, we found Hemingway straddling a chair in a far corner, the old Spaniard explaining an intricate manoeuvre. The boy had to repeat it again and again; his father was a difficult taskmaster, and Bumbi's face was puckered with apprehension. He was very nearly ready for tears. Our advent seemed a happy interruption, to him at least.

Hemingway got up, arranged with the *torero* for another lesson, told his son that he would have to do better next time, and led us all out to the terrace, where Pauline was waiting and where we drank sherry, and ate what I think was a ragout of kid, cooked in Marsala wine. Ernest had engaged a box for the fight next to the President's, and every bit as good, and to my delight I found myself rubbing elbows with Charlie Chaplin, who was in the grand official box. When the ear was cut from the final bull, the torero offered it with historic ritual to the purposely flustered Chaplin, who waved and kissed his hands to applauding thousands in his most coy Chaplinesque manner. It was a wonderful day. We left Franklin and Hemingway waiting for Chaplin at the same corner bistro, where we had met earlier. We were sorry to leave, but there was to be a fancy dress ball that night in Biarritz. . . .

"Caresse Crosby a inventé le Soutien Gorge et Hemingway" announced the headline in a Paris paper when I visited France in '48. I was on my way home from the Italian elections at the time. My readers by now know that I *did* invent the brassiére, but for their peace of mind they should know that I did *not* invent Hemingway, although I managed to make him whopping mad. . . .

I had already published *Torrents of Spring* in the Crosby Continental Editions, but that was a "first" for Europe only—it may be said that Europe was delighted not with the Hemingway alone, but with all the other American titles in the series, Faulkner's *Sanctuary,* Dorothy Parker's *Laments for the Living,* Kay Boyle's *Year Before Last,* etc., etc. However, I coveted a really honest-to-Hemingway original, a limited edition de luxe, just so many copies signed by the author, at an elevated price—the Press had done it before with Joyce, Lawrence, Crane, MacLeish—why not Hemingway?

It was on my return from Spain that I decided the Black Sun should have one legitimate Hemingway to its credit.

He and Pauline were stopping at a little left-bank hotel about halfway between the Press in the rue Cardinale and my apartment in the rue de Lille.

Hemingway in Billings, Montana, after his 1 November 1930 auto accident

Narcisse and I walked over one fine noon and found the Hemingways still not up (much the best way to be at noon). On the big bed between them was propped a painting by Juan Gris, of a guitar player, it was a beauty, and Ernest had just acquired it the day before. He ruefully remarked that it took nearly all the passage money for their return trip to the United States, scheduled for a few weeks later, they were hurrying to get back home, Pauline said, so that their next son could be born with the benefit of presidency.

With true publisher instinct I saw my opening, here was a fine gambit. "I could pay you for the story at once," I suggested, "if you do need money for the tickets." But Ernest was not to be taken that easily. "I'll have to know just what you want first, and see what I have to give you." I answered that I know he was doing a book on bullfighting. "But it's not written yet." "What about writing some of it for me? I could publish part of it as I did with Joyce's *Work in Progress*." This seemed to interest him. "How many words would you want?" (An echo of Joyce's voice in my ear) and I answered as Harry and I had answered Joyce.

"Whatever you care to give me, but enough to make a book, it will be a limited edition, and if you will sign a hundred copies I can sell them extra high so that we need not print over five hundred in all which can only delight your publishers."

"Scribners," he said.

"I know," I rejoined, "Perkins won't mind."

He wouldn't say yes, but he didn't say anything, so I only asked him to let me know in plenty of time before he sailed.

"Sure," he acknowledged, and put his arms protecting around his Gris, as though to say "to hell with the B.S.P." Pauline kept very quiet. Narcisse and I stalked down the cabbage-perfumed stairs not quite as cockily as we had pranced up!

It was two days later that I received a rather frantic call. "I am here at the Line," he told me. "I'm having difficulty over the passage. The sailings are crowded, they want me to pay now, and I'm a little short. Could you let me have the advance this morning?"

"Then I'll get the manuscript," I answered.

"Sure you'll have it by the first of the week." He picked up the cheque at noon and I showed him *The Escaped Cock* by Lawrence, and Joyce's *Tales Told of Shem and Shaun,* so he'd have an idea of what I was planning. I said I would have the sub-title page set up before he sailed so he could sign a hundred copies, and he swore that I'd get the necessary text in less than a week. He had it written, he admitted, but he wanted to work it up a bit. It was part of the new book.

Monday came and no manuscript. I was not idle, however, for the edition was taking form in my imagi-

nation, and I believed that if de Chirico (I was being untrue to Grosz) could be persuaded to do a frontispiece (matador subject seemed right for him) the edition would leap in value. I went round to Le Divan, a small gallery near the Deaux Magots Café on the Place St. Germain about two hundred yards from my office, for it was there that de Chirico exhibited his work from time to time–but the artist himself was rarely seen in Paris. I explained the idea to the lady in charge of the *boutique* and she was delighted, but thought it would be very difficult to make a rendezvous. Could I not write him? I was sure that my written French would be incomprehensible, I'd have to show de Chirico some of the Black Sun Books and also I guessed I would have to wave my hands a good deal to get the idea across. She invited me to return the next day at five and to bring Hemingway's text with me, she'd do her best to trap de Chirico at that hour. He was known to be unmanageable.

Tuesday came and no manuscript, and Tuesday was dwindling. I knew that the Hemingways had to sail on Saturday. I sent them round a note and waited, still nothing happened. Disappointed, but determined, I went to meet de Chirico. I was half an hour late, the voluble saleslady was beside herself with anxiety. She had, it seems, frantically shut the man up in her office. "He's dangerous," she hissed, and shaking her head she locked the street door behind her and prodded me ahead of her as though he were the bull and I was to be the toreador–when the office door opened, out burst de Chirico head down, tail up and charged me–he was in riding boots and corduroy jacket, his hair fell over his eyes like a forelock, he looked ferocious, and in his hand he held (and cracked) a short-thonged whip–the attack, God be praised, was only verbal–just what did I want and why?

I thought to myself what a fine pair of Miura (bulls) Ernest and Giorgio would make, and what a miserable thing was a publisher after all! Luckily, Narcisse tried to bite my quarry and that calmed him down at once. I tied up my pet and he discarded his whip, and we both plopped down on the divan–in a few minutes I had an amenable collaborator in hand. His price would be lofty, but so were my ideas. We shook hands on it (the whip hand) and I promised to bring him, the story and the author together that Thursday.

I returned about noon and was waiting in fury at the Press when a messenger arrived. With agitated fingers I tore open a slim envelope to discover only a few pages of typescript, it seemed to be mostly one-word lines of four-letter words. The whole thing amounted to about one thousand words and had nothing to do with toreadors. It looks to me like a discarded passage from *A Farewell to Arms*. I was so indignant and disappointed

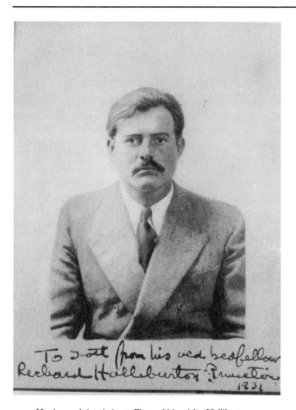

Hemingway's inscription to Fitzgerald is a joke. Halliburton, a Princetonian, was a popular travel-book writer and was alleged to be homosexual (Matthew J. and Arlyn Bruccoli Collection, University of South Carolina).

that I wanted to cry. Instead I sat down and wrote the author a red-hot letter in which, among other things, I said that a five-page edition de luxe of Hemingway, signed, at ten dollars a throw, would appear mighty "precious" to the public. With this letter the printer himself ran round to Hemingway's hotel.

The answer came back in a flash like a flash. "No one can call Hemingway 'precious' and get away with it." Would I please return the manuscript to him at once. He implied that any other publisher would offer a million on bended knees and he also added that he could not return the advance as they had to sail and their tickets were bought. I called Jacques Porel to my assistance and he was the bearer-back of the manuscript. He was to tell Hemingway that instead of the "precious" bit I would accept the Continental rights to one of his novels for the C.C.E. This he had offered before the special edition was discussed and he had suggested *Farewell to Arms*. I instructed Jacques to sign for *In Our Time* which I then considered (and still do) Hemingway's best. The barter was accomplished without too much compromise, but Jacques told me that as

he left the hotel he could hear Ernest muttering a four-letter word and "precious" over and over as the banging of trunks grew to a mighty din.

I have never regretted my decision, but it makes it quite obvious that I did not invent Hemingway: moreover, I like to think that it was Gris and not the steamship line that crashed that cheque, and I had already published this laudatory introduction to *Torrents of Spring!*

Paris, December, 1931.

Dear Ernest,

I have a confession to make to you. Do you remember that torrential day in Spain last August, "Torrents of Summer" when we all foregathered after the corrida, you, your wife, Jacques and I and the boot-black in the little posada behind the arena? I was feeling pretty sick after the fight and would have felt more so if it hadn't been that the matador now and then forgot his bull in admiration of Charlie Chaplin who was throwing gold cigarette cases from the box of honour to the pigtailed heroes. The place was full of English and Americans; you and Charlie were the focus of many admiring eyes and I felt very jealous of you. It must be thrilling to be famous and I wondered how to set about it. (Don't smile! There are, they say, a hundred gateways to the Temple of Fame, and woman-like, I fondly hoped to wedge my way in by one of them!) Above all, I wanted to do something as you two had done something; I wanted to make something out of all this Anglo-Saxon alertness and zest for discovery of new things in ancient lands. Every American fancies himself a new Columbus rediscovering Europe. And Europe seems to welcome their curiosity with open arms.

The barrier that separates us and always will (I am not Esperanto-minded, are you?) is the difference in language. Local colour, bulls and blood, are all very well, but one wants to know what the people are saying and thinking. You have told us and told us very convincingly how it all strikes you, but how about bull-fighting from the Spaniard's point of view? We are always hearing how Paris appeals to the American, or Berlin strikes the Briton—but Paris as the Parisians see it? (Do you know, for instance, that in proportion to its population Iceland publishes more newspapers than any country in the world?)

That is why I was thinking of, across the din and pageantry of that afternoon—my thoughts were revolving round a new idea, to give all these eager travellers a glimpse into the consciousness that makes and mixes the colour, as the painter mixes the paints on his palette. I remember saying something to you about it after the second (or was it the third?) absinthe; and you answered "swell". You have probably forgotten, but that "swell" of yours was a prelude to a rising tide. Aprés vous, le déluge . . . In other words the C.C.E.

As you know I have for some years been publishing de luxe editions at my Black Sun Press (for subscribers only!) Now I am venturing on something much less luxurious in form and at prices more in keeping with the times . . . Cheap editions in English of the masterpieces of the modern world, books that will express the genius of every country in the language we all understand, at a price we all can afford.

I am beginning the collection with an American book, your book, because I admire it and because I know I am not the only one to admire what you write; a few million others do to . . . The next book will be Kay Boyle's translation of "Le Diable au Corps" by Raymond Radiquet (Aldous Huxley has written the introduction to it), a masterpiece in its English form as well as in the original; and when I send you a copy I have an idea you will repeat that "swell". After the "Devil in the Flesh" will follow "Bubu de Montparnasse", that classic of the Paris underworld. I am amazed that our compatriots, for all their enthusiasm for Montparnasse life, have never been able to read in their own language this magnificent human document. Last month, during a voyage of literary exploration to Scandinavia, I was lucky enought to secure the rights to an amazing psychological crime story that has just won the Inter-Scandinavian prize contest, "Two Living and One Dead" by Christiansen—and also the rights to quite a different but very unusual type of work, stories of Corsica by Prince Wilhelm of Sweden.

"Of the making of books there is no end" (or so I am assured on good authority) and there are many beginnings, too many, far too many, as over-worked critics are fond of telling us, but of the re-making of really good books there can never be enough—or that is how I look at it. Europeans who wish to keep up with Anglo-American literature will be, I hope, delighted to find a supply at the same low prices as their own novels. Until now the prices of so many translations have been prohibitive.

I am going to publish books that I like, that have merit, and that interest or amuse me personally, books for the serious reader as well as mystery stories to while away the hours on the Mauretania or the Ile-de-France, and fascinating cosmopolitan tales of adventure and travel for the Train Bleu.

I hope very shortly to secure books for this series by such leading authors as Lawrence, Joyce, Kafka, Colette, Maurois, Thomas Mann, Tozzi, Dos Passos, Sackville-West, Aldington, McAlmon, Huxley, Maugham, Kay Boyle, Katherine Mansfield, et al—and I have just evolved a brilliant idea that the colours of the titles should match the countries, Red for Russia, Blue for Peru, but green for the "Torrents of Spring" in honour of Diana and the woods of Michigan!

Everyone tells me that I am lucky to begin my collection with a book of yours. If they only knew all that I have confessed in this letter, they would realize that you and those Miura bulls are, between you, responsible, not only for this edition of "Torrents of Spring" but for many C.C.E.'s to come.

Good fishing, and again many thanks.

Caresse Crosby

This article was published in the Kansas City Star, *21 October 1931, p. 17. The identity of the Hemingway impostor was never determined, but the impostor was rumored to be the son of an American admiral and, according to Hemingway, "a psychopathic case."*

THE GHOST OF A WRITER

ERNEST HEMINGWAY SEEKS HIS "DOUBLE" IN SEVERAL PLACES.

So Far the Imposter Hasn't Turned Bad Check Author, but He Disconcerts the Novelist When Proof Becomes Necessary.

Ernest Hemingway, writer, who is in Kansas City, is engaged in a leisurely and haphazard quest of a man who has been impersonating him for the last year and who has been practicing the deception in many parts of the world.

"I don't know when I'll find him, or what I'll do about it when I do encounter him, but I am eager to have a look at anyone dumb enough to want to pass himself off as me," Mr. Hemingway laughed in commenting on the case to friends on The Star's staff, of which he was a member before he went away to war and later wrote "Men Without Women" and "A Farewell to Arms."

FAR AWAY FROM NEW YORK.

"The first time I ever heard of my other self was in January of this year," Mr. Hemingway explained. "At that time I was in Florida and received a letter from an editor friend in New York in which he made reference to my having been in New York the previous December.

"Actually, I hadn't been in New York since the previous summer.

"The next time I heard about this Mr. Hyde Hemingway was in Paris last month. I met a couple of young Americans there who told me ruefully of having been duped by the impostor, who gave one of them a long interview about the Hemingway views on literature, which the young man published. It was quite a scoop, as I never give interviews on my work or what I think about literature.

"And the third time I heard about my unseen self also was in Paris last month. This time a Mr. Lewin telephoned me at my hotel and gave me hell (the use of

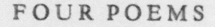

Front Cover

FOUR POEMS

By

ERNEST HEMINGWAY

On August 31, 1930 There were printed privately for the presentation of persons 1 copies of Four Poems, for E. H. by L. H. C. This is Number

Inside front cover

THE AGE DEMANDED

The age demanded that we sing
and cut away our tongue.
The age demanded that we flow
and hammered in the bung.
The age demanded that we dance
and jammed us into iron pants.
And in the end the age was handed
the sort of shit that it demanded.

THE EARNEST LIBERAL'S LAMENT

I know monks masturbate at night
That pet cats screw
That some girls bite
And yet
What can I do
To set things right?

1st page of text

THE LADY POETS WITH FOOT NOTES

One lady poet was a nymphomaniac and wrote for Vanity
Fair. (1)

One lady poet's husband was killed in the war. (2)

One lady poet wanted her lover but was afraid of having
a baby. When she finally got married, she found
she couldn't have a baby. (3)

One lady poet slept with Bill Reedy got fatter and fatter
and made half a million dollars writing bum plays. (4)

One lady poet never had enough to eat. (5)

One lady poet was big and fat and no fool. (6)

2nd page

Proof for Louis Henry Cohn's projected booklet of Hemingway poems that had appeared in Der Querschitt. *The marginal notes are in Hemingway's hand. The pamphlet was never published (Louis Henry Cohn Collection, University of Delaware).*

the word "hell" here proves that the real Mr. Heming-way was speaking, as anyone who reads his books will know) for having stood him up in front of the National City Bank in New York one previous midnight.

WORSE TO HAVE TO PROVE IT.

"Mr. Lewin and I got together and he seemed very indignant that I was not the man who had stood him up, as he called it. He didn't seem to believe that I was the real Hemingway, and was rather disagreeable about it. In fact, he was so dis-agreeable that I got kind of 'sore,' because it's bad enough to be Ernest Hemingway without having to prove it.

"Anyway, I learned from Mr. Lewin that my other self had used my name aboard the Roma on a trip from Italy to New York, had autographed books with a fair replica of my signature, and had been extended the privileges of a club because of his pos-ing as me.

"The last time I ran across his trail was just the other day in a station bookshop in St. Louis, where some time previously the other 'Mr. Hemingway' had casually mentioned to the proprietress that he was on the way to visit my wife's people in Arkan-sas. He certainly has me tagged, hasn't he?"

NOT A CHECK WRITER.

Mr. Hemingway is rather tolerant of his impos-tor just now because he doesn't appear to have writ-ten any bad checks on the Hemingway account. But the author believes that one of these days he and the impostor will be in the same town at the same time and then something might be done about it.

In the meantime Mr. Hemingway and his wife plan an indefinite stay in Kansas City, where they are guests of Mr. and Mrs. W. Malcom Lowry, 6435 Indian Lane. The author has not decided upon a title for the book he is now completing, which is not a novel, which is about bull-fighting, and which won't be published for a year.

Dos Passos wrote a letter to Hemingway offering advice for edit-ing Death in the Afternoon *(1932), and Hemingway followed most of his directions. From* The Fourteenth Chronicle: Let-ters and Diaries of John Dos Passos, *edited and with a bio-graphical narrative by Townsend Ludington (Boston: Gambit, 1973), pp. 402–403.*

[February 1932]

Dear Hem—

We certainly had a fine four days in Key West. Damn consoling to find you in such swell shape—well housed, catching sail fish, able to eat and drink. The boys dont seem to me to be holding up like I'd hoped on the whole—Never enjoyed anything more than the three days on the gulfstream—only it was rotten luck missing Pauline.

The Bullfight book—is absolutely the best thing can be done on the subject—I mean all the description and the dope—It seems to me an absolute model for how that sort of thing ought to be done—And all the accounts of individual fighters towns etc, are knockout. I'm only doubtful, like I said, about the parts where Old Hem straps on the longwhite whiskers and gives the boys the lowdown. I can stand the old lady—but I'm pretty doubtful as to whether the stuff about Waldo Frank (except the line about shooting an owl) is as good as it ought to be. God knows he ought to be deflated—or at least Virgin Spain—(why not put it on the book basis instead of the entire lecturer?) and that is certainly the place to do it. And then later when you take off the make up and assure the ladies and gents that its really only old Uncle Hem after all and give them the low down about writing and why you like to live in Key West etc. I was pretty doubtful—Dont you think that's all secrets of the profession—like plaster of paris in a glove and oughtn't to be spilt to the vulgar? I may be wrong—but the volume is so hellishly good. (I'd say way ahead of anything of yours yet) and the language is so magnificently used—(why right there sitting in Bra's boat reading the type-written pages I kept having the feeling I was reading a classic in the Bohn library like Rabelais or Harvey's Circulation of the Blood or something and that's a hell of a good way to feel about a book not even published yet) that it would be a shame to leave in any unnecessary tripe—damn it I think there's always enough tripe in anything even after you've cut out—and a book like that can stand losing some of the best passages—After all, a book ought to be judged by the author according to the excellence of the stuff cut out. But I may be packed with prunes with all this so for God's sake dont pay too much attention to it—the Books damn swell in any case—

We were laid low again by our typhoid and paraty-phoid, but now better and getting ready to land at Progreso this afternoon. Say why dont you plan to come up to Prov-incetown or Truro in the spring before going out West? I'll have a small sailboat and it won't be so bad there—

Wish I was going down to Cuba with you—strafe the finnies and love to Pauline

Yrs
Dos

Manuscript page from Death in the Afternoon *(Harry Ransom Humanities Research Center, University of Texas at Austin)*

Hemingway's revised typescript for the opening of his treatise on bullfighting (Harry Ransom Humanities Research Center, University of Texas at Austin)

Hemingway was a superstitious person and often reacted violently to perceived insults and curses. Even Perkins was not safe from Hemingway's rage. Alfred Dashiell was editor of Scribner's Magazine. From The Only Thing That Counts, *pp. 171–172.*

28 June 1932
Tuesday–
Box 406
Key West

Dear Max: . . .

Have done 233 pages of the page proof and all the captions. Will go right on through it and send it off to you with the list of fixed dates of fights in Spain–Central and South Am and Mexico. Would prefer not to call these appendices–Limitations of space and costs have aborted any attempt to make the book exhaustive so as it is appendices are only pretentious–So list them in the table of contents by their titles–removing the designations Appendix A, B and C. . . .

Will try and find contract and send it to you to protect you against worry in case of any such future contingencies. Know neither you nor I worry about the contract or would have sent it before–

But listen Max could you bawl out please or raise hell with the son of a bitch who slugged all those galleys Hemingway's Death? You know I am superstitious and it is a hell of a damn dirty business to stare at that a thousand times even to haveing it (in this last filthy batch) written in with red and purple ink–If I would have passed out would have said your Goddamned lot put the curse on me–

About the combining of pictures–You dont want to open the illustrations with a double page–Also that seed bull and ox are too good to combine–That's why I sent you the wire–the two Villaltas combine much better–

22 and 23

Saw a publicity sheet sent out by Benjamin Hauser presumably rehashing Scribner publicity–Mostly ballyhooing stuff I had cut out–What you will do is get everyone disappointed–I put all that stuff in so that anyone buying the book for no matter what reason would get their money's worth–All that story, dialogue, etc is thrown in extra–The book is worth anybody's 3.50 who has 3.50 as a straight book on bull fighting–If you go to advertizing that it is so many damned other things all you will do is make people disappointed because it hasnt a cook book and a telephone directory as well.

If you try to sell it as a great classic Goddamned book on bull fighting rather than some fucking miscellany you may be able to sell a few–Let the critics claim it has something additional–But suppose all chance of that is gone now with that lovely Hauser stuff–If you want to try to find someone to speak well of it ask Dos Passos–

But thats your business–not mine–

About the words–Youre the one who has gone into that–If you decide to cut out a letter or two to keep inside the law that is your business–I send the copy and you are supposed to know what will go to jail and what will not–F-ck the whole business–that looks all right–Its legal isnt it–

Max I feel damned sick still, but I could break the neck of the punk that slugged those galleys–

Oh yes–What about that Modern Library money? I'm flat broke–What is Mr. Dashiell's budget for stories now? Please answer these last two.

Also will you please have three sets of these corrected page proof galleys drawn as want one for Cape, one for Germany and one for my self–Best to you always–Ernest

If they feel disappointed and still want my "literary credo" in a book on bull fighting they can run an insert saying "F-ck the whole goddamned lousy racket"–Hemingway–

If you want some pictures will get some taken but for Christ sake no more of those open mouth open collar wonders–Promise me that–

And NIX on that one of me lying with the sick steer–

Will send you painting by Luis Quintanilla who did the frescoes in the Casa del Pueblo that you can use–

[In the right margin of page one] Not going to Africa this year–Wouldnt want to miss the literary teas

----

In explaining what the writer must do, and how and why he must do it, Hemingway presents his "iceberg theory" in Death in the Afternoon *(New York: Scribners, 1932), pp. 191–192.*

When writing a novel a writer should create living people; people not characters. A *character* is a caricature. If a writer can make people live there may be no great characters in his book, but it is possible that his book will remain as a whole; as an entity; as a novel. If the people the writer is making talk of old masters; of music; of modern painting; of letters; or of science then they should talk of those subjects in the novel. If they do not

4 Gal 1—3404 Hemingway's Death 11½-14-Scotch

DEATH IN THE AFTERNOON

CHAPTER ONE

At the first bullfight I ever went to I expected to be horrified and perhaps sickened by what I had been told would happen to the horses. Everything I had read about the bull ring insisted on that point; most people who wrote of it condemned bullfighting outright as a stupid brutal business, but even those that spoke well of it as an exhibition of skill and as a spectacle deplored the use of the horses and were apologetic about the whole thing. The killing of the horses in the ring was considered indefensible. I suppose, from a modern moral point of view, that is, a Christian point of view, the whole bullfight is indefensible; there is certainly much cruelty, there is always danger, either sought or unlooked for, and there is always death, and I should not try to defend it now, only to tell honestly the things I have found true about it. To do this I must be altogether frank, or try to be, and if those who read this decide with disgust that it is written by some one who lacks their, the readers', fineness of feeling I can only plead that this may be true. But whoever reads this can only truly make such a judgment when he, or she, has seen the things that are spoken of and knows truly what their reactions to them would be.

Once I remember Gertrude Stein talking of bullfights spoke of her admiration for Joselito and showed me some pictures of him in the ring and of herself and Alice Toklas sitting in the first row of the wooden barreras at the bull ring at Valencia with Joselito and his brother Gallo below, and I had just come from the Near East, where the Greeks broke the legs of their baggage and transport animals and drove and shoved them

Galley proof for Hemingway's treatise on bullfighting. On 27 June 1932 Hemingway wired Maxwell Perkins, "DID IT SEEM VERY FUNNY TO SLUG EVERY GALLEY HEMINGWAYS DEATH OR WAS THAT WHAT YOU WANTED HAVE BEEN PLENTY SICK" (Louis Henry Cohn Collection, University of Delaware).

talk of those subjects and the writer makes them talk of them he is a faker, and if he talks about them himself to show how much he knows then he is showing off. No matter how good a phrase or a simile he may have if he puts it in where it is not absolutely necessary and irreplaceable he is spoiling his work for egotism. Prose is architecture, not interior decoration, and the Baroque is over. For a writer to put his own intellectual musings, which he might sell for a low price as essays, into the mouths of artificially constructed characters which are more remunerative when issued as people in a novel is good economics, perhaps, but does not make literature. People in a novel, not skillfully constructed *characters,* must be projected from the writer's assimilated experience, from his knowledge, from his head, from his heart and from all there is of him. If he ever has luck as well as seriousness and gets them out entire they will have more than one dimension and they will last a long time. A good writer should know as near everything as possible. Naturally he will not. A great enough writer seems to be born with knowledge. But he really is not; he has only been born with the ability to learn in a quicker ratio to the passage of time than other men and without conscious application, and with an intelligence to accept or reject what is already presented as knowledge. There are some things which cannot be learned quickly and time, which is all we have, must be paid heavily for their acquiring. They are the very simplest things and because it takes a man's life to know them the little new that each man gets from life is very costly and the only heritage he has to leave. Every novel which is truly written contributes to the total of knowledge which is there at the disposal of the next writer who comes, but the next writer must pay, always, a certain nominal percentage in experience to be able to understand and assimilate what is available as his birthright and what he must, in turn, take his departure from. If a writer of prose knows enough about what he is writing about he may omit things that he knows and the reader, if the writer is writing truly enough, will have a feeling of those things as strongly as though the writer had stated them. The dignity of movement of an ice-berg is due to only one-eighth of it being above water. A writer who omits things because he does not know them only makes hollow places in his writing. A writer who appreciates the seriousness of writing so little that he is anxious to make people see he is formally educated, cultured or well-bred is merely a popinjay. And this too remember; a serious writer is not to be confounded with a solemn writer. A serious writer may be a hawk or a buzzard or even a popinjay, but a solemn writer is always a bloody owl.

Critic Ben Ray Redman wrote this review of Hemingway's Death in the Afternoon *for the* Saturday Review of Literature, *9 (24 September 1932), p. 121. Unlike many American reviewers, Redman was not shocked by the subject of the book or by Hemingway's enjoyment of bullfighting.*

Blood and Sand, and Art

This book will meet with three kinds of reviewers, those who dislike bullfighting, those who like it, and those who know nothing about it; and the reviews will be consequently conditioned. To expose the conditioning factors of the present review, let me say at the outset that I like bullfighting to the point of loving it when it is good, and that I know a little about it. I have seen Marcial Lalanda, "the most complete and masterly fighter in bullfighting today," during the seasons of 1929 and 1930, which Hemingway marks as the first of his great years; and Nicanor Villalta when he was at his best, or at least what I thought must be his best, and at his worst; and Chicuelo, when both cowardly and inspired; and Felix Rodriguez, before he became ill; and Nino de la Palma, and Cagancho, and Bejarano, and Manolo Bienvenida, and Algabeno; and Sidney Franklin, whose cape work struck me, even when I was only guessing at what Hemingway has now told me, as the perfection of classical restraint and beauty. And—with "Death in the Afternoon" before me to furnish reminders and hints on almost every page—I remember the individual performances of these men, their tricks of style and technique, their weakness and their strength, their successes and failures, as the amateur of symphony concerts remembers the performances of various conductors.

But, let me repeat, my practical experience has been very limited,—only a few men, killing a few bulls in a few ways; whereas Hemingway has, with technical knowledge increasing through the years, watched more than fifteen hundred bulls killed (and too many men killed also) in all the ways at the command of contemporary fighters. Besides, he has lived with bullfighters at work and at play, and watched them die in the infirmary; he has got at the thoughts behind the foreheads of managers, breeders, horse contractors, professional bullfight critics, and sword handlers; he has visited the great farms on which the fighting bulls are bred, seen them branded, watched them being tested at the age of two, witnessed their fights among themselves, and followed their progress in the ring; he has tried his hand at amateur fights, when the horns were padded, and dis-

Chapter Three: 1930–1935

Charles Thompson and Pauline Hemingway's wealthy uncle, Gustavus Adolphus Pfeiffer, Dry Tortugas, 1932. Uncle Gus was especially generous toward his favorite niece and her husband, for whom he bought a car and a home in Key West and financed their 1933–1934 safari.

covered that he "was too old, too heavy, and too awkward," and that his "figure was the wrong shape, being thick in all the places where it should be lithe." In short, his knowledge of the art has grown to match his instinctive love of it; and he has written a book in which technical explanations burn with emotion because of the passion that is mated with the science. And I, having read this book with close attention and continuous

excitement, must testify that of the little I now know about bullfighting ten per cent is due to personal experience, and ninety per cent to "Death in the Afternoon," which has clarified the significance of that experience, and transformed into scientific and esthetic certainties many intuitions.

So I take it that, in one case at least, this book has precisely performed half of its intended function: to explain to the person who has seen bullfighting, without really knowing much about it, just what it is that he has seen. The other half, of course, is to prepare those who have never seen a bullfight for their first encounter with the art. This half is the more difficult; just how difficult Hemingway himself admits when he reaches his seventh chapter:

> There are two sorts of guide books; those that are read before and those that are to be read after and the ones that are to be read after the fact are bound to be incomprehensible to a certain extent before; if the fact is of enough importance in itself. So with any book on mountain ski-ing, sexual intercourse, wing shooting, or any other thing which it is impossible to make come true on paper, or at least impossible to attempt to make more than one version of at a time on paper, it always being an individual experience, there comes a place in the guide book where you must say do not come back until you have ski-ed, had sexual intercourse, shot quail or grouse, or been to the bullfight so that you will know what we are talking about. So from now on it is inferred that you have been to the bullfight.

But, difficult or not, Hemingway has done his best to write a book that will prove at least intelligible to the reader who has not seen a bullfight, that will prepare him for the spectacle and properly orientate his thinking; a book that will truly serve as an emotional and technical introduction to its subject. And he has so written it that, if it is intelligible before, it is nothing less than a revelation afterward. He has written of the art in all its aspects, from every point of view: historical, critical, emotional, and esthetic. He has revealed its glory and its baseness; he has pointed to the heights which the art can reach, and uncovered the depths to which, because it is a commercial art, it descends. He has explained the ways in which bulls are bred and selected; the tricks of breeders who would breed their animals down in size, and length of horn, and courage, for the convenience of the fighters. He has exposed the wiles of the horse contractor bargaining with the picador, and the corruption of the peone who leads wounded horses from the ring, that they may be sewn up to fight again, instead of killing them when he should. He has explained the formal divisions of the bullfight, and the significance and importance of each: the first act with the picadors, the second act with the planting of the

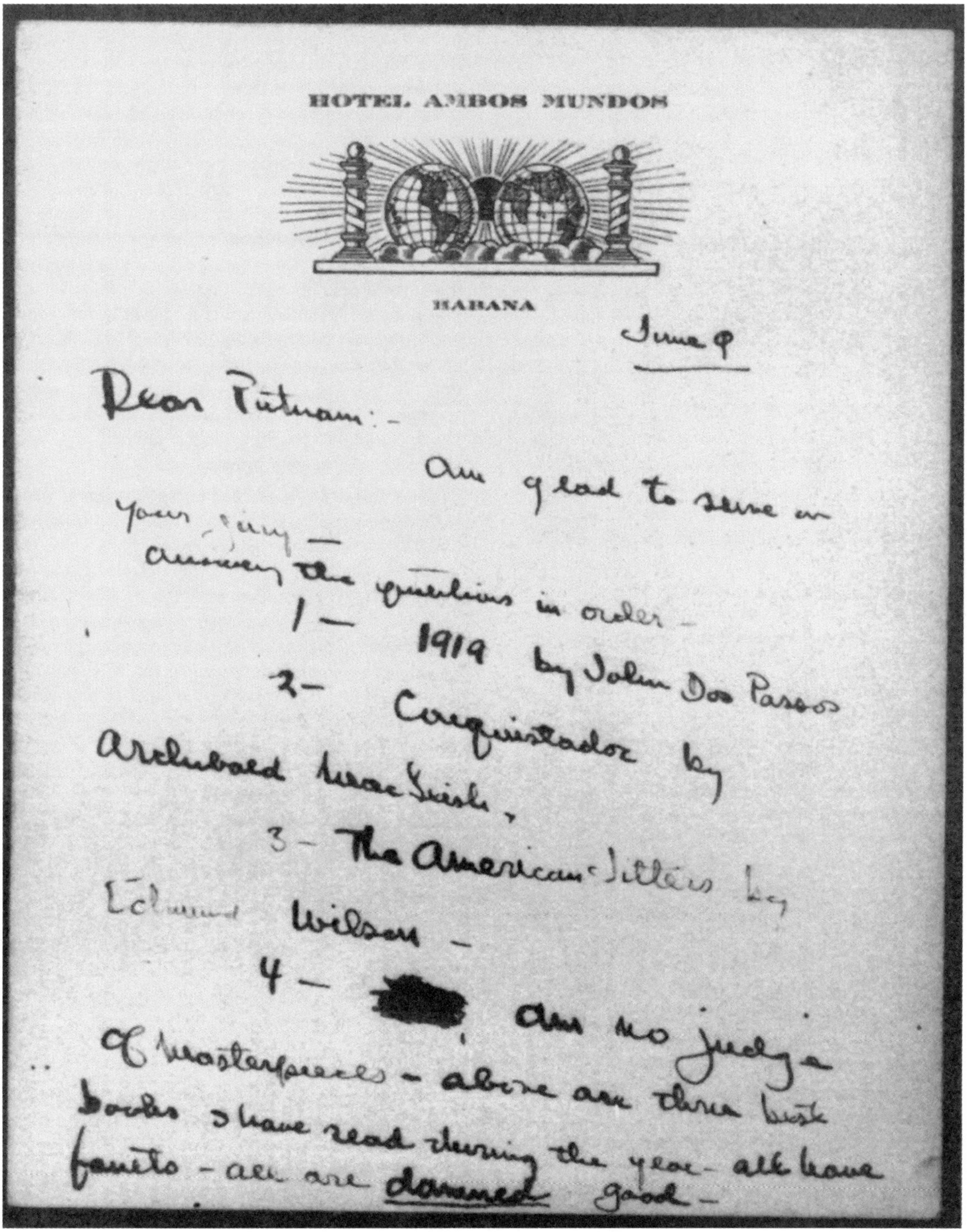

HOTEL AMBOS MUNDOS

HABANA

June 9

Dear Putnam:—

    Am glad to serve on your jury— Answering the questions in order—

1— 1919 by John Dos Passos

2— Conquistador by Archibald MacLeish,

3— The American Jitters by Edmund Wilson—

4— ▬, am no judge of masterpieces—above are three best books I have read during the year—all have faults—all are *damned* good—

Hemingway's reply to Samuel Putnam's request for his opinion on the best books of 1932 (Clifton Waller Barrett Library, University of Virginia)

banderillas or darts, and the third act of death, which ends with the actual killing that the Spaniards call "the moment of truth." He has described all the customs, costumes, weapons, and living factors in the spectacle; he has told us how to distinguish the really brave bull from the pawing, snorting animal that only appears so; how to distinguish between true danger, and danger that is faked by the fighter for the benefit of his more ignorant public; how to tell when the picador (the man on horseback armed with the spiked pole) is doing his work well, and when he is doing it ill; how to estimate the work done by the banderillero (who places the darts); how to evaluate the work with the muleta (the scarlet cloth which the matador uses as a lure in the last act, and with which he should dominate the bull, and place him in position for the kill), differentiating between the difficulty of its use in the right or the left hand; how to judge the final work with the sword, honest or faked, brilliant or merely competent or wretched. And these things he does in a book written entirely to his own liking (he is permitted to say things that no English or American publisher has let an author say before), stuffed with savage wit and enlivened by amusing digressions, and couched in a prose that must be called perfect because it states with absolute precision what it is meant to state, explains what it is meant to explain beyond possibility of misunderstanding, and communicates to the reader the emotion with which it is so heavily charged. . . .

This, I submit, is very clear and very fine writing; and Hemingway describes every phase of the bullfight, from the first trailing of the first cape as the bull enters the arena to the final death thrust, in prose of the same quality. As for the emotion of which I have spoken, any reader who ruffles a few pages will encounter it; but if he is in a hurry for samples he may turn to the death of Gitanillo on page 218, or to the death of Todo on page 239.

Throughout this review I have spoken steadily of bullfighting as an art, and the passage quoted is that of an art critic writing of the technique of an art. This is the first point which must be driven home to the Anglo-Saxon reader: that bullfighting is not a contest, and only secondarily a sport, but an art. It is hard to persuade him of this, for the vulgar notion of bullfighting is that it is a contest between a man and a bull to see which will emerge from the ring alive, and that it is a very unfair contest because a Joselito kills fifteen hundred bulls, while it takes that number of bulls finally to kill one Joselito. And this vulgar notion is completely wrong. The man's object is not merely to kill the bull, but to kill him in a certain way, in a very beautiful way (sculpturally speaking) which has become formalized by tradition and convention, and in the most exciting

way because it is precisely the way which compels the man to expose himself to the greatest danger. The perfect bullfight is the one which combines the maximum of daring, beauty, and danger on the man's part, with the maximum of bravery, endurance, speed, and directness on the bull's part. This ideal is seldom realized, and the difference between a good fight and a bad one is the difference between a masterpiece and a daub, but unless the bullfighter does his best to approximate this ideal he will be driven from the ring with shrieks and catcalls or pelted from it with cushions and other solid but throwable objects. All these things, however, are said perfectly, patiently, and at length in Hemingway's book; and no reader can put down that book ignorant of the fact that bullfighting is a tragic art, operating upon the initiated spectators with the cathartic power of tragedy, a tragedy not only beautiful at its best, but one which communicates, at its highest moment, a sense of immortality in the very presence of death.

Of this book I have said only a fraction of what I wished to say, and said it less well than I would have liked. I have not mentioned the many remarkable photographs, admirably chosen, wisely grouped, and captioned with as much wit as expert knowledge; nor the very useful glossary of Spanish words and terms used in bullfighting, into which sardonic wit also enters; nor the exceedingly amusing group of case histories illustrating various initial reactions to bullfighting, which the author has compiled; nor a brief and just estimate of the American Sidney Franklin, as fighter and artist. Nor have I mentioned "The Old Lady," invented on page 64, and thrown out of the book (much to my regret) on page 190, with whom Hemingway conducts the most sprightly, various, informative, and scandalous conversations. Nor have I referred to his startling frankness in treating the personalities, and professional characteristics, of living bullfighters. Indeed, looking back, I see that I have barely hinted at the fun which "Death in the Afternoon" affords. It was probably a mistake. But the fun is incidental to the serious work of a serious literary artist; it is the comic relief to a genuine work of artistic criticism; the froth on the surface of a book that will confirm many readers in their belief that Ernest Hemingway, in the handling of words as an interpretation of life, is not a brilliant and ephemeral novillero, but a matador possessed of solid and even classic virtues.

Hemingway disliked H. L. Mencken, the most influential literary critic of his day, perhaps because Mencken never wrote a wholly positive review of his work. Although Mencken dismissed A

Farewell to Arms *by saying that Hemingway's "tricks begin to wear thin," he wrote his most positive assessment of any Hemingway book when he reviewed* Death in the Afternoon *in* American Mercury, *27 (December 1932), pp. 506–507.*

The Spanish Idea of a Good Time

Mr. Hemingway has been before the public for ten years and in that time he has published seven books. He has been praised very lavishly, but has somehow failed to make his way into the first rank of living American authors. Nevertheless, he has made some progress in that direction, and his last novel, "A Farewell to Arms," was unquestionably his best. In the present book, which is not fiction but fact, his characteristic merits and defects are clearly revealed. It is, on the one hand, an extraordinarily fine piece of expository writing, but on the other hand it often descends to a gross and irritating cheapness. So long as the author confines himself to his proper business, which is that of describing the art and science of bullfighting, he is unfailingly clear, colorful and interesting. Unfortunately, he apparently finds it hard to so confine himself. Only too often he turns aside from his theme to prove fatuously that he is a naughty fellow, and when he does so he almost invariably falls into banality and worse. The reader he seems to keep in his mind's eye is a sort of common denominator of all the Ladies' Aid Societies of his native Oak Park, Ill. The way to shock this innocent grandam, obviously, is to have at her with the ancient four-letter words. Mr. Hemingway does so with moral industry; he even drags her into the story as a character, to gloat over her horror. But she is quite as much an intruder in that story as King George V would be, or Dr. Irving Babbitt, or the Holy Ghost, and the four-letter words are as idiotically incongruous as so many boosters' slogans or college yells.

Mr. Hemingway's main purpose in "Death in the Afternoon" is to describe bullfighting as he has observed it in Spain. He admits frankly that he enjoys it, and he conveys a good deal of that enjoyment to the reader. The sport is brutal, but there is no evidence that it is any more brutal than football. The common American idea, I suppose, is that the bull is a senile and sclerotic beast with no chance against the matador, but Mr. Hemingway shows that this is very far from the truth. The bull, in fact, is always a youngster, and he is selected for his stamina and warlike enterprise. If he shows no pugnacity the fight is a flop, and the fans indicate their discontent by bombarding the matador with empty bottles. Moreover, the matador is not permitted to kill his antagonist in the safest way possible, which would probably also be the easiest. On the contrary, he must expose himself deliberately to the maximum of risk, and his rank in his profession is determined very largely by his ingenuity in devising new hazards, and his courage in facing them. When the formal jousting prescribed by the canon is over and he prepares to kill, he must approach the bull so closely and so openly that a miscalculation of half an inch may well cost him his life.

Mr. Hemingway has seen hundreds of fights, and no less than 3,000 bulls have been dispatched before his eyes. He has cultivated bullfighters and studied the immense literature of their mystery, and at one time he even ventured into the ring himself. Thus he knows everything about bullfighting that anyone save an actual matador can hope to learn, and this large and particular knowledge is visible on every page of his book. No better treatise on the sport has ever been written in English, and there is not much probability that better ones are to be had in Spanish. The narrative is full of the vividness of something really seen, felt, experienced. It is done simply, in English that is often bald and graceless, but it is done nevertheless with great skill. Take out the interludes behind the barn, for the pained astonishment of the Oak Park *Damenverein,* and it would be a really first-rate book. Even with the interludes it is well worth reading. Not many current books unearth so much unfamiliar stuff, or present it so effectively. I emerge cherishing a hope that bullfighting will be introduced at Harvard and Yale, or, if not at Harvard and Yale, then at least in the Lynching Belt of the South, where it would offer stiff and perhaps ruinous competition to the frying of poor blackamoors. Years ago I proposed that brass bands be set up down there for that purpose, but bullfights would be better. Imagine the moral stimulation in rural Georgia if an evangelist came to town offering to fight the local bulls by day and baptize the local damned by night!

Mr. Hemingway's main text fills about half of his book. There follows a series of excellent full-page photographs of bullfighters in action, including several which show the bull getting the better of it. There is also an elaborate and amusing glossary of bullfighting terms, running to nearly a hundred pages, and at the end is a calendar of the principal bullfights of Spain and Latin-America, for the convenience of tourists. A four-page note on Sidney Franklin, the Brooklyn matador, completes the book. Señor Franklin first came to fame in Mexico, but of late he has been enjoying great success in Spain. Mr. Hemingway says that "he kills easily and well. He does not give the importance to killing that it merits, since it is easy for him and because he ignores the danger." But ignoring it has not enabled him to avoid it, for he has been gored twice, once very badly. Mr. Hemingway describes his principal wounds in plain English. They will give the Oak Park W.C.T.U. another conniption fit. The Hemingway boy is really a case.

Chapter Three: 1930–1935

Hemingway usually did not respond publicly to adverse criticism. In late 1932, however, he made statements about two critical articles. The first—a reply to Lawrence Leighton's "An Autopsy and a Prescription," a negative assessment of the work of Hemingway, Dos Passos, and Fitzgerald that had been published in Hound and Horn, 5 *(July–September 1932)—appeared in* Hound and Horn *on 6 October 1932. Hemingway's second response, published in the 5 November 1932 issue of* The New Yorker, *was to Robert Coates—author of the Dada novel* The Eater of Darkness *(1926) and a resident of Paris in the 1920s—who had reviewed* Death in the Afternoon *for* The New Yorker *on 1 October 1932.*

27 August 1932

Sirs:

Referring to Mr. Lawrence Leighton's very interesting and revealing autopsy on Mr. Dos Passos, Mr. Fitzgerald and myself, may I take exception to one sentence:

"One feels behind Radiguet, Mme. de Lafayette, Benjamin Constant, Proust, even Racine."

Surely this should read "Radiguet behind Mme. de Lafayette." The rest of the sentence might stand although it would be more just to place Cocteau behind Radiguet and give Racine the benefit of the doubt. But perhaps Mr. Leighton has a feeling for Racine and would not wish to deprive him of his place.

Yours very truly
Ernest Hemingway

5 October 1932

Dear Bob:

There weren't any cracks against Faulkner. You read it over and you will see. Your interpretations, opinions and judgments are naturally none of my god-damned business-es and would not comment on them. This only is question of fact. There was a mention, a pretty damned friendly mention. There was a crack at Cocteau (who is a public character and perfectly crackable), there was re-buttal to W. Frank, Eliot and [Aldous] Huxley.

The Eliot thing has been back and forth for a long time. Frank is a twirp (pen in hand), no matter how admirable politically. Huxley is a smart fellow, a very smart fellow.

I don't really think of you as a critic—no disparagement, I mean I think of you as a writer—or would not make any explanations. Certainly, books should be judged by those who read them—not explained by the writer.

But I'm damned if I wrote any petulant jibes against Faulkner and the hell with you telling citizens that I did.

All the petulant jibes you like against Waldo Frank (or yourself even, if you're looking for them), or anyone for whom I have no particular respect. But I have plenty of respect for Faulkner and wish him all luck. That does not mean that I would not joke about him. There are no subjects that I would not jest about if the jest was funny enough (just as, liking wing shooting, I would shoot my own mother if she went in coveys and had a good strong flight). If it was not funny to you that is my, or perhaps your, hard luck.

Always,
Your friend
Ernest Hemingway

When Everett H. Perry, City Librarian of Los Angeles, wrote Hemingway on 28 January 1933 to ask why he used words considered to be obscene in Death in the Afternoon, *Hemingway offered this response. From* Selected Letters, *pp. 380–384.*

c. 7 February 1933

Dear Mr. Perry:

Thank you for your letter. The fundamental reason that I used certain words no longer a part of the usual written language is that they are very much a part of the vocabulary of the people I was writing about and there was no way I could avoid using them and still give anything like a complete feeling of what I was trying to convey to the reader. If I wrote any approximation even of the speech of the bullring it would be unpublishable. I had to try to get the feeling by the use of two or three words, not using them directly, but indirectly as I used the Natural History of the Dead to make a point that you may have noticed.

I am trying, always, to convey to the reader a full and complete feeling of the thing I am dealing with; to make the person reading feel it has happened to them. In doing this I have to use many expedients, which, if they fail, seem needlessly shocking. Because it is very hard to do I must sometimes fail. But I might fail with one reader and succeed with another.

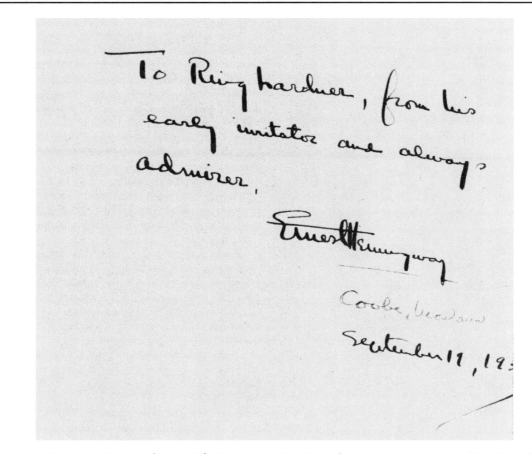

Inscription in Death in the Afternoon *(Courtesy of The Lilly Library, Indiana University). Hemingway mentions that he sent his book to Lardner in "Defense of Dirty Words" (*Esquire, *September 1934).*

My use of words which have been eliminated from writing but which persist in speech has nothing to do with the small boy chalking newly discovered words on fences. I use them for two reasons. 1st as outlined above. 2nd when there is no other word which means exactly the same thing and gives the same effect when spoken.

I always use them sparingly and never to give gratuitous shock–although sometimes to give calculated and what to me seems necessary shock.

Yours very truly,
Ernest Hemingway

Max Eastman's review of Death in the Afternoon *aroused Hemingway's undying wrath. From* The New Republic, *7 June 1933, pp. 94–97.*

BULL IN THE AFTERNOON

There are gorgeous pages in Ernest Hemingway's book about bullfights–big humor and reckless straight talk of what things are, genuinely heavy ferocity against prattle of what they are not. Hemingway is a full-sized man hewing his way with flying strokes of the poet's broad axe which I greatly admire. Nevertheless, there is an unconscionable quantity of bull–to put it as decorously as possible–poured and plastered all over what he writes about bullfights. By bull I mean juvenile romantic gushing and sentimentalizing of simple facts.

For example, it is well known and fairly obvious that bulls do not run and gallop about the pasture; they stand solid "dominating the landscape with their confidence" as Hemingway brilliantly says. Therefore when they have dashed about the ring some minutes, tossed a few horses, repeatedly charged and attempted to gore a man and thrown their heads off because he turned out

Chapter Three: 1930–1935

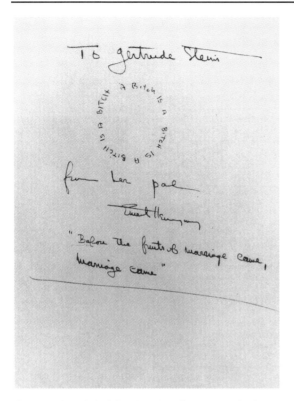

Hemingway's inscription in Death in the Afternoon *parodies Stein's "Rose is a rose is a rose." Hemingway was angered by comments Stein makes about him in* The Autobiography of Alice B. Toklas *(1933)*

to be a rag, they soon get winded and their tongues hang out and they pant. Certain bulls, however, for reasons more or less accidental, go through the ordeal in a small area without much running and therefore get tired in the muscles before they get winded. These bulls do not hang their tongues out and pant. This plain fact, which would be obvious to anybody without smoke in his eyes, is romanticized by Hemingway to mean that some bulls are so "brave" that they will never let their tongues out, but hold their mouths "tight shut to keep the blood in" even after they are stabbed to death and until they drop. This is not juvenile romanticism, it is child's fairy-story writing. And yet Hemingway asks us to believe that what drew him to bullfights was the desire to learn to put down "what really happened in action; what the actual things were which produced the emotion that you experienced."

In pursuit of this rigorous aim he informs us that bullfights are "so well ordered and so strongly disciplined by ritual that a person feeling the whole tragedy cannot separate the minor comic-tragedy of the horse

so as to feel it emotionally." And he generalizes: "The *aficionado,* or lover of the bullfight, may be said, broadly, then, to be one who has this sense of the tragedy and ritual of the fight so that the minor aspects are not important except as they relate to the whole." Which is just the kind of sentimental poppycock most habitually dished out by those art nannies and pale-eyed professors of poetry whom Hemingway above all men despises. Hemingway himself makes plain all through his book that the performance itself is not an artistic tragedy as often as one time out of a hundred. When it is, there is about one man out of a thousand in the grandstand who would know what you were talking about if you started in on "the whole tragedy" as opposed to the "minor comic-tragedy of the horse." The *aficionado,* or bullfight fan, is the Spanish equivalent of the American baseball fan. He reacts the same way to the same kind of things. If you could get the authorization to put on a bullfight in the Yankee Stadium, you would see approximately the same crowd there that you do now, and they would behave, after a little instruction from our star reporters and radio announcers, just about the way the Spanish crowd behaves. And they would not be—"broadly"—the kind of people, if there are such people, who can see an infuriated bull charge across a bull ring, ram his horns into the private end of a horse's belly and rip him clear up to the ribs, lifting and tossing his rider bodily in the air and over against the fence with the same motion, and keep their attention so occupied with the "whole tragedy" that they cannot "separate" this enough to "feel it emotionally." Bullfights are not wholly bad, but sentimentalizing over them in the name of art-form and ritual is.

Whatever art may be, the thing which exempts it from those rules of decent conduct which make life possible and civilization a hope, is that its representations are not real. A bullfight—foolishly so called by the English, since it does not except for a moment resemble a fight—is real life. It is men tormenting and killing a bull; it is a bull being tormented and killed.

And if it is not "art" in a sense to justify Hemingway's undiscriminating recourse to that notion, still less is it "tragedy" in a sense to sustain the elevated emotions which he hopes to erect over it with this portentous term.

Suppose that you attend a bullfight with your eyes and emotional receptors recklessly wide open, as a poet should. What do you see to admire and what to despise? Men moving in the risk of wounds and death with skill, grace, suavity and courage. That is something to admire—and the wild free fighting force of the animal as he charges into the arena, a sight so thrilling that words fail utterly. They fail Hemingway. Until

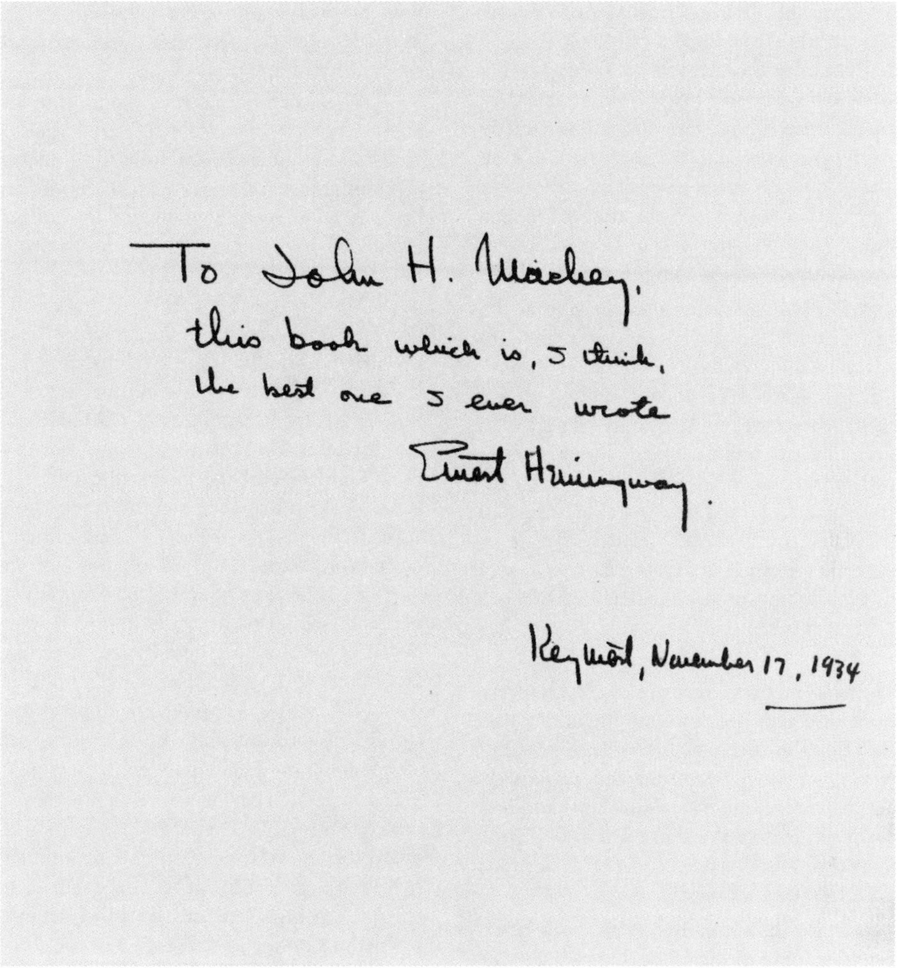

To John H. Mackey,
this book which is, I think,
the best one I ever wrote

Ernest Hemingway.

Key West, November 17, 1934

Inscription in John H. Mackey's copy of Death in the Afternoon *(McKeldin Library, University of Maryland)*

Christians thought up the sickly idea of worshipping a lamb, this noble creature symbolized the beauty of divine power in a good half of the great religions of the earth.

Here, then, are two things to admire and they command admiration; they command sympathy. And then you see these admirable brave men begin to take down this noble creature and reduce him to a state where they can successfully run in and knife him, by a means which would be described in any other situation under the sun as a series of dirty tricks, these tricks being made possible by his well known and all too obvious stupidity—the limitations of his vision and rigidity of his instincts—this stupidity being further assured by breeding, by keeping him in a dim light before the running and by never giving him a second chance in the ring. You see this beautiful creature, whom you despise for his stupidity and admire because he is so gorgeously equipped with power for wild life, trapped in a ring where his power is nothing, and you see him put forth his utmost in vain to escape death at the hands of these spryer and more flexible monkeys, whose courage you admire and whose mean use of their wit you despise. You see him baffled, bewildered, insane with fright, fury and physical agony, jabbed, stabbed, haunted, hounded, steadily brought dreadfully down from his beauty of power, until he stands horribly torpid, sinking leadlike into his tracks, lacking the mere strength of muscle to lift his vast head, panting, gasping, gurgling, his mouth too little and the tiny black tongue hanging out too far to give him breath, and faint falsetto cries of anguish, altogether lost-baby-like now and not bull-like,

133

coming out of him, and you see one of these triumphant monkeys strike a theatrical pose, and dash in swiftly and deftly—yes, while there is still danger, still a staggering thrust left in the too heavy horns—and they have invented statistics, moreover, and know exactly how much and how little danger there is—dash in swiftly and deftly and plunge a sword into the very point where they accurately know—for they have also invented anatomy, these wonderful monkeys—that they will end that powerful and noble thing forever.

That is what a bullfight is, and that is all it is. To drag in notions of honor and glory here, and take them seriously, is ungrown-up enough and rather sophomoric. But to pump words over it like tragedy and dramatic conflict is mere romantic nonsense and self-deception crying to heaven. It is not tragic to die in a trap because although beautiful you are stupid; it is not tragic to play mean tricks on a beautiful thing that is stupid, and stab it when its power is gone. It is the exact opposite of tragedy in every high meaning that has ever been given to that word. It is killing made meaner, death more ignoble, bloodshed more merely shocking than it has need to be.

Fortunately it is no great trick to close one's receptors in a certain direction, to deaden sympathies that are unfruitful. We all go through life with these emotional blinders on; we could not go through otherwise. You remember the anxious mother whose husband had taken their infant son into one of those sidewalk horror exhibitions—it was an illuminated view of a "famous painting of Nero throwing Christians to the lions."

"George, George, how could you subject Bobby's tender little growing mind to that shocking experience? What *did* he do? What *did* he say?"

"He said, 'Oh, Papa, there's one poor lion hasn't got any Christian!'"

This being the nature of the human infant, it is obvious that if you grow up in a society which does not extend sympathy to bulls in the bull ring, barring some heightened consciousness or gift of reflection in you amounting to an eccentricity, you will not do so either. For this reason the idea that bullfights prove Spaniards to be cruel, or as Havelock Ellis says, "indifferent to pain both in themselves and others," seems to me—with all respect to that eminent authority—the veriest nonsense. The appetites to which bullfighting appeals are a universal human inheritance, and if its survival in Spain must have some explanation other than cultural accident, I should associate it with the almost feminine gentleness of character to be felt in that country which seems to have need of this stoical over-protest of courage without mercy. At any rate, we expect an American poet who goes down there to see more and not less

than a Spanish adolescent, whose one-sided obtundity in this matter is as inevitable as the misshapen callus on the bottom of any man's foot.

Why then does our iron advocate of straight talk about what things are, our full-sized man, our ferocious realist, go blind and wrap himself up in clouds of juvenile romanticism the moment he crosses the border on his way to a Spanish bullfight? It is of course a commonplace that anyone who too much protests his manhood lacks the serene confidence that he *is* made out of iron. Most of us too delicately organized babies who grow up to be artists suffer at times from that small inward doubt. But some circumstance seems to have laid upon Hemingway a continual sense of the obligation to put forth evidences of red-blooded masculinity. It must be made obvious not only in the swing of the big shoulders and the clothes he puts on, but in the stride of his prose style and the emotions he permits to come to the surface there. This trait of his character has been strong enough to form the nucleus of a new flavor in English literature, and it has moreover begotten a veritable school of fiction-writers—a literary style, you might say, of wearing false hair on the chest. Nevertheless I think it is inadequate to explain the ecstatic adulation with which Hemingway approaches everything connected with the killing of bulls in the bull ring.

He says that he went to see these spectacles because he was trying to learn how to write, and he wanted something "simple" to write about; violent death, he thought, was one of the simplest things; he had seen a great deal of violent death in the War, but the War being over and he still learning to write, it seemed necessary to see some more. I do not think you can call it psychoanalysis to remark that the only simple thing here is Ernest Hemingway. A man writes about—and travels over the earth to see—what he likes to dwell on. Moreover, it is not death Hemingway writes about or travels to see, but killing. Nobody above fourteen years old will contend that he has got into his book that "feeling of life and death" which he says he was working for. He has got into it an enthusiasm for killing—for courage and dominating and killing. Hemingway cannot feel—he cannot even see—the hero of his "tragedy" staggering toward death in blood loss and bewilderment. He withdraws automatically from any participation in that central fact. He did once feel, he tells us, the surprise of pain which makes the animal toss awkwardly like a great inflexible box when the banderillas are jabbed into his withers, but this live feeling vanished instantly and by an extraordinary magic the moment he learned that the bull is more and not less dangerous after he has been "slowed" in this way, and will now make better aimed, because more desperate, efforts to defend his life. After learning this, Heming-

Galley proofs for God Rest You Merry Gentlemen *(New York: House of Books, 1933), revised by Hemingway (Louis Henry Cohn Collection, University of Delaware)*

way felt no more sympathy for the bull "than for a canvas or the marble a sculptor cuts or the dry powder snow your skis cut through." Which is a clear statement—is it not?—of indifference to "the feeling of life and death," and total preoccupation with the art of courageous killing.

A like numbness of imagination afflicts this poet when the life and death of the matador is in question. The climax of his enterprise of learning how to write, at least the last mention of it, occurs on page 20, where after seeing a matador gored by a bull, he wakes in the night and tries to remember "what it was that seemed just out of my remembering and that was the thing that I had really seen and, finally, remembering all around it, I got it. When he stood up, his face white and dirty and the silk of his breeches opened from waist to knee, it was the dirtiness of the rented breeches, the dirtiness of his slit underwear and the clean, clean, unbearably clean whiteness of the thigh bone that I had seen, and it was that which was important." Is the clean whiteness of a man's thigh bone the "important" thing to a poet working for the feeling of life and death, or is it merely the most shocking thing, and therefore the most sought after by an ecstatic in the rapture of killing?

"Do you know the sin it would be," he says, "to ruffle the arrangement of the feathers on a hawk's neck if they could never be replaced as they were? Well, that would be the sin it would be to kill El Gallo." And we turn the page with a shudder for El Gallo.

It seems, then, that our ferocious realist is so romantic about bullfights, and so blind to much of what they "actually are," because he is enraptured with courageous killing. He is athirst after this quality of act and emotion with that high-fevered thirst of the saint after the blood of the living God, so that little else can open its way into his eyes or down to his heartstrings. He is himself, moreover, courageous enough—and with a courage rarer than that of toreros—to state plainly that he loves killing, and try to state why. It is because killing makes him feel triumphant over death.

"Killing cleanly and in a way which gives you esthetic pride and pleasure," he says, "has always been one of the greatest enjoyments of a part of the human race. . . . One of its greatest pleasures . . . is the feeling of rebellion against death which comes from its administering. Once you accept the rule of death thou shalt not kill is an easily and a naturally obeyed commandment. But when a man is still in rebellion against death he has pleasure in taking to himself one of the godlike attributes; that of giving it. This is one of the most profound feelings in those men who enjoy killing."

Hemingway is quite right about the pleasure derived by a part of our race, and in imagination, indeed, by all of it, from killing. One need only read the Old Testament to see how easy it was for our most pious ancestors in morality to cut a whole people out of the tiny circle of their tribal sympathy like the ring of light round a campfire, and enjoy with free hearts the delight of slaughtering them "so that there was none left in that city, man, woman or child." And one need only remark the popularity of murder stories—or of Hemingway's own book so gorgeously full of horses' blood and bulls' blood, and matadors' blood, and carpenters' blood, and even the blood of "six carefully selected Christs" crucified in his riotous imagination to make a holiday for his readers, in order to see that this littlesatisfied thirst is wellnigh universal.

Had men not enjoyed killing, they would not be here, and the bulls would be doing it all. That is a significant fact. But nevertheless the important part of the killing has been done, and the present tendency is to suppress, to sublimate in representative art, even in some measure to breed out, this dangerous taste. For this we have the authority of Gene Tunney, a writer who stands at the opposite pole from Hemingway, having abundantly established his prowess in action, and in literature therefore being somewhat concerned, strangely enough, to establish his sensibility. Speaking in his biography of the "killer-instinct boys," he remarks that "the higher in human development one goes, the more controlled one finds this reaction." And if that is true in the prize ring, it is more certainly true among poets and artists and sensitive young men generally.

It is so true that the nervous horror of these young men, and their mental and moral sickness, after forcing themselves through the insensate butchery of the World War, may be said almost to have created an epoch in our literature. One by one they have recovered their tongues and stood up during these fifteen years, those stricken poets, and confessed that they were devastated and quite utterly shattered by that forced discipline in the art of wholesale killing—those have, that is, who were not too shattered to speak. And their speech, with the silence of the others, is the true aftermath in poetry of the Great War—not the priggish trivialities of the Cult of Unintelligibility, not the cheap moral of decorum (that shallow cult so admirably exterminated root and branch by Ernest Hemingway in a paragraph of this book), not the new Bohemianism of the synthetic-gin period, not the poetry of the new scientific hope in Russia, for it has had no poetry—but the confession in language of blood and tears of the horror unendurable to vividly living nerves of the combination of civilized life with barbaric slaughter.

Will it be too much like a clinic if I point out that Ernest Hemingway is one of the most sensitive and keen-feeling of these poets, one of the most passionately intolerant, too, of priggery and parlor triviality and old maids' morals and empty skulls hiding in unintelligibility? I am not strong for literary psychoanalysis, but I must record a guess rising toward the middle of his book and growing to conviction in the end, that *Death in the Afternoon* belongs also among those confessions of horror which are the true poetry or the weightiest poetry of this generation. It does not matter much whether Ernest Hemingway knows this fact or not. We may hope he will find out, for a man cannot grow to his height without self-knowledge. But the important thing is for us to know.

We took this young man with his sensitive genius for experience, for living all the qualities of life and finding a balance among them—and with that too obvious fear in him of proving inadequate—and we shoved him into our pit of slaughter, and told him to be courageous about killing. And we thought he would come out weeping and jittering. Well, he came out roaring for blood, shouting to the skies the joy of killing, the "religious ecstasy" of killing—and most pathetic, most pitiable, killing as a protest against death.

Hemingway responded to Eastman's "Bull in the Afternoon" in this 1933 letter to Maxwell Perkins. From The Only Thing That Counts, *pp. 190–191.*

June 13/

Dear Max: . . .

Eastman has given me a new slant on my so-called friends in N.Y. If he ever gets a solvent publisher to publish that libel between covers it will cost the publisher plenty of money and Eastman will go to jail. Moe Speiser [Hemingway's lawyer] will see to that. I could use some of that dough.

If I ever see him anywhere or anytime, now or in the future, I will get my own redress myself.

I am tempted never to publish another damned thing. The swine arent worth writing for. I swear to Christ they're not. Every phase of the whole racket is so disgusting that it makes you feel like vomiting. Every word I wrote about the Spanish fighting bull was absolutely true and result of long and careful and exhaustive observation. Then they pay Eastman, who knows nothing about it, to say I write sentimental nonsense. He really knows how bulls are. They are like this—(he explains) I am like this—etc. (he explains) I have seen 50 bulls do what that fool says—from his ignorance—no bull can do—Its Too disgusting to write about—

And it is a commonplace that I lack confidence that I am a man—What shit—And I'm supposed to go

around with your good friends spreading that behind my back—And they imagine they will get away with it. Mr Crichton—Mr Eastman etc. Why dont you give them space to write it in the magazine? Whenever and wherever I meet any one of them their mouths will make a funny noise when they ever try to say it again after I get through working over them Mr. Crichton— the brave man who tells everybody things to their faces—We'll see—

They're a nice lot—The professional male beauties of other years—Max Eastman—a groper in sex (with the hands I mean) a traitor in politics and—hell I wont waste it on them.

It certainly is damned fine to have friends—They hear you are out of the country and they open up. Good. Bring on some more friends. I'll be a long way out of the country and they will all get very brave and say every thing they wish were true—Then I'll be back and we will see what will happen.

You see what they cant get over is 1 that I <u>am</u> a man (2) that I can beat the shit out of any of them 3 that I can write. The last hurts them the worst. But they dont like any of it. But Papa will make them like it. Best to you—Ernest.

In January 1933 at Captain Louis Henry Cohn's House of Books in New York, Hemingway met Arnold Gingrich, who was planning to launch Esquire, *a new magazine for men, and asked Hemingway to contribute to it. Although he was reluctant at first, Hemingway agreed to contribute a monthly letter; through the years he published twenty-five essays and six stories, including "The Snows of Kilimanjaro," in* Esquire.

3 April 1933

Dear Mr. Gingrich:

You write a very good letter.

First about the prospective benefits from the advertisers. The collar size is 17½, 44 in jackets but 46 as good or better. Shoes are wide 11. Trousers 34 by 34. Don't imagine they send many sizes that dimension to photograph. If you ever have anything like that and send it parcel post collect will promise to wear them out.

I don't worship Joyce. I like him very much as a friend and think no one can write better, technically, I learned much from him, from Ezra, in conversation principally, from G. Stein, who was a fine woman until she went professionally patriotically goofily complete lack of judgment and stoppage of all sense lesbian with the old menopause. Until then she was damned smart. Then she started taking herself seriously rather than her work seriously and because she had always been that way began to take that seriously too rather than as an accident of what she happened to be. Then she got the idea that anybody who was any good must be queer, if they did not seem to be they were merely concealing it. But what was worse she got the idea that anybody who was queer must be good. Learned a lot from her before she went haywire. Learned nothing from old Ford except mistakes not to make that he had made. Although he was damned generous about writing things about what I wrote. Learned from Anderson but it didn't last long. Imitated Ring Lardner as a kid but didn't learn from him. Nothing to learn because he doesn't know anything. All he has is a good false ear and has been around. The poor guy really hates everything but Purity. Learned from D. H. Lawrence about how to say what you felt about country. What the hell is this, confession, benedeteme parde porque ha aprendido.

The non-commercial magazines are nearly always run to make a career for the editors or editress-es. The only one that was ever worth a damn was the Little Review. They work out as good things, however, nearly all of them, in the long run. Kids feel they have to publish, and they have to to get the stuff behind them.

It is too cockeyed bloody hot today to write anything else and now it is too hot to write a letter even.

Still must go on and finish about the letters for your quarterly. I'll write the four. First one from Cuba. 2nd from Spain. 3rd and 4th from Africa. If anything should happen to Africa will write 3rd and 4th from somewhere else. Will surely be somewhere if I'm still on tap. You send me the first 250 when I write for it and so on. Getting the money will make me write the piece. If you will have enough money you can send me the advance for two and two ie 500 at a time. . . .

About what you say about humor. The bastards don't want you to joke because it disturbs their categories. Most people will not even read the Torrents but Joyce and Ezra like it and so does everybody that knows a damned thing about what I'm trying to do.

This is a very I, me, mine letter but you said you were interested. Capt. Cohn after saying 200 copies announced 350. When called by old Papa he wrote the usual sad letter about how he could have made a little money which needed badly out of 350 copies but needed 250 to pay his expenses and would not do anything against my wishes but would I wire him he could print 250. I wired him ok for 300. But why in christ's name not say 350 at the start rather than get it onto that sort of basis? For christ sake never mention this to him because if wished to offend him would do myself. . . .

I wanted to work today but it has been too bloody hot. This letter probably shows it. Working on a title for

book of stories now. With enough time you can always get a good title. The hell of it is that you always have a lot that seem good and that it takes time to tell which one is right.

Good luck to you,

yours always,
Ernest Hemingway

Hemingway enjoyed inviting people, especially Gingrich and Scribner editor Maxwell Perkins, to Key West for fishing. On the Pilar, *Hemingway was in charge. In the September 1965 issue of* Playboy, *pp. 123, 256–258, Gingrich published an article about these fishing trips with Hemingway.*

HORSING THEM IN WITH HEMINGWAY

"Gingrich is a pretty keen fisherman," I said.
"I started him," said Hemingway.
–ROBERT EMMETT GINNA
in a May 1958 interview
with Ernest Hemingway

He didn't, and even if he had, the deep-sea fishing I did with Ernest Hemingway would have been a false start, never leading to any real appreciation of the deepest satisfaction of angling. We fished out of Key West and out of Bimini, first in '34 on the Anita, the boat that belonged to Josie Russell, and later in '35 and '36 on the Pilar, the boat Ernest bought when *Esquire* advanced him the money he lacked to complete the deal. Most of that fishing was hard work, calling for a great deal of back-bending exertion, and though some of it was fun, none of it was what I later came to consider real angling.

Ernest was a meat fisherman. He cared more about the quantity than about the quality, and was more concerned with the capture of the quarry than with the means employed to do it. He was also–and this is what no true angler is–intensely competitive about his fishing, and a very poor sport. If the luck was out, then nobody around him could do any right, and he was ready to blame everybody in sight, ahead of himself. When things were going right, he was quick to promote everybody in his company to high rank as good fellows, and was jovially boastful about their every least accomplishment, as well as his own. But let a hook pull out and his attitude was never to praise the fish that managed to bend it, but only to blame the hookmaker.

Arnold Gingrich

In Bimini in June of '36, when the Atlantic record for marlin stood at 736 pounds, Ernest hooked a beautiful bright silver marlin with the coloration of a young fish. It was big, and as it leaped again and again, with a long, low trajectory like that of a horse going over steeplechase barriers, its faint lavender stripings glistened in the sun like the light flashing off a diamond. Big fish, up in the 600- and 700-pound class, usually looked dark, of an allover blue that almost verged on black. So Jane Kendall Mason, who had pioneered the Cuban marlin fishing with Hemingway some five years earlier, who had a boat of her own and at least as much big-game-fishing experience as he had, ventured the guess that the fish might go about 450 pounds.

The fish was still on, and still in sight—to me it looked about the size of a tank car—when she spoke. Hemingway bridled as if he'd been hit, turned his head to make an angry answer, and in that same instant felt the heavy line go slack. Back came the hook, a new one from Hardy, hand-forged and monstrous, looking as if it could do in a pinch as a spare anchor for the Queen Mary or the Normandie. It was pulled out to an angle of about 130 degrees, like a bent hairpin. Hemingway began shaking it in Jane Mason's face, so vigorously that he might well have been about to claw her with it.

"Four hundred fifty, huh? Look at that hook—just look at it—fourteen hundred pounds if it was an ounce."

He was beside himself, shrieking about the marlin Zane Grey had landed in Tahiti that went over a thousand pounds even though sharks had taken huge hunks out of its tail section, and insisting that this one would have surpassed that, not merely for a new Atlantic record, but for a world record as well. His wife Pauline and her sister Virginia tried to calm him down. Pauline pressed a drink into his hand, to make him stop brandishing the bent hook, while Ginny wound up her Liberty-phone to drown him out with *You're the Top*. I finally managed the diversion, like the successful one of three *banderilleros* trying to distract a goring bull, by at last getting him to hear me say that Jane hadn't made the slighting 450-pound estimate herself, but had only been echoing, in astonished disagreement, my own ignorant guess at the weight of the fish.

"She didn't say it was four-fifty—I did, and what the hell do *I* know about it?" As a gambit, it compared to Peter Lorre's later line, in the film *Casablanca*: "What right do I have to think?"

His wrath turned, in the instant, upon the Messrs. Hardy. They would certainly hear from him, and in certain colorfully specified terms.

He was more fun to fish with when there were fewer people aboard for him to show off for.

On its inaugural trip, there were just three of us fishing aboard the Pilar, because the fourth, who was supposed to have been F. Scott Fitzgerald, had refused to come, saying: "I can't face Ernest again, when he's so successful and I'm such a failure." The third man in the boat was John Dos Passos, who was even less of a fisherman than Scott Fitzgerald, but mixed a mean drink which he called a Gulf Stream Special. As I remember it, it was a poor country cousin to Pimm's Cup. Dos Passos mixed it in a zinc pail, to which he gave full marks for its contribution to the mixture's peculiar pungency.

The gin gave out at Dry Tortugas, where there were no facilities to acquire any more, but a search of the boat uncovered a case of John Jameson's Irish Whisky up in the bow, which somebody had thoughtfully put aboard as a christening present to the Pilar. It was over the Irish, that evening, that Ernest confided to Dos Passos and me his high opinion of Gary Cooper as Lieutenant Henry in the screen version of *A Farewell to Arms,* and his correspondingly low opinion of Helen Hayes as the choice to portray Catherine Barkley.

"Who would you have liked, Hem?" asked Dos Passos.

Expecting him to nominate somebody like Dietrich, though she wasn't Scottish, I was utterly unprepared, at least by the book itself, for his answer that there couldn't possibly be any other logical choice, for Christ's sake, than a girl named Jean Harlow. Dos Passos, it seemed, had never heard of her, so Hemingway gave him an animated demonstration, worthy of the Hindu dancer Shan-Kar, of her salient points of personality.

On the run back from Dry Tortugas, in a most unlikely spot, we came upon a school of big barracuda, and Dos Passos, between his eyesight and the Irish, and coupled with his less than passionate addiction to fishing in the first place, seemed to Hemingway to be lousing up what might have proved an excellent chance to break the rod and reel record for barracuda, which back then, in early '35, stood not too much above the record of 69 pounds and some ounces for muskellunge. Dos Passos and Hemingway were both into fish at the same time, but Dos appeared to be more the victim than the master of his, so Hemingway asked me to hand him the Colt Woodsman automatic that was in the cabin. He shot both fish, to avert the threatened foul-up of the lines that might cause us to lose either or both of them in getting them aboard. The more orthodox method would have been to brain them, once they were up over the stern, with a sawed-off baseball bat, but there were signs of so many other fish, any one of which might have broken the record, that he didn't want to waste another moment of fishing time. So Dos Passos was benched, and I was drafted to fill the other fishing chair, and admonished to for Christ's sake horse 'em in fast and not frig around like Dos, to see if we couldn't bring in enough of them that one might break the record. We managed to get some six or seven more before the school let out, but though all weighed in high in the 60s, none went over the 70-pound mark.

After the barracuda explosion, nothing else seemed to be happening for a considerable interval, so as a dead soldier out of the case of Irish went over the stern and bobbed away in the wake where our filleted mullet baits were dragging, Ernest passed me the Colt Woodsman and asked me if I shot. By the time I figured out where the safety catch was and how it worked, the bobbing bottle began to look as far away as a ship on the horizon. But without raising the pistol to sight it—shooting from the lap, as it were—I sheered off its neck with the first tentative and diffident shot. Hemingway, jumping up out of the fishing chair beside me, burbled excitedly that there weren't a dozen men in the world who could make a shot like that, and Jesus Christ if he'd known I shot that well we'd have done some shooting at Dry Tortugas.

My enthusiasm for shooting being somewhat less than that of Dos Passos for fishing, I tried to explain the

shot away as a lucky punch, but Hemingway, with the recent eyewitness knowledge to the contrary, refused to believe my disclaimers, so we had to turn around and go back to Dry Tortugas. There our quarry was sandpipers on the shore, delicate tiny birds on toothpick legs. It seemed to me, as a sporting proposition, tantamount to attacking butterflies with a tank, but although we blasted away at them until the ammunition was exhausted, neither of us even nicked one. Hemingway was generally credited with being an excellent shot with rifle and shotgun, but a pistol is something else again.

In all the fishing I did with Hemingway over the three winter seasons of '34, '35 and '36, I never once tied into a marlin, which is, of course, the apex of deep-sea fishing, as salmon is of stream fishing. I would work hours on tuna, however, pumping and reeling to get one up for what seemed like forever, only to have the fish sound like an elevator when the cable breaks, and then pump and reel again until I could barely see, except for red and orange balloons at the corners where my sweat-congealed eyelids seemed to be coming unhinged, and my mouth began to taste of a weird cocktail, compounded of all the elements of sheer fatigue.

Part of that fishing was fun, of course, because any fishing is more fun than no fishing; but most of it was the worst kind of work, the kind of work for which the worker is not in condition. I would fly down from Chicago to Key West or Bimini, in the days when night flights were slow and arduous, having had in the interim no more exercise than that involved in the waving of a pocket handkerchief, and would get back home utterly exhausted. . . .

Henry Seidel Canby published this review of Hemingway's third story collection, Winner Take Nothing *(1933), in* Saturday Review of Literature, *10 (28 October 1933), p. 217.*

FAREWELL TO THE NINETIES

We have accustomed ourselves to Ernest Hemingway, and therefore it becomes more possible to estimate his values and to place him in the literary show. His staccato style has had the compliment of much imitation. His themes, drawn from the wreckage of war, or from ruthless analysis of youthful memories, or from the upsurge of savagery or brutal egoism in supposedly civilized man, have become as expected and familiar as the Cinderella plot of the conventional short story. Hemingway, like Ring Lardner, like O. Henry, like

Manuscript page for "A Clean, Well-Lighted Place" (Ernest Hemingway Collection, John F. Kennedy Library)

Kipling, has created his world and his technique of making it articulate. He is no longer one of the youngsters, and we must praise him now, not for his novelties as such, but for their merit as renderings of life, and for the qualities of that life itself.

And what does one find in a collection of short stories such as "Winner Take Nothing"? On the plus side, an extraordinary power of observation, worthy of comparison with Kipling's, an observation that knows no inhibitions, but is as limited as was that earlier master's—who could do the sensational, but not nuances and subtleties of a matured culture. An observation, however, that, because it is not inhibited, brings a fresh range of subjects into the light. I find nothing in this volume as poignant as certain sketches of trout fishing (a passionate subject for Hemingway) in earlier writing, or as beautifully organized as the retreat from Caparetto in "A Farewell to Arms," unless it be the dangerously macabre descriptions of horrid death in "A Natural History of Death," or the hysterical account of fornication in "Fathers and Sons." Yet no one can read of the brute who looks through his water glass at the sunken steamer, with bodies floating inside the port holes, his rudimentary pity only felt, not realized like the frustration of his greed, without hailing one of the most skillful writers of our generation.

And yet, and yet, the comparison with Kipling persists. Now that the novelty is off these studies of egoism, brutality, cold lust, and pathetic demoralization, it becomes clearer and clearer that we have not changed so much from the Nineties as we supposed. Then it was what somewhere East of Suez had to say to smug Victorianism which excited the younger readers. The lid was on in genteel America and England—even Mark Twain had not dared to lift it; but under the old Chinese pagoda at Mandalay the Westerner became primitive man again. He fell in love with Dinah Shadd but could not step out to tell her so without worse than philandering on the way. He lived a brute's life and paid for it. He was usually drunk, usually lusting for women, and sadly willing to tell about it. Of course Kipling threw a glamor over it all—removed it by half a world from the complacent West. His Mulvaneys were romantic figures in a cleaner, greener land than ours. The raw shocks to our sensibilities were cushioned by humor and restraint in language, for one remembers that the Soldiers Three told their stories to a gentleman and pruned their language to suit. And unquestionably Hemingway has come a step further along the road. Kipling could never have handled his cold killers, for the war had not yet drained humanitarianism from the imagination. Kipling was incapable of such unadorned brutality of natural speech between men and women who have only their vulgar selves with no overtones of humane possibilities given to them by the writer.

Yet Kipling, with more humor, was far less sentimental than Hemingway. He never is so sorry for himself as this man who records struggle where the winner gets nothing. His norm is still a hearty, courageous world in which brutality or degeneracy is an aberration, romantic because it releases the inhibited in man, but transitory. And Kipling is the better story-teller. When you cannot reread with the old pleasure a story of Kipling's it is because he so gloats upon and overemphasizes the sensations. His style is sometimes all exclamation mark. Yet even then the brilliant plot remains. When you are bored by Hemingway, as I frankly am by a half dozen of these new stories, which are repetitive with the slow pound, pound of a hammer upon a single mood, there is nothing to revive you except flashes of excellent observation. The younger man is at his best precisely when (if one insists upon regarding him as a novelist) he is at his worst,—when he takes one episode, one phase of a temperament, one mood, one moment, and eliminating all context, all verbiage, cuts a stencil of it and stamps it on the page with unforgettable incisiveness.

And yet I cannot see much difference in the history of art between the two sensationalisms, except that Kipling (like his business contemporaries) had Asia to exploit, and Hemingway, after the breakup of the great war, finds his horrors at home, and makes his romance out of reversions instead of adventures. Neither man is a novelist, both men deal in specialties eminently suitable to the sketch or the short story. Both depend upon overemphasis. Both will suffer heavily from a change in taste, as Kipling has already suffered from the shift in interest away from the romance of imperialism. Kipling, of course, has a far greater endowment as a writer. Yet I do not believe that it is merely the franchise to speak plainly of things not written about in nineteenth century English which has given Hemingway his great success. His dialogue is limited. It is good only for special people—especially for primitive passionates, for wounded sophisticates where the primitive shows through like an exposed bone, for pathetic inarticulates, and for men of abnormal simplicity whose love of wine, of women, or of murder so dominates as to run the whole machine—but for these it is a superb instrument. Whether Kipling's humor and his superb apprehensions of the beauty of heroism, of the fundamental decencies, of patriotism, of love not merely sexual, do not make him the greater man, depends upon whether the brutality in which the world is just now indulging is, in truth, further from the heart of human desire than what other ages have longed for.

Hemingway's explanation for the "C" and "M" reference in "The Light of the World" (Swann Galleries, 6 June 1996 Public Auction Sale 1727, Item 91)

But the two belong to the same wave of historical culture. Kipling began what Hemingway, perhaps, is ending. The path seems to lead into a swamp.

The British notices of Hemingway's third short-story collection were mostly positive. This review of Winner Take Nothing *was published in the* Times Literary Supplement, *8 February 1934, p. 90.*

WINNER TAKE NOTHING

The somewhat pessimistic title of Mr. Ernest Hemingway's new collection of stories–WINNER TAKE NOTHING (Cape, 7s. 6d. net)–is appropriate enough: a melancholy note predominates in these tales. The protagonist of the first, "After the Storm," literally takes nothing, and that is the burdon of the story he tells. He is a fisherman of Havana who is the first to discover a liner which has sunk in shallow water with all hands, but is unable to turn his discovery to account. He reflects that "there must have been some scenes inside because she settled fast," but it is the thought of so much wealth just beyond his reach which upsets him: the tragic implications of his blunt narrative are the reader's affair; and presented in this way they have certainly a force which no sympathetic emphasis could have given them.

A similar effect is more starkly contrived in "God Rest You, Merry Gentlemen," a really terrible story in which two doctors describe a case of self-mutilation to a friend. In "A Natural History of the Dead" (reprinted from "Death in The Afternoon") Mr. Hemingway observes human suffering with a bitterness which his elaborate irony can scarcely contain. "A Way You'll Never Be" is a story of the War on the Italian front, and skilfully explores the aberrations of shell-shock. Suffering is still the theme in "One Reader Writes," and is more subtly evoked in "A Clean, Well-lighted Place" and "The Gambler, the Nun, and the Radio." In the last-mentioned story–which is laid in the accident ward of a hospital–the depression of both the hero and reader is lightened by the enthusiasm of the nun, Sister

Dust jacket for Hemingway's third short-story collection

Cecilia, who goes to chapel to pray earnestly for the success of a baseball team. We are reminded in this story how sensitive is Mr. Hemingway's ear for dialogue. "Wine of Wyoming" is among the pleasanter stories. In this study of a charming elderly couple we can enjoy Mr. Hemingway's talent for communicating simple pleasures—the pleasures of vague and genial talk, of courtesy and hospitality. After a few pages in the company of Fontan and his wife we can appreciate how great a misfortune it really was that the narrator and his friend did not turn up one evening when Fontan had made preparations to entertain them. In "Fathers and Sons" we learn something of the antecedents of Nicholas Adams—of his father who taught him to love fishing and shooting and who "was as sound on those tow things as he was unsound on sex," and of his education, frankly described, in the matters on which his father was unsound. There is perhaps nothing in this collection so good as the best in "Men Without Women" and "In Our Time." One or two stories are unsuccessful: "The Sea Change," for example, in which the main characters are too little developed for their situation to be interesting. But on the whole Mr. Hemingway's singular merits as a story-teller are well sustained.

Negative reviews of Winner Take Nothing *and Hemingway's perception that Perkins and Scribners had failed to support the book aroused his anger. From* The Only Thing That Counts, *pp. 201–204.*

> November 17 1933
>
> c/o Guaranty Trust Co. of N.Y
>
> 4 Place de la Concorde
>
> Paris
>
> Cable address HEMINGWAY
>
> GARRITiS
>
> PARIS

Dear Max:

Thanks for your two cables—of a week and two weeks ago and your letter of Nov. 6 enclosing some of the reviews. I cabled you yesterday because I had been seeing the N.Y Times, Herald Tribune and Sat Review of Lit and they all were full of ads of a book of stories by Dotty Parker but nothing about this book. There was an ad in Sunday Times and I believe Daily Times the week the book came out. Then nothing. No follow up at all. Saw No mention of book in Sunday Herald Trib in number it was reviewed in. An ad in with your fall list in the week after. Believe there was an ad in Herald Trib the day it came out. The advertizing is your business—not mine. But if a publisher seems to give no importance to a book and make no Boom Ha Ha the public takes the cue from the publisher very quickly.

One of the reasons I always stuck by you was (in a commercial way) because you kept on pushing The Sun Also Rises through a terrificly slow start—And one of the things I did not care much about was the way after a wonderful start they dropped Death In The Afternoon absolutely cold. You know yourself.

This happens to be a book <u>you</u> have to do a little work to push—But in the end it doesnt do anyone any particular harm to publish literature once in a while—Especially as I have always paid my way.

You mention a review by Soskins in your letter but you didnt send it.

Also I have never had any August royalty reports—nor any accounting since I saw you in N.Y (May have had a royalty report in the Spring) Will you please send them.

The bird, when he labelled me as approaching middle-age was trying to get rid of me that way—Others having failed. So the advertizing department siezes on that to advertize the book by. If I write about <u>any-</u>

body—automatically they label that character as me—when I write about somebody that can't possibly be me—as in After The Storm, that unfortunate convert to Economics religion Mr. Chamberlain, says it is unusually imaginative or more imaginative than anything I've attempted. What shit.

When does Middle Age commience? That story—Wine of Wyoming is nothing but straight reporting of what heard and saw when was finishing A Farewell To Arms out in Sheridan and Big Horn—How old was I then? That was 1928 and I was just 30 years old while I was out there. Yet that bird says it is about middle aged people because he himself is middle-aged. I was 17 when first went to the war. (This for your own information) I write some stories absolutely as they happen ie. Wine of Wyoming—The letter one, A Day's Wait The Mother of a Queen, Gambler, Nun, Radio, and another word for word as it happened, to Bra, After The Storm,; (Chamberlain found that more imaginative than the others) others I invent completely Killers, Hills Like White Elephants, The Undefeated, Fifty Grand, Sea Change, A Simple Enquiry. Nobody can tell which ones I make up completely. The point is I want them all to sound as though they really happened. Then when I succeed those poor dumb pricks say they are all just skillful reporting.

I invented every word and every incident of A Farewell To Arms except possibly 3 or 4 incidents. All the best part is invented—95 per cent of The Sun Also was pure imagination. I took real people in that one and I controlled what they did—I made it all up—

A fool like Canby thinks I'm a reporter. I'm a reporter and an imaginative writer. And I can still imagine plenty and there will be stories to write As They Happened as long as I live. Also I happen to be 35 years old and the last two stories I wrote in Havana were the best in the book—And this 15,000 word one is better than either of them. Several miles better.—So if you let all the people who want me over with kid you into believing Im through—or let the business office start to lay off me as a bad bet—You will be making a very considerable mistake because I havent started to write yet—(wont ever write you this again—)

I cant write better stories than some that I have written—What Mr. Fadiman asks for—because you cant write any better stories than those—and nobody else can—But every once in a long while I can write one as good— And all the time I can write better stories than anybody else writing. But they want better ones and as good as anyone ever wrote.
God damn it. There cant be better ones. The one they pick out as "classic" Hills Like White Elephants not a damn critic thought anything of when it came out. I

always knew how good it was but I'll be Goddamned if I like to have to say how good my stuff is in order to give the business office confidance enough to advertize it after they have read an unfavorable review and think I'm through.

So I wont Ever Again. Will do something else. . . .

Does it seem of any significance to you that they all say there are 3 really good stories and nearly all pick 3 different ones? That Mr. Harry Hansen who doesnt understand these didnt understand A Farewell To Arms when it came out—Panned it—Now thinks it great novel etc. Oh hell—why go on. Why write as far as that goes? Because I have to. . . .

Yours always,
Ernest

Humorist Robert Benchley wrote this piece for The Colophon, *a magazine for book collectors, in September 1934.*

WHY DOES NOBODY COLLECT ME?
Queried by Robert Benchley

Some months ago, while going through an old box of books looking for a pressed nasturtium, I came across a thin volume which, even to my dreamer's instinct, seemed worth holding out, if only for purposes of prestige.

It was a first edition of Ernest Hemingway's *In Our Time,* the edition brought out in Paris by the Three Mountains Press in 1924, while Hemingway was just "Old Ernie" who lived over the saw-mill in the rue Notre Dame des Champs. I knew that it must be worth saving, because it said in the front that the edition consisted of one hundred and seventy copies, of which mine was Number Thirty-nine. That usually means something.

It so happened that, a few weeks later, "Old Ernie" himself was using my room in New York as a hide-out from literary columnists and reporters during one of his stop-over visits between Africa and Key West. On such all-too-rare occasions he lends an air of virility to my dainty apartment which I miss sorely after he has gone and the furniture has been repaired.

More to interrupt his lion-hunting story than anything else, I brought out my copy of *In Our Time* and suggested that, in memory of happy days around the Anise Deloso bowl at the Closerie des Lilas, it might be the handsome thing for him to inscribe a few pally sentiments on the fly-leaf. Not, as I took pains to explain to

Charles Thompson with Jack, Ernest, and Pauline Hemingway, en route to Europe, August 1933
(Courtesy of The Lilly Library, Indiana University)

him, that I was a particular admirer of his work, so much as that I wanted to see if he really knew how to spell.

Encouraged by my obviously friendly tone, he took a pen in his chubby fist, dipped it in a bottle of bull's blood, and wrote the following:

> To Robert ("Garbage Bird") Benchley,
> hoping that he won't wait for prices
> to reach the peak——
> from his friend,
> Ernest ("—— ———") Hemingway

The "Garbage Bird" reference in connection with me was a familiarity he had taken in the past to describe my appearance in the early morning light of Montparnasse on certain occasions. The epithet applied to himself, which was unprintable except in *Ulysses*, was written deliberately to make it impossible for me to cash in on the book.

Then, crazed with success at defacing *In Our Time*, he took my first edition of *A Farewell to Arms* and filled in each blank in the text where Scribner's had blushed and put a dash instead of the original word. I think that he supplied the original word in every case. In fact, I am sure of it.

On the fly-leaf of this he wrote:

> To R.(G).B. from E.(–).H.
> Corrected edition. Filled-in blanks.
> Very valuable. Sell quick.

Now, oddly enough, I had never considered selling either book. I had known, in a general way, that a first edition of the Gutenberg Bible would be worth money, and that, if one could lay hands on an autographed copy of *Canterbury Tales,* it would be a good idea to tuck it away, but that a first edition of one of Ernie's books could be the object of even Rabelaisian jesting as to its commercial value surprised and, in a vague sort of way,

Inscription on the front free endpaper of In Our Time *(McKeldin Library, University of Maryland)*

depressed me. Why are not *my* works matters for competitive bidding in the open market?

I am older than Hemingway, and have written more books than he has. And yet it is as much as my publishers and I can do to get people to pay even the list-price for my books, to say nothing of a supplementary sum for rare copies. . . .

Hemingway informs his editor that he has completed Green Hills of Africa *(New York: Scribners, 1935), the account of his African safari. From* The Only Thing That Counts, *pp. 214–216.*

Tuesday–Nov. 20–1934

Dear Max:

Thanks for the wire. I'm glad you liked the Esquire piece. Wrote them another one Sunday and sent it off yesterday. Have been having a terrible lot of energy–Bad as disease–Have worked all day every day since we got back from Cuba–Maybe it's that worry to get your work done we always feel in the fall when the year dies–

I've just been looking at this I've finished to get an idea of the length. . . . There are 491 pages which would make it 73,650 words–

I've been over a little more than half of it 3 times re-writing and cutting so I dont imagine will cut more than 3 or 4 thousand words out of the last.

I started it as a short story about while we were hunting in Africa, wanting it to be a damned fine story to go at the end of the First Fifty Four and it kept going on and on–Until now it is as long as I tell you–But it has a beginning and an end–it the action covers almost a month–and after you have read it I think you will have been there–

It is more like the story at the end of In Our Time–Big Two Hearted river than anything else–in quality–It is as much landscape painting, making the country come alive, but a hell of a lot happens in this one and there is plenty of dialogue and action. There is plenty of excitement, I think–But you will know when you read it–I had never read anything that could make me see and feel Africa–It was not at all as I had imagined it or like any thing I'd ever read–When I started the story that was what I wanted to make–But just the straight story, the actual things that happened on that wonderful Goddamned kudu hunt–the relation between the people and the way it all worked up to a climax–seemed to me a very fine story. Anyway I have it done now–

Been starving me to do it for 8 months.

One thing I have learned this last year is how to make a story move–So that it seems short when it is really very long. I think this has that–Anyway we will see–

I've written it absolutely truly. absolutely with no faking or cheating of any kind but I think I have learned to make it smoother without sacrificing any honesty–This is as honest as the Big Two Hearted River and much more exciting–I make the excitement with the country–But there is so much more going on too–

Then we will have to figure how to handle it–I suppose 70,000 words is a little long for a story–It can

Hemingway on safari, Kenya, December 1933

be a book by its-self <u>Is</u>! but because I <u>know</u> how good it is I would like to throw it in free with something else to give them their supreme bloody moneys worth—I want to be <u>un</u>-pompous and give them what is really literature without being pretentious while your pompous guys blow themselves up like balloons and burst.

I notice you didnt say anything about it when I mentioned collecting the Esquire articles—What was the matter? Didnt you like them? I have 11 of them now—The 2 on big game in Africa are the only two that are weak. And they are O.K. But I didnt want to get into something there I was going to use—It would be possible to run this long one and follow it with the Esquire articles—calling it—say—The Highlands of Africa—
and Other Pieces

It is a swell thing, Max—I think the best Ive written—True narrative that is exciting and still is literature is very rare Because first it has to happen

Then the person that it happens to has to be equipped to make it come true ie to realize it, so that it has all the dimensions You have to <u>make</u> the country—not describe it. It is as hard to do as paint a Cezanne—and I'm the only bastard right now who can do it. Because I've been working, learning how to do it all this time.

There's one way to handle it—another way would be to run it either as a story in or as the Introduction to The First Fifty-Four or whatever we call it—(For Christ sake keep that title <u>absolutely</u> to yourself or somebody will grab it for something else).

It is a hell of a good book by its-self—but I want to get out a book of <u>super value</u> for the money—That is the best way to sell a hell of a bloody lot of them—After whichever is published first—either the collected stories or the collected Essays—I want to follow with a novel that will knock them cold. But I am not in a hurry about it—And can always publish both books first—I'd even write another novel and let this one wait There is no hurry on anything that is any good. The hell of it is my mother and my fathers brother being alive (That's a hell of a sentence to

Hemingway's fishing cruiser, the Pilar. *Hemingway is standing immediately to the left of the swordfish (Ernest Hemingway Collection, John F. Kennedy Library).*

write isn't it? Let us wish my mother luck Hope she lives forever. Maybe that will take the curse off.)

Anyway So long, Max. Thanks for the books, the Lee the Gordon (Paulines read it I havent had time yet) the Henry James and The Duck book. Youre the only publisher that ever sends free books that are worth a damn. Thanks <u>very</u> much. . . .

Best luck always, Ernest . . .

—————

In Key West in Transition: A Guide Book for Visitors *(Key West, Fla.: Key West Administration, 1934), the Hemingways' home is listed as one of the local attractions and described thus: "One of the older houses on the island, built shortly after the Civil War, is now occupied by Ernest Hemingway, author and*

sportsman. Hemingway stopped here a few years ago, expecting to spend a day awaiting travel connections. He felt the magnetic charm of the Island City, purchased the house he now occupies, and makes this his permanent residence." The letter Hemingway published in the April 1935 issue of Esquire *reveals his reaction to this listing in the guidebook. The 1935 edition of the guidebook lists Hemingway's home as "Closed to Visitors."*

The Sights of Whitehead Street: A Key West Letter

The house at present occupied by your correspondent is listed as number eighteen in a compilation of the forty-eight things for a tourist to see in Key West. So there will be no difficulty in a tourist finding it or any other of the sights of the city, a map has been prepared by the local F.E.R.A. authorities to be presented to each arriving visitor. Your correspondent is a modest and retiring chap with no desire to compete with the Sponge Lofts (number 13 of the sights), the Turtle Crawl (number 3 on the map), the Ice Factory (number 4), the Tropical Open Air Aquarium containing the 627 pound jewfish (number 9), or the Monroe County Courthouse (number 14). The ambition of your correspondent does not even run to competition with Typical Old House (number 12), the Ley M.E. Church, South (number 37), or Abandoned Cigar Factory (number 35). Yet there your correspondent is at number 18 between Johnson's Tropical Grove (number 17) and Lighthouse and Aviaries (number 19). This is all very flattering to the easily bloated ego of your correspondent but very hard on production.

To discourage visitors while he is at work your correspondent has hired an aged negro who appears to be the victim of an odd disease resembling leprosy who meets visitors at the gate and says, "I'se Mr. Hemingway and I'se crazy about you." Of course a visitor who really knows much about leprosy is not at all terrified by this aged negro and after examining him in a cursory fashion dismisses him as an imposter and demands to be introduced into the presence of his master. But tourists with a limited knowledge of leprosy are often easily discouraged and can be seen running down the street toward Fort Taylor (number 16) with the aged negro hobbling after them on his crutches shouting out to them tales of how he caught gigantic marlin and sailfish and details of his sporting exploits with animals whose names he has a lamentable habit of confusing. Lately the poor old chap has taken to telling such visitors as will listen stories for which your correspondent can really, in no way, be responsible.

The other afternoon sitting on the verandah enjoying a cheroot your correspondent heard the old fellow regaling a group of rather horror stricken tourists with a tale of how he wrote a book which he insisted on calling "De Call to Arms." In some odd way he had confused the plot with that of another best seller, Uncle Tom's Cabin, and his description of how he wrote the passage where Missy Catherine Barkley pursues the Italian army with blood hounds over the ice would have been mirth provoking if it had not been so realistic. One of his rather reluctant audience asked him why he always wrote in the first person and the old man seemed stumped for a moment but finally answered, "No sir. You're wrong, sir. I don't write in the first person. I don't fool with no person at all. I write direct on the typewriter."

"But were you really in Italy during the war, Mr. Hemingway? Or was the background of your best seller purely imaginative?"

This always sets the old man off for he loves to talk about Italy which he describes as the place where "he first get that leppacy disease," but his audience rarely stay to hear the end of that story and drawing deeply on my cheroot I enjoyed seeing them get a good bit of exercise as they strung out along Whitehead Street toward the Cable House (number 22) with the old man making not bad time after them on the not un-gruesome remains of his legs.

On the old man's day off or on national holidays visitors will sometimes get into the house itself. Since his home has been listed as an official attraction your correspondent feels that he owes it to the F.E.R.A. to give such visitors their money's worth. Such a visitor was Mr. Questioner, a prominent business man and fellow member of the Player's Club who honored us with his visit lately. Your correspondent had just finished a hard day's work and was feeling rather fatigued when the door opened and looking up he saw Mr. Questioner.

"Why, hello Questioner, old pal," you say.

"I just dropped in," said Questioner. "Saw the door was open and noticed you sitting there reading. Not fishing today?"

"No. Been working."

"Ha. Ha. Call that working. What do they pay you for those things?"

"Oh it varies. Sometimes a dollar a word. Sometimes seventy-five cents. Sometimes you bid them up to two dollars when you have something on them. Of course the stuff the kids do is a little cheaper."

"I didn't know your children wrote."

"Well, of course, there's only one of them really writes. That's the oldest boy, Bumby. The others just dictate."

"And you can sell their stuff as yours?"

"Every word of it. Of course you have to touch up the punctuation a bit."

"It's a regular business," says Questioner, very interested now. "I had no idea there was that much money in it. What does the little boys' stuff bring?"

"We get about three for a quarter for the eldest boy. The others are in proportion."

"Even at that it's money."

"Gad yes," you say. "If you can keep the little bastids at work."

"Is it hard?"

"It's not easy. When you over-beat them they write such damned sad stuff there's no market for it until you get down around a dime a word. And I want to keep their standards up."

"My word, yes," said Questioner. "Tell me more about it. I had no idea this writing business was so

The Hemingways' home at 907 Whitehead Street, Key West, where he lived from 1931 to 1939

interesting. What do you mean when you 'have something on' an editor?"

"It's rather like the old badger game," you explain. "Of course we have to give quite a cut to the police though. So there's not the money in it there used to be. Say an editor comes down, a married editor, we get him off to one of those—well you know—or we just surprise him in his room sometime and then of course the price goes up. But there's really no money in that anymore. The N.R.A. has practically put a stop to it."

"They've tried to stop everything," said Questioner.

"Johnson cracked down on us about the kids," you say. "Tried to call it child labour, and the oldest boy over ten. I had to go to Washington on it. 'Listen, Hugh,' I said to him. 'It's no skin off the ants of conscience in my pants what you do to Richberg. But the little boy works, see?' Then I walked out on him. We got the little fellow up to around ten thousand words a day after that but about half of it was sad and we had to take a loss on that."

"Even at that," said Questioner, "It's money."

"It's money, yes. But is isn't real money."

"I'd like to see them working."

"We work them nights," you tell him. "It's not so good for the eyes but they can concentrate better. Then in the morning I can go over their stuff."

"You don't mind putting it all out under your name?"

"No, of course not. The name's sort of like a trade-mark. The second rate stuff we sell under other names. You've probably seen some of it around. There was quite a lot of it around at one time. Now there's not so much. We marketed it under too many names and it killed the market."

"Don't you write any yourself anymore?"

"Just a little to keep it going. The boys are doing fine and I'm proud of the boys. If they live I'm going to turn the business over to them. I'll never forget how proud I was when young Patrick came in with the finished manuscript of Death In The Afternoon. He had done the whole thing from a single inspiration. Damned odd story. He saw a negro funeral going by of the Sons and Daughters of Rewarded Sorrow, a sort of insurance agency that's quite popular down here, and as it was the afternoon at the time that gave him his title. The little chap went right ahead and dictated the whole thing straight off to his nurse in less than a week."

"Damned amazing," said Questioner. "I'd like to get in on something like that."

"I said to him, 'Pat there's a picture in this if we can get some moron to buy it.' And do you know what the little fellow answered? 'Daddy let Williams who cleans out the garage buy it. I heard you call him a black moron when he threw away the beer bottles you wanted to return to Mr. Josie.' Shows you how up to snuff they are."

"Did Williams buy it?"

"Yes. He's out on the coast now. He's trying to sell it to Jock Whitney for Technicolor. Of course Williams is colored himself."

"Do you ever write any stories about negroes?"

"Well we've tried to avoid it on account of the instability of the southern market but this year we're about ready to shoot the works."

"What do you mean about instability?"

"Well you just get a character popularized and he makes some mistake and they lynch him. But we're avoiding that by using genuine negro dialect with certified white characters, many of them daughters of the Confederacy. What do you think of it?"

"I'm for it. Tell me some more about it."

"Well we're going to write an epic. They're working on it now day and night. Bumby has the historical sense, Pat does the dialogue and Gregory does plot. You see we've got a new angle. It's an epic about the Civil War but the trouble with most epics is they weren't long enough but what somebody would be able to read the epic and pass the word it was lousy. We figure to run to three thousand pages. If it nets a million we're going to send Gregory to school, he's always crying to go to school, and let Pat open up an office on the coast. That's all he keeps talking about. 'Daddy when can I go out to the coast?' until I get so I can't listen to it. So I said to him today, 'Finish the epic and if it goes over as it should you can go to the coast.' He claims he wants to see Donald Ogden Stewart. Funny isn't it? I said to him, 'I'll go with you Pat. Because I want to see Dotty Parker. I really do.' But he says, 'No Daddy I want to go to the coast alone to open up our office and I want to see Stewart. Alone.' What do you suppose has got into a hard-working kid like that? What does he want to see Stewart about? Maybe an old debt or something like that. Kids are funny that way. Now I forgot anything we owed Stewart years ago."

"You know, I think I ought to go," Mr. Questioner said, and there is a new respect in his tone. "You may be busy."

"Never too busy to see you, Questioner old sod. Come by any time when we've knocked off. Nathaniel can always get you a quick one."

"Goodbye Hoggelway," says Questioner. "You don't know how interesting this is to me."

"Details of a man's work are always interesting."

"Goodbye and thank you so much."

"Goodbye."

Questioner is gone and you call Nathaniel.

Nathaniel: "Yes, Mr. Emmings."

You: "Nathaniel, make a practice of locking the front door at all times."

Nathaniel: "Yes sir. It wasn't my fault Mr. Questioner got in this time."

You: "I understand, Nathaniel. But make a practice of locking it, Nathaniel. If one strains the imagination so late in the day, one is always liable to rupture it. Yes, thank you Nathaniel. Yes, another."

Ivan Kashkin was a Soviet critic and translator who did more than anyone else to promote Hemingway's reputation in the U.S.S.R. Hemingway paid homage to him by giving his name to a Russian officer in For Whom the Bell Tolls *(New York: Scribners, 1940). In the letter he first wrote to Kashkin, Hemingway develops his views of the writer's proper position, views reiterated in* Green Hills of Africa. *From* Selected Letters, *pp. 417–421.*

19 August 1935

Dear Kashkeen:

Thank you for sending the book and the article in *International Literature*. They came, forwarded by [William] Saroyan today. A little while ago the article came forwarded by *Esquire* and I read it.

It is a pleasure to have somebody know what you are writing about. That is all I care about. What I seem to be myself is of no importance. Here criticism is a joke. The bourgeois critics do not know their ass from a hole in the ground and the newly converted communists are like all new converts; they are so anxious to be orthodox that all they are interested in are schisms in their own critical attitudes. None of it has anything to do with literature which is always literature, when it is, no matter who writes it nor what the writer believes. Edmund Wilson is the best critic we have but he no longer reads anything that comes out. Cowley is honest but still very much under the impression of being con-

Maxwell Perkins and Hemingway in Key West, 1935. Perkins made the trip to read the typescript of Green Hills of Africa.

verted. He is also tending to stop reading. The others are all careerists. I do not know one that I would want with me, or trust with me, if we ever had to fight for anything. I've forgotten Mike Gold. He is honest too.

This is the way most criticism goes. Isidor Schneider will write a piece about me, say. I will read it because I am a professional and so do not care for compliments. Only to see what I can learn. The article will be very stupid and I learn nothing. I am not indignant; only bored. Then some friend of mine (Josephine Herbst) will write to Schneider and say why do you say such and such, what about *A Farewell To Arms,* what about what Hem says in *Death in the Afternoon,* etc. Schneider will write her in answer that he never read anything of mine after *The Sun Also Rises* which seemed to him to be anti-semitic. Yet he will write a serious article on your work. And not read your three last books. It is all balls.

Your article is very interesting. The only trouble, to me, is that it ends with me as Mr. Frazer out in Bill-

ings Montana with right arm broken so badly the back of my hand hung down against the back of my shoulder. It takes five months to fix it and then is paralyzed. I try to write with my left hand and can't. Finally the musculo-spiral nerve regenerates and I can lift my wrist after five months. But in the meantime one is discouraged. I remember the study in pain and the discouragement, the people in the hospital and the rest of it and write a story *Gambler, Nun and Radio.* Then I write *Death in the Afternoon.* Then I write the other stories in the last book. I go to Cuba and there is a little trouble. I go to Spain and write a damned good story about necessity which maybe you did not see called *One Trip Across.* In the meantime I write that stuff in *Esquire* to eat and support my family. They do not know what I am going to write and it gets to them the day before they go to press. Sometimes it is better than others. I write it in one day each time and I try to make it interesting and to tell the truth. It is not pretentious. We go to Africa and have the best time I have ever had. Now have finished a

Key West Monday Feb 4 – 1935

Dear Arnold :
        I was asleep when you called up that night and guess
I never woke up properly during the conversation . Glad to hear your voice
though and thought you were very thoughtful to worry about the lousy disease.
Have been fairly sick with it . Max Perkins was down here and a bastard
from Cosmopolitan that would buy it for plenty money if I would cut it
to 45,000 words (I can't) and you can't do business or refuse to do
business and fill up on emetine and entertain a publisher while taking
castor oil every two hours . So the disea e got the jump on me . But have
been in bed yest . and on the oil etc. today and am getting it whipped
but have no pep and can't think .

        As I read that paragraph in the Trib there is nothing
for me to do but turn over whatever money you get for those mss. to
various writers and painters . I can't get mixed up in anything
like that or not follow the letter of it . So will give you a list of who to
send dough to . If they announce a sale for idigent writers to indigent
writers it bloody well goes .
        What I had hoped to do was to raise some jack for myself
to replace the $200. $250. $400 . and $200 . I have let various
writers take since last March plus the $500. and so I have spent on the
Quintanilla . But reading that Trib item I can't touch that money .

        In the meantime I am broke pending selling serial rights
to the book and need m ney for my taxes and three hundred bucks I had
promised to send for Bumby's schooling the end of th last month . So will
have to raise that somewhere else. You tell me what Mss. money you get
and I will write you how to dispose of it or give you a receipt and an
accounting of Max is crazy to serialize the book in Scribners but they
won't be able to pay much jack . I doubt if I could get ten grand .
Would you be interested in it ? I know you haven't serialized kmt
anything yet but you are at a stage where you can make your policy as you go
along . I have been held up sending it waiting for Max to get through
with it and then Dos wanted it before I had chance for Pauline to correct the
carbon .   Max and Dos both were very strong for it and Max would not
be if it wasn't good as all he would have to do would be pick faults to save
money . Dos has always been honest with me and very critical . I hope you
will like it . Have divided it into three parts and xxx it has
thirteen chapters . Have a good title and it has shaped well . I really
ought to get some good money out of it as it is worth it .
        I hope you don't think I am being righteous or
ymca about the manuscript thing . I will run liquor or   and
will kill if necessary to help something I believe in bad enough but I
can't do anything about my goddamned writing that isn't honest and I
can't help it . It is simply my bad luck that it was handled that way
and I thank you very much and don't blame you in the least . And also therexx
are guys that need it worse than I do even though I need it .

        After you wrote about reading Farewell to Arms again
I read some of it myself and it's good all right . But it is very
ghostly to read your own stuff after a long time . How many the hell love
stories do they want a guy to write ?

        Max will run the book in either six or seven installments .
Cosmop wanted to run it in four . I couldn't cut it to that and keep
the story and why in gods name cut it at all . I don't need jack that
bad but by God I could use some . I'd like to get about twenty grand for it .
Or even fifteen . Anything under ten won't do me any good .

Letter to Arnold Gingrich discussing the serialization of Green Hills of Africa *in* Scribner's Magazine *(Sotheby Parke Bernet, Goodwin Collection, Item 717, 12 April 1978)*

book and will send it to you. Maybe you will think it is shit and maybe you will like it. Anyway it is the best I can write. If you like it and want any of it for the magazine to translate you can use it. It may be of no interest to you. But I think it will be, perhaps, to yourself if not to the magazine.

Everyone tries to frighten you now by saying or writing that if one does not become a communist or have a Marxian viewpoint one will have no friends and will be alone. They seem to think that to be alone is something dreadful; or that to not have friends is to be feared. I would rather have one honest enemy than most of the friends that I have known. I cannot be a communist now because I believe in only one thing: liberty. First I would look after myself and do my work. Then I would care for my family. Then I would help my neighbor. But the state I care nothing for. All the state has ever meant to me is unjust taxation. I have never asked anything from it. Maybe you have a better state but I would have to see it to believe it. And I would not know then because I do not speak Russian. I believe in the absolute minimum of government.

In whatever time I had been born I could have taken care of myself if I were not killed. A writer is like a Gypsy. He owes no allegiance to any government. If he is a good writer he will never like the government he lives under. His hand should be against it and its hand will always be against him. The minute anyone knows any bureaucracy well enough he will hate it. Because the minute it passes a certain size it must be unjust.

A writer is an outlyer like a Gypsy. He can be class conscious only if his talent is limited. If he has enough talent all classes are his province. He takes from them all and what he gives is everybody's property.

Why should a writer expect reward or the appreciation of any group of people or any state? The only reward is in doing your work well and that is enough reward for any man. There is nothing more obscene to me than a man posing himself as a candidate for the French Academy or any Academy.

Now if you think this attitude leads to sterility and the individual's becoming nothing but human waste I believe you are wrong. The measure of a man's work is not quantity. If you can get as much intensity and as much meaning in a story as some one can get in a novel that story will last as long as it is any good. A true work of art endures forever; no matter what its politics.

If you believe one thing and work at it always, as I believe in the importance of writing, you have no disillusion about that unless you are ambitious. All you have is hatred for the shortness of the time we have to live and get our work done.

A life of action is much easier to me than writing. I have greater faculty for action than for writing. In action I do not worry any more. Once it is bad enough you get a sort of elation because there is nothing you can do except what you are doing and you have no responsibility. But writing is something that you can never do as well as it can be done. It is a perpetual challenge and it is more difficult than anything else that I have ever done—so I do it. And it makes me happy when I do it well.

I hope this does not bore you. I write it to you because of the care and the accuracy you have used in studying what I write so that you might know something of what I think. Even though it makes you think me a worse shit when you read it. I do not give a damn whether any U.S.A. critic knows what I think because I have no respect for them. But I respect you and I like you because you wished me well.

Yours very truly,
Ernest Hemingway

P.S. Do you ever see Malraux? I thought *La Condition Humaine* was the best book I have read in ten years. If you ever see him I wish that you would tell him so for me. I meant to write to him but I write French with so many misspelled words that I was ashamed to write.

I had a cable signed by him, Gide and Rolland forwarded to me by mail from London asking me to some writers congress. The cable came to me in the Bahama Islands two weeks after the Congress was over. They probably think I was rude not to answer.

This new book is out in October. I'll send it to you then. I can always be reached through Key West, Florida, USA. They forward when we are away.

E.H.

P.P.S. Don't you drink? I notice you speak slightingly of the bottle. I have drunk since I was fifteen and few things have given me more pleasure. When you work hard all day with your head and know you must work again the next day what else can change your ideas and make them run on a different plane like whisky? When you are cold and wet what else can warm you? Before an attack who can say anything that gives you the momentary well being that rum does? I would as soon not eat at night as not to have red wine and water. The only time it isn't good for you is when you write or when you fight. You have to do that cold. But it always helps my shooting. Modern life, too, is often a mechanical oppression and liquor is the only mechanical relief. Let me know if my books make any money and I will come to Moscow and we will find somebody that drinks and drink my royalties up to end the mechanical oppression.

Unlike American critics, Kashkin—whose work on Hemingway remains among the better assessments of his style—had analyzed all the writer's works to date and believed that they presented a consistent philosophy. He sent this article to Hemingway. From International Literature, *No. 5 (May 1935), pp. 72–90.*

Ernest Hemingway: A Tragedy of Craftsmanship

1

We have never seen Hemingway. In his wanderings over the world he has never visited our country and in order to imagine what he is like we have to rely, though not without reservation, on what others say. And from what they say there arises a legendary figure: Hemingway—the hero and favorite of the young literary crowd in Paris and New York, "one of the gang," a boon companion at the Dingo Café in Paris or at Greenwich Village bars. Here is the evidence of his English friend, the well-known Ford Madox Ford:

Into the animated din would drift Hemingway, balancing on the point of his toes, feinting at my head with hands as large as hams . . . At last Hemingway extended an enormous seeming ham under my nose. He shouted. What he shouted I could not hear: under the shadow of that vast and menacing object.

Other witnesses recall Hemingway taking part in Spanish bullfights and the memorable fiesta when he had the good luck of rescuing that clumsy amateur-torero John Dos Passos from a "sudden violent death."

They recall skiing parties in Switzerland, the sensational knockout at the *Salle Wagram* Hemingway gave a boxer for foul play. And while reading such testimonies you fancy a strong, fullblooded athlete, an excellent tennis-player, a first rate boxer, an inveterate skier, hunter and fisherman, a fearless torero, a distinguished front line soldier, an arrogant bully, and in addition to all that—on second thought as it were—a world famous writer. And under this impression of the legendary hero, the famous "Hem the Great" of a "lost generation," you open his books.

You read the joyless tale of Hemingway's favorite hero—ever the same under his changing names—and you begin to realize that what had seemed the writer's face is but a mask, and by degrees you begin to discern a different face, that of Nick Adams, Tenente Henry, Jake Barnes, Mr. Johnson, Mr. Frazer.

Then you think of another testimony of Ford Madox Ford's:

When, in those old days, Hemingway used to tell stories of his Paris landlords he used to be hesitant, to pause between words and then to speak gently but with great decision. His mind selecting the words to employ. The impression was one of a person using restraint at the biddings of discipline. It was the right impression to have had.

And you imagine the man, morbidly reticent, always restrained and discreet, very intent, very tired, driven to utter despair, painfully hearing the too heavy burden of life's intricacies. This conception of "Hem the Tragic" may be legendary as well, but such as we see him in his books and one-sided as this conception may be it affords the possibility of a different sidelight on Hemingway and his writings. We accept it merely as a working hypothesis that might help us make out what he is actually like.

Hemingway shows us how complicated he is by his very attempts to be simple. A tangle of conflicting strains and inconsistencies, a subtle clumsiness, a feeling of doubt and unrest are to be seen even in Hemingway's earlier books as early as his presentation of Nick Adams's cloudless young days, but as he proceeds on the way of artistic development these features show increasingly clear and the split between Hemingway and reality widens.

Closely following the evolution of his main hero you can see how at first Nick Adams is but a photo film fixing the whole of life in its simplest tangible details. Then you begin to discern Nick's ever growing instinct of blind protest, at which the manifestations of his will practically stop.

Home with its bible, a copy of *Science and Health* on the table, Indians wrangling with Doc about logs he is supposed to have stolen, his mother's sugary, "Are you going out, dear," and the stench of the fire in which during a fit of housecleaning she destroys the collections of snakes and other specimens treasured by Nick's puerile father. In a word—the stuffy, stale atmosphere of provincial existence.

And beyond home—the meeting with the prize-fighter, the trip to the Indian camp, the sight of that living corpse Ole Andreson and the consequent longing "to get out of this town" into another mysteriously alluring world of boxers, killers, soldiers. And soon we see Nick along with many boys of his age escaping to the front.

Of his youthful impressions there remain the memories of the time when "he felt sure that he would never die," a liking for sound, simple people (Indians, the battler's Negro companion, and later—Romero, wrestlers, toreros); there also remains the hunter's sharp eye and the firm grip of the future artist.

Tenente Henry—the next incarnation of the same hero is Nick Adams, grown into a man wearing a uniform. His relations with Cat are still youthfully fresh and spontaneous. When he recalls his past ("Now I Lay Me") it bears a striking likeness to the past of Nick Adams. At the front he is glad to find everything so simple. "It was simple and you were friends."

Tenente Henry enjoys the definite, clear-cut relations between people, the good comradeship "We felt held together by there being something that had happened, that they did not understand," and the feeling of risk while it lasts.

But soon along with the debâcle at Caporetto he finds himself faced by the cruelty of the rear, choked by its lies and filth, hurt by the hatred of the working people to *gli ufficiali*. And as his shellshock had lost him his sleep so does the stronger shock of war make him a different man. By the time the war is over he has learned to discern "liars that lie to nations" and to value their honeyed talk at what it is worth.

I was always embarrassed by the words sacred, glorious, and sacrifice and the expression in vain. We had heard them, sometimes standing in the rain almost out of earshot, so that only the shouted words came through, and had read them, on proclamations that we slapped up by billposters over other proclamations, now for a long time, and I had seen nothing sacred, and the things that were glorious had no glory and the sacrifices were like the stockyards at Chicago, if nothing was done with the meat except to bury it. . . . Abstract words such as glory, honor, courage, were obscene beside the concrete names of villages, the numbers of roads, the names of rivers, the numbers of regiments and the dates (*A Farewell to Arms*).

His illusions about the war gone, Tenente Henry means to get through with the "glorious conflict."

Disgusted with the rôle of a mute in this infamous show, willing to be used as cannon fodder in the Caporetto slaughter, the man admittedly brave, now feels rising within him the instinct for self-preservation, and fiercely struggles to save life by every means possible down to desertion. Catherine's tragic death puts a sudden stop to the short lived idyll of life's simpler joys.

Nick's youthfully fresh outlook on life is now overcast by the ghastly shadow of a close acquaintance

with death in its ugliest forms, his mind is laid waste. The man of the front has no hopes or faith left.

Such he comes back home only to be immersed once more in the old familiar but now hopelessly alien things. "Nothing was changed in the town. But the world they were in was not the world he was in." Everything was awfully mixed up and one had to keep lying, lying about the war, about heroism, about the German machine-gunners chained to their guns, and one had to kneel by mother's side and pray God to make him a good boy again. Was this then the way to keep the promise made in the trenches of Fossalta? Really things were awfully mixed up.

After a stay at home, Hemingway's contemporary flees to Europe again, to wander, to live a bohemian life. But there also life seems too complicated after the front and the new milieu is barren and revolting, Hemingway knows this milieu to perfection; he depicts "our boys abroad" with a pity alternating with lashing irony. Every line of Hemingway's poignantly reserved story about the Eliots is an insult flung at their bourgeois-aesthetic marriage and in his "A Canary for One" he mockingly offers the lonely and languishing Juliet a caged canary by way of substitute for a glimpsed Romeo. Hemingway's hero has no use for happiness, he is busy getting through his divorce-suit and when in 1933 Hemingway himself recalls this time in his triptych "Homage to Switzerland," he seems to see this philistine Eden as a sort of theatre stage with puppet-people acting in it, their dialogue adopted from Berlitz's *Spoken English*.

The grave bitterness of the middle panel of the triptych is further accentuated by the figure of Mr. Wheeler—that prudent bourgeois tourist,—and by the brutal practical joke played on that harmless crank, the geographer.

Hemingway knows the value of the *plaisirs et les jeux* of the rich, he tells about them with undisguised sarcasm. But as for making sure of his own position, as for drawing the necessary conclusions from his instinctive disgust at the world of the philistine—that he cannot do, it is all too complicated.

What is left him is to wander over the world, "look at things and try new drinks." What is left him is surely the wrong path—simplify things as much as possible, play a solitary game of hide and seek, "eat, drink, copulate, fight the bull, take the dope"—in a word—be just like everybody.

The well trained athletic body is full of strength, it seeks for moments of tension that would justify this sort of life and finds them in boxing and skiing, in bull fighting and lion hunting, in wine and women. He makes a fetish of action for action, he revels in "all that threatens to destroy." (Pushkin).

But the mind shocked by the war, undermined by doubt, exhausted by a squandered life, the poor cheated, hopelessly mixed up mind fails him. The satiated man with neither meaning nor purpose in life is no longer capable of a prolonged consecutive effort. "You oughtn't to ever do anything too long" and we see the anecdote of the lantern in the teeth of the frozen corpse ("An Alpine Idyll") grow into a tragedy of satiety when nothing is taken in earnest any longer, when "there is no fun anymore."

As the process of decomposition goes on, strength itself, unapplied and unnecessary, becomes a weakness and a burden.

Action turns into its reverse, into the passive pose of a stoic, into the courage of despair, into the capacity of keeping oneself in check at any cost, no longer to conquer, but to give away, and that smilingly. The figure of Jake mutilated in the war grows into a type. It is the type of a man who has lost the faculty of accepting all of life with the spontaneous ease of his earlier days. And taken from this point of view the otherwise normal characters of the story "Hills Like White Elephants" may be said to stand on the verge of a similar moral disaster. Every last bit of effort now goes into hiding their pain, into keeping the stiff upper lip, into being the "undefeated" as before, though secretly they know that their strength is not what it used to be. Sick old Belmonte puts into his toothed wolf-jawed lipless grin all his pain and hatred, all his contempt for the mob ever crying for blood and impossible victories—and then goes out to kill another bull.

This "grin and bear it" attitude towards danger and death calls to mind the conception of the heros in ancient tragedies. We know from the very first that there is no hope for Oedipus, the chorus knows it, he himself comes to know it, we see how inexorably things rush to the destined doom.

Though doomed the heroes continue their fight, and attain a tragic beauty and repose, facing the unavoidable bravely and in full armour. But Hemingway has no pity, he leads us onto the next stage. "The undefeated" are followed by the "baited."

Like the mob around the arena, like the obliging friends—the killers—life has no mercy, life relentlessly and steadily drives the weak into an impasse, turning the pose of the stoic into the "lie down and have it" torpor of the giant Ole Andreson with his hopeless "There ain't anything to do now."

And then there are those whom life has ensnared, and those who shun it. Disbelieving their power to affect what is bound to happen the weaker ones commit a number of accidental, inconsistent acts.

What's the use—there's no escape anyway.

The incapacity to find his way through questions he cannot solve, his reticence the admission of his own weakness,—those familiar steps on the path of the individualist–bring Hemingway's contemporary to desertion on principle. The theme of desertion is not new to Hemingway. Long ago Nick Adams fled from his home town, then he fled to the front. But here too the brave arditti decorated with all sorts of medals is a potential deserter at heart.

The wounded Nick says to Rinaldi "You and me we've made a separate peace. We're not patriots." Tenente Henry kills the Italian sergeant when the latter, refusing to fulfill his order, renounces his part in the war, but inwardly he is a deserter as well and on the following day we actually see him desert. "In the fall the war was always there, but we did not go to it any more" ("In Another Country"). This theme of sanctioned treason, or desertion in every form, so typical of the extreme individualist, recurs throughout Hemingway's work.

The mental confusion and vacuum of Hemingway's contemporary, and his self absorption logically lead him down to the last form of desertion. The task of saving the world is either impossible, or else too much for him to shoulder. Then let it be saved by those who wish,—Hemingway's characters say,—as for us—let's have some lunch. And here is what Hemingway himself says:

Let those who want to save the world if you can get to see it clear and as a whole. Then any part you make will present the whole if it's made truly. The thing to do is work and learn to make it (*Death in the Afternoon*).

But to learn to do it is no easy job, especially for one whose sight is limited by the blinders of sceptical individualism. Life is too complicated and full of deceit. The romance of war had been deceit, it is on deceit that the renown of most writers rests. The felicity of the Eliot couple is but self-deceit; Jake is cruelly deceived by life; for Mr. Frazer everything is deceit or self-deceit, everything is dope—religion, radio, patriotism, even bread. There is despair in the feeling of impending doom, and morbidity in the foretaste of the imminent loss of all that was dear.

Madame, all stories if continued far enough end in death, and he is no true-story teller who would keep that from you. Especially do all stories of monogamy end in death, and your man who is monogamous while he often lives most happily, dies in the most lonesome fashion. There is no lonelier man in death except the suicide, than that man who has lived many years with a good wife and then outlives her. If two people love each other there can be no happy end to it. (*Death in the Afternoon*).

The theme of the end recurs in Hemingway's works with a growing persistence, the obsession of death is there, not to be driven off. . . .

The best of them are gone and in his memories he IS among them. This business of conversing with friends that are dead is a gruesome affair, and one can't live on it long. Unless death be welcome—and one still holds on to life by instinct—one has either to find some definite purpose that would make life worth living or else look for stable values, for firm ground to stand on. "If he is to lose everything . . . he should find things he cannot lose" ("In Another Country").

In pursuit of solace Hemingway's hero seeks support in Catholicism. "Technically" he is a Catholic, only he does not know what that really means. He regrets being such a rotten Catholic, he wishes he could feel religious, expects to become more devout as he grows older like Count Greffi does, or to become a tin saint, like his nun. But somehow it does not come. Somehow we put little faith in the faith of this sceptic. "With a disposition to wonder and adore can no branch of Natural History be studied without increasing the faith, love and hope," Hemingway quotes from Bishop Stanley and he shows us one of the branches—studying the dead—which has filled him with unbelief and scepticism. For Hemingway "One of the simplest things of all and the most fundamental is violent death," but in his "Natural History of the Dead" we see this last thing wickedly stripped of all halo.

Even a Harry Crosby could hardly lean on such a notion of death. Love is another thing of value but for Hemingway it is of short duration and involves the inevitable loss of the beloved. And besides he is always prepared to question the feeling, however sincere or poetical, and seeks to degrade it in a way that verges on mania.

And so the ultimate value—"A clean well lighted place." There should be a place for a man to go to, mustn't there? And he pictures a neat and cleanly cage where he could hide from himself. But it appears that in that clean and well lighted cage things look dark and doubtful. Well, then every thing under the sun is nonsense or Nothing. Nada on earth. Nada in heaven as well. "Our Nada who art in Nada." Perhaps there is rest to be found here, the sort of rest that comes after despair and the frustration of all hopes, but you see that Hemingway's hero unlike the waiter of the just quoted story, doesn't rest here. He goes on. Mr. Frazer, and the characters of the story "Wine of Wyoming," show us glimpses of acknowledging their past mistakes, of regretting things they have spoiled and broken, things that are gone never to return again. All the long sought values lose their worth when we see included among

them the cheap solace of the sovereign bottle, while the very search for values results in their successive degradation and denial, in the scepticism of the cynic.

Each of Hemingway's stories is a perfectly-finished work of art. But perfect as his stories are when taken separately, their full meaning and depth appear only when we take them in connection with all the rest of his work, and include them in the main stream of his artistic evolution. "A Very Short Story" acquires a new meaning after you have read *A Farewell to Arms*. The suite: "Hills Like White Elephants," "Cat in the Rain," "A Canary for One," "Homage to Switzerland" can be fully understood only when placed against the settings of *The Sun Also Rises*; the stories about Nick form a natural cycle, each of them being a self-sufficing sketch for an unwritten novel.

If on closing Hemingway's books you recall and assort the disjoined pieces of the biography of his main hero you will be able to trace the decisive points of his life. Nick—first a tabula rasa, then turning away from too cruel a reality; Henry struggling for his life and trying to assert its joys, Jake and Mr. Johnson—already more than half broken and Mr. Frazer—a martyr to reflection and growing passivity. So we witness both the awakening and the ossification of the hero whose psychology is so intimately known to Hemingway himself, and as opposed to it a file of brave and stoic people—the Negro in "Battler," the imposing figures of Belmonte and Manola, the broken giant Ole Andreson; in a word—those people for whom Hemingway's double has so strong an instinctive liking, first worshipped as heroes and then brought down to earth.

Those brave and simple people seem to be living only in so far as Hemingway's main hero retains his vitality, and although placed in a different higher plane, to walk the way he walks. A way from an assertion of life however elementary, to the pseudo-stoical scepticism of despair. And as you turn the last page of Hemingway's latest book, as you recall his "Natural History of the Dead," the thoughts of Mr. Frazer and Mr. Johnson, the prayer "Our nada," the talk between Nick Adams and his son in the story "Fathers and Sons"—you see the face of the hero stiffen into a horrible grimace. What had seemed to be prosperity in the case of Richard Cory and Henry Crosby turned out but a show. It will deceive no one any longer. When the mind is fatally injured, the body however strong it might seem turns into a well embalmed mummy, a walking corpse that needs but a slight push to fall to dust. . . .

Hemingway's hero wants to be simple and sane, but the sore trial to which he subjects himself doesn't pass unavenged.

Chapter Three: 1930–1935

The artist's power to see is perverted and broken by the obsession of death. His what-the-hell tonic, his affected stoicism, his would be indifference—are nothing but a pose taken on to hide the weariness, the refined scepticism, the despair. It is by them that Hemingway is driven to mere craftsmanship, often aimless and to our mind following the wrong trend.

> Pamplona is changed, of course, but not as much as we are older. I found that if you took a drink that it got very much the same as it was always. I know things change now and I do not care. It's all been changed for me. Let it all change. We'll all be gone before it's changed too much and if no deluge comes when we are gone it still will rain in summer in the north and hawks will nest in the Cathedral at Santiago and in La Granja, where we practised with the cape on the long gravelled path between the shadows; it makes no difference if the fountains play or not. . . . We've seen it all go and we'll watch it done and see and hear and learn and understand; and write when there is something that you know; and not before; and not too damned much after. . . . The thing to do is work and learn to make it (*Death in the Afternoon*).

This is not the devil-may-care, the *après nous le déluge* attitude, whatever Hemingway himself may have said a few lines before; it is merely the statement of the fact that his powers are limited. And it is not the apology of quietism, but rather the familiar gesture of hopeless simplification. Not to save the world, but so see it and to remake at least a tiny part of it, that's what Hemingway wants and calls upon others to do. *Il faut cultiver notre jardin,* he seems to repeat after Candide and as his aim he selects the attainment of craftsmanship. In this he radically differs from his idle heroes, but nevertheless for an artist of Hemingway's scope, for the head of a literary school to turn his back on really important themes and problems may only be qualified as an escape into seclusion, as desertion.

Still it is a good sign that in working for the sake of work, in fulfilling the prisoner's task he set himself, he remains the ever scrupulous professional. And it is this honest attitude towards his work, blind though it may appear to us, that has earned Hemingway the right to be classed among the masters.

2

In the best of his works Hemingway attains the simplicity of a great master. You believe in the simplicity of the pathetic Negro, in the imposing and genuine simplicity with which Belmonte, Manola and the entire fiesta is presented. You even believe in the ultimate primitiveness of the youthful memories of Nick Adams.

We are all in favor of simplicity, we have been, for a long time.

> My straw hat was almost filled with nuts, when I suddenly heard a noise. I looked round: Indians! An old man and a young one took hold of me and dragged me away. One of them threw the nuts out of my hat and stuck it on my head. After that I remember nothing. I probably swooned, for I came to under a tall tree. The old man was gone. Some people were arguing animatedly. My protector shouted. The old man and four other Indians came running. The old chief seemed to be talking very severely to the one that had threatened to kill me.

Who is it all about? Hemingway's Indians? No, as early as a hundred years ago this simplicity was noted by Pushkin who included in one of his articles long passages from the memoirs of John Tanner.

We highly appreciate the intentional indigence born out of abundance, the costly simplicity of Leo Tolstoi—the artist. In his *Cossacks and Hadji Mourat* he is as simple as his hunters and mountaineers whose dandified rags worn with the huntsman's peculiar smartness only serve to accentuate the necessary luxury of their expensive arms. We know that this sort of simplicity may be the result of either ancient culture or personal genius. The culture of the mountaineer, the genius of Yeroshka, the culture and genius of Tolstoi himself. We were highly pleased to read that Chekhov thought the best definition of the sea the one given by a schoolgirl—"The sea was big." We have seen Gorki resolutely strip the later versions of his early stories of all the romantic adornments and work out the cleansed style of his memoirs, or of *The Artamonoffs*. We shared the joy of the journalist Koltsov when he was telling us, how after casting about for all possible attributes for "snow"—the snow was marble, the snow was violet, the snow was blue, the snow was like sugar—he delightfully caught at the "delicious white word" "the snow was white" and rejoiced in the joy of his future readers. We couldn't remain indifferent when reading bolshevist documents of such highly-convincing simplicity as the January 1905 proclamations or speeches by Lenin and Stalin. They, as well as our best masters of literature, are in favor of simplicity, that costly synthetic simplicity of socialist realism, which necessarily implies a high degree of professional craftsmanship. But there also exists another sort of simplicity. We know the affected simplicity of a Shklovski, a Hausner, a Gabrilovich, tortured, strained ever in search of new forms of conception and style. But Gabrilovich and Hausner have a purpose. They know what they are after, when stamping out the inertia of verbosity. They want to find a new language for the new themes and the new experiences of man in second birth. It is the simplicity of the period of transition.

Even in the elaborate, naïve simplicity of John Dos Passos, by means of which he occasionally tries to cover up his helplessness and his inability to find his way through the complexity of our time, ever in this helpless simplicity we can detect a desire to see and understand those who are out to save the world and those who desperately interfere with their efforts.

In this respect Hemingway's simplicity is often affected, not unfrequently vicious, and always hopeless.

Hemingway's perception of the world is keen to the extreme, but his understanding of it as reflected in his works is intentionally primitive. It is a sort of muscular and tactual perception. He feels the world as the weight of a trout pulling at the line. "Ag was cool and fresh in the hot night." "The grass was wet on his hands as he came out"—this to mean that Nick has just got out of the tent on all fours, in a word—"The snow was white." And this is not bad at all.

His crudity is not bad in itself either, the more so as it is only seeming: "It is awfully easy to be hard-boiled about everything in the daytime, but at night it is another thing." (*The Sun Also Rises*). "Hard-boiled but mild-hearted"—Hemingway certainly is, and if the latter quality shows particularly in his novels, he seems to be trying to make up for it in the short stories. In most of these he is above all afraid of sounding sentimental and strives to be utterly simple, dry and affectedly clumsy. Let's open one of his books at random, and we are sure to bump into something like this:

"Let's get drunk," Bill said.
"All right," Nick agreed.
"My old man won't care," Bill said.
"Are you sure?" said Nick.
"I know it," Bill said.
"I'm a little drunk now," Nick said.
"You aren't drunk," Bill said.
He got up from the floor and reached for the whisky bottle.

After reading Hemingway's parodies of himself like the one just quoted we see how easy it must have been for Curtis H. Reider to ridicule his affected clumsiness. Indeed, such a dialogue by Reider as:

Then I turned and saw Gerty.
"Hello," she said.
"Hello," Ernie said.
"Hello," I said. . . .
"Tweedleboom the rumdum," Joyce said.
"Hello, I said," Ernie said. . . .
"Sit down down," Gerty said.
I sat down. Ernie sat down. We all sat down.

is but a cliché of many similar passages from Ernie Hemingway and his forerunners. Stopping to look more attentively you will see that Hemingway's clumsiness and audacity hide the wary reticence of a man whose nerves are taut, a man shellshocked by life and ready to scream on the slightest provocation. He can talk of the simplest things alone and that only in undertones, if not a whisper. Even when all is boiling within him, even when like Jake he has just given away his love to another man or has hopelessly twisted his own life as his heros so often do. At times this reserve becomes merely infantile simplification or, as in the case of Krebs—downright crudity.

Hemingway's heroes are infantile American fashion. Theirs is not the weak-minded lisping of the "ramolis" admirers of pseudo-childish nonsense, it is simply the fancy of a strong and healthy youngster for the playthings of men—the pipe, the gun, the bottle, the fishing nets, the brothel, to a certain point the badge of an arditti. Which alone would not matter so much. What matters is that these whims blind him to the greater, the truer problems of life, that they screen out life itself by the blinders of self restriction, the devil-may-care tone, the resort to gastronomy. "Say," said John, "how about eating?" "All right," I said—this being the solution Hemingway professes to offer for many a truly tragic situation. What matters is that as time goes on we perceive more and more of the snobism of the too-subtle primitive in Hemingway's treatment of the hopelessly tangled complexity and the cynically stripped image of death. More and more often we see him present horror and perversion in pseudo-simple tones. And in the long run this simplicity turns into its reverse—into a desperate complication; Hemingway no longer deals directly and simply with things either simple or complex, but deliberately simplifies things making them yet more complicated.

Hemingway's simplicity is nothing new to the American reader who has his own tradition of honest simplicity. When reading the manifestoes of the imagists, the interpretations of American culture by Waldo Frank, Mumford and others one is ready to believe that the spirit of Thoreau is alive in American literature and his influence will yet bear fruit. In our days the wanton growth of the machine age, disfigured by the clutches of capitalism and the sinister ghost of philistine comfort and contentment have driven the American intellectual to Rousseauism, to intellectual vagabondage, to the simple life.

A liberation from abstract rhetoric and convention was advocated by the American imagist poets as early as 1912. Even earlier than that Gertrude Stein made her first experiments with analytical prose. Immediately after the war Sherwood Anderson produced specimens of lyrical prose of the same pseudo-simple sort.

But imagist poetry was food for writers and poets only. Gertrude Stein was hopelessly unintelligible. To go through the boredom of reading her affected sing-song incantations was a hard job, they were a revelation of a new art fit only to be studied by professionals. Sherwood Anderson was obsessed by the mysticism of sex, was floundering in the swamp of static psycho-analysis, thus screening from sight his new, though not consciously realised intonation and manner. In Hemingway's writings one hears at times both the artless intonation of Sherwood Anderson, and the complicated primitive of Gertrude Stein, but the thing to be noted is that this technique, so deliberately and brilliantly assimilated, is part and parcel of Hemingway's intrinsic self. Nick Adams, still alive in Hemingway, wields this technique in an easy and natural way, thus bringing the experiments of Gertrude Stein and the psycho-analytical studies of Sherwood Anderson into the sphere of genuine art.

Maybe it is just the Nick Adams part of Hemingway that is so much in arms against the bloodless scholastic simplicity of the neo-humanists, wearing the garb of antiquity and reactionary ideology; also against the cold-blooded virtuosity of that specialist in nightmares Faulkner and of his kind. In *Death in the Afternoon* Hemingway draws a definite line beyond which he leaves both "the long preserved sterility" of the "children of decorous cohabitation" and the prolific thrill-monger William Faulkner. Coming as it did in the postwar years, the simplicity of Hemingway was very much to the taste of American readers who, their eyes now open to the reality and deceit of the Wilsonian era and starving for simple truth, were delighted to welcome the precise, laconic, lucid and refreshing stories of Hemingway's first book, stories that, like the icy water from a brook, made your teeth ache. Hemingway became the pet and the prophet of the Lost Generation but nothing could make him swerve one inch from his lonely path. He did not care for permanent seclusion in the "ivory tower" of the esthetes; settling in it for a time only he cut the windows wider, hung the walls with fishing–nets, rods, hunting bags, boxing-gloves and banderillas; but he used it only as his working-room, and didn't stay in it long, for he was busy hunting and fishing and boxing and wandering all over the world. Still he didn't make a single step to meet the tastes of the readers of the *Saturday Evening Post*. He didn't lower his art. He didn't condescend to provide explanatory notes for his transparently-clear cryptograms.

Year after year Hemingway steadily elaborated his main lyrical theme, creating the peculiar indirectly personal form of his narrative (Soldier's Home, Now I Lay Me), sober on the surface, yet so agitated; and as the years went by, the reader began to perceive the tragic side of his books.

It became more and more apparent that his health was a sham, that he and his heroes were wasting it away. Hemingway's pages were now reflecting all that is ugly and ghastly in human nature, it became increasingly clear that his activity was the purposeless activity of a man vainly attempting not to think, that his courage was the aimless courage of despair, that the obsession of death was taking hold of him, that again and again he was writing of the end—the end of love, the end of life, the end of hope, the end of all. The bourgeois patrons and the middle-class readers tamed by prosperity, were gradually losing interest in Hemingway. To follow him through the concentric circles of his individualistic hell was becoming a bit frightening and a bit tedious. He was taking things too seriously. In early days both critics and readers had highly admired the "romantic" strength, the "exotic" bull-fights, "the masculine athletic style;" but now Hemingway's moments of meditation, his too intent gazing at what is horrible, his self confessed weakness, the tenseness of his despair disturbed their balance, so essential to them "in the conditions of the crisis they were living through." They were not long in discovering new pets. They found the icily-academical Thornton Wilder and that cold virtuoso Faulkner more to their taste. Hemingway was perfectly aware of this coolness. In *Death in the Afternoon* we find a few significant dialogues with the patronising old lady. In the end of each chapter Hemingway entertains her with stories and talk. At first the old lady is interested and asks quite a number of questions; but by and by she gets bored with Hemingway's professionally honest attitude to the cruel Spanish sports and his too frank exposition of its seamy side. She makes faces and begs to be told something "amusing yet instructive." Hemingway makes her listen to a chapter of his "Natural History of the Dead." In answer to a similar request from the "jolly critic"–

Why do you frown? Now leave this freakish strain
And with gay songs the people entertain–
Pushkin said in his "A Joke"–*Look what a view is there* and proceeded to draw a nihilist picture of the bare and stripped country-side. Hemingway's cruel parody of "A familiar history of the birds"–his blood-curdling Natural History of Cannon-Fodder is in its way still more nihilistic.

On hearing it to the end the old lady acidly remarks: "This is not amusing at all. You know I like you less and less the more I know you," and soon she disappears for good from the pages of *Death in the Afternoon* accompanied by the author's "aside." "What about the Old Lady? She's gone. We threw her out of the book finally. A little late you say. Yes, perhaps a little late."

Hemingway's latest books in which he has given up entertaining old ladies and is developing his main lyrical theme with a frightening seriousness are no longer enjoyed by old ladies, or critics or the bourgeois readers in general. A vacuum is forming about Hemingway. He has squared his accounts with the philistine, has given a good dressing down to the Neo-humanist esthetes; he hasn't the courage to join the ranks of his former brothers in arms—now "proletarians of art"—for they have taken upon themselves the tremendous and for him unbearable task of saving the world. Solitude, a path through the vacuum—lion hunting, dwelling on morbid subjects, the motto: *Winner Take Nothing*. And we see the book thus entitled met with indifference by the critics and readers and with a sense of alarm by those who are fond of Hemingway and realise which way he is tending. And it is exactly "the proletarians of art" whom the crisis has taught many a lesson that realised it most painfully. The erstwhile esthetes are now members of writers' committees; they have visited the mining districts of Kentucky, they have received a piece of first hand knowledge of the theory and practice of class-struggle. It is the first time that the "proletarians of art" have clearly understood that class struggle is no "idle invention" of Karl Marx's, that it is bound to draw them in and to grind them between its mill-stones. And having understood that much, many of them have decided to cast their lot with the real proletariat, with the working class: their first step was to change from nonsocial esthetes to radicals. And for these who had once been in the same camp with Hemingway, his books acquire a new value, that of a document fixing and condemning the wrong course that brought the writer to an impasse. For this class of readers Hemingway's books are a warning of the peril that threatened their own artistic growth. They are a memento that in our time even a perfectly sound man is in danger of social and artistic decay if he follows the individualistic way and remains within the confines of bourgeois society; that new courses and a new way out of the impasse are now to be sought.

First the pet of the American youth that had seen the war at the front or in the rear,—then the prophet of the "lost generation" and the impertinent favorite of his bourgeois patrons—then a maniac alarming with his growing unrest and finally a vicious degenerate and a bogey for some, and for others—a man in supreme distress, sending out SOS signals. This is how from far away we picture the evolution of Hemingway in the eyes of his American readers.

Is there really no way out of the impasse to which Hemingway has come? His writings of the last years are few and strained, or else extremely special, such as his treatise on bull fighting. Another circle has come to completion. The question is which way Hemingway will turn now. Will it be another concentric circle of his individual hell or a step up leading from under the ground to the open spaces of realism to which he is obviously tending. In the story "Fathers and Sons" there is a promise of a novel about his father and his own boyhood. Even if in writing it he should embrace the course of naïve autobiographism as so many American writers have done, his craftsmanship, applied to simple and well-known material, is in itself a pledge of success: and one might "wish him luck, and hope that he will keep writing," a wish he vainly expects from his bourgeois critics; still writing not about Death, alone, but about work and craft and life as well.

The Nick Adams in Hemingway is an incorrigible realist. He can stand no lie or sham—either in life or in art.

> If a man writes clearly enough any one can see if he fakes. If he mystifies to avoid a straight statement, which is very different from breaking so-called rules of syntax or grammar to make an effect which can be obtained in no other way, the writer takes a longer time to be known as a fake and other writers who are afflicted by the same necessity will praise him in their own defence (*Death in the Afternoon*).

Hemingway himself, when he finds it necessary, has courage to break the traditional intonations and forms. He knows every device of his writer's trade to perfection but in this case he is an idealist like his Mexican gambler, who unfortunately for himself loves the risk of an honest game for its own sake and "suffers great losses thereby," at least in the opinion of the orthodox modernist innovators, who don't seem to relish Hemingway's taste for intelligible simplicity.

When necessary he knows no fear or compunction whatever. No theme however risqué or repulsive can become obscene when handled in his straightforward and precise manner. And this first of all because he doesn't wallow in it. Hemingway's indecency is either an experienced nightmare which he must put on paper in order to get rid of it or else a deliberate insult at all the old and young ladies and gentlemen that turn up their noses at the Chicago and Verdun stockyards alike. He points at what he feels must be pointed at and does it straightforwardly. "So far, about morals, I know only that what is. Moral is what you feel good after and what is immoral is what you feel bad after."

But the trouble is that his courage is limited and in some fields as for instance the social one, deliberately so; his values are as profoundly sceptical and cynical as bourgeois society itself.

A bull has gored a picador's horse and the entrails hang down between its legs in a blue bunch, while blood pumps from the gored belly. "I wish they didn't have the horse part"–Hemingway makes one of the spectators say. "They are not important"–his companion answers, "after a while you never notice anything disgusting." Hemingway's sight is confined to his walled in world. He is wearing blinders.

When in his first book he makes an attempt at sketching the portrait of a Hungarian revolutionist you hardly recognise Hemingway, so flat the result is. But within his chosen field he is invulnerable.

He knows how to name things, how to make us feel them, how to reveal new features in them. His books can teach you the technique of trout fishing, skiing or boxing, bullfighting and above all–the trade of a writer.

"The Old Newsman" Hemingway relates that in the days of the Greco-Turkish war "his correspondent's output–something on this order: 'Kemal inswards unburned Smyrna guilty Greeks,' was to appear as, copyrighted by Monumental News Service, 'Mustapha Kemal in an exclusive interview today with the correspondent of the Monumental News Service denied vehemently that the Turkish forces had any part in the burning of Smyrna. The city, Kemal stated, was fired by incendiaries in the troops of the Greek rear guard before the first Turkish patrols entered the city,'" you could almost believe that Hemingway is unconsciously comparing his crisp and weighty stammer to the trite academical verbosity of Booth Tarkington & Co. Like Hemingway the reporter of the olden days, Hemingway the writer is now sending us telegraphic versions of his stories. And back of the sober and dark grotesque of his puzzling text you often hear a cry of despair or at least a signal of coming disaster.

This newsman, unlike the free and easy know-nothings of the editorial offices, is very exigent to himself.

The trouble with our former favorite is that he started his education too late. There is no time for him now, to learn what a man should know before he will die. . . . First you have to know the subject; then you have to know how to write. Both take a lifetime to learn" ("Old Newsman Writes").

Hemingway takes up an extremely honest stand with regard to his material, he spares no pains in order to approach it closely just as the brave and scrupulous matador is not afraid to work "close to the bull." This is adequately illustrated by his depressingly conscientious treatise on bull fighting. At first it seems a pity that in order to master a subject like that so much labor should have been wasted. But then you remember the remarkable though peculiar literary qualities of *Death in the Afternoon*. You remember that it was while studying bull fighting that Hemingway found the material for many an unforgettable page in his other works, you remember the description of the fiesta in *The Sun Also Rises*.

And you see that to be able to produce these pages he was bound to go through the strenuous laboratory work which he describes on page 10 of his treatise: *Death in the Afternoon:*

I was trying to write . . . mentally shut his eyes.

Hemingway is reserved and frugal–he keeps to the strict self-discipline of the exacting master. He is never tired pruning off all that can be dispensed with: convention, embellishment, rhetoric, leaving only what is essential and indispensable. You won't find one ounce of "metaphorical fat" in the prose of this sportsman. You won't find more than one image or simile in a whole story, sometimes in a whole novel.

Hemingway knows how to be brief. In his story "The Killers" he might easily have told at great length what offense it was the obliging fellows had come to avenge or how they ran Ole Andreson from town to town, from state to state. But Hemingway has no wish to do so and produces a theory to explain why he usually drops a number of links that go to make his stories. See *Death in the Afternoon* page 183 ("If a writer of prose . . . hollow places in his writing.")

He has no faith in the power of the word. Whatever you say and however you say it you will express nothing anyway. A good formula for this idea that Hemingway never put into words is Tyutchev's line. "Each thought when utter'd, is a lie." (Silentium).

The application of this theory is Hemingway's method of using the strictly worded hint, the combination of precision and laconicism, of *demi-mot* and *mot juste;* it is the canonization of expressive suggestions that he uses to avoid the necessity of either giving up the world for good or definitely accepting it. He doesn't adhere to the pure keys of the literary "well-tempered Clavichord." He is in search of new harmonies, unstable yet convincing, of novel means of expression by hints, by merely fixing external gestures and situations. Whole stories are nothing but a euphemism, the entire story "Hills Like White Elephants" for instance, pivoting on one unspoken word.

The awkward tone of everyday talk, halting and hesitating, is the best way to tell an intimacy about to be broken, or of the increasingly painful feeling of life and love going, with the sensation that "we are cut of it all," and that all that is left is "look at things, and try new drinks." The talk is over. The low mild-looking wave has passed leaving nothing but a swell, but somewhere at the shore it will turn into a fierce surf. And it will catch up the boat and hurl it on the rocks.

Only a writer of Hemingway's rank can thus convey the most intimate, the most subtle moods by an accumulation of external details; not by the word which is powerless, but by an opposition of words; not by directly expressed thought which is inexpressible, but by an impulse, by pulling a bell that is to reverberate later in the reader's mind; by a scrupulous selection of external and trivial things, i.e., in fact by straining to restrict his power to see.

Even the reader used to the obviously unintelligible style of Joyce or Gertrude Stein wants a key to solve Hemingway's puzzles simple though they look on the surface. Even to him this puzzling question may occur: "What's it all about?" Hemingway supplies the key though it is not easy to find it. The accumulation of detail in his stories looks unnecessary—naturalistic until suddenly you perceive a phrase thrown in as if inadvertently to blend the "unnecessary" details into a single logical chain thus creating a complete and very essential background. The main theme shows through the trivial talk and it is in most cases an uncanny and significant theme.

On careful reading you are sure to find in most of Hemingway's works such a key disclosing the hints and the implications of this or that story. Take the unspoken word "abortion" in "White Elephants"; or the casual remark "You oughtn't to ever do anything too long" (An Alpine Idyll), or "He didn't want it. It wasn't worth it . . . While the boys are all settling down" (Soldier's Home), and so on. But in their own way the average readers who fail to find this key and reproach Hemingway with writing on nothing are still right. So are the shrewder readers who accuse him of deliberately veiling his meaning. Hemingway is indeed to be blamed, for he doesn't care for being easily understood, he wishes to meet his reader on equal terms, to lift him up to the heights of his own shrewd art.

The same theory of expressive suggestion leads Hemingway to project the dénouement of his stories into the future as if expecting the reader himself to supply the end. And this is certainly not the right thing to offer to bored readers like the old lady we have already met; the natural question for them to ask is, "And what then?" On hearing out one of the stories the old lady drops the disappointed remark:

"And is that all of the story? Is there not to be what we called in my youth a wow at the end?"—Ah, madame, it is years since I added the wow to the end of a story. Are you sure you are unhappy if the wow is omitted? (*Death in the Afternoon*)

The typical American story with a plot, like those of Aldrich, O. Henry and others may be compared to a box of surprises, to a thrilling chess game with an intriguing opening, a tense mid-play and a brilliant and unexpected end-play. We are sure to see their dénouement for the social function of this sort of story is to captivate, divert and lull to sleep, whether by admiration or pity, by genuine harmony or by harmony that is false. Now the surprises that Hemingway's stories contain are not in their plot but in their psychological development. They are rather like chess problems—the chessmen being practically brought up to the decisive point but the problem ending in what looks like a stalemate. Actually however they imply a mate and in most cases the mate to the hero is so well prepared dialectically that any trifle can supply the decisive impetus and once the impetus is given and things have been set in motion, the mate is inevitable at whatever move the author chooses to stop the game.

The social function of such stories is not to solve or even to set any questions but rather to evoke them in the reader's mind. They convey the unrest and confusion that obsess the author and there can be no harmonious solution. Most of the stories break off at half-time. In "The Killers" for instance, the chessmen are shown in the "end-play," without any digressions into their past and the game begins with the check to the hero. Any moment he may turn up in Henry's lunch room to meet the instantaneous mate. But the game is artificially prolonged; unlike the traditional "murder story" this tale has no apparent ending although the end is clearly foreseen. Whatever will happen—whether or not Ole Andreson is ultimately run down by the Killers—he is a finished man, the passive anticipation of death has already killed him.

Hemingway has really learned to construct his stories. His very short stories are not loose sketches but sometimes *very* short novels.

He has parted with metaphor only to pay the more attention to composition. "Prose is architecture, not interior decoration, and the Baroque is over."

There is a solid backbone to all of his stories. At about the time when Dos Passos wrote *Manhattan Transfer*, Hemingway, too, introduced into American literature—the type of book interspersed and held together by impressionist epigraphs.

At first sight there seems to be no connection whatever between the epigraphs of *In Our Time*, and the basic stories that go to make that book, but then you begin to perceive that a certain connection actually exists between them, sometimes based on analogy and sometimes on contrast.

For instance in Chapter I what might connect the story and the epigraph is the theme of expected and much dreaded death and the different ways men find to escape the fear. Darkness for the adjutant; death itself for the Indian.

In Chapter VII in the epigraph the shock of war amid a fit of naïve religious feeling imbibed in early days; in the story–Krebs feeling an alien at home as a result of the shock and a conscious revolt against the false prayer that is being imposed on him.

In Chapter XII–the acme of craftsmanship and technique–a praise to bull fighting and skiing.

In Chapter XIV and XV–the greatest contrast imaginable between the grim epigraph and the idyllic story.

The book as a whole is held together by the introductory epigraph and the tail-piece. In the epigraph the author's American friends question him about Europe and the French girls. In the tail-piece Greeks want to go to America; an ironical transfusion and the emphasised vanity of meeting aspirations.

The same function of compositional clamp is borne by the identical setting recurring three times in Hemingway's triptych "Homage to Switzerland" and by the numerous parallelisms in stories such as "Soldier's Home" and "Cat in the Rain."

But besides serving as backbones these persistent repetitions of external details fulfill a psychological function as well. They are a means for the author to reflect in his style the utter boredom of the philistine Eden: "I want a cat" (Cat in the Rain), "He didn't want it. It wasn't worth it" (Soldier's Home), "Would you like a drink of something" (Homage to Switzerland), and similar intense reiterations recur again and again taking the place of psychological analysis.

The leit-motif is the principle on which Hemingway builds all of his works, or rather all of his art. Hemingway's leit-motif is either his general basic theme–the theme of war, the theme of the end of human relationships, the theme of death and void, or else it is the special backbone of this or that work. Thus repeated fragments of the phrases "everybody was drunk," "going along the road in the dark" hold together the first epigraph of the book *In Our Time*. Thus the story "Cross Country Snow" seemingly so simple is held together by the parallelism–the pregnant girl at the inn and Nick's pregnant wife–and by the basic theme of free snow-swept spaces, all of it being but a prologue to the impending complication–the skiing trip over, back to the States, the kid born–farewell to freedom. The mournful "there ain't anything to do now"–is the burden of "Killers"; so is the ominous sound of the rain in "Cat in the Rain" and especially in *A Farewell to Arms*. Hemingway uses this method with great skill, but even here the skill turns into weakness. His themes are few, they break into fragments.

Book after book brings him to his starting point, the concentric circles lead back to the underground. "An Alpine Idyll" repeats the motifs of "Cross Country Snow," "White Elephants" shows the explosion of what you felt brewing underneath the inaction of "Cat in the Rain." The theme of the loss of things most dear, the theme of death is to be found in nearly every story. True, each time the theme recurs, it gains in depth and intensity but to break free of the enchanted circle either the force or the wish is lacking.

There was a time when Hemingway knew how to laugh. Let us remember for instance the softly-humorous scene, when Nick Adams thoroughly drunk but thoroughly practical converses with Bill on a "high plane" in the story "The Three Day Blow," or the amusing tippler Peduzzi in "Out of Season." But as the years go by we see Hemingway more and more often basing his restless stories on a pointed contrast, verging on a ghastly grotesque.

If they still have any humor left it is a direful and morbid humor. We may say of Hemingway what Victor Hugo once said of Baudelaire: *Il a creé un nouveau frisson,*–the shudder at the simple horror of everyday existence.

In line with his book *Men Without Women* where female characters indeed appear in only two of the stories, Hemingway writes a book about the poignant love affair between the mutilated Jake and a woman of Brett's temperament.

Even in his earliest stories he liked to oppose the keen sensation of life to the sudden intrusion of peril or death (Indian Camp); his later stories remind you more and more often of grim jokes, suffice it to recall "The Killers," "An Alpine Idyll," "Homage to Switzerland."

Most of all Hemingway is interested in people. "The hardest thing in the world to do is to write straight honest prose on human beings." He makes but a sparing use of settings giving only as much as is necessary for action to develop. As a rule his landscape has a psychological function to fulfill. In "An Alpine Idyll" Hemingway wants to show people incapable of sustained purposeful effort, people who seek to avoid questions that cannot be solved, who want to be lulled to sleep. And we see all the setting every detail of it taking part in the lulling.

You are tired of skiing, blinded by the snow and the sun, hypnotised by the sawmill you see from the window with the saw constantly moving back and forth, by the drowsy crows, and by the sun reflected in empty glasses; you are stunned by the appalling anecdote about the lantern in the teeth of the dead woman and dulled by the dinner with its inevitable dose of wine; and from a certain point of view all this is not so bad for it leaves no time to think.

The landscape in *A Farewell to Arms* is in itself an acting character—it is the ominous rain. In other cases it is the Maritza "running yellow almost up to the bridge," and the rain again, as a background for the stream of refugees flowing along the muddy roads. Or a car-window view of France in the story "A Canary for One," the arrivals and departures of which remind you by the laconic and impetuous manner in which they are presented of similar arrivals and departures in the books of John Dos Passos. But in the rare cases when Hemingway develops his method of description to its full length it is apt to tire the unhardened reader. After following Nick four or five times down the hill or passing a dozen bends of the river in search of trout you begin to feel as tired as Nick himself, much as you admire the author's perfect precise manner of fixing the stream of perceptions.

Hemingway's art is as contradictory as his nature. He stubbornly adheres to his creative principles with no guiding idea to relieve them, no high purpose to justify them, no faith in victory to quicken them. So he often slips into a parody of himself, he comes to an impasse. Art for art's sake only serves to reveal and emphasise the void and desolation that have formed within him.

3

Summing up we see in Hemingway his affirmation of life and a torpor at the vision of death, his full-blooded pessimism and his restrained despair, the cynical sincerity of many of his pages and his sceptical Catholicism, his skillful clumsiness and complicated simplicity, the tautological brevity of his dialogues and the precision of his hints, finally his mirthless spasmodic smile—all this tangle of conflicts has its roots in the tragic disharmony *mens morbida in corpore sano,* the mental discord that threatens to bring about the disintegration of the body and its decay.

A latent supply of reticence and of optimism not yet fully spent distinguishes Hemingway from the "writers of hatred," "engineers of death." There is not much in him to be compared to the blaspheming Celine sadist frenzy and his affected longing for nonentity. Hemingway merely looks unblinking at what awaits us all—at death. He has seen the front. He knows the taste of death too well to relish it. And perhaps it is Aldington, that other, even more harassed and sophisticated man from the front who of all the writers of this group may be placed nearest to him.

And then again he may have moments of envy at the quiet ironical hopelessness of T. S. Eliot who has taught him more than merely quoting Andrew Marvell.

The orthodox innovators have for Hemingway a feeling of wary distrust. They particularly dislike the taste this rebellious disciple shows for intelligible simplicity. "He looks modern, but smells of museum," says Gertrude Stein who on the whole is very fond of him. Hemingway has known a passing infatuation for decadent art, but he realises perfectly well that it is impossible to approach the problems set and solved by the classics if one's method and possibilities are those of decadent art. . . .

While fully appreciating the high skill of the modern matador and the modern decadent poet he himself keeps aloof of the tasks the decadents are out to solve. In his best works he has shown that he can be genuine, simple and integral almost to the point of classicism. But the people he depicts are broken and crippled by life however simple and realistic the method of their presentation. They are in constant search of some support, even if it is only unsuccessful technical Catholicism and what they find is the mental discord, the scepticism and nihilism of a Mr. Frazer. Hemingway wants to see the world as a whole in that particular tiny part of it on which he is working. But he cannot achieve this aim by fusing the scattered things he knows into a single unbroken world philosophy. The necessary illusion is created by a gradual chopping off of all the roots holding him to the ground and by a seclusion in the stone cell of the "Ivory Tower."

The balance of the half-healthy man is permanently disturbed, the man has torn himself away from life, he is uprooted and drying up. All that was good in him turns into evil. Art is there, it has been achieved but there seems to be nothing for him to speak about except himself and the void within him. Hemingway's fate is a tragical illustration of what awaits the stragglers, those individuals who have lost their way through the period of transition. In his books Hemingway seems to be more and more hopelessly admitting that if he should follow this course he will really take nothing even though he win. Hemingway is now facing Flaubert's old problem—the never ending torture of dissatisfaction on the way to achieving art for art's sake. Although he has never formulated his doubts as to his art, or the course he is following, these doubts have for a long time been persistently materialising in his works, in the recurring images of impotence of body and soul and of nihilistic scepticism.

In some of Hemingway's latest works we detect signs showing that for him "the time of stern maturity is nearing" (Bagritski). A mental crisis is at hand, a crisis in his outlook. Thoughts are beginning to obsess Hemingway. True, so far these are but the ravings of sick Mr. Frazer suffering from insomnia, but nevertheless it is a step forward as compared to the nights when that same Mr. Frazer having silenced his radio to a whisper was learning to listen to its murmur without thinking.

Now he thinks. Naturally, enough, his thoughts turn on all sorts of dope. We have no delusions whatever.

It would be hard to expect a precise and consistent way of thinking of a man who has just said, "Many times I don't follow myself with pleasure." But time will not wait. Let Mr. Frazer not imagine that the nihilistic nightmares that haunt his sleepless nights are "only insomnia that many must have." The way from the trenches to the confessional, from the bullfighting arena to the ring where even the winner takes nothing, from Big Two Hearted River to a Clean Well-lighted Place—this is indeed a terrible war. The war of Stavrogin that we know so well from Dostoyevski. Let Mr. Frazer not put too much faith in his failing powers.

And to conclude with:—reading Hemingway is a bitter and instructive business. His problem is to us an illustration of how the bourgeois machine uses first-class human raw material to turn out perfectly manufactured and skilfully disguised human waste—a consummate literary craftsman, a perfect sportsman and globe trotter, a man reduced to stupor by having gazed too long at the repelling and yet fascinating mask of Nada.

On 2–3 September 1935 a hurricane hit Matecumbe Key, killing 458 veterans who were constructing a road to connect the Keys. Hemingway assisted in the cleanup and was deeply affected by what he saw. On 7 September he wrote to Maxwell Perkins that the veterans had been "practically murdered," and on 17 September he published the following article in the New Masses, pp. 9–10.

Who Murdered the Vets?
A First-Hand Report on the Florida Hurricane

KEY WEST, FLA.

I have led my ragamuffins where they are peppered; there's not three of my hundred and fifty left alive, and they are for the town's end to beg during life.

Shakespeare.

Yes, and now we drown those three.

Whom did they annoy and to whom was their possible presence a political danger?

Who sent them down to the Florida Keys and left them there in hurricane months?

Who is responsible for their deaths?

The writer of this article lives a long way from Washington and would not know the answers to those questions. But he does know that wealthy people, yachtsmen, fishermen such as President Hoover and President Roosevelt, do not come to the Florida Keys in hurricane months. Hurricane months are August, September and October, and in those months you see no yachts along the Keys. You do not see them because yacht owners know there would be great danger, unescapable danger, to their property if a storm should come. For the same reason, you cannot interest any very wealthy people in fishing off the coast of Cuba in the summer when the biggest fish are there. There is a known danger to property. But veterans, especially the bonus-marching variety of veterans, are not property. They are only human beings; unsuccessful human beings, and all they have to lose is their lives. They are doing coolie labor for a top wage of $45 a month and they have been put down on the Florida Keys where they can't make trouble. It is hurricane months, sure, but if anything comes up, you can always evacuate them, can't you?

This is the way a storm comes. On Saturday evening at Key West, having finished working, you go out to the porch to have a drink and read the evening paper. The first thing you see in the paper is a storm warning. You know that work is off until it is past and you are angry and upset because you were going well.

The location of the tropical disturbance is given as east of Long Island in the Bahamas and the direction it is traveling is approximately toward Key West. You get out the September storm chart which gives the tracks and dates of forty storms of hurricane intensity during that month since 1900. And by taking the rate of movement of the storm as given in the Weather Bureau Advisory you calculate that it cannot reach us before Monday noon at the earliest. Sunday you spend making the boat as safe as you can. When they refuse to haul her out on the ways because there are too many boats ahead, you buy $52 worth of new heavy hawser and shift her to what seems the safest part of the submarine base and tie her up there. Monday you nail the shutters on the house and get everything movable inside. There are northeast storm warnings flying, and at five o'clock the wind is blowing heavily and steadily from the northeast and they have hoisted the big red flags with a black square in the middle one over the other that mean a hurricane. The wind is rising hourly and the barometer is falling. All the people of the town are nailing up their houses.

You go down to the boat and wrap the lines with canvas where they will chafe when the surge starts, and believe that she has a good chance to ride it out if it comes from any direction but the northwest where the opening of the sub-basin is; provided no other boat smashes into you and sinks you. There is a booze boat seized by the Coast Guard tied next to you and you notice her stern lines are only tied to ringbolts in the stern, and you start belly-aching about that.

"For Christ sake, you know those lousy ringbolts will pull right out of her stern and then she'll come down on us."

"If she does, you can cut her loose or sink her."

"Sure, and maybe we can't get to her, too. What's the use of letting a piece of junk like that sink a good boat?"

From the last advisory you figure we will not get it until midnight, and at ten o'clock you leave the Weather Bureau and go home to see if you can get two hours' sleep before it starts, leaving the car in front of the house because you do not trust the rickety garage, putting the barometer and a flashlight by the bed for when the electric lights go. At midnight the wind is howling, the glass is 29.55 and dropping while you watch it, and rain is coming in sheets. You dress, find the car drowned out, make your way to the boat with a flashlight with branches falling and wires going down. The flashlight shorts in the rain and the wind is now coming in heavy gusts from the northwest. The captured boat has pulled her ringbolts out, and by quick handling by Jose Rodriguez, a Spanish sailor, was swung clear before she hit us. She is now pounding against the dock.

The wind is bad and you have to crouch over to make headway against it. You figure if we get the hurricane from there you will lose the boat and you never will have enough money to get another. You feel like hell. But a little after two o'clock it backs into the west and by the law of circular storms you know the storm has passed over the Keys above us. Now the boat is well-sheltered by the sea wall and the breakwater and at five o'clock, the glass having been steady for an hour, you get back to the house. As you make your way in without a light you find a tree is down across the walk and a strange empty look in the front yard shows the big old sappodillo tree is down too. You turn in.

That's what happens when one misses you. And that is about the minimum of time you have to prepare for a hurricane; two full days. Sometimes you have longer.

But what happened on the Keys?

On Tuesday, as the storm made its way up the Gulf of Mexico, it was so wild not a boat could leave Key West and there was no communication with the Keys beyond the ferry, nor with the mainland. No one knew what the storm had done, where it had passed. No train came in and there was no news by plane. Nobody knew the horror that was on the Keys. It was not until late the next day that a boat got through to Matecumbe Key from Key West.

Now, as this is written five days after the storm, nobody knows how many are dead. The Red Cross, which has steadily played down the number, announcing first forty-six then 150, finally saying the dead would not pass 300, today lists the dead and missing as 446, but the total of veterans dead and missing alone numbers 442 and there have been seventy bodies of civilians recovered. The total of dead may well pass a thousand as many bodies were swept out to sea and never will be found.

It is not necessary to go into the deaths of the civilians and their families since they were on the Keys of their own free will; they made their living there, had property and knew the hazards involved. But the veterans had been sent there; they had no opportunity to leave, nor any protection against hurricanes; and they never had a chance for their lives.

During the war, troops and sometimes individual soldiers who incurred the displeasure of their superior officers, were sometimes sent into positions of extreme danger and kept there repeatedly until they were no longer problems. I do not believe anyone, knowingly, would send U.S. war veterans into any such positions in time of peace. But the Florida Keys, in hurricane months, in the matter of casualties recorded during the building of the Florida East Coast Railway to Key West, when nearly a thousand men were killed by hurricanes, can be classed as such a position. And ignorance has never been accepted as an excuse for murder or for manslaughter.

Who sent nearly a thousand war veterans, many of them husky, hard-working and simply out of luck, but many of them close to the border of pathological cases, to live in frame shacks on the Florida Keys in hurricane months?

Why were the men not evacuated on Sunday, or, at latest, Monday morning, when it was known there was a possibility of a hurricane striking the Keys *and evacuation was their only possible protection?*

Who advised against sending the train from Miami to evacuate the veterans until four-thirty o'clock on Monday so that it was blown off the tracks before it ever reached the lower camps?

These are questions that someone will have to answer, and answer satisfactorily, unless the clearing of Anacostia Flats is going to seem an act of kindness compared to the clearing of Upper and Lower Matecumbe.

When we reached Lower Matecumbe there were bodies floating in the ferry slip. The brush was all brown as though autumn had come to these islands where there is no autumn but only a more dangerous summer, but that was because the leaves had all been blown away. There was two feet of sand over the highest part of the island where the sea had carried it and all the heavy bridge-building machines were on their sides. The island looked like the abandoned bed of a river where the sea had swept it. The railroad embankment was gone and the men who had cowered behind it and finally, when the water came, clung to the rails, were all gone with it. You could find them face down and face up in the mangroves. The biggest bunch of the dead were in the tangled, always green but now brown, mangroves behind the tank cars and the water towers. They hung on there, in shelter, until the wind and the rising water carried them away. They didn't all let go at once but only when they could hold on no longer. Then further on you found them high in the trees where the water swept them. You found them everywhere and in the sun all of them were beginning to be too big for their blue jeans and jackets that they could never fill when they were on the bum and hungry.

I'd known a lot of them at Josie Grunt's place and around the town when they would come in for pay day, and some of them were punch drunk and some of them were smart; some had been on the bum since the Argonne almost and some had lost their jobs the year before last Christmas; some had wives and some couldn't remember; some were good guys and others put their pay checks in the Postal Savings and then came over to cadge in on the drinks when better men were drunk; some liked to fight and others liked to walk around the town; and they were all what you get after a war. But who sent them there to die?

They're better off, I can hear whoever sent them say, explaining to himself. What good were they? You can't account for accidents or acts of God. They were well-fed, well-housed, well-treated and, let us suppose, now they are well dead.

But I would like to make whoever sent them there carry just one out through the mangroves, or turn one over that lay in the sun along the fill, or tie five together so they won't float out, or smell that smell you thought you'd never smell again, with luck. But now you know there isn't any luck when rich bastards make a war. The lack of luck goes on until all who take part in it are gone.

So now you hold your nose, and you, you that put in the literary columns that you were staying in Miami to see a hurricane because you needed it in your next novel and now you were afraid you would not see one, you can go on reading the paper, and you'll get all you need for your next novel; but I would like to lead you by the seat of your well-worn-by-writing-to-the-literary-columns pants up to that bunch of mangroves where there is a woman, bloated big as a balloon and upside down and there's another face down in the brush next to her and explain to you they are two damned nice girls who ran a sandwich place and filling

station and that where they are is their hard luck. And you could make a note of it for your next novel and how is your next novel coming, brother writer, comrade s—t?

But just then one of eight survivors from that camp of 187 not counting twelve who went to Miami to play ball (how's that for casualties, you guys who remember percentages?) comes along and he says, "That's my old lady. Fat, ain't she?" But that guy is nuts, now, so we can dispense with him and we have to go back and get in a boat before we can check up on Camp Five.

Camp Five was where eight survived out of 187, but we only find seventy-seven of those plus two more along the fill makes sixty-nine. But all the rest are in the mangroves. It doesn't take a bird dog to locate them. On the other hand, there are no buzzards. Absolutely no buzzards. How's that? Would you believe it? The wind killed all the buzzards and all the big winged birds like pelicans too. You can find them in the grass that's washed along the fill. Hey, there's another one. He's got low shoes, put him down, man, looks about sixty, low shoes, copper-riveted overalls, blue percale shirt without collar, storm jacket, by Jesus that's the thing to wear, nothing in his pockets. Turn him over. Face tumefied beyond recognition. Hell he don't look like a veteran. He's too old. He's got grey hair. You'll have grey hair yourself this time next week. And across his back there was a great big blister as wide as his back and all ready to burst where his storm jacket had slipped down. Turn him over again. Sure he's a veteran. I know him. What's he got low shoes on for then? Maybe he made some money shooting craps and bought them. You don't know that guy. You can't tell him now. I know him, he hasn't got any thumb. That's how I know him. The land crabs ate his thumb. You think you know everybody. Well you waited a long time to get sick, brother. Sixty-seven of them and you got sick at the sixty-eighth.

And so you walk the fill, where there is any fill and now it's calm and clear and blue and almost the way it is when the millionaires come down in the winter except for the sandflies, the mosquitoes and the smell of the dead that always smell the same in all countries you go to—and now they smell like that in your own country. Or is it just that dead soldiers smell the same no matter what their nationality or who sends them to die?

Who sent them down there?

I hope he reads this—and how does it feel?

He will die too, himself, perhaps even without a hurricane warning, but maybe it will be an easy death, that's the best you get, so that you do not have to hang onto something until you can't hang on, until your fingers won't hold on, and it is dark. And the wind makes a noise like a locomotive passing, with a shriek on top of that, because the wind has a scream exactly as it has in books, and then the fill goes and the high wall of water rolls you over and over and then, whatever it is, you get it and we find you, now of no importance, stinking in the mangroves.

You're dead now, brother, but who left you there in the hurricane months on the Keys where a thousand men died before you in the hurricane months when they were building the road that's now washed out?

Who left you there? And what's the punishment for manslaughter now?

Hemingway's "Monologue to the Maestro: A High Seas Letter," published in Esquire *in October 1935 (pp. 21, 174A–174B), is one of his best statements about writing and art. "The Maestro" is Arnold Samuelson, a young man who worked for him in 1935. Samuelson published his account of that year as* With Hemingway: A Year in Key West and Cuba *(New York: Random House, 1984).*

Monologue to the Maestro:
A High Seas Letter

About a year and a half ago a young man came to the front door of the house in Key West and said that he had hitch-hiked down from upper Minnesota to ask your correspondent a few questions about writing. Arrived that day from Cuba, having to see some good friends off on the train in an hour, and to write some letters in the meantime, your correspondent, both flattered and appalled at the prospect of the questioning, told the young man to come around the next afternoon. He was a tall, very serious young man with very big feet and hands and a porcupine hair-cut.

It seemed that all his life he had wanted to be a writer. Brought up on a farm he had gone through high school and the University of Minnesota, had worked as a newspaper man, a rough carpenter, a harvest hand, a day laborer, and had bummed his way across America twice. He wanted to be a writer and he had good stories to write. He told them very badly but you could see that there was something there if he could get it out. He was so entirely serious about writing that it seemed that seriousness would overcome all obstacles. He had lived by himself for a year in a cabin he had built in North Dakota and written all that year. He did not show me anything that he had written then. It was all bad, he said.

I thought, perhaps, that this was modesty until he showed me a piece he had published in one of the Minneapolis papers. It was abominably written. Still, I thought, many other people write badly at the start and this boy is so extremely serious that he must have something; real seriousness in regard to writing being one of the two absolute necessities. The other, unfortunately, is talent.

Besides writing this young man had one other obsession. He had always wanted to go to sea. So, to shorten this account, we gave him a job as night watchman on the boat which furnished him a place to sleep and work and gave him two or three hours work each day at cleaning up and a half of each day free to do his writing. To fulfill his desire to go to sea, we promised to take him to Cuba when we went across.

He was an excellent night watchman and worked hard on the boat and at his writing but at sea he was a calamity; slow where he should be agile, seeming sometimes to have four feet instead of two feet and two hands, nervous under excitement, and with an incurable tendency toward sea-sickness and a peasant reluctance to take orders. Yet he was always willing and hard working if given plenty of time to work in.

We called him the Maestro because he played the violin, this name was eventually shortened to the Mice, and a big breeze would so effectually slow up his co-ordination that your correspondent once remarked to him, "Mice, you certainly must be going to be a hell of a good writer because you certainly aren't worth a damn at anything else."

On the other hand his writing improved steadily. He may yet be a writer. But your correspondent, who sometimes has an evil temper, is never going to ship another hand who is an aspirant writer; nor go through another summer off the Cuban or any other coast accompanied by questions and answers on the practice of letters. If any more aspirant writers come on board the Pilar let them be females, let them be very beautiful, and let them bring champagne.

Your correspondent takes the practice of letters, as distinct from the writing of these monthly letters, very seriously; but dislikes intensely talking about it with almost anyone alive. Having had to mouth about many aspects of it during a period of one hundred and ten days with the good old Maestro, during much of which time your correspondent had to conquer an urge to throw a bottle at the Mice whenever he would open his mouth and pronounce the word writing, he hereby presents some of these mouthings written down.

If they can deter anyone from writing he should be deterred. If they can be of use to anyone your correspondent is pleased. If they bore you there are plenty of pictures in the magazine that you may turn to.

Your correspondent's excuse for presenting them is that some of the information contained would have been worth fifty cents to him when he was twenty-one.

Mice: What do you mean by good writing as opposed to bad writing?

Your Correspondent: Good writing is true writing. If a man is making a story up it will be true in proportion to the amount of knowledge of life that he has and how conscientious he is; so that when he makes something up it is as it would truly be. If he doesn't know how many people work in their minds and actions his luck may save him for a while, or he may write fantasy. But if he continues to write about what he does not know about he will find himself faking. After he fakes a few times he cannot write honestly any more.

Mice: Then what about imagination?

Y.C.: Nobody knows a damned thing about it except that it is what we get for nothing. It may be racial experience. I think that is quite possible. It is the one thing beside honesty that a good writer must have. The more he learns from experience the more truly he can imagine. If he gets so he can imagine truly enough people will think that the things he relates all really happened and that he is just reporting.

Mice: Where will it differ from reporting?

Y.C.: If it was reporting they would not remember it. When you describe something that has happened that day the timeliness makes people see it in their own imaginations. A month later that element of time is gone and your account would be flat and they would not see it in their minds nor remember it. But if you make it up instead of describe it you can make it round and whole and solid and give it life. You create it, for good or bad. It is made; not described. It is just as true as the extent of your ability to make it and the knowledge you put into it. Do you follow me?

Mice: Not always.

Y.C. (crabbily): Well for chrisake let's talk about something else then.

Mice (undeterred): Tell me some more about the mechanics of writing.

Y.C.: What do you mean? Like pencil or typewriter? For chrisake.

Mice: Yes.

Y.C.: Listen. When you start to write you get all the kick and the reader gets none. So you might as well use a typewriter because it is that much easier and you enjoy it that much more. After you learn to write your whole object is to convey everything, every sensation, sight, feeling, place and emotion to the reader. To do this you have to work over what you write. If you write with a pencil you get three different sights at it to see if the reader is getting what you want him to. First when you read it over; then when it is typed you get another

chance to improve it, and again in the proof. Writing it first in pencil gives you one-third more chance to improve it. That is .333 which is a damned good average for a hitter. It also keeps it fluid longer so that you can better it easier.

Mice: How much should you write a day?

Y.C.: The best way is always to stop when you are going good and when you know what will happen next. If you do that every day when you are writing a novel you will never be stuck. That is the most valuable thing I can tell you so try to remember it.

Mice: All right.

Y.C.: Always stop while you are going good and don't think about it or worry about it until you start to write the next day. That way your subconscious will work on it all the time. But if you think about it consciously or worry about it you will kill it and your brain will be tired before you start. Once you are into the novel it is as cowardly to worry about whether you can go on the next day as to worry about having to go into inevitable action. You *have* to go on. So there is no sense to worry. You have to learn that to write a novel. The hard part about a novel is to finish it.

Mice: How can you learn not to worry?

Y.C.: By not thinking about it. As soon as you start to think about it stop it. Think about something else. You have to learn that.

Mice: How much do you read over every day before you start to write?

Y.C.: The best way is to read it all every day from the start, correcting as you go along, then go on from where you stopped the day before. When it gets so long that you can't do this every day read back two or three chapters each day; then each week read it all from the start. That's how you make it all of one piece. And remember to stop while you are still going good. That keeps it moving instead of having it die whenever you go on and write yourself out. When you do that you find that the next day you are pooped and can't go on.

Mice: Do you do the same on a story?

Y.C.: Yes, only sometimes you can write a story in a day.

Mice: Do you know what is going to happen when you write a story?

Y.C.: Almost never. I start to make it up and have happen what would have to happen as it goes along.

Mice: That isn't the way they teach you to write in college.

Y.C.: I don't know about that. I never went to college. If any sonofabitch could write he wouldn't have to teach writing in college.

Mice: You're teaching me.

Y.C.: I'm crazy. Besides this is a boat, not a college.

Inscription in Gustavus Pfeiffer's copy of Green Hills of Africa *(Courtesy of The Lilly Library, Indiana University). He paid for the Hemingways' safari as a gift.*

Mice: What books should a writer have to read?

Y.C.: He should have read everything so he knows what he has to beat.

Mice: He can't have read everything.

Y.C.: I don't say what he can. I say what he should. Of course he can't.

Mice: Well what books are necessary?

Y.C.: He should have read *War and Peace* and *Anna Karenina* by Tolstoi, *Midshipman Easy, Frank Mildmay* and *Peter Simple* by Captain Marryat, *Madame Bovary* and *L'Education Sentimentale* by Flaubert, *Buddenbrooks* by Thomas Mann, Joyce's *Dubliners, Portrait of the Artist* and *Ulysses, Tom Jones* and *Joseph Andrews* by Fielding, *Le Rouge et le Noir* and *La Chartreuse de Parme* by Stendhal, *The Brothers Karamazov* and any two other Dostoevskis, *Huckleberry Finn* by Mark Twain, *The Open Boat* and *The*

Blue Hotel by Stephen Crane, *Hail and Farewell* by George Moore, *Yeats's Autobiographies,* all the good De Maupassant, all the good Kipling, all of Turgenieff, *Far Away and Long Ago* by W. H. Hudson, Henry James' short stories, especially *Madame de Mauvers* and *The Turn of the Screw, The Portrait of a Lady, The American—*

Mice: I can't write them down that fast. How many more are there?

Y.C.: I'll give you the rest another day. There are about three times that many.

Mice: Should a writer have read all of those?

Y.C.: All of those and plenty more. Otherwise he doesn't know what he has to beat.

Mice: What do you mean "has to beat"?

Y.C.: Listen. There is no use writing anything that has been written better before unless you can beat it.

What a writer in our time has to do is write what hasn't been written before or beat dead men at what they have done. The only way he can tell how he is going is to compete with dead men. Most live writers do not exist. Their fame is created by critics who always need a genius of the season, someone they understand completely and feel safe in praising, but when these fabricated geniuses are dead they will not exist. The only people for a serious writer to compete with are the dead that he knows are good. It is like a miler running against the clock rather than simply trying to beat whoever is in the race with him. Unless he runs against time he will never know what he is capable of attaining.

Mice: But reading all the good writers might discourage you.

Y.C.: Then you ought to be discouraged.

Mice: What is the best early training for a writer?

Y.C.: An unhappy childhood.

Mice: Do you think Thomas Mann is a great writer?

Y.C.: He would be a great writer if he had never written another thing than *Buddenbrooks*.

Mice: How can a writer train himself?

Y.C.: Watch what happens today. If we get into a fish see exactly what it is that everyone does. If you get a kick out of it while he is jumping remember back until you see exactly what the action was that gave you the emotion. Whether it was the rising of the line from the water and the way it tightened like a fiddle string until drops started from it, or the way he smashed and threw water when he jumped. Remember what the noises were and what was said. Find what gave you the emotion; what the action was that gave you the excitement. Then write it down making it clear so the reader will see it too and have the same feeling that you had. That's a five finger exercise.

Mice: All right.

Y.C.: Then get in somebody else's head for a change. If I bawl you out try to figure what I'm thinking about as well as how you feel about it. If Carlos curses Juan think what both their sides of it are. Don't just think who is right. As a man things are as they should or shouldn't be. As a man you know who is right and who is wrong. You have to make decisions and enforce them. As a writer you should not judge. You should understand.

Mice: All right.

Y.C.: Listen *now*. When people talk listen completely. Don't be thinking what you're going to say. Most people never listen. Nor do they observe. You should be able to go into a room and when you come out know everything that you saw there and not only that. If that room gave you any feeling you should know exactly what it was that gave you that feeling.

Try that for practice. When you're in town stand outside the theatre and see how the people differ in the way they get out of taxis or motor cars. There are a thousand ways to practice. And always think of other people.

Mice: Do you think I will be a writer?

Y.C.: How the hell should I know? Maybe you have no talent. Maybe you can't feel for other people. You've got some good stories if you can write them.

Mice: How can I tell?

Y.C.: Write. If you work at it five years and you find you're no good you can just as well shoot yourself then as now.

Mice: I wouldn't shoot myself.

Y.C.: Come around then and I'll shoot you.

Mice: Thanks.

Y.C.: Perfectly welcome, Mice. Now should we talk about something else?

Mice: What else?

Y.C.: Anything else, Mice, old timer, anything else at all.

Mice: All right. But—

Y.C.: No but. Finish. Talk about writing finish. No more. All gone for today. Store all close up. Boss he go home.

Mice: All right then. But tomorrow I've got some things to ask you.

Y.C.: I'll bet you'll have fun writing after you know just how it's done.

Mice: What do you mean?

Y.C.: You know. Fun. Good times. Jolly. Dashing off an old masterpiece.

Mice: Tell me—

Y.C.: Stop it.

Mice: All right. But tomorrow—

Y.C.: Yes. All right. Sure. But tomorrow.

Hemingway's Green Hills of Africa *(New York: Scribners, 1935) is as much about art as it is about hunting. These are some of his comments on writers and writing from that safari narrative (pp. 18–27, 72–73, 108–109).*

"We have books," he said. "I cannot buy new books now but we can always talk. Ideas and conversation are very interesting. We discuss all things. Everything. We have a very interesting mental life. Formerly, with the shamba, we had the *Querschnitt*. That gave you a feeling of belonging, of being made a part of, to a very brilliant group of people. The people one would see if one saw whom one wished to see. You know all of those people? You must know them."

"Some of them," I said. "Some in Paris. Some in Berlin."

I did not wish to destroy anything this man had, and so I did not go into those brilliant people in detail.

"They're marvellous," I said, lying.

"I envy you to know them," he said. "And tell me, who is the greatest writer in America?"

"My husband," said my wife.

"No. I do not mean for you to speak from family pride. I mean who really? Certainly not Upton Sinclair. Certainly not Sinclair Lewis. Who is your Thomas Mann? Who is your Valery?"

"We do not have great writers," I said. "Something happens to our good writers at a certain age. I can explain but it is quite long and may bore you."

"Please explain," he said. "This is what I enjoy. This is the best part of life. The life of the mind. This is not killing kudu."

"You haven't heard it yet," I said.

"Ah, but I can see it coming. You must take more beer to loosen your tongue."

"It's loose," I told him. "It's always too bloody loose. But *you* don't drink anything."

"No, I never drink. It is not good for the mind. It is unnecessary. But tell me. Please tell me."

"Well," I said, "we have had, in America, skillful writers. Poe is a skillful writer. It is skillful, marvellously constructed, and it is dead. We have had writers of rhetoric who had the good fortune to find a little, in a chronicle of another man and from voyaging, of how things, actual things, can be, whales for instance, and this knowledge is wrapped in the rhetoric like plums in a pudding. Occasionally it is there, alone, unwrapped in pudding, and it is good. This is Melville. But the people who praise it, praise it for the rhetoric which is not important. They put a mystery in which is not there."

"Yes," he said. "I see. But it is the mind working, its ability to work, which makes the rhetoric. Rhetoric is the blue sparks from the dynamo."

"Sometimes. And sometimes it is only blue sparks and what is the dynamo driving?"

"So. Go on."

"I've forgotten."

"No. Go on. Do not pretend to be stupid."

"Did you ever get up before daylight—"

"Every morning," he said. "Go on."

"All right. There were others who wrote like exiled English colonials from an England of which they were never a part to a newer England that they were making. Very good men with the small, dried, and excellent wisdom of Unitarians; men of letters; Quakers with a sense of humor."

"Who were these?"

"Emerson, Hawthorne, Whittier, and Company. All our early classics who did not know that a new classic does not bear any resemblance to the classics that have preceded it. It can steal from anything that it is better than, anything that is not a classic, all classics do that. Some writers are only born to help another writer to write one sentence. But it cannot derive from or resemble a previous classic. Also all these men were gentlemen, or wished to be. They were all very respectable. They did not use the words that people always have used in speech, the words that survive in language. Nor would you gather that they had bodies. They had minds, yes. Nice, dry, clean minds. This is all very dull, I would not state it except that you ask for it."

"Go on."

"There is one at that time that is supposed to be really good, Thoreau. I cannot tell you about it because I have not yet been able to read it. But that means nothing because I cannot read other naturalists unless they are being extremely accurate and not literary. Naturalists should all work alone and some one else should correlate their findings for them. Writers should work alone. They should see each other only after their work is done, and not too often then. Otherwise they become like writers in New York. All angleworms in a bottle, trying to derive knowledge and nourishment from their own contact and from the bottle. Sometimes the bottle is shaped art, sometimes economics, sometimes economic-religion. But once they are in the bottle they stay there. They are lonesome outside of the bottle. They do not want to be lonesome. They are afraid to be alone in their beliefs and no woman would love any of them enough so that they could kill their lonesomeness in that woman, or pool it with hers, or make something with her that makes the rest unimportant."

"But what about Thoreau?"

"You'll have to read him. Maybe I'll be able to later. I can do nearly everything later."

"Better have some more beer, Papa."

"All right."

"What about the good writers?"

"The good writers are Henry James, Stephen Crane, and Mark Twain. That's not the order they're good in. There is no order for good writers."

"Mark Twain is a humorist. The others I do not know."

"All modern American literature comes from one book by Mark Twain called *Huckleberry Finn*. If you read it you must stop where the Nigger Jim is stolen from the boys. That is the real end. The rest is just cheating. But it's the best book we've had. All American writing comes from that. There was nothing before. There has been nothing as good since."

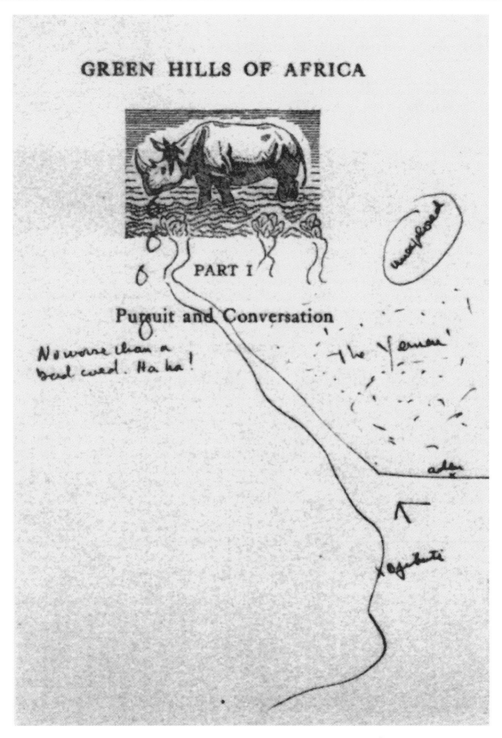

Hemingway's inscription in Gerald and Sara Murphy's copy of Green Hills of Africa *(Collection of Honoria Murphy Donnelly)*

"What about the others?"

"Crane wrote two fine stories. *The Open Boat* and *The Blue Hotel*. The last one is the best."

"And what happened to him?"

"He died. That's simple. He was dying from the start."

"But the other two?"

"They both lived to be old men but they did not get any wiser as they got older. I don't know what they really wanted. You see we make our writers into something very strange."

"I do not understand."

"We destroy them in many ways. First, economically. They make money. It is only by hazard that a writer makes money although good books always make money eventually. Then our writers when they have made some money increase their standard of living and they are caught. They have to write to keep up their establishments, their wives, and so on, and they write slop. It is slop not on purpose but because it is hurried. Because they write when there is nothing to say or no water in the well. Because they are ambitious. Then, once they have betrayed themselves, they justify it and you get more slop. Or else they read the critics. If they believe the critics when they say they are great then they must believe them when they say they are rotten and they lose confidence. At present we have two good writers who cannot write because they have lost confidence through reading critics. If they wrote, sometimes it would be good and sometimes not so good and sometimes it would be quite bad, but the good would get out. But they have read the critics and they must write masterpieces. The masterpieces the critics said they wrote. They weren't masterpieces, of course. They were just quite good books. So now they cannot write at all. The critics have made them impotent."

"Who are these writers?"

"Their names would mean nothing to you and by now they may have written, become frightened, and be impotent again."

"But what is it that happens to American writers? Be definite."

"I was not here in the old days so I cannot tell you about them, but now there are various things. At a certain age the men writers change into Old Mother Hubbard. The women writers become Joan of Arc without the fighting. They become leaders. It doesn't matter who they lead. If they do not have followers they invent them. It is useless for those selected as followers to protest. They are accused of disloyalty. Oh, hell. There are too many things happen to them. That is one thing. The others try to save their souls with what they write. That is an easy way out. Others are ruined by the first money, the first praise, the first attack, the first time they find

they cannot write, or the first time they cannot do anything else, or else they get frightened and join organizations that do their thinking for them. Or they do not know what they want. Henry James wanted to make money. He never did, of course."

"And you?"

"I am interested in other things. I have a good life but I must write because if I do not write a certain amount I do not enjoy the rest of my life."

"And what do you want?"

"To write as well as I can and learn as I go along. At the same time I have my life which I enjoy and which is a damned good life."

"Hunting kudu?"

"Yes. Hunting kudu and many other things."

"What other things?"

"Plenty of other things."

"And you know what you want?"

"Yes."

"You really like to do this, what you do now, this silliness of kudu?"

"Just as much as I like to be in the Prado."

"One is not better than the other?"

"One is as necessary as the other. There are other things, too."

"Naturally. There must be. But this sort of thing means something to you, really?"

"Truly."

"And you know what you want?"

"Absolutely, and I get it all the time."

"But it takes money."

"I could always make money and besides I have been very lucky."

"Then you are happy?"

"Except when I think of other people."

"Then you think of other people?"

"Oh, yes."

"But you do nothing for them?"

"No."

"Nothing?"

"Maybe a little."

"Do you think your writing is worth doing—as an end in itself?"

"Oh, yes."

"You are sure?"

"Very sure."

"That must be very pleasant."

"It is," I said. "It is the one altogether pleasant thing about it."

"This is getting awfully serious," my wife said.

"It's a damned serious subject."

"You see, he is really serious about something," Kandisky said. "I knew he must be serious on something besides kudu."

"The reason every one now tries to avoid it, to deny that it is important, to make it seem vain to try to do it, is because it is so difficult. Too many factors must combine to make it possible."

"What is this now?"

"The kind of writing that can be done. How far prose can be carried if any one is serious enough and has luck. There is a fourth and fifth dimension that can be gotten."

"You believe it?"

"I know it."

"And if a writer can get this?"

"Then nothing else matters. It is more important than anything he can do. The chances are, of course, that he will fail. But there is a chance that he succeeds."

"But that is poetry you are talking about."

"No. It is much more difficult than poetry. It is a prose that has never been written. But it can be written, without tricks and without cheating. With nothing that will go bad afterwards."

"And why has it not been written?"

"Because there are too many factors. First, there must be talent, much talent. Talent such as Kipling had. Then there must be discipline. The discipline of Flaubert. Then there must be the conception of what it can be and an absolute conscience as unchanging as the standard meter in Paris, to prevent faking. Then the writer must be intelligent and disinterested and above all he must survive. Try to get all these in one person and have him come through all the influences that press on a writer. The hardest thing, because time is so short, is for him to survive and get his work done. But I would like us to have such a writer and to read what he would write. What do you say? Should we talk about something else?" . . .

What I had to do was work. I did not care, particularly, how it all came out. I did not take my own life seriously any more, any one else's life, yes, but not mine. They all wanted something that I did not want and I would get it without wanting it, if I worked. To work was the only thing, it was the one thing that always made you feel good, and in the meantime it was my own damned life and I would lead it where and how I pleased. And where I had led it now pleased me very much. This was a better sky than Italy. The hell it was. The best sky was in Italy and Spain and Northern Michigan in the fall and in the fall in the Gulf off Cuba. You could beat this sky; but not the country.

All I wanted to do now was get back to Africa. We had not left it, yet, but when I would wake in the night I would lie, listening, homesick for it already.

Now, looking out the tunnel of trees over the ravine at the sky with white clouds moving across in the wind, I loved the country so that I was happy as you are after you have been with a woman that you really love, when, empty, you feel it welling up again and there it is and you can never have it all and yet what there is, now, you can have, and you want more and more, to have, and be, and live in, to possess now again for always, for that long, sudden-ended always; making time stand still, sometimes so very still that afterwards you wait to hear it move, and it is slow in starting. But you are not alone, because if you have ever really loved her happy and untragic, she loves you always; no matter whom she loves nor where she goes she loves you more. So if you have loved some woman and some country you are very fortunate and, if you die afterwards it makes no difference. Now, being in Africa, I was hungry for more of it, the changes of the seasons, the rains with no need to travel, the discomforts that you paid to make it real, the names of the trees, of the small animals, and all the birds, to know the language and have time to be in it and to move slowly. I had loved country all my life; the country was always better than the people. I could only care about people a very few at a time. . . .

P. O. M. was reading *Spanish Gold*, by George A. Birmingham, and she said it was no good. I still had the Sevastopol book of Tolstoi and in the same volume I was reading a story called "The Cossacks" that was very good. In it were the summer heat, the mosquitoes, the feel of the forest in the different seasons, and that river that the Tartars crossed, raiding, and I was living in that Russia again.

I was thinking how real that Russia of the time of our Civil War was, as real as any other place, as Michigan, or the prairie north of town and the woods around Evans's game farm, of how, through Turgenieff, I knew that I had lived there, as I had been in the family Buddenbrooks, and had climbed in and out of her window in *Le Rouge et Le Noir,* or the morning we had come in the gates of Paris and seen Salcède torn apart by the horses at the Place de Grèves. I saw all that. And it was me they did not break on the rack that time because I had been polite to the executioner the time they killed Coconas and me, and I remember the Eve of St. Bartholomew's and how we hunted Huguenots that night, and when they trapped me at her house that time, and no feeling more true than finding the gate of the Louvre being closed, nor of looking down at his body in the water where he fell from the mast, and always, Italy, better than any book, lying in the chestnut woods, and in the fall mist behind the Duomo going across the town to the Ospedale Maggiore, the nails in my boots on the cobbles, and in the Spring sudden showers in the mountains and the smell of the regiment like a copper coin in your mouth. So in the heat the train stopped at Dezenzano and there was Lago de Garda and those troops are the Czech Legion, and the next time it was raining, and the next time it was in the dark, and the next time you passed it riding in a truck, and the next time you were coming from somewhere else, and the next time you walked to it in the dark from Sermione. For we have been there in the books and out of the books—and where we go, if we are any good, there you can go as we have been. A country, finally, erodes and the dust blows away, the people all die and none of them were of any importance permanently, except those who practised the arts, and these now wish to cease their work because it is too lonely, too hard to do, and is not fashionable. A thousand years makes economics silly and a work of art endures forever, but it is very difficult to do and now it is not fashionable. People do not want to do it any more because they will be out of fashion and the lice who crawl on literature will not praise them. Also it is very hard to do. So what? So I would go on reading about the river that the Tartars came across when raiding, and the drunken old hunter and the girl and how it was then in the different seasons.

Bernard DeVoto, editor of the Saturday Review of Literature, *wrote the following review of Hemingway's safari memoir for that magazine, 26 October 1935, p. 5. While DeVoto admired how Hemingway presents the people on the safari, he found those parts about hunting and literature to be boring.*

Hemingway in the Valley

"The writer has attempted to write an absolutely true book to see whether the shape of a country and the pattern of a month's action can, if truly presented, compete with a work of the imagination." So Mr. Hemingway describes his intention, in a preface that is shorter than the average sentence that follows it. Later, in one of the "bloody literary discussions," he praises prose that is "without tricks and without cheating"—a phrase which sums up an ambition that has been constant in all his work. Then he records his satisfaction "when you write well and truly of something and know impersonally you have written in that way and those who are paid to read it and report on it do not like the subject so they say it is all a fake." In another passage, "the lice who crawl on literature will not praise" a work of art. Either the reviewers have been getting under his skin or he is uneasy about this book.

Mr. Hemingway should have his answer: "Green Hills of Africa" cannot compete with his works of the imagination. It is not exactly a poor book, but it is certainly far from a good one. The trouble is that it has few fine and no extraordinary passages, and long parts of it are dull. And being bored by Ernest Hemingway is a new experience for readers and reviewers alike. The queer thing is that this novelty springs from the same intense literary self-consciousness that has been a large part of the effectiveness of his books up to now. He kills this one by being too assiduously an experimental artist in prose, out to register sensation and find the right words for the countryside and activity and emotion, and, by way of the bush and the campfires and the rhinoceros dung, carry his prose to the "fourth and fifth dimension that can be gotten." He has reverted to his café-tabletalk days, he is being arty, and Africa isn't a good place for it.

Only about forty percent of the book is devoted to the shape of the country and the pattern of action. That part isn't too good. He is magnificent when he is rendering the emotions of the hunt and the kill, but those passages are less frequent than long, confusing, over-written descriptions, and these are lush and very tiresome. Besides, there are a lot of tricks and some cheating. Mr. Hemingway plunges into the rhetoric he has monotonously denounced, and he overlays a good many bits of plain brush-work with very eloquent and highly literary researches into past time.

The rest of it runs about twenty percent literary discussion, twenty percent exhibitionism, and twenty percent straight fiction technique gratefully brought into this unimaginative effort. The literary discussion, though it contains some precious plums, is mostly bad; the exhibitionism is unfailingly good. Mr. Hemingway is not qualified for analytical thought. His flat judgments and especially his papal rules and by-laws are superficial when they aren't plain cockeyed. He has written about writing, probably, more than any other writer of his time; he is much better at writing and we should all be richer if he would stick to it. But he is a first-rate humorist, and the clowning is excellent. When he gives us Hemingway in the sulks, Hemingway with the braggies, Hemingway amused or angered by the gun-bearers, Hemingway getting tight, Hemingway at the latrine, Hemingway being hard-boiled, or brutal, or swaggering, or ruthless, Hemingway kidding someone or getting sore at someone—the book comes to life. It comes to life, in fact, whenever he forgets about the shape of the country and the pattern of action, and brings same people on the stage.

Working with real people, Pop, P.O.M., Karl, the casuals, he is quite as effective a novelist as he is with imaginary ones. He imparts the same life to the natives, some of whom do not even speak. Droopy, Garrick, and The Wanderobo are splendid creations; one sees and feels them, accepts them, experiences them. They live. And that is creation of a high order, a *tour de force* all the more remarkable since it is done without the dialogue that is Mr. Hemingway's most formidable weapon. When he is being a novelist, he achieves his purpose. His book has the life and validity he tells us he set out to give it; he gets the experience itself into prose. It successfully competes with the imagination—because it uses the tools and technique of an imaginative artist.

The big news for literature, however, is that, stylistically, there is a new period of Hemingway. He seems to be fighting a one-man revolution to carry prose back to "The Anatomy of Melancholy" or beyond. There have been omens of it before now, of course, and Mr. Hemingway, in his café-table days, pondered Gertrude Stein to his own gain. The repetitious Stein of "Tender Buttons" doesn't show up here, but the Stein who is out to get four or five dimensions into prose is pretty obvious. But he also appears to have been reading a prose translation of "The Odyssey" too closely, and something that sounds like a German translation of Hemingway. With the result that whereas the typical Hemingway sentence used to run three to a line it now runs three to a page. And whereas he used to simplify vocabulary in order to be wholly clear, he now simplifies grammar till the result looks like a marriage between an e. e. cummings simultaneity and one of those ground-mists of Sherwood Anderson's that Mr. Hemingway was burlesquing ten years ago.

The prize sentence in the book runs forty-six lines, the one I should like to quote as typical ("Now, heavy socks. . ." p. 95), though less than half that long is still too long, and a comparatively straightforward one must serve. "Going downhill steeply made these Spanish shooting boots short in the toe and there was an old argument, about this length of boot and whether the boot-maker, whose part I had taken, unwittingly, first, only as interpreter, and finally embraced his theory patriotically as a whole and, I believed, by logic, had overcome it by adding onto the heel."

This is simpler than most, but it shows the new phase. Usually the material is not so factual as this and we are supposed to get, besides the sense, some muscular effort or some effect of color or movement that is latent in pace and rhythm rather than in words. But, however earnest the intention, the result is a kind of etymological gas that is just bad writing. The five-word sentences of "The Sun Also Rises" were better. You know where you stood with them, and what Mr. Hemingway was saying. He ought to leave the fourth dimension to Ouspensky and give us prose.

An unimportant book. A pretty small book for a big man to write. One hopes that this is just a valley and that something the size of "Death in the Afternoon" is on the other side.

Carl Van Doren published the following review of Green Hills of Africa *in* New York Herald Tribune Books, *27 October 1935, p. 3.*

Ernest Hemingway, Singing in Africa

This is a chapter of the post-war history of Ernest Hemingway, who does not mean to be a soldier again . . .

But an artist must have a subject which is important to him, and Mr. Hemingway returns to what is for him the most important subject. The death of soldiers, the death of bulls in the ring, the death of wild animals. "Green Hills of Africa" is his account of hunting in the country around Lake Manyara in Tanganyika. Such accounts, as a rule, he says, bore him. He has attempted "to write an absolutely true book to see whether the shape of a country and the pattern of a month's action can, if truly presented, compete with a work of the imagination."

Of course they can and his book does. If he had called it a novel it would have made little difference. Most of his readers will read it as if it were. They will not know how truthful he is about the African landscape or about the habits of the men and animals that live there. They will not know whether the persons of the story are actual or invented, what they do and say and appear to feel and think. The story is built like a novel, goes back like one after beginning in the middle and then moves forward to a calculated climax of romantic ecstasy and ironic disappointment. The persons talk like characters in a novel; that is, a Hemingway novel. All it lacks is lovers, and Mr. Hemingway in his Foreword says that "any one not finding sufficient love interest is at liberty, while reading it, to insert whatever love interest he or she may have at the time."

What makes "Green Hills of Africa" history or autobiography, not fiction, is that Mr. Hemingway is in his own person the hero. The minor figures, his wife, the other hunters, and the various natives, are characterized and differentiated with lively skill. The country through which he hunts not only looks real, but sounds, feels, smells, and tastes real. He has used all his senses in perceiving it and he communicates it to all the senses of his readers. But it frankly exists as it existed for him. He is the center of the action, the sensorium on which the action is recorded. His book about Africa is a book about Ernest Hemingway in Africa.

This would be true about any book of the sort. The hunter telling his story can bring back only what has become a part of him. What distinguishes Mr. Hemingway from ordinary hunters is the candor with which he reports his own sensations: his excitements, his defeats, his chagrins, his uncontrollable momentary jealousy of Karl, the lucky hunter, his bragging, his admission that he brags.

"Green Hills" makes it plain once more that Mr. Hemingway is not tough and strong, as in the legend about him. The strongest kind of man, like Pop in the story, would not have such ups and downs of spirit as Mr. Hemingway's. The next strongest kind would not be so conscious of them, if he had them, as to be able to turn them to literary use. Mr. Hemingway belongs to a third class of strong men. Or rather, he is what is better for him to be, a very sensitive man, subtle and articulate beneath his swaggering surfaces. He is an artist who likes best to deal with the deeds of strong men, because they stir him and fit his talents.

When he reflects or argues he is often as boyish as Byron, and he is often tiresome when he goes in for talking and writing tough. He is mature only as an artist, expounding his own art and exhibiting it in prose that sings like poetry without ever ceasing to be prose, easy, intricate, and magical.

Sinclair Lewis, author of Main Street *(1920) and* Arrowsmith *(1925), found* Green Hills of Africa *to be boorish and beneath Hemingway's talent—as indicated by the following poem from his essay, "Rambling Thoughts on Literature as a Business," in* Yale Literary Magazine, *101 (February 1936), pp. 43–47, and the subsequent parody that Lewis published in "Literary Felonies" in the* Saturday Review of Literature, *14 (3 October 1936), p. 3.*

Lines to a College Professor

Mister Ernest Hemingway
Halts his slaughter of the kudu
To remind you that you may
Risk his sacerdotal hoodoo
If you go on, day by day,
Talking priggishly as you do.
Speak up, man! Be bravely heard
Bawling the four-letter word!
And wear your mind décolleté
Like Mr. Ernest Hemingway.

Obtaining Game under False Pretenses

The kudu was a good 470 meters away. I grabbed up my Mannlicher, muttering to the Laconic Limey, "Thoreau is lousy—Willa Cather is a bum—Josephine Johnson is an illiterate brat." I threw down the Mannlicher and grabbed up my Sharp's. The n.g. with his usual native-guide surliness said, "N'bo?" which meant, "Why, in the name of the crocodile god, don't you try a Thompson submachine gun—that's the only wagon you can hit that kudu with now!"

"Go to the devil, n.g. Dos Passos is all right, though, and I suppose e. e. cummings is, even if Bunny Wilson did boost him." And I chucked the Sharp's and grabbed my Winchester four-gauge shotgun.

By now the kudu was 516 meters away. I aimed pretty carefully. "You're a swell woodchuck killer!" jeered the L.L. I went on aiming. It was swell. I felt fine. The o.l. shouted, "It's certainly swell! I feel fine! You're a swell shot!" And maybe I was, for the kudu, hit in the belly, was crawling, his guts dragging, while he made a foolish noise like a woman dying in agony.

"Isn't it swell and melancholy, the way the kudu groans! Like something at twilight. Like the Sonata Appassionata at twilight," said the o.l.

"Santayana is lousy. He never slaughters any animals. None at all. Thornton Wilder is terrible. So was Emerson," I said.

The kudu stopped and died. We all had a drink of beer. We felt fine.

"You're a first-rate woodchuck killer. Swell!" said the L.L.

Hemingway liked the reviews for the English edition of Green Hills of Africa *(London: Cape, 1936) much more than those for the American edition. As this review in the* Times Literary Supplement *(4 April 1936, p. 291) shows, the British reviewers were not bothered by the hunting in the book.*

GREEN AFRICA

The fascination of East Africa and the thrill of big game shooting find real expression in Ernest Hemingway's new book. "The Green Hills of Africa" is a promising title, to begin with, for it evokes at once a typical aspect of the country, and one that may be surprising; for in the untravelled imagination Africa is apt to be all yellow ochre. Tanganyika was the happy hunting ground, and we get a real impression of its atmosphere and appearance with very little actual description. The

Dust jacket for the account of Hemingway's safari, 1935

little black-and-white drawings of the chapter headings contribute no small part to the general impression; they manage to convey the sense of dazzling light and shimmering heat haze. By their design, and by the device of using very light lines of even thickness, giving transparency of shadow, they suggest a lack of solidity which is very typical of that country in the heat of the day.

Africa has a very special appeal for many people, and Mr. Hemingway has felt that appeal strongly. He has something to say in this book beyond telling a tale of hunting big game. In the first chapter a chance meeting with an Austrian traveller gives him an opportunity of explaining a favourite theme, which runs on as an undertone throughout the book. The Austrian is a serious-minded man of intellectual ambitions, who is shocked to find an author whom he admires leading the life of a man of action—killing for sport like any unregenerate dullard. The author holds that life should be lived and enjoyed to the full—not only in the intellect, for that would cramp and desiccate the mind—it would be a kind of intellectual cannibalism.

I thought about Tolstoy and about what a great advantage an experience of war was to a writer. It was one of the major subjects, and those writers who had not seen it were always jealous and tried to make it seem unimportant, or abnormal, or a disease as a subject, while really it was something quite irreplaceable that they had missed.

It is death to his genius, he argues, for a writer to write when there is no "water in the well"—to write except when he feels he must; it should be the overflow, as it were, of a full life. "I have a good life, but I must write because if I do not write a certain amount I do not enjoy the rest of my life."

This may all seem rather self-conscious, but it is part of the general design. The book has definite design; it is arranged in four sections called "Pursuit and Conversation," "Pursuit Remembered," "Pursuit and Failure," and "Pursuits Happiness," each written in a rather different mood and tempo, the conversation with the Austrian being given as a prelude, although in the time sequence of the tale it really takes place near the end.

Hemingway with his publisher, Charles Scribner III, and his editor, Maxwell Perkins, November 1935

Lions, rhino, buffalo and sable were hunted and shot, but the main high light of the tale is centred on the kudu hunt. For successful and happy hunting unlimited time and patience are needed, but in Mr. Hemingway's case a time limit was set by the approach of the rainy season, and no greater kudu were found until very near the end of their time. The kudu hunt takes on a new seriousness, but every time the author gets within hope of a kudu, something frightens it, or it proves to be a cow. One misfortune after another spoils his chances, and the agony gets worse and worse, until at the very last moment success greater than nay he had dreamed of crowns his efforts and he gets two super kudu bulls. On his return to camp there is a grand anticlimax when he finds that one of his companions has shot a yet more stupendous kudu during his absence.

The party consists of the author and his wife and a friend or two, a "white hunter" and two native trackers, besides porters and servants, and various local tribesmen who attach themselves temporarily as guides to the party. We get to know all these people very well during the expedition and the dialogue is in Mr. Hemingway's best vein. In the heat of the day the party rests under shady trees and talk or read or think, and in the evening round the camp fire they talk more and think less. There is a tendency after a few drinks to brag of hunting prowess, but ironic and teasing remarks from the other check that at the outset.

Certainly the book is the expression of a deep enjoyment and appreciation of being alive—in Africa. Hunting game is an intense part of that enjoyment, but there is more to it than that; it is the feeling of the dew on the grass in the morning—the shape and colour and smell of the country, the companionship of friends and particularly that of his wife, the skill of the trackers, and the feeling (before the anxiety of the kudu hunt) that time has ceased to matter. It is the memory of other pleasant days, and of good books read. All these factors contribute in their various degrees to the complete pattern of appreciation.

Chapter Four: 1936–1940

1936

ca. 20 February   Hemingway gets into a fistfight with poet Wallace Stevens, who is vacationing in Key West.

11 July   Hemingway tells Maxwell Perkins that he is working on a novel set in Key West and Havana.

18 July   General Francisco Franco leads a revolt of Fascists in the Spanish Army against the government, as the Spanish Civil War begins.

August   *Esquire* publishes "The Snows of Kilimanjaro."

Late November   Hemingway agrees to cover the Spanish Civil War for the North American Newspaper Alliance.

Late December   Hemingway meets writer Martha Gellhorn in Sloppy Joe's Bar in Key West.

1937

ca. 17 February   Hemingway meets with Dos Passos, Archibald MacLeish, and Lillian Hellman in New York City to discuss making a film documentary to promote the cause of the Spanish Republic.

14 March   Hemingway arrives in Spain, where for two months he observes the course of the war, assists director Joris Ivens, and spends time with Gellhorn.

4 June   Hemingway delivers a speech, "Fascism Is a Lie," before the American Writer's Congress in New York City.

5 July   *The Spanish Earth,* narrated by Hemingway, premieres in New York City; three days later Hemingway, Gellhorn, and Ivens are at the White House to show the film to the Roosevelts.

11 August   Hemingway scuffles with critic Max Eastman in Perkins's office.

6 September   Hemingway and Gellhorn return to Spain.

15 October   Scribners publishes *To Have and Have Not.*

28 December   Hemingway joins his wife, Pauline, in Paris.

1938

31 March   Hemingway and Gellhorn go to Perpignan, near the Spanish border; Hemingway leaves Spain on 3 May.

14 October   *The Fifth Column and the First Forty-nine Stories* is published in New York; in addition to the previously published stories, it includes Hemingway's play about the Spanish Civil War and four stories not previously collected in a Hemingway volume.

3 November	Hemingway makes his fourth and final trip to Spain to cover the war; he returns to Paris by 17 November.

1939

ca. 14 February	In Havana, Hemingway begins writing a novel about the war.
28 March	The Spanish Civil War ends with the surrender of all Spanish Republican forces.
April	Hemingway and Gellhorn move into La Finca Vigía, a house outside Havana.
1 September	World War II begins, as Germany invades Poland.
ca. 19 December	Hemingway moves his belongings from Key West to Havana.
7 March	*The Fifth Column* opens on Broadway.

1940

May	Pauline Hemingway files for divorce.
July	Hemingway completes *For Whom the Bell Tolls*.
21 October	Scribners publishes *For Whom the Bell Tolls*. More copies of this Hemingway book have been sold than any other.
21 November	Hemingway and Gellhorn are married.
21 December	F. Scott Fitzgerald dies of a heart attack in Hollywood.
28 December	Hemingway buys La Finca Vigía.

Following the publication of *Green Hills of Africa,* Hemingway returned to fiction writing. In 1936 he published two short stories based on his African experiences, "The Short Happy Life of Francis Macomber" and "The Snows of Kilimanjaro." He also began work on his third story about Key West boatman Harry Morgan, who is the central character of "One Trip Across" (1934) and "The Tradesman's Return" (1936). In July he decided to incorporate these three stories about Morgan into a novel instead of publishing them in a proposed collection, and he worked on this novel for the rest of the year. The first draft was completed in early January 1937.

Hemingway spent much of 1937 in Spain. In July 1936 the Spanish Civil War had begun, when fighting had broken out between forces loyal to the Spanish Republic (Loyalists or Republicans) and those of General Francisco Franco (Fascists). The war became international when Germany and Italy began providing troops and equipment to Franco and the Soviet Union gave military assistance to the Loyalists. Hemingway supported the Republic and traveled to Spain four times in 1937 and 1938 to cover the war. During his first trip, in March 1937, he assisted in the writing of *The Spanish Earth,* a motion-picture documentary pro-duced to raise funds for the Loyalist cause. He also began an affair with Martha Gellhorn, a journalist he had met in Key West in December 1936.

After returning to the United States in May 1937, Hemingway traveled to New York; Washington, D.C.; and Los Angeles to promote the Loyalist cause. In June he gave his first public speech, at the Second American Writers' Congress. Not all his newsworthy activities concerned international politics: on 11 August 1937 he scuffled with Max Eastman in Maxwell Perkins's office after Eastman had written "Bull in the Afternoon," an unfavorable review of *Death in the Afternoon.*

To Have and Have Not, Hemingway's third novel, was published on 15 October 1937. Most reviewers found the book to be uneven, but they welcomed Hemingway's return to writing fiction. Leftist reviewers were the most enthusiastic, seeing the story of Harry Morgan's struggle to make a living during the Depression as a sign that Hemingway was going to devote his writing to promoting social and political causes. Thirty-seven thousand copies of the novel were sold.

In the first part of 1938 Hemingway tried unsuccessfully to arrange for the Broadway production of *The Fifth Column,* the play about the war he had written in Madrid in 1937. The play was produced in 1940, after

Hemingway at The Stork Club with proprietor Sherman Billingsley and author John O'Hara, late 1935

he and Perkins had decided in 1938 to publish it in an omnibus collection of his stories. In addition to the play and the stories of his three previous collections, the book included "The Short Happy Life of Francis Macomber," "The Capital of the World," "The Snows of Kilimanjaro," "Old Man at the Bridge," and "Up in Michigan" (a story that had been written in the early 1920s but had not been published in America). When *The Fifth Column and the First Forty-nine Stories* was published on 14 October 1938, most reviewers praised the stories but thought that the play failed as a drama. Scribners sold more than 15,000 copies of the collection between 1938 and 1940.

In March 1939, soon after the Fascist victory, Hemingway began writing a novel set during the Spanish Civil War. The next month he left Pauline and

moved to Cuba, where he settled with Gellhorn in La Finca Vigía (Lookout Farm) outside Havana. Pauline soon began divorce proceedings.

In Cuba, Hemingway continued writing his new novel, the first draft of which he completed in July 1940 at Sun Valley, Idaho. He chose *For Whom the Bell Tolls* (a phrase from John Donne's "Meditation XVII") for the title of the book. The novel was chosen as the main selection for October by the Book-of-the-Month Club and was the first Hemingway work to be sold to a book club. Scribners published it on 21 October 1940; reviews were overwhelmingly positive, except for those written by leftist critics who thought that Hemingway had betrayed the Republican cause by including scenes of Loyalist sympathizers committing atrocities and by depicting some Russian leaders as being incompetent and murderous. Within five years 500,000 copies had been sold, making it Hemingway's most financially successful work. He ended 1940 by marrying Gellhorn on 21 November and buying La Finca Vigía on 28 December.

Hemingway's summary of his career up to 1936 was published, along with a drawing of him, in Georges Schreiber's Portraits and Self-Portraits *(Boston: Houghton Mifflin, 1936), p. 57.*

The author, whose portrait, drawn by a man who has never seen him, appears opposite this, is thirty-eight years old, married, the father of three sons, and has published two novels, three books of short stories, a treatise on the Spanish bull ring, a satirical novel, and an account of a hunting trip in Tanganyika. He has made his own living since he was sixteen years old and has worked, before it was fashionable, as a day laborer, farmhand, dishwasher, waiter, sparring partner, newspaper reporter, foreign correspondent, and, since 1926, has supported himself and his family as a writer. From 1919 to 1927 he sent stories to American magazines without being able to sell one until the *Atlantic Monthly* published a story called "Fifty Grand." During this time the *Little Review* published several things, but were unable to pay for them, and he was selling stories, articles, and poems to magazines published in France and in Germany. Since he was a young boy he has cared greatly for fishing and shooting. If he had not spent so much time at them, at ski-ing, at the bull ring, and in a boat, he might have written much more. On the other hand, he might have shot himself.

He would rather read than do anything else except write, and nothing can make him so happy as having written well. He has been very lucky in his life and would like his luck to hold a little while longer.

In this letter to his editor Hemingway outlines his initial plan for his novel, To Have and Have Not *(New York: Scribners, 1937). The story collection was published as* The Fifth Column and the First Forty-nine Stories *(New York: Scribners, 1938). From* The Only Thing That Counts, *pp. 243–244.*

July 11 [1936]

Dear Max:

Gingrich was down here and I showed him the 30,000 words I had done on the Key West–Havana novel of which One Trip Across and The Tradesman's Return were a part–I had taken these for the book of stories and he seemed to think that was crazy–I hadnt even looked at the 30,000 since I left off to finish the book of stories–Anyway Ive decided to go on and finish that book now when we go out West–That will only take 2 stories from a book–and will have plenty of others by the time you want the stories, and it can come out after this book–

The book contrasts the two places–and shows the inter-relation–also contains what I know about the mechanics of revolution and what it does to the people engaged in it–There are two themes in it–The decline of the individual–The man Harry–who shows up first in One Trip Across–and then his re-emergence as Key West goes down around him–and the story of a shipment of dynamite and all of the consequences that happened from it–There is a hell of a lot more that I wont inflict on you–But with luck it is a good book–Gingrich was very steamed up about what he read and wanted me to promise not to bring out the stories until I'd finished this–I got the last stuff I needed for it on my last trip across–Also have the hurricane and the vets in it.

I owe you as I recall 1100 dollars advance on the book of stories–I have enough stories for a book but not if I take out One Trip Across and The Tradesman's Return–I can return you the 1100 if you want–or you can let that ride on the next book of stories–or let it ride on this new book–Tell me which you prefer? Have arranged with Gingrich to write only 6 pieces a year for Esquire instead of what I was doing so as not to interfere–Am to get same amount for six as formerly for 12–But do not have to have them in if let him know in advance and I refused an advance so I wouldnt <u>have</u> to turn them out if busy on any of this other–Did you read The Snows of Kilimanjaro and The Short Happy Life of Francis Macomber?) Would have written you this before but had to get it all straightened out–I stink so to the N.Y critics that if I bring out a book of stories no matter how good this fall they will all try to kill it– Well I will be able to give them both barrels next Spring and Fall with a book and a book of stories if you want to play it that way–Meantime the stuff I publish will not hurt my reputation any–All I want to do is get out west and settled down in a cabin writing–We caught a 514 and a 610 lb of tuna–So far have been bitched on marlin–Lost one over 700 and one over 1000–He straightened the hook straight as a pencil! Well what the hell I really have another trade beside marlin fishing and am very anxious to get back to work at it–We will stay out west until Oct or so. Then back to K.W to work hard before the bloody sons of bitching winter visitors come.

I hope I've not let you down about the story book.

Please let me know to K.W. Leave here Thursday if catch some decent weather–It's been blowing a gale for 3 days–Will try to get this off on plane today–Dont think Im trying to stall on the story book as have

Up In Michigan
One Trip Across
The Horns of the Capitol
Tradesman's Return
Short Happy Life of Francis Macomber
The Snows of Kilimanjaro

besides whats new and unnamed–But if I can lift those 2 and finish this other then with only a couple more stories I have 2 books instead of one and one of them that thing the pricks all love–a novel–

Best always–
Ernest/

Hemingway's preface to Jerome Bahr's All Good Americans *(New York: Scribners, 1937) shows his understanding of the economic realities of publishing.*

These stories by Jerome Bahr need no preface. Their solid, youthful worth, their irony, their humor, their peasant lustiness, and the Pieter Brueghel quality of the country and the people that Mr. Bahr has made, need no comment by another writer. Along with many other excellencies they will be apparent to any one who reads the book. Why, then, should the book have a preface? It should not have one.

But, when you are a young writer, the only way you can get a book of stories published now is to have some one with what is called, in the trade, a name write a preface to it. Otherwise you must write a novel first. A novel, even if it fails, is supposed to sell enough copies to pay for putting it out. If it succeeds, the publisher has a property, and when a writer becomes a property he will be humored considerably by those who own the property. He will be, that is, as long as he continues to make them money, and sometimes for a long time afterwards on the chance that he will produce another winner. But when he is starting out he is not humored at all and many natural, good story writers lose their true direction by having to write novels before they are ready to if they want to earn enough at their trade to eat; let alone to marry and have children. It is the same system by which young prizefighters are overmatched and destroyed because their managers need the money that the fight, which the fighter does not yet know enough to win, will bring.

So I am very glad to write a preface to Mr. Bahr's book if doing so will get it published. I think he is a fine honest writer with a talent which is both sturdy and delicate, and I apologize to the reader for the economic necessity of pointing out qualities that would be perceived without any pointing. Mr. Bahr, I am sure, will write a fine novel eventually–maybe he has it planned already–and I hope it will have great success and that he will live to become a gigantic publisher's property of the most enormous kind. In the meantime, he writes very good stories full of irony and empty of bitterness, writing them under the usual impossible circumstances of youth, and I feel very good that they are to be published and ask you to excuse the preface.

From March to May 1937, Hemingway wrote and narrated the commentary for Joris Ivens's movie The Spanish Earth *(1937). In this article Hemingway recounts the production of the movie and some events of his first trip to cover the Spanish Civil War. From* Verve, *1 (Spring 1938), p. 46.*

THE HEAT AND THE COLD

REMEMBERING TURNING THE SPANISH EARTH, THE IVENS-HEMINGWAY FILM OF THE SPANISH WAR

Afterwards, when it is all over, you have a picture. You see it on the screen; you hear the noises and the music; and your own voice, that you've never heard before, comes back to you saying things you'd scribbled in the dark in the projection room or on pieces of paper in a hot hotel bedroom. But what you see in motion on the screen is not what you remember.

The first thing you remember is how cold it was; how early you got up in the morning; how you were always so tired you could go to sleep at any time; how hard it was to get gasoline; and how we were always hungry. It was also very muddy and we had a cowardly chauffeur. Nothing of that shows on the screen except the cold when you can see the men's breath in the air in the picture.

What I really remember clearest about that, the cold part of the picture, is that I always carried raw onions in the pockets of my lumberman's jacket and would eat them whenever I was really hungry much to the disgust of Joris Ivens and John Ferno. No matter how hungry they were they would not eat raw spanish onions. It has something to do with their being Dutchmen. But they would always drink out of the large, flat, silver flask of whiskey which was always empty by four o'clock in the afternoon. The greatest technical discov-

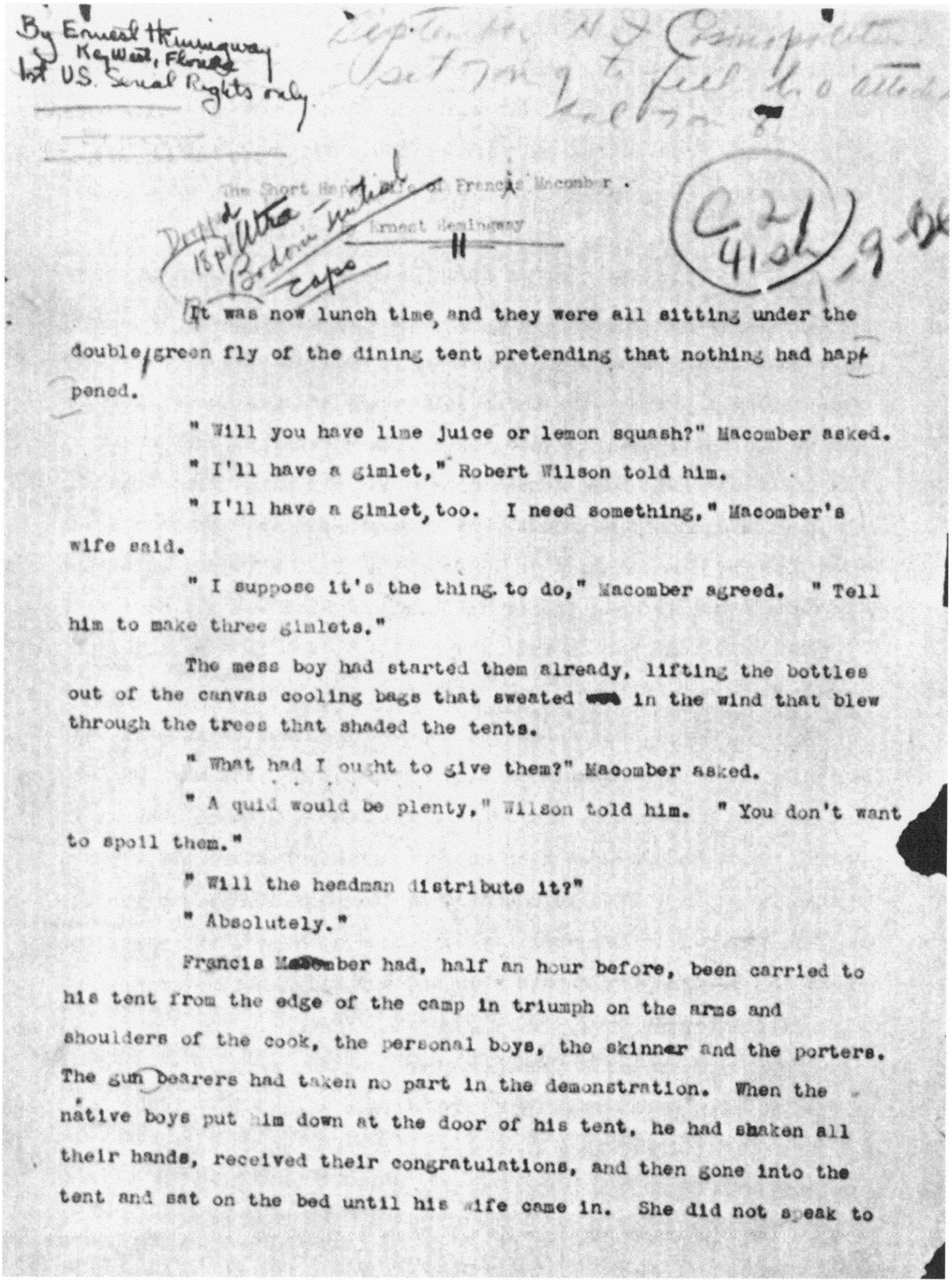

By Ernest Hemingway
Key West, Florida
for U.S. Serial Rights only

The Short Happy Life of Francis Macomber.

by Ernest Hemingway

It was now lunch time, and they were all sitting under the double green fly of the dining tent pretending that nothing had happened.

" Will you have lime juice or lemon squash?" Macomber asked.

" I'll have a gimlet," Robert Wilson told him.

" I'll have a gimlet, too. I need something," Macomber's wife said.

" I suppose it's the thing. to do," Macomber agreed. " Tell him to make three gimlets."

The mess boy had started them already, lifting the bottles out of the canvas cooling bags that sweated wet in the wind that blew through the trees that shaded the tents.

" What had I ought to give them?" Macomber asked.

" A quid would be plenty," Wilson told him. " You don't want to spoil them."

" Will the headman distribute it?"

" Absolutely."

Francis Macomber had, half an hour before, been carried to his tent from the edge of the camp in triumph on the arms and shoulders of the cook, the personal boys, the skinner and the porters. The gun bearers had taken no part in the demonstration. When the native boys put him down at the door of his tent, he had shaken all their hands, received their congratulations, and then gone into the tent and sat on the bed until his wife came in. She did not speak to

Printer's copy for "The Short Happy Life of Francis Macomber" (Morris Library, Southern Illinois University at Carbondale)

ery we made at that time was to carry a bottle to refill the flask with and the greatest non-technical discovery we made was Warner Heilbrun.

After we met Heilbrun, who was medical officer for the Twelfth International Brigade, we always had gasoline, his gasoline. All we had to do was to get out to a brigade hospital to eat well and fill with gasoline. He always had everything marvelously organized. He furnished us with transport. He took us to attacks, and a big part of the film that I remember is the slanting smile, the cap cocked on the side, the slow, comic Berlin Jewish drawl of Heilbrun. When I would go to sleep in the car coming back from somewhere to Madrid at night Heilbrun would tell Luis his chauffeur to take a short way out to the hospital at Moraleja. When I would wake it would be to see the gates of the old castle and at three in the morning we would have a hot meal in the kitchen. Then, when all the rest of us were dead with sleep, Heilbrun would do his work; the work he did so well, so intelligently, so painstakingly so delicately and skillfully, and always with the languid air of doing nothing.

The big part of that section of the picture, for me, is Heilbrun. But he doesn't show in it and he and Luis now are buried in Valencia.

Gustav Regler shows in the picture. You see and hear him make a speech, a fine speech, and again you see, not speech making, but in the line under fire, very calm, very cheerful and a good officer pointing out an immediate objective just before a counter-attack. Regler was a big part of the picture that I remember.

Lucasz shows just for a moment bringing up the Twelfth Brigade to deploy along the Arganda road. You do not see him late at night on that great party on the first of May in Moraleja playing the tune he only played so very late at night on a pencil held against his teeth; the music clear and delicate like a flute. You only see a little glimpse of Lucasz when he was working.

After the cold part of the picture I remember the hot part very well. In the hot part you ran with cameras, sweating, taking cover in the folds of the terrain on the bare hills. There was dust in your nose, and dust in your hair and in your eyes, and you had the great thirst for water, the real dry-mouth that only battle brings. Because you had seen a little war when you were young you knew that Ivens and Ferno would be killed if they kept on because they took too many chances. And your moral problem was always to get clear how much you were holding them back from necessary and just prudence, based on experience, and how much was simply the not so pretty prudence of the burnt monkey who dreads the hot soup. That part of the film that I remember was all sweat and thirst and blowing dust; and in the film I think that shows a little.

So now when it is all over you sit in a theater and suddenly the music comes and then you see a tank come riding like a ship and clanking in the well remembered dust and your mouth dries again. When you were young you gave death much importance. Now you give it none. You only hate it for the people that it takes away.

Death is still very badly organized in war, you think, and let it go at that. But it is a remark you would like to make to Heilbrun, who would grin, and to Lucasz, who would understand it very well. So if it's all the same to you I won't go to see the Spanish Earth any more. Nor will I write about it. I don't have to. Because we were there. But if you weren't there I think you ought to see it.

British poet Stephen Spender went to Spain to promote anti-Fascist propaganda. While there in the spring of 1937 he met Hemingway, an event he recorded in his memoir, World Within World *(New York: Harcourt, Brace, 1951), pp. 208–210.*

One of the writers to arrive at the Press office was Ernest Hemingway, a black-haired, bushy-mustached, hairy-handed giant, who did not belie the impression one might have of his appearance from his novels. In his behavior he seemed at first to be acting the part of a Hemingway hero.

I wondered how this man, whose art concealed under its apparent huskiness a deliberation and delicacy like Turgenev, could show so little of his inner sensibility in his outward behavior. But one afternoon, when he and I were walking through the streets of Valencia, I caught a glimpse of the esthetic Hemingway, whose presence I suspected. I had happened to mention that I had no books in Valencia and that the bookshops were empty of all but Spanish and a little French literature. In one bookshop, I went on, I had seen a novel which I had never read, Stendhal's *La Chartreuse de Parme,* and I did not know whether to buy it. Hemingway said that he thought the account at the beginning of the hero, Fabrice, wandering lost in the middle of the Battle of Waterloo, with which *La Chartreuse* opens is perhaps the best, though the most apparently casual, description of war in literature. For war is often really like that, a boy lost in the middle of an action, not knowing which side will win, hardly knowing that a battle is going on. He warmed to the theme of Stendhal, and soon I realized that he had that kind of literary sensibility which the professional critic, or the don, nearly always lacks. He saw literature not just as "good writing," but as the

lived he would never write about her, he knew now. Nor about any of
them. The rich were dull and they drank too much, or they played
too much backgammon. They were dull and they were repetitious. He
remembered poor Scott FitzGerald and his romantic awe of them and how
he had started a story once that began, The very rich are different
from you and me. And how had said to Scott, Yes, they have more
money. But that was not humorous to Scott. He thought they were a
special glamorous race and when he found they weren't it wrecked him
just as much as any other thing that wrecked him.

He had been contemptuous of those who wrecked. You did not have
to like because you understood. He could beat anything, he thought,
because no thing could hurt him if he did not care.

All right. Now he would not care for death. One thing he had
always dreaded was the pain. He could stand pain as well as any man,
until it went on too long, but here he had something that had hurt
frightfully and just when he had felt it breaking him the pain had
stopped.

He remembered long ago when Williamson, the bombing officer,
had been caught coming in through the wire that night and screaming,
had begged everyone to kill him. He was a fat man, very brave, and
a good officer, although addicted to fantastic shows. But that night
he was caught in wire, with a flare lighting him up and his bowels
spilled out into the wire, so when they brought him in, alive, they
had to cut him loose. Shoot me, Harry. For Christ sake shoot me.
They had had an argument obe time about the Lord never sending you
anything you could not bear and some one's theory had been that
meant that at a certain time the pain passed you out automatically..
But he had always remembered Williamson, still this now, that he
had, was very easy; and if it was no worse as it went on there was

Hemingway's revised typescript for "The Snows of Kilimanjaro" (Harry Ransom Humanities Research Center, University of Texas at Austin). The reference to "poor Scott Fitzgerald" was changed to "poor Julian" when the story was collected in The Fifth Column and the First Forty-nine Stories *(New York: Scribners, 1938).*

AUGUST 1936

Esquire
• THE MAGAZINE FOR MEN

FICTION • SPORTS • HUMOR
CLOTHES • ART • CARTOONS

PRICE FIFTY CENTS

Cover of the magazine issue that included "The Snows of Kilimanjaro" and F. Scott Fitzgerald's "Afternoon of an Author"

unceasing inter-relationship of the words on the page with the life within and beyond them—the battle, the landscape or the love affair. For him, writing was a kind of wrestling of the writer armed with a pen, as a huntsman with his spear, with his living material. I mentioned the battle scenes in Shakespeare. "Why do you talk to me about Shakespeare?" he asked with annoyance. "Don't you realize I don't read books?" and he changed the conversation to—was it boxing? Shortly after this he was saying that his chief purpose in coming to Spain was to discover whether he had lost his nerve under conditions of warfare which had developed since Caporetto. By now we had reached a *taverna* on the shore. We went in and found some gypsy players. Hemingway seized a guitar and started singing Spanish songs. He had become the Hemingway character again.

He told me often that I was "too squeamish," by which, I suppose, he meant "yeller." Yet on one occasion he came down heavily on my side. K—, on sick leave from the Brigade, used to hobble around the cafés where the journalists met, leaning on a stick. Whenever there were arguments about Communism this man attacked me viciously, and most people knew that his motive was to draw attention to the fact that my name

was linked with that of Jimmy. As K— was believed by all the journalists to be a hero, these attacks were humiliating. After a particularly acrimonious discussion, Hemingway took me aside and said: "Stephen, don't you worry about K—. I know his type. He's just a malingerer. He's yeller." He then gave me an outline of K—'s story, which became, in the telling, such excellent Hemingway that I begged him to write it. He said: "I give the idea to you. Why don't you write it?" And from that we went on to make a compact that we would both write the same story. Of course, neither of us did so, and now I forget what it was. All I remember is the curious fact of receiving Hemingway's support in a situation where I should never have expected it. For I had to accept the humiliation of knowing that I was not on the side of the heroes. This was a difficult attitude to maintain, because as my experience of Spain deepened I found myself more and more appreciative of the difficulties of the people, like Kerrigan and Springhall, who were strong, even whilst I wrote often in defense of the weak.

This account of Hemingway's reading at Shakespeare and Company was published in the European edition of the New York Herald Tribune, *14 May 1937, p. 5.*

Hemingway Curses, Kisses, Reads At Sylvia Beach Literary Session

By FRANCIS SMITH

Ernest Hemingway once defined courage as "grace under pressure." He was under pressure Wednesday night at Sylvia Beach's Shakespeare and Company Library, and he knew it. As he threw his 210 pounds into the little room and kissed Adrienne Monnier on both cheeks, he cursed, said that this was the first time he had ever read any of his works, and he would never do it again, even for Sylvia Beach.

He sat down at the little table and started nervously to thumb the bright, white pages of his yet unpublished novel. "I don't know whether I can do this," he said. His voice was only a whisper. A few ladies told him to speak more lightly. He did.

He got through the first chapter all right which dealt with Harry, a pretty tough guy who took fishermen out from Havana to get marlin in the Gulf, Mr. Johnson, the passenger, and an awful rummy named Eddie, always bleary-eyed from drink and who walked as if his joints were turned inside out.

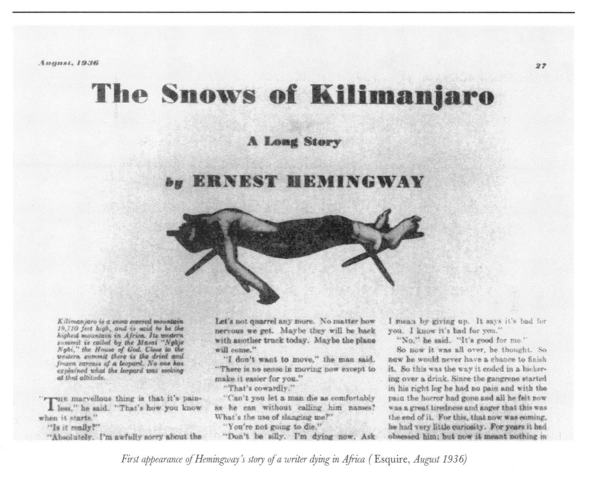

First appearance of Hemingway's story of a writer dying in Africa (Esquire, *August 1936)*

By the time he reached the third chapter, his voice had lost the monotonous pitch, his mouth and half-moon mustache twitched even more. He began to put expression in the clean, terse phrases. He was beginning to show some grace under pressure. As his big head and full face ducked to disappear in a stein of foamy beer which Miss Beach pulled from the cupboard, the picture of him which must have been taken some twelve years ago, when he was twenty-seven and very handsome, could be seen on the wall behind. He continued on about Mr. Sing and the twelve Chinks. When the fourth chapter was finished, he took another bottle of beer and stopped. And when the applause had become a patter, James Joyce, who had been sitting in the shadows in the back of the room, got up and walked out.

Stephen Spender, the tall, rumple-haired English poet and critic, who, like Hemingway, has just returned from Spain, read five poems, expressing his opinion about war in general, not "about this war." He read in a peculiarly definite tone: "I have an appointment with a bullet at seventeen hours, minus a split second, and I

shall not be late," and many other lines. When he was through, he asked Hemingway for some beer. The latter assented and then the evening came to an end.

On 4 June 1937 Hemingway gave this speech to the American Writers' Congress in New York. It was published in the New Masses, *22 June 1937, p. 4.*

Fascism Is a Lie

A writer's problem does not change. He himself changes, but his problem remains the same. It is always how to write truly and, having found what is true, to project it in such a way that it becomes a part of the experience of the person who reads it.

There is nothing more difficult to do, and because of the difficulty, the rewards, whether they

Hemingway (center) in Spain (1937), where he supported the Loyalist forces of the Spanish Republic in its struggle against the Fascist revolt led by General Francisco Franco (Ernest Hemingway Collection, John F. Kennedy Library)

come early or late, are usually very great. If the rewards come early, the writer is often ruined by them. If they come too late, he is probably embittered. Sometimes they only come after he is dead, and then they cannot bother him. But because of the difficulty of making true, lasting writing, a really good writer is always sure of eventual recognition. Only romantics think that there are such things as unknown masters.

Really good writers are always rewarded under almost any existing system of government that they can tolerate. There is only one form of government that cannot produce good writers, and that system is fascism. For fascism is a lie told by bullies. A writer who will not lie cannot live or work under fascism.

Because fascism is a lie, it is condemned to literary sterility. And when it is past, it will have no history except the bloody history of murder that is well known and that a few of us have seen with our own eyes in the last few months.

A writer, when he knows what it is about and how it is done, grows accustomed to war. That is a serious truth which you discover. It is a shock to discover how truly used to it you become. When you are at the front each day and see trench warfare, open warfare, attacks, and counter-attacks, it all makes sense no matter what the cost in dead and wounded—when you know what the men are fighting for and that they are fighting intelligently. When men fight for the freedom of their country against a foreign invasion, and when these men are your friends—some new friends and some of long standing—and you know how they were attacked and how they fought, at first almost unarmed, you learn, watching them live and fight and die, that there are worse things than war. Cowardice is worse, treachery is worse, and simple selfishness is worse.

In Madrid, where it costs every British newspaper £57 or say $280 a week to insure a correspondent's life, and where the American correspondents work at an average wage of $65 a week uninsured, we of the working press watched murder done last month for nineteen days. It was done by German artillery, and it was highly efficient murder.

Joris Ivens, Hemingway, and Dr. Werner Heilbrun in Madrid, April 1937

being fought to a standstill at Bilbao. Every time they are beaten in the field, they salvage that strange thing they call their honor by murdering civilians.

You have seen this murder in Joris Ivens's film, so I will not describe it. If I described it, it would only make you vomit. It might make you hate. But we do not want hate. We want a reasoned understanding of the criminality of fascism and how it should be opposed. We must realize that these murders are the gestures of a bully, the great bully of fascism. There is only one way to quell a bully, and that is to thrash him; and the bully of fascism is being beaten now in Spain as Napoleon was beaten in that same peninsula a hundred and thirty years ago. The fascist countries know it and are desperate. Italy knows her troops will not fight outside of Italy, nor, in spite of marvelous material, are they the equal as soldiers of the new Spanish regiments. There is no question of them ever equaling the fighters of the international brigades.

Germany has found that she cannot depend on Italy as an ally in any sort of offensive war. I have read that von Blomberg witnessed an impressive series of maneuvers yesterday with Marshal Badoglio, but it is one thing to maneuver on the Venetian plain with no enemy present, and another to be outmaneuvered and have three divisions destroyed on the plateau between Brihuega and Trijueja, by the Eleventh and Twelfth International Brigades and the fine Spanish troops of Lister, "Campesino," and Mera. It is one thing to bombard Almeria and take an undefended Málaga given up by treachery, and another to lose seven thousand troops before Cordoba and thirty thousand in unsuccessful assaults on Madrid. It is one thing to destroy Guernica and another to fail to take Bilbao.

I have talked too long. I started to speak of the difficulty of trying to write well and truly, and of the inevitable reward to those who achieve it. But in a time of war—and we are now in a time of war, whether we like it or not—the rewards are all suspended. It is very dangerous to write the truth in war, and the truth is also very dangerous to come by. I do not know just which American writers have gone out to seek it. I know many men of the Lincoln Battalion. But they are not writers. They are letter writers. Many British writers have gone. Many German writers have gone. Many French, and Dutch writers have gone; and when a man goes to seek the truth in war he may find death instead. But if twelve go and only two come back, the truth they bring will be the truth, and not the garbled hearsay that we pass as history. Whether the truth is worth some risk to come by, the writers must decide themselves. Cer-

I said you grow accustomed to war. If you are interested enough in the science of it—and it is a great science—and in the problem of human conduct under danger, you can become so encompassed in it that it seems a nasty sort of egotism even to consider one's own fate. But no one becomes accustomed to murder. And murder on a large scale we saw every day for nineteen days during the last bombardments of Madrid.

The totalitarian fascist states believe in the totalitarian war. That, put simply, means that whenever they are beaten by armed forces they take their revenge on unarmed civilians. In this war, since the middle of November, they have been beaten at the Parque del Oeste, they have been beaten at the Pardo, they have been beaten at Carabanchel, they have been beaten on the Jarama, they have been beaten at Brihuega, and at Cordoba, and they are

Invitation to Hemingway and Stephen Spender's 1937 reading (Sylvia Beach Collection, Princeton University Library)

tainly it is more comfortable to spend their time disputing learnedly on points of doctrine. And there will always be new schisms and new fallings-off and marvelous exotic doctrines and romantic lost leaders, for those who do not want to work at what they profess to believe in, but only to discuss and to maintain positions—skillfully chosen positions with no risk involved in holding them, positions to be held by the typewriter and consolidated with the fountain pen. But there is now, and there will be from now on for a long time, war for any writer to go to who wants to study it. It looks as though we are in for many years of undeclared wars. There are many ways that writers can go to them. Afterward there may be rewards. But that need not bother the writer's conscience. Because the rewards will not come for a long time. And he must not worry about them too much. Because if he is like Ralph Fox and some others he will not be there to receive them.

This account of the fight between Hemingway and journalist Max Eastman was published in The New York Times, *14 August 1937, p. 15.*

HEMINGWAY SLAPS EASTMAN IN FACE

Both Authors Agree on This, but Ernest Denies He Was Then 'Stood on His Head'

RETURN BOUT IS SOUGHT

Clash in Publisher's Office Has to Do With 'Bull' and 'Death,' Both 'in Afternoon'

Ernest Hemingway says he slapped Max Eastman's face with a book in the offices of Charles Scribner's Sons, publishers, and Max Eastman says he then threw Hemingway over a desk and stood him on his head in a corner.

They both tell of the face-slapping, but Mr. Hemingway denies Mr. Eastman threw him anywhere or stood him on his head in any place, and says that he will donate $1,000 to any charity Mr. Eastman may name—or even to Mr. Eastman himself—for the pleasure of Mr. Eastman's company in a locked room with all legal rights waived.

Mr. Eastman's most recent book was "The Enjoyment of Laughter," published by Simon & Schuster.

He was sitting in Max Perkins's office at Scribner's Wednesday—Mr. Perkins is editor for that firm—discussing a new book called "The Enjoyment of Poetry," when Mr. Hemingway walked in, he said yesterday.

Using a few "Death in the Afternoon" phrases in what he describes as a "kidding manner," Mr. Hemingway commented on an essay by Mr. Eastman that had been entitled "Bull in the Afternoon."

Mr. Eastman had written:

"Come out from behind that false hair on your chest, Ernest. We all know you."

The volume containing this essay happened to be on Mr. Perkins's crowded desk, "and when I saw that," says Mr. Hemingway, "I began to get sore."

Writers Compare Chests

In what he hoped was a playful manner, he said, he bared his chest to Mr. Eastman and asked him to look at the hair and say whether it was false.

He persuaded Mr. Eastman to bare his chest and commented on the comparatively hairless condition.

"We were just fooling around, in a way," Mr. Hemingway said yesterday. "But when I looked at him and I thought about the book, I got sore. I tried to get him to read to me, in person, some of the stuff he had written about me. He wouldn't do it. So that's when I socked him with the book."

"Was he in a chair or standing up?"

"He was standing over there," pointing to a window with a window seat in Mr. Perkins's office. "I didn't really sock him. If I had I might have knocked him through that window and out into Fifth Avenue. That would be fine, wouldn't it? That would have got me in wrong with my boss, and he might have had me arrested. So, though I was sore, I just slapped him. That knocked him down. He fell back there on the window seat."

"But how about throwing you over the desk?" Mr. Hemingway was asked, "and standing you on your head in a corner?"

"He didn't throw anybody anywhere. He jumped at me like a woman—clawing, you know, with his open hands. I just held him off. I didn't want to hurt him. He's ten years older than I am."

Mr. Perkins's office retains the somewhat Old World atmosphere that it had in the days—not long past—when it was the rule that gentlemen should not smoke in Scribner's because women were employed in the offices.

"How about books and papers being knocked off the desk?" Mr. Hemingway was asked. "Mr. Eastman says——"

"Sure, some books were knocked off. He jumped at me, I held him off, there was a little, a little wrestle."

According to the Eastman version, after Mr. Hemingway was knocked down he patted Mr. Eastman's shoulder in an embarrassed fashion and smiled.

Hemingway Felt Sorry

Mr. Hemingway explained that he had felt sorry for Mr. Eastman, for he knew that he had seriously embarrassed him by slapping his face.

"The man didn't have a bit of fight. He just croaked, you know, at Max Perkins. 'Who's calling on you? Ernest or me?' So I got out. But he didn't do any throwing around. He just sat and took it."

"I felt sorry for him. Max Perkins told me, he said 'no man has any right to humiliate a man the way you have.' And I guess he's right. I feel kind of sorry, but he shouldn't go around telling these lies."

Mr. Hemingway had a large swelling over his left eye, high up on his forehead. Asked if this was a result of the battle of Thursday he grinned and shook his head.

He pulled off his coat and showed a deep scar in the biceps of his right arm.

"Max Eastman didn't do that to me, either," he said. He showed another scar. "Or that."

Mr. Hemingway gave his present weight at a little under 200 pounds, said that Mr. Eastman was narrower at the shoulders, just as big around the waist.

"Here's a statement," he offered as the interview closed. "If Mr. Eastman takes his prowess seriously—if he has not, as it seems, gone in for fiction—then let him waive all medical rights and legal claims to damages, and I'll put up $1,000 for any charity he favors or for himself. Then we'll go into a room and he can read his book to me—the part of his book about me. Well, the best man unlocks the door."

Mr. Hemingway is sailing for Spain today. It is understood that Mr. Eastman left yesterday to spend a week-end at Martha's Vineyard.

Mr. Perkins and other members of the Scribner staff refused to do more than verify the fact that the affair had taken place, taking the stand that "this is a personal matter between the two gentlemen in question."

Two manuscript pages for the speech Hemingway delivered before the Second American Writers' Congress in New York, 4 June 1937 (Glenn Horowitz, Library of Clinton J. Smullyan, *Item 33, 1992)*

they cannot bother him. But because of the

difficulty of his trade a writer making... is always sure of eventual recognition only romantics think that there are really good writers are always rewarded under any system of government... but now really good writers are a rarity. In a time of war and... the trade of writing it is to be followed...

...element. That element is danger. To find out what is true in a war you must first go to the war. Then you must go in the lines. Then you must be in battle. Until you have done that you can, be as a writer, believe nothing that you

They have nothing to

There is only one system of government that cannot produce good writers

Sinclair Lewis's review of Hemingway's To Have and Have Not *was published in* Newsweek, *10 (8 October 1937), p. 34.*

Glorious Dirt

It is interesting and significant that President Roosevelt, in his Cleveland speech of Oct. 5, and Ernest Hemingway in his new novel, "To Have and Have Not," published Oct. 15 (Scribners, $2.50), should have united in giving America a new philosophy. Philosopher Roosevelt said: "In respect to national problems, the excellently educated man and woman form the least worthwhile opinions." Philosopher Hemingway goes farther, and in this alleged novel, which is not a novel at all but a group of thinly connected tales of tough seafaring and tougher drinking ashore, on the Florida Keys, he demonstrates that all excellently educated men and women are boresome and cowardly degenerates, while unlettered men engaged in rum running and the importation of Chinese coolies are wise and good and attractive—although it seems that they do not really run rum to gain virtue, but because there is nowhere in America any industrial chance for a decent man.

Following these spiritual guidances, it is easy to see that to produce a nation of noble and blissful people we have only to eliminate Groton, Harvard, and all reading—including the novels of Mr. Ernest Hemingway.

My friend Mr. Hemingway was recently reported by the public prints as demonstrating to my friend Mr. Max Eastman that he had a lot of hair on his chest, and that anybody who didn't believe it was a lot of things to be expressed in a home journal only by the ——. He needn't have been so violent. Why, Mr. Hemingway is so virile and hairy that the hairs stick right through the pages of his book and positively bruise the fingers. He makes it clear that no real man ever thinks of anything save adultery, alcohol, and fighting—preferably fighting with a submachine gun, ending in such quantities of blood that the saloon porter has to clean it up in buckets.

Now this would all be very good if the killings were nice exciting killings, as in Mr. Dashiell Hammett. But while one killing is—as Mr. Hemingway gloatingly and often points out—very jolly and inspirational, two killings are commonplace, three are annoying, and four in a row are pretty dull. And that is the eventual criticism of this "novel"; not that Hemingway has a barbaric love of violence, not that all his characters are writhing knots of neurotic misery, not that he feels that it is brave and original to make poor Messrs. Scribners print out in his book all the four-letter words which 45 years ago, in Sauk Center, we also thought to be brave

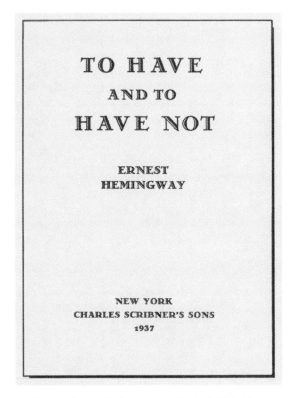

TO HAVE
AND TO
HAVE NOT

ERNEST
HEMINGWAY

NEW YORK
CHARLES SCRIBNER'S SONS
1937

Title page for the only Hemingway novel set in the United States

and original, but that after a few pages, these yarns become irritatingly dull.

And this thin screaming, this little book of not more than 75,000 words, is Mr. Hemingway's first novel in eight years—the first since the rich and exhilarating "Farewell to Arms." It continues logically the combination of puerile slaughter with senile weariness which was betrayed a couple of years ago in his hunting chronicle "The Green Hills of Africa."

Please, Ernest! You could have been the greatest novelist in America, if you could have come to know just one man who wasn't restricted to boozing and womanizing. Perhaps you still can be. Please quit saving Spain and start saving Ernest Hemingway.

V. S. Pritchett published this review of To Have and Have Not *in the British periodical* Now & Then, *no. 58 (Winter 1937), pp. 29–30.*

While every other American writer of importance was up to the neck in Left-wing politics, Mr. Hemingway went big game hunting in Africa and experimented with prose style. How long would he be able to resist direct reference to the social troubles of his country? Not long, as his new book shows. He has reacted to the prevailing wind and in his own fashion; and you can see that he has too great a dose of American herd instinct in him, to care for prolonged thought about anything. Thought leads to radicalism and he is American enough to pretend to himself that he doesn't like that because radicals are not generally noted for being tough.

The traditional American way of dealing with this awkward temperament is to revive pioneer feeling and get right away from civilization to where men are men and generally refer to each other as sons of bitches. And you measure your contempt for present society or civilization by showing that, rotten as it is for, say, the textile workers, it is worse still for that cream of humanity, the son of a bitch. When these dogs can't make a go of it, then society and civilization must be in a mess.

The advantage of taking this line is that you are still not a radical nor an intellectual, nor anything that anyone can put a finger on. So Harry Morgan is created, a huge ugly perfect animal, trying to make money out of his boat down at Key West. He takes a holiday-maker out deep-sea fishing and the holiday-maker swindles him; he goes in for smuggling Chinese and does a murder, a distinctly gratuitous murder. With his boat gone, the bootleg trade gone, fishing gone, money gone, he agrees at last to taking over a party of Cuban assassins and revolutionaries. He takes a Thomson gun too, and that is the end of him. His wife, like some monumental Sophie Tucker, laments him; and millionaires and writers sit around in their yachts in the harbour worrying about income tax, drinking too much, drugging too much, exchanging too many wives and brooding upon their respective sexual capacities. In the tough world, rutting is everything.

This is all rather like Lawrence but written in the vernacular. Our roving camera reports . . . that Mr. Hemingway finds men are no longer men in American civilization. He is a herd man, he glories in being a herd man, but the herd has got foot and mouth or something like it and the few remaining healthy bulls are dying out. This makes him very angry. Somewhere there must be triumphant simplicity. If not in the towns, then in the hunter's struggle with nature; if not there, then perhaps in prose style. He became a Roman Catholic in Spain and so simplicity has become something conceived as ritual. It is strange to find this enemy of the artifices of present society—birth control is one—writing the most completely unsimple prose; indeed, consciously intoning his matter as if he were groping his way toward a method of writing the great American

saga or epic. One looks at the work of all young writers of importance and sees in Hemingway the generic traits; an escape from the sensitive civilized personality into the vernacular, lowest-common-denominator personality, desire to be a mere first person singular, a unit, an anonymous singer. There is this craving of the educated to be uneducated, to destroy the *bourgeois* in oneself so that the subject may be more than life size, epic and magnificent and not whittled away by private sensibility. Whether Harry Morgan is of that dimension will be a matter of opinion; but there is no doubt that Mr. Hemingway's new book shows this literary dilemma in a new and interesting phase; and that he maintains the modern Catholic tradition of pungent criticism in very lively fashion.

Most reviewers of To Have and Have Not, *such as George Stevens, who published this review in the* Saturday Review of Literature, *16 (16 October 1937), pp. 6–7, considered it Hemingway's weakest work of fiction.*

Two Kinds of Life

Down in Key West the have-nots can take their choice of working for the F.E.R.A. at $6.50 a week like Albert Tracy, or going into the smuggling business, like Harry Morgan. The haves are all a bunch of contemptible parasites who lie around the harbor in their yachts, drinking, promiscuating, and evading the Bureau of Internal Revenue. The have-nots are the real people; they've got guts, and they know how to take it.

Hemingway is at his best with Harry Morgan, who tries to make an honest living with his 38-foot power boat, gets cheated out of $825 by one of the haves who chartered the boat for a month's fishing, and then goes in for rum-running and coolie-smuggling between Havana and Key West. Harry can kill a man when he has to without being either too casual or too introspective about it. The story of Harry is so fast and exciting that you read it without caring, at the time, whether it's just a glorified pulp or whether it really says something. What gives you is Harry's character, inside out, and always in Harry's own words. Harry's speech, and that of the Negro and the rummy who ship with him, cannot be improved upon for vigorous, natural American. It is the talk as much as the action that carries you along, if not breathless, certainly well stimulated.

But Harry is a very simple character. There is not much about him, or about the three short stories in which he figures—and which do not quite add up to a

Hemingway and journalist Martha Gellhorn in New York during the late 1930s. They were married on 21 November 1941 (Ernest Hemingway Collection, John F. Kennedy Library)

novel—to stick with you. There is an excellent two-page scene between Harry and his wife, written in human terms, which illuminates the subhumanity of many other scenes. But on the whole I remember less about "To Have and Have Not" after two weeks than about "A Farewell to Arms" after eight years or "The Sun Also Rises" after eleven. The idea of the book seems to be that you either live dangerously or you walk around dead. This idea doesn't have to be phony, as it was in "The Green Hat," for instance, and it isn't phony in Hemingway; but it is less than profound and short of impressive. In the third volume of "Men of Good Will," "The Proud and the Meek," Jules Romains explored the same dichotomy of haves and have-nots, with incomparably more subtlety, and with immeasurably superior results, both intellectually and artistically.

Hemingway has such vituperative contempt for people who do not live dangerously that he presents all of them—the "haves"—in caricature. These rich people are not without actual counterparts among the lunatic fringe of economic royalty, but as object lessons in Hemingway's book they are tiresome, because they are all alike. There is one in the beginning of the book named Johnson, and another in the closing section named Johnston; there is no evidence except the change in spelling that they are meant to be two different people, and the suspicion lurks with the reader that the change in spelling just might have been a careless mistake. The scenes in "To Have and Have Not" which do not involve Harry Morgan seem like interruptions, as if they didn't belong in the book at all. One such episode, concerning a third-rate but wealthy writer on the skids, is not so much bad Hemingway as bad John O'Hara. Hemingway's implicit, but belligerent, intolerance of complex personalities has come nearer and nearer the surface in his last three books, but he seems to have abandoned the 450-word sentence; so whatever it may not be, "To Have and Have Not" is good reading.

In this review of To Have and Have Not *from the* Saturday Review of Literature, *16 (16 October 1937), p. 8, Bernard DeVoto reiterates the charge that Hemingway's characters lack psychological complexity.*

Tiger, Tiger!

So far none of Ernest Hemingway's characters has had any more consciousness than a jaguar. They are physiological systems organized around abdomens, suprarenal glands, and genitals. They are sacs of basic instinct. Their cerebrums have highly developed motor areas but are elsewhere atrophied or vestigial. Their speech is rudimentary, they have no capacity for analytical or reflective thought, they have no beliefs, no moral concepts, no ideas. Living on an instinctual level, they have no complexities of personality, emotion, or experience.

Working exclusively with such people, Mr. Hemingway has created the most memorable prize-fighters, bull-fighters, literary hangers-on, fishermen, duck-shooters, and thugs that American literature has ever seen. With Frederic Henry, a man without consciousness caught up in a catastrophic mob-panic, and Catherine Barkley, a woman who lives in completely unconscious obedience to instinct, he has composed a novel that will last as long as any in its generation. No one else writing in America today can give a scene the reality that Mr. Hemingway gives it, or can equal his dialogue, which reaches the reader as living speech.

That is an achievement on which any writer who ever lived might well rest, but Mr. Hemingway seems uneasy about it. He has grown, as our reviewer says, increasingly belligerent about personalities more complex than those he creates, about ideas, about every kind of experience that is not localized in or near the viscera. But if his characters are incapable of ideas, Mr. Hemingway is not. Their mindlessness is itself the assertion of an idea. It is one of Mr. Hemingway's root ideas and has come to dominate his work. Every so often it should be taken out and scrutinized.

Since the thinking of the Hemingway characters has been confined to a form of omphalic irritation, they have not usually had any social awareness. The social significance of "To Have and Have Not" is also negligible. The dice which Mr. Hemingway is rolling are so openly and flagrantly loaded that he cannot mean us to think of his sterile millionaires and his gonadotropic "conchs" in economic terms. The social assertions and findings are so naive, fragmentary, and casual that they cannot be offered as criticism of the established order: beside them, the simplest of the blue-jeans-and-solidarity Cinderella stories that *The New Masses* was praising three or four years ago would seem profound. The significance of the title is not sociological: it is one with the significance of Jake's wound in "The Sun Also Rises" and with the symbolism of the plaster cast in which the hero of "A Farewell to Arms" had to make love. The millionaires and the literary lice are not the "haves"– they are the "have-nots." The "haves" are the conchs, and particularly Harry Morgan. Just what it is that Harry Morgan has and his oppressors lack we are told specifically and repeatedly. Mr. Hemingway has given us the supporting argument before.

It is curious where that argument takes you– where it has taken Mr. Hemingway. "Since he was a boy," one of his companions says of Harry Morgan, "he never had no pity for nobody. But he never had no pity for himself either." Quite clearly, for Mr. Hemingway the second half of that antithesis is a complete justification of the first half. If you do not pity yourself you need not pity anyone, and conversely you must not pity yourself lest you grow weak by pitying someone else. Yet one wonders whether a man is completely vindicated and sufficiently praised when it is said of him that he does not pity himself. One wonders if refusal to pity himself is enough to make Harry Morgan so admirable as Mr. Hemingway considers him. He breaks faith with and murders the Chinaman who employs him; after rum-running and miscellaneous violence, he becomes an accessory to bank robbery and more murder; and he finishes up with a quadruple murder. But floods of adrenalin are always surging into his blood stream, and, when he is wounded, both his central and his sympathetic nervous systems are polarized in support of his will to live. Mr. Hemingway is in the position of saying that nothing else matters.

"He never had no pity for nobody. But he never had no pity for himself either." It is not by chance that that analysis summons up an image of a trapped animal escaping by gnawing off its foot. "She watched him go out of the house, tall, wide-shouldered, flat-backed, his hips narrow, moving, still, she thought, like some kind of animal, easy and swift and not old yet." Also, "Him, like he was, snotty and strong and quick, and like some kind of expensive animal." We have reached the end of a path that Mr. Hemingway has been traveling for a long time. The highest praise he can give a man is to say that he is like an animal.

You see, it is only the animals who never deny life by forsaking the level of pure instinct. They are clean, honest, unpitying. They live in the reality of blood-consciousness, immersed in primary and direct experience: hunger, thirst, desire, alertness, wariness, aggressiveness. When they couple they do not weave a dishonest poetry over the clean delight of physiological function. When they kill, they kill without guilt, without remorse, without rationalization. They do not pose; they do not talk nobly; they do not live in a fog of thought, in the diseased secretion of the mind that betrays and enfeebles man. They do not kid themselves with ideas; they do not delude themselves with reason or reverie; instead, they are clean, sure, and very strong. They pity neither themselves nor other animals. They live instinctively, they defend themselves to the death, and every mammal pleases but only man is vile. What gave the death of the bull its tragic beauty was the fact that it perished at the moment of total aggressiveness, charging at its mortal enemy with all the physiology of its animal nature concentrated in the instinctive, self-justifying act of destruction. And now, compared with the human world which gives the sterile dominion over the potent, how beautiful is the long curve of the shark diving for gouts of blood.

Every man to his preference. Mr. Hemingway is certainly entitled to fall in love with sharks if he wants to, and our literature is the richer for his admiration. There has been, of course, much anthropophobia in modern literature. If the admirers of D. H. Lawrence, for instance, have not consciously loved alligators, they are at least accustomed to praise the faculties of alligators that may be discerned in man. But it is hard to see just how man himself may profitably employ the idea and just what reference either the alligator or the bull has to the problems man is working with in the modern world. And it will be interesting to see how the literary left, which temporarily regards Mr. Hemingway as an ally, will adapt his conclusions when adopting them. The cult of blood-consciousness and holy violence, as well as the clean beauty of the shark, has so far been the property of their political opponents.

It would be even more interesting to find out what Mr. Hemingway thinks of Mr. Robinson Jeffers. Utilizing the diseased secretion of thought to the utmost, Mr. Jeffers has also reached the conclusion that the animals are superior to man, but he finds the waving grasses still more admirable. Unpitying alligator or undeluded chlorophyll—which shall we prefer, which shall be the measure of things?

In addition to reporting the Spanish Civil War for the North American Newspaper Alliance (NANA), Hemingway also wrote articles about it for Arnold Gingrich's short-lived politically aware periodical, Ken. *This article, published on 7 April 1938 (pp. 36–37), was Hemingway's first contribution to this liberal magazine.*

THE TIME NOW, THE PLACE SPAIN

It takes just under sixteen minutes from the time the big Italian naval bombers leave their bases on the Island of Mallorca until they are over the port of Valencia. In one minute and a half from the time they are sighted they are over the center of the city. In that time they can dump their stuff and go. There is not any time to get pursuit planes up, and German anti-aircraft is the only anti-aircraft I've seen yet that is really worth a damn. So the Italians love to bomb Valencia. And they love to bomb Barcelona, which is the same business, and easier, because bigger, with more sprawled out workers' districts to hit.

They even let one of Mussolini's boys come and bomb these two cities until the Spanish government bombed the Italian air-base at Mallorca. Then they decided there was danger involved and sent him home. He has probably been decorated by now. For the Italians decorate as easily as they panic; and they can panic with the specialists; with the very, very best. Small bodies of Portuguese infantry, some of whom were captured by the Germans, had their backsides painted green by their captors, and were returned to the Allied lines during the 1914–18 war bearing large signs lettered NOT WORTH KEEPING; may have exceeded the Italian average troops in sheer velocity of retreat. But if you hide the bicycles, my money will still go on the Italians.

This does not mean that Italian troops cannot fight. They fought well for two days at Guadalajara. But it was an eight-day battle. And on the tenth day we could not find them on our maps of that district and had to go into Madrid for new maps.

We found the dead, and the best ones were the dead ones, as always; and by the way they lay they showed the merit of their dying. We found vast quantities of cartridges, automatic rifles, machine guns, trench mortars, shells, trucks, tractors, tanks, guns, piled and scattered all along the roads, in dumps and in the fields and scrub oak forests. We found many prisoners hidden in caves, barns, straw-stacks and sometimes just cowering in ditches. But we could not find the Italian army on that map. They had pulled out. And no one could find them for a long time after that.

Now that is the weak link in the fascist chain. Mussolini has forged a people into a war machine. Some of them are good fighters, and he has some excellent troops. His Alpine troops are as good as any in the world. But he needs those good troops to defend his frontiers, and in a war good troops have a way of getting killed early. Mussolini, to make war, as soon as he has used up his elite, has to depend on the ordinary run of the mine conscripts. The average Italian conscript is only a passable soldier, even if he is exceptionally well-led, and there never have been enough brave, cool, non-panicky Italians in Italy, not even in Caesar's time, to officer an army of the size Mussolini has built.

The Italian peasantry are a sound, solid, hard working, peaceful, very wise and excellent people. Italian workers are capable and skillful and I have seen them many times both generous and brave. The middle class are like any other middle class except that they are more patriotic and now have less money. Their upper class are either very good or very, very stinko. Also they are prac-

tically extinct. But the sum of this people does not add up as soldiers.

Fascism in Italy is the bluff of a bully playing at soldier. You have to have known the man Mussolini beforehand; before he was in power and made his legend, to know this. You have to know that he was not hot stuff in the war; that he was never even decorated on a front where they decorated plenty of times for attacking when the order was to attack; that he was never wounded in action but took advantage of slight wounds caused by the explosion of an Italian trench mortar to leave the front permanently early in the war; although he was featuring his prowess as an athlete and duelist in 1918 while good men were dying.

You have to realize that Italian militarism is not, like German militarism, the expression of a people that history has shown to be suited to be soldiers. Italian militarism is the romantic thinking of men who were not brave and want to be; of men who were not in the war, and would like to have been; of a race of patriots who like to imagine themselves as soldiers; and are not good at it.

Hemingway with Loyalist soldiers at the Ebro River, April 1938

<u>Ernest Hemingway</u>

First U.S. serial Rights only
10,497 wds

NIGHT BEFORE BATTLE.

At this time we were working in a shell smashed house
that over-looked the Casa del Campo in Madrid. Below us a
battle was being fought. You could see it ~~spread out across~~,
spread out below you and over the hills, could smell it, could
~~taste the~~ dust of it, and the noise of it was one great
glittering
~~splittering~~ sheet of rifle and automatic rifle fire rising and
dropping and in it came the crack of the guns and the bubbly
rumbling of the outgoing shells fired from the batteries behind
us, the thud of their bursts and then the rolling yellow clouds
But
of dust ~~it~~ It was just too far to film well.

We had tried working closer but they kept sniping at
the camera and you could not work. The big camera was the most
expensive thing we had and if it was smashed we were through.
We were making the film on almost nothing and all the money was
in the cans of film and the cameras. We could not afford to
waste film and you had to be awfully careful of the cameras.

The day before we had been sniped out of a good place
to film from and I had to crawl back holding the small camera
to my belly, trying to keep my head lower than my shoulders,
hitching along on my elbows, the bullets whocking into the
brick wall over my back and twice spurting dirt *over me.*

Our heaviest attacks were made in the afternoon, God
knows why, as the fascists then had the sun at their backs,
and it shone on the camera lenses and made them blink like a
helio and the moors would open up on the flash. They knew all

Typescript for the opening of one of Hemingway's Spanish Civil War stories (Sotheby Parke Bernet, Goodwin Collection, Item 156, 29 March 1977)

There is a leavening in Italian militarism, of men who were suited to war; there are some fair generals and one excellent general, Badoglio. They also have a really first rate engineer corps. But the war in Spain has shown again that average Italian troops only really flourish in battle when the conditions can be brought as nearly as possible to approximate those of assassination.

In this last year I have watched them run too far at Guadalajara; have seen too many Fiat pursuit planes hang up in the sun afraid to dive because that dive might lead to death; have seen too many prisoners lie and crawl to save their hides (where good soldiers simply would have kept their mouths shut), later to change their stories and become so very brave and patriotic when they knew their hides were safe; and seen too much of that great, spouting, roaring murder that Italians love to do (see little Mussolini's book) when they think nobody will come amurdering back; to believe that fascism has strengthened their characters very much.

No, they are still Italians. They are the ones who are afraid to die and still want to be soldiers (you can be afraid to die and *not* want to be a soldier and still be a good one); and they still cry and moan for "*Mama mia*" when they're hit. An officer still has to put them so they almost touch each other. He can't scatter them very widely, because if he does they won't be there when he comes back. They need a feeling of fraternal contact, and I guess they really need *Mama mia* too. You can't take them too far away from *Mama mia* and have them fight on strange hillsides the way the French fought over a thousand strange hills they did not know under Napoleon. And that does not mean that one does not think mother love an admirable virtue; nor that one does not know that a man who is a good soldier in battle is often a bastard at any other time.

This year you have seen the Garibaldi Battalion fight, so that you know there are still good Italian fighters; you've seen them calm and cold and brave, as fine troops as ever lived, and Pacciardi, gay and beautiful in action, the way that Ney must have been; but that is five hundred out of a nation. In Italy there might be a hundred thousand troops out of a million and a half that would be that good. And there might not be fifty thousand. I know what they've sent to Spain in flyers and in troops have stunk.

The bombers assassinate very well. But they will not fight. If they had wanted to fight they could have come, protected by pursuit planes, or taking chances by themselves if their pursuit was too frightened to take off, and cut the Spanish government

main communications only forty miles from Sagunto, a coast town on the main road to Teruel. They could have almost paralyzed operations in that battle by bombing three different towns and blocking that road. But there was danger in the operation so they never tried it. They just bombed Sagunto every night—killing non-combatants, women and children, and having good clean Italian Fascist fun the way it was in Abyssinia where they had no planes against them. They are terrific when they have no planes against them.

So what? Have you read Hitler's speech? If you have you know there is going to be war. One thing can delay it. If Hitler loses confidence in his allies.

So why not beat the Italians in Spain? There still is time and you're fighting on somebody else's home grounds. It is the only chance to avoid war and they are not hard to beat. I remember a general saying to me at Guadalajara, he's dead now and so are most of the friends you made last year, "So, knowing they were Italians, we initiated a maneuver that we would never have attempted against other troops."

Why not try to beat them in Spain now? The Spaniards will do it gladly if they can only be allowed to buy planes, artillery and munitions. The Spaniards do not take the Italians very seriously and they will beat them any time Mussolini sends them into action. I went to bed for the last five months hoping every night, before I went to sleep, that they would attack again. But they never attacked. They never made the offensive that they always threatened.

They simply moved, in trucks, into the undefendable towns in the lost North; into Santander and Gijon. They followed in the wake of the destruction the German planes and the German and Italian artillery caused among the defending Basque, Montanese and Asturian militia men and occupied hills when the defenders had been blasted off them. Often the defenders counterattacked and drove the Italians back. One hill, defending Gijon, they retook five times without artillery support and with no planes.

With planes and artillery to back them, the men of the North could have given Mussolini his second Guadalajara and Italy her third Caporetto. But they had no planes—that's a story for another time—and finally no ammunition; so Santander is an Italian victory. It is the favorite type of Italian victory; where troops move in in trucks after the fighting's over; and there are more telegrams of congratulation than there are casualties. And all this time, while the fascists were looking for easy, sure victories in the north to borrow money on, the gov-

Dust jacket for Hemingway's narration for the soundtrack of the movie directed by Joris Ivens and produced to raise money for Spanish Loyalists

ernment was forging an army. That's another story too.

One thing is certain now. If you want to break fascism you have to hit it at its weakest link. Its weakest link is Italy. It will take them some time to form another chain if that link goes. It will take plenty of time if the other allies, Germany and Japan, lose confidence in that link. Fascism can still be beaten in Spain the same way Napoleon was beaten in Spain.

Right now there is a lot of talk about oceans. It seems we are protected by the oceans so we do not need to care what happens. But, brother, when a war starts we will be put in it. And you'll hate those oceans, both the Atlantic and the Pacific, when you ride over them in the good old vomit-stink of transports. There is only one way to avoid, or to postpone, that ride. That is to beat Italy, always beatable, and to beat her in Spain, and beat her now. Otherwise you will have to fight tougher people than the Italians, and don't let anybody ever tell you that you won't.

Eugene Jolas, editor of transition, *a Paris-based little magazine that ceased publication in 1938, posed questions to contemporary writers; Hemingway's response to the questionnaire was published in the April-May 1938 issue, p. 237.*

Inquiry Into The Spirit And Language of Night

I have asked a number of writers to answer the following questions:

1. *What was your most recent characteristic dream (or day-dream, waking-sleeping hallucination, phantasma)?*
2. *Have you observed any ancestral myths or symbols in your collective unconscious?*
3. *Have you ever felt the need for a new language to express the experiences of your night mind?*

EUGENE JOLAS

Ernest Hemingway:

Answering your first question–I usually dream about whatever am doing at the time or what I have read in the paper; i.e., run into grizzly with wrong caliber shells for rifle; trigger spring sometimes broken, etc. when shooting; sometimes shoot very large animal of some kind I've never seen; or very detailed fighting around Madrid, house to house fighting, etc., after the paper; or even find myself in bed with Mrs. S... (not too good). Have had lovely experiences with Miss Dietrich, Miss Garbo and others in dreams too, they always being awfully nice (in dreams).

2. Second question, don't know much about.

3. I haven't ever felt this as would like to be able to handle day and night with same tools and believe can be done but respect anyone approaching any problem of writing with sincerity and wish them luck.

Hemingway wrote these prefaces for All the Brave *(New York: Modern Age Books, 1938), a volume of paintings by Spanish artist Luis Quintanilla.*

THREE PREFACES

March 10, 1938. Key West

A year ago today we were together and I asked Luis how his studio was and if the pictures were safe.

"Oh it's all gone," he said, without bitterness, explaining that a bomb had gutted the building.

"And the big frescoes in University City and the Casa del Pueblo?"

"Finished," he said, "all smashed."

"What about the frescoes for the monument to Pablo Iglesias?"

"Destroyed," he said. "No, Ernesto, let's not talk about it. When a man loses all his life's work, everything that he has done in all his working life, it is much better not to talk about it."

These paintings that were destroyed by the bomb, and those frescoes that were smashed by artillery fire and chipped away by machine gun bullets were great Spanish works of art. Luis Quintanilla, who painted them, was not only a great artist but a great man. When the Republic that he loved and believed in was attacked by the fascists, he led the attack on the Montaña Barracks that saved Madrid for the government. Later, studying military books at night while he commanded troops in the daytime, he fought in the pines and the gray rocks of the Guadar-

Dust jacket for Hemingway's drama, adapted by Benjamin Glaser and produced in New York, 6 March through 18 May 1940. Contrary to the claim, the play was not a success.

rama; on the yellow plain of the Tagus; in the streets of Toledo, and back to the suburbs of Madrid where men with rifles, hand grenades, and bundled sticks of dynamite faced tanks, artillery, and planes, and died so that their country might be free.

Because great painters are scarcer than good soldiers, the Spanish Government ordered Quintanilla out of the army after the fascists were stopped outside Madrid. He worked on various diplomatic missions, and then returned to the front to make these drawings. The drawings are of war. They are to be looked at; not written about in an introduction.

There is much to say about Quintanilla, but the drawings say all they need to say themselves.

ERNEST HEMINGWAY

I wrote this and left for Spain on the eighteenth of last March. Mr. Elliot Paul, who has known Quintanilla's work for many years and is much better qualified to write of it than I would ever be, had agreed to write a long critical introduction. I had promised to write a short one of a thousand words or less.

On the boat going over I tried to write this but it was quite impossible. I found that I had said what I felt about Luis Quintanilla in three hundred and fourteen words and in the face of what was happening just then in Spain the other thousand would not come. I did not worry particularly about the matter because I knew that, even if I should never be able to furnish a further introduction, there was this short one, and there would be a fine long one by Elliot Paul. Then, too, the things to see were Luis's drawings.

For a while in the months of March and April the Spanish war went very badly. I was always sure of an ultimate victory by the government; but there were many days when it looked as though long before that victory should be achieved a great many of us would be released from any necessity to write prefaces.

It was on one of those days, one of the very worst of those days, that I received a cable from New York saying that unless the publisher received the introduction by a certain date he would cancel the contract. So that night I wrote the introduction which follows and sent it off.

April 18, 1938, Somewhere in Spain

They are marvelous drawings. Quintanilla is a great Spanish artist and an old friend. He fought in the revolution and he fought in the war. I should now sit at the typewriter and write about how great he is as an artist, man, soldier, and revolutionary. But the typewriter is not going very well this evening.

Elliot Paul will write you all about the great painter Quintanilla is and I will bear testimony that his work has all been destroyed. I have seen the wreck a bomb made of his studio and looked at what artillery and machine gun fire did to his frescoes in University City. They are gone, all right, along with a lot of other things; along with too many other things. And what is there to be done about all this? Nothing. You can shut up and forget it. Which Quintanilla has done. Also he has gone on working.

Now if there were three candles to write this by instead of two candles it would probably be a brighter and more cheery introduction. You need good light to write introductions by. That is how they differ from dispatches. You can write dispatches by any sort of light but introductions need a better light and more time. So if anybody does not like this introduction, let

them write an introduction of their own and I will be glad to sign it for them.

At this point in the introduction there should be a little literature about what it means to a man to have all his life's work destroyed. So at this point we will omit that bit of literature and take it for granted that nobody thinks it is funny for all the work a man has done in his life to be destroyed. Is that all right?

We will just take it for granted that it is unfortunate.

Now what comes next in an introduction? Certainly; that is it. The comparison with Goya. So let us just skip that too. Enough people will make that without our having to put it into this introduction and the candles are getting low.

So what comes now in an introduction to drawings of war? There certainly should be some reference to war itself. What do you think of war, Mr. Hemingway? Answer: I find it unpleasant. I have never liked it. But I have a small talent for it.

Do you like drawings of war? Answer: no. But these are very good ones. You probably will like them.

What do you like in war? Answer: to win it and get it over with and have peace.

What would you do in that event? Answer: I would go to The Stork Club.

You are evidently not a serious fellow. Answer: perhaps not.

You should not speak with such levity on such serious subjects. Answer: just where are you talking from, yourself?

That was New York speaking, but this is Barcelona, and yesterday was Tortosa, and tomorrow will be Tortosa again, and it is very difficult to write an introduction when the only thing you can think about is holding the line of the Ebro. Compared to the necessity of holding the line of the Ebro everything, including drawings of war by a great artist and one of your best friends, seems like chicken crut, and that is what makes this an unpleasant and churlish piece of writing.

If it was not for that you could remember the old days when we worked hard in Madrid together. That summer—when I wrote a book and Quintanilla did his great etchings and we all worked hard in the day and met in the evening to drink beer in the Cervecería in the Pasaje Alvarez and Quintanilla explained quietly and simply to me the necessity for the revolution—is a long way away now. It seems so far away that it is like a different world. It is like the old world there was once when, seeing a sign-board saying 350 kilometers to such and such a town, you knew that if you followed that road you would get to that town. While now you know that if you follow that road you will get killed.

All that makes a little difference in you, and tonight the writing is not easy.

But the publishers demand an introduction, or they will cancel a contract. That is all right. They will get their introduction. It is coming out on the paper all the time. A letter at a time. A word at a time, a page at a time it comes out as well as any toothpaste squeezes and probably reads as attractively as some of the viler toothpastes taste. All that is necessary is for the candles to hold out so you can see the keys. But here she comes, publishers, here comes the good old introduction and if you want five thousand words there are different forms of the same word that could be written five thousand times and still quite a lot of contempt be unexpressed.

So now let's see. How many words are there to be? Put in a few more words for the publisher. The reader does not need them because the reader can look at the pictures. They are nice pictures, too. Are they not, reader? That is something of what war looks like; a very small part of it. And you must not be shocked at the dead Moors or think that they are disgusting because there is one thing that you learn in war and that is that a dead enemy always smells good.

So now we are getting to the end of the candles and the end of the introduction, I hope you like the introduction, I hope you like the pictures; I hope the publisher has not been annoyed, it was just kidding you know, publisher old boy, old boy. I hope you like Mr. Quintanilla; if you meet him, give him my regards.

You see there are quite a lot of Americans strung out along the Ebro too, along with Belgians, Germans, Frenchmen, Poles, Czechs, Croats, Bulgarians, Slovenes, Canadians, British, Finns, Danes, Swedes, Norwegians, Cubans, and the best Spaniards in the world. They are all waiting there for the decisive battle of the war to commence. So now if the introduction stops, please don't mind. It could easily go on much longer if I had learned the touch system so that I could write in the dark. But it would all be very much the same. Because everything except the Ebro seems very unimportant tonight.

ERNEST HEMINGWAY

May, 1938, Somewhere in Spain

At best an introduction is only a literary curiosity so we will let that particularly churlish piece of writing stand. It is a good example of the peculiar, unattractive, surly righteousness which certain phases of war can produce in people. It is peculiarly unjust because I was angry at Luis when I wrote it. I was angry at him, I suppose, because he was alive and too many other people you were fond of died that month.

Luis Quintanilla is one of the bravest men that I have ever known. War is not his trade and there is no reason for him ever to do any more of it. He did enough of it. But this was the time when the Italians had been beaten again up the Ebro above Cherta. They had been beaten by Lister's division, and another division, the Third, of the old Fifth Army Corps, in a bitter ten-day battle; and we knew that they would never take Tortosa. We also knew that there was something rotten on the left flank and it went, very suddenly, with old Duran holding all the mountains in between, and after ten days you had to give them what they never could have taken. At such times people become very bitter and unjust. Afterwards you apologize. So I apologize to Luis, and to Luis only. He knows the sort of thing we are talking about and he understands.

Then there is the reference to The Stork Club. That looks like levity and levity is unpardonable in a serious writer. I have learned that, because when I have committed levity it has never been pardoned. A serious writer should be quite solemn. If you joke about things, people do not take you seriously. These same people do not know there are many things you could not go through and keep sane if you do not joke, so it will be well to explain that levity has not been committed. The reference to The Stork Club is serious.

When you have sat at a table and been served a plate of water soup, a single fried egg and one orange after you have been working fourteen hours, you have no desire to be anywhere but where you were, nor to be doing anything but your work, but you would think, "Boy, I'll bet you could get quite a meal at The Stork tonight."

And when you would lie in the dark sometimes, with no company but the pictures in your head of what you had seen that day and all the other days, it was all right and there was always plenty to think about—military, political and personal. But sometimes you would think about how nice and noisy it would be at The Stork now, and that if you were at The Stork you would not have to think at all. You would just watch the people and listen to the noise.

In the old days in Madrid when Quintanilla and Elliot Paul and Jay Allen and I lived there, there were many places where you could eat as well as you could do at The Stork and have just as pleasant a time. But food is scarce in Madrid now and there are very few good things to drink. Hunger is a marvelous sauce and danger of death is quite a strong wine, they say, but under hunger the stomach shrinks so that when you finally get a chance at a series of decent meals you have much appetite in the eyes but no capacity for eating; and you become so used to danger that there is no exhilaration in it, only annoyance.

You keep The Stork, though, as a symbol of how well you would like to eat. Because this war in Spain is not being fought so that everyone will be reduced to a level of blockade rations but so that everyone can eat as well as the best.

There should be a lot about the old days in this, but a strange thing about the war is that it destroys the old days. Each day wipes out each other day and by the time you have two or three hundred days of it in the same scene where once you lived in peace, the memories, finally, are as smashed as the buildings. The old days and the old people are gone and nostalgia is something that you read about in books.

Later on, perhaps, it all rebuilds just as the buildings are rebuilt. It was all very simple in the old days. The old days were so simple that now they seem almost pitiful. If you want to have it simple now, you can do one thing: take orders and obey them blindly. That is the only simplicity that is left now.

If you are a writer and, now that you have seen it, you want to get some of it down before it should cauterize itself away, you must renounce the luxury of that simplicity. In writing you have to make your own mistakes. So now you are all ready to make them for awhile.

I would like to hope that, in writing from now on about this war, I will be able to do it as cleanly and as truly as Luis Quintanilla draws and etches. War is a hateful thing. It is inexcusable except in self-defense. In writing of it, a writer should be absolutely truthful because, of all things, it has had the least truth written of it.

There are various reasons for this. One is that it is very dangerous to see much of it, and anyone seeing very much of it at first hand will be either wounded or killed. If those at it are not wounded or killed, they are apt to become brutalized so that they lose their sensitivity to normal reactions. Or they can become so frightened that their reactions are not normal either. To write about it truly you have to know a great deal about cowardice and heroism. For there is very much of both, and of simple human endurance, and it is a long time since anyone has balanced them truly.

I envy Quintanilla very much that he has his drawings made. For now I have to try to write my stories.

This review of Hemingway's The Fifth Column and the First Forty-nine Stories *(New York: Scribners, 1938) was written by Malcolm Cowley for the* New Republic, *97 (2 November 1938), pp. 366–367. Like most reviewers, Cowley*

disliked the play but praised the four stories that had not previously appeared in a Hemingway collection: "The Short Happy Life of Francis Macomber," "The Capital of the World," "The Snows of Kilimanjaro," and "Old Man at the Bridge."

Hemingway in Madrid

Hemingway says in his preface, "This is only a play about counter espionage in Madrid. It has the defects of having been written in wartime, and if it has a moral it is that people who work for certain organizations have very little time for home life. There is a girl in it named Dorothy but her name might also have been Nostalgia." I should judge that "The Fifth Column" would need a little play-doctoring before production. There is too much commotion offstage, there are scenes that wouldn't be effective for lack of the proper timing, and no great skill is shown in the playwright's business of getting people in and out of doors. But the play reads like one of Hemingway's short stories, which is to say that it reads very well. The plot jumps ahead, the dialogue is sometimes tough, sometimes outrageously funny, and the minor characters are real creations—especially Max, the secret agent with a very tender heart and a face horribly deformed by torture.

The hero, Philip Rawlings, is the latest in a long line of Hemingway heroes, all of them brutal and reckless by day but wistful as little boys when alone at night with the women they love. As compared with Harry Morgan, of "To Have and Have Not," he shows an interesting development. Morgan, the lonely freebooter, had died in discovering the fellowship of the dispossessed: "No matter how, a man alone ain't got no bloody f———g chance." Philip is putting that discovery into action. He has the reputation of being a fancy war correspondent who spends his working hours wherever he can find women or whiskey. He likes to drink, that much is true. But in reality he is a hard-working agent in the counter-espionage service, acting under Communist Party orders. If he haunts the cafés along the Gran Via—"and the embassies and the Ministerio and Vernon Rodgers' flat and that horrible Anita"—it is because he is looking for spies.

He longs for the carefree life he used to lead in the 1920s. You can hear the bitterness in his voice when he tells a very young and virtuous American volunteer, "We of the older generation have certain leprous spots of vice which can hardly be eradicated at this late date. But you are an example to us." Again he says, "After this is over, I'll get a course of discipline to rid me of any anarchistic habits I may have acquired. I'll probably be sent back to working with pioneers." It is as if he were talking over the heads of the audience, to the editors of The New Masses. But in the midst of these sallies and asides, Hemingway is discussing an important theme, that of the individual serving an organization in which he believes, but not without moments of skepticism. Philip questions the means that must be employed—notably when there are prisoners to be given a third degree or fascist spies to be shot—and sometimes he questions the ends for which he is fighting. He wants to forget the war and take his girl to Kitzbühel for the skiing. Then suddenly a boy is killed from ambush, or a dog is wounded by shellfire and howls in the street, and Philip submits himself once more to party discipline. At the end, he decides to leave Dorothy because he loves her so much that she is interfering with his work. "I do not ask that," says poor tortured Max, his comrade. "No. But you would sooner or later. There's no sense babying me along. We're in for fifty years of undeclared wars and I've signed up for the duration."

The trouble is that although long-legged, bright-haired Dorothy is a symbol of the hero's nostalgia, and might be a symbol of ours if we saw her in the flesh, she is nothing of the sort when we read "The Fifth Column." She is presented there as a chattering, superficial fool, a perfect specimen of the Junior Leaguer pitching woo on the fringes of the radical movement, with the result that she keeps the play from being a tragedy or even a valid conflict between love and duty. If Philip hadn't left her for the Spanish people, he might have traded her for a flask of Chanel No. 5 and still have had the best of the bargain.

This same big book contains Hemingway's forty-nine short stories, the entire contents of "In Our Time," "Men Without Women" and "Winner Take Nothing," in addition to four new ones collected for the first time. Among them is "The Snows of Kilimanjaro," the only story in which he has allowed himself to be conventionally poetic; it describes the death of a writer, with disquieting touches of self-loathing and self-pity. Another story is his very latest, "Old Man at the Bridge," which was cabled from Barcelona in 1938. Six pages beyond it comes one of his oldest, "On the Quai at Smyrna," written, I think, in 1921. Essentially they are the same story, that of people caught in the aftermath of a great military defeat.

During the seventeen years of his literary career, Hemingway's short stories have changed very little. He has broadened the range of his technical effects, and his geographical background, and to some extent his human sympathies. The new stories

are not published like a few of the earlier ones, in the effort to be lurid or shocking. Yet those first stories defined his talent as a writer, and some of them I still prefer to his more recent work. When he wrote them he seemed to be closer to his material and more directly moved by it. Has he ever shown more compassion than in "The Battler" and "Indian Camp" and "My Old Man," all included in his first volume?

Reading the stories over again, you are impressed by how well they stand up in the face of a thousand products advertised to be just as good. You are also impressed by the number of them that deal with lust or violent death. In the first story—taking the order in which they are printed, not the order of writing—a rich woman shoots her husband in the back of the head with a hunting rifle. In the second, a Spanish boy plays at bull-fighting and is killed by an accidental thrust from a butcher knife. In the third, a writer dies of gangrene after reliving his violent past. In the fourth, an old man waits for death in the midst of a general retreat. Some of the others deal with suicide, abortion, self-mutilation, wartime insanity, lesbianism, death on the racetrack, death in the bull ring; one story is called "A Natural History of the Dead." People used to say that this choice of subjects was due to some unhealthy quirk, but I think there is another explanation. Every great writer—as Robert Cantwell said in his fine essay on Henry James—is a prophet in spite of himself. He tries to express the underlying spirit of his age, and that spirit will sometimes be carried into action. Hemingway's violence seemed excessive during the relatively quiet decade that followed the War. But now, after the fighting in Spain and China and the great surrender at Munich, it seems a simple and accurate description of the world in which we live.

Elmer Davis, like many other reviewers of The Fifth Column *and the First Forty-nine Stories, believed that Hemingway's omnibus collection of his short stories was better than* To Have and Have Not. *Davis's comments at the end of the review allude to Hemingway's preface to the collection. From the* Saturday Review of Literature, *18 (15 October 1938), p. 6.*

He Has Ground a New Edge

The news is that Hemingway is back again, and you can write off "To Have and Have Not" along with "The Prodigal Parents," "A Double-Barreled Detective Story," and other errors by men with a high fielding average. "The Fifth Column" is a play which was not produced because the first man who was going to produce it died and the next couldn't raise the money. (Let us hope the jinx wore out before it reached Mr. Maxwell Perkins at Scribner's.) But Hemingway had it published because he thought it might read well, and he is right. Also, his preface would serve as a pretty good review, except that he only says "if it is good." Well, it is good; no need to worry about that.

The fifth column, as people who follow the Spanish war news probably know, was the organization of rebel sympathizers in Madrid who were going to help Franco's four attacking columns take the town; and the play is about the counter-espionage organization that fights them. Among the group of Americans living in the Hotel Florida is Philip Rawlings, who posed as a barfly but actually was somebody of consequence in that organization. Next door to him was Dorothy Bridges ("her name," says Hemingway, "might also have been Nostalgia") who had come over to write magazine articles and was about fed up with Robert Preston—"one of those men who just use their wife-and-children as an opening wedge to get into bed with some one and then immediately afterwards they club you with them." By the time Philip had slept with her once or twice he began to think how good it would be to go some place where there was enough to eat and plenty of hot water and no war, and marry Dorothy and see what the kids would look like. But, says Hemingway, "the moral is that people who work for certain organizations have very little time for home life."

Enough about the plot; the point is that these people are all alive—Philip and Dorothy, and Antonio the hard-boiled Colonel in command of counter-espionage, and Max the German revolutionary whose face had been spoiled by the Nazis. Max and Antonio didn't like people who weakened; but Max at least could understand it. These people (except Dorothy) are all doing something; whether you agree with what they are doing a hundred per cent, or only fifty-one per cent, or no per cent, they are worth reading about. So far as a layman can see, the story ought to play well too.

Just for good measure are included Hemingway's forty-nine published short stories. There is not much to say about them, except that nobody else now living could show forty-nine stories that good. Hemingway says that while he was writing the play, more than thirty high-explosive shells hit the Hotel Florida, and that if the play is good, perhaps those shells helped write it. Maybe and maybe not; of his last four stories two were written in Africa where

things were peaceful, two in Spain; the two from Spain are only so-so, the two from Africa, "The Short Happy Life of Francis Macomber" and "The Snows of Kilimanjaro"—are right up among the best. Every middle-aged author has played with the idea of the man who dies before he got around to doing the things he always meant to do, but I cannot recall anybody else who has done it so well as it is done in "The Snows of Kilimanjaro."

"In going where you have to go," says Hemingway, "and doing what you have to do, and seeing what you have to see, you dull and blunt the instrument you write with. But I would rather have it bent and dulled and know I had to put it on the grindstone again and hammer it into shape and put a whetstone to it, and know that I had something to write about, than to have it bright and shining and nothing to say, or smooth and well-oiled in the closet, but unused." Well, he has got an edge on the instrument again—a real edge, not tinfoil; and maybe he doesn't have to go to Spain to get something to write about. He could probably write a good novel about his home town, if he sat down and really tried.

This review seems to have been written mostly by the author of the book, but that won't hurt it.

Hemingway published "The Writer as a Writer" in Direction, *2 (May–June 1939), p. 3. James Lardner, the son of author Ring Lardner, was killed in September 1938.*

The Writer as a Writer

It was in a room on the fifth floor of the Majestic Hotel in Barcelona last April and Jim Lardner, pale, good looking, immensely serious about himself and the world and the world and himself, but always quick smiling if you made a joke about either one, was going over and over the same question, "Where and how do you think I would really be most useful here in the Spanish War?"

He had not yet made up his mind to join the International Brigade and part of the time he wanted you to argue him out of that intention and part of the time he hoped to be argued into it. It was very interesting to him and you can see how it would be. It was he who was doing the joining or the not joining. I did not think he should go into the Brigade at that time, although I believed he had a perfect right to if he wanted to.

ERNEST HEMINGWAY

THE FIFTH COLUMN
AND THE FIRST
FORTY-NINE
STORIES

Dust jacket for the first publication of Hemingway's play; the volume also includes four stories that had not previously appeared in a collection of Hemingway's work—"The Short Happy Life of Francis Macomber," "The Snows of Kilimanjaro," "The Capital of the World," and "Old Man at the Bridge"

"You really want to know where you would be most useful? Really useful? Not just to have someone argue with you?"

"Of course."

"Then go to Madrid and stay in it until it falls and after it falls stay on and then come out and write the truth about what happened. You have no registered political beliefs, you are not down as a sympathiser with the loyalist cause and you can stay there, see what happens and write the truth when all those who have either politics or are considered loyalist sympathisers will have to get out, be locked up, or shot."

"But you don't think Madrid will fall, do you?"

"No," I said. "But it always can fall. It can fall either through treachery or, if they make a big offensive with as much stuff as they used here in Catalonia, they can encircle it and starve it out. You would have to wait for that chance; go through the siege and be there to write about what happens when the Fascists come in. Otherwise no one will ever know. I think that is the most important thing any man in your position can do."

"It sounds very far fetched to me," Jim said. "I don't like to even talk about the possibility of them taking Madrid."

"Neither do I. But you asked me where I thought you could be most truly useful and I told you what I thought."

"How long would I have to be there?"

"Maybe a year. Maybe longer."

"And what if they never took Madrid?"

"Why you'd be o.k. If they never took Madrid the Government would have won the war. That's what you want, isn't it?"

"Yes. But I don't want to be a cheer leader. I want to take an active part."

"O.K.," I said. "You asked me where I thought you would be most useful. I told you. If you want to argue about joining the Brigade go on down and argue with Jimmy Sheean. I tell you in this war you do not have to write any propaganda for the side you believe in. All you have to do is write the truth and be there where you can write it. That is the most difficult thing to do. If no honest man is in Madrid to write about what really happens if it ever falls it will be one of the tragedies of history. You're ideal for the job and I think it's the absolutely most useful thing you could do. I'd do it but they would throw me in the can the minute they came in and all I could do would be write another book like Knoestler's. That's as good a book as can be written on that subject. You could see it all."

"It sounds sort of like defeatist talk to me," said Jim. "And I think it is very far fetched."

Well, he joined the Brigade and soldiered well and everybody liked him and he was a fine kid and he ran into a fascist patrol, or onto a fascist post by mistake, in the night on the last night the Fifteenth Brigade was in the lines in the Sierra de Pandols and he was killed. His joining the Brigade was a fine example and he was a brave and cheerful soldier, if not a particularly skillful soldier, and he is dead.

There was no one in Madrid to do the job he could have done when the City fell to Franco and we have to depend for the truth on what happened there, and is happening there every day, on the dispatches of Mr. William Carney. As Jim said it seemed very far fetched at the time. But then writing is a very far fetched business and to be a writer you have to write even though you have to go far away or wait a long time to fetch the truth.

Critic and translator Samuel Putnam, an associate of Hemingway in Paris during the 1920s, published this evaluation of Hemingway's career in We Moderns: Gotham Book Mart, 1920–1940 *(New York: Gotham Book Mart, 1939), p. 35.*

ERNEST HEMINGWAY

Ernest Hemingway is not only one of the masters of modern English prose; he is one of the few, perhaps two or three, who in this generation have notably contributed to the shaping, and above all to the *purifying*, the *cleansing*, of our literary speech. With a surgical directness and unflinchingness he has pared away its fatty excesses and degenerations, bringing it back to something that is near at times to the King James Version of the Old Testament (one suspects that this may have been one of his models), and at other times to the geometric austerity of a Cubist painting of the classic period. For just as painting at the end of the nineteenth century, in the hands of the Post-Impressionists and particularly the early Matisse and the Fauves, had ended in an amorphous blurb and riot of color, so with the language that writers used—there was need of a Hemingway and a Stein with their palette-knives to remove the smudge and restore the blurred outlines, the *form*, of simple, direct, honest meaning.

But *meaning* there must be. Hemingway knew this when he wrote *The Sun Also Rises,* before he wrote *The Sun Also Rises,* and he has never once forgotten it. With the other sad young men of his hard living generation he preferred the truth that comes out the neck of a bottle to the lies that pass as truths. With the young Frenchmen of the *après-guerre* Hemingway and his kind might have exclaimed: "Nothing is left us but love for the night and our desire for *purity*." Hemingway, however, was not to stop here. He was not to be satisfied with the "purity" of an expatriate bar in the rue Delambre, or with that purity which comes from evading the best-seller list and substantial checks. No Ivory Tower could hold him long, not even one furnished with a cocktail bar. He was too deep in life, and the capacities for growth of man and artist in him were too big; he had to move on with his age. He was too used, for one thing, to getting at the meaning behind words. Purity was not enough. He had to ask: purity *for what*? Purity of meaning? What *was* the meaning? He began to find the answer, among the vets in the Florida quake, on the battlefields of Spain. He is still finding the answer. He tried to put the answer, a part of it, into his *To Have and Have Not*. But he is not done with the job yet. It is a big job, a big answer. Meanwhile, compare *To Have and Have Not* with *The Sun Also Rises,* and you will have the measure of a great artist's growth in a little more than a decade—a great artist and a brave one, brave enough to risk not writing a masterpiece once in a while, big enough to see the thing through.

Gene Van Guilder, a publicity man for the Sun Valley, Idaho, ski lodge, became friends with Hemingway in 1939. After Van Guilder was killed in a hunting accident on 29 October 1939, his widow asked Hemingway to deliver the eulogy, which was published in the Idaho Statesman, *2 November 1939, p. 4.*

Eulogy to Gene Van Guilder

You all know Gene. Almost every one here is better equipped to speak about him and has more right to speak of him than I have. I have written down these thoughts about him because if you trusted yourself simply to speak about Gene there might be a time when you would be unable to go on.

You all know that he was a man of great talent. He had great talent for his work, for writing and for painting. But he had something much more than that. He had a great talent for living and for communicating his love and enjoyment of life to others.

If it was a fine bright day and you were out in the hills with Gene, he made it into a better day. If it was a dark gloomy day and you saw Gene, he made it a lot less gloomy. There weren't any bad days when Gene was around. He gave something of himself to all those who knew him or worked with him. And what he gave us all was very precious because it was compounded of the rarest elements. It was made up of true goodness, of kindliness, of fairness and generosity, of good humor, of tolerance and of the love of life. What he gave us he gave for good.

We have that from him always. When I heard that Gene had died I could not believe it. I cannot believe now. Yes, technically he is dead. As we all must be. But the thing he gave to those who knew him was not a thing that ever perishes and the spirit of Gene Van Guilder is not a thing that will perish, either.

Gene loved this country. He had a true feeling and understanding of it. He saw it with the eyes of a painter, the mind of a trained writer, and the heart of a boy who had been brought up in the west, and the better he saw it and understood it, the more he loved it.

He loved the hills in the spring when the snows go off and the first flowers come. He loved the warm

Scene from the Theatre Guild production of
The Fifth Column *(1940)*

Hemingway had to wait two years for his play about the Spanish Civil War, The Fifth Column, *to be produced on Broadway. George Jean Nathan's review of the play (adapted by Benjamin F. Glazer and produced by the Theatre Guild) was published in* Newsweek, *15 (18 March 1940), p. 52. The play closed, after eighty-seven performances, on 18 May 1940.*

Oscar Bait

Some strange bedfellows are presently rolling around in the show business hay at the Alvin. Benjamin Glazer, a Hollywood scenario writer and quondam play collaborator with Vicki Baum, is found bundling with Ernest Hemingway, and Billy Rose, the boy-meets-mermaid impresario, is discovered cuddling with the Theatre Guild. The result of this miscellaneous literary-dramatic and financial amour is an adaptation of Hemingway's published play of anti-Franco connivance in the Spain of 1938, THE FIFTH COLUMN, and what eventually emerges from the several flirtations is an exhibit which, save for intermittent flashes of authentic and driving Hemingway, not only suffers from such an arbitrary Hollywood prettying up of its love interest that the enterprise seems rather less Ernest than Violet Hemingway but which on the whole for inner organization and clear directness might benefit from the dramaturgical form and clarity of even a William Saroyan.

As Hemingway wrote it, the play, as anyone who read it appreciates, was far from being dramatically satisfactory. As Glazer has amended it, it is not only equally far from being dramatically satisfactory but is critically even a bit farther. Attempting to develop the stage action around an emphasis on the boy-meets-girl element in the story, the adaptor finds himself in much the same difficulty that Laurence Stallings observed himself when he attempted, with infinitely sounder justification, to do the same thing some years ago in the dramatization of "A Farewell To Arms." When the voice of Hemingway is allowed its solo say, the play now and again has an honest ring, but when that voice is retailed through Mr. Glazer lodged Charlie McCarthy-like on Hemingway's lap the honesty takes on a mechanical birds-eye maple quality. As a playwright, Hemingway may unconversantly throw his bonnet over the windmill. As his adaptor, Glazer goes chasing the bonnet and essays safely to put it back on Hemingway's head. Neither may be right, but of the two I incline toward the Hemingway gesture, wherever it may or may not get him theatrically.

sun of summer and the high mountain meadows, the trails through the timber and the sudden clear blue of the lakes. He loved the hills in the winter when the snow comes.

Best of all he loved the fall. He told me that the other night riding home in the car from pheasant hunting, the fall with the tawny and grey, the leaves yellow on the cottonwoods, leaves floating on the trout streams and above the hills the high blue windless skies. He loved to shoot, he loved to ride and he loved to fish.

Now those are all finished. But the hills remain. Gene has gotten through with that thing we all have to do. His dying in his youth was a great injustice. There are no words to describe how unjust is the death of a young man. But he has finished something that we all must do.

And now he has come home to the hills. He has come back now to rest well in the country that he loved through all the seasons. He will be here in the winter and in the spring and in the summer, and in the fall. In all the seasons there will ever be. He has come back to the hills that he loved and now he will be a part of them forever.

The staging and acting, however, are quite as they should be. Lee Strasberg has maneuvered the indecisive script with considerable skill and has handled the rape and love business with a minimum of its melodramatic greasepaint content. Franchot Tone, Lenore Ulric, Katherine Locke, and, particularly, Lee Cobb, the last named as the anti-Nazi fighting Franco fascism, are capital. But the play, to repeat, for all its occasional bombs of eloquent indignation, remains strained synthesis.

In the preface he wrote for Gustave Regler's The Great Crusade *(New York & Toronto: Longmans, Green, 1940) Hemingway reflects on the lessons of the war in Spain.*

The Spanish civil war was really lost, of course, when the Fascists took Irun in the late summer of 1936. But in a war you can never admit, even to yourself, that it is lost. Because when you will admit it is lost you are beaten. The one who being beaten refuses to admit it and fights on the longest wins in all finish fights; unless of course he is killed, starved out, deprived of weapons or betrayed. All of these things happened to the Spanish people. They were killed in vast numbers, starved out, deprived of weapons and betrayed.

But this novel deals with the golden age of the International Brigades when all their gold was iron. It deals with the days when the Eleventh and Twelfth Brigades fought in defense of Madrid, at Boadilla del Monte, at the Arganda Bridge, in the Pardo, at Algora and Mirabueno, and finally at Guadalajara. No one has more right to write of these actions which saved Madrid than Gustav Regler. He fought in all of them.

You see the Eleventh Brigade was really the First Brigade. The Twelfth was the Second and so on. There were no first nine Brigades and there were never more than five. The Fifteenth Brigade, which in the time this novel deals with, contained the American Abraham Lincoln Battalion, was really the Fifth Brigade. It later became a very fine Brigade; one of the best in the army. But at the epoch this book deals with it had been almost destroyed in one single, idiotic, stupidly conceived and insanely executed attack in the hills above the Jarama River and, its morale low, it was holding a quiet stretch of front while a new Brigade was being built at the base.

The man who planned and ordered that attack was afterward shot when he returned to Russia. He should have been shot at the time. He was a Hungarian and he hated newspaper men. He had good reason to. For conditions on his front were so deplorable that as soon as they became known he was removed. General

Lucasz, who is the General Paul of this book, asked me to make him a confidential report on what I saw when visiting this Hungarian general's front to make some film for a picture. I hope the report may have had something to do with his removal.

But while the Fifteenth Brigade spent their long, moral calvary of ninety-some days without being relieved in the now quiet hills above the Jarama, the Eleventh and Twelfth were fighting constantly. I was privileged to be with them a good part of this time.

They were two great Brigades. The Eleventh was German. They had nearly all had military training or fought in the war. They were all anti-Nazis. Most of them were Communists and they marched like the Reichswehr. They also sang songs that would break your heart and the last of them died on the Muela of Teruel which was a position that they sold as dearly as any position was ever sold in any war. But they were a little serious to spend much time with. Unless, of course, you were with Hans the Commander. Hans is a book to himself. We have too much together for me ever to risk losing any of it by trying to write about it. There is something about him in this book.

The Twelfth Brigade was where my heart was. There was Regler, who is the Commissar of this book. There was Lucasz, the General. There was Werner Heilbrun, who is the Doctor in this book. There were all the others. I will not name them. Some were Communists, but there were men of all political beliefs. They are all in this novel of Regler's and most of them are dead now. But until they died there was not one of them (that's a lie, there were a few) who could not make a joke in the imminent presence of death and who could not spit afterward to show the joke was real. We introduced the spitting test because it is a fact, which I discovered in early youth, that you cannot spit if you are really frightened. In Spain I very often could not spit after quite a good joke.

The jokes were never bravado. The jokes were because really brave men are almost always very gay and I think I can truly say for all those I knew as well as one man can know another, that the period of fighting when we thought that the Republic could win the Spanish civil war was the happiest period of our lives. We were truly happy then for when people died it seemed as though their death was justified and unimportant. For they died for something that they believed in and that was going to happen. Lucasz and Werner died as they die in this book. I never think of them as dead. I think I cried when I heard Lucasz was dead. I don't remember. I know I cried once when somebody died. It must have been Lucasz because Lucasz was the first great loss. Everyone else who had been killed was replaceable. Werner was the most irreplaceable of all;

but he was killed just afterward. And about crying let me tell you something that you may not know. There is no man alive today who has not cried at a war if he was at it long enough. Sometimes it is after a battle, sometimes it is when someone that you love is killed, sometimes it is from a great injustice to another, sometimes it is at the disbanding of a corps or a unit that has endured and accomplished together and now will never be together again. But all men at war cry sometimes, from Napoleon, the greatest butcher, down.

Gustav should have been killed when Lucasz was. It would have saved him much trouble, including the writing of this book. He would not have had to see the things that we have seen; nor the ones that we will have to see. He would not have had to be cured of a hole in the small of his back which uncovered the kidneys and exposed the spinal cord and that was so big, where the pound and a half piece of steel drove through Gustav's body from side to side, that the doctor pushed his whole gloved hand through in cleaning it.

He would not have lived to be put in a French concentration camp after he had fought France's battle in Spain and helped delay Germany's war on France, by the greatest holding attack in history. The Soviet Union was not bound by any pact with Hitler when the International Brigades fought in Spain. It was only after they lost any faith in the democracies that the Alliance was born.

If Gustav had been killed he would have been spared much suffering and much trouble. But he does not mind suffering, nor trouble, nor poverty, for himself. To Gustav those are only bad things to happen to others. He has, intelligently and unselfishly, the same bravery and immunity to personal suffering that a fighting cock has, which, wounded repeatedly, fights until it dies.

So Gustav will be all right as long as he is alive. The French have released him from concentration camp and admitted it was a mistake to have put him there. But Regler deserves to have a place to live and work: to be able to write and live with his wife and eat three meals a day. The best citizens we had came in the German migration of 1848, after another revolution failed. America is a big enough country to receive the Reglers who fought in Germany and in Spain; who are against all Nazis and their allies; who would honor America as much by living in it as we would aid them by granting them the right of asylum we have always accorded to those who have fought in their own land against tyranny and been defeated.

I have not written much about this book. It is to be read; not written about. Alvah Bessie wrote a book, a true, honest, fine book about the Fifteenth Brigade in the last phase the Brigade went through. In spite of the heroism and the wonderful fight they made in the Ebro

diversion, it is no more typical or true account of the complete role of the International Brigades than an account of the retreat from Moscow would give you a true picture of Austerlitz or Wagram. We never had any Austerlitz. But we did have Madrid, Arganda, and Guadalajara. A great part of the men who made the good Brigades (there were bad ones too) immortal as some of the finest fighting units in history, were dead before Mr. Bessie joined what was left of the Fifteenth Brigade on their retreat from Aragon. The Brigades had the same numbers after Teruel, but the men were different.

The Ebro diversion was a great thing and Bessie writes truly and finely of all that he could see of it and he saw enough for one man. But Guadalajara, Arganda and Madrid were victories, and it is a good thing, to give those people who are opposed to Fascism hope, that these victories should be told now as Regler tells them: truly.

The greatest novels are all made-up. Everything in them is created by the writer. He must create from knowledge, of course, unless his book is to be a tour de force. There have been great tours de force too: *The Red Badge of Courage* and *Wuthering Heights*. But the authors of such books are usually poets who happen to be writing prose. But there are events which are so great that if a writer has participated in them his obligation is to try to write them truly rather than assume the presumption of altering them with invention. It is events of this importance that have produced Regler's book.

Harry Burton, the editor of Cosmopolitan, *was considering serializing* For Whom the Bell Tolls *(1940) but did not do so. In his memoir,* Feet First *(New York: Crown, 1971), Ben Finney confirms this account that Hemingway gave Maxwell Perkins about Finney reading the manuscript. From* The Only Thing That Counts, *pp. 280–282.*

[*Mid-April 1940*]

Dear Max;

Harry Burton should have gotten those 32 chapters last Saturday. I sent him 28 on Monday and he got them on Wed. Sent the other on Thursday and he should have had them on Saturday. Since it is now in the pay or not pay stage they become very cagy and the usual hurrah, hurrah, hurrah telegrams are suspended.

I wrote him to turn it over to you. You can show it to Cape. But for Christ sake Max not to Alvah Bessie and every other bastard that will want to see it. You read it. Charley. Bill Webber. Meyer if you want. But for Christ sake don't let any of those communists read it just because you like them and trust everybody you like.. Don't please argue with me on this. And please see no one outside of office reads it and that the Mss. doesn't leave office.

I was laid up five days. My heart was only hitting 52 at noon and Dr. said I was shot with over-work and should lay off for two months or so. Stayed in bed 2 days. Loafed three and went back to work last Wednesday. This is sat. Have been going good. Am on Chap. 35 (almost finishedthat chap) Yest. Ben Finney good tough guy F.F.V Captain in Marines at 20 last war, first guy to ever run the Cresta from the top first try etc. Old friend. Came out here at 4 p.m. Started to read Mss. Read straight through without stopping until eleven o'clock and then I let him take it out to the yacht with him to finish. He thought it was the best and most exciting book I'd ever written. Twice while he was reading he called me in to see that he had an erection about the girl. Good sign because Finney pretty well fucked out. My desk swamped with cigarrette butts from Finney's reading.

He tried to make me admit I'd seen all that stuff. Hell no, I made it up, I told him. You're a goddamn liar, said Finney.

That is what you want to do with writing. What I did once with Caporetto.

Christ I am tired though, Max. Me in the third person for a year and going on two months. Me that the third person can beat to death in a thousand words.

Will consult with you on all serialization angles before doing anything.

Also no need to deposit that $500. Will size up how play goes and let you know. But it is an open and shut thing with Revenue Bureau. That's how they told it should be done. Can deposit thousand or fifteen hundred another month and be same.

Once I get this all cleared up am going to work with Author's League on tax situation to get a juster treatment for all writers. Went into that with Revenue Agent to get his advice. Ideal would be if we could get it on a crop basis the way farmers have. But would have to have some straight authors who are not gyppers and crooks meet with the department and talk things over. Then take various cases and carry them through and get rulings. I would be glad to do it when am in the clear again and not writing a novel. Trouble is that there are so many kind of writers. The law works to the advantage of the straight commercial writers. . . .

Have worked two whole days with Bible, Shakespear etc. on title. (Worked plenty before. But this was on account your 22nd date.)

The Undiscovered Country is the nearest I can get with the necessary counter-point. But still it isn't right.

Cover for the issue that included Hemingway's last contribution to this party-line magazine (14 February 1939)

Have 24 others. None right. Still working. Will get it right.

> Best always.
> Ernest/

Robert Van Gelder published this interview in The New York Times *on 11 August 1940 (p. 2), while Hemingway was revising* For Whom the Bell Tolls *in New York.*

Ernest Hemingway Talks Of Work and War

Ernest Hemingway was here in New York copyreading and delivering to Scribners, his publishers, at the rate of 300 pages a day, the final draft of his longest novel. People who have read the manuscript agree that it is his best. Said one such reader encountered as he waited, rather bemused, for a chance to cross a cross-street on which there was no traffic, one afternoon some months ago: "I've just read the first three-quarters of the new Hemingway and you might as well believe me because you're going to find out that it's true—it is even better than *Farewell to Arms*."

Mr. Hemingway's stay here was supposed to be all for work, but cheerfulness kept breaking in. On the eleventh day of July's heat wave his rooms at the Hotel Barclay saw as lively company as any rooms in town. An electric fan droned on the coffee table, flanked by bottles of White Rock and fronted by a superb bowl of ice. A fifth of Scotch rested hospitably on the floor where it could be handily reached from three of the four chairs. Lawyers, old friends and visiting soldiers came and went. The telephone rang not quite continuously. Mr. Hemingway wore an unbuttoned pajama coat affording a view of chest that—if Max Eastman still is interested—would have made the eyes of a fur trapper pop.

"I've worked at it solid for seventeen months," said Hemingway of his new novel. "This one had to be all right or I had to get out of line, because my last job, *To Have and Have Not,* was not so good. For seventeen months I wrote no short stories or articles—nothing to earn a penny. I'm broke."

A friend said: "Ernest, if I am paid $200 for the job I am doing tonight we will have a wonderful time tomorrow." "Don't worry about $200," said Hemingway. "Whether you get it or I get it we'll *still* have a wonderful time tomorrow. Charley Scribner isn't broke."

The talk was a mixture of Spanish, French and English. Each comment that Hemingway made on his writing he prefaced with an explanatory speech to Gustavo Duran, the former pianist and composer, who had developed as one of the most brilliant of the army

Hemingway writing For Whom the Bell Tolls, *his novel about the Spanish Civil War and his longest book*

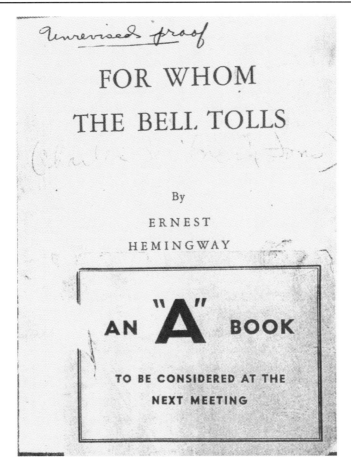

Proof copy of Hemingway's fourth novel, prepared for Book-of-the-Month Club judges

corps commanders on the Loyalist side of the civil war in Spain.

"Sorry, Gustavo, but Bob has to ask these questions, it's his job, and I'm supposed to answer them, see?" And then, rapidly: "I start work each morning at 7:30 and work until about 2:30. The first thing I do when I'm writing a novel is read back through all that has gone before. That way I break the back of the job. Then I put the words in—like laying bricks. I write in longhand and don't try to make much time. I've tried this speed writing, getting it all down and then going over it, but the trouble is if you speed too much you don't know if you have a book or not when you've finished the first draft."

"About how many words do you write each day?" Duran asked, seriously. Hemingway looked at him, not sure whether or not he was being ribbed. "I don't know, Gustavo. Some days a lot, some days a little. I never write to fit a thesis or a plan. I start with blank paper and put all that I know at the time on the paper. Most of the time it is tough going. You can't figure any average. Why in hell do you want to know, Gustavo?"

Duran shrugged: "I don't know. It is interesting." He talked of his own job as a commander. He said that in his army regulations the first sentence was the seemingly meaningless one that roughly translated into "the first duty of the commander is to make decisions."

"It seems simple when you read it. You think, 'What is decision? Each day I decide what color shoes to wear, what to eat.' But decision, when the life or death of hundreds of men depend on your decision, that is much else. In Spain I was assigned, as you know, to hold a position. My cowardice told me to draw in my left flank so that if I failed I would be near the French border and the lives of thousands would be saved if we lost. My judgment said perhaps that is right but perhaps it would be better to turn my right flank, though if we lost we

476   FOR WHOM THE BELL TOLLS

Granja when they had been ordered up after the first report of the attack on the lower post. They had ridden hard and had then had to swing back because the bridge had been blown, to cross the gorge high above and come around the timber. Their horses were wet and blown and they had to be urged into the trot.

Lieutenant Berrendo, watching the trail, came riding up, his thin face serious and grave. His sub-machine gun lay across his saddle in the crook of his left arm. Robert Jordan lay behind the tree, holding onto himself very carefully and delicately to keep his hands steady. He was waiting until the officer reached the sunlit place where the first trees of the pine forest joined the green slope of the meadow. He could feel his heart beating against the pine needle floor of the forest.

Two short chapters, amounting to 1,500 words in all, will bring the book to a conclusion. In the first of these Karkov and Goltz meet after the failure of the attack, and in driving back from the front they talk together about it, and about Robert's message and his success in blowing up the bridge. In the second, Andrés and Gomez motorcycle back to the outpost and then Andrés makes his way over the ground he covered before, and eventually reaches the abandoned camp, sees the ruined bridge, and knows all that has happened there.

These chapters are written, but not yet to the complete satisfaction of the author. He wished to wait until after reading the proof up to this point before perfecting the end.

EDITOR

Typescript note pasted in the proof copy to describe the proposed ending that Hemingway never wrote
(Louis Henry Cohn collection, University of Delaware)

would be cut off from safety. That is a decision that hurts all through your body; you cannot sleep, you ache. There is nothing more difficult in life."

"Which flank did you turn?"

"My right flank. But that is not important. The decision is important."

"Do you suppose all commanders feel that way? Did Napoleon?"

"Napoleon was a victor. When you are a victor, what can hurt you? But when you must fight a long defensive action with no chance of winning, only of holding the enemy off, then with every decision you are in hell," said Duran. "You ache with wanting—but what you want cannot quite be reached. It is like my sitting in this chair wanting to rip that necktie from your neck. I reach, I almost seize it. It is just beyond my hand. Always in war there are possibilities plain to be seen, but materials are lacking, the men fail, a mistake is made somewhere along the line—and frustration eats your stomach."

It was suggested that perhaps because the military decision is so difficult to make, that is why when it is made rightly it pays off so well. There is nothing in finance, for example, to compare with it, or in internal politics, and perhaps for twenty years the importance of the military decision has been underestimated and aims that are practically inferior have been mistakenly rated above the real pay-off, which still is strength at arms. Hemingway exclaimed: "That's what the new novel is about!" and then another visitor arrived, and the talk took another turn.

Much of the conversation ran to questions of survival or failure to survive. "Where is so-and-so?" "He went back to Russia and was shot." "And so-and-so?" "He also was shot." Another Spanish fighter had landed in a German concentration camp. A married pair "tried to get to Chile but were turned away. They finally were admitted to Buenos Aires." Duran himself escaped from Spain aboard a British destroyer, was taken to Marseille, transported across France in a sealed train, and shipped to England. He was on his way here during the Blitzkrieg in Flanders.

"The world now is very confusing. It is amazing how sure we once were, Ernest, that our ideas were right."

"The fight in Spain will have to be fought again," Hemingway said.

Duran looked at his hands.

"I don't know."

Telephone calls, visitors ushered in and out, another rather hesitant question about writing and another apology to Duran.

"The thing wrong with *To Have and Have Not* is that it is made of short stories. I wrote one, then another when I was in Spain, then I came back and saw Harry Morgan again and that gave me the idea for a third. It came out as a new novel, but it was short stories, and there is a hell of a lot of difference. A novel—when you do a novel"—he couldn't find the phrase he wanted. "I don't know how many more I'll do. But they say that when you're in your forties you ought to know enough and have enough stuff to do one good one. I think this is it."

After his long session of work Hemingway looked elephant-big, enormously healthy. His talk is unevenly paced, a quick spate and then a slow search for a word. His chair keeps hitching across the floor toward the other chairs, and then as he reaches a point, a conclusion, he shoves his chair back to the edge of the group again. While Duran was telephoning in the next room he said that Duran was a character in the new novel, which is set in Spain during the civil war, and that while he was writing the book he badly wanted to see Duran, "to straighten things out, to get information."

"Now that I've finally found him the book is on its way to the printer, can't be changed. But I've questioned him and the stuff I used was all right. You write what should be true as, with what knowledge you have, it seems to you. And that's the best you can do, anyway."

Dorothy Parker's review of Hemingway's novel of the Spanish Civil War was published in Ralph Ingersoll's liberal tabloid PM, *20 October 1940, p. 42. In early 1941 Hemingway covered the Second Sino-Japanese War for* PM.

Mr. Hemingway's Finest Story Yet

Once I knew a woman who, by a set of circumstances which has been denied my understanding, got herself among people who chanced to be discussing *War and Peace*. "Now, let me see," she said. *"War and Peace,* now, did I read that, or didn't I? I sort of think I did, but I'm not really sure."

I shall meet that woman again, for I have little luck in such matters. It will be with those who are talking about Ernest Hemingway's latest book. "Now, let me see," she will say. *"For Whom the Bell Tolls.* Oh, yes, of course I read that. It's one of those books about the Spanish War, isn't it?"

I let her go, on the *War and Peace* affair. But this time she shall die like a dog.

Ernest Hemingway's new book, that took two years in the writing, spans three days of the war in

Ernest Hemingway

Don't Lose This For Christ's Sake. 8/26

EH

Memorandum on corrections of proof For Whom The Bell Tolls
These corrections may not have been made on this set of galleys due to lack of space .They
are uniform and each word and   usage should be checked throughout all the galleys .

Throughout the book use Heinkel for planes --never Henkel .

It is Golz ——— never Goltz

It is Estremadura -   never Extremadura .

Rafael is the gypsy - never the Gypsy(except at the beginning of a sentence)

Maria is referred to as guapa —— not Guapa (except at the beginning of
a sentence .)

Maria is referred to as rabbit ₤ - not Rabbit   (except at beginning of
a sentence .)

It is viejo (l.c.) never Viejo (except at beginning of a sentence .)

It should be máquina —— never machina

In Qué va the accent aigu should be used in every instance .

~~Saghiiipexxxaxeaidxxaxxipaixaad~~
guerrillero   should be in italics throughout the book .

partizan   should be   italics and laxl.c. through the book .

It should be Agustin throught the book—— never Augustin

Gredos
In some places   the Sierra de ~~Sragan~~ is referred to as the Gredos

(Robert Jordan always refers to them thus)   Sordo and Pablo would simply say Gredos
. Follow my corrected galleys on this without querying them . I have checked all usage
carefully .

Since I have cut chapter three into chapters three and four the numeration
of all subsequent chapters should be advanced by one . Check this carefully .

Please check with some one who is familiar with Russian names as to
whether Kashkeen   should be spelled Kashkin . (I do not have my Russians here)
If it should be spelled Kashkin correct. the spelling to this through-out the book .

I will wire you the name of a proper cavalry regiment to insert in the blank
left in galley 9I

The dedication is to read :

This book is for Martha Gellhorn .

Check carefully my corrections on the passage from Donne . In the
galleys it was full of errors which I have corrected from the original .

Hemingway's style sheet for For Whom the Bell Tolls *(Charles Scribner's Sons Archive, Princeton University Library)*

The New York Times Book Review *advertisement for Hemingway's top-selling novel to that time (20 October 1940)*

Spain. The war, they all know now, that should have been won against Fascism, so that this war could never be. Many did not know it then, and that is not terrible of them. For they were not told, and they read lies and heard them. But some who were high in power did know, and for their own brief advantage they lied and said it was not like that and everybody should do nothing about it. And theirs is the deed that cannot be forgotten.

Of All Time

This is a book, not of three days, but of all time. This is a book of all of us alive, of you and me and ours and those we hate. That is told by its title, taken from one of John Donne's sermons: "No man is an *Iland*, intire of its selfe; every man is a peece of the *Continent*, a part of the maine; if a *Clod* bee washed away by the *Sea*, *Europe* is the lesse, as well as if a *Promontorie* were, as well as if a *Mannor* of thy friends or of *thine owene* were: any mans death diminishes me, because I am involved in *Mankinde*. And therefore never send to know for whom the *bell* tolls. It tolls for *thee*."

This is a book about love and courage and innocence and strength and decency and glory. It is about stubbornness and stupidity and selfishness and treachery and death. It is a book about all those things that go on in the world night and day and always; those things that are only heightened and deepened by war. It is written with justice that is blood brother to brutality. It is written with a wisdom that washes the mind and cools it. It is written with an understanding that rips the heart with compassion for those who live, who do the best they can, just so that they may go on living.

About Love

It is a great thing to see a fine writer grow finer before your eyes. *For Whom the Bell Tolls* is, and beyond all comparison, Ernest Hemingway's finest book. It is not necessary politely to introduce that statement by the words "I think." It is so, and that is all there is to it. It is not written in his staccato manner. The pack of little Hemingways who ran along after his old style cannot hope to copy the swell and flow of his new one. I cannot imagine what will become of those of them who are too old for the draft.

There are many authors who have written about love, all along the gamut from embarrassment to enchantment. There are many who have written about sex and have got rich and fat and pale at the job. But nobody can write as Ernest Hemingway can of a man and a woman together, their completion and their fulfillment. And nobody can make melodrama as Ernest Hemingway can, nobody else can get such excitement upon a printed page. I do not feel that the creation of excitement is a minor achievement.

For Whom the Bell Tolls is nothing to warrant a display of adjectives. Adjectives are dug from soil too long worked, and they make sickly praise and stumbling reading. I think that what you do about this book of Ernest Hemingway's is point to it and say, "Here is a book." As you would stand below Everest and say, "Here is a mountain."

Playwright Robert Sherwood reviewed Hemingway's Spanish Civil War novel for "The Atlantic Bookshelf," Atlantic Monthly, 166 (November 1944), front section.

One must be hesitant to apply the word "artist" to a virile American writer. He is apt to feel that he has been ticketed as an escapist, or a literary embroiderer. However—here goes: Ernest Hemingway is an artist, and his new novel *For Whom the Bell Tolls* is a rare and beautiful piece of work. It contains all the strength and brutality, the "blood and guts" of all the previous Hemingway books (and more skillfully rendered profanity and obscenity than any of them); and it is written with a degree of delicacy which proves that this fine writer, unlike some other fine American writers, is capable of self-criticism and self-development. Hemingway has not been content merely to go on expending the huge natural force that is his, but has worked, and worked hard and intelligently, to give it form as well as substance.

He has succeeded magnificently and hearteningly and at the right moment.

There is in *For Whom the Bell Tolls* not only the immediate stimulus of which Hemingway has always been an open-handed provider; there is in it a curious sense of permanence and nobility of spirit. Its characters are not represented as exceptional, as strange refugees from space and time. They are the eternal fighters of all wars, and the eternal victims. Theirs is the lost cause that can never be lost, the sacrifice that can never be futile. Thus the novel justifies the John Donne quotation from which came the title. . . .

For Whom the Bell Tolls is another story of the Spanish Civil War, and its extraordinary merits seem all the more extraordinary because of that. Hemingway was there, in that war, in that prologue to war, and he felt it with a degree of intensity which was felt, God knows, by too few others. He now writes of it with detachment and objectivity, and with hardly a trace of rancor. I know that too much detachment and objectivity and too little rancor can be fatal to creation. But in this book he has achieved the true union of passion and reason, and that is why it is so preeminently a work of art.

He has painted on a small canvas. He has not attempted to sweep over a vast panorama, as in the retreat from Caporetto in *A Farewell to Arms*. He tells of an exceedingly minor operation in the war; his central characters are few in number, and we see them during only seventy-two hours of their lives. But it seems to me that he tells the whole story of what was behind the Spanish tragedy, and what was to come of it for Spain and Europe and the rest of us. In one tremendous chapter (the tenth) he gives the story of how the movement started in one small town. Again, he tells of how an important message is delivered through the lines, and the difficulties involved in that delivery form the story of the centrifugal leadership of the Loyalist cause, which dissipated the hopes of the innocents of Spain. In these passages, Hemingway provides a masterpiece in the brief characterization of Comrade Marty, the political commissar, who was more eager to verify his own suspicions of his own associates than to gain victory over Fascism.

Hemingway's hero is named Robert Jordan. He bears a superficial resemblance to other Hemingway heroes, the clever ones and the dumb ones alike, in that he is resolutely resistant to illusion. But I should say that he is a better man than any of them. He is more grown-up. His consciousness is clearer. The love scenes between Robert Jordan and the girl Maria, to whom the Fascists had done "bad things," are complete love scenes. Complete love scenes are rare in modern literature. Any writer with knowledge of his craft can write skillfully about sex, but it takes an artist to write thus beautifully and truly about love.

When I said that Hemingway has written without rancor, I meant that he wrote with aching sympathy for all the victims of Fascism, including the Fascists themselves. He took no time out for denunciatory editorials. He did not feel the need to insult the reader's intelligence by telling him that Fascism is that which kills the spirit of man, which forbids man to be an artist. He has done his finest work, and, what is perhaps more important, he has dispelled any fears concerning his own limitations.

Novelist Alvah Bessie, a member of the Abraham Lincoln Brigade, reviewed For Whom the Bell Tolls *in New Masses, 37 (5 November 1940), pp. 25–29. His reaction is typical of responses by Communists or critics who were sympathetic to the Communist cause.*

Hemingway's "For Whom the Bell Tolls"

The author, Alvah Bessie says, has written a book about Spain without the Spanish people, and without illuminating the cause of the republic Hemingway championed.

"No man is an *Iland,* intire of it selfe; every man is a peece of the *Continent,* a part of the *maine;* if a *Clod* bee washed away by the *Sea, Europe* is the lesse, as well as if a *Promontorie* were, as well as if a *Mannor* of thy friends or of *thine owne* were; any mans *death* diminishes me, because I am involved in *Mankinde;* And therefore never send to know for whom the *bell* tolls; It tolls for *thee.*"

This is the quotation from John Donne which Ernest Hemingway sets as a rubric for his new novel, and this is the touchstone by which that novel must be evaluated. Since we must assume that Donne was speaking of the universal brotherhood of man, of the inter-relationship of human life and its indivisibility, we have a right to expect that Hemingway's long novel of the war in Spain will illuminate that text and not obscure it, will demonstrate the novelist's realization of the significance of that war, and find him at the peak of his achievement. For that war, which Hemingway witnessed at close hand, is being revealed with every day that passes to have been a touchstone and a turning point in human history which those who had foresight in 1936 stated it would be: "the cause of all advanced and progressive mankind."

Ernest Hemingway's relationship to that war was intimate and varied. In many senses he was as much a participant as those men he knew and loved who now are gone—Lucasz, Werner Heilbrunn, and the many anonymous dead of the glorious Twelfth International Brigade. The novelist gave freely of his substance and his spirit in the cause of Spain; he wrote and he spoke and he acted. And he commanded the admiration and respect of the men of many nationalities who fought there and who knew his name. It was during that war that he wrote a novel that represented what should have been—and what many thought was—a transition book: *To Have and Have Not.* It was both interesting and inevitable that that novel should have been the first work from his hand that was *not* greeted with unanimous enthusiasm by the critical fraternity of the bourgeois press. For in its pages a new note had been sounded. The old Hemingway of the postwar what-the-hell-boys and the old let's-have-another-drink was gone. A new Hemingway made his appearance, a new theme emerged. Whereas in his short stories and in two previous novels the author had exasperated his most perspicacious admirers by his inconclusive treatment of the necessity for manliness and the pervasive horror of death, a maturing artist found another subject—the problem of making a living, the necessity for human solidarity. "One man alone ain't got," whispered the dying Harry Morgan, an honest man who had found that he could not feed his wife and children by honest labor. "No man alone now." He stopped. "No matter how a man alone ain't got no bloody –––ing chance."

The critics deplored this new and serious note in their pet disillusioned author, an author they had praised for being above the political arena, who dealt with eternal realities in a "lean, athletic prose." It was whispered freely among these objective gentlemen that Hemingway was slipping; he was a member of the League of American Writers; he had discovered that non-existent figment of the Reds' imagination—the Class Struggle. But many who had thought Hemingway was dead (for more valid reasons) took new hope with the appearance in his work of this wider realization of man's humanity, this deeper understanding of his struggle. Sex and death were eternal verities, but it was not until 1937 that Hemingway discovered taxes.

Dust jacket for Hemingway's love story set during the Spanish Civil War and dedicated to Martha Gellhorn

To Have and Have Not was a vastly imperfect work; the author's satirical treatment of the human parasites who lived on luxury yachts off the Florida keys was both brittle and jejune, and his old limitations were amply manifest: the interchangeability of his conversation; his feeble understanding of female character; his inability to fully explore and *plumb* character at all. For with the rarest of exceptions few characters that Hemingway has dealt with up to date have been more than pegs on which to hang those moods and intimations of mortality which have been the author's forte, and which reveal his greatest gifts.

That those gifts are considerable no sensitive person could doubt. He has an ear for the language (in dialogue) that is unique. No human being ever talked the way Hemingway's characters talk, but every word they speak makes the reader say, "How true to life." This is a real artistic triumph. This man can create moods and crystallize certain fundamental emotions in a way few writers have ever been privileged to achieve. And it is these moods and these emotions that the reader gener-

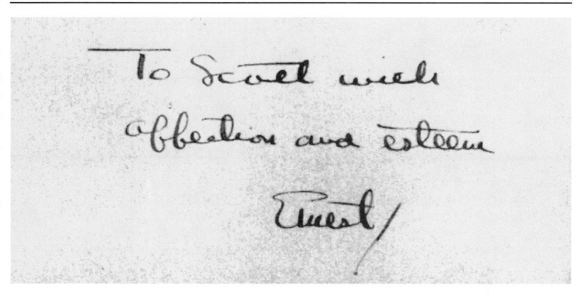

Inscription in F. Scott Fitzgerald's copy of For Whom the Bell Tolls *(Matthew J. and Arlyn Bruccoli Collection, University of South Carolina)*

ally remembers, not the people who live through them—the futility of the life of the expatriate, his emptiness and his frantic search for a kick; the horror of the retreat from Caporetto; the loneliness that surrounds the death in childbed of the heroine of *A Farewell to Arms,* the brutality of *The Killers,* and the frustration of *Fifty Grand;* the loneliness and incongruity of drunkenness, and the sense of decay that pervaded all his work up to *To Have and Have Not,* where the wider significance of living made a momentary appearance.

Many expected that Hemingway's experience in Spain would so inflame his heart and his talents, that his long-announced novel of that war would be both his finest achievement and "the" novel about Spain. It is not. It is his finest achievement only in the sense that he has now perfected his extraordinary technical facility and touched some moments of action with a fictional suspense that is literally unbearable. But depth of understanding there is none; breadth of conception is heartbreakingly lacking; there is no searching, no probing, no grappling with the truths of human life that is more than superficial. And an astounding thing has happened, that anyone who was even remotely concerned with what happened in Spain will find almost incredible: Hemingway has treated that war (in an essential way) exactly as he treated the first world war in *A Farewell to Arms.* Touched in his own flesh and spirit by the horror of that first great imperialist conflict, struck into a mood of impotent despair by its utter lack of meaning and its destruction of everything all decent human beings value, Hemingway proclaimed the futil-

ity of life and love and happiness. He killed his heroine and in a memorable evocation of utter human loneliness, his hero "walked home in the rain." The *Farewell* was so bitter a condemnation of imperialist war that it aroused the ire of Archibald MacLeish, who found that it had been largely responsible for destroying the new generation's faith in its misleaders.

Let us examine *For Whom the Bell Tolls,* and see what the author (who only recently aptly replied to MacLeish) has done with one of the greatest human facts of our century—the two and a half years during which the Spanish people held in check, with their bare hands, the forces of international fascism. His hero this time is Robert Jordan, American volunteer in Spain who is a *partizan* fighter—one of that small band of extremely courageous men who worked behind the fascist lines. Jordan is sent behind the lines again to blow up a strategic bridge—his signal for the explosion is to be the beginning of a government attack upon Segovia.

The action takes place in three days' time. Jordan makes contact with a group of Spanish *guerilleros,* meets a Spanish girl who had been captured and raped by the fascists, falls in love with her, makes his plans to blow the bridge—a difficult enterprise in which he fully expects to lose his life. His guerrillas attack the fascist garrisons, and he blows the bridge as what is to be a futile attack gets under way—for the fascists have learned of the plans for the offensive and are prepared to meet it. In escaping, Jordan's horse is wounded, falls upon the man, and breaks his leg. He is too badly injured to be carried, and must be left behind to do

Scribners bindery card for For Whom the Bell Tolls *(Charles Scribner's Sons Archive, Princeton University Library)*

what damage he can with a light machine-gun, and then to end his life.

This is a story of action, and the action is fast and furious, fused with a suspense that is magnificently handled in every incident. But this is also *A Farewell to Arms,* slightly in reverse. For the total implication of the novel is, again, the necessity for virility, the pervasive horror of death, the futility–nay, the impossibility of love. Given only seventy-two hours in which to live, Robert Jordan must live his life within that span. He accepts that fate, but the reader's disappointment in his fate is Hemingway's disappointment with life–for there is no tragedy here, merely pathos. Here, again, are long and fruitless and somewhat meaningless disquisitions upon the significance of death and killing (in war, in murder, in the bull-ring, by accident, by design). Here again is the small and personal (and the word *personal* is the key to the dilemma of Ernest Hemingway's persistent lack of growth) frustration of the individual, and here again is the author's almost pathological preoccupation with blood and mutilation and sex and death–they all go together and are part and parcel of his attitude toward life, and they are the *only* facts of life with which he has consistently dealt. I do not mean to imply that these subjects are unworthy or incapable of profound treatment, singly or together; I do mean to insist that in Hemingway's hands they have never achieved the stature of universality, perhaps because Hemingway cannot see them in perspective, cannot see them more than sentimentally.

It must be clearly stated that Hemingway's position in this novel is unequivocally on the side of the Spanish people; there can be no question of his defection from that cause. It is, however, a tragic fact that the cause of Spain does not, in any *essential* way, figure as a motivating power, a driving, emotional, passional force in this story. In the widest sense, that cause is actually *irrelevant* to the narrative. For the author is less concerned with the fate of the Spanish people, whom I am certain that he loves, than he is with the fate of his hero

Poster publicizing a meeting led by veterans of the Spanish Civil War to protest Hemingway's novel (Milton Wolff Collection)

strated in permitting his play, *The Fifth Column,* to be mutilated and distorted out of all semblance of what he originally wanted to say, to the point where it was actually a slander of the Spanish people.

There are many references in the *Bell* to various political aspects of the struggle in Spain. And few of these references do more than *obscure* the nature of that struggle. Robert Jordan, his American anti-fascist fighter, wonders "what the Russian stand is on the whole business." If Jordan, who is pictured as an utterly inflexible anti-fascist, did not understand what the Soviet Union felt about Spain, surely his creator did and does. And just as in his story *Below the Ridge,* Hemingway's sins of omission in the *Bell* allow the untutored reader to believe that the role of the Soviet Union in Spain was sinister and reprehensible. For certainly he must himself know—and it is his obligation to clearly state—that that role was clear and well-defined, and so honest as to command the entire respect and adherence of the Spanish people, who hung banners in their towns which read: *Viva La U.R.S.S.; Mejor Amigo del Pueblo Espanol* (Long Live the Soviet Union, Best Friend of the People of Spain!).

Now this concentration, this constriction of Hemingway's indubitable genius, to the purely personal, has resulted in a book about Spain that is not about Spain at all! It has resulted in the intensification of his idiosyncratic tendencies to the point where he, an inflexible supporter of the loyalists and an avowed admirer of the International Brigades, can conceive and execute as vicious a personal attack upon Andre Marty, the *organizer* of the International Brigades, as could be and has been delivered upon him by French fascist deputies themselves! This attack upon Marty, who is portrayed in the novel under his own name, and upon whom Hemingway exercises the presumption (both personal and artistic) of *thinking for him,* is entirely irrelevant to the narrative. To understand it at all, one would have to know, at first hand, the nature of Hemingway's personal contact with this man—a revolutionary figure of the first magnitude, organizer of the Black Sea mutiny of the French navy (an achievement that could scarcely have been conceived and executed by the criminal imbecile Hemingway portrays), a monolithic representative of the French working class, and the man who was the organizational genius and spirit of the Brigades Hemingway makes such protestation of admiring. Both as novelist and reporter Hemingway had an obligation to understand this man, whatever his personal experience with Marty, whatever his personal opinion of Marty's personality might have been. He cannot plead that his intentions in attacking Marty were good; that it was his honest conviction that Marty was a part of the incompetence, the red tape, and the outright treachery that strangled Spain, for such "facts" simply will not hold water;

and his heroine, who are *himself.* They are Hemingway and Hemingway alone, in their (say rather *his,* for Jordan is the mainspring of the narrative, and the girl Maria is only lightly sketched) morbid concentration upon the meaning of *individual* death, *personal* happiness, *personal* misery, *personal* significance in living and their personal equation is not so deeply felt or understood as to achieve wide significance. For all his groping, the author of the *Bell* has yet to integrate his individual sensitivity to life with the sensitivity of every living human being (read the Spanish people); he has yet to expand his personality as a novelist to embrace the truths of other people, everywhere; he has yet to dive deep into the lives of others, and there to find his own.

This personal constriction has long been evident and has made inevitable other aspects of Hemingway's personality that are, to say the least, reprehensible. I refer to his persistent chauvinism, as referred to the Italian people, and to women; to the irresponsibility he has shown in publishing in Hearst's *Cosmopolitan* such a story as *Below the Ridge,* a story whose implications gave deadly ammunition to the enemy—Hemingway's enemy, the fascist-minded of America; to the irresponsibility he demon-

they are lies. And I am afraid that Hemingway will live to see his book hailed by our universal enemy *precisely because* of his attack upon Marty; I am afraid he will live to see every living and dead representative of the Abraham Lincoln Battalion attacked and slandered because of the great authority that attaches to Hemingway's name and his known connection with Spain.

Yet this man Marty is the man the author portrays as a fool, a madman, and categorically indicts as a murderer! And I wonder, when he wrote these pages, whether he considered for a moment that he was attacking him with the very terms that have been leveled at him by the French fascists who sold France down the river to Hitler. I wonder if he considered he was accusing him in the very same way and with the very same words that were used by American deserters who appeared before the Dies committee and attempted to smear the Veterans of the Lincoln Brigade, with the very words of the Hearst press which, throughout the war in Spain, characterized the Internationals as the scum of the earth, international bums, gangsters, and murderers.

This is the trap into which the individualism Hemingway's bourgeois critics so admired, has led a man who is still one of our most greatly endowed creative artists. For he has written a novel of Spain without the Spanish people, a *Hamlet* without the Dane. And he has forgotten the words he wrote earlier this year: "There are events which are so great that if a writer has participated in them his obligation is to try to write them truly rather than assume the presumption of altering them with invention." For the author of the *Bell* does not convince us, with this novel, that "any mans death diminishes me, because I am involved in Mankinde." He only convinces us—no matter how tenderly he may write of the love of Robert Jordan and Maria—that the imagination of his own death may yet destroy him as an artist.

It seems certain that Hemingway did not intend to write a *Cosmopolitan* love story against a background of the Spanish Civil War; yet this is what he has done. It is certain that he did not intend to slander the Spanish people or the Soviet Union; yet his method of telling the story has resulted in both. With minor exceptions, the Spanish people portrayed here are cruel, vindictive, brutalized, irresponsible. Throughout the long narrative there is evidence of much confusion: Hemingway praises the individual heroism of individual Communists, and impugns and slanders their leadership, their motives, and their attitudes. He admires the Brigades, and assails their leadership (and surely he knows enough about military affairs to realize that no soldier can fight well unless his officer commands his respect).

Already this greatly endowed writer, who on innumerable occasions has placed himself without equivocation on the side of the people against their enemies, has

been readmitted by the most reactionary critics to the Valhalla of the Literary Giants. J. Donald Adams of the New York *Times* has forgiven him for writing *To Have and Have Not;* the defected liberal, John Chamberlain, absolves him for having (in the same novel) made "a common murderer of inferior sensibility and no moral sense whatever . . . do duty as a symbol of downtrodden humanity," cheers the fact that "If Archibald MacLeish still thinks of Hemingway as an underminer of the soldierly virtues he will have to change his mind," and becomes shrill with joy over the attack on Marty, Hemingway's "turn (ing) on the politicos of Moscow" and finally arriving at the point announced by John Dos Passos in *Adventures of a Young Man.* (This should be news to Hemingway, for Dos Passos ultimately became an avowed enemy of the republican government of Spain.) Edmund Wilson also points the Dos Passos parallel in the *New Republic,* lauds Hemingway for being more interested in "The *kind* of people . . . rather than their social-economic relations. . . ."

But this is strange company for a man like Hemingway, a man who transcended the futility created in him by the first world war, was vitalized, as a man and as an artist, by Spain; a man who won the respect and admiration of almost every International Brigade man who met him, and who gave liberally to these men of his own substance. For at the moment he is found in bad company; in the company of his enemies, and the people's enemies—clever enemies who will fawn upon him and use him, his great talents and his passion for the people's cause, to traduce and betray those talents and those people.

Sinclair Lewis wrote this introduction to For Whom the Bell Tolls *(Princeton: Printed for the Members of the Limited Editions Club by the Princeton University Press, 1942).*

In November 1941 the judges who had accepted responsibility for The Limited Editions Club's Gold Medal Award—they were Sterling North, Clifton Fadiman and Sinclair Lewis—gave the medal to Ernest Hemingway for writing FOR WHOM THE BELL TOLLS, which they believed to be the American book published during the three years which was most likely to survive, to be known fifty years from now, or possibly a hundred. These ponderous professors presented for their decisions three entirely different reasons, all contradictory of the others and all correct.

To one, FOR WHOM THE BELL TOLLS was a truly great book because it was a great "love story."

Another judge asserted that it was essentially a galloping chronicle in the tradition of *A Tale of Two Cities* or *Ivanhoe*. But the third, and naturally the soundest, of the court trumpeted that FOR WHOM THE BELL TOLLS might just possibly be a masterpiece, a classic, because here was a crystallization of the world revolution that began long ago—perhaps in 1776, perhaps in 1848—and that will not cease till the human world has either been civilized or destroyed—perhaps in 1976, perhaps in 2848.

It is dangerous to use the terms "great" and "masterpiece" about any contemporary book. The literary reviews of thirty years ago are funnier than the women's hats of that vintage. But I shall not much care if thirty years from now it seem ridiculous to have agreed noisily that FOR WHOM THE BELL TOLLS is indeed that most unusual and most desirable luxury, a great love story.

Here are a man and a girl, healthy, fighting, passionate, without the inhibitions of either Main Street or the Stork Club. They are natural human beings with natural longings. Yet they are not fictional barbarians who have always lived in a pine tree and never heard what it is all about. They have been reared in the dangerous exactitudes of a revolution; the man has read, and the girl has heard comrades reading, Rimbaud and Karl Marx and the *Handy Manual of Anatomy for First Aid,* to an accompaniment of machine-gun firing. Their life is urgent, their love is urgent, with death and torture and ecstasy the triune priest at their unchurched wedding.

Yes, and it is a great tale, too; an "adventure story," if you will, and there is haste and the joy of violence in it. Ernest Hemingway is one author who can be counted upon not to decline into literary teas or radio studios or the choice cottage in Connecticut. He is a jolly and amiable fellow to meet, yet he is also a lone scarred tree, for the lightning of living has hit him. He hunts, skiis, fishes for shark in the Gulf Stream, flies from Paris to Idaho to Havana to China, not to be sporting and different but because to him a heightened sort of experimental existence is habitual. And that gallantry is in his story.

The feeling of lurking murder that runs through FOR WHOM THE BELL TOLLS accomplishes what clever detective stories try to accomplish, and Robert's plan to blow up the bridge and halt the Spanish Fascist troops is to the reader almost painful in the perfection of its suspense.

Yes, it is a great love story, and a great *story*. But it is also a dramatization of the revolution that is now altering the whole world. And what is unheard-of is that it is revolutionary without a whisper of "propaganda."

The hero of the novel is one of ten million (maybe a hundred million) intelligent strong young men who today will bet with their lives on the chance of the world being transmuted from traditional oppression to true commonwealth. He is for the Communists when they furnish courage and devotion; he is acidly against them when they become power-hungry intriguers. Robert Jordan is a fighter, trained and formidable, but he indicates how the world is changing by his freedom from all the phony heroics of Kipling and Richard Harding Davis. He proves that we are living in the first age of history that is really romantic and interesting, so that we need no gilt and costuming to trick it out.

This young man of the story is by choice a scholar, who would be sufficiently content with a teacher's cottage near the campus of Midwest College—provided he could have a little dangerous skiing, and the detail of a world grown just. He has quietly turned from textbooks to the skilled use of dynamite, which he applies to bridges as carefully and usefully as one might apply manure to a garden patch.

The hero of any novel of thirty years ago was solid in proportion as he believed that his world was going to be essentially the same always; that it was there to be faced and conquered. Now he is solid precisely as he sees that he must forever adapt himself to change and peril.

Robert in this book is not a revolutionary dogmatist, but he does begin to have a notion of what the fighting is about. The Spanish hillmen are in profoundest truth his brothers. His battles and his love are exciting, yes, but they mean something, they are part of a scheme that means something—a notion that mankind must plan and fight for a world in which all men's lives will mean something.

The world today is jammed with greasily articulate public figures who write and shout that democracy must prevail, that justice shall be established, that freedom must be courageously won. Some of them mean well, and some of them like to be seen around, and quite a lot manage to combine the two. But though their doctrine is true, their words are dry and dead, their words are empty bombs. Not by pulpiteering shall the people be stirred to resolution and combative common sense. But when the reader, identifying himself with Robert Jordan, actually smells the fighting, then freedom may become an activity to live for, to die for, and brotherhood may become inevitable.

That is what Ernest Hemingway has done here.

Chapter Five: 1941–1952

1941

11 February–   The Hemingways travel to China to cover the Japanese invasion.
6 May

7 December   Japan attacks Pearl Harbor, Hawaii, an act that brings the United States into World War II.

1942

March   Hemingway agrees to edit and write an introduction for *Men at War,* an anthology about war.

July   Using the *Pilar* as a Q-boat, Hemingway begins hunting German submarines. Despite searching until September 1943, he never encounters an enemy vessel.

October   *Men at War* is published by Crown in New York.

1943

25 October   Martha Hemingway leaves Havana to report on the war in Europe.

1944

March   Hemingway agrees to go to Europe as a correspondent for *Collier's Weekly.*

17 May   Hemingway flies to London, where he soon meets correspondent Mary Welsh Monks.

28 May   Martha Hemingway comes to London to visit Ernest; by the end of the visit, she tells Hemingway that she never wants to see him again.

6 June   Hemingway covers the D-Day landings from a correspondents' transport. He does not go ashore.

19–20 June   Hemingway goes on an RAF bombing mission.

18 July   Hemingway goes to France, where, on 28 July, he joins Colonel Charles "Buck" Lanham's 22nd Regiment (4th Infantry Division). He and Lanham become lifelong friends.

18–28 August   Hemingway joins a group of French partisans to gather intelligence. The group "liberates" the Traveler's Club, Café de la Paix, the Ritz Hotel, the Negre de Toulouse, Lipp's Brasserie, and Shakespeare & Company.

18 September   Viking publishes *The Portable Hemingway,* edited by Malcolm Cowley.

October   Charged with acting as a combatant and bearing arms, Hemingway is ordered to report to the Third Army for Court of Inquiry. He is cleared of the charges in late November.

| 15 November | Hemingway rejoins Lanham's regiment for the Hürtgenwald offensive. He returns to Paris on 4 December. |

1945

6–8 March	Hemingway flies to New York.
2 May	Mary Welsh arrives at La Finca Vigía.
7 May	The surrender of Germany to Allied Forces ends World War II in Europe.
14 August	World War II ends, as the atomic bombing of Hiroshima (6 August) and Nagasaki (9 August) by the United States causes Japan to surrender.
21 December	Ernest and Martha Hemingway are divorced.

1946

| January | Hemingway begins writing a novel set on the French Riviera in the 1920s. |
| 14 March | Hemingway marries Mary Welsh. |

1947

| 13 June | Hemingway is awarded the Bronze Star for his service in France in 1944. |
| 17 June | Maxwell Perkins dies in New York. |

1948

September	Hemingway probably begins writing *Islands in the Stream*.
Late October	The Hemingways travel to Venice.
Late December	In Venice, Hemingway meets Adriana Ivancich, the model for Renata in *Across the River and Into the Trees*.

1949

March	Hemingway contracts erysipelas; doctors fear that the infection may spread to his brain.
April	After recovering from his illness, Hemingway begins a story about Venice; it eventually becomes the novel *Across the River and Into the Trees*.
5 September	Hemingway meets *Cosmopolitan* editor A. E. Hotchner.
17–18 November	Lillian Ross interviews Hemingway for an article in *The New Yorker*.
Early December	While staying at the Ritz Hotel in Paris, Hemingway completes *Across the River and Into the Trees*.

1950

February	*Cosmopolitan* begins serializing *Across the River and Into the Trees*.
13 May	Ross's profile of Hemingway, "How Do You Like It Now, Gentlemen?," is published.
7 September	Scribners publishes *Across the River and Into the Trees*.
24 December	Hemingway says that he has finished *Islands in the Stream*.

Chapter Five: 1941–1952

1951

17 February   Hemingway finishes the first draft of *The Old Man and the Sea*.

2 October   Pauline Hemingway dies in Los Angeles.

1952

11 February   Charles Scribner III, Hemingway's publisher and editor, dies in New York City.

1 September   *Life* publishes *The Old Man and the Sea*. More than 5,000,000 copies of this issue are printed.

8 September   Scribners publishes *The Old Man and the Sea*.

Hemingway wrote no fiction during the first half of the 1940s. From February to May 1941 he traveled with Martha to China, where he reported the Japanese invasion for *PM*, a liberal New York newspaper. He and Martha disagreed about whether she should cover the war in Europe; Hemingway wanted her to stay with him.

The only literary project he undertook was an introduction for an anthology about war for Crown Publishers. After he persuaded editor Nat Wartels to change the contents of the book, *Men at War* was published in October 1942—with most of the weakest selections removed.

That same year Hemingway undertook one of his more foolhardy endeavors. With the support of the U.S. embassy in Havana he outfitted his boat, the *Pilar,* as a Q-boat to hunt German submarines in the Caribbean Sea. He patrolled intermittently from June 1942 to July 1943 without ever engaging the enemy.

When Martha left for London as a correspondent for *Collier's* in November 1943, Hemingway remained in Cuba, fishing and drinking heavily. Then in May 1944 he, too, left for Europe to cover the war for *Collier's*. After a party following his arrival in London, he was injured when his driver hit a water tank. In his hospital room he and Martha quarreled about his behavior before she left for an assignment, and Hemingway consoled himself by beginning an affair with Mary Welsh, a writer for *Time*.

Hemingway covered the D-Day landings and wrote articles about RAF operations before going to France on 18 July to report the advance on Paris. Attached to the 22nd Regiment of the 4th Infantry Division, he quickly became friends with its commander, Colonel Charles "Buck" Lanham. In August he accompanied a group of French partisans, for whom he was an unofficial liaison with the U.S. Army, during the last stages of their advance on Paris. The group entered the city on 25 August and "liberated" the Ritz Hotel, Shakespeare and Company, and other establishments. He rejoined the 22nd Regiment on 1 September for the advance on Germany and witnessed its heavy casualties in the Hürtgen Forest in November before returning to Paris, where he remained until he went back to Cuba in March 1945.

Martha had asked for a divorce in November 1944, and in May 1945 Mary Welsh joined Hemingway at La Finca Vigía. His divorce from Martha became final in December, and he and Welsh were married on 14 March 1946.

In early 1946 Hemingway began writing a novel, *The Garden of Eden*. The book was set in France in the 1920s and focused on two couples: a writer, David Bourne, and his wife, Catherine, on their honeymoon on the Riviera; and a painter, Nick Sheldon, and his wife, Barbara, in Paris. By June Hemingway claimed to have written more than 1,000 pages, but he stopped working on the novel in 1947. In late 1948 he began a different novel about World War II that was based on his experiences hunting German submarines, flying with the RAF, and reporting on combat with the 22nd Regiment—a book he called his "land, sea and air novel." But he stopped work on this book in 1949 to begin yet another one about a dying American colonel's last visit to postwar Venice, where he and Mary had recently sojourned. It is likely that he borrowed material about the land war in Europe (material based on his experience with Lanham's unit) from the "land, sea and air novel" and incorporated it into his new novel, *Across the River and Into the Trees*.

This narrative was serialized in *Cosmopolitan* in five installments beginning in February 1950. It was Hemingway's first novel in ten years, and most critics were disappointed with it. Reviewers disliked Colonel Cantwell's conduct and his implausible affair with Renata, the eighteen-year-old contessa. Although more than 93,000 copies of the book were sold soon after publication, it was considered a literary failure.

In May 1950 Hemingway had written to his publisher, Charles Scribner III, about a novella that he had begun before he had started *Across the River and Into the Trees.* He completed this work, which he titled *The Old Man and the Sea,* in February 1951. At first he planned to use it as the epilogue for his "land, sea, and air novel," but he decided in May 1952 to publish it simultaneously as a magazine story and as a book. *Life* paid Hemingway $40,000 for the magazine rights and published *The Old Man and the Sea* in the 1 September 1952 issue. Scribners and the Book-of-the-Month Club released the book a week later. The praise for the book was overwhelming, and most critics wrote that it was a welcome return to the old Hemingway style after his last book had been so disappointing. Scribners and the book club printed more than 280,000 copies; *Life* had to print more than 5,000,000 copies of its 1 September issue to meet demand. It proved to be the last new book that Hemingway published.

In early 1941 Hemingway traveled to China to cover the Japanese invasion for Ralph Ingersoll's newspaper, PM. *This interview in* PM *(9 June 1941, pp. 6–10) introduced Hemingway's series of articles.*

Story of Ernest Hemingway's Far East Trip

Ernest Hemingway left for China in January. He had never been in the Orient before. He went to see for himself—how Chiang Kai-shek's war against Japan was going; how much truth there was to the reports that the Chinese position was menaced by threat of civil war; what would be the effect of the then imminent Russo-Japanese pact and—most important of all—what was our own position in the Orient. What was our position both as a leading anti-Fascist power and as a nation of 130,000,000 people with vital trade interests in other parts of the world—or were they vital?—and if they were vital, were they menaced?

Hemingway wanted to find out for himself, and for you and for me, what pattern of events might lead us into war with Japan—what alternate sequence of circumstances might possibly keep Japan in her place in the Pacific without us having to fight her.

Most people know Ernest Hemingway as America's No. 1 novelist. His reputation as a novelist is so great in fact that it overshadows two other reputations, either one of which gives him international recognition.

Long before he was a novelist, Ernest Hemingway was a noted war correspondent. He covered the fighting in the Mediterranean in the last war, the whole of the Spanish war—in which the present war was fought in miniature.

Of sufficient stature to be distinct from his reputation as a war correspondent is his reputation as a mili-

tary expert. He is a student of war in its totality—everything about war, from machine gun emplacements to tactics and maneuvers to civilian morale and industrial organization for war. These things he has studied for 20 years.

So when Ernest Hemingway went to China he went as no casual visitor but as a student and an expert—he went with a reputation which made it possible for him to visit fronts that had not been visited by foreign journalists until now, and to talk with people who are running the war in the Orient on a unique basis.

When Ernest Hemingway went to the Orient, *PM* made this agreement with him: that if action broke out he was to remain there and cover the war by cable, but if no action broke out, he was to make notes as he went but not to write until he finished this study—until all the returns were in and he had time and the perspective to analyze everything he had seen and heard, and render a report of more lasting value than day-to-day correspondence.

This is the report that will be published here beginning tomorrow.

In the meantime, I have talked with Mr. Hemingway about his trip. Here is where he went and what he did and what he saw—the background from which his report is drawn:

Ernest Hemingway went to China with his wife, Martha Gellhorn. Mrs. Hemingway carried credentials as correspondent for *Collier's* where her articles have already begun appearing. The two flew to Hong Kong by Pan American Clipper.

Hemingway stayed a month in Hong Kong, where he could talk not only with the Chinese but with their opposition. The Japanese come in and out of Hong Kong quite freely—in fact, they celebrated the Emperor's birthday in their frock coats and with a formal toast. The British naval and military intelligence is there—and our own naval and military intelligence. The local Communist opposition is there and so are the Chinese pacifists who play Japan's game.

We asked Hemingway what it is like in Hong Kong. He said that danger had hung over the place so long it had become absolutely commonplace. People had completely adjusted themselves to the tension. He said that the city was very gay. The stabilizing element in any British colony are the British womenfolk, who keep life on a formal basis. But they had been evacuated and in general morale was high and morals low.

"There are at least 500 Chinese millionaires living in Hong Kong—too much war in the interior, too much terrorism in Shanghai to suit a millionaire. The presence of the 500 millionaires has brought about another concentration—of beautiful girls from all parts of China.

Gregory, Jack, Ernest, Martha, and Patrick Hemingway in Sun Valley, Idaho, September 1941

The 500 millionaires own them all. The situation among the less beautiful girls is very bad because it is the British position that prostitution does not exist there, and therefore its control is no problem. This leaves about 50,000 prostitutes in Hong Kong. Their swarming over the streets at night is a war-time characteristic."

How many troops there are in Hong Kong is, of course, a military secret. Hemingway knows the exact number. That is the type of censorship *PM* does not try to beat. But Hemingway reports Hong Kong is "excellently defended.

"In case of attack Hong Kong's problem would be food. There are 1,500,000 people there now and they would have to be fed."

He continued: "Even more serious would be the sewage disposal problem—for in Hong Kong there are neither flush toilets nor drains. Sewage is disposed of by night soil coolies who collect and sell it to farmers. In case of a blackout sewage will be dumped in the streets and a cholera epidemic would be inevitable. This is known because two nights of practice blackout did produce a cholera epidemic.

"At present, however," Hemingway continued, "the food is plentiful and good, and there are some of the finest restaurants in the world in Hong Kong—both European and Chinese. There's also horse racing, cricket, rugby, association football."

After Hemingway had been in Hong Kong a month, he and Mrs. Hemingway flew to Nam Yung by Chinese air line. This flight took him over the Japanese lines. From Nam Yung, the Hemingways drove to Shaikwan, headquarters of the 7th War Zone.

The Chinese front is divided into eight war zones. Hemingway chose the 7th because he "wanted to make

La Finca Vigía, Hemingway's home in Cuba from 1940 to 1960 (photo by Roberto Herrera Sotolongo)

an intensive study of what a typical Chinese war zone was like, and the 7th has, ultimately, the greatest offensive potentiality."

Here he studied the complete organization of a Chinese war zone from headquarters through the army corps, divisions, brigades, regiments and down to the forward echelons.

The army Hemingway visited is a Kuomintang army. That is, it is part of the regular Chinese Army and not part of the Chinese Communist Army. The Chinese Communist armies have welcomed journalists and there has been much written about them. But this is the first time an American journalist has done extensive work at the front with the regular Chinese Army.

We asked Hemingway about this situation. He said:

"There are 300 divisions in the Chinese Army, 200 of which are first-class divisions and 100 secondary divisions. There are 10,000 regular troops in each division. Out of these 300 divisions three are Communist divisions. The area that the Communist divisions hold is an extremely important one and they have done marvelous fighting. But the 297 other divisions, occupying about the same amount of terrain per division, have not been visited at all before. Whereas the Communists have welcomed correspondents, there has been very strict censorship on the regular Chinese Army. Passes have been impossible to get, and correspondents have not been allowed into the forward echelons at all."

Hemingway said he went to see the regular Chinese Army because the Communist troops have already been excellently described by people like Edgar Snow, Agnes Smedley and others.

News of the Kuomintang army is important not simply because it has received no publicity but because the Kuomintang comprises the bulk of the troops on which we, in America, must depend to keep the Japanese divisions occupied in China while we are preparing to defend the Pacific.

Hemingway spent a month at the front, living with the troops, going everywhere with them. He traveled down the river by sampan first, then on horseback, and finally on foot. There were 12 days during a wet spell when he and Mrs. Hemingway never had dry clothes to put on.

They also discovered such delicacies as snake wine and bird wine. Hemingway described snake wine as "a special rice wine with a number of small snakes coiled up at the bottom of the bottle. The snakes are dead," he said. "They are there for medicinal purposes. Bird wine is also rice wine, but at the bottom of its bottle there are several dead cuckoos."

Hemingway liked the snake wine better. He says it cures falling hair and he is going to have some bottled for his friends.

After a month at the front, the Hemingways went back overland by sampan, car and train to Kweilin. This trip had not been planned, but everywhere they had gone for two months they had been told Kweilin was the most beautiful place in China. And they reported that it is the most beautiful place they saw. "There are thousands of miniature mountains there which look like a huge mountain range but are only 300 feet high. Many of the lovely imaginative scenes you see in Chinese prints and paintings, and think are made up out of an artist's imagination, are really almost photographic likenesses of Kweilin. There is also a famous cave there which is now used for an aid raid shelter. It holds 30,000 people."

To get from there to Chungking they arranged to be picked up by a freight plane which was carrying bank notes to the capital. The plane was a Douglas DC-3—the kind that flies on most of our air lines here—and all the other seats were occupied by shipments of bank notes.

All the air lines in China are owned by a company called the CNAC, or China National Aviation Corp. The Chinese Government owns 51 per cent and our own Pan American Airways owns 49 percent and does the operating. Hemingway said:

"They used DC-2's and 3's and old Condor biplanes which can only fly on short hauls where the mountains are under 7,000 feet high. There are passenger flights from Hong Kong to Chungking three times a week, for instance. But the idea of buying tickets on them is an academic one—for the waiting list is months long and only priority counts."

When it did not look as if the priority was coming through in time, Hemingway chartered a Vultee sin-gle-motored low-wing monoplane. But then the priority came through.

By the time the Hemingways got to Chungking they had learned a good deal about China. They spent some time with Chiang Kai-shek and in an all-afternoon interview, Mme. Chiang Kai-shek did the interpreting. But Hemingway reports that when the talk was on military subjects the Generalissimo understood military terms in English. He saw and got to know China's Minister of Finance, Dr. Kung, the Minister of Education, the Minister of Communications, the Minister of War, as well as various generals and the General Staff.

"Chungking," he reports, "had not been bombed seriously from August 25 until May 3—there is no bombing in Chungking during the winter because of low visibility."

He found the hotels in Chungking excellent—the food plentiful and the water hot. Everywhere he went in China, in fact, he found food sold without restrictions—even in the villages. At no time, he reports, did he see any of the signs you see when the war is being lost for lack of food. At no time did he see anything like the conditions he saw in Spain.

"But," he said, "the food in China is expensive. Moreover, China is such a huge country that there are sections where the food situation gets bad locally—when due to a local drought a crop has failed. And communications are so bad that it is difficult to ship in food from other parts of the country. Such a condition prevails at present in South Shansi province and in other parts of the northern provinces. On the whole, the food situation this year is very good."

We asked Hemingway what people meant when they came back and said the ec2onomic situation in China was "very bad."

He said: "When people come into China from America and see signs of a monetary inflation there, they think everything is going to pot, whereas the situation is actually very good, considering China is in the fourth year of war. The inflation there is no worse than occurs in any other country that fights for four years. In the fourth year of the last war no European country was in better shape."

He felt that "China has to make some radical currency reforms—but principally to prevent the Japanese from buying up their money. The Japanese sell their own money short and buy Chinese money—now that America is backing China's money," he said. "I don't think this will be hard to control. My personal opinion is that eventually China will have to adjust its currency on a rice standard. Rice is the gold of China and only a currency based on a rice standard will prevent the kind of inflation in which people are not able to buy food."

Martha and Ernest during their trip to China, 1941

The first time the Hemingways were in Chungking they stayed about eight days, constantly talking with people. Hemingway dined, lunched and breakfasted with Government people.

At the end of the eight days he flew up to Chengtu to visit the Chinese military academy—where Chiang Kai-shek trains his officers and cadets. And he inspected the flying schools and the new airdromes that are being constructed in this district. Here again, as a guest of the military academy, he had an opportunity to study the whole Chinese military system.

"The military academy," he said, "is in full swing. It was set up by a German General Alexander Von Faulkenhausen, and its professors are German-trained Chinese."

Hemingway flew back from the Chinese West Point to Chungking and then took another plane south over the Burma Road. He saw the trucks passing up and down the road.

We asked him whether reports that the Road was all banged up were true. He said: "Some of the bridges were out, but the Chinese have a very efficient ferry system to replace them. The Road is being bombed regularly—Kunming practically every day—but the bombing of bridges is not effective, partly because of the ferries and partly because they rebuild the bridges so quickly."

Hemingway said: "The control organization of the China section of the Burma Road is now in the charge of a committee which includes Dr. Harry Baker, former head of the American Red Cross in China. If Dr. Baker is not hamstrung by his fellow committee members he will be able to put through many traffic reforms."

From Lashio, which, you will see by the map, is far up on the Burma Road route, Hemingway went to Mandalay by car and then down to Rangoon by train. All along this route he studied the Burma Road problem, and gave us this picture of it:

"The first part of the problem is getting materials from the coast up to the beginning of the Road. Here there are two methods of transportation available. One is via the Burma railway, the other is via the river. So far most of the material has gone up over the railway which is Burmese owned and very jealous of river traffic. The river traffic is transported by an organization called the Irrawaddy Flotilla, which belongs to a Scottish-owned company.

"The Irrawaddy is navigable as far as Bhamo. You should look at the map here because Bhamo is becoming very important. At Bhamo a connecting road is being completed through to the Burma Road. You will see that not only does it cut off a good part of the Burma Road—and a difficult and mountainous part—but it permits goods to be transported up from the coast all the way by river. In effect this new route—from Rangoon to Bhamo by water and from Bhamo by short cut to well up on the Burma Road—constitutes a cut-off which is almost impossible for the Japanese to damage.

"The old route," he continued, "by rail from Lashio to Kunming, remains available, and shippers can also use the river up from Rangoon to Mandalay to Lashio.

"This makes two ways in.

"A third way," he went on, "is now being developed. This way uses first water and then rail to a place called Myitkyina—pronounced Michina—which, if you are interested in the Burma Road problem, you should locate for yourself on the map. Because you will see that by using Myitkyina as a railhead, a 200-mile air shuttle service from Myitkyina to Tali cuts off 509 miles of the Burma Road and leaves only 197 miles to travel to Kunming.

"This 197 miles—from Tali to Kunming—is downhill and there are no bridges and gorges which the Japanese can turn into bottlenecks by bombing. On a 200-mile hop the freight planes will not have to refuel in China at all.

"Thus," Hemingway explained, "the Chinese have what amounts to three alternate routes of supply from the south, not counting the constant bootlegging of supplies in from the whole China Coast."

Hemingway studied this traffic and says it is of enormous extent. He does not write about it in detail because he does not want to give information to the Japanese.

Now, remembering that the overland route into Russia is still open and that the Chinese are still getting supplies from Russia—as Hemingway explains in one of his articles—one realizes for the first time just what an enormous problem the Japanese have in interrupting Chinese communications.

"If the Japanese interruptions on the Road were as one, the interruptions due to inefficiency, graft and red tape would be as five. That is, take the whole route from Rangoon into Chungking—inefficiency, graft and red tape cause five times as much trouble as Japanese bombings. This is the problem which Dr. Baker has to solve."

We were startled by this figure and asked Hemingway to tell us more about it. He said:

"All projects in China move very quickly until money is involved. The Chinese have been doing business for many centuries and when things are a business matter to them they move very slowly. The Generalissimo can order something done—something in which money doesn't enter—and it is done practically, immediately. But the minute it becomes a financial thing it slows right up. No one person is responsible for this. It is the age-old Chinese custom of squeeze.

"There have been cases of truck drivers selling their gasoline, which they were hauling over the Burma Road, to private concerns. There have been cases of dumping whole loads to carry passengers. I saw with my own eyes tires being thrown off trucks loaded with them—evidently to be picked up by confederates later.

"There's no efficient policing of the Road. Of course every load should be checked as it goes in, and all the way through, and as it comes out. That is what Dr. Baker's Commission has to fix. After they opened the Road things ran wild for a while. Some people, operating transportation companies from outside of China, had no efficient control of their organizations on the Road. Now the Generalissimo realizes the importance of this. Something is being done about it."

Hemingway told us that the situation in Burma doesn't make things any better. He said: "Burma is a land of complete and utter red tape. Everything there is slowed up as much as it can be. If a military attaché comes to Rangoon to get a load of food to take back up to Kunming, it takes him two days in Rangoon just to clear through red tape. It is worse than France was before the fall. It is entirely administered by the Burmese, who combine the worst features of the Hindu Babu and the French pre-fall functionary. On the other hand, the British in Burma, not the Burmese, were efficient and uniformly helpful. Censorship was realistic and intelligent."

We asked Hemingway what it was like visiting romantic-sounding places like Mandalay and Rangoon. He said Rangoon was an English colonial city, "96 degrees at night and 103 degrees in the day, in the hot months when we were there. The flying fish were not playing. Kipling was talking about a place further down—Moulmein, below Rangoon, near the mouth of the river."

Hemingway went all the way down to Rangoon and stayed there for about a week. Then he flew back via Lashio and Kunming to Hong Kong and stayed there again for a week before leaving for America. Mrs. Hemingway continued on to Batavia and the Dutch East Indies while Hemingway worked between Clippers in Manilla. She rejoined him on the next Clipper.

As this is being written Mr. Hemingway is completing his last piece for *PM*. We asked him a few final questions: What about the Chinese arsenals? If, by any mischance, the supply routes were cut, could they go on fighting?

He said: "I visited arsenals near Chungking and saw that they were manufacturing small arms and small arms ammunition, and were very self-sufficient. Moreover, much material can come right through Japanese lines. The guerrillas had been running trucks through the Japanese lines by completely dismantling them—into the smallest possible pieces—and carrying them by hand. An American motor company representative in Hong Kong was delivering trucks through the Japanese lines to Free China making a $450 service charge for delivery." Hemingway has more news of the latest developments in guerrilla fighting.

News from the Orient has been confusing and contradictory to most people. Russia supposedly offers the hand of friendship to Japan—and at the same time continues to ship supplies to China.

America gives China a $100,000,000 credit—and at the same time sells oil to China's enemy. What's it all about?

Hemingway told us. He traced for us the probable consequences of each move we were making, and each Japanese move.

He showed us how Russia was playing a devious hand in this gigantic game of Chinese checkers which anybody might win.

Must America fight Japan? Hemingway told us why it's a matter of timing. As far as America is concerned, time itself is fighting on our side. As for Japan, time is running out on her—and no one, not even the Japanese, knows when the last strategic moment will have come. Or whether she should extricate herself from China at any price before challenging us. If Britain should fall it would be the signal for Japan aggressively to pursue her conquests in new directions. And this may well mean war with the U.S.A.

If England grows stronger and America is able to keep the fleet in the Pacific, war between the United States and Japan may never occur. And further, Hemingway tells us, we may thus beat Japan without ever firing a gun.

No one interview such as this, however—no one article—can give you the full impact, can piece together the complete pattern of this tremendously significant picture.

———————————

In 1942 Hemingway was asked to edit and write an introduction for Men At War, *an anthology of writing about war to be published by Crown. In this letter to his editor at Scribners he discusses the contents of the volume. From* The Only Thing That Counts, *pp. 318–320.*

May 30, 1942

Dear Max: . . .

I have never been any good at writing those kind of advertisements that you sent in the letter, but I suppose if you have to do it, you have to do it, although by the time the back jacket of my book comes out the whole thing may be compulsory and that will solve the problem. I have decided, or rather I decided several months before it started, or may be several years say, not to write any propaganda in this war at all. I am willing to go to it and will send my kids to it and will give what money I have to it but I want to write just what I believe all the way along through it and after it. It was the writers in the last war who wrote propaganda that finished themselves off that way. There is plenty of stuff that you believe absolutely that you can write which is useful enough without having to write propaganda. Do you remember poor old Owen Wister? Such a good man, and Mr. Britling sees It Through" and other things the last time? We have had Steinbeck's book [*Bombs Away,* 1942] so far and I would rather cut three fingers off my throwing hand than to have written it. If we are fighting for what we believe in we might as well always keep on believing in what we have believed, and for me this is to write nothing that I do not think is the absolute truth. So stall along about me writing that stuff. . . .

Now, about the war anthology man. I was very disappointed in his contents too. I have read over 370 galleys and have thrown out much of the worst stuff. I have also gotten him to include Frank Tinker's account of the Italian debacle at Guadalajara. Have got him to put in some good flying stuff. Have gotten him to include all the wonderful part about Waterloo from, "The Chartreuse de Parma" and got him to put in the account of the battle of Shiloh from that Lloyd Lewis book, "Sherman, Fighting Prophet", and I am insisting on him publishing an account of the first battle of Ypres by Frank Richards in, "Old Soldiers never Die", and an account of the fight on the Somme in 1916 by the same man. Have also had him throw out Ralph Bates' phoney story about the women machine gunners at Brunete as well as, "The Moment of Victory" by O'Henry, "The War Years" by James Hilton, "The Square EGg", by Saki, Arthur Guy Empey, the early life of your pal Winston by Richard Harding Davis (his, "The River War", would have been damned good to include), a terrible selection from, "Death of a Hero", by Richard Aldington, and a very phony, disorganized bit called, "West Canada Creek", from "Drums Along the Mohawk".

I hope the above hasn't confused you completely. Take your time and go over it and see if they were some of the weak things that you said he had included in his table of contents. If you have the table of contents, will you please check them.

Will you also, Max, please write me by return airmail what were the things you suggested to him which he did not include. Also, do you know what Charlie Sweeney suggested to him and he did not include? I think John Thomlinson must have suggested other things than just those pieces of his from, "Lone Star Preacher". They are very good, but, my God, that is not the story of our civil war. Please let me know about this as soon as possible as I do not want to have anything to do with the book unless it is as good a book as can be made. I still think it is a big mistake for us not to have taken the whole thing over and you have me edit it and write the introduction. Or had me edit and have John write the introduction. Wartels in his last letter said that he wanted to publish it as being edited with an introduction by Ernest Hemingway. I wrote him that I would not consider that as I had not edited it. But if I write an introduction to it I want it to be as good a book as can be gotten out and it is very much to the interests of everyone engaged in the present war that it be a really good book which can do some good. So, even though it is a bother for you, will you answer by return mail on the questions that I have asked you.

About my book of stories, I still have two long stories to complete. I am into both of them but was interrupted by this damned war anthology. I thought that it might do some active good if it was gotten out really well and so have been concentrating on it and my other work has suffered. Perhaps on account of that you should figure to publish in the spring rather than in the fall. Both stories are very long and very good. I had to stop on one while I waited to get some stuff that I needed for it to be really accurate. Then I got going on the other and I held it up when this war anthology came along. When they are finished I have enough stories for the book and the title will be either that of the best story or I will get as good a title as I can, as usual. I don't want you to count on anything and not deliver

Katina Paxinou (Pilar), Mikhail Rasumny (Rafael), Gary Cooper (Robert Jordan), and Vladimir Sokoloff (Anselmo) in For Whom the Bell Tolls *(Paramount, 1943)*

exactly when I should. Usually you have needed to have the stuff by July in order to publish in the fall. Personally, I do not care anything about publishing this fall as will need whatever money the book brings in to keep my family and this house going next year wherever I am. I would rather turn the book over to you complete in the fall so you could bring it out whenever you wanted next year so that there would be enough money from it to handle the overhead wherever I am. I think there is going to be some sort of arrangement that if you are in the army your income tax can be deferred. Anyhow I need the book as a source of income for next year to handle necessary expenses and contingencies. Whenever the picture [*For Whom the Bell Tolls*] is released there will be some money, coming in from that edition too. Could you tell me what the sale has been since you gave me the $4,000 in February to pay on the income tax? Approximately what amount of cash is due to me now?

I am very sorry, Max, if you are disappointed in not having the manuscript by the end of June or early July as I had planned. It is that damned war anthology which has held me up. I take it you also know the difficulty of working in these times. I can really do it though but it involves putting yourself into a sort of temporary vacuum, and you do not feel very happy in that place. I have to do it though in order to be free to do what I want and I will do it and finish it.

Please write me right away about the war anthology and read this letter over carefully so you know what the points are I asked you about. If you see Charlie (Martha who has gone up to see her mother, talked to him on the phone and he may be down here next week), ask him what the things were that he suggested so I can force Wartels to take them. Would it be too much to ask you to write John Thomlinson to ask him what he suggested to Wartels too. I would write him but I do not know him as well as you do. Tell him my excuse in bothering him is to try to make this book into a good weapon. . . .

Best always,
Ernest
Ernest Hemingway . . . .

Patrick and Gregory Hemingway were fourteen and eleven years old, respectively, at the time Hemingway attempted to hunt for submarines with the Pilar *as a Q-boat. From Gregory Hemingway's* Papa: A Personal Memoir *(Boston: Houghton Mifflin, 1976), pp. 70–89.*

Don Quixote Vs. the Wolf Pack

In the summer of 1943, when I was twelve, my father convinced the American Ambassador to Cuba that the forty-foot *Pilar* could be converted into a sub-destroyer, and that she could easily sink one of the German submarines that were preying on Allied shipping in the straits of Florida. By the time Pat and I arrived for the summer, the *Pilar* was armed to the teeth.

Two men were stationed in the bow with submachine guns and two in the stern with BARs and hand grenades. Papa steered on the flying bridge and up there with him was "The Bomb," a huge explosive device, shaped like a coffin, with handles on each end. The idea was to maneuver the *Pilar* next to a sub—how, exactly, wasn't quite clear—whereupon a pair of over-the-hill jai alai players with more guts than brains would heave The Bomb into the open hatch of the conning tower. And then The Bomb would presumably blow the submarine to kingdom come.

As soon as she heard of the scheme, Marty expressed her feelings intelligently, if not dispassionately.

"What if The Bomb misses, Ernest? The conning tower is slightly higher than the bridge of the *Pilar*, and that conning tower is about six feet in diameter while the width of the hatch is only thirty inches across. If the bomb doesn't go down the hatch it won't blow up the sub. It will rattle around until it goes off and blows the conning tower right into you. That will cause some confusion on the sub, of course, but she'll recover and pull away to a thousand yards or so and then her six-inch deck gun will blow the *Pilar* right out of the water."

Marty didn't give papa time to answer. "Kitten, you need a vacation," she continued. "Maybe we could go down the coast to Guanabacoa and you could do that piece you wanted to write on the Chinese watering the human feces they sell to the truck farmers—the one you promised *Collier's* about how the buyers have to sample the stuff with a straw to decide whether it's thick enough."

"Don't you think I know the realities of war?" he said. "I had enough time to contemplate them while the doctors picked those two hundred thirty-seven (or was it two hundred thirty-eight?) pieces of shrapnel out of my leg in the hospital in Milan during World War One."

"Love, this time, if that bomb misses, they won't find two hundred thirty-eight pieces of *you*."

"I know, darling. But the whole project's gone so far now I can't stop it. We have all the equipment on board and signed for, and the crew is terribly excited. Besides, they're all fine men. Neville is not the intellectual type of course—the other day I asked him why he was reading the life of Christ so fast and he said he couldn't wait to see how it ended. But he's basically a good man and loyal, and he fits in perfectly."

"Yes," Marty said, "I think his uncle went down on the *Titanic*."

Papa let that one pass. "Frankly, Hammer, that marine gunner the U.S. naval attaché lent us, is the only one of the crew I have my doubts about. All he does is read comic books. During yesterday's practice run, when we threw the hand grenades at that big green turtle, I called for battle stations and Hammer just said, 'Fuck that. My superior officer said my duties were to operate this here radio and *nothing* else. Why do you think I took this fucking job? I want a rest from the real war. Say, any more of the Scotch left, Ernie? The good Black and White?'"

Papa's imitation of Hammer made them both laugh, Marty a little less loudly, though.

"But I think he's all right," papa said. "He's got combat experience. Maybe he's just had too much war—has battle fatigue or something. Maybe jungle rot, too, from the way his feet smell. You know, that fungus they get in the Pacific. We'll have to get those feet fixed up before we cram nine people . . ."

"Nine? I thought you said seven."

"Well, the boys . . ."

"You're not taking the boys!" Marty screamed.

"Of course not, darling, but they'll be on the boat for the four days' run down to Cayo Confitis, our base island. We'll leave them with Gregorio during the day while we're out on patrol. Of course, if we sight a sub on the way down or back we won't engage it. But I may not let the boys know that. I'll see how they take to the idea of sub-hunting first, and if they aren't frightened it might be great fun and very exciting for them to feel a part of a Q-boat crew."

And it was. My station was in the bow. I was issued my mother's old Mannlicher Schoenauer. She had used it in Africa hunting lions and I felt very proud with it up against my shoulder. But it made a godawful noise and kicked like hell, so I only fired it once.

I'd stay in the bow and practice with a .22, shooting at flying fish which were frightened by the large boat and would take off on incredibly long runs, propelling themselves out of the water with their fins and then gliding for about fifty yards. Sometimes they would flick the water again with their tails and glide for what seemed like an eternity. They were great to practice on because you could see just where your shots were hitting the water, and I learned that even with a rifle, it was necessary to lead a moving target, if the target was far enough away.

The sea was very rough when we left Havana and headed toward the south coast of Cuba and the island of Confitis. The boat was pounding, pounding, pounding into the waves, but when we were about half an hour out the monotony was broken by Gregorio shouting, "Feesh, papa! Feesh!"

Papa jumped down off the flying bridge as the fish knocked the bait out of the outrigger with its bill. Then papa took off the drag from the reel, letting the line run freely, and continued: "One chimpanzee, two chimpanzee, three chimpanzee, four chimpanzee . . ." all the way up to fifteen.

Papa brought in the fish in eighteen minutes flat. It was a marlin, and weighed about 600 pounds.

Gregorio took some fillets and we threw the rest overboard. Within about fifteen minutes he gave another cry. It was a marlin, again. I noticed papa only counted to five before striking the rod after the bait had come out of the outrigger and this fish jumped an awful lot more. He'd propel himself into the air, coming out long and beautiful, then make a series of jumps like a ballet dancer, out of the water, back in, out, back in, in a straight line for three hundred yards or so. It was the longest run of a fish jumping I'd ever seen.

This one was a lot harder to bring in because he was hooked in the mouth, papa not having waited so long to strike him. He finally got the fish in. Then he did something I'd never seen him do before. Papa told Gregorio to release the hook.

"We'll always remember those jumps," papa said. "I'd rather release him and give him his life back and have him enjoy it, than 'immortalize him' in a photograph."

The second day out we saw a whale shark, the largest fish in the sea, sixty feet long, with black and white polka dots on his dorsal side. He was just basking on the surface, docile and harmless. We went right up beside him, and Gregorio poked him in the side with an oar, to see if he could make him move, but it was like poking the side of a building.

"Christ," he said, "that thing's enormous."

"Yes," papa said. "Almost a third the size of the sub we're looking for."

Papa said that this huge fish lives entirely on plankton, a form of minute marine life which it takes in through its mouth and strains like a sieve through some mechanism in its gills. I could see how that is a good way for them to feed as they are so huge that they could never live off other fish if they had to hunt for them.

The following day we saw a school of killer whales. I couldn't express it at the time, but in retrospect they seemed to represent all the evil in nature. But then they just frightened me. Papa said we should give them a wide berth because they had been known to attack fishing boats, breaking them up with their ramrodlike heads and sometimes eating the crew. He said they'd go into a school of tuna and just kill for the fun of it, sometimes not stopping even to eat what they had killed.

They weren't very big for whales, only about eighteen to twenty feet long. But they were built for speed, like porpoises, and they kept moving in synchronization, back and forth, breaking the water together, turning in unison, always moving, always hunting. When I was older I saw wild dogs in Africa which reminded me of these killer whales in the way they, too, were constantly on the move. One knew they had to do a lot of killing and eating to fuel such a frenzied pace.

In the evening we'd pull into shore at some harbor or cove. The first night I was assigned to a berth down below, next to Hammer, and his feet smelled terrible. I almost threw up all over him before I got out of there, but as he was always drunk by six o'clock, the poor bastard probably would not have noticed. When we went up topside for a breather it was really beautiful. The stars seem brighter in those latitudes, especially when you're out on the water, away from pollution. There must have been millions of them, some much,

much brighter than others. Pat was interested in astronomy and had told me something about Orion's Belt and other constellations. I tried to pick out the North Star, too, but there were so many stars that I couldn't be sure that I'd found it.

Papa had bought Pat a beautiful telescope, as he always encouraged our interests, but papa himself wasn't really interested in astronomy and would say, never to Pat of course, "Sure, they're up there and they're beautiful and they're a great aid to navigation at night, but to make one's life work studying them seems sort of pointless. How can they help us any more than they already have? Star-gazing is just what the term implies."

The next morning, on the second day out, the country started to get beautiful too. It looked the way the Florida Everglades must have looked in the old days, with colors the hues of a Turner painting, and flocks of flamingos standing in the shallow waters, sometimes rising like undulating pink clouds floating over the early morning mist still covering the water. It was like the dawn of creation and it put papa in a religious mood.

"Can you look at this country and doubt there's a God, Gig?" I knew he didn't expect an answer.

"But I've seen other country, too," he went on. "Perhaps God has his good and bad days . . ."

"I thought you said it was blasphemy to joke about God," I said.

"I joke a lot about organized religion because I don't think Bible pushers have the Word any more than I do. I wouldn't kid Our Lord, for example, if He was on the Cross, but I would try to joke with Him if I ran into Him chasing the money-changers out of the Temple.

"But never joke about a man's religion in front of him," he warned me. "A hell of a lot of people get comfort from their religion. Who knows, they might even be right."

Then we hit bottom.

"Jesus Christ!" Papa immediately stopped all engines, put the *Pilar* in reverse, and backed off slowly, with the screws churning up mud; there was an awful sound as if the boat were human and in agony. Next to us and his wife and his cats, I think my father loved the *Pilar* more than anything on earth and I felt sick as we went around opening all the floorboard coverings to see if water was coming in.

But there weren't any leaks. Papa said there had been a slight mistake in the chart which showed the depth at low tide to be three feet higher than it actually was. Perhaps. Sometimes sand shifts and time obliterates landmarks, but it was also conceivable that papa had made a slight mistake.

We reached Cayo Confitis just before dark. The whole island couldn't have been much larger than the skating rink at Rockefeller Center, maybe 100 yards in diameter. It was flat and unoccupied except for a shack in the center, with a radio antenna on top, and a huge flagpole next to the shack.

Cuba's proud colors were still aloft but at sunset three bored-looking little men marched out in formation from the shack, waved to us, and with great ceremony proceeded to haul down the flag. One man worked the ropes; the officer, identified as such by some rusty braid loosely attached to one shoulder, stood at attention, and the third man stood slightly behind the officer, picking his nose.

It was the sort of post the officer might have been assigned to if he was suspected of having an affair with the commandant's wife—or the other two, of committing petty thievery. The officer always showed his rank by wearing a faded tunic; the soldiers just wore khaki shorts coming apart at the seams.

Papa could see that Pat and I were glum at the prospect of spending two months on the island, and he immediately tried to cheer us up.

"I know it looks bleak, guys, and I am not happy either to be separated from you all day while we are out on patrol. But there are some wonderful reefs for spear fishing around here (involuntary twitch of my facial muscles at the mention of scuba diving) and there are plenty of interesting birds to identify, Pat, and you can shoot the edible ones, Gig, after he has identified them. We'll have fun in the evening, reading and playing cards. You'll see, it won't be so bad."

Next day Pat and I stayed on the island fishing, collecting seashells, and skin diving, while papa went out on patrol. Gregorio, who had five kids, kept us company and in the evening rowed us out to join papa when he returned. Everybody on the *Pilar* was tired but in amazingly good humor. We sat around playing cards. We played for what seemed like thousands of dollars and it was pretty exciting if you had a good hand.

There was surprisingly little drinking at first, partly because the supply of alcohol was low, partly because the crew wanted to be in good shape if they spotted a sub. Papa reached for a book more often than a bottle. He had a bag crammed with detective stories, *War and Peace,* and Fraser's *The Golden Bough.* . . .

Papa couldn't have been more pleasant or a better father on that trip. He was wonderfully cheerful with everyone, and keeping several people cramped in a boat in good humor all the time was no easy trick. He talked about subjects that interested the different crew members. To me it was baseball. One time I got into an argument with Neville about Ty Cobb's lifetime batting average and Neville said, "I bet you a hundred dollars it wasn't as high as three sixty-seven."

And I looked him in the eye and said, "Neville, I wouldn't want to take your money." Papa laughed; he appreciated my generosity.

It was great fun for a while–until Hammer won everybody's money at cards and the books ran out, and until it became apparent that the ocean out there was awfully big and that the chances of spotting a sub on it were pretty small.

The submarines were there all right, we would hear them talking back and forth in German at night, but as none of us could speak German very well, this wasn't much help. And, in any event, we had no triangulation device to pin them down. Subs would almost never surface during the day. Thank God they didn't, or I might still be on that bloody island living off shellfish and watching the Cubans raise and lower that flag. . . .

Hammer's feet finally put an end to the trip. The fungus rot got so bad that he couldn't wear shoes anymore and the combined sight and smell of those feet began to elicit pity from all of us, the first pity we'd felt for him since he'd won our money.

Papa, who knew some medicine, was afraid that Hammer's feet might have to be amputated unless he got treatment, so we called off the chase and headed back to Havana. The Cubans showed little emotion when we left. They were beyond that, poor devils. . . .

Everyone was a little hung over the next morning. It was past seven when the *Pilar* reached open sea, and we were all on the flying bridge when Neville saw it.

"Submarine! Submarine! About ten points off the starboard bow and closing. Approximate range one thousand yards. She must have just surfaced. I scoured that area a few minutes ago."

"Battle stations," papa said, almost inaudibly. "But take it easy. Normal movements. No rushing. Try to make your faces seem calm. We don't know how powerful their binoculars are."

Once below decks, though, I moved fast, got my Mannlicher Schoenauer from under my bunk and loaded it. Pat was up in the bow, ahead of me, on the starboard side, loading his 303 Lee-Enfield. We grinned at each other, too excited to be afraid. War is a great game for boys.

Hammer murmured, "Fighting's not in my fucking orders!" But he finally limped to his post.

The Bomb was already on the flying bridge and the two jai alai players were unloosening its fastenings.

"Christ," Neville said, staring through his binoculars. "She's as big as a battleship."

"But she doesn't seem to be getting any bigger," papa said, and took the glasses from Neville. After a few seconds he handed the glasses back.

"Neville, it's not closing. It's heading AWAY from us," he said with cold, furious control in his voice. "And not only that. It's PULLING away from us. Our max speed is twelve knots. Hers is a lot more than that. She looks to be about fifteen hundred yards away now."

Then papa laughed and said in Spanish to Patche, "Can you throw The Bomb fifteen hundred yards?"

By now no one needed field glasses to tell that the sub was losing us fast, moving majestically on the dead-calm sea.

Everybody was cursing. Patche yelled, "Come back and fight, you yellow sons of whores!" By now the sub was just a dot on the horizon. We were stunned; the last thing we had expected was to be ignored by the enemy.

In the silence that followed we could hear the radio operator flushing the john.

Later that evening papa told me, "I had decided that we wouldn't close with you and Pat on board." And in a lower voice, "I bet some of the U-boat crew are just kids, too. It's trite to talk about war: Sherman said it all. War is necessary sometimes. Maybe. You wonder."

He was mocking orators now:

"Someone else will fight for me on the beaches. December seven, a day that will live in infamy, will be avenged by younger men. Hell, fix me a gin and tonic, will you, Gig? We're heading home."

This interview, conducted in London, was published in Hulton's National Weekly Picture Post, *24 (15 July 1944), pp. 20–21.*

HEMINGWAY LOOKS AT THE WAR IN EUROPE

"Good morning, gentlemen. Have you had breakfast?"

The author of *For Whom the Bell Tolls* squats on his bed in white pyjamas and a khaki shirt. His hotel room is littered with books and military kit.

He throws a timorous glance at the camera.

"Well, what do you want me to do? I'm not an actor you know. I'm a writer."

We look at the man as he reclines massively against the headboard, one hand plucking at the patriarchal beard which encroaches on his ruddy, boyish

Hemingway recuperating in a London hospital after the May 1944 car crash in which his driver hit a water tank during a blackout

cheeks. He looks like a mixture of prophet and mountain shepherd, prepared to do a little fighting in the intervals. He watches carefully as the cameraman gets ready.

"Is that a Leica? I always use a Rolleiflex; used it a lot in the Spanish Civil War. I don't now, of course. I just write war reports for Collier's Magazine. Someone else takes the pictures. And now the others are doing the fighting too."

"Will you be writing war reports for long, do you think?"

Hemingway's large face spreads into a quick smile.

"I don't know, and I wouldn't tell you if I did. There are some things about it I like, and some I don't. I like going out with the men and watching the action. But I hate the writing part of it. I'd rather write books. You see," he continues warming up and raising himself on his pillow, "when I work on a book, I only write about 350 words at a time. Now I have to cable them 6,000 words a day. As a matter of fact I have rather a tough time with this punctuation for cables," and before

I can stop him he has slid off the bed, stalked to a corner cupboard, and handed me one of his typescripts, in which every question-mark is written out in its full dozen letters.

The typescript tells part of the story of D-Day, with American assault boats carrying men from transports to the most bitterly contested beach in Normandy.

"Were you in one of these?"

"From three in the morning until late in the afternoon. It was the longest battle I'd ever been through without a drink. That's why I'm not likely to forget it."

"Did you get that there?" nodding at the gash across the dome of his forehead.

"No, I got that when my car ran against a static water tank. Fifty-two stitches but very unromantic, I'm afraid."

There's a knock at the door and a waiter comes in, wheeling the breakfast. With a puzzled look Hemingway gazes at his bacon, mushroom, toast and rhubarb, but does not stir. He seems not to realise what it's all doing here, or who can have ordered it.

"You're quite sure you've had your breakfast?"

"Positive."

So the breakfast must be his. He takes a roll and breaks it reluctantly. Still not quite certain. But as he looks his face lightens. "This is a typical good hotel breakfast," he says. "Always the same, but excellent. Much better than at home. But I do feel a perfect pig eating like this, with you fellows just sitting round working."

The howl of a siren interrupts him. He points his fork at the door and says: "Some people don't seem to mind these things, and others don't care for them at all. It seems to worry the women most."

The meal over, he sits down at the typewriter, reads over yesterday's script and sets about removing commas that should have been spelled out. Then he turns to us once more.

"You don't suppose I could have some of those photographs, do you? I should like to send some to my boys. I've got one in Italy, you know. The other two are at school back home. Normally I'd be with them now."

We promise to send them, and say good-bye. Before we are out of the door Hemingway is back at his work. He is still wearing a khaki shirt and pyjama trousers, and he's got another 3,000 words to do for Collier's before the next knock at the door brings another equally unexpected meal.

These comments by Hemingway were used as captions for the photographs in the article.

"Of course it was different in the Spanish war. I wasn't there to watch—but to fight. I liked that a lot better."

"Back Home I Start Work At Five. I've been working since five. I like to start things early. It comes of living in the country."

"What? Sure You've Had Enough? I Hate Eating Alone." A large, genial, impressive figure—surprisingly gentle and extremely friendly—makes his unusual breakfast: bacon, mushroom, rhubarb, toast and whiskey.

"Isn't That One of Those Flying Bombs Just Going Over?" In his bedroom in "Southern England," Ernest Hemingway hears the flying bomb—latest weapon in the war between humanity and Fascism. That war, so far as he's concerned, has been going on since the Spanish fighting began in 1936.

"Clothes? I Wear What's Around." A khaki shirt and white pyjama trousers are Hemingway's outfit for this morning's writing.

Hemingway published this account of the taking of Paris in Collier's, 114 (7 October 1944), pp. 65–66.

How We Came to Paris

Never can I describe to you the emotions I felt on the arrival of the armored column of General Leclerc southeast of Paris. Having just returned from a patrol which scared the pants off of me and having been kissed by all the worst element in a town which imagined it had been liberated through our fortuitous entry, I was informed that the general himself was just down the road and anxious to see us. Accompanied by one of the big shots of the resistance movement and Colonel B, who by that time was known throughout Rambouillet as a gallant officer and a *grand seigneur* and who had held the town ever since we could remember, we advanced in some state toward the general. His greeting—unprintable—will live in my ears forever.

"Buzz off, you unspeakables," the gallant general said, in effect, in something above a whisper, and Colonel B, the resistance king and your armored-operations correspondent withdrew.

Later the G-2 of the division invited us to dinner and they operated next day on the information Colonel B had amassed for them. But for your correspondent that was the high point of the attack on Paris.

In war, my experience has been that a rude general is a nervous general. At this time I drew no such deductions but departed on another patrol where I could keep my own nervousness in one jeep and my friends could attempt to clarify the type of resistance we could encounter on the following day between Toussus le Noble and Le Christ de Saclay.

Having found out what this resistance would be, we returned to the Hotel du Grand Veneur in Rambouillet and passed a restless night. I do not remember exactly what produced this restlessness but perhaps it was the fact that the joint was too full of too many people, including, actually, at one time two military police. Or perhaps it was the fact that we had proceeded too far ahead of our supply of Vitamin B_1, and the ravages of alcohol were affecting the nerves of the hardier guerrillas who had liberated too many towns in too short a time. At any rate I was restless and I think, without exaggeration, I may truly state that those whom Colonel B and I by then referred to as "our people" were restless.

The guerrilla chief, the actual fighting head of "our people," said, "We want to take Paris. What the hell is the delay?"

The Cross Roads   - 7

German prisoners who had been taken by ~~the~~ irregulars

were often as cooperative as head waiters or minor diplomats. ~~In~~ Something

general ~~we~~ regarded the Germans as perverted Boy Scouts. This is

~~Sometimes they regarded them less tenderly~~

another ~~way of saying they were splendid soldiers. We were~~ not

~~splendid soldiers.~~ ~~We were~~ specialists in a dirty trade. In French

we said, "un metier tres sale."

We knew, from repeated questionings, that all Germans

coming through on this escape route were making for Aachen and I

knew that all we killed now we would not have to fight in Aachen

nor behind the West Wall. ~~We, in the Division, were racing them~~ This was simple

~~to the West Wall and we ranged ahead of the Division and fought~~ on

~~a personal basis every day.~~

He Germans ~~that we~~ saw coming now were on bicycles.

There were four of them and they were in a hurry too but they were

very tired. They were not cyclist troops. They were just Germans

on stolen bicycles. The leading rider saw the fresh blood on the

road and then he turned his head and saw the vehicle and he put his

weight hard down on his right pedal with his right boot and we

opened on him and on the others. A man shot off a bicycle is always

a sad thing to see, although not as sad as a horse shot with a

Typescript for Hemingway's World War II story "Black Ass at the Crossroads," written in 1956 (auctioned by Charles Hamilton Galleries, Sale Number 19, 24 May 1967)

"There is no delay, Chief," I answered. "All this is part of a giant operation. Have patience. Tomorrow we will take Paris."

"I hope so," the guerrilla chief said. "My wife has been expecting me there for some time. I want to get the hell into Paris to see my wife, and I see no necessity to wait for a lot of soldiers to come up."

"Be patient," I told him.

That fateful night we slept. It might be a fateful night but tomorrow would certainly be an even more fateful day. My anticipations of a really good fight on the morrow were marred by a guerrilla who entered the hotel late at night and woke me to inform me that all the Germans who could do so were pulling out of Paris. We knew there would be fighting the next day by the screen the German army had left. But I did not anticipate any heavy fighting, since we knew the German dispositions and could attack or by-pass them accordingly, and I assured our guerrillas that if they would only be patient, we would have the privilege of entering Paris with soldiers ahead of us instead of behind us.

This privilege did not appeal to them at all. But one of the big shots of the underground insisted that we do this, as he said it was only courteous to allow troops to precede and by the time we had reached Toussus le Noble, where there was a short but sharp fight, orders were given that neither newspapermen nor guerrillas were to be allowed to proceed until the column had passed.

The day we advanced on Paris it rained heavily and everyone was soaked to the skin within an hour of leaving Rambouillet. We proceeded through Chevreuse and St. Rémy-lès-Chevreuses where we had formerly run patrols and were well known to the local inhabitants, from whom we had collected information and with whom we had downed considerable quantities of armagnac to still the ever-present discontent of our guerrillas, who were very Paris-conscious at this time. In those days I had found that the production of an excellent bottle of any sort of alcoholic beverage was the only way of ending an argument.

After we had proceeded through St. Rémy-lès-Chevreuses, where we were wildly acclaimed by the local *charcutier,* or pork butcher, who had participated in previous operations and been cockeyed ever since, we made a slight error in preceding the column to a village called Courcelle. There we were informed that there were no vehicles ahead of us and, greatly to the disgust of our people who wished to proceed on what they believed to be the shortest route into Paris, we returned to St. Rémy-lès-Chevreuses to join the armored column

which was proceeding toward Châteaufort. Our return was viewed with considerable alarm by the local *charcutier.* But when we explained the situation to him he acclaimed us wildly again and, downing a couple of quick ones, we advanced resolutely toward Toussus le Noble where I knew the column would have to fight.

At this point I knew there would be German opposition just ahead of us and also on our right at Le Christ de Saclay. The Germans had dug and blasted out a series of defense points between Châteaufort and Toussus le Noble and beyond the crossroads. Past the airdrome toward Buc they had 88s that commanded all that stretch of road. As we came closer to where the tanks were operating around Trappes I became increasingly apprehensive.

The French armor operated beautifully. On the road toward Toussus le Noble, where we knew there were Germans with machine guns in the wheat shocks, the tanks deployed and screened both of our flanks and we saw them rolling ahead through the cropped wheat field as though they were on maneuvers. No one saw the Germans until they came out with their hands up after the tanks had passed. It was a beautiful use of armor, that problem child of war, and it was lovely to see.

When we ran up against the seven tanks and four 88s the Germans had beyond the airfield, the French handled the fight prettily, too. Their artillery was back in another open wheat field, and when the German guns—four of which had been brought up during the night and were firing absolutely in the open—cut loose on the column, the French mechanized artillery slammed into them. You could not hear with the German shells coming in, the 20-mm. firing, and the machine-gun fire cracking overhead, but the French underground leader who had correlated the information on the German dispositions shouted in French into my ear, "The contact is beautiful. Just where we said. Beautiful."

It was much too beautiful for me, who had never been a great lover of contact anyway, and I hit the deck as an 88 shell burst alongside the road. Contact is a very noisy business and, since our column was held up at this point, the more forceful and active of the guerrillas aided in reconstructing the road which had been churned into soup by the armor. This kept their minds from the contact taking place all around us. They filled in the mudholes with bricks and tiles from a smashed house, and passed along chunks of cement and pieces of house from hand to hand. It was raining hard all this time, and by the time the contact was over, the column had two dead and five wounded, one tank burned up, and had knocked out two of the seven enemy tanks and silenced all of the 88s.

"*C'est un bel accrochage,*" the underground leader said to me jubilantly.

This means something like "We have grappled with them prettily" or "We tied into them beautifully," searching in mind for the exact meaning of *accrochage,* which is what happens when two cars lock bumpers.

I shouted, "Prettily! Prettily!"

At which a young French lieutenant, who did not have the air of having been mixed up in too many *accrochages* in his time but who, for all I know, may have participated in hundreds of them, said to me, "Who the hell are you and what are you doing here in our column?"

"I am a war correspondent, monsieur," I replied.

The lieutenant shouted: "Do not let any war correspondents proceed until the column has passed. And especially do not let this one proceed."

"Okay, my lieutenant," the M.P. said. "I will keep an eye on them."

"And none of that guerrilla rabble, either," the lieutenant ordered. "None of that is to pass until all the column has gone through."

"My lieutenant," I said, "the rabble will be removed from sight once this little *accrochage* is finished and the column has proceeded."

"What do you mean—this little *accrochage*?" he demanded, and I feared hostility might be creeping into his voice.

Since we were not to advance farther with the column, I took evasive action at this point and waded down the road to a bar. Numerous guerrillas were seated in it singing happily and passing the time of day with a lovely Spanish girl from Bilbao whom I had last met on the famous two-way, or wide-open patrol point just outside the town of Cognières. This was the town we used to take from the Germans whenever one of their vehicles pulled out of it, and they would return whenever we stepped off the road. This girl had been following wars and preceding troops since she was fifteen and she and the guerrillas were paying no attention to the *accrochage* at all.

A guerrilla chief named C said, "Have a drink of this excellent white wine." I took a long drink from the bottle and it turned out to be a highly alcoholic liqueur tasting of oranges and called Grand Marnier.

A stretcher was coming back with a wounded man on it. "Look," a guerrilla said, "these military are constantly suffering casualties. Why do they not allow us to proceed ahead in a sensible manner?"

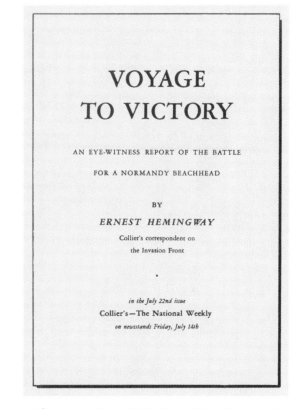

VOYAGE TO VICTORY

AN EYE-WITNESS REPORT OF THE BATTLE

FOR A NORMANDY BEACHHEAD

BY

ERNEST HEMINGWAY

Collier's correspondent on
the Invasion Front

·

in the July 22nd issue
Collier's—The National Weekly
on newsstands Friday, July 14th

Title page from the pamphlet Collier's *published that recounts the D-Day landings. The magazine distributed this article to promote sales of its issues.*

"Okay, okay," said another guerrilla in G.I. fatigue clothes, with the brassard of the *francs-tireurs* on his sleeve. "What about the comrades who were killed yesterday on the road?"

Another said, "But today we're going into Paris."

"Let's go back and see if we can make it by Le Christ de Saclay," I said. "The law has arrived and they won't let us go on any farther until the column has passed. The roads are too muddy and torn up here. We could push the light touring cars through, but the truck might bog down and stall things."

"We can push through by a side road," the guerrilla chief named C said. "Since when do we have to follow columns?"

"I think it is best to go back as far as Châteaufort," I said. "Maybe we can go much faster that way."

On the crossroads outside Châteaufort we found Colonel B and Commander A, who had become detached from us before we had run into the

Ernest Hemingway read
Fathers and Sons from this copy of
Winner take Nothing on May. 12th 1937
for the Friends of Shakespeare and Company

Lu et approuvé

Ernest Hemingway
Paris august 25
1944:

Hemingway added this note to Sylvia Beach's copy of Winner Take Nothing *after "liberating" Shakespeare and Company, August 1944 (Sylvia Beach Collection, Princeton University Library)*

accrochage, and told them about the beautiful contact up the road. The artillery was still firing in the open wheat field, and the two gallant officers had found some lunch in a farmhouse. French troops from the column were burning the wooden boxes that had held the shells the artillery had been blasting with, and we took off our wet clothes and dried them at the fire. German prisoners were drifting in, and an officer in the column asked us to send the guerrillas up to where a group of Germans had just surrendered in the wheat shocks. They brought them back in good military style, all the prisoners alive and well.

"This is idiotic, you know, my captain," the oldest one of the band said. "Now someone has to feed them."

The prisoners said they were office workers in Paris and had only been brought out and put in the positions at one o'clock this morning.

"Do you believe that sort of stuff?" asked the oldest guerrilla.

"It could be possible. They weren't here yesterday," I said.

"This entire military nonsense disgusts me," the oldest guerrilla said. He was forty-one and had a thin, sharp face with clear blue eyes, and a rare but fine smile. "Eleven of our group were tortured and shot by these Germans. I have been beaten and kicked by them, and they would have shot me if they knew who I was. Now we are asked to guard them carefully and respectfully."

"They are not your prisoners," I explained. "The military took them."

The rain turned to a light drifting mist and then the sky cleared. The prisoners were sent back to Rambouillet in the big German truck that the underground big shot quite rightly was anxious to get out of the column for the moment. Leaving word with the M.P. on the crossroads where the truck could rejoin us, we drove on after the column.

We caught up with the tanks on a side road this side of the main Versailles-Paris highway and moved with them down into a deeply wooded valley and out into green fields where there was an old château. We watched the tanks deploy again, like watching dogs outside a moving band of sheep. They had fought once up ahead of us while we had gone back to see if the road through Le Christ de Saclay was free, and we passed a burned-out tank and three dead Germans. One of these had been run over and flattened out in a way that left no doubt of the power of armor when properly used.

On the main Versailles-Villacoublay highway the column proceeded past the wrecked airdrome of Villacoublay to the crossroads of the Porte Clamart. Here, while the column was stopped, a Frenchman came running up and reported a small German tank on the road that led into the woods. I searched the road with my glasses but could not see anything. In the meantime, the German vehicle, which was not a tank but a lightly armored German jeep mounting a machine gun and a 20-mm. gun, made a turn in the woods and came tearing up the road, firing at the crossroads.

Everyone started shooting at it, but it wheeled and regained the woods. Archie Pelkey, my driver, got in two shots at it but could not be sure that he had hit. Two men were hit and were carried into the lee of the corner building for first aid. The guerrillas were happy now that shooting had started again.

"We have nice work ahead of us. Good work ahead of us," the guerrilla with the sharp face and the light blue eyes said. "I'm happy some of the b————s are still here."

"Do you think we will have much more chance to fight?" the guerrilla named C asked.

"Certainly," I said. "There's bound to be some of them in the town."

My own war aim at this moment was to get into Paris without being shot. Our necks had been out for a long time. Paris was going to be taken. I took cover in all the street fighting—the solidest cover available—and with someone covering the stairs behind me when we were in houses or the entrances to apartment houses.

From now on, the advance of the column was something to see. Ahead of us would be a barricade of felled trees. The tanks would pass around them or butt them around like elephants handling logs. You would see the tanks charge into a barricade of old motorcars and go smashing on ahead with a jalopy bouncing along, its smashed fenders entangled in the tracks. Armor, which can be so vulnerable and so docile in the close hedgerow country where it is a prey to antitank guns, bazookas and anyone who does not fear it, was smashing round like so many drunken elephants in a native village.

Ahead and on our left, a German ammunition dump was burning, and the varicolored antiaircraft projectiles were bursting in the continuous rattle and pop of the exploding 20-mm. stuff. The larger projectiles started to explode as the heat increased, and gave the impression of a bombardment. I couldn't locate Archie Pelkey, but later I found he had advanced on the burning munitions dump, thinking it was a fight.

"There wasn't nobody there, Papa," he said; "it was just a lot of ammunition burning."

"Don't go off by yourself," I said. "How did you know we didn't want to roll?"

"Okay, Papa. Sorry, Papa. I understand, Papa. Only, Mr. Hemingway, I went off with *Frère*—the one who is my brother—because I thought he said there was a fight."

"Oh, hell!" I said. "You've been ruined by guerrillas."

We ran through the road where the munitions dump was exploding, with Archie, who has bright red hair, six years of regular Army, four words of French, a missing front tooth, and a *Frère* in a guerrilla outfit, laughing heartily at the noise the big stuff was making as it blew.

"Sure is popping off, Papa," he shouted. His freckled face was completely happy. "They say this Paris is quite a town, Papa. You ever been into it?"

"Yeah."

We were going downhill now, and I knew that road and what we would see when we made the next turn.

"*Frère*, he was telling me something about it while the column was held up, but I couldn't make it out," Archie said. "All I could make out was it must be a hell of a place. Something about he was going to *Paname*, too. This place hasn't got anything to do with Panama, has it?"

"No, Arch," I said, "the French call it *Paname* when they love it very much."

"I see," Archie said. "*Compris*. Just like something you might call a girl that wouldn't be her right name. Right?"

"Right."

"I couldn't make out what the hell *Frère* was saying," Archie said. "I guess it's like they call me Jim. Everybody in the outfit calls me Jim, and my name is Archie."

"Maybe they like you," I said.

"They're a good outfit," Archie said. "Best outfit I ever been with. No discipline. Got to admit that. Drinking all the time. Got to admit that. But plenty fighting outfit. Nobody gives a damn if they get killed or not. *Compris?*"

"Yeah," I said. I couldn't say anything more then, because I had a funny choke in my throat and I had to clean my glasses because there now, below us, gray and always beautiful, was spread the city I love best in all the world.

The U.S. Army investigated charges that Hemingway had carried weapons and led French partisans during the fight for Paris in August 1944, and in Nancy on 17 November 1944 he was interrogated by the Inspector General of the Third Army. Staff Sergeant George Blam transcribed this examination, after which Hemingway was cleared of all charges (Blam Manuscripts, Lilly Library, Indiana University).

INVESTIGATION INTO THE ACTIVITIES OF ERNEST HEMINGWAY, WAR CORRESPON-DENT FOR COLLIERS, DURING WORLD WAR II IN THE EUROPEAN THEATER OF OPERATIONS IN RAMBOUILLET, FRANCE, IN AUGUST, 1944.

PRESENT:

COLONEL PARK, INSPECTOR GENERAL OF THE THIRD ARMY.
ERNEST HEMINGWAY
STAFF SERGEANT GEORGE BLAM

ERNEST HEMINGWAY,
being first duly sworn, was examined and testified as follows:

EXAMINATION BY COLONEL PARK:

Q: Please state your name, occupation and station.

A: Ernest Hemingway, War Correspondence, Colliers Weekly, APO 887.

Q: I am required to caution each witness during an investigation of his rights with respect to the 24th Article of War. It is as follows.

(The 24th Article of War was read.)

Q: Do you understand your rights as a witness?

A: I understand them.

Q: Were you in Rambouillet about August 22nd to 25th just before the French Armored Division entered Paris?

A: I was.

Q: Will you state briefly what you were doing there?

A: On August 19th I stopped at the Command Post of the 22nd Infantry Regiment of the 5th Division just outside of Maintenon in my capacity as War Correspondent accredited to the Third Army to ask for information on the front this regiment was holding.

The G2 and 3 of this regiment showed me the disposition of their battalions and of their most advanced outpost at a point a short distance beyond Epernon on the road to Rambouillet. At the Regimental Command Post I was informed there was heavy fighting in progress outside of Rambouillet.

I knew the country and the roads around Epernon, Rambouillet, Trappes, and Versailles well as I have bicycled, walked and driven a car through this part of France for many years.

At the forward outpost of the 22nd Infantry Regiment I encountered some French civilians who had just come in from Rambouillet by bicycle.

I was the only person at the outpost who spoke French. These civilians informed me that the last Germans had left Rambouillet at 3:00 o'clock that morning but that the roads into the town were mined. They reported that contrary to the information given me at the C.P. of the 22nd Infantry Regiment. There was no fighting in progress outside of Rambouillet at all.

I started to return to Regimental Headquarters with this information which seemed to be necessary to be placed in the hands of the proper authorities as soon as possible, but after driving a short way down the road back to Maintenon I decided it would be better to return and get the French civilians and take them to the Regimental C.P. so they themselves could be interrogated and give fuller information.

When I reached the outpost again I found two cars full of French guerrilla fighters, most of whom were naked to the waist. They were armed with pistols and two sten guns they received by parachute. They just came from Rambouillet and their story of the German withdrawal tallied with the information the French civilians had given.

They also possessed additional information and I conducted them back to the Regimental Command Post of the 22nd Infantry where I translated their information on the town and the state of the roads to the proper authorities.

I then returned to the outpost in my capacity as War Correspondent to wait for a mine clearing detail and a reconnaissance troop that were to make rendezvous with these French guerrillas who were to conduct them to the mined area which they had already reconnoitered.

I was proceeding toward Rambouillet as a War Correspondent but would act as an interpreter for the

THESE SPACES FOR MESSAGE CENTER ONLY

TIME FILED   MSG CEN No.   HOW SENT

MESSAGE (SUBMIT TO MESSAGE CENTER IN DUPLICATE)   PRECEDENCE

NO. 1   DATE 20 AUG 44

TO DYNAMITE ORD OR DYNAMITE UNITS.

THIS IS AUTHORITY FROM THE CG DYNAMITE TO PROVIDE MR EARNEST HEMINGWAY WITH SMALL ARMS GRENADES OR OTHER CAPTURED ARTICLES HE DESIRES.

OFFICIAL DESIGNATION OF SENDER   TIME SIGNED 1030

SIGNATURE AND GRADE OF WRITER R. L. Norling Maj

Authorization for Hemingway to be issued weapons from U.S. Army forces operating near Rambouillet (Ernest Hemingway Collection, John F. Kennedy Library)

troops which were being sent on mine clearing and reconnaissance.

After waiting for some time and no one coming up, the French guerrilla fighters became very impatient. They had placed themselves under my command ignorant of the fact that a War Correspondent cannot command troops, a situation which I explained to them at the earliest moment. They wished to proceed to the mine field and establish a guard to prevent any American vehicles which might advance from running into it.

I agreed that this seemed an intelligent thing for them to do, and we were proceeding toward Rambouillet when we were joined by Lieutenant Irving Krieger of East Orange, New Jersey, from the 2nd Infantry Regiment. Lieutenant Krieger, aided by these French guerrilla fighters, who placed themselves under his orders, cleared the mine field which was composed of a mixture of French and German mines. The field had been hastily laid and many of the American mines were placed upside down. The source of the American mines was ascertained when mention was made of an American truck which had formed part of an American reconnaissance unit which had been ambushed outside of Rambouillet by anti-tank and machine-gun fire two days before. The truck had been shot up and two jeeps had also been hit. Seven American personnel had been killed and were buried by the French alongside the road. The leading car of the reconnaissance unit had been allowed to pass before the truck and the two jeeps were fired upon. Some American personnel escaped and some who were wounded were later recovered. I was never able to ascertain the names of these men, but during the time that we were in Rambouillet an officer from their unit came to the town to ascertain the place of their burial and requesting what papers had been taken from them by the civilian population when they were buried.

In addition to the mine field there were two German self-propelled anti-tank weapons in position to impede an American advance down the road. They were in the form of miniature tanks and I was informed by Lieutenant Krieger each one carried 200 pounds of TNT in it and that they were controlled electrically. One was in the road pointing straight up the hill. In order to take any column descending the hill head-on, and the other was on the left side of the shoulder of the road. As you looked up the hill on the right side of the shoulder of the road, looking uphill, there was a high wall and any column descending the hill encountering the first of these miniature tanks would have had to swerve to their right and would have been taken in the flank by the second of these self-propelled anti-tank weapons. This weapon is called by the Germans the Goliath self-propelled tank and was one of their vaunted, secret weapons.

Lieutenant Krieger severed the wires controlling these tanks and placed a guard over them. After the clearing of this roadblock the French guerrilla fighters still wished to place themselves under my command.

I explained that I was unable to accept this as a correspondent is forbidden by the Geneva Convention to command troops, but that I would be glad to give them the benefit of my advice on any matters that came up if I could do so without violating the Geneva Convention.

When my advice was requested by them, I suggested they should aid in the preservation of law and order until the arrival of the proper constituted authorities. There was no disorder in Rambouillet of any kind.

I also suggested to them that it might be useful for them to make a reconnaissance on the two main roads beyond the town pending the arrival of the reconnaissance troop commanded by Lieutenant Peterson of Cleveland, Ohio.

When the French guerrillas asked my advice as to what capacity they would be most useful, I suggested that they might aid in screening the approachers to the town. Lieutenant Peterson was in sufficient force only to hold the center of the town at this time. This also was done.

After arrival of Colonel David R.E. Bruce, CO, OSS, ETOUSA, I explained to him what had taken place in the town up to this time and offered my services to him in any way in which I might be useful provided that my actions did not violate the Geneva Convention or that any of them should in any way prejudice my fellow War Correspondents.

As senior American officer present in the town, Colonel Bruce had a great many problems to deal with. These problems were greatly increased when the American reconnaissance forces were withdrawn on the 20th, thus leaving the town, which had been occupied by American troops, without the presence of any

troops except those who were there on special missions. These troops consisted entirely, to my knowledge, of British and Allied parachuters, agents employed on missions into enemy territory and other men engaged in secret intelligence activities.

After the withdrawal of the American combat units the problem arose of the disposal of this American personnel and whether there was a possibility of the town being screened or defended in order that the enemy should not re-enter it when they became aware of the withdrawal of the American Army reconnaissance units.

Q.: This phase of the Rambouillet incident is covered by a statement by James W. Thornton, a Major AC, IS9 (WEA), American, G-2 Division, SHAEF, APO 757. This statement is hereby appended.

This statement will be marked Exhibit C in this report of investigation. Please proceed.

A: The following problems existed at this point:

The presence of German troops in both small and large bodies throughout the forest of Rambouillet. Many of these bodies of troops had no desire to fight but wished to surrender. They were residue of troops which had been defeated at Chartres. Other bodies of German troops were attempting to join the German forces which were intact between Rambouillet and Paris. It was necessary for the proper authorities to establish priorities for dealing with the problems presented by these different types of German forces.

Second, there was the problem of the possibility of the defense of the town.

Third, there was a problem of obtaining precise and accurate information as to the enemy disposition between Rambouillet and the Versailles Road in order that this information might be delivered to the proper authorities if, in case, they advanced through this sector.

In all of these problems I served only in an advisory capacity to Colonel Bruce, who was the senior American officer present. I didn't command troops nor give orders but only transmitted orders given by a senior American officer who was occupied with multiple problems at this time.

In regard to the value of any information obtained, I offer the statements by Colonel Bruce, GSC, CO, OSS, a statement by S.L.A. Marshall, Lieutenant Colonel GSC, G2, Historical Branch, WDGS, who were in Rambouillet at this time.

Q.: They will be marked Exhibits D and E respectively to this report of investigation.

A: All information received as to location of enemy mine fields, the emplacement of enemy artillery and anti-tank pieces, the location of enemy radar, anti-aircraft batteries, the enemy defense line, the strong points of which were blasted out the day before the arrival of the Second French Armored Column, and the movement of enemy tanks and troops in this area were evaluated, checked and delivered by Colonel Bruce to the proper military authorities.

Q: Were your activities observed or known by a number of other correspondents?

A: My actual activities were not known to a number of other correspondents. My obvious activities as passing information, helping in organization of the hotel, attempting to provide billets for the correspondents who arrived during the latter part of our tenure at Rambouillet were quite obvious, well known and frequently misunderstood.

Q: In accordance with Paragraph 7 AR2O-30 it is appropriate that I acquaint you with the allegations which I am required to investigate. They are included in a report to the effect that Mr. Hemingway stripped off correspondent's insignia and acted as a colonel, French resistance troops; that he had a room with mines, grenades and war maps; that he directed resistance patrols which action is believed to violate prudential rights of correspondents. Is there further comment you desire to make with respect to those allegations?

A: In reply to above allegations I wish to state that all correspondents who were in Rambouillet can testify to the fact that I was wearing correspondent's insignia except at such times as I was in my shirt sleeves during warm weather. Correspondents are frequently seen in their shirt sleeves and even in their underwear without the proper insignia being exhibited. It is customarily worn on the blouse or on a gray coat in bad weather.

In regard to being a Colonel, if I was ever referred to as a Colonel it was in the same way that citizens of the State of Kentucky are sometimes addressed as Colonel without it implying any military rank, just as all Chinese who have followed the trade of war up to a certain age are always addressed as General. These terms mean nothing and one might be addressed affectionately as Captain, Colonel or General without it having any military significance.

Any arms or armament seen by anyone in my room was stored there by French resistance men who were operating under the orders of the proper authorities and left these arms or armament in my room for security purposes.

At this time various prisoners and suspects were being guarded in the courtyard of the hotel, and it would be impossible to leave any arms or armament otherwise than in a secure place.

In regard to a war map, I don't understand this phrase clearly. I have been accustomed to operate from maps ever since I have been an accredited correspondent. As I understand it, the only thing that a correspondent must not do is to carry marked maps where they can fall into the possession of the enemy. I have never done this.

As far as the question of directing resistance patrols, I believe that has been covered in my previous statement.

Q: Were there mines in your room?

A: There were no mines in my room. I would greatly prefer not to have mines in my room at any time.

Q: Did you tell any correspondents that you had removed your insignia so as not to prejudice them?

A: I didn't tell correspondents that I had removed my insignia not to prejudice them, to the best of my knowledge.

Q: You accompanied the 4th Infantry Division for some time, did you not?

A: I accompanied the 4th Infantry Division from the time of the break-through until the 25th of September of this year except for the short time that I was in Rambouillet.

Q: Were you usually accompanied by a Public Relations officer from the 4th Infantry Division?

A: I was accompanied by a Public Relations officer from the 4th Infantry Division or was in the company of their officers in that division.

Q: Who was the Public Relations officer?

A: Captain Marcus O. Stevenson.

Q: Did you have one chauffeur most of this time?

A: I had various chauffeurs at this time, but during the start of the time I was with the 4th Infantry Division Captain Stevenson usually drove himself and I accompanied him.

Q.: Did you at any time tell some correspondents that while with the 4th Infantry Division you removed your correspondent's insignia and fought with the men?

A: I didn't tell correspondents this and didn't fight with the men.

Q.: With respect to your activity with the French resistance groups, do I understand that this consisted primarily of interpreting reports and orders and offering suggestions when asked for them?

A: My activities so consisted. I also occasionally accompanied patrols in order to obtain direct information to aid me in evaluating information received and to give me necessary information for the writing of my articles. It is perfectly permissible for a correspondent to go on an infantry patrol.

Q.: Did you, when in company with these French resistance groups, consider yourself as or act in the capacity of a commander directing them?

A: It was impossible for me to so consider myself due to the fact that I was an accredited correspondent.

Q.: Is there any other information you wish to add?

A: Only the fact that in Rambouillet I wasn't armed, a fact which, as far as I know, has not been disputed. That is all.

Q.: Did you state to anyone at about this time, "I am no longer a correspondent"?

A: I didn't make any such statement in a serious sense. I may have said jokingly, "I am now a hotel manager, the unthanked billeting clerk, a general errand boy around the establishment," but in the serious sense that I wasn't a correspondent, it would be impossible for me to make such a statement since I am an accredited correspondent for Colliers Weekly through whom I am earning my living.

Q.: Is there anything else you deem appropriate to add at this time?

Hemingway with Col. Charles T. "Buck" Lanham on the Siegfried Line, 18 September 1944

A: Nothing unless there are any further points you wish cleared up.

(Statement concluded.)

Hemingway's foreword to Treasury for the Free World, *edited by Ben Raeburn (New York: Arco, 1946), presents his opinions about the postwar world and the atomic bomb.*

Now that the wars are over and the dead are dead and we have bought whatever it is we have it is a good time to publish books like this.

We have come out of the time when obedience, the acceptance of discipline, intelligent courage and resolution were most important into that more difficult time when it is a man's duty to understand his world rather than simply fight for it.

To understand we must study. We must study not simply what we wish to believe. That will always be skillfully presented for us. We must try to examine our world with the impartiality of a physician. This will be hard work and will involve reading much that is unpleasant to accept. But it is one of a man's first duties now.

It will be our duty, when we have sufficient valid knowledge, to disagree, to protest, even to revolt and to rebel and still work always toward finding a way for all men to live together on this earth.

It has been necessary to fight. It has been necessary to kill, to maim, to burn and to destroy. Certainly for a country whose continent has never been bombed we have done our share of bombing. We have possibly killed more civilians of other countries than all our enemies did in all the famous massacres we so deplore. There is really very little favorable difference to a man or a woman between being burned alive or stood against a wall and shot.

We have waged war in the most ferocious and ruthless way that it has ever been waged. We waged it against fierce and ruthless enemies that it was necessary to destroy. Now we have destroyed one of our enemies and forced the capitulation of the other. For the moment we are the strongest power in the world. It is very important that we do not become the most hated.

First page of Hemingway's letter of apology to Milton Wolff, a member of the Abraham Lincoln Brigade. Wolff had provoked Hemingway's anger after the publication of For Whom the Bell Tolls *when he called Hemingway a "tourist" during the Spanish Civil War (Sotheby's New York, Item 136, Sale Number 7001, 3 June 1997).*

It would be easy for us, if we do not learn to understand the world and appreciate the rights, privileges and duties of all other countries and peoples, to represent in our power the same danger to the world that Fascism did.

We have invented the sling and the pebble that will kill all giants; including ourselves. It is simple idiocy to think that the Soviet Union will not possess and perfect the same weapon.

This is no time for any nation to have any trace of the mentality of the bully. It is no time for any nation to become hated. It is no time for any nation even to swagger. Certainly it is no time for any nation to jostle. It is no time for any nation to be anything but just.

In this new world all of the partners will have to relinquish. It will be as necessary to relinquish as it was necessary to fight. No nation who holds land or dominion over people where it has no just right to it can continue to do so if there is to be an enduring peace. The problems this brings up can not be examined in this foreword. But we must examine them and examine them intelligently, impartially and closing our eyes to nothing.

This book has one advantage. The various articles are not full of the knowledge after the fact of the use of the release of atomic energy. We need to study and understand certain basic problems of our world as they were before Hiroshima to be able to continue, intelligently, to discover how some of them have changed and how they can be settled justly now that a new weapon has become a property of a part of the world. We must study them more carefully than ever now and remember that no weapon has ever settled a moral problem. It can impose a solution but it cannot guarantee it to be a just one. You can wipe out your opponents. But if you do it unjustly you become eligible for being wiped out yourself.

In Germany our military courts have sentenced a sixty year old German woman to be hanged as one of a mob which brutally murdered American aviators who had parachuted to the ground in Germany. Why hang her? Why not burn her at the stake if we wish to make martyrs?

For the Germans know whether any sixty year old German women were ever killed by fighter pilots, on their way back from missions, coming down to strafe German villages. As far as I know we never hanged any pilots for going down on the deck and doing a little strafing. German civilians, strafed in Germany, feel much the same about it as Spanish civilians strafed in Spain by Germans or as American civilians would feel if the Germans had ever been able to strafe them.

Say you've been down on the deck; sometimes there were comic incidents. Often they looked comic from the air. Nothing blew up like ambulances (which proved the Germans carried munitions in them). Always plenty comic instances when you have command of the air. Comic to you. I believe in shooting up everything, myself, and getting it over with. (You shouldn't say that. That's too much like war.) But you cannot expect them not to be excited if you fall into their hands.

Air-Marshal Harris is on record as to what he wished to do to the German people. We were fighting the German people as well as the German army. The Germans fought the British people as well as the British army. The German army fought the Russian people and the Russian people fought back. That is war and to fight a war any other way is playing dolls.

But the secret of future peace is not in hanging sixty year old women because they killed fliers in hot blood. Hang or shoot those who starved and beat and tortured in cold blood. Hang or shoot those who planned the war and would plan another. Hang or shoot deliberate war criminals. Deal with the S.S. and the voluntary Party members as they should be dealt with. But do not make martyrs of sixty year old women who killed in anger against force which had become so strong it no longer had any conscience or any feeling of evil doing.

To win a war you have to do things that are inconceivable in peace and that are often hateful to those who do them. That is they are hateful for a while. Afterwards some people get used to them. Some get to like them. Everyone wants to do everything, no matter what, to get it over with. Once you are involved in a war you have to win it by any means.

The military, in order to maintain their status and certain safeguards of their status, would like to have war fought by rules. The air-forces steadily smashed through all these rules and developed a realistic war in which nations fought nations; not armies armies.

An aggressive war is the great crime against everything good in the world. A defensive war, which must necessarily turn to aggressive at the earliest moment, is the necessary great counter-crime. But never think that war, no matter how necessary, nor how justified, is not a crime. Ask the infantry and ask the dead.

We have fought this war and won it. Now let us not be sanctimonious; nor hypocritical; nor vengeful nor stupid. Let us make our enemies incapable of ever making war again, let us re-educate them, and let us learn to live in peace and justice with all countries and all peoples in this world. To do this we must educate and re-educate. But first we must educate ourselves.

Ernest Hemingway

San Francisco de Paula, Cuba
September 1945

Malcolm Cowley was one of the most influential critics in the United States and in 1944 had edited The Viking Portable Hemingway. *In this letter Hemingway shares his opinions about some of his contemporaries. From* Selected Letters, *pp. 603–605.*

17 October and 14 November 1945
Dear Cowley:

It was awfully good to hear from you. A few days after I got the book and liked the introduction very much. See what you mean about the nocturnal thing now. Hope will have some luck writing now to get you some good new specimens to get the old scalpel to work on.

You see it's awfully hard to talk or write about your own stuff because if it is any good you yourself know about how good it is—but if you say so yourself you feel like a shit. My kids are the only people I ever talk to about my stuff or what have always been trying to do. They know Dos and they love to hear about Scott and Jim Joyce and how things truly were instead of the accepted version. There surely is a great difference. They will ask, "Papa what is the *true* gen on so and so or such and such." The gen is RAF slang for intelligence, the hand out at the briefing. The *true* gen is what they know but don't tell you. The true gen very hard to obtain.

Had no idea we had so much early life in common. It was a fine life wasn't it? Feel very bad to hear you are having trouble with deafness. If we have to lose one, though, that is the one to lose. But no fun to lose any of them.

I'd no idea Faulkner was in that bad shape and very happy you are putting together the Portable of him. He has the most talent of anybody and he just needs a sort of conscience that isn't there. Certainly if no nation can exist half free and half slave no man

can write half whore and half straight. But he will write absolutely perfectly straight and then go on and on and not be able to end it. I wish the christ I owned him like you'd own a horse and train him like a horse and race him like a horse—only in writing. How beautifully he can write and as simple and as complicated as autumn or as spring.

I'll try and write him and cheer him up.

We'll have to get together and talk when get up to N.Y. Don't know when that will be though. I'm working good now. Work every morning; haven't had a drink in the night nor until after finish work for a couple of months. That's the hardest thing to do when you come back from a war. You get to useing the old Giant Killer and it is able to fix up practically anything. I remember in Spain I'd have to have about two shots before I could even look at the map but after the two shots it didn't look so bad as all that—even when it was awful. Then after it is over you have to boil it all out of your system and only take what is useful to you to relax after working and not lie to yourself nor kid yourself and it is always a tough process. . . .

You know I could never read Katherine Ann P[orter]. I just can't read it. Seems so terribly dull. Not phony like that Carson McCullers but just too dull to live.

When Kenneth Burke was writing well I was too uneducated to understand him. Would like to re-read it now. You see when you guys were first writing I had only been through high school. I knew Italian from the war and had kept on with it and knew a little German. Was getting start on education in Paris same time as was learning to write (mostly books from Sylvia Beach's until I learned French) and then, after, Spanish. Every year keep on studying, keep on reading and every year study something new to keep head learning. Learning is a hell of a lot of fun. Don't see why can't keep it up all my life. Certainly plenty to learn.

November 14
Certainly didn't do very well at getting that letter off!

Been working every day and going good. Makes a hell of a dull life too. But it is more fun than anything else. Do you remember how old Ford was always writing how Conrad suffered so when he wrote? How it was un metier du chien [a dog's trade] etc. Do you suffer when you write? I don't at all. Suffer like a bastard when don't write, or just before, and feel empty and fucked out afterwards. But never feel as good as while writing.

Chapter Five: 1941–1952

Hemingway, director Henry Hathaway, Gary Cooper, and Ingrid Bergman in Sun Valley, Idaho, 1947 (Courtesy of The Lilly Library, Indiana University)

Sent for the Portable Poe after I had your letter. What an awful bloody life he had. He had more self propelled bad luck than Scott even. If he'd been born in our time he would probably have been one of Oswald Moseley's gang. They would have put up the money for the magazine and it would have been the only good Fascist magazine. I looked forward to reading Poe. Thought that would be good to do this winter. Then found I'd read it all before ever went to Italy and remembered it so clearly that I couldn't re-read. Had forgotten them all but they were all there—intact. He seems a lot like Evan. Of course he was doing it first too. You know Evan is a hell of a good writer? Don't think anybody realizes how good.

Does Archie still write anything except Patri-otic? I read some awfully lifeless lines to a Dead Soldier by him in that Free World anthology. I thought good old Allen Tate could write the lifeless-est lines

to Dead Soldiers ever read but Archie is going good. You know his bro. Kenny was killed in last war flying and I always felt Archie felt that sort of gave him a controlling interest in all deads.

What is going to be done about Pound? Did he continue to broadcast after we went to war? I think they should shave his head as a collaborator. Any other punishment would be excessive. He was a great poet and the most generous friend and looker-after of people and so flattered at being respected in Italy instead of being made fun of that he swallowed Fascism whole (No one but an idiot with Ezra's type of ego would but he did: as simple as that, and then set out to justify it.) In 1933 Joyce (James) swore to me Ezra was crazy and asked me to come to be with him at something he had invited Ezra to because he said "Ezra's mad now and I don't know what he will do." I don't think his thinking has

264

been normal for a long time. Those broadcasts of his I read were so silly and insane that they, themselves, if presented in entirety would be his best defense.

Do you know what they want to do about him? William (Haw-Haw) Joyce was a very dangerous business. It would be wicked to consider Ezra who was a traitor but a silly, and a crazy and a harmless traitor in the same category.

[Ernest]

After Maxwell Perkins died on 17 June 1947, Hemingway wrote this letter of condolence to his publisher, Charles Scribner

III. Hemingway dedicated The Old Man and the Sea *(New York: Scribners, 1952) to Perkins and Scribner. From* The Only Thing That Counts, *pp. 344–346.*

June 28 1947

Dear Charlie:

Don't worry about me kid. . You have troubles enough without that. I didn't write you after I cabled because what the hell can you say. We don't need to talk wet about Max to each other. The bad was for him to die. I hadn't figured on him dying; I'd just thought he might get so completely damn deaf we'd lose him that way Anyway for a long time I had been trying to be less of a nuisance to him and have all the fun with him possible. We had a hell of a good time this last time in New York and wasn't it lucky it was that way instead of a lot of problems and arguments. Anyway he doesn't have to worry about Tom Wolfe's chickenshit estate

Hemingway with Marlene Dietrich (whom he called "The Kraut") in New York, November 1949. The two first met in 1934 and remained warm friends.

anymore, or handle Louise's business, nor keep those women writers from building nests in his hat. Max had a lot of fun, anyway I know we had a lot of fun together, but useing up all his resistance that way by not taking some lay offs to build up is a good lesson to us and don't you get to overworking now, at least until young Charlie gets to know the business for quite a long time because I want to be able to see your alcohol ravaged face when I come in the office for at least the next twenty two years to help me feel someone in N.Y has a worse hangover than I have.

Charlie don't worry about me at all. I never liked that son of a bitch Darrow but he's out. Wallace and I like and understand each other very well. You and I get along damn well. A lot better than people know and you don't have to worry about writing me letters. I'd have to work and try to write well if I were in jail, or if I had 20 million dollars, or if I was broke and working at something else to keep going, or if I was going to die, or if I had word I was going to live forever. So don't worry about me. I'm not going to succomb to any temptations and I don't flatter easy any more. You've got enough dough to back me to extent that I have to ask for it while I write this book and I will borrow as little as I can and write as good as I can. Have been working out ways for my existant stories to be sold to pictures on a non-whoreing basis to keep me going while write, same as always, with no regard for whether it is to sell; but only on a basis of how well I can write it. At least have been working on that and if Speiser doesn't blow it up by over-extending his negociatory ability should be o.k. within this month. However things go I have dough now to last me until Sept. But if the deal with Hellinger goes through I am set for all the time I will need on the book and some afterwards.

If it would do any good you might let it be known that while Max was my best and oldest friend at Scribners and a great, great editor he never cut a paragraph of my stuff nor asked me to change one. One of my best and most loyal friends and wisest counsellors in life as well as in writing is dead. But Charles Scribners Sons are my publishers and I intend to publish with them for the rest of my life.

Malcom Cowley can tell you what he and Max and I and later he and Max were lineing up of getting out a three vol. edition of Farewell To Arms, Sun Also Rises, and For Whom The Bell Tolls showing the relationship between the three with illustrations and an introduction by Cowley. That might come after the new edition of A Farewell To Arms you said you and Max were talking about. I think it is g od policy to keep these books going in our own editions and the three comeing out together with the Cowley tie-up of them

would insure g od reviews. Might do better hitting with all three than throwing in piecemeal.

If only the boys hadn't done away with Ben Siegal we might have put him in charge of getting me the Nobel prize. He asked me one time, "Ernie why don't you ever get any of these prizes? I see other writers getting prizes what's the trouble Ernie? There's certainly someway that can be rigged."

Won't bother you with any more of this with everything you have on your hands. If young Charlie is going good in the advertizing end why not leave him there for a while instead of yanking him? . . .

We have real Gordon's gin at 50 bucks a case and real Noilly Prat and have found a way of makeing ice in the deep-freeze in tennis ball tubes that comes out 15 degrees below zero and with the glasses frozen too makes the coldest martini in the world. Just enough vermouth to cover the bottom of the glass, ounce 3/4 of gin, and the spanish cocktail onions very crisp and also 15 degrees below zero when they go in the glass.

This has been rugged as I said but there are better ways of sweating it out than putting your head on the wailing wall.

Did Max get the invitation to the Bronze Star thing? Gen. Lanham who I was with from Normandy on when he was commanding 22nd Inf. Regt. said I should have turned it down but I thought that would be rude and also imply I thought I should have something better which I thought sort of chickenshit. One time in the war got drunk at a dinner because was to get DSC but it got turned down at the top. So thought better take this before it got cancelled.

So long Charlie. Take care of yourself.

Best always
Ernest

Have you heard anything from Martha? I havent heard from her since Christmas. Have a new house-maid named Martha and certainly is a pleasure to give her orders. Marty was a lovely girl though. I wish she hadnt been quite so ambitious and war crazy. Think it must be sort of lonesome for her without a war.

In a talk at the University of Mississippi, William Faulkner had said that Hemingway was his fourth most important contemporary and added, "he has no courage, has never climbed out on a limb. He has never used a word where the reader might check his usage by a dictionary." When Faulkner's comments were reported in the New York Herald Tribune, *Hemingway exploded and*

Villa Aprile
Cortina D'Ampezzo
Italy
March 7 1949

Dear Jack :
    Thanks for the letters and the   columns . Think you did
very good   job on the xxxxxxxxxx columns . "Hardly a man is now alive who
remembers that famous day and year " They were good reading .
    About the letters ie. anything that should be answered . Don't
know what mystery there is about the Willard Saunders fight . Mike
Lerner saw it . But can understand his Secretary's caution in ducking it
if thought they might get sued or something . She probably has it
mixed up with the Joe Knapp fight . Anyway skip them all . Ask Mike , if you
ever see him , just out of curiosity, about the Willard Saunders fight . He
didn't see the Joe Knapp one . I'm not running as a fighter anyway .
You just asked me for anecdotes   and the best ones I could tout you onto
were around Bimini   and the Bar Florida or old Sloppy Joe's in Key West .
You don't need that stuff anyway to make a column .

    About the book of pieces : I think they should pay
something unless they publish them for some charity . Somebody stands
to make some money and when the book is written by professional
writers they should get their cut . We threw plenty for nothing learning
how to throw . Afterwards the hell with pitching for honor if there is
money involved and it isn't a benefit . If the other people do it for
nothing they are dopes and somebody should set them an example . My
dough can go to the heart disease fund they named after Hellinger
or The Hundred Neediest Cases but when put something between stiff
covers it makes money for somebody, and   I should say how my share
of it is used .
    Hope you agree . with my name attached,

    Plenty people it helps . OK let. them do it for nothing .
For me a re-publishing what I wrote under censor-ship and to get it out
really fast xxxxx , publishing that between stiff covers , is just as
helpful to me as getting hit in the head by a pitched ball or breaking
a finger or a toe .

    If wouldn't join The Institute of Arts and Letters ,
which is supposed to be an honor and also free , why should let
somebody publish me as an honor ? The only honors I know that
respect at all are the V.C. and Congressional Medal of Honor . Since will
never have either one of those   why fool with the chicken ones ?
    If there is any dough involved let them pay . The hell with
the honor .
    Sorry you had that ptomaine and the trip wasn't better . If you
see Granny Rice give him my best . Write this in a hurry to get it off
. Cables very expensive from here and air-mail fast .

    Best wishes to you always ,

                    Ernest

    Ernest Hemingway

Hemingway's comments to a New York journalist about including one of Hemingway's Spanish Civil War articles in A Treasury of Great Reporting *(Matthew J. Bruccoli and C. E. Frazer Clark Jr., eds.,* Hemingway at Auction 1930–1973*)*

Chapter Five: 1941–1952

asked General Lanham to write Faulkner to tell him of Hemingway's behavior under fire. Faulkner apologized to Hemingway, explaining that he had meant courage in writing. This is Hemingway's response to Faulkner. From Selected Letters, *pp. 623–625.*

23 July 1947

Dear Bill:

Awfully glad to hear from you and glad to have made contact. Your letter came tonight and please throw all the other stuff away, the misunderstanding, or will have to come up and we both trompel on it. There isn't any at all. I was sore and Buck was sore and we were instantly unsore the minute we knew the score.

I know what you mean about T. Wolfe and Dos and still can't agree. I never felt the link-up in Wolfe except with the N.C. stuff. Dos I always liked and respected and thought was a 2nd rate writer on acct. no ear. 2nd rate boxer has no left hand, same as ear to writer, and so gets his brains knocked out and this happened to Dos with every book. Also terrible snob (on acct. of being a bastard) (which I would welcome) and very worried about his negro blood when could have been our best negro writer if would have just been negro as hope *we* would have.

You picked a very cold one of mine to make the comparison on about the great thing we would all like to do. To make it really how it was any really good morning–but I tried to get way past that like when they are fucking comeing back from makeing contact with the other outfit about the bridge, when the Pilar woman knows what the hell it is all about; again where she is talking about her man, before, and Valencia and the fun they had (which think will stand); where she is talking about smell of death (which is no shit) and all the part with her man who was in bull fight business and where we kill the fascists in the village. Probably bore the shit out of you to re-read but as brother would like to know what you think. Anyway is as good as I can write and was takeing all chances (for a pitcher who, when has control, can throw fairly close) could take. (Probably failed.)

Difference with us guys is I always lived out of country (as mercenary or patriot) since kid. My own country gone. Trees cut down. Nothing left but gas stations, sub-divisions where we hunted snipe on the prairie, etc. Found good country outside, learned language as well as know English, and lost it the same way. Most people don't know this. Dos always came to us as a tourist. I was always makeing a liveing, paying my debts and always stayed to fight. Been chickenshit dis-placed person since can remember but fought each time before we lost (and this last time we fought with

COULD HE LIVE WITHOUT THE POWER TO LOVE?

Ernest Hemingway

717

THE SUN ALSO RISES

"You gave more than your life," the Colonel had said. It was a rotten way to be wounded.

A BANTAM BOOK, Complete and Unabridged

Contrary to the claim on the cover, Bantam expurgated the anti-Semitic remarks from this 1949 paperback edition.

most stuff and it was the easiest and we lost the worst). Things never been worse than now.

You are a better writer than Fielding or any of those guys and you should just know it and keep on writing. You have things written that come back to me better than any of them and I am not dopy, really. You shouldn't read the shit about liveing writers. You should always write your best against dead writers that we know what stature (not stature: evocative power) that they have and beat them one by one. Why do you want to fight Dostoevsky in your first fight? Beat Turgenieff–which we both did soundly and for time which I hear tick too with a pressure of 205 over 115 (not bad for the way things have run at all). Then nail yourself DeMaupassant (tough boy until he got the old rale. Still dangerous for three rounds). Then try and take Stendhal. (Take him and we're all happy.) But don't fight with the poor pathological characters of our time (we won't name). You and I can both beat Flaubert who is our most respected, honored master. But to do that you have to be able to accept the command of a battalion

when it is given (when you are a great company commander), to relinquish it to be second in command of a regiment (walk with shits nor lose the common touch) and
then be able to take a regiment when you loathe the takeing
of it and were happy where you were (or were unhappy
but didn't want to go over Niagara Falls in a barrell) (I can't
go up higher in this hierarchy because have no higher experience and anyway probably bore the shit out of you). Anyway I am your Bro. if you want one that writes and I'd like
us to keep in touch. My middle kid (Pat) very sick now 4
months. Had to feed rectally 45 days. Now eats and sleeps
OK but not out of woods. Please excuse if write stupidly.
This most talented boy. Oldest very . . . nice. Capt Para-
troops 3 times wounded etc. Prisoner 6 months. We
mounted attack to get him out of hock when first taken
P.O.W. and accessible (drop) but was cancelled. This boy
(sick) good painter, head smashed in auto accident his kid
bro. driveing. Excuse chickenshit letter. Have much regard
for you. Would like to keep on writing [letters].

Ernest Hemingway

―――――――――

The 4 August 1947 issue of Time *(p. 8) included this interview
with Hemingway, one of several conducted with American writers.*

Hemingway in the Afternoon

Most of the authors who answered TIME's questions on
the state of U.S. writing were interviewed by correspondents. Ernest Hemingway answered his questions by mail.
He requested that both TIME's questions & his answers be
published "since this has to do with my trade. You can say
that when you saw me I was unshaven, needed a haircut,
was barefoot, wearing a pyjama bottom and no top." The
questions, and his replies:

Q: What do you find wrong with present-day writing–or good about it? Why aren't we getting more significant writing?

A: "Really good writing very scarce always. When
comes in quantities everybody very very lucky."

Q: Has postwar or atomic era had any influence on
writers; has it had a tendency to dry them up creatively?

A: "Writers dry up when their juice dries up. Atomic
bomb probably as fatal to writers as cerebral hemorrhage

or senility. Meantime good writers should keep on writing."

Q: Which U.S. writers in your opinion are doing
good work?

A: "Writers my generation mostly dead except Dos
Passos, going very good with *Number One.* Robert Penn
Warren writing very well. First rate books by new writers
that have read are *All Thy Conquests,* Alfred Hayes–*Never
Come Morning,* Nelson Algren–*The Big Sky,* A. B. Guthrie
Jr.–*The Assault,* Allen R. Matthews."

Q: Which once-prominent ones have slipped or
failed to measure up to early promise?

A: "Prefer not to answer this question. A writer has
no more right to inform the public of the weaknesses and
strengths of his fellow professionals than a doctor or a lawyer has.

"Writers should stick together like wolves or gypsies
and they are fools to attack each other to please the people
who would exploit or destroy them. Naturally I know the
weaknesses of my fellow professionals but that information
is not for sale nor for free."

Q: How much has the big money of slicks, Hollywood, radio, etc., taken writers away from serious personal
themes?

A: "Most whores usually find their vocations."

Q: Is a writer-Hollywood combination capable of
doing good literary work?

A: "So far hasn't. But Hollywood has proven can
make good pictures from good stories honestly written."

Q: What is your own attitude toward writing for
Hollywood?

A: "Never done it."

Q: Do you detect any trends, or any new schools in
recent U.S. writing? If so, what are they?

A: "Ask a professor."

Q: Has the "Hemingway influence" declined? If so,
what kind of writing are we heading for?

A: "Hemingway influence only a certain clarification
of the language which is now in the public domain."

Chapter Five: 1941-1952

Hemingway and his fourth wife, Mary, in Venice, 1949

Hemingway wrote this introduction to Elio Vittorini's In Sicily *(New York: New Directions, 1949).*

Elio Vittorini is one of the very best of the new Italian writers. He was born July 23, 1908, in Syracuse in Sicily and spent his boyhood in various parts of Sicily where his father was a station master on the railways of that island. He is not a regional writer, for Italy is certainly not a region, and Vittorini from the time he was old enough to leave home without permission at seventeen learned his Italy in the same way American boys who ran away from home learned their own country.

The Italy that he learned and the America that the American boys learned has little to do with the Academic Italy or America that periodically attacks all writing like a dust storm and is always, until everything shall be completely dry, dispersed by rain.

Rain to an academician is probably, after the first fall has cleared the air, H$_2$O with, of course, traces of other things. To a good writer, needing something to bring the dry country alive so that it will not be a desert where only such cactus as New York literary reviews grow dry and sad, inexistent without the watering of their benefactors, feeding on the dried manure of schism and the dusty taste of disputed dialectics, their only flowering a desiccated criticism as alive as stuffed birds, and their steady mulch the dehydrated cuds of fellow critics; such a writer finds rain to be made of knowledge, experience, wine, bread, oil, salt, vinegar, bed, early mornings, nights, days, the sea, men, women, dogs, beloved motor cars, bicycles, hills and valleys, the appearance and disappearance of trains on straight and curved tracks, love, honor and disobey, music, chamber music and chamber pots, negative and positive Wassermanns, the arrival and non-arrival of expected munitions and/or reinforcements, replacements or your brother. All these are a part of rain to a good writer along with your hated or beloved mother, may she rest in peace or in pieces, porcupine quills, cock grouse drumming on a bass-wood log, the smell of sweet-grass and fresh smoked leather and Sicily.

In this book the rain you get is Sicily. I care nothing about the political aspects of the book (they were many at the time) nor about Vittorini's politics (I have examined them carefully and to me they are honorable). But I care very much about his ability to bring rain with him when he comes if the earth is dry and that is what you need.

He has more books about the north of Italy that he knows and loves and about other parts of Italy. This is a good one to start with.

If there is any rhetoric or fancy writing that puts you off at the beginning or the end, just ram through it. Remember he wrote the book in 1937 under Fascism and he had to wrap it in a fancy package. It is necessarily wrapped in cellophane to pass the censor. But there is excellent food once you unwrap it.

ERNEST HEMINGWAY
Cortina D'Ampezzo, 1949

Between 1950 and 1952 Hemingway contributed lists to the "Books I Have Liked" column published in the Christmas Book Issue of the New York Herald Tribune Book Review.

3 December 1950

Collected Stories of William Faulkner; Mixed Company, by Irwin Shaw; *Out of the Red,* by Red Smith.

9 December 1951

Too late to appear with other "Books I Have Liked" lists in the Christmas Book Issue last week, the following letter from Cuba has arrived in the offices of this Review:

To the Editor:
> Here are three:
> The Consul at Sunset—Gerald Hanley
> The Broken Root—Arturo Barea
> Nobody Asked Me—Jimmy Cannon

This is naming three is hard as you know. It was very hard to choose between Jimmy Cannon's book and Air Power in War by Lord Tedder. But since Lord Tedder's book had not been published in America, I choose Mr. Cannon's. Runner-up was The American Racing Manual—1951.

Books I would have enjoyed reading but could not obtain here were:
> Longevity Pays: The Life of Arthur Mizener—by F. Scott FitzGerald
> The Shulberg Incident—by F. Scott FitzGerald
> The Critics: An Harpooner's Story—by Herman Melville

Other fine books I was unable to get my hands on were:

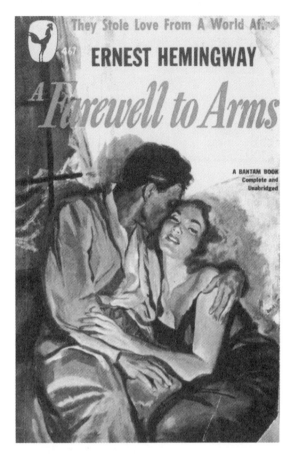

They Stole Love From A World Af... ERNEST HEMINGWAY A Farewell to Arms

A BANTAM BOOK
Complete and Unabridged

First U.S. paperback edition of Hemingway's 1929 novel (New York: Bantam, 1949)

> He and Lillian: The Story of a Profile—by Mary Hemingway
> Wisdom, Culture, God and I (3 vol.)—by André Malraux
> It Went Thataway: The Story of Existentialism—by Jean-Paul Sartre

I will stop now as there are *so* many good books one does not get to read these days.

ERNEST HEMINGWAY
7 December 1952

Picture, by Lillian Ross; *Rumor and Reflection,* by Bernard Berenson; *The Shores of Light,* by Edmund Wilson.

Died 640 Sept 6.
Ed.

Jedut mail Chas by

FINCA VIGIA   SAN FRANCISCO DE PAULA   CUBA

September First 1949   0600

Maybe we should do the Quiel

Dear Charlie :

       Early morning animal situation report on the Finca :

       Dogs are trumps but cats are the longest suite we hold .

Then
       Re-read your letter in the   first light and saw I had not written anything about book clubs . May be wrong but suggest we submit nothing to no-one and split with no one . (*May be wrong on this . you tell me .*) Would like to play this horse to win and pile it on . If we don't win we are ok because we have a sure winner in   the next book and we can lay off a little with the Book Clubs . But this time let's try to hit one on the actual nose . Hope this use of gambling terms does not shock you .

and   If the critics don't like it (and I have many such *old enemies* lumpen-proletariat adversaries   who would love to ham-string you (only am not a ham) it is more or less their ass because   we run the bulldozer over them with the next book . Hope this doesn't sound over-confident . Am a man without any ambition ,except to be champion of the world . I wouldn't fight Dr. Tolstoi   in a 20 round bout because I know he would knock my ears off . The Dr. had terrific wind and could go forever and then some . But I would take him on for six and he would never hit me and would knock the shit out of him and maybe knock him out . He is easy to hit . But boy how he can hit . *if I can live to 60 I can beat him* . (MAYBE)

       For your information I started out trying to beat dead writers that I knew how good they were .(Excuse vernacular) I tried for Mr. Turgenieff first   and it wasn't   too hard . Tried for Mr. Maupassant (won't concede him the de) and it took four   of the best stories to beat him . He's beaten and if he was around he would know it . Then I tried for another guy (am getting embarrassed and bare-assed now   from bragging ; or stateing ; and I think I fought a draw with him . *this other dead crusader .*

       Mr. Henry James I would just thumb him once the first time he grabbed and then hit him once where he had no balls   and ask the referee to stop it .

       There are some guys nobody could ever beat like Mr. Shakespeare (The Champion) and Mr. Anonymous . But would be glad any time , if in training , to go twenty with Mr. Cervantes in his own home town (Alcala de Henares)   and beat the shit out of him .Although Mr. C. very smart and would be learning all the time and would probably beat you in a return match . *The third fight people would pay to see . Plenty peoples .*

       But these Brooklyn jerks are so ignorant that they start off fighting Mr. Tolstoi . And they announce they have beaten him before the fight starts . They should be hung by the balls until dead for ignorance . I can write good and I would not get into the ring with Mr. T. over the long distance unless I and my family were not eating .

       In the big book I hope to *and* take Mr. Melville and Mr. Doestoevsky ,they are coupled as a stable entry ,throw lots of mud in their faces because the track isn't fast . But you can only run so many of those kind of races . *They take it out of you .*

       Know this sounds like bragging but Jeezoo Chrise   you have to have confidence   to be a champion and that is   the only thing I ever wished to be . And it was not until I was one half one hundred years old that I realized had never turned the horse loose and let him run .He's going to run now until the son of a bitch breaks something or dies .

later —   With which pious sentiment I leave you and get to work ,

    PS. *Did 1149 Friday Shipped Sat-Sun and Guest. wrote letters .*

Diel 587 today Sept 5, Monday .

that cleaned up our business

Hemingway's letter to his publisher, Charles Scribner III, expressing his competitive feelings about other writers (Charles Scribner's Sons Archive, Princeton University Library)

Hemingway with Adriana Ivancich, model for Renata in Across the River and Into the Trees, *at a party in her honor at La Finca Vigía (photograph by Roberto Herrera Sotolongo)*

Harvey Breit published this interview in The New York Times Book Review *on 17 September 1950 (p. 14), two weeks after the publication of Hemingway's fifth novel.*

Talk with Mr. Hemingway

This department has gradually, over a period of seventy-five weeks or so, solidified more or less into a set of conventions. The question is asked, the answer is given; a brief physical description is arrived at; the interlocutor prods, the interlocutee replies by monologue or monosyllable; a brief, very transient sense of the object under surveillance is (it is to be supposed) attained. Let us, then, for this once depart from the conventions. For this week it is Ernest Hemingway who is introduced to the reader, and the tested means are unsuited to presenting that unorthodox, uncompromising figure. The following opinions—some intense, some relaxed, but all profoundly true of Mr. Hemingway—are extracts from a series of exchanges between Mr. Hemingway and this reporter.

On big questions. Honest to God, I don't know the answers to such questions. I am embarrassed by nearly all big pictures—like big questions—except for Tintoretto's "Crucifixion of Our Lord," in Venice. From it I learned principally how to crucify, and how wonderfully the thief on the right behaved. On the right when you look at it. Actually on the left of our Lord.

On Contemporary Themes. That is a lot of deletion. The themes have always been love, lack of it, death and its occasional temporary avoidance which we describe as life, the immortality or lack of immortality of the soul, money, honor and politics. That is an oversimplification. But nobody has employed me to write 150,000 words between covers on any of these themes this morning.

On Country, Culture, Politics, etc. The country that a novelist writes about is the country he knows; and the country that he knows is in his heart. Culture is good to have. It is like a good 1/10,000 map. But you have to make your own attack and remember that no classic resembles another.

We work in our time; which happens to be the worst time I've ever seen or heard about. But you can have plenty fun in it and still know how bad it is. Politics I would rather not be quoted on. All the contact I have had with it has left me feeling as though I had been drinking out of spittoons. The self-confessed patriot, the traitor and the regulator of other people's lives, beliefs, etc. and the Regimentator all run in a photo-finish. The Senate may develop the picture if they can find a photographer who can photograph a photo-finish. Otherwise they could get a seeing-eye dog. Think it might be a good idea if we could provide all our statesmen and several other characters with such dogs.

On Boxing. Anybody could hit Joe Louis who had the guts to try it. Look at the people who had him down. But he was a good getter-upper. Jack Blackburn could never teach him how not to get hit by left hands. After the first Schmeling fight he taught Louis how to avoid a right. (What you learn in kindergarten.) But Louis hit so hard and beautifully with both hands, he never learned to box.

If you fight a great left-hooker, sooner or later he will knock you on your deletion. He will get the left out where you can't see it, and in it comes like a brick. Life is the greatest left-hooker so far, although many say it was Charley White of Chicago.

On Poetry. Well, I guess some of us write and some of us pitch, but so far there isn't any law a man has to go and see *The Cocktail Party,* by T. S. Eliot from St. Louis, where Yogi Berra comes from. A damned good poet and a fair critic, but he would not have existed except for dear old Ezra, the lovely poet and stupid traitor.

Be a good boy and keep on writing those pieces and maybe they will let you interview the Robert Brownings and the Leigh Hunts and if ever you need relief that will be me you will see moving in from the bullpen with the sorest arm in the world.

On the Novel. Sure, they can say anything about nothing happening in *Across the River,* but all that happens is the defense of the lower Piave, the breakthrough in Normandy, the taking of Paris and the destruction of the 22d Inf. Reg. in Hurtgen forest plus a man who loves a girl and dies.

Only it is all done with three-cushion shots. In the last one I had the straight narrative: Sordo on the hill for keeps; Jordan killing the cavalryman; the village; a full-scale attack presented as they go; and the unfortunate incident at the bridge.

Should I repeat myself? I don't think so. You have to repeat yourself again and again as a man but you should not do so as a writer.

In writing I have moved through arithmetic, through plane geometry and algebra, and now I am in calculus. If they don't understand that, to hell with them. I won't be sad and I will not read what they say. They say? What do they say? Let them say.

Who the hell wants fame over a week-end? All I want is to write well.

Novelist John O'Hara's review of Across the River and Into the Trees *(New York: Scribners, 1950) was the most positive notice of Hemingway's novel. From* The New York Times Book Review, *10 September 1950, pp. 1, 30–31.*

The Author's Name Is Hemingway

The most important author living today, the outstanding author since the death of Shakespeare, has brought out a new novel. The title of the novel is *Across the River and Into the Trees.* The author, of course is Ernest Hemingway, the most important, the most outstanding author out of the millions of writers who have lived since 1616.

Ernest Hemingway was born in Oak Park, Ill., U.S.A., on July 21, 1898. That makes him an American whose age is fifty-two. His father was a physician named Clarence Edmonds Hemingway; his mother's maiden name was Grace Hall.

Hemingway went to Oak Park High and not to college. He got into the newspaper business, went to France as a Red Cross ambulance driver when he was nineteen years old and a year later was badly shot up in Italy. After World War I he spent most of his time in Europe, with visits to the United States and Africa for hunting, fishing, and seeing friends and acquaintances.

He anticipated World War II, and took part in the actions in Spain. In 1944 he participated in the invasion of the European continent. (He was anti-Fascist in the Spanish hostilities and anti-Hitler in the subsequent activities. It may seem that these things should go without saying, but nowadays nothing goes without saying. These comments are meant to be straightforward, but there must be no lingering doubt.)

Between War One and War Two Ernest Hemingway produced the following books: *Three Stories and Ten Poems* (1923); *In Our Time* (1924); *The Torrents of Spring* (1926); *The Sun Also Rises* (1926); *Men Without Women* (1927); *A Farewell to Arms* (1929); *Death in the Afternoon* (1932); *Winner Take Nothing* (1933); *The Green Hills of Africa* (1935); *To Have and Have Not* (1937); *The Fifth Column* (1938); *For Whom the Bell Tolls* (1940).

HEMINGWAY

ACROSS THE RIVER
AND
INTO THE TREES

Dust jacket for Hemingway's 1950 novel. The illustration is by Adriana Ivancich.

Books do not necessarily represent an author's activity, but the new novel is Hemingway's thirteenth book in what appears to be twenty-seven years of writing and knocking around, for a rough average of one book every two years. Hemingway has not been idle, and most of the items in his bibliography come alive by merely calling up their titles.

The reasons that Ernest Hemingway is important are not easy to search for, although they are easy to find. Once you have skipped the remarks of the pedants, the college professors, the litterateurs, and of Hemingway himself, and have examined his background and his still immediate history, you can relax down to the fine, simple, inexplicable acceptance of being in the world-presence of a genius. The college professors (no can do; can teach pretty good) are ready out of their chunky erudition to prove that Ernest Hemingway got that way because he had a sister whose middle name was Xerxes. Or they, the pundits, may have got by hearsay a remote rumor that one day in Montreal a man who looked very much like Ernest Hemingway was seen to have in the left-hand pocket of

his tweed jacket a small volume not too dissimilar from an *Anabasis.*

The chances are that Ernest Hemingway in the formative years didn't read much but Ring Lardner's sport stories in the Chicago papers, Caesar's Gallic Wars and the literature that any high school boy skips over. Over or through. He was a big kid with not very good eyesight, with enormous, ill-controlled strength of muscle, and, apparently, an enviable admiration for an enviable father. Ernest went to the rehearsal war, and, after it, got some rude experience in cablese, a frustrating discipline that almost lost us all an artist. There was, it must be remembered, a phase during which Hemingway could have been found guilty of poetry of a sort.

Miss Gertrude Stein, who was as inevitable as the Albany night boat, did Hemingway no harm. She was living in Paris, France, and she was a good influence. I have a theory, which I have offered before, that all you need to know about the influence of Miss Stein on the young Ernest Hemingway is to pretend that you are, say, a Chinese who never has read English: you look at some pages of the *Autobiography of Alice B. Toklas,* then look at the superb Caporetto retreat writing in *A Farewell to Arms.* You will think they were written by the same person.

In the new novel (as in some earlier ones) the big block paragraph is not employed by the artist as it was in *A Farewell to Arms.* I have not been able to find a paragraph longer than fourteen uninterrupted slugs of type. Whatever influence Gertrude Stein had on Hemingway has been accepted, studied, utilized, and rejected. Ernest Hemingway is and really always was his own man. We now can forget about Gertrude Stein. Thank you very much, and so long.

The outsize boy, the doctor's son, the brittle bones, the halting speech (completely different from that of Dr. Maugham), the defective eyesight–they all had and have their part in the mental and physical makeup of a great author. But who has not known a stammering, gangling gawk of a doctor's embarrassment who couldn't go past M in the alphabet? Ernest Hemingway, the sternly self-edited artist, had young people in the 1930s marrying on no more than "We'll have a fine life." Why? Because Ernest Hemingway, the artist, had put just those words in his lines of type at just the right time.

The truculent, self-pitying hero of *Across the River and Into the Trees* is a busted one-star general called Col. Richard Cantwell. He seems to have traversed the same territory as the charming Lieutenant Henry of *A Farewell to Arms.* It is impossible to believe that the lieutenant and the colonel are the same man, and therefore the autobiographical aspect must be ruled out one time or the other. The present reviewer, whose age is forty-five, is unwilling to concede that Enrico and Ricardo are the same infant with years piled on. In any event, Colonel Cantwell is in Venice to see his girl, a beautiful and quite incredible countess named Renata. The colonel is full of junk, against the bad heart condition he has, and the story is hardly more than a report of their last love-making, to the accompaniment of a threnody on and by the dying warrior. That great, great man and fine actor, Walter Huston, was in my mind all the time I read this book. Huston, singing "September Song," you know. But Hemingway, the inimitable, has written a 308-page novel out of a "September Song" situation, and not one syllable of what Hemingway has written can or will be missed by any literate person in the world.

Before you ever see the girl, the countess, you are taken through some duck-shooting that makes you want to let go at a boatman with both barrels. At the same time you somehow are rooting for a second duck. The colonel is understandably angry with the inefficient boatman; he also is rather swaggeringly proud of getting two ducks. I, myself, a rifle man, wanted to kill the colonel while he was in the barrel that you shot ducks from, but that certainly is nothing against Hemingway's writing. He probably meant it that way.

The novel opens with the colonel on his way to his ultimate rendezvous with the countess. Cantwell, the colonel, is pulling rank on the rather nice little T-5 who is driving the colonel's Cadillac. The little fellow is somebody named Jackson, from the state of Wyoming. My own personal experience with Wyoming characters has been that Jackson would have twirled the colonel out of the automobile and reported him dead. The colonel insists upon giving Jackson, a noncommissioned officer, a Michelin-Baedeker course in how to appreciate Venice, Italy. The course goes back quite a few years, several centuries, in fact. It not only had to do with the colonel's serving in the Italian Army in War One, but 'way, 'way before. Jackson, who seemed to the present reviewer to be one of those Wyoming skinny boys whose father might have been a pal of Senator Cary's, should have stopped the Cadillac and said, "Colonel, you got any prayers, you say them, because you bore me." Then, to be sure, we'd have had no novel. Or not the same novel.

After the patronizing travelog, the noncom and Colonel Cantwell get to Venice, and the colonel has the rendezvous with his girl, the countess. She is, on this reviewer's oath, practically all that a middle-aged man with a cardiac condition could ask for. Not yet nineteen years old, a countess who need not worry about consequences, Renata (whose name sounds like lasso to me) is so much in love with the colonel that she takes his rudeness and gives him emeralds in return.

It is so easy to kid that aspect of Hemingway's writing and it is so foolish to do so. Go ahead and disbelieve in Catherine Barkley, as I disbelieve now in the Countess Renata, as I did too in Maria, of *For Whom the Bell Tolls*. But the Hemingway heroines, as distinguished from the Sinclair Lewis ones, have a way of catching up with you after you have passed them by. You read them; you see them played by Helen Hayes, Elissa Landi, Ingrid Bergman; you put them away. And yet in later years you form your own nontheatrical picture of them out of what you remember of what Hemingway wrote, and what you have seen of living women. If Rita Hayworth or Ava Gardner should play Renata it will be easy to understand why either actress was cast, but it will probably only postpone a personal picture of the heroine of *Across the River and Into the Trees*. There are not many real things about Renata, in fact, she has so few individual characteristics and attributes that after the inevitable movie has been made, it may be much easier to form your own idea—and almost entirely your own—of what Renata was intended to be.

It is not unfair or unjustifiable, this casting of the novel's characters. The novel was written as a serial for *Cosmopolitan,* whose demands and restrictions are, I should say, almost precisely those of the movies. Now that the novel is available between boards, a great many touches that most likely were in Hemingway's working manuscript have been restored. They don't add much, they don't take much away. At the same time they do make a difference, they make the bound volume authentically Hemingway, and not Hemingway plus (or maybe minus is the word) the *Cosmopolitan* editors. And in any case the touches never would appear in the movies. They would not even appear in the most rudimentary "treatment" that might be submitted to the Johnston Office.

The reasons Hemingway is important are not easy to search for, but they are easy to find. They are hard to search for, because he is so competent and deceivingly simple and plain. It is not enough to say that simplicity itself is rare. People are always mailing authors their nine-year-old children's compositions as examples of beautiful simplicity. Simplicity is not rare. And fancy, complicated writing isn't rare either. Every author gets fancy writing in the form of letters and manuscripts from jailbirds, psychopaths, and students.

But what Hemingway has—and Steinbeck has it too—is pre-paper discipline. It means, first of all, point of view. A great many nonwriters have it without having to reveal it, but with an author it is not only revealing; it often is exposing. A possibly oversimplified definition of point of view would be "feeling and preference" and, in an author's case, the expression of an attitude. It is in the manner and method of the expression of the atti-

Galley proof for Across the River and Into the Trees, *with Hemingway's revisions (Norberto Fuentes,* Hemingway in Cuba*)*

tude that writers vary, and before that, the pre-paper discipline—the thinking, the self-editing—gets its test.

An author may seem to lead a ruggedly simple life, but the fact that he is an author makes him not a simple individual. The personality therefore requires enormous discipline in putting the uncomplicated thinking down on paper. The ostensibly simple lives led by men like Hemingway and Steinbeck tell practically nothing about the personalities, although the writing is simple too. The ostensibly simple life led by William Faulkner tells nothing about him either, for the writing comes out plain but complicated, with so little change in the process between first thought and final printed page that Faulkner, while a genius, may not be an artist. It makes damn small difference to him or to me.

It shouldn't to Hemingway, although it may, because he permits himself practically no private life, or at any rate gets none. The most recent, and most disgusting, example of the intrusions into Hemingway's private life was made by a publication that reported on Hemingway's drinking habits, somewhat in the manner of a gleeful parole officer. It also included some direct quotes, in tin-ear fashion, of what were passed off as Hemingway's speech, but sounded more like the dialogue written for the Indian chief in *Annie Get Your Gun.*

The inability to write the way people talk is a common affliction among writers. But for Eustace Tilley to raise an eyeglass over anybody's drinking is one for the go-climb-a-lamppost department. The magazine had printed numerous little attacks on Hemingway by a semi-anonymous staffman who has gone to his heavenly reward, just as it printed attacks on Faulkner by a critic who has returned to his proper chore on the radio. With the long piece on Hemingway the magazine achieved a new low in something.

In the new novel, Hemingway, rather regrettably, has done nothing to protect himself against personal attack, or, more accurately, counterattack. He has named some names, and made easily identifiable some others: Patton, Eisenhower, Montgomery, Ney, Custer, Truman, Dewey, as well as an author or two, a journalist or two, and probably a few noncelebrated individuals who will recognize themselves or think they do.

This does not sound like a *roman à clef,* any more than it is an autobiography (Hemingway is still alive, and Dick Cantwell ends the book by dying), and that doesn't matter either way. What matters is that Ernest Hemingway has brought out a new book.

To use his own favorite metaphor, he may not be able to go the full distance, but he can still hurt you. Always dangerous. Always in there with that right cocked.

Real class.

Critic Maxwell Geismar reviewed To Have and Have Not *in the* Saturday Review of Literature, *33 (9 September 1950), pp. 18–19. Like most American and British reviewers, Geismar finds this novel to be Hemingway's weakest.*

To Have and To Have and To Have

This is an unfortunate novel and unpleasant to review for anyone who respects Hemingway's talent and achievement. It is not only Hemingway's worst novel; it is a synthesis of everything that is bad in his previous work and it throws a doubtful light on the future.

It is so dreadful, in fact, that it begins to have its own morbid fascination and is almost impossible, as they say, to put down. The story concerns an American officer, a professional soldier, in Italy. He has a bad heart and is about to die. He is in love with an Italian countess whom he calls Daughter. But Colonel Richard Cantwell is a caricature of such figures as the Lieutenant Henry of "A Farewell To Arms" or the Jake of "The Sun Also Rises." The love story is a "romance" and written mainly in what I can only describe as Indian prose: "They stood there and kissed each other true."

The sex is oral and anatomical mainly; the passion, so far as I can see, is purely verbal. There is not one scene of genuine feeling; what is even more curious on the part of the artist who could understand Lady Brett or Catherine Barkley is the heroine's complete lack of sensuousness or feminine perception. She is a fantasy of the completely docile, pliant child bride and is useful in the novel merely as interlocutor for the Colonel's overwhelming narcissism. Petting her, the Colonel reflects that he is assisting "at the only mystery that he believed in except the occasional bravery of man," but the true mystery of "Across the River and Into the Trees" is Hemingway's concept of love.

Although the dialogue has become so stylized that it is impossible to carry on a serious conversation, the Colonel also offers us (usually in bed) a set of opinions about modern life which may be summarized as follows. The GI's are all "sad Americans," while their commanding officers are politicians and frauds. The only professional soldiers were the Germans. The United States is now "governed in some way, by the dregs," including an amateur pianist and unsuccessful haberdasher. But the French are even worse, mainly jerks. Everybody who has written about the last war to date is either a journalist or a jerk. Etc. In a moment of

FINCA VIGIA, SAN FRANCISCO DE PAULA, CUBA

April 19 1951

Dear Malcolm :

It was good to hear from you . I had the same re-action you did about what a shame it was for Scott not to be around for his own revival . But to be revived by such strange people : First Schulberg , a very nice guy everybody says , and most pleasant when I met him once in Key West , writes something that really balls up everything about Scott and Zelda . I never saw Scott in that stage of his life. But the way Zelda is handled makes the whole thing sort of pointless .

Mizener deceived me completely by his letters . I thought he was a straight guy and then came that unspeakable piece of grave robbery he wrote for LIFE . When a man , and fellow writer , has a daughter ,married and with children liveing to hang a heritage of insanity onto them ,for money , seems hardly a Christian act .

Poor Scott ; what robes, or shroud , he had we re torn and sold by very strange people . I hope to hell you will be able to set some things right . As you know only a few of the short stories are good . Gatsby is good and Tender Is The Night is mixed up but absolutely excellent . The Last Tycoon is very good .But it was more a beautifully organized scheme to borrow advances on than a completed novel . I am sure Scott would have fought to complete it . But from what I heard from the people who were with him at the end ; especially one man I knew and who told me very detailed things , he was quite incapable of finishing it . But Scott tried hard and did not die from dear old Dartmouth nor on the playing fields of Princeton and I am afraid I think both Schulberg and Mizener are swine ; no matter how plausible .

You are a decent man and whatever you do ,according to Scott's wishes , about Tender In The Night is ok . People have a choice of reading either version . But that Schulberg - Mizener Axis could well be hanged ,head down , in front of any second rate garage .

Wish you luck with your other projects . I have only one : this novel .Never worked harder ,nor better , nor happ ier in my life .Knocked blood-pressure down to 140 over 70 and I can pitch as many days a week as it needs . I wish you could see some of it . Always plenty of problems . But my only true problem is this one .

Who is Young and what sort of a book is he doing on me ? If it is literary criticism let it be however it is and be damned . But if it is about my private life; since I asked you not to write that , nor Harvey Breit , nor Carlos Baker I think I ought to know about it . Can you tell me about who Philip Young is and for whom he is undertaking this project ?

I am very glad your family are well. Give my best to Muriel and to Rob . Pat is doing well at Harvard I believe and is going to Madrid this summer . Last summer they were in southern Italy and Greece . Gigi is AI or IA in the draft . Bumby just lost a son in Berlin on a surprize midnight caesrean . The baby lived five hours . Mother ok. He has a very fine daughter .Mary is fine and very happy . Tell Rob not to read A Farewell To Arms too much .

Best to you always

Ernest

Hemingway's letter to critic Malcolm Cowley on the F. Scott Fitzgerald revival (Sotheby Parke Bernet, Goodwin Collection, Item 425, 25 October 1977)

insight the Colonel does describe himself as "the unjust bitter criticizer who speaks badly of everyone," and this is indeed a sterile bitter, disappointed, and distasteful point of view.

What is even more distressing than the articulation of this morbid and infantile egotism (the Colonel has a habit of referring to himself as a good boy or a bad boy) is the implicit set of values in the novel. "The hell with anything American except me," the Colonel says, but could anything be more American than his notion of "fun" and his rigid code of behavior? The ideological background of the novel is a mixture of *True Romances,* Superman, and the Last Frontier. And the setting of the novel is a perfect instance of Veblen's conspicuous consumption. The Colonel drinks to Leclerc's death with a magnum of Perrier-Jouet Brut 1942 and knows the feeding habits of lobsters from the Dalmatian coast. His companion, the young countess, speaks casually of her butler and maid while she impulsively slips her lover the family jewels. But the Colonel moves warily from duck shoot to duck shoot and even at his favorite cafe, after the tourists and diplomats have gone, he is alert for plots, intrigues, sudden death, and makes sure he has both his flanks covered.

As in the case of Sinclair Lewis, the late phase of Hemingway's work—this vulgar and snobbish vision of social superiority and luxury—is essentially middle class. And yet what marks this psychological universe is precisely the lack of any sort of middle ground. Just as the Colonel's friends range from waiters to the Italian nobility, but exclude an average citizen, the only alternative to "fun" is desperation. He is himself either barbarous or kind, a good boy or a bad boy; everything is either wonderful or dreadful, and the love affair oscillates between these precarious poles of emotion. The Colonel indeed lives in fear that the "spell," such as it is, will be broken.

"Do not let anything spoil it. . . . Let's not think about anything at all." Don't speak. Don't think. This is, of course, a familiar refrain in Hemingway's work from "In Our Time" to "For Whom the Bell Tolls." It is the motif of the great dark stories of the 1930's, and one remembers the author in "The Gambler, the Nun, and the Radio"—the writer who never permitted himself to think except when he was writing. It is in one sense the secret of Hemingway's art because at his best he expressed so well the intuitive values of life, and because the "wound" in his work—the sense of hidden suffering and of shared anguish—was actually what gave it the complex, ambiguous rich tone.

But all that is left here is the scab and the pus, as it were, of the true insights. The suffering and anguish are a mark of superiority, not of human communion; the double identification in Hemingway's best work with both the hunter and the hunted has been resolved into the code of the snob and the killer. This is a cosmos of jerks, this is Winner Take Everything, this is to Have and to Have and to Have. There are still good things in "Across the River and Into the Trees," and it is possible that the novel will serve as an emotional release for an intricate and tormented talent, very much as "The Torrents of Spring" did in the earliest phase of Hemingway's career.

But surely this, to use his new lingo, is not the work of the man who was there. Nor did Walt Whitman's original phrase of compassion—"I was the man. I was there"—mean what Hemingway now means.

Across the River and Into the Trees received the worst criticism of all of Hemingway's novels. English novelist Evelyn Waugh defended the work in Commonweal, 53 *(3 November 1950), pp. 97–98.*

The Case of Mr. Hemingway

Mr. Ernest Hemingway's long-expected novel has been out for some weeks, and has already been conspicuously reviewed by all the leading critics. It is now impossible to approach it without some prejudice either against the book itself or against its critics, for in England their disapproval has been unanimous. They have been smug, condescending, derisive, some with unconcealed glee, some with an affectation of pity; all are agreed that there is a great failure to celebrate. It is the culmination of a whispering campaign of some years' duration, that "Hemingway is finished."

I read the reviews before I read the book, and I was in the mood to make the best of it. Mr. Hemingway is one of the most original and powerful of living writers. Even if he had written a completely fatuous book, this was not the way to treat it. What, in fact, he has done is to write a story entirely characteristic of himself, not his best book, perhaps his worst, but still something very much better than most of the work to which the same critics give their tepid applause.

It is the story of the death of an old soldier. He knows he is mortally ill, and he chooses to spend his last days in and near Venice, shooting and making love. The book is largely a monologue. The veteran ruminates bitterly over old battles. He exults in his young mistress. And all is written in that pungent vernacular which Mr. Hemingway should have patented.

It may be conceded at once that the hero is not an attractive character. He is a boor and a bore, jocular, humorless, self-centered, arrogant; he rose to command a brigade, but he is consumed by the under-dog's resentment of his superiors both in the army and elsewhere; the last man, in fact, to choose as one's companion in Venice. But these reviewers have been telling us for years that we must not judge novels by the amiability of their characters, any more than we must judge pictures by the beauty of their subjects. Mr. Hemingway makes a full, strong portrait of his obnoxious hero.

The heroine, a very young Venetian, is strangely unchaperoned. If social conventions have indeed relaxed so much since I was last in that city, this young lady's behavior provides ample evidence that the traditional, rigid code was highly desirable. But are our reviewers the right people to complain of her goings-on? I think it is the troubador in Mr. Hemingway which impels him to ennoble his heroines. He did the same thing in his first, startlingly brilliant *Fiesta*. There is a strong affinity between that book and this. How it delighted and impressed us a quarter of a century ago! How flatly we accept the same gifts today!

Of course, between then and now there have been the shoals of imitators. It was so easy. You have to be an accomplished writer to imitate Henry James. Any journalist can produce a not quite passable imitation of Mr. Hemingway. But it was not only the inventions in technique that impressed us in *Fiesta*. It was the mood. English literature is peculiarly rich in first-class Philistine novelists—Surtees and Mr. P. G. Wodehouse, for example. But their characters were always happy. Mr. Hemingway has melancholy, a sense of doom. His men and women are as sad as those huge, soulless apes that huddle in their cages at the zoo. And that mood is still with us.

Across the River and Into the Trees is the nemesis of the philistine. The hero is fifty-one years of age, when the civilized man is just beginning the most fruitful period of his life. But the philistine is done for, a "beat-up old bastard," as he expresses it. He has lived for sport and drink and love-making and professional success, and now there is nothing left for him. He has to be decorated with a physical, mortal illness as with a medal. In accentuation of the pathos of his position, he regards himself as rather cultured and sophisticated. He has been places. He is one with that baffled, bibulous crew of *Fiesta* who thought they were plunging deep into the heart of Europe by getting on friendly terms with barmen; who thought their café pick-ups the flower of decadent European aristocracy. He believes he is the sort of guy for whom the Old Masters painted, and to hell with the art experts.

All of the faults of this latest book were abundantly present in the first; and most of the merits of the

first are here again. Why has there been this concerted attack on Mr. Hemingway?

It began a few months ago with a softening-up blitz in the *New Yorker*. That widely-read paper attached a female reporter to Mr. Hemingway to study him while he was on a holiday in New York. She ate and drank, went shopping and visited art galleries with him, and took careful note of every silly or vulgar thing he said or did during his spree. One might suppose that only a megalomaniac or a simpleton would expose himself to such an ordeal. She made a complete ass of him, of course; not altogether a lovable ass, either. I have never met Mr. Hemingway, but I think it probable that his own boisterous manners have contributed to his present unpopularity.

He has really done almost everything to render himself a "beat-up old bastard." His reputation was unassailable in 1936. Then with much trumpeting, he went to Madrid and Barcelona. Here was something greater than bull-fights and *bistros*. The greatest modern writer was devoting his art to the greatest modern theme. Picasso had painted Guernica; Messrs. Auden and Spender had written something or other; now the great warrior-artist of the New World was going to write the Modern Epic. But it did not turn out like that. *For Whom the Bell Tolls* was not at all what the Socialists wanted. They had been busy denying atrocities; Mr. Hemingway described them in detail with relish. They had denied the presence of Russians; Mr. Hemingway led us straight into the front-door of the Gaylord Hotel. He made Marty and la Passionaria as comic as any *New Yorker* correspondent could have done. From then on he was on the wrong side of the barricades for the Socialists, while his pounding revolutionary heart still drove him from civilization.

His sense of superiority to Americans combined with his sense of inferiority to Europeans to give him the sort of patriotism which pleased no one. He could not abide the urban commercial development of his own country; he supposed, rather rightly, that the English were snooty about him, and the French wanted only his dollars. He had a Kiplingesque delight in the technicalities of every trade but his own. He remained, of course, an admirable technician, but, while he could talk for nights to fishermen about their tackle, he was nauseated by the jargon of other writers. Indeed, in this book he uses an American novelist as the typic contrast to his hero; a seedy, industrious fellow in the same hotel, sober, with no young mistress and no scars of battle, and no rollicking jokes with the servants.

When the second war came Mr. Hemingway could not be a soldier, and he despised war-correspondents; he became a war-correspondent. There is plenty to account for the bitterness and frustration of his

S. F. de P.

June 18 1952

Dear Mr. Fenton :

I'm sorry my letter made you sore and that you wrote the letter you sent . Last night I wrote you a three page letter . But I will try now , at first light, to write you cold and straight and not in anger . We will let the stuff about haveing the wind up etc. go by . I have seen enough people blow up to understand it and I know how straight I tried to help you on what you said your project was and I know from many first lights that I am not too windy a character . Dry-mouthed many times Not likeing it ; sure . But windy; no and usually cheerful .

Here is the point . I had a wonderful novel to write about Oak Park and would never do it because I did not want to hurt liveing people . I did not think that a man should make money out of his father shooting himself nor out of his mother who drove him to it nor out of his poor pitiful brother . Tom Wolfe wrote only of his own life with rhetoric added . I wanted to write about the whole damned world if I could get to know it . When I started I wrote some short stories about actual things and two of them hurt people . I felt bad about it . Later if I used actual people I used only those for whom I had completely lost respect and then I tried to give them a square shake . I know this all sounds very noble but it is not really horse-shit . The man who indentifies himself as Cohn in The Sun Also Rises once said to me ," But why did you make me cry all the time ?"

I said , "listen, if that is you then the narrator must be me ? Do you think that I had my prick shot off or that if you and I had ever had a fight I would not have knocked the shit out of you ? We boxed often enough so you know that . And I'll tell you a secret : you do cry an awful lot for a man ."

So now we get back to Oak Park where you feel it your duty as a scholar (when does a writer get to be a scholar and have these obligations ?) to dig into my family while I am still alive , to question my poor bloody ass of a kid brother who I never knew until after my father had shot himself , and the rest of it . Nobody in Oak Park likes me I should suppose . The people that were my good friends are dead or gone . I gave Oak Park a miss and never used it as a target . You wouldn't like to bomb your home town would you ? Even if it ceased to be your home town the day you could leave it ?

When you go into my family , etc. it is to me an invasion of privacy and I gave you the cease and desist . There are defensible interpretations for any violation of ethics or good taste . But I think you will agree that if I had written about Oak Park you would have a point in studying it . But I did not write about it .

I know it is better to have a straight guy write about your work than a crook . I think of you as a straight guy . But nobody likes to be tailed . That is not a sign that you are windy . It is a sign that you do not like to be tailed , investigated , queried about , by any amateur detective no matter how scholarly or how straight . You ought to be able to see that Fenton . It was one of the rights that was agreed upon, in principle at least , when our ancestors set up the country .

Then take the Moise thing . I tried to remember if I had ever helped get Moise home when he was stabbed by either a whore or somebody's husband and whether I was present when he threw a typewriter through the window of the press room at police headquarters and I honestly could not . In newspaper work you have to learn to forget every day what happened the day before . Everything was wonderful to me in Kansas City (that sounds like a line from a song) but I was working on a newspaper and so I cannot remember as I should . You might note for your book that newspaper work is valuable up until the point that it forcibly begins to destroy your memory . A writer must leave it before that point . But he will always have scars from it . Just as any experience of war is invaluable to a writer . But it is destructive if he has too much . You could probably write on this better than I could . If you had not served as well and as long as you did you would probably be writing instead of teaching writing and rideing herd on my childhood .

But I know too bloody well that Hurtgen Forest was much more destructive to me than instructive . But I have tried hard to train back out in the first place .

Let's drop Dave Randall . I never should have picked it up not

Hope you take this in the spirit in which it is written . I trusted you completely on your project . But it was getting out of hand . The proof of that is the extent to which you wrote me had been urged to extend it . Do you agree

write me what you think and lay off the words that provoke with guys like ourselves ...Maybe I should include myself in people like us . But I have certain ethical standards about prose in spite of my marriages , my blunders etc. as you list them . Maybe when you are 52 going on 53 you will have some blunders too . There are usually some reasons for the marriages and I hope to Christ I never give them . The writing published in books is what I stand on and I would like people to leave my private life the hell alone . what right has

anyone to go into it? I may be right of all

Best luck

Hemingway's letter to Charles Fenton (author of The Apprenticeship of Ernest Hemingway, *1954) recounting details of the writer's early career (Sotheby Parke Bernet, Item 157, Sale Number 3968, 29 March 1977)*

present work. But our critics thrive on bitterness and frustration. They have forgotten that they once raised clenched fists to the red flag in Barcelona. Not more than a handful have been physically assaulted by the man. Why do they all hate him so?

I believe the truth is that they have detected in him something they find quite unforgivable–Decent Feeling. Behind all the bluster and cursing and fisticuffs he has an elementary sense of chivalry–respect for women, pity for the weak, love of honor–which keeps breaking in. There is a form of high, supercilious caddishness which is all the rage nowadays in literary circles. That is what the critics seek in vain in this book, and that is why their complaints are so loud and confident.

Life printed 5,000,000 copies of this issue.

Hemingway's reaction to the mostly negative reviews of Across the River and Into the Trees *was published in Harvey Breit's column in* The New York Times Book Review, *3 December 1950, p. 58.*

Success, It's Wonderful!

After I have written a book I only wish to see it published exactly as I wrote it and have as many people read it as possible. You write for yourself and for others. This last book was written for people, too, who had lived and would die and be capable of knowing the difference between those two states. It was also written for all people who had ever fought or would be capable of fighting or interested in it. It was written, as well, for people who had ever been in love or were capable of that happiness.

The fact that many people read the book of their own accord and that it is not a packaged product made me very happy. It has not, however, altered my way of life or any plans I may have. I hope to write as well as I can as long as I live. And I hope now to live quite a long time.

Many times critics do not understand a work when a writer tries for something he has not attempted before. But eventually they get abreast of it. The critic, out on a limb, is more fun to see than a mountain lion. The critic gets paid for it so it is much more just that he should be out on that limb than the poor cat who does it for nothing. Altogether I believe it has been quite healthy and the extremely dull thuds one hears as the critics fall from their limbs when the tree is shaken slightly may presage a more decent era in criticism–

when books are read and criticized, rather than personalities attacked.

These comments appeared in an advertisement on the back cover of the 25 August 1952 issue of Life, *the issue immediately before that in which* The Old Man and the Sea *was first published.*

From Ernest Hemingway To the Editors of LIFE

"I'm very excited about *The Old Man and the Sea* and that it is coming out in LIFE so that many people will read it who could not afford to buy it. That makes me much happier than to have a Nobel Prize. To have you guys being so careful and good about it and so thoughtful is better than any kind of prize. . . .

"Whatever I learned is in the story but I hope it reads simply and straight and all the things that are in it do not show but only are with you after you have read it. . . .

"I had wanted to write it for more than 15 years and I never did it because I did not think I could. . . . Now I have to try to write something better. That is sort of rough. But I had good luck with this all the way and maybe I will have luck again. . . .

"Don't you think it is a strange damn story that it should affect all of us (me especially) the way it does? I have had to read it now over 200 times and everytime it does something to me. It's as though I had gotten finally what I had been working for all my life. . . ."

Carlos Baker, author of the first scholarly biography of Hemingway, Ernest Hemingway: A Life Story *(New York: Scribners, 1969), reviewed* The Old Man and the Sea *in the* Saturday Review, 35 *(6 September 1952), pp. 10–11.*

The Marvel Who Must Die

The admirable Santiago, Hemingway's ancient mariner and protagonist of this triumphant short novel, enters the gallery of permanent heroes effortlessly, as if he had belonged there from the beginning.

Indeed he has. His story belongs as much in our time as that of Nick Adams. He is one of the men without women, fighting it out alone with only a brave heart for company. He is one of the winners who takes nothing. Though he does not die he is one of those for whom the bell tolls. What Santiago has at the close of his story is what all the heroes of Hemingway have had—the proud, quiet knowledge of having fought the fight, of having lasted it out, of having done a great thing to the bitter end of human strength.

Santiago, in the sum of things, is a tragic hero. His story, architectonically speaking, shows a natural tragic pattern. After eighty-four days without a strike, the old man rises in the cool dark morning and rows out alone towards the mile-deep Gulf Stream. It is the month of September, the time of the big fish. Towards noon of this eighty-fifth day, trolling his baits at various levels, he hooks a huge marlin down in the green dark of a hundred fathoms. Then through that long afternoon, and the night, and another day and another night, he hangs on with the line over his shoulder while his skiff is towed slowly north-eastward through the calm September sea.

Living on strips of raw bonito, a flying fish, and part of a dolphin, washed down with nips from his water-bottle, Santiago takes and endures almost infinite pains. Twice the fish leaps clear of the water, trying to throw the hook. But it is not until noon of the third day

out that Santiago manages to bring his great trophy finally to the surface and to drive his harpoon into that other fighting heart. The marlin is two feet longer than the skiff, too big to hoist aboard even if the old man's strength were still equal to the task. He lashes it alongside, comes about, and sets his patched old sail for home.

An hour later the first shark comes. The tragedy of subtraction begins. Number One is a handsome Mako, big and voracious, with eight raking rows of teeth. Santiago kills him with the harpoon, which is lost when the Mako sinks. Also lost, like a piece of the courageous old man's heart, is a great forty-pound bite from the side of the prize fish. What is worse, the scent of its blood spreads through the water like a lure for all the sea's rapacious attackers. Two more presently close in—ugly, shovel-nosed Galanos sharks, rending and tearing what the old man has earned by the sweat of his brow, the blood of his hands, and the indomitable pride of his endurance. Like the first, these are killed. But others follow: one, then a pair, and finally in the night a whole anonymous pack. Santiago fights them off with all he has (his knife lashed to an oar-butt, the boat's club, the tiller) until these break or are lost and there are no more weapons. Yet now there is no more trophy, either. If the old man were to look overside in the dark, he would see only the bony head, the proud perpendicular tail, and the picked white skeleton of his prize. The old man does not bother to look. He knows too well what has happened.

Once more, in his lengthening career as one of the few genuine tragic writers of modern times, Hemingway has memorably engaged a theme familiar to tragic literature. Santiago belongs among all those who have the strength and dignity to fight against great odds and to win moral victories, even though the tangible rewards may be lost in the process of the battle. On the heroic level, one thinks of Melville's Ahab, Whitman's Columbus, Sandburg's Lincoln. But the great skill here has been to take a simple fisherman and by setting his struggle against the background of the ancient and unchanging sea, and pitting him against an adversary worthy of his strength, to bring out his native ability and indomitability until, once having known him, we can never afterwards lose sight of him. Wordsworth's Michael and his leech-gatherer are pastoral types, artfully projected against the English hills and plains, and showing the resolution and independence which always tugged at Wordsworth's heart-strings, as Santiago's tug at ours. Yet the pitch here attained and held to is several degrees above the plane of pastoral tragedy. It approaches, as a tragic pattern, the story of King Lear, whose shark-hearted daughters bled him of his dominions and his hundred knights, yet left his dignity unimpaired and his

Announcement for Hemingway's novella about an old Cuban fisherman

trope in which every man may locate some of the profounder aspects of his own spiritual biography.

The second point enters the region of religious experience. The theme of what is Christlike in every good man has grown in upon Hemingway since 1940, when the Christian Anselmo, another aged man, was established as the moral norm in "For Whom the Bell Tolls." The ancient Santiago, stumbling out of his boat with dried blood on his face from a partly healed wound, and with the deep cord-cuts like stigmata on his hands, carries the mast over his shoulder up the hill. Sleeping exhaustedly face down on the spread newspapers that cover the springs of his bed, he lies cruciform, with arms out straight and palms turned upwards. *In hoc signo vinces.* He has entered the Masonic order of Christian heroes. In short, Hemingway has enhanced the native power of his tragic parable by engaging, though unobtrusively, the further power of Christian symbolism. Somewhere between its parabolical and its Christian meaning lies one important explanation of this book's power to move us.

"The Old Man and The Sea" is a great short novel, told with consummate artistry and destined to become a classic in its kind. It is a good kind of present for a man to give the world on or about his fifty-third birthday.

William Faulkner's review of The Old Man and the Sea, *the only review of a Hemingway novel that he wrote, was published in* Shenandoah, *2 (Autumn 1952), p. 55.*

His best. Time may show it to be the best single piece of any of us, I mean his and my contemporaries. This time, he discovered God, a Creator. Until now, his men and women had made themselves, shaped themselves out of their own clay; their victories and defeats were at the hands of each other, just to prove to themselves or one another how tough they could be. But this time, he wrote about pity: about something somewhere that made them all: the old man who had to catch the fish and then lose it, the fish that had to be caught and then lost, the sharks which had to rob the old man of his fish; made them all and loved them all and pitied them all. It's all right. Praise God that whatever made and loves and pities Hemingway and me kept him from touching it any further.

---

native courage unshaken. "I will show him what a man can do," says Santiago of his marlin, "and what a man endures." The thousand times he has proved his worth before mean nothing. Now, climactically, he is proving it again, and earning nothing more tangible than our sympathy and admiration.

"One cannot hope to explain," says the publisher's commentary, "why the reading of this book is so profound an experience." One can, however, at least begin to explain the essence of the experience by making two related observations about it. The first is that the story not only shows a natural tragic pattern (which is no doubt why Hemingway was drawn to it); it develops also as a kind of natural parable. Like human life, for which it easily stands as an extended image, the struggle commences, grows, and subsides between one sleep and another. The parable of Santiago Agonistes works upon our sensibilities like a heroic metaphor achieved naturally and without manifest heroics. The result, a dividend above and beyond the pleasure of reading a fine story, is the discovery of an open-sided

Poet Delmore Shwartz's review of The Old Man and the Sea *was published in the* Partisan Review, *19 (November-December 1952), pp. 702–703.*

The ovation which greeted Hemingway's new novel was mostly very nice. For it was mostly a desire to continue to admire a great writer. Yet there was a note of insistence in the praise and a note of relief, the relief because his previous book was extremely bad in an ominous way, and the insistence, I think, because this new work is not so much good in itself as a virtuoso performance which reminds one of Hemingway at his best. The experience of literature is always comparative, and we have only to remember a story like "The Undefeated," which has almost the same theme as *The Old Man and the Sea,* or the account of the Caporetto retreat in *A Farewell To Arms,* to see exactly how the new book falls short. Whenever, in this new book, the narrative is concerned wholly with fishing, there is a pure vividness of presentation. But when the old man's emotions are explicitly dealt with, there is a margin of self-consciousness and a mannerism of assertion which is perhaps inevitable whenever a great writer cannot get free of his knowledge that he is a great writer. Perhaps this is why the old fisherman is too generalized, too much without a personal history; the reader cannot help but think at times that Hemingway, the publicized author and personality bewitched by his own publicity and an imitator of his own style, is speaking to him directly.

Nevertheless this book does not exist in isolation from the author's work as a whole, which gives it a greater significance and to which it gives a new definition and clarity. We see more clearly how for Hemingway the kingdom of heaven, which is within us, is moral stamina; experience, stripped of illusion, is inexhaustible threat. Which should make the reader recognize how purely American a writer Hemingway is. For what is this sense of existence but the essential condition of the pioneer? It is the terror and the isolation of the pioneer in the forest that Hemingway seeks out in his prizefighters, gunmen, matadors, soldiers and expatriate sportsmen. The hunting and fishing which were necessities of life for the pioneer may be merely sports and games now, but they are pursued with an energy and passion absent in other areas of existence because only within the conditions of sport can a man be truly himself, truly an individual, truly able to pit an isolated will and consciousness against the whole of experience. In *To Have and To Have Not,* Hemingway tried to repudiate this sense of existence; in *For Whom the Bell Tolls* he tried to go beyond it, but he wrote with all of his power under control only when the hero was contained within guerilla warfare, which is obviously Daniel Boone again; in *Across the River and Into the Trees* there is an hysterical fury against modern warfare, for in modern warfare the isolated individual can have no role purely as an isolated individual. Now, after the bluster, bravado and truculence of that book, his fresh possession of his own sensibility suggests the possibility of a new masterpiece.

This statement was published in "I Wish I Had Written That," The New York Times Book Review, *7 December 1952, p. 4.*

Joyce Cary ("Prisoner of Grace")

Of the books I have read this year, Hemingway's "The Old Man and the Sea" struck me as the most complete job. Hemingway at his best is unique: He tells a folk tale, but it is a sophisticated folk tale. It has been said that this great artist belongs essentially to the world of the strip cartoon and there is something in judgement for those who understand the difference between Lear and Silver King. Both are melodramas for barnstormers but one is tailored by genius and the other is a reach-me-down from the slop-shop. They are different in effect because they are different in cause. Lear's tragedy was written by a man who loved melodrama for its richness of theme. Silver King began and ended as a tear-jerker. It is stale now because it was a dead thing then. It had no root in experience or reflection. Hemingway's old man is profoundly original. It deals with fundamentals, the origins. Its form, so elaborately contrived, is yet perfectly suited to the massive shape of a folk theme.

Chapter Six: 1953–July 1961

1953

4 May — *The Old Man and the Sea* wins the Pulitzer Prize in fiction.

ca. 4 July — Making his first trip to Spain since 1938, Hemingway arrives in Pamplona.

6 August — The Hemingways leave Marseilles for Africa.

September — *The Hemingway Reader,* edited by Charles Poore, is published by Scribners.

1954

1 Sept. 1953– 21 Aug. 1954 — With Patrick Hemingway and Philip Percival as white hunters, the Hemingways go on safari in Africa.

23–24 January — Following two plane crashes, in the second of which Hemingway badly injures his head, newspapers around the world report that he has been killed.

24 March — Hemingway accepts a $1,000 Award of Merit from the American Academy of Arts and Letters.

28 October — Hemingway wins the Nobel Prize in literature. He says that he is too ill to go to Stockholm for the ceremony.

1955

4 May — Hemingway is writing a book about his 1953–1954 safari.

September — Hemingway assists in the production of fishing sequences for the movie of *The Old Man and the Sea.*

1956

April — Hemingway reports that he has finished his African book.

17 November — Hemingway discovers trunks that he had left at the Paris Ritz twenty years earlier; he claims that they contain parts of *A Moveable Feast.*

1957

September — Hemingway reports that he is working on his memoirs of Paris in the 1920s.

December — Hemingway begins revising *The Garden of Eden.*

Chapter Six: 1953–July 1961

1958

April   *The Paris Review* publishes George Plimpton's interview with Hemingway.

1959

1–2 January   Fidel Castro takes power in Cuba. Hemingway decides to buy a house in Ketchum, Idaho.

May–September   Hemingway covers the *mano a mano* competition between matadors Antonio Ordóñez and Luis Miguel Dominguín for *Life*.

3 November   Hemingway delivers his Paris memoirs to Scribners.

1960

5 September   The first of three installments of *The Dangerous Summer* is published in *Life*.

30 November   Hemingway enters the Mayo Clinic for treatment of paranoia, depression, and other illnesses. After undergoing electroshock, he is discharged on 22 January 1961.

1961

21 April   Hemingway makes his first suicide attempt. On 23 April he tries again.

25 April   Hemingway is readmitted to the Mayo Clinic; he is discharged on 26 June.

2 July   At his home in Ketchum, Hemingway kills himself. The family announces that his death is an accident.

By 1953 Hemingway was the most famous writer in the world. *The Old Man and the Sea* won the Pulitzer Prize in fiction that year, and the next year Hemingway was awarded the Nobel Prize in literature. In 1953 he made his first trip to Spain since the civil war, and he received a warm welcome. Later that year he and Mary went to Africa for a five-month safari, and he was made Honorary Game Warden for the Kimana Swamp region in Kenya. In January 1954 he and Mary were in two plane crashes in Africa. Newspapers around the world reported that he had been killed, but Hemingway, although he suffered burns and internal injuries, survived.

Upon his return to Cuba, Hemingway began working on a book about his 1953–1954 safari. His work was interrupted when he assisted in the filming of *The Old Man and the Sea*. He also began work on a Nick Adams novel but soon set it aside, as well. Part of this novel was published as "The Last Good Country" in *The Nick Adams Stories* in 1972. In the second half of the 1950s he began working again on *The Garden of Eden* but could not complete it. His work was impaired by poor health: high blood pressure, diabetes, and the lingering effects of the concussions he had received. He also showed symptoms of depression. These problems destroyed Hemingway's ability to edit his work.

In 1957 Hemingway began a new literary project. Alleged to have been inspired by the discovery of notebooks and manuscripts in a trunk he had placed in storage at the Paris Ritz in 1937, he began writing a series of sketches about his life in Paris in the 1920s. The trunk material has not been identified. He worked on this book for the rest of the decade and delivered it to Scribners in 1960 but decided to postpone publication.

During the last year of the decade Hemingway agreed to go to Spain to cover for *Life* the *mano a mano* series of bullfights by Luis Miguel Dominguín and Antonio Ordóñez. Although the article was supposed to be only about 35,000 words long, Hemingway's first draft was 120,000 words. "The Dangerous Summer" was cut and published in three issues of *Life* (5, 12, and 19 September 1960). It was the last work Hemingway published during his lifetime.

In 1960 Hemingway's health continued to deteriorate, a process that was accelerated when the Hemingways left Cuba following the takeover by Fidel Castro. Hemingway became increasingly paranoid and suicidal. In November he was admitted to the Mayo Clinic for a two-month stay for treatment of his depression and other health problems. He was released after showing a slight improvement but had to be readmitted in April after he tried to kill himself. He persuaded his doctors to release him in June and returned with Mary to their home in Ketchum, Idaho. On the morning of 2 July 1961 he shot himself in the head with one of his shotguns.

Hemingway liked the reviews of his work that Charles Poore had written for The New York Times, *and he selected Poore to edit* The Hemingway Reader *(New York: Scribners, 1953). Poore wrote this foreword for the volume.*

This book is planned for the pleasures and rewards of reading. The selections are arranged chronologically. They were chosen mainly to give variety and balance. Other hands, I am aware, would make other choices; no doubt they duly will. The field of choice is as wide as the world the men and women who live in these stories wander over, in peace and in war.

There is the full text of a novel that set the flags for a generation, *The Sun Also Rises,* and a freely sketched satire on the eternal pomposities of unconventionality, *The Torrents of Spring.* There are complete episodes from five other novels in Hemingway's chronicle of modern chivalry: *A Farewell to Arms, To Have and Have Not, For Whom the Bell Tolls, Across the River and Into the Trees,* and *The Old Man and the Sea.* There are chapters on Spain and the art of the torero, "the only art in which the artist is in danger of death and in which the degree of brilliance in the performance is left to the fighter's honor," from *Death in the Afternoon,* and the wonderful dialogue on American writing from *Green Hills of Africa.* There are eleven short stories. These, alone, would be worth a book.

The stories and the novels together represent a body of work that has changed the course of storytelling and given new cadences to the language. They are not gathered here, though, to illustrate academic principles or to pepper elegies. They are alive, a part of experience that tells us more vividly than any casual actuality ever can, where men and women have been, and what they have done and left undone in this brightest and bloodiest of centuries.

Excellence is never as recent as its discovery. The elements of what we admire in a late story, toward the end of this book, are unmistakably present in an early one. It is the field of operations that broadens, from Michigan to the Gulf Stream, from Spain and Paris to the Hurtgen Forest, from Tanganyika to the Venetian Plain; it is the perception that deepens as all that is not essential is burned away to make a story like *The Old Man and the Sea.*

The clarity, the intensity, the humor, valor, grace and love of life in an age that happens through no particular fault of Hemingway to be much concerned with death, were always there. The rough passages of our day's hallowed and unhallowed forages, pilgrimages and crusades are rendered as scrupulously as the smooth ones along the way. These are qualities that have given him his place as the outstanding storyteller, the finest stylist, of his time.

It is idle to observe that he has written no three-generation dynastic family novels, no romances in which Napoleon wins the Civil War and marries Mary Queen of Scots. We have many eminently available novelists for those occasions; we can depend on other authors to create for us private counties and principalities of their own devising. The measure of Hemingway's stature is that he shows us what he has seen of the world as it is, with its gallantry and havoc, its dreams of fair women and hopes of peace.

The age of Hemingway is as shaken and open to adventure as the end of the Middle Ages and the Renaissance. We are all Tudors now, whether we like it very much or not. Yet these pages also remind us that we always have marked Napoleonic characters around in hot, close pursuit of destiny; wars civil and uncivil, and heroines as appealing as the Scottish Queen. He might have written his own chronicle of chivalry in the manner he used when he composed the inscription for a book of stories, *Winner Take Nothing:*

> Unlike all other forms of lutte or combat the conditions are that the winner shall take nothing; neither his ease, nor his pleasure, nor any notions of glory; nor, if he win far enough, shall there be any reward within himself.

Instead, he created his own prose for a new time.

It is for him, I imagine, a process without ending. After service in the first World War on the Italian Front where he was severely wounded before he was 19 and won the Medaglia d'Argento al Valore Militare and three Croces al Merito di Guerra, he came back to America and then went abroad as a correspondent for Canadian and American papers, serving in Europe and the Middle East. "I was trying to write then," he said in *Death in the Afternoon,* "and I found the greatest difficulty, aside from knowing truly what you really felt, rather than what you were supposed to feel . . . was to put down what really happened in action; what the actual things were which produced the emotion that you experienced. . . . The real thing, the sequence of motion and fact which made the emotion and which would be as valid in a year or in ten years or, with luck and if you stated it purely enough, always, was beyond me and I was working very hard to try to get it."

Then there were the years when none would pay money to publish stories that now are in a hundred anthologies, the times he remembered in *Green Hills of*

Africa, living in Paris: "in Notre Dame des Champs in the courtyard with the sawmill (*and the sudden whine of the saw, the smell of sawdust and the chestnut tree over the roof with a mad woman downstairs*) and the year worrying about money (*all of the stories back in the mail that came in through a slit in the sawmill door, with notes of rejection that would never call them stories, but always anecdotes, sketches, contes, etc. They did not want them, and we lived on poireaux and drank cahors and water*) and how fine the fountains were at the Place de L'Observatoire (*water sheen rippling on the bronze of horses' manes, bronze breasts and shoulders, green under thin-flowing water*) and when they put up the bust of Flaubert in the Luxembourg on the short cut through the gardens on the way to the rue Soufflot (*one that we believed in, loved without criticism, heavy now in stone as an idol should be*)."

The years of fame have not banked the fire. He will say, I think, "Aún aprendo," like Goya, "I'm still learning," in his eighties.

Ford Madox Ford pointed out in an introduction to *A Farewell to Arms* that "the aim—the achievement—of the great prose writer is to use words so that they shall seem new and alive because of their juxtaposition with other words. This gift Hemingway has supremely. . . . You cannot throw yourself into a frame of mind and just write and get that effect. Your mind has to choose each word and your ear has to test it until by long disciplining of mind and ear you can no longer go wrong. That disciplining through which you must put yourself is all the more difficult in that it must be gone through in solitude. You cannot watch the man next to you in the ranks smartly manipulating his side-arms nor do you hear any word of command by which to time yourself. On the other hand a writer holds a reader by his temperament. That is his true 'gift'—what he receives from whoever sends him into the world. It arises from how you look at things. If you look at and render things so that they appear new to the reader you will hold his attention. If what you give him appears familiar or half familiar his attention will wander."

It was Ford who defined the style many have bumbled through a volume trying to define when he said: "Hemingway's words strike you, each one, as if they were pebbles fetched fresh from a brook. They live and shine, each in its place. So one of his pages has the effect of a brook-bottom into which you look down through the flowing water. The words form a tessellation, each in order beside the other." That judgment, made early in Hemingway's career, sets Ford apart from those who cherish the simple notion that the style is all a matter of simple sentences. The simplicity is there—but few things are more complex than Hemingway's simplicity. It is about as simple as a Bach fugue or a Cézanne landscape and it is as clearly,

cleanly present in this book's first story, the classic "Big Two-Hearted River" ("the river shallow ahead entering the woods, curving into the woods, shallows, light glittering, big water-smooth rocks, cedars along the bank and white birches") as it is in the 424-words-long sentence about all our yesterdays, todays and tomorrows in *Green Hills of Africa.*

It is in *Across the River and Into the Trees,* a novel of man's experience that can best be experienced by those who have known girls as lovely as Renata and worn Cantwell's armor, where dusk and dawn seem to happen on the page, somehow, as he thinks, "I could be part of the ground where the children play in the evenings, and in the mornings, maybe, they would still be training jumping horses and their hoofs would make the thudding on the turf, and trout would rise in the pool when there was a hatch of fly." And in the memory of the West in "The Snows of Kilimanjaro," ". . . the ranch and the silvered gray of the sage brush, the quick, clear water in the irrigation ditches, and the heavy green of the alfalfa. The trail went up into the hills and the cattle in the summer were shy as deer. The bawling and the steady noise and slow moving mass raising a dust as you brought them down in the fall. And behind the mountains, the clear sharpness of the peak in the evening light and, riding down along the trail in the moonlight, bright across the valley."

The observation is always miraculously precise, as in *The Sun Also Rises,* where Jake, crossing the Seine, notices "a string of barges being towed empty down the current, riding high, the bargemen at the sweeps as they came toward the bridge"; Pilar, in *For Whom the Bell Tolls* remembering Finito, "as he furled the heavy flannel cloth around the stick; the flannel hanging blood-heavy from the passes where it had swept over the bull's head and shoulders and the wet streaming shine of his withers and on down and over his back as the bull raised into the air and the banderillas clattered." That is writing, isn't it?—the "sequence of motion and fact which made the emotion," as it is in the unforgettable opening sentence of "The Light of the World": "When he saw us come in the door the bartender looked up and then reached over and put the glass covers on the two free-lunch bowls."

I do not hold with those who are comparing Chaucer favorably to Hemingway these days. Nor do I think it is wise to expend spirit in trying to move him farther away from the Browning Automatic Rifle, closer to the circle of Robert Browning. One world at a time, please. There is still reason to wish that he had begun *The Sun Also Rises* at Chapter III, that he had left stuff about Radiguet and his band out of *Death in the Afternoon,* and that Colonel Cantwell were less touched with vainglory. But I am most certain that he will stand with

Yeats and Joyce as one of the three principal men of letters of our time. And since clocks and calendars move forward, not backward, from here on out he may be the strongest influence in literature that this age will give to posterity.

The readers of this era have passed many worthy authors by to choose in Hemingway's books their emblems. He gives us grace and fortitude to face the Toynbee-paced calamities of modern history and a measure of laughter to deal with follies and pomposities. His standards of writing are severe and arduous. They are serious. But they specifically exclude solemnity. . . .

He is more at home in the world beyond American borders than any writer of his stature since Henry James and Stephen Crane, and he has given us aspects of that world they could not have known as contemporaries, for Crane died young and James would scarcely be the man to help Hemingway move into Rambouillet. Nor go with him on the 4th Division's run north from Paris that led to St. Quentin and Le Cateau, crossed the Ardennes, and broke the Siegfried Line in the Schnee Eifel. In the second World War he was called a war correspondent by masterly understatement. In actual fact, his activities had a somewhat longer trajectory. He began amphibious action by hunting German submarines in the Caribbean when their sinkings of our oil tankers were making those waters a sea of fire. Then he went on to fly combat missions with the Royal Air Force. Officers and enlisted men of the 4th Infantry Division, those who survived out of the more than 24,000 casualties that Division suffered, speak of him with affection and remember how he tried to be of service to that Division in any way that he was able to, in more than one hundred days of combat.

He had already seen more of war, in Italy and Spain, than some of the leading novelists of the second World War would ever see. His books were records— and prophecies. A rout, a long march in the dark backwash of defeat, is one of the tragic commonplaces of our era. There have been many, all over the world since Caporetto. It is not easy to find on ordinary maps. In *A Farewell to Arms* Lieutenant Henry had first seen it as "a little white town with a campanile in a valley. It was a clean little town and there was a fine fountain in the square." But the world knows Caporetto better than many more famous battles now because it remembers Lieutenant Henry and the retreat to which it gave the name, and the way "the whole country was moving, as well as the army," and the battle police, the questioners who "had that beautiful detachment and devotion to stern justice of men who are dealing in death without being in any danger of it."

In Hemingway's books the dialogue, the famous dialogue, varies more subtly than any hasty reading

shows. The cadences change not only from speaker to speaker, but also in the way the same person will discuss the same subject with different people. Lieutenant Henry discussing matters of love and religion with Rinaldi, the young Italian Army doctor he has served with for two years so that they understand each other ribaldly and completely, changes when he speaks to Count Greffi, the old diplomat with the beautiful manners who had been a contemporary of Metternich and was living to be one hundred years old.

"All my life I encounter sacred subjects," Rinaldi says, "but very few with you." And Lieutenant Henry challenges: "I can say this about your mother and that about your sister?" They both laugh as Rinaldi says swiftly: "And that about *your sister*." It gets rough. When Lieutenant Henry is talking to Count Greffi, though, the difference is like the difference between the captured enemy cognac Rinaldi pours into what he calls "your old toothbrushing glass" and the cold dry champagne Count Greffi serves in stemmed crystal.

Lieutenant Henry has asked the Count whether he would like to live after death, and Count Greffi says: "This life is very pleasant. I would like to live forever." He smiles. "I very nearly have." Count Greffi asks Lieutenant Henry to pray for him, if he ever becomes devout; "I am asking several of my friends to do that. I had expected to become devout but it has not come." Like Jake Barnes and others in Hemingway's books, Lieutenant Henry is more deeply concerned with matters of faith than the glib salvationists who have never prayed in true humility in the Duomo or at Santiago de Compostella. He tells the Count that his own devotion comes and goes. "I might become very devout. Anyway, I will pray for you." And the Count says: "Then too you are in love. Do not forget that is a religious feeling."

Catherine gives Lieutenant Henry the faith of love, as Renata brings the faith of love to Cantwell in *Across the River and Into the Trees*. It is Catherine he is thinking of in a passage from *A Farewell to Arms* that became a part of the belief of a generation: "If people bring so much courage to this world the world has to kill them to break them, so of course it kills them. The world breaks every one and afterward many are strong at the broken places. But those that will not break it kills. It kills the very good and the very gentle and the very brave impartially. If you are none of these you can be sure it will kill you too but there will be no special hurry."

When Hemingway was writing it, he said, "the fact the book was a tragic one did not make me unhappy since I believed that life was a tragedy and knew it could only have one end. But finding you were able to make something up; to create truly enough so that it made you happy to read it; and to do this every day you worked was something that gave a greater pleasure than any I had ever known. Beside it nothing else mattered."

The tragic sense of life is always present in the minds of thinking men. It is a part of existence to Harry Morgan in *To Have and Have Not,* a novel that answered stingingly those who had said Hemingway was not enough concerned with the state of his own country. It is in "The Short Happy Life of Francis Macomber" and "The Snows of Kilimanjaro" and "A Clean, Well-Lighted Place" and "Old Man at the Bridge" and "The Capital of the World," the story of the boy who "died, as the Spanish phrase has it, full of illusions. He had not had time in his life to lose any of them, nor even, at the end, to complete an act of contrition."

Yet even in the face of death the pleasures of life are remembered. El Sordo, dying on the hill in *For Whom the Bell Tolls,* hates the idea of death but has no fear of it: "But living was a field of grain blowing in the wind on the side of a hill. Living was a hawk in the sky. Living was an earthen jar of water in the dust of the threshing with the grain flailed out and the chaff blowing. Living was a horse between your legs and a carbine under one leg and a hill and a valley and a stream with trees along it and the far side of the valley and the hills beyond."

There are two inscriptions on the flyleaf of *The Sun Also Rises.* One, naming the lost generation, ascribed to Gertrude Stein, was mindlessly taken up by many strange people who somehow seemed to think it forgave them their trespasses forever. The other, the longer one, is taken from the Book of Ecclesiastes, the words of the Preacher, the Son of David, King of Jerusalem, who gave his heart "to seek and search out by wisdom concerning all things that are done under heaven," and it may well have led a few readers back to read Ecclesiastes on vanity and responsibilities. A part of the iceberg-depth of the novel that on the surface concerns Lady Brett Ashley, who at 34 is a little old for her generation, is to be found in her despairing efforts to share Barnes' faith. She wants to go to church when he does. Once he says, "I'm pretty religious," and she asks him not to start proselyting, and at the end Jake reminds her that "Some people have God. Quite a lot." These are not points that were emphasized when the book was published in the Nineteen Twenties, though they may be a part of the reason why the book is still read, just as Jake prays for the bullfighters in the cathedral and the bullfighters pray before they go into the ring.

The dialogues give the story its incomparable vitality. A thousand writers have tried to imitate the conversations between Jake and Bill Gorton, Brett, Mike (who upon being offered a chance to go into the bullring grandly said: "It wouldn't be fair to my creditors"), and Robert, in a thousand books.

At one place Hemingway now seems to have an uncanny air of having parodied ahead of time what vicarious moralists would say for years about his work. "You know what's the trouble with you?" the slightly sauced Gorton happily asks that reasonably diligent correspondent, Jake. "You're an expatriate. One of the worst type. Haven't you heard that? Nobody that ever left their own country ever wrote anything worth printing. . . . You've lost touch with the soil. You get precious. Fake European standards have ruined you. You drink yourself to death. You become obsessed by sex. You spend all your time talking, not working. You are an expatriate, see? You hang around cafés." "It sounds like a swell life," Jake suggests. "When do I work?"

A few decades later, the uproars over prolonged residence abroad that once made livid the little reviews and large ones had grown hazy. Several million Americans had since then served their years of expatriation in South Pacific former-paradises and the European Theater of Operations, U.S. Army. The effect on the styles of those who wrote was the least of their concerns, but they were often in very close touch with the soil.

The Torrents of Spring, which mentions expatriation, Mencken, rustic fertility rites and other institutions, is a satire of many devices. It has a plot of awesome, Benchleyan complexity. The author obviously can't quite follow it, but others may try. At one time I thought it might be meant as an antidote to Franz Kafka's fatal allegories. Many savants have noticed that it holds in no reverence Sherwood Anderson's dairy tales; some have charged that Hemingway was trifling with Gertrude Stein's massive affections. The bedeviled existence of Scripps O'Neil is shrewdly paralleled by the bewildering fate of Yogi Johnson. Academicians who conduct scholarly safaris through Hemingway's subconscious will find a challenge here. In one place we are told that O'Neil's father was a great composer, his mother an Italian lady from Northern Italy. In another place we learn that his father was a Civil War general and that Sherman himself put the match to his mansion. Now here is the question for psychoanalytical exegetes to ponder: *What part of Northern Italy did O'Neil's mother come from?* For if it can be proved that she came from one region she may be significantly related to one aspect of the Hemingway canon; if she came from another, she may even be the great-aunt of the post-war Milanese rich in *Across the River and Into the Trees.* Who knows? Who cares?

The chair of Hemingway studies will have many far more irrelevant matters brought before it in the years ahead, and some that only seem irrelevant to those they do not interest. Somewhere, right now, I hope, a student inspired by the wonderful references to Mr. DiMaggio in *The Old Man and the Sea,* is tracing other ballplayers in other stories, such as Frankie Fritsch in *The Sun Also Rises* and Heinie Zimmerman in "The Three-Day Blow." There is an interesting study to be made of the amazingly wide range of painters mentioned throughout Hemingway's works, and I have entertained the idea that Colonel Cantwell and the Countess Renata might be considered as an allegory of Goya and the Duchess of Alba, only slightly deterred by Bernard Berenson, speaking of another book in the chronicle of chivalry.

"Hemingway's *The Old Man and the Sea,*" Berenson said, "is an idyll of the sea as sea, as un-Byronic and un-Melvillian as Homer himself, and communicated in a prose as calm and compelling as Homer's verse. No real artist symbolizes or allegorizes—and Hemingway is a real artist—but every real work of art exhales symbols and allegories."

No part of Hemingway's work, in Donne's words that stand at the beginning of *For Whom the Bell Tolls,* is only an island, entire in itself; every part is a piece of a continent, a part of a main, created in a new prose for a new world.

Alone among so many of his earliest and best contemporaries, Hemingway has never needed a revival.

This letter to Jack Hirschman was published in The Mark Twain Journal, 9 *(Summer 1962), p. 10.*

Letter to a Young Writer
Ernest Hemingway

At the peak of his career, Ernest Hemingway took time to read a story sent to him by an aspiring young writer, and to indite the youth a warm personal letter. In 1953 the young and unpublished writer sent the story to Hemingway, asking for his advice about it.

Within ten days a reply came back from Hemingway at his estate in Cuba.

"Thank you for the letter," it read, "and for letting me read the story.

"I can't help you, kid. You write better than I did when I was nineteen. But the hell of it is you write like me. That is no sin. But you won't get anywhere with it.

"When I was your age I guess I wrote like Kipling. I thought he was the best short story writer that ever lived and I still know some of the short stories are the best, but later on I knew I had to try to break

the language down and start new. When you do that it gets to be personal and it sounds personal. That is the hell of it.

"Why don't you start again at the beginning and read Kipling-i.e. 'The End of the Passage', 'The Strange Ride of Maraby Jukes', 'The Mark of the Beast' for three De Maupassant's 'Boule De Souif' and 'Le Maison Tellier' Stevie Crane's 'The Open Boat' and 'The Blue Hotel'; Ambrose Bierce's 'An Occurrence at Owl Creek Bridge;' Flaubert's 'Un Coeur Simple,' and read 'Madame Bovary'.

"That will hold you for awhile. If you've read them, then reread them. Read a story by Thomas Mann called 'Disorder and Early Sorrow'. Read 'Buddenbrooks.' Skip all late Mann.

"Then see the things you write about not through my eyes and my ears but through your own with your language conditioned not by me but by the above characters all of whom wrote well. But write it your own way.

"You don't have to hate me or say Hemingstein [one of Hemingway's nicknames] is a bum or anything. Just go to work for a new firm. Wish me luck too.

"I don't know how long we will be here as I am overdue to leave for Africa. You have a lot of luck to be nineteen no matter how things go. I would as soon start it over at nineteen anytime. Instead I am going to play it as well as I know now from fifty-three on in. Nobody's but fools ever thought it was an easy ride.

"I'll be glad to see you anytime when I'm not working. But this is about as straight as I can think your problem out; this is your problem as you have stated it and according to the story.

"Your friend
Ernest Hemingway."

Newspapers around the world reported that Hemingway had been killed in a plane crash on 23 January 1954. This article was published in The New York Times *on 26 January 1954, pp. 1, 25. Hemingway's statements inspired Ogden Nash to write the novelty song "A Bunch of Bananas and a Bottle of Gin."*

Hemingway Out of the Jungle; Arm Hurt, He Says Luck Holds
By The United Press

ENTEBBE, Uganda, Jan. 25—Ernest Hemingway arrived in Entebbe today after having survived two plane crashes in the elephant country of Uganda.

Chapter Six: 1953–July 1961

Mary and Ernest Hemingway on safari, 1953 (courtesy of The Lilly Library, Indiana University)

His head was swathed in bandages and his arm was injured, but the novelist, who is 55 years old, quipped: "My luck, she is running very good."

He was carrying a bunch of bananas and a bottle of gin. With him was his wife, the former Mary Welsh. She had two cracked ribs and was limping as Mr. Hemingway helped her from an automobile that brought them here from Butiaba, 170 miles away.

Although he declined an offer to fly out of the jungle after his second crash yesterday, Mr. Hemingway said with a grin that he would fly again as soon as he had found another plane.

He waved a swollen arm, wrapped in a torn shirt, and appeared to be in high spirits as he shrugged off the crashes.

He joshed his wife, saying her snoring had attracted elephants as they camped overnight near the wreckage of the first plane that crash-landed Saturday near Murchison Falls on the upper Nile near Lake Albert.

"We held our breath about two hours while an elephant twelve paces away was silhouetted in the moonlight, listening to my wife's snores," Mr. Hemingway roared.

Mrs. Hemingway, a former war correspondent, smiled.

Mr. Hemingway was examined by a doctor at Butiaba, scene of the second plane crash. An X-ray was advised, but he apparently was not badly hurt.

The first accident occurred when a Cessna, piloted by Roy Marsh, cracked up near a 400-foot falls while making an emergency landing. Search pilots who flew over reported herds of elephants near.

The second accident occurred Sunday after the Hemingways had been taken by a tourist steamer to Butiba. There a plane, piloted by T. R. Cartwright, ground-looped into a sisal plantation and caught fire.

Mr. Hemingway said the blue and silver single-engine Cessna they had hired for the flight to Murchison Falls crashed when Mr. Marsh dived at low altitude to avoid hitting a flying flock of ibises—black and white jungle birds big enough to smash the canopy of the plane.

Landed on Elephant Track

Mr. Hemingway said that to miss the ibises the plane had to land either on a sandpit where six croco-

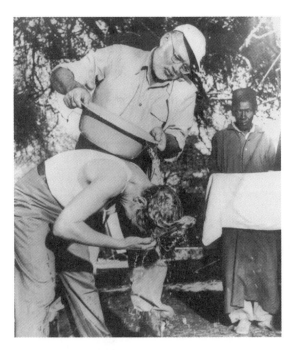

Ernest and Mary Hemingway in camp during their safari, Kenya, 1953

Hemingway and natives with a lion he killed during his 1953–1954 safari

Hemingway, in Venice, showing the burns on his hand after the second of two plane crashes in Africa

diles lay basking in the sun or on an elephant track through thick scrub.

Mr. Marsh chose the scrub and landed the plane with minor damage. They spent Saturday night around a camp fire surrounded by the elephant herd and caught a ride yesterday morning in a launch filled with tourists back to Butiaba and Lake Albert.

When the second plane ground-looped and caught fire, Mr. Hemingway said he butted open the rear door and scrambled out. His wife and the pilot also escaped, but all their luggage was destroyed.

Even when the first crash stranded them overnight in the jungle, Mr. Hemingway said he was not worried. "We had emergency goods, but were short on water," he said. "We took turns going to the river, but the elephants were very stuffy about it. There were lot of hippos and crocs wandering around the river bank."

Their trip around Africa, he said, is his wife's Christmas present.

Mr. Cartwright, who flew here from Butiaba, brought the first details of the two crashes. He said that when he asked Mr. Hemingway about his adventures the novelist merely replied that he was "very impressed" by the wealth of big game.

The Hemingways found big brush fires burning near the edge of the Upper Nile when they first landed and set backfires to save themselves and the plane, Cartwright said.

At twilight they were forced to move back from the banks of the Nile, tormented by swarms of mosquitos.

For the last few weeks he and his wife have been on a safari on which he is writing a series of articles for Look Magazine. One of his first stops on his return to Africa after twenty years was the towering peak of Kilimanjaro.

It was Kilimanjaro that signified death to one of his heroes.

Hemingway won the Nobel Prize in literature in 1954. Claiming that he was too ill to travel to Sweden to receive the award, he had his acceptance speech read by John C. Cabot, U.S. Ambassador to Sweden, at the ceremony on 10 December 1954.

Nobel Prize Acceptance Speech

Members of the Swedish Academy, Ladies and Gentlemen:

Having no facility for speech-making and no command of oratory nor any domination of rhetoric, I wish

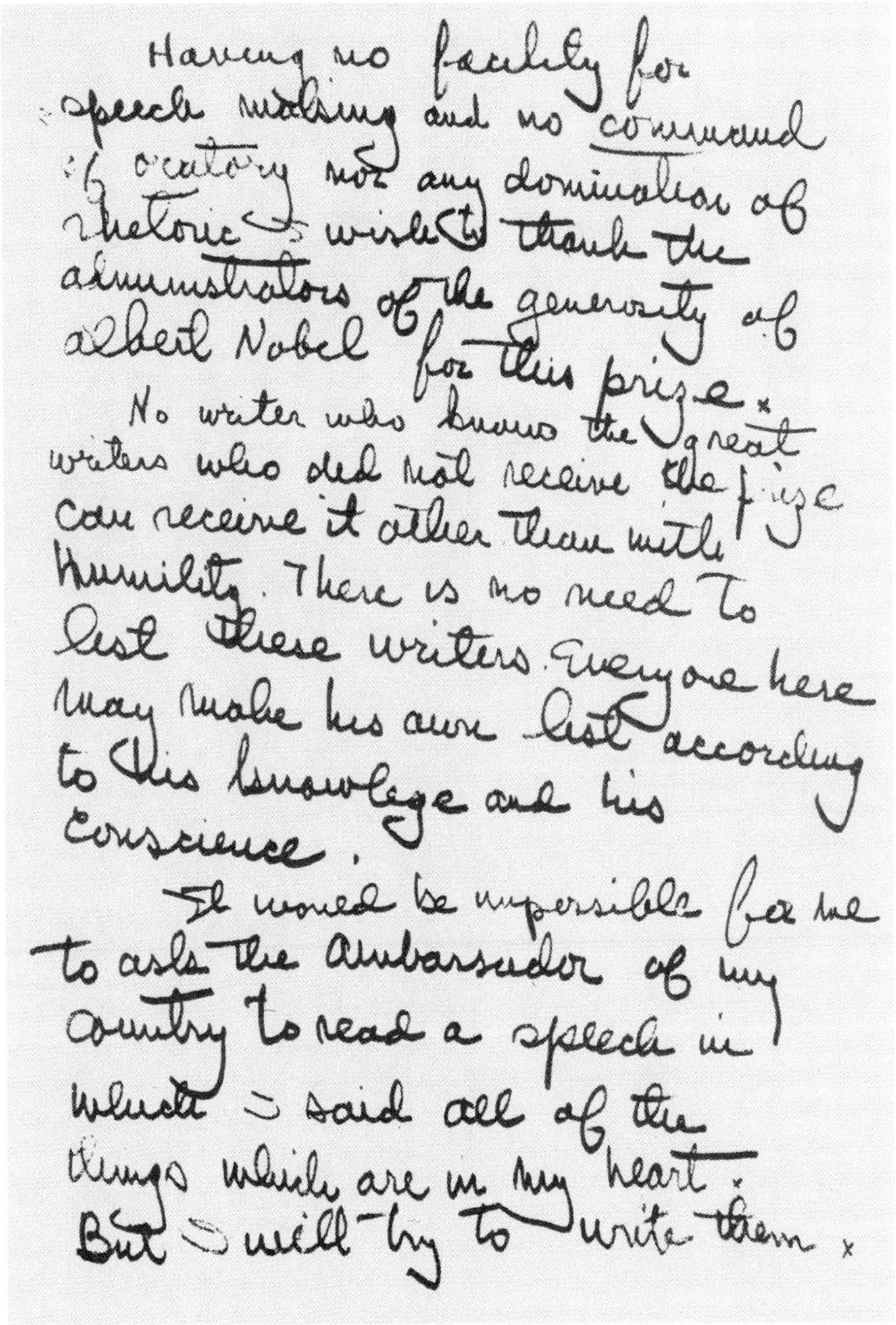

Having no facility for
speech making and no command
of oratory nor any domination of
rhetoric I wish to thank the
administrators of the generosity of
Albert Nobel for this prize.

No writer who knows the great
writers who did not receive the prize
can receive it other than with
humility. There is no need to
list these writers. Everyone here
may make his own list according
to his knowlege and his
conscience.

It would be impossible for me
to ask the Ambassador of my
country to read a speech in
which I said all of the
things which are in my heart.
But I will try to write them.

Manuscript page of Hemingway's Nobel Prize acceptance speech (Ernest Hemingway Collection, John F. Kennedy Library)

to thank the administrators of the generosity of Alfred Nobel for this prize.

No writer who knows the great writers who did not receive the prize can accept it other than with humility. There is no need to list these writers. Everyone here may make his own list according to his knowledge and his conscience.

It would be impossible for me to ask the Ambassador of my country to read a speech in which a writer said all of the things which are in his heart. Things may not be immediately discernible in what a man writes, and in this sometimes he is fortunate; but eventually they are quite clear and by these and the degree of alchemy that he possesses he will endure or be forgotten.

Writing, at its best, is a lonely life. Organizations for writers palliate the writer's loneliness but I doubt if they improve his writing. He grows in public stature as he sheds his loneliness and often his work deteriorates. For he does his work alone and if he is a good enough writer he must face eternity, or the lack of it, each day.

For a true writer each book should be a new beginning where he tries again for something that is beyond attainment. He should always try for something that has never been done or that others have tried and failed. Then sometimes, with great luck, he will succeed.

How simple the writing of literature would be if it were only necessary to write in another way what has been well written. It is because we have had such great writers in the past that a writer is driven far out past where he can go, out to where no one can help him.

I have spoken too long for a writer. A writer should write what he has to say and not speak it. Again I thank you.

George Plimpton's interview with Hemingway includes important statements about his aesthetic theories and his writing. The questions were submitted in written form, and Hemingway responded in writing. The interview was published in The Paris Review, *5 (Spring 1958), pp. 60–89.*

The Art of Fiction, XXI: Ernest Hemingway

Hemingway: You go to the races?
Interviewer: Yes, occasionally.
Hemingway: Then you read the *Racing Form* . . . there you have the true Art of Fiction.

—Conversation in a Madrid café, May, 1954

Ernest Hemingway writes in the bedroom of his home in the Havana suburb of San Francisco de Paula. He has a special workroom prepared for him in a square tower at the south-west corner of the house, but prefers to work in his bedroom, climbing to the tower-room only when "characters" drive him up there.

The bedroom is on the ground floor and connects with the main room of the house. The door between the two is kept ajar by a heavy volume listing and describing "The World's Aircraft Engines." The bedroom is large, sunny, the windows facing east and south letting in the day's light on white walls and a yellow-tinged tile floor.

The room is divided into two alcoves by a pair of chest-high bookcases that stand out into the room at right angles from opposite walls. A large and low double-bed dominates one section, over-sized slippers and loafers neatly arranged at the foot, the two bedside tables at the head piled seven-high with books. In the other alcove stands a massive flat-top desk with two chairs at either side, its surface an ordered clutter of papers and mementos. Beyond it, at the far end of the room, is an armoire with a leopard skin draped across the top. The other walls are lined with white-painted bookcases from which books overflow to the floor, and are piled on top amongst old newspapers, bullfight journals, and stacks of letters bound together by rubber bands.

It is on the top of one of these cluttered bookcases—the one against the wall by the east window and three feet or so from his bed—that Hemingway has his "work-desk"—a square foot of cramped area hemmed in by books on one side and on the other by a newspaper-covered heap of papers, manuscripts, and pamphlets. There is just enough space left on top of the bookcase for a typewriter, surmounted by a wooden reading-board, five or six pencils, and a chunk of copper ore to weight down papers when the wind blows in from the east window.

A working habit he has had from the beginning, Hemingway stands when he writes. He stands in a pair of his oversized loafers on the worn skin of a Lesser Kudu—the typewriter and the reading-board chest-high opposite him.

When Hemingway starts on a project he always begins with a pencil, using the reading-board to write on onion-skin typewriter paper. He keeps a sheaf of the blank paper on a clipboard to the left of the typewriter, extracting the paper a sheet at a time from under a metal clip which reads "These Must Be Paid." He places the paper slantwise on the reading-board, leans against the board with his left arm, steadying the paper with his hand, and fills the paper with handwriting which in the years has become larger, more boyish,

FINCA VIGIA, SAN FRANCISCO DE PAULA, CUBA
24/7/56

Dear Mr. Rider:

Thank you very much for your letter. The most readable of Faulkner is Sanctuary and Pylon. I think he is a no good. Son of a bitch myself. But some of the Southern stuff is good and some of the negro stuff is very good. also a short story called The Bear is worth reading. His last book A Fable isn't pure shit. It is impure diluted shit and there isn't a shit tester in the at Ichang where they ship the night soil from chungking to but would found it.

We used to smoke. sail fish too in the smokehouse here on the Finca and before that at K.W. It is very good.

Good luck to you and don't bend any more airplanes.

Best always,

Ernest Hemingway

Hemingway's comments about William Faulkner (Hemingway at Auction)

with a paucity of punctuation, very few capitals, and often the period marked with an x. The page completed, he clips it face-down on another clipboard which he places off to the right of the typewriter.

Hemingway shifts to the typewriter, lifting off the reading-board, only when the writing is going fast and well, or when the writing is, for him at least, simple: dialogue, for instance.

He keeps track of his daily progress—"so as not to kid myself"—on a large chart made out of the side of a cardboard packing case and set up against the wall under the nose of a mounted gazelle head. The numbers on the chart showing the daily output of words differ from 450, 575, 462, 1250, to 512, the higher figures on days Hemingway puts in extra work so he won't feel guilty spending the following day fishing on the Gulf Stream.

A man of habit, Hemingway does not use the perfectly suitable desk in the other alcove. Though it allows more space for writing, it too has its miscellany: stacks of letters, a stuffed toy lion of the type sold in Broadway nighteries, a small burlap bag full of carnivore teeth, shotgun shells, a shoe-horn, wood carvings of lion, rhino, two zebras, and a wart-hog—these last set in a neat row across the surface of the desk—and, of course, books. You remember books of the room, piled on the desk, bedside tables, jamming the shelves in indiscriminate order—novels, histories, collections of poetry, drama, essays. A look at their titles shows their variety. On the shelf opposite Hemingway's knees as he stands up to his "work-desk" are Virginia Woolf's *The Common Reader*, Ben Ames Williams' *House Divided*, *The Partisan Reader*, Charles A. Beard's *The Republic*, Tarle's *Napoleon's Invasion of Russia*, *How Young You Look* by one Peggy Wood, Alden Brook's *Shakespeare and the Dyer's Hand*, Baldwin's *African Hunting*, T. S. Eliot's *Collected Poems*, and two books on General Custer's fall at the battle of the Little Big Horn.

The room, however, for all the disorder sensed at first sight, indicates on inspection an owner who is basically neat but cannot bear to throw anything away—especially if sentimental value is attached. One bookcase top has an odd assortment of mementos: a giraffe made of wood beads, a little cast-iron turtle, tiny models of a locomotive, two jeeps and a Venetian gondola, a toy bear with a key in its back, a monkey carrying a pair of cymbals, a miniature guitar, and a little tin model of a U.S. Navy biplane (one wheel missing) resting awry on a circular straw placemat—the quality of the collection that of the odds-and-ends which turn up in a shoebox at the back of a small boy's closet. It is evident, though, that these tokens have their value, just as three buffalo horns Hemingway keeps in his bedroom have a value dependent not on size but because during

the acquiring of them things went badly in the bush which ultimately turned out well. "It cheers me up to look at them," Hemingway says.

Hemingway may admit superstitions of this sort, but he prefers not to talk about them, feeling that whatever value they may have can be talked away. He has much the same attitude about writing. Many times during the making of this interview he stressed that the craft of writing should not be tampered with by an excess of scrutiny—"that though there is one part of writing that is solid and you do it no harm by talking about it, the other is fragile, and if you talk about it, the structure cracks and you have nothing."

As a result, though a wonderful raconteur, a man of rich humor, and possessed of an amazing fund of knowledge on subjects which interest him, Hemingway finds it difficult to talk about writing—not because he has few ideas on the subject, but rather that he feels so strongly that such ideas should remain unexpressed, that to be asked questions on them "spooks" him (to use one of his favorite expressions) to the point where he is almost inarticulate. Many of the replies in this interview he preferred to work out on his reading-board. The occasional waspish tone of the answers is also part of this strong feeling that writing is a private, lonely occupation with no need for witnesses until the final work is done.

This dedication to his art may suggest a personality at odds with the rambunctious, carefree, world-wheeling Hemingway-at-play of popular conception. The point is, though, that Hemingway, while obviously enjoying life, brings an equivalent dedication to everything he does—an outlook that is essentially serious, with a horror of the inaccurate, the fraudulent, the deceptive, the half-baked.

Nowhere is the dedication he gives his art more evident than in the yellowtiled bedroom—where early in the morning Hemingway gets up to stand in absolute concentration in front of his reading-board, moving only to shift weight from one foot to another, perspiring heavily when the work is going well, excited as a boy, fretful, miserable when the artistic touch momentarily vanishes—slave of a self-imposed discipline which lasts until about noon when he takes a knotted walking stick and leaves the house for the swimming pool where he takes his daily half-mile swim.

Interviewer: Are these hours during the actual process of writing pleasurable?

Hemingway: Very.

Interviewer: Could you say something of this process? When do you work? Do you keep to a strict schedule?

Hemingway: When I am working on a book or a story I write every morning as soon after first light as possible. There is no one to disturb you and it is cool or cold and you come to your work and warm as you write. You read what you have written and, as you always stop when you know what is going to happen next, you go on from there. You write until you come to a place where you still have your juice and know what will happen next and you stop and try to live through until the next day when you hit it again. You have started at six in the morning, say, and may go on until noon or be through before that. When you stop you are as empty, and at the same time never empty but filling, as when you have made love to someone you love. Nothing can hurt you, nothing can happen, nothing means anything until the next day when you do it again. It is the wait until the next day that is hard to get through.

Interviewer: Can you dismiss from your mind whatever project you're on when you're away from the typewriter?

Hemingway: Of course. But it takes discipline to do it and this discipline is acquired. It has to be.

Interviewer: Do you do any re-writing as you read up to the place you left off the day before? Or does that come later, when the whole is finished?

Hemingway: I always re-write each day up to the point where I stopped. When it is all finished, naturally you go over it. You get another chance to correct and re-write when someone else types it, and you see it clean in type. The last chance is in the proofs. You're grateful for these different chances.

Interviewer: How much re-writing do you do?

Hemingway: It depends. I re-wrote the ending to *Farewell to Arms,* the last page of it, thirty-nine times before I was satisfied.

Interviewer: Was there some technical problem there? What was it that had stumped you?

Hemingway: Getting the words right.

Interviewer: Is it the re-reading that gets the "juice" up?

Hemingway: Re-reading places you at the point where it *has* to go on, knowing it is as good as you can get it up to there. There is always juice somewhere.

Interviewer: But are there times when the inspiration isn't there at all?

Hemingway: Naturally. But if you stopped when you knew what would happen next, you can go on. As long as you can start, you are all right. The juice will come.

Interviewer: Thornton Wilder speaks of mnemonic devices that get the writer going on his day's work. He says you once told him you sharpened twenty pencils.

Hemingway: I don't think I ever owned twenty pencils at one time. Wearing down seven No. 2 pencils is a good day's work.

Interviewer: Where are some of the places you have found most advantageous to work? The Ambos Mundos hotel must have been one, judging from the number of books you did there. Or do surroundings have little effect on the work?

Hemingway: The Ambos Mundos in Havana was a very good place to work in. This Finca is a splendid place, or was. But I have worked well everywhere. I mean I have been able to work as well as I can under varied circumstances. The telephone and visitors are the work destroyers.

Interviewer: Is emotional stability necessary to write well. You told me once that you could only write well when you were in love. Could you expound on that a bit more?

Hemingway: What a question. But full marks for trying. You can write any time people will leave you alone and not interrupt you. Or rather you can if you will be ruthless enough about it. But the best writing is certainly when you are in love. If it is all the same to you I would rather not expound on that.

Interviewer: How about financial security? Can that be a detriment to good writing?

Hemingway at work at La Finca Vigía, 1950s

Hemingway: If it came early enough and you loved life as much as you loved your work it would take much character to resist the temptations. Once writing has become your major vice and greatest pleasure only death can stop it. Financial security then is a great help as it keeps you from worrying. Worry destroys the ability to write. Ill health is bad in the ratio that it produces worry which attacks your subconscious and destroys your reserves.

Interviewer: Can you recall an exact moment when you decided to become a writer?

Hemingway: No, I always wanted to be a writer.

Interviewer: Philip Young in his book on you suggests that the traumatic shock of your severe 1918 mortar wound had a great influence on you as

a writer. I remember in Madrid you talked briefly about his thesis, finding little in it, and going on to say that you thought the artist's equipment was not an acquired characteristic, but inherited, in the Mendelian sense.

Hemingway: Evidently in Madrid that year my mind could not be called very sound. The only thing to recommend it would be that I spoke only briefly about Mr. Young's book and his trauma theory of literature. Perhaps the two concussions and a skull fracture of that year had made me irresponsible in my statements. I do remember telling you that I believed imagination could be the result of inherited racial experience. It sounds all right in good jolly post-concussion talk, but I think that is more or less where it belongs. So until the next liberation trauma, let's leave it there. Do you agree? But thanks for leaving out the names of any relatives I might have implicated. The fun of talk is to explore, but much of it and all that is irresponsible should not be written. Once written you have to stand by it. You may have said it to see whether you believed it or not. On the question you raised, the effects of wounds vary greatly. Simple wounds which do not break bone are of little account. They sometimes give confidence. Wounds which do extensive bone and nerve damage are not good for writers, nor anybody else.

Interviewer: What would you consider the best intellectual training for the would-be writer?

Hemingway: Let's say that he should go out and hang himself because he finds that writing well is impossibly difficult. Then he should be cut down without mercy and forced by his own self to write as well as he can for the rest of his life. At least he will have the story of the hanging to commence with.

Interviewer: How about people who've gone into the academic career? Do you think the large number of writers who hold teaching positions have compromised their literary careers?

Hemingway: It depends on what you call compromise. Is the usage that of a woman who has been compromised? Or is it the compromise of the statesman? Or the compromise made with your grocer or your tailor that you will pay a little more but will pay it later? A writer who can both write and teach should be able to do both. Many competent writers have proved it could be done. I could not do it, I know, and I admire those who have been able to. I would think though that the academic life could put a period to outside experience which might possibly limit the growth of knowledge of the world. Knowledge, however, demands more responsibility of a writer and makes writing more difficult. Trying to write something of permanent value is a full-time job even though only a few hours a day are spent on the actual writing. A writer can be compared to a well. There are many kinds of wells as there are writers. The important thing is to have good water in the well and it is better to take a regular amount out than to pump the well dry and wait for it to re-fill. I see I am getting away from the question, but the question was not very interesting.

Interviewer: Would you suggest newspaper work for the young writer? How helpful was the training you had with the *Kansas City Star*?

Hemingway: On the *Star* you were forced to learn to write a simple, declarative sentence. This is useful to anyone. Newspaper work will not harm a young writer and could help him if he gets out of it in time. This is one of the dustiest cliches there is and I apologize for it. But when you ask someone old tired questions you are apt to receive old tired answers.

Interviewer: You once wrote in the *Transatlantic Review* that the only reason for writing journalism was to be well-paid. You said: "And when you destroy the valuable things you have by writing about them, you want to get big money for it." Do you think of writing as a type of self-destruction?

Hemingway: I do not remember ever writing that. But it sounds silly and violent enough for me to have said it to avoid having to bite on the nail and make a sensible statement. I certainly do not think of writing as a type of self-destruction though journalism, after a point has been reached, can be a daily self-destruction for a serious creative writer.

Interviewer: Do you think the intellectual stimulus of the company of other writers is of any value to an author?

Hemingway: Certainly.

Interviewer: In the Paris of the twenties did you have any sense of "group feeling" with other writers and artists?

Hemingway: No. There was no group feeling. We had respect for each other. I respected a lot of painters, some of my own age, others older—Gris, Picasso, Braque, Monet, who was still alive then—and a few writers: Joyce, Ezra, the good of Stein . . .

Interviewer: When you are writing, do you ever find yourself influenced by what you're reading at the time?

Hemingway: Not since Joyce was writing *Ulysses*. His was not a direct influence. But in those days when words we knew were barred to us, and we had to fight for a single word, the influence of his work was what changed everything, and made it possible for us to break away from the restrictions.

Interviewer: Could you learn anything about writing from the writers? You were telling me yesterday that Joyce, for example, couldn't bear to talk about writing.

Hemingway: In company with people of your own trade you ordinarily speak of other writers' books. The better the writers the less they will speak about what they have written themselves. Joyce was a very great writer and he would only explain what he was doing to jerks. Others writers that he respected were supposed to be able to know what he was doing by reading it.

Interviewer: You seem to have avoided the company of writers in late years. Why?

Hemingway: That is more complicated. The further you go in writing the more alone you are. Most of your best and oldest friends die. Others move away. You do not see them except rarely, but you write and have much the same contact with them as though you were together at the cafe in the old days. You exchange comic, sometimes cheerfully obscene and irresponsible letters, and it is almost as good as talking. But you are more alone because that is how you must work and the time to work is

Hemingway writing letters in Havana, 1957

shorter all the time and if you waste it you feel you have committed a sin for which there is no forgiveness.

Interviewer: What about the influence of these people—your contemporaries—on your work? What was Gertrude Stein's contribution, if any? Or Ezra Pound's? Or Max Perkins'?

Hemingway: I'm sorry but I am no good at these post-mortems. There are coroners literary and non-literary provided to deal with such matters. Miss Stein wrote at some length and with considerable inaccuracy about her influence on my work. It was necessary for her to do this after she had learned to write dialogue from a book called *The Sun Also Rises*. I was very fond of her and thought it was splendid she had learned to write conversation. It was no new thing to me to learn from everyone I could, living or dead, and I had no idea it would affect Gertrude so violently. She already wrote very well in other ways. Ezra was extremely intelligent on the subjects he really knew. Doesn't this sort of talk bore you? This backyard literary gossip while washing out the dirty clothes of thirty-five years ago is disgusting to me. It would be different if one had tried to tell the whole truth. That would have some value. Here it is simpler and better to thank Gertrude for everything I learned from her about the abstract relationship of words, say how fond I was of her, re-affirm my loyalty to Ezra as a great poet and a loyal friend, and say that I cared so much for Max Perkins that I have never been able to accept that he is dead. He never asked me to change anything I wrote except to remove certain words which were not then publishable. Blanks were left, and anyone who knew the words would know what they were. For me he was not an editor. He was a wise friend and a wonderful companion. I liked the way he wore his hat and the strange way his lips moved.

Interviewer: Who would you say are your literary forebears— those you have learned the most from?

Hemingway: Mark Twain, Flaubert, Stendhal, Bach, Turgeniev, Tolstoi, Dostoevsky, Chekhov, Andrew Marvell, John Donne, Maupassant, the good Kipling, Thoreau, Captain Marryat, Shakespeare, Mozart, Quevedo, Dante, Virgil, Tintoretto, Hieronymus Bosch, Breughel, Patinier, Goya, Giotto, Cézanne, Van Gogh, Gaughuin, San Juan de la Cruz, Gongora—it would take a day to remember everyone. Then it would sound as though I were claiming an erudition I did not possess instead of trying to remember all the people who have had an influence on my life and work. This isn't an old dull question. It is a very good but a solemn question and requires an examination of conscience. I put in painters, or started to, because I learn as much from painters about how to write as from writers. You ask how this is done? It would take another day of explaining. I should think what one learns from composers and from the study of harmony and counterpoint would be obvious.

Interviewer: Did you ever play a musical instrument?

Hemingway: I used to play cello. My mother kept me out of school a whole year to study music and counterpoint. She thought I had ability, but I was absolutely without talent. We played chamber music—someone came in to play the violin; my sister played the viola, and mother the piano. That cello—I played it worse than anyone on earth. Of course, that year I was out doing other things too.

Interviewer: Do you re-read the authors of your list. Twain, for instance?

Hemingway: You have to wait two or three years with Twain. You remember too well. I read some Shakespeare every year, *Lear* always. Cheers you up if you read that.

Interviewer: Reading, then, is a constant occupation and pleasure.

Hemingway: I'm always reading books—as many as there are. I ration myself on them so that I'll always be in supply.

Interviewer: Do you ever read manuscripts?

Hemingway: You can get into trouble doing that unless you know the author personally. Some years ago I was sued for plagiarism by a man who claimed that I'd lifted *For Whom the Bell Tolls* from an unpublished screen scenario he'd written. He'd read this scenario at some Hollywood party. I was there, he said, at least there was a fellow called "Ernie" there listening to the reading, and that was enough for him to sue for a million dollars. At the same time he sued the producers of the motion-pictures *North-West Mounted Police* and the *Cisco Kid,* claiming that these, as well, had been stolen from that same unpublished scenario. We went to court

and, of course, won the case. The man turned out to be insolvent.

Interviewer: Well, could we go back to that list and take one of the painters—Hieronymus Bosch, for instance? The nightmare symbolic quality of his work seems so far removed from your own.

Hemingway: I have the nightmares and know about the ones other people have. But you do not have to write them down. Anything you can omit that you know you still have in the writing and its quality will show. When a writer omits things he does not know, they show like holes in his writing.

Interviewer: Does that mean that a close knowledge of the works of the people on your list helps fill the "well" you were speaking of a while back. Or were they consciously a help in developing the techniques of writing?

Hemingway: They were a part of learning to see, to hear, to think, to feel and not-feel, and to write. The well is where your "juice" is. Nobody knows what it is made of, least of all yourself. What you know is if you have it, or you have to wait for it to come back.

Interviewer: Would you admit to there being symbolism in your novels?

Hemingway: I suppose there are symbols since critics keep finding them. If you do not mind I dislike talking about them and being questioned about them. It is hard enough to write books and stories without being asked to explain them as well. Also it deprives the explainers of work. If five or six or more good explainers can keep going why should I interfere with them? Read anything I write for the pleasure of reading it. Whatever else you find will be the measure of what you brought to the reading.

Interviewer: Continuing with just one question on this line: One of the advisory staff editors wonders about a parallel he feels he's found in *The Sun Also Rises* between the dramatis personae of the bull ring and the characters of the novel itself. He points out that the first sentence of the book tells us Robert Cohn is a boxer; later, during the desencajonada, the bull is described as using his horns like a boxer, hooking and jabbing. And just as the bull is attracted and pacified by the presence of a steer, Robert Cohn defers to Jake who is emasculated precisely as is a steer. He sees Mike as the picador, baiting Cohn repeatedly. The editor's thesis goes on, but he wondered if it was your conscious intention to inform the novel with the tragic structure of the bullfight ritual.

Hemingway: It sounds as though the advisory staff editor was a little bit screwy. Who ever said Jake was "emasculated precisely as a steer?" Actually he had been wounded in quite a different way and his testicles were intact and not damaged. Thus he was capable of all normal feelings as a *man* but incapable of consummating them. The important distinction is that his wound was physical and not psychological and that he was not emasculated.

Interviewer: These questions which inquire into craftsmanship really are an annoyance.

Hemingway: A sensible question is neither a delight nor an annoyance. I still believe though that it is very bad for a writer to talk about how he writes. He writes to be read by the eye and no explanations nor dissertations should be necessary. You can be sure that there is much more than will be read at any first reading and having made this it is not the writer's province to explain it or run guided tours through the more difficult country of his work.

Interviewer: In connection with this, I remember you have also warned that it is dangerous for a writer to talk about a work-in-progress, that he can "talk it out" so to speak. Why should this be so? I only ask because there are so many writers—Twain, Wilde, Thurber, Steffens come to mind—who would seem to have polished their material by testing it on listeners.

Hemingway: I cannot believe Twain ever "tested out" *Huckleberry Finn* on listeners. If he did they probably had him cut out good things and put in the bad parts. Wilde was said by people who knew him to have been a better talker than a writer. Steffens talked better than he wrote. Both his writing and his talking were sometimes hard to believe, and I heard many stories change as he grew older. If Thurber can talk as well as he writes he must be one of the greatest and least boring talkers. The man I know who talks best about his own trade and has the pleasantest and most wicked tongue is Juan Belmonte, the matador.

Interviewer: Could you say how much thought-out effort went into the evolvement of your distinctive style?

Hemingway: That is a long-term tiring question and if you spent a couple of days answering it

Hemingway in his library at La Finca Vigía. He read widely and owned a large collection of books.

you would be so self-conscious that you could not write. I might say that what amateurs call a style is usually only the unavoidable awkwardness in first trying to make something that has not heretofore been made. Almost no new classics resemble other previous classics. At first people can only see the awkwardness. Then they are not so perceptible. When they show so very awkwardly people think these awkwardnesses are the style and many copy them. This is regrettable.

Interviewer: You once wrote me that the simple circumstances under which various pieces of fiction were written could be instructive. Could you apply this to "The Killers"—you said that you had written it, "Ten Indians" and "Today is Friday" in one day—and perhaps to your first novel *The Sun Also Rises*?

Hemingway: Let's see. *The Sun Also Rises* I started in Valencia on my birthday, July 21st. Hadley, my wife, and I had gone to Valencia early to get good tickets for the Feria there which started the 24th of July. Everybody my age had written a novel and I was still having a difficult time writing a paragraph. So I started the book on my birthday, wrote all through the Feria, in bed in the morning, went on to Madrid and wrote there. There was no Feria there, so we had a room with a table and I wrote in great luxury on the table and around the corner from the hotel in a beer place in the Pasaje Alvarez where it was cool. It finally got too hot to write and we went to Hendaye. There was a small cheap hotel there on the big long lovely beach and I worked very well there and then went up to Paris and finished the first draft in the apartment over the sawmill at 113 rue Notre-Dame-des-Champs six weeks from the day I started it. I showed the first draft to Nathan Asch, the novelist, who then had quite a strong accent and he said "Hem, vaht do you mean saying you wrote a novel? A novel huh. Hem you are riding a travhel büch." I was not too discouraged by Nathan and rewrote the book, keeping in the travel (that was the part about the fishing trip and Pamplona) at Schruns in the Vorarlberg at the Hotel Taube.

The stories you mention I wrote in one day in Madrid on May 16 when it snowed out the San Isidro bullfights. First I wrote "The Killers" which I'd tried to write before and failed. Then after lunch I got in bed to keep warm and wrote "Today is Friday." I had so much juice I thought maybe I was going crazy and I had about six other stories to write. So I got dressed and walked to Fornos, the old bull fighter's cafe, and drank coffee and then came back and wrote *Ten Indians*. This made me very sad and I drank some brandy and went to sleep. I'd forgotten to eat and one of the waiters brought me up some Bacalao and a small steak and fried potatoes and a bottle of Valdepeñas.

The woman who ran the Pension was always worried that I did not eat enough and she had sent the waiter. I remember sitting up in bed and eating, and drinking the Valdepeñas. The waiter said he would bring up another bottle. He said the Señora wanted to know if I was going to write all night. I said no, I thought I would lay off for a while. Why don't you try to write just one more, the waiter asked. I'm only supposed to write one, I said. Nonsense, he said. You could write six. I'll try tomorrow, I said. Try it tonight, he said. What do you think the old woman sent the food up for?

I'm tired, I told him. Nonsense, he said (the word was not nonsense). You tired after three miserable little stories. Translate me one.

Leave me alone, I said. How am I going to write it if you don't leave me alone. So I sat up in bed and drank the Valdepeñas and thought what a hell of a writer I was if the first story was as good as I'd hoped.

Interviewer: How complete in your own mind is the conception of a short story? Does the theme, or the plot, or a character change as you go along?

Hemingway: Sometimes you know the story. Sometimes you make it up as you go along and have no idea how it will come out. Everything changes as it moves. That is what makes the movement which makes the story. Sometimes the movement is so slow it does not seem to be moving. But there is always change and always movement.

Interviewer: Is it the same with the novel, or do you work out the whole plan before you start and adhere to it rigorously?

Hemingway: *For Whom The Bell Tolls* was a problem which I carried on each day. I knew what was going to happen in principle. But I invented what happened each day as I wrote.

Interviewer: Were the *Green Hills of Africa*, *To Have and Have Not*, and *Across the River and Into the Trees* all started as short stories and developed into novels? If so, are the two forms so similar that the writer can pass from one to the other without completely revamping his approach?

Hemingway: No, that is not true. The *Green Hills of Africa* is not a novel but was written in an attempt to write an absolutely true book to see whether the shape of a country and the pattern of a month's action could, if truly presented, compete with a work of the imagination. After I had written it I wrote two short stories, "The Snows of Kilimanjaro" and "The Short Happy Life of Francis Macomber." These were stories which I invented from the knowledge and experience acquired on the same long hunting trip one month of which I had tried to write a truthful account of in the *Green Hills*. *To Have and Have Not* and *Across the River and Into the Trees* were both started as short stories.

Interviewer: Do you find it easy to shift from one literary project to another or do you continue through to finish what you start?

Hemingway: The fact that I am interrupting serious work to answer these questions proves that I am so stupid that I should be penalized severely. I will be. Don't worry.

Interviewer: Do you think of yourself in competition with other writers?

Hemingway: Never. I used to try to write better than certain dead writers of whose value I was certain. For a long time now I have tried simply to write the best I can. Sometimes I have good luck and write better than I can.

Interviewer: Do you think a writer's power diminishes as he grows older? In the *Green Hills of Africa* you mention that American writers at a certain age change into Old Mother Hubbards.

Hemingway: I don't know about that. People who know what they are doing should last as long as their heads last. In that book you mention, if you look it up, you'll see I was sounding off about American literature with a humorless Austrian character who was forcing me to talk when I wanted to do something else. I wrote an accurate account of the conversation. Not to make deathless pronouncements. A fair percent of the pronouncements are good enough.

Interviewer: We've not discussed character. Are the characters of your work taken without exception from real life?

Hemingway: Of course they are not. *Some* come from real life. Mostly you invent people from a knowledge and understanding and experience of people.

Interviewer: Could you say something about the process of turning a real-life character into a fictional one?

Hemingway: If I explained how that is sometimes done, it would be a handbook for libel lawyers.

Interviewer: Do you make a distinction—as E. M. Forster does—between "flat" and "round" characters?

Hemingway: If you describe someone, it is flat, as a photograph is, and from my standpoint a failure. If you make him up from what you know, there should be all the dimensions.

Interviewer: Which of your characters do you look back on with particular affection?

Hemingway: That would make too long a list.

Interviewer: Then you enjoy reading over your own books—without feeling there are changes you would like to make?

Hemingway: I read them sometimes to cheer me up when it is hard to write and then I remember that it was always difficult and how nearly impossible it was sometimes.

Interviewer: How do you name your characters?

Hemingway: The best I can.

Interviewer: Do the titles come to you while you're in the process of doing the story?

Hemingway: No. I make a list of titles *after* I've finished the story or the book—sometimes as many as 100. Then I start eliminating them, sometimes all of them.

Interviewer: And you do this even with a story whose title is supplied from the text—"Hills Like White Elephants," for example?

Hemingway: Yes. The title comes afterwards. I met a girl in Prunier where I'd gone to eat oysters before lunch. I knew she'd had an abortion. I went over and we talked, not about that, but on the way home I thought of the story, skipped lunch, and spent that afternoon writing it.

Interviewer: So when you're not writing, you remain constantly the observer, looking for something which can be of use.

Hemingway: Surely. If a writer stops observing he is finished. But he does not have to observe consciously nor think how it will be useful. Perhaps that would be true at the beginning. But later everything he sees goes into the great reserve of things he knew or has seen. If it is any use to know it, I always try to write on the principle of the iceberg. There is seven-eights of it underwater for every part that shows. Anything you know you can eliminate and it only strengthens your iceberg. It is the part that doesn't show. If a writer omits something because he does not know it then there is a hole in the story.

The Old Man and the Sea could have been over a thousand pages long and had every character in the village in it and all the processes of how they made their living, were born, educated, bore children, etc. That is done excellently and well by other writers. In writing you are limited by what has already been done satisfac-

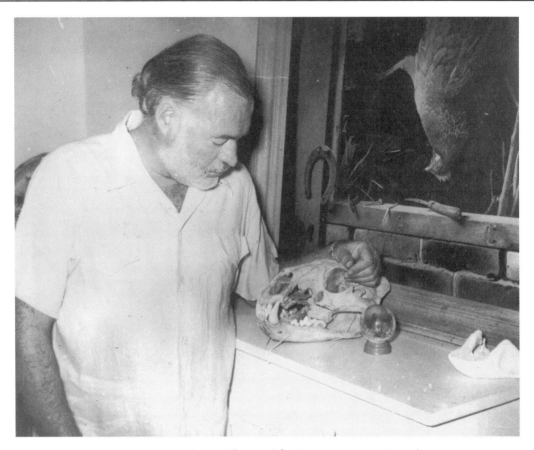

Hemingway with a lion's skull (courtesy of The Lilly Library, Indiana University)

torily. So I have tried to learn to do something else. First I have tried to eliminate everything unnecessary to conveying experience to the reader so that after he or she has read something it will become a part of his or her experience and seem actually to have happened. This is very hard to do and I've worked at it very hard.

Anyway, to skip how it is done, I had unbelievable luck this time and could convey the experience completely and have it be one that no one had ever conveyed. The luck was that I had a good man and a good boy and lately writers have forgotten there still are such things. Then the ocean is worth writing about just as man is. So I was lucky there. I've seen the marlin mate and know about that. So I leave that out. I've seen a school (or pod) of more than fifty sperm whales in that same stretch of water and once harpooned one nearly sixty feet in length and lost him. So I left that out. All the stories I know from the fishing village I leave out. But the knowledge is what makes the underwater part of the iceberg.

Interviewer: Archibald MacLeish has spoken of a technical device you discovered which would seem to do with conveying experience to a reader. He said you developed it while covering baseball games back in those *Kansas City Star* days. It was simply that a writer should concentrate during moments of apparent inactivity—that what he described of those moments had an effect, and a powerful one, of making the reader conscious of what he had been aware of only subconsciously . . .

Hemingway: The anecdote is apocryphal. I never wrote baseball for the *Star*. What Archie was trying to remember was how I was trying to learn in Chicago in around 1920 and was searching for the unnoticed things that made emotions such as the way an outfielder tossed his glove without looking back to where it fell, the squeak of resin on canvas under a fighter's flat-soled gym-shoes, the gray colour of Jack Blackburn's skin when he had just come out of stir and other

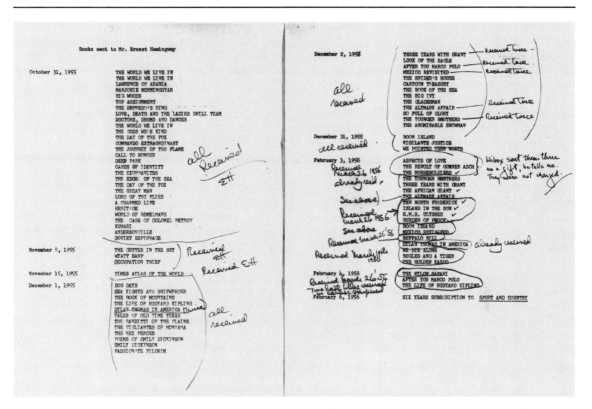

List of books sent from the Scribner Bookstore with Hemingway's notes (Charles Scribner's Sons Archive, Princeton University)

things I noted as a painter sketches. You saw Blackburn's strange colour and the old razor cuts and the way he spun a man before you knew his history. These were the things which moved you before you knew the story.

Interviewer: Have you ever described any type of situation of which you had no personal knowledge?

Hemingway: That is a strange question. By personal knowledge do you mean carnal knowledge? In that case the answer is positive. A writer, if he is any good, does not describe. He invents or *makes* out of knowledge personal and impersonal and sometimes he seems to have unexplained knowledge which could come from forgotten racial or family experience. Who teaches the homing pigeon to fly as he does; where does a fighting bull get his bravery, or a hunting-dog his nose? This is an elaboration or a condensation on that stuff we were talking in Madrid that time when my head was not to be trusted.

Interviewer: How detached must you be from an experience before you can write about it in fictional terms? The African air-crashes, for instance?

Hemingway: It depends on the experience. One part of you sees it with complete detachment from the start. Another part is very involved. I think there is no rule about how soon one should write about it. It would depend on how well adjusted the individual was and on his or her recuperative powers. Certainly it is valuable to a trained writer to crash in an aircraft which burns. He learns several important things very quickly. Whether they will be of use to him is conditioned by survival. Survival, with honor, that outmoded and all-important word, is as difficult as ever and as all important to a writer. Those who do not last are always more beloved since no one has to see them in their long, dull, unrelenting, no quarter given and no quarter received, fights that they make to do something as they believe it should be done before they die. Those who die or quit early and easy and with every good reason are preferred because they are understandable and human. Failure and well-disguised cowardice are more human and more beloved.

Interviewer: Could I ask you to what extent you think the writer should concern himself with the socio-political problems of his times?

309

Hemingway: Everyone has his own conscience and there should be no rules about how a conscience should function. All you can be sure about in a political-minded writer is that if his work should last you will have to skip the politics when you read it. Many of the so-called politically enlisted writers change their politics frequently. This is very exciting to them and to their political-literary reviews. Sometimes they even have to rewrite their view-points . . . and in a hurry. Perhaps it can be respected as a form of the pursuit of happiness.

Interviewer: Has the political influence of Ezra Pound on the segregationalist Kasper had any effect on your belief that the poet ought to be released from St. Elizabeth's Hospital.

Hemingway: No. None at all. I believe that Ezra should be released and allowed to write poetry in Italy on an undertaking by him to abstain from any politics. I would be happy to see Kasper jailed as soon as possible. Great poets are not necessarily girl guides nor scoutmasters nor splendid influences on youth. To name a few: Verlaine, Rimbaud, Shelley, Byron, Baudelaire, Proust, Gide should not have been confined to prevent them from being aped in their thinking, their manners or their morals by local Kaspers. I am sure that it will take a footnote to this paragraph in ten years to explain who Kasper was.

Interviewer: Would you say, ever, that there is any didactic intention in your work?

Hemingway: Didactic is a word that has been misused and has spoiled. *Death in the Afternoon* is an instructive book.

Interviewer: It has been said that a writer only deals with one or two ideas throughout his work. Would you say your work reflects one or two ideas.

Hemingway: Who said that? It sounds much too simple. The man who said it possibly *had* only one or two ideas.

Interviewer: Well, perhaps it would be better put this way: Graham Greene said in one of these interviews that a ruling passion gives to a shelf of novels the unity of a system. You yourself have said, I believe, that great writing comes out of a sense of injustice. Do you consider it important that a novelist be dominated in this way—by some such compelling sense?

Hemingway: Mr. Greene has a facility for making statements that I do not possess. It would be impossible for me to make generalizations about a shelf of novels or a wisp of snipe or a gaggle of geese. I'll try a generalization though. A writer without a sense of justice and of injustice would be better off editing the Year Book of a school for exceptional children than writing novels. Another generalization. You see; they are not so difficult when they are sufficiently obvious. The most essential gift for a good writer is a built-in, shock-proof, shit detector. This is the writer's radar and all great writers have had it.

Interviewer: Finally, a fundamental question: namely, as a creative writer what do you think is the function of your art? Why a representation of fact, rather than fact itself?

Hemingway: Why be puzzled by that? From things that have happened and from things as they exist and from all things that you know and all those you cannot know, you make something through your invention that is not a representation but a whole new thing truer than anything true and alive, and you make it alive, and if you make it well enough, you give it immortality. That is why you write and for no other reason that you know of. But what about all the reasons that no one knows?

In 1959 Hemingway's publisher, Charles Scribner Jr., asked him to write an introduction to a proposed student edition of his stories. Hemingway worked on it in Spain during the summer. Scribner did not like the introduction, and the edition was not published. The introduction first appeared in The Paris Review, *79 (1981), pp. 85–102.*

The Art of the Short Story

Gertrude Stein who was sometimes very wise said to me on one of her wise days, "Remember, Hemingway, that remarks are not literature." The following remarks are not intended to be nor do they pretend to be literature. They are meant to be instructive, irritating and informative. No writer should be asked to write solemnly about what he has written. Truthfully, yes. Solemnly, no. Should we begin in the form of a lecture designed to counteract the many lectures you will have heard on the art of the short story?

Many people have a compulsion to write. There is no law against it and doing it makes them happy

ERNEST HEMINGWAY *says:*

"Each generation of Americans needs to re-discover Europe

...*Why? Because you'll see your own country's destiny more clearly if you spend your next vacation abroad"*

Signed at the Finca Vigia, Cuba, Dec. 1st. 1956

"*Pan American and I are old friends*"

"We started flying commercially about the same time. They did the flying and I was the passenger. It turned out to be a good partnership.

"After the old Key West-Miami-Havana-Bahamas early days, there was the Pacific when you took a day to Midway—another to Wake—one more to Guam—one to Manila—then Hongkong.

"Flying in China you had to sweat out many things. But you never worried about equipment, maintenance nor any Pan American pilot. I feel as safe with Pan American as I do any morning I wake up to a good working day."

Only Pan American offers **overnight** service from New York, Boston, Philadelphia, Detroit, and Chicago to 25 European cities... Fly Now—Pay Later!

FLY NOW—PAY LATER

Pan American originated "Pay Later" and now—thru March 31—has a new money-saving Family Fare plan. Ask for details.

	Tourist round trip fare New York	Minimum 10% down payment
Shannon	44	23
London	49	26
Paris	52	28
Frankfort	56	30
Rome	61	33
Nice	58	31
Istanbul	79	42
'Round the World	135	73

The Romans tried, but couldn't bridge the mighty floods of the Rhône River at Avignon. Here in the South of France, in the year 1177, Saint Benezet built the famous stone bridge which lasted until 1680. Today, in a morning's drive from the Pan American airport at Nice, you can be dancing before lunch on the bridge when seven generations of Americans have sung: "Sur le pont d'Avignon..."

PAN AMERICAN
WORLD'S MOST EXPERIENCED AIRLINE

Hemingway's endorsement illustrates the level of his celebrity in the 1950s (Holiday, February 1956). He also endorsed Parker pens and Ballantine ale.

while they do it and presumably relieves them. Given editors who will remove the worst of their emissions, supply them with spelling and syntax and help them shape their thoughts and their beliefs, some compulsive writers attain a temporary fame. But when shit, or *merde*–a word which teacher will explain–is cut out of a book, the odor of it always remains perceptible to anyone with sufficient olfactory sensibility.

The compulsive writer would be advised not to attempt the short story. Should he make the attempt, he might well suffer the fate of the compulsive architect, which is as lonely an end as that of the compulsive bassoon player. Let us not waste our time considering the sad and lonely ends of these unfortunate creatures, gentlemen. Let us continue the exercise.

Are there any questions? Have you mastered the art of the short story? Have I been helpful? Or have I not made myself clear? I hope so.

Gentlemen, I will be frank with you. The masters of the short story come to no good end. You

query this? You cite me Maugham? Longevity, gentlemen, is not an end. It is a prolongation. I cannot say fie upon it, since I have never fied on anything yet. Shuck it off, Jack. Don't fie on it.

Should we abandon rhetoric and realize at the same time that what is the most authentic hipster talk of today is the twenty-three skidoo of tomorrow? We should? What intelligent young people you are and what a privilege it is to be with you. Do I hear a request for authentic ballroom bananas? I do? Gentlemen, we have them for you in bunches.

Actually, as writers put it when they do not know how to begin a sentence, there is very little to say about writing short stories unless you are a professional explainer. If you can do it, you don't have to explain it. If you can not do it, no explanation will ever help.

A few things I have found to be true. If you leave out important things or events that you know about, the story is strengthened. If you leave or skip something because you do not know it, the story will be worthless. The test of any story is how very good the stuff is that you, not your editors, omit. A story in this book called "Big Two-Hearted River" is about a boy coming home beat to the wide from a war. Beat to the wide was an earlier and possibly more severe form of beat, since those who had it were unable to comment on this condition and could not suffer that it be mentioned in their presence. So the war, all mention of the war, anything about the war, is omitted. The river was the Fox River, by Seney, Michigan, not the Big Two-Hearted. The change of name was made purposely, not from ignorance nor carelessness but because Big Two-Hearted River is poetry, and because there were many Indians in the story, just as the war was in the story, and none of the Indians nor the war appeared. As you see, it is very simple and easy to explain.

In a story called "A Sea Change," everything is left out. I had seen the couple in the Bar Basque in St.-Jean-de-Luz and I knew the story too too well, which is the squared root of well, and use any well you like except mine. So I left the story out. But it is all there. It is not visible but it is there.

It is very hard to talk about your work since it implies arrogance or pride. I have tried to get rid of arrogance and replace it with humility and I do all right at that sometimes, but without pride I would not wish to continue to live nor to write and I publish nothing of which I am not proud. You can take that any way you like, Jack. I might not take it myself. But maybe we're built different.

Another story is "Fifty Grand." This story originally started like this:

"How did you handle Benny so easy, Jack?" Soldier asked him.

"Benny's an awful smart boxer," Jack said. "All the time he's in there, he's thinking. All the time he's thinking, I was hitting him."

I told this story to Scott Fitzgerald in Paris before I wrote "Fifty Grand" trying to explain to him how a truly great boxer like Jack Britton functioned. I wrote the story opening with that incident and when it was finished I was happy about it and showed it to Scott. He said he liked the story very much and spoke about it in so fulsome a manner that I was embarrassed. Then he said, "There is only one thing wrong with it, Ernest, and I tell you this as your friend. You have to cut out that old chestnut about Britton and Leonard."

At that time my humility was in such ascendance that I thought he must have heard the remark before or that Britton must have said it to someone else. It was not until I had published the story, from which I had removed that lovely revelation of the metaphysics of boxing that Fitzgerald in the way his mind was functioning that year so that he called an historic statement an "old chestnut" because he had heard it once and only once from a friend, that I realized how dangerous that attractive virtue, humility, can be. So do not be too humble, gentlemen. Be humble after but not during the action. They will all con you, gentlemen. But sometimes it is not intentional. Sometimes they simply do not know. This is the saddest state of writers and the one you will most frequently encounter. If there are no questions, let us press on.

My loyal and devoted friend Fitzgerald, who was truly more interested in my own career at this point than in his own, sent me to Scribner's with the story. It had already been turned down by Ray Long of Cosmopolitan Magazine because it had no love interest. That was okay with me since I eliminated any love interest and there were, purposely, no women in it except for two broads. Enter two broads as in Shakespeare, and they go out of the story. This is unlike what you will hear from your instructors, that if a broad comes into a story in the first paragraph, she must reappear later to justify her original presence. This is untrue, gentlemen. You may dispense with her, just as in life. It is also untrue that if a gun hangs on the wall when you open up the story, it must be fired by page fourteen. The chances are, gentlemen, that if it hangs upon the wall, it will not even shoot. If there are no questions, shall we press on? Yes, the unfireable gun may be a symbol. That is true. But with a good enough writer, the chances are some jerk just hung it there to look at. Gentlemen, you can't be sure. Maybe he is queer for guns, or maybe an interior decorator put it there. Or both.

So with pressure by Max Perkins on the editor, Scribner's Magazine agreed to publish the story and pay me two hundred and fifty dollars, if I would cut it to a length where it would not have to be continued into the back of the book. They call magazines books. There is significance in this but we will not go into it. They are not books, even if they put them in stiff covers. You have to watch this, gentlemen. Anyway, I explained without heat nor hope, seeing the built-in stupidity of the editor of the magazine and his intransigence, that I had already cut the story myself and that the only way it could be shortened by five hundred words and make sense was to amputate the first five hundred. I had often done that myself with stories and it improved them. It would not have improved this story but I thought that was their ass not mine. I would put it back together in a book. They read differently in a book anyway. You will learn about this.

No, gentlemen, they would not cut the first five hundred words. They gave it instead to a very intelligent young assistant editor who assured me he could

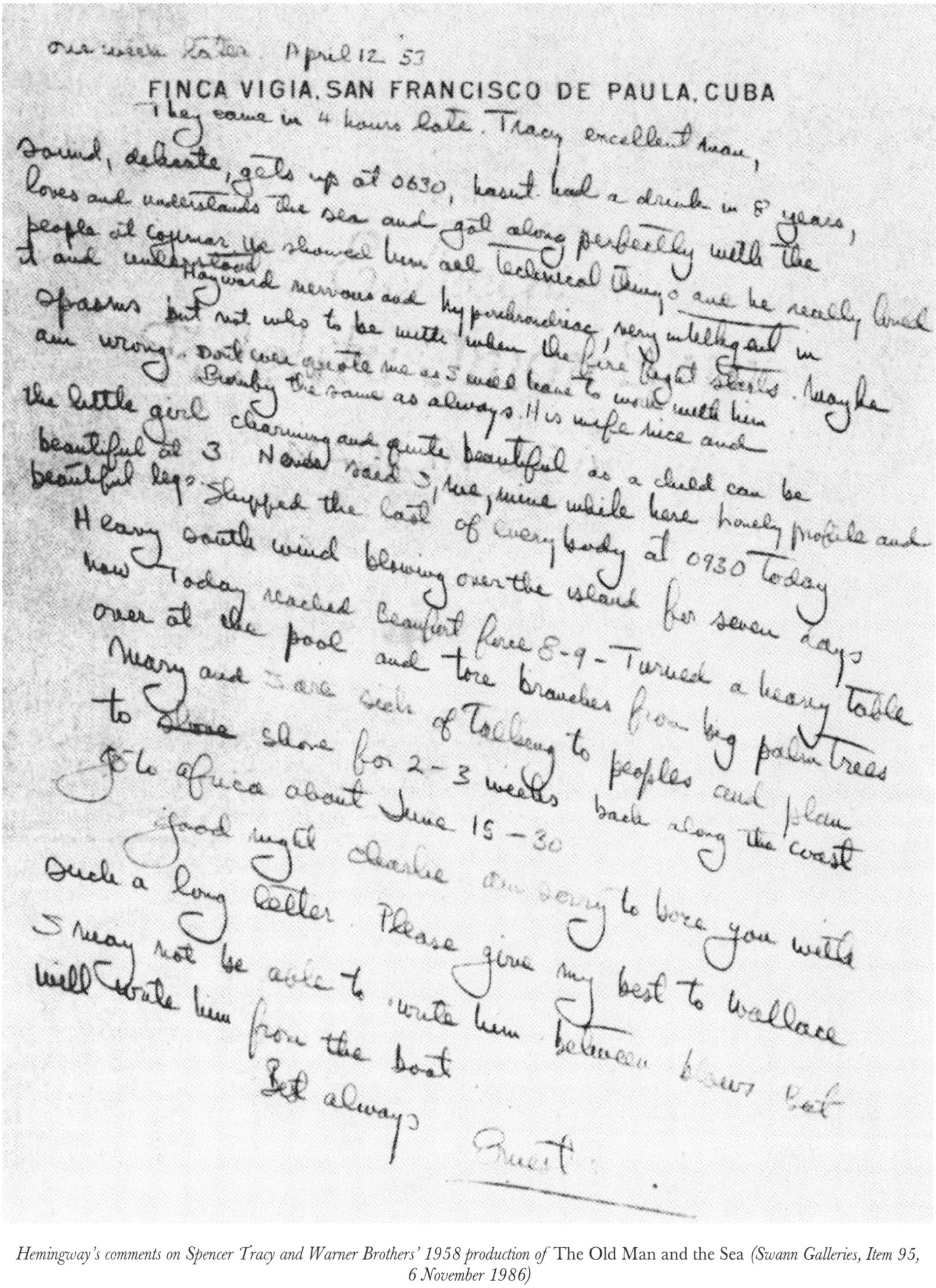

one week later. April 12 '53

FINCA VIGIA, SAN FRANCISCO DE PAULA, CUBA

They came in 4 hours late. Tracy excellent man, sound, delicate, gets up at 0630, hasn't had a drink in 8 years, loves and understands the sea and got along perfectly with the people at Cojimar. He showed him all technical things and he really loved it and understood. Hayward nervous and hypochondriac, very intelligent in spasms but not who to be with when the fire fight starts. Maybe am wrong. Don't ever quote me as I will have to work with him. Bromby the same as always. His wife nice and the little girl charming and quite beautiful as a child can be beautiful at 3. Never said I, me, mine while here. Lovely profile and beautiful legs. Shoved the last of everybody at 0930 today

Heavy south wind blowing over the island for seven days now. Today reached Beaufort force 8-9 — Turned a heavy table over at the pool and tore branches from big palm trees. Mary and I are sick of Tobsing to peoples and plan to shore shore for 2-3 weeks back along the coast. Go to Africa about June 15 - 30

Good night Charlie am sorry to bore you with such a long letter. Please give my best to Wallace. I may not be able to write him between blows but will write him from the boat

So always

Ernest

Hemingway's comments on Spencer Tracy and Warner Brothers' 1958 production of The Old Man and the Sea *(Swann Galleries, Item 95, 6 November 1986)*

cut it with no difficulty. That was just what he did on his first attempt, and any place he took words out, the story no longer made sense. It had been cut for keeps when I wrote it, and afterwards at Scott's request I'd even cut out the metaphysics which, ordinarily, I leave in. So they quit on it finally and eventually, I understand, Edward Weeks got Ellery Sedgwick to publish it in the *Atlantic Monthly*. Then everyone wanted me to write fight stories and I did not write any more fight stories because I tried to write only one story on anything, if I got what I was after, because Life is very short if you like it and I knew that even then. There are other things to write about and other people who write very good fight stories. I recommend to you "The Professional" by W. C. Heinz.

Yes, the confidently cutting young editor became a big man on *Reader's Digest*. Or didn't he? I'll have to check that. So you see, gentlemen, you never know and what you win in Boston you lose in Chicago. That's symbolism, gentlemen, and you can run a saliva test on it. That is how we now detect symbolism in our group and so far it gives fairly satisfactory results. Not complete, mind you. But we are getting in to see our way through. Incidentally, within a short time *Scribner's Magazine* was running a contest for long short stories that broke back into the back of the book, and paying many times two hundred and fifty dollars to the winners.

Now since I have answered your perceptive questions, let us take up another story.

This story is called "The Light of the World." I could have called it "Behold I Stand at the Door and Knock" or some other stained-glass window title, but I did not think of it and actually "The Light of the World" is better. It is about many things and you would be ill-advised to think it is a simple tale. It is really, no matter what you hear, a love letter to a whore named Alice who at the time of the story would have dressed out at around two hundred and ten pounds. Maybe more. And the point of it is that nobody, and that goes for you, Jack, knows how we were then from how we are now. This is worse on women than on us, until you look into the mirror yourself some day instead of looking at women all the time, and in writing the story I was trying to do something about it. But there are very few basic things you can do anything about. So I do what the French call *constater*. Look that up. That is what you have to learn to do, and you ought to learn French anyway if you are going to understand short stories, and there is nothing rougher than to do it all the way. It is hardest to do about women and you must not worry when they say there are no such women as those you wrote about. That only means your women aren't like their women. You ever see any of their women, Jack? I have a couple of times and you would be appalled and I know you don't appall easy.

What I learned constructive about women, not just ethics like never blame them if they pox you because somebody poxed them and lots of times they don't even know they have it—that's in the first reader for squares—is, no matter *how* they get, always think of them the way they were on the best day they ever had in their lives. That's about all you can do about it and that is what I was trying for in the story.

Now there is another story called "The Short Happy Life of Francis Macomber." Jack, I get a bang even yet from just writing the titles. That's why you write, no matter what they tell you. I'm glad to be with somebody I know now and those feecking students have gone. They haven't? Okay. Glad to have them with us. It is in you that our hope is. That's the stuff to feed the troops. Students, at ease.

This is a simple story in a way, because the woman, who I knew very well in real life but then invented out of, to make the woman for this story, is a bitch for the full course and doesn't change. You'll probably never meet the type because you haven't got the money. I haven't either but I get around. Now this woman doesn't change. She has been better, but she will never be any better anymore. I invented her complete with handles from the worst bitch I knew (then) and when I first knew her she'd been lovely. Not my dish, not my pigeon, not my cup of tea, but lovely for what she was and I was her all of the above which is whatever you make of it. This is as close as I can put it and keep it clean. This information is what you call the background of a story. You throw it all away and invent from what you know. I should have said that sooner. That's all there is to writing. That, a perfect ear—call it selective—absolute pitch, the devotion to your work and respect for it that a priest of God has for his, and then have the guts of a burglar, no conscience except to writing, and you're in, gentlemen. It's easy. Anybody can write if he is cut out for it and applies himself. Never give it a thought. Just have those few requisites. I mean the way you have to write now to handle the way now is now. There was a time when it was nicer, much nicer and all that has been well written by nicer people. They are all dead and so are their times, but they handled them very well. Those times are over and writing like that won't help you now.

But to return to this story. The woman called Margot Macomber is no good to anybody now except for trouble. You can bang her but that's about all. The man is a nice jerk. I knew him very well in real life, so invent him too from everything I know. So he is just how he really was, only he is invented. The White Hunter is my best friend and he does not care what I

Spencer Tracy (Santiago) in a scene from The Old Man and the Sea *(Warner Brothers, 1958)*

write as long as it is readable, so I don't invent him at all. I just disguise him for family and business reasons, and to keep him out of trouble with the Game Department. He is the furthest thing from a square since they invented the circle, so I just have to take care of him with an adequate disguise and he is as proud as though we both wrote it, which actually you always do in anything if you go back far enough. So it is a secret between us. That's all there is to that story except maybe the lion when he is hit and I am thinking inside of him really, not faked. I can think inside of a lion, really. It's hard to believe and it is perfectly okay with me if you don't believe it. Perfectly. Plenty of people have used it since, though, and one boy used it quite well, making only one mistake. Making any mistake kills you. This mistake killed him and quite soon everything he wrote was a mistake. You have to watch yourself, Jack, every minute, and the more talented you are the more you have to watch these mistakes because you will be in faster company. A writer

who is not going all the way up can make all the mistakes he wants. None of it matters. He doesn't matter. The people who like him don't matter either. They could drop dead. It wouldn't make any difference. It's too bad. As soon as you read one page by anyone you can tell whether it matters or not. This is sad and you hate to do it. I don't want to be the one that tells them. So don't make any mistakes. You see how easy it is? Just go right in there and be a writer.

That about handles that story. Any questions? No, I don't know whether she shot him on purpose any more than you do. I could find out if I asked myself because I invented it and I could go right on inventing. But you have to know where to stop. That is what makes a short story. Makes it short at least. The only hint I could give you is that it is my belief that the incidence of husbands shot accidentally by wives who are bitches and really work at it is very low. Should we continue?

315

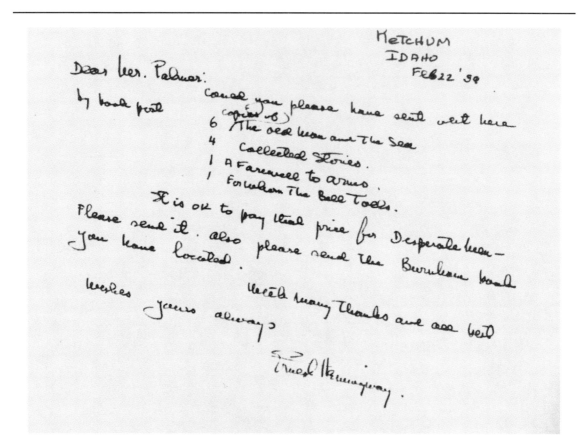

Hemingway was probably ordering these copies of his own work to give as gifts to friends (Swann Galleries, Sale 1601, Item 144, 17 September 1992)

If you are interested in how you get the idea for a story, this is how it was with "The Snows of Kilimanjaro." They have you ticketed and always try to make it that you are someone who can only write about theirself. I am using in this lecture the spoken language, which varies. It is one of the ways to write, so you might as well follow it and maybe you will learn something. Anyone who can write can write spoken, pedantic, inexorably dull, or pure English prose, just as slot machines can be set for straight, percentage, give-away or stealing. No one who can write spoken ever starves except at the start. The others you can eat irregularly on. But any good writer can do them all. This is spoken, approved for over fourteen I hope. Thank you.

Anyway we came home from Africa, which is a place you stay until the money runs out or you get smacked, one year and at quarantine I said to the ship news reporters when somebody asked me what my projects were that I was going to work and when I had some more money go back to Africa. The different wars killed off that project and it took nine-

teen years to get back. Well it was in the papers and a really nice and really fine and really rich woman invited me to tea and we had a few drinks as well and she had read in the papers about this project, and why should I have to wait to go back for any lack of money? She and my wife and I could go to Africa any time and money was only something to be used intelligently for the best enjoyment of good people and so forth. It was a sincere and fine and good offer and I liked her very much and I turned down the offer.

So I get down to Key West and I start to think what would happen to a character like me whose defects I know, if I had accepted that offer. So I start to invent and I make myself a guy who would do what I invent. I know about the dying part because I had been through all that. Not just once. I got it early, in the middle and later. So I invent how someone I know who cannot sue me—that is me—would turn out, and put into one short story things you would use in, say, four novels if you were careful and not a spender. I throw everything I had been saving into the story and spend it all. I really throw it away, if you know what I mean. I am not gambling with it. Or maybe I am. Who knows? Real gamblers don't gamble. At least you think they don't gamble. They gamble, Jack, don't worry. So I make up the man and the woman as well as I can and I put all the true stuff in and with all the load, the most load any short story ever carried, it still takes off and it flies. This makes me very happy. So I thought that and the Macomber story are as good short stories as I can write for a while, so I lose interest and take up other forms of writing.

Any questions? The leopard? He is part of the metaphysics. I did not hire out to explain that nor a lot of other things. I know, but I am under no obligation to tell you. Put it down to *omertá*. Look that word up. I dislike explainers, apologists, stoolies, pimps. No writer should be any one of those for his own work. This is just a little background, Jack, that won't do either of us any harm. You see the point, don't you? If not it is too bad.

That doesn't mean you shouldn't explain for, apologize for or pimp or tout for some other writer. I have done it and the best luck I had was doing it for Faulkner. When they didn't know him in Europe, I told them all how he was the best we had and so forth and I over-humbled with him plenty and built him up about as high as he could go because he never had a break then and he was good then. So now whenever he has a few shots, he'll tell students what's wrong with me or tell Japanese or anybody they send him to, to build up our local product. I get tired of this but I figure what the hell he's had a few shots and maybe he even believes it. So you asked me just now what I think about him, as everybody does, and I always stall, so I say you know how good he is. Right. You ought to. What is wrong is he cons himself sometimes pretty bad. That may just be the sauce. But for quite a while when he hits the sauce toward the end of a book, it shows bad. He gets tired and he goes on and on, and that sauce writing is really hard on who has to read it. I mean if they care about writing. I thought maybe it would help if I read it using the sauce myself, but it wasn't any help. Maybe it would have helped if I was fourteen. But I was only fourteen one year and then I would have been too busy. So that's what I think about Faulkner. You ask that I sum it up from the standpoint of a professional. Very good writer. Cons himself now. Too much sauce. But he wrote a really fine story called "The Bear" and I would be glad to put it in this book for your pleasure and delight, if I had written it. But you can't write them all, Jack.

It would be simpler and more fun to talk about other writers and what is good and what is wrong with

Hemingway with matador Antonio Ordoñez in Spain, summer 1959 (Ernest Hemingway Collection, John F. Kennedy Library)

them, as I saw when you asked me about Faulkner. He's easy to handle because he talks so much for a supposed silent man. Never talk, Jack, if you are a writer, unless you have the guy write it down and have you go over it. Otherwise, they get it wrong. That's what you think until they play a tape back at you. Then you know how silly it sounds. You're a writer aren't you? Okay, shut up and write. What was that question?

Did I really write three stories in one day in Madrid, the way it said in that interview in *The Paris Review* and *Horizon*? Yes sir. I was hotter than a—let's skip it, gentlemen. I was laden with uninhibited energy. Or should we say this energy was canalized into my work. Such states are compounded by the brisk air of the Guadarramas (Jack, was it cold) the highly seasoned bacalao vizcaíno (dried cod fish, Jack) a certain vague loneliness (I was in love and the girl was in Bologna and I couldn't sleep anyway, so why not write.) So I wrote.

"The stories you mention I wrote in one day in Madrid on May 16 when it snowed out the San Isidro bullfights. First I wrote 'The Killers' which I'd tried to write before and failed. Then after lunch I got in bed to

keep warm and wrote 'Today is Friday.' I had so much juice I thought maybe I was going crazy and I had about six other stories to write. So I got dressed and walked to Fornos, the old bull fighter's cafe, and drank coffee and then came back and wrote 'Ten Indians.' This made me very sad and I drank some brandy and went to sleep. I'd forgotten to eat and one of the waiters brought me up some bacalao and a small steak and fried potatoes and a bottle of Valdepeñas.

"The woman who ran the Pension was always worried that I did not eat enough and she had sent the waiter. I remember sitting up in bed and eating, and drink the Valdepeñas. The waiter said he would bring up another bottle. He said the Señora wanted to know if I was going to write all night. I said no, I thought I would lay off for a while. Why don't you try to write just one more, the waiter asked. I'm only supposed to write one, I said. Nonsense, he said. You could write six. I'll try tomorrow, I said. Try it tonight, he said. What do you think the old woman sent the food up for?

"I'm tired, I told him. Nonsense, he said (the word was not nonsense). You tired after three miserable little stories. Translate me one.

"Leave me alone, I said. How am I going to write it if you don't leave me alone. So I sat up in bed and drank the Valdepeñas and thought what a hell of a writer I was if the first story was as good as I'd hoped."

I have used the same words in answering that the excellent Plimpton elicited from me in order to avoid error or repetition. If there are no more questions, should we continue?

It is very bad for writers to be hit on the head too much. Sometimes you lose months when you should have and perhaps would have worked well but sometimes a long time after the memory of the sensory distortions of these woundings will produce a story which, while not justifying the temporary cerebral damage, will palliate it. "A Way You'll Never Be" was written at Key West, Florida, some fifteen years after the damage it depicts, both to a man, a village and a countryside, had occurred. No questions? I understand. I understand completely. However, do not be alarmed. We are not going to call for a moment of silence. Nor for the man in the white suit. Nor for the net. Now gentlemen, and I notice a sprinkling of ladies who have drifted in attracted I hope by the sprinkling of applause. Thank you. Just *what* stories do you yourselves care for? I must not impose on you exclusively those that find favor with their author. Do *you* too care for any of them?

You like "The Killers"? So good of you. And why? Because it had Burt Lancaster and Ava Gardner in it? Excellent. Now we are getting somewhere. It is always a pleasure to remember Miss Gardner as she was then. No, I never met Mr. Lancaster. I can't tell you what he is really like but everyone says he is terrific. The background of that story is that I had a lawyer who had cancer and he wanted cash rather than any long term stuff. You can see his point I hope. So when he was offered a share in the picture for me and less cash, he took the more cash. It turned out badly for us both. He died eventually and I retained only an academic interest in the picture. But the company lets me run it off free when I want to see Miss Gardner and hear the shooting. It is a good picture and the only good picture ever made of a story of mine. One of the reasons for that is that John Huston wrote the script. Yes I know him. Is everything true about him that they say? No. But the best things are. Isn't that interesting.

You mean background about the story not the picture? That's not very sporting, young lady. Didn't you see the class was enjoying itself finally? Besides it has a sordid background. I hesitate to bring it in, on account of there is no statute of limitations on what it deals with. Gene Tunney, who is a man of wide culture, once asked me, "Ernest, wasn't that Andre Anderson in 'The Killers'?" I told him it was and that the town was Summit, Illinois, not Summit, N.J. We left it at that. I

Hemingway and Fidel Castro, 15 May 1960. The Cuban dictator was the winner of the individual championship at Hemingway's fishing tournament (photograph by Roberto Herrera Sotolongo).

thought about that story a long long time before I invented it, and I had to be as far away as Madrid before I invented it properly. That story probably had more left out of it than anything I ever wrote. More even than when I left the war out of "Big Two-Hearted River." I left out all Chicago, which is hard to do in 2951 words.

Another time I was leaving out good was in "A Clean Well-Lighted Place." There I really had luck. I left out everything. That is about as far as you can go, so I stood on that one and haven't drawn to that since.

I trust you follow me, gentlemen. As I said at the start, there is nothing to writing short stories once you get the knack of it.

A story I can beat, and I promise you I will, is "The Undefeated." But I leave it in to show you the difference between when you leave it all in and when you take it out. The stories where you leave it all in do not re-read like the ones where you leave it out. They understand easier, but when you have read them once

or twice you can't re-read them. I could give you examples in everybody who writes, but writers have enough enemies without doing it to each other. All really good writers know exactly what is wrong in all other good writers. There are no perfect writers unless they write just a very little bit and then stand on it. But writers have no business fingering another writer to outsiders while he is alive. After a writer is dead and doesn't have to work any more, anything goes. A son of a bitch alive is a son of a bitch dead. I am not talking about rows between writers. They are okay and can be comic. If someone puts a thumb in your eye, you don't protest. You thumb him back. He fouls you, you foul him back. That teaches people to keep it clean. What I mean is, you shouldn't give it to another writer, I mean really give it to him. I know you shouldn't do it because I did it once to Sherwood Anderson. I did it because I was righteous, which is the worst thing you can be, and I thought he was going to pot the way he was writing and that I could kid him out of it by showing him how awful

FINCA VIGIA, SAN FRANCISCO DE PAULA, CUBA

June 1 1960

My Monique mia.

How is everything? Here it seems now for the 5th day and grey beer is growing on all the leather, + an color trying to form in the Yucatan channel. am very tired of being in the tropics the way the weather has been. Crazy cold weather and then jump directly to hurricane weather. Have not written because working every day until dead house in the head. Finished first draft of 110,000 words two days ago and had to start immediately on Income Tax. Used up my eyes too much writing on book and they make trouble now for a month + maybe only over-strain - Hope so.

Hope the Plane Trees did well. Juanito Quintana sent me a review that was quite good + I think you can write better than that book. But maybe it only seems it was not as good because I am reparado de la vista or berries or straw in my eyes. I cabled Knapp something about Juan's book and also talked to critics about him when was North. Hope did some good. Sometimes talking does good.

Now that I am doing Income Tax I must know how much gallemard paid to Mary and report it. I do not think I have to report what they paid

First page of Hemingway's letter to French writer Monique Lange. *The first draft he mentions is probably for* The Dangerous Summer *(Charles Hamilton Auctions, Sale Number 82, Item 176, 14 November 1974).*

it was. So I wrote *The Torrents of Spring*. It was cruel to do, and it didn't do any good, and he just wrote worse and worse. What the hell business of mine was it if he wanted to write badly? None. But then I was righteous and more loyal to writing than to my friend. I would have shot anybody then, not kill them, just shoot them a little, if I thought it would straighten them up and make them write right. Now I know that there is nothing you can do about any writer ever. The seeds of their destruction are in them from the start, and the thing to do about writers is get along with them if you see them, and try not to see them. All except a very few, and all of them except a couple are dead. Like I said, once they're dead anything goes as long as it's true.

I'm sorry I threw at Anderson. It was cruel and I was a son of a bitch to do it. The only thing I can say is that I was as cruel to myself then. But that is no excuse. He was a friend of mine, but that was no excuse for doing it to him. Any questions? Ask me that some other time.

This brings us to another story, "My Old Man." The background of this was all the time we spent at the races at San Siro when I used to be in hospital in Milan in 1918, and the time put in at the tracks in Paris when we really worked at it. Handicapping I mean. Some people say that this story is derived from a story about harness racing by Sherwood Anderson called "I'm a Fool." I do not believe this. My theory is that it is derived from a jockey I knew very well and a number of horses I knew, one of which I was in love with. I invented the boy in my story and I think the boy in Sherwood's story was himself. If you read both stories you can form your own opinion. Whatever it is, it is all right with me. The best things Sherwood wrote are in two books, *Winesburg, Ohio* and *The Triumph of the Egg*. You should read them both. Before you know too much about things, they are better. The best thing about Sherwood was he was the kind of guy at the start his name made you think of Sherwood Forest, while in Bob Sherwood the name only made you think of a playwright.

Any other stories you find in this book are in because I liked them. If you like them too I will be pleased. Thank you very much. It has been nice to be with you.

June 1959
La Consula
Churriana
Malaga, Spain

These statements about Hemingway's life and work were published in The New York Times *on 3 July 1961, p. 6.*

Authors and Critics Appraise Works

Following are estimates of Ernest Hemingway's work given to The New York Times:

ARCHIBALD MacLEISH, poet and playwright–He was a master of English prose, the great stylist of his generation. He had an English idiom of his own, which imposed itself by its own validity on his contemporaries. Like all true idioms it was an idiom of the human spirit, not of the language alone. Writers in other tongues were influenced almost as much as those who wrote in English. Hemingway felt the pulse of the time and gave it an equivalent in words.

LIONEL TRILLING, critic and Professor of English at Columbia University–His place in American literature is secure and pre-eminent. There is no one in the whole range of literature of the modern world who has a better claim than he to be acknowledged as a master, but it is in his short stories rather than in his novels that his genius most truly and surely showed itself.

ALFRED KAZIN, author and critic–Probably no other American writer of our time has set such a stamp on modern literature. Hemingway was one of our true poets. He gave a whole new dimension to English prose by making it almost as exact as poetry, by making every word sound, by reaching for those places of the imagination where the word and the object are one.

JAMES THURBER, author and playwright–Hemingway was unquestionably one of the greatest writers of the century. It was once said accurately of him that his contribution to literature was a certain clarification of the English language. Of himself, he once said, "The thing to do is last and get your work done." I met him only once and we went over to Tim Costello's and had a wonderful time and became brothers.

JOHN DOS PASSOS, novelist–He was one of the best of our time. I believe his original short stories will certainly last. He was a great stylist and a magnificent writer. I am sure that all of his work that I have read will stand up. He was indeed a magnificent writer and his contributions were large.

VAN WYCK BROOKS, author and literary historian, Chancellor of the American Academy of Arts and Letters–His destiny has been to symbolize an age of unparalleled violence as no other American has symbolized it. He was in his way a typical American, and there was something permanently adolescent about him that stood for certain immaturity in the American mind. He was a twentieth-century

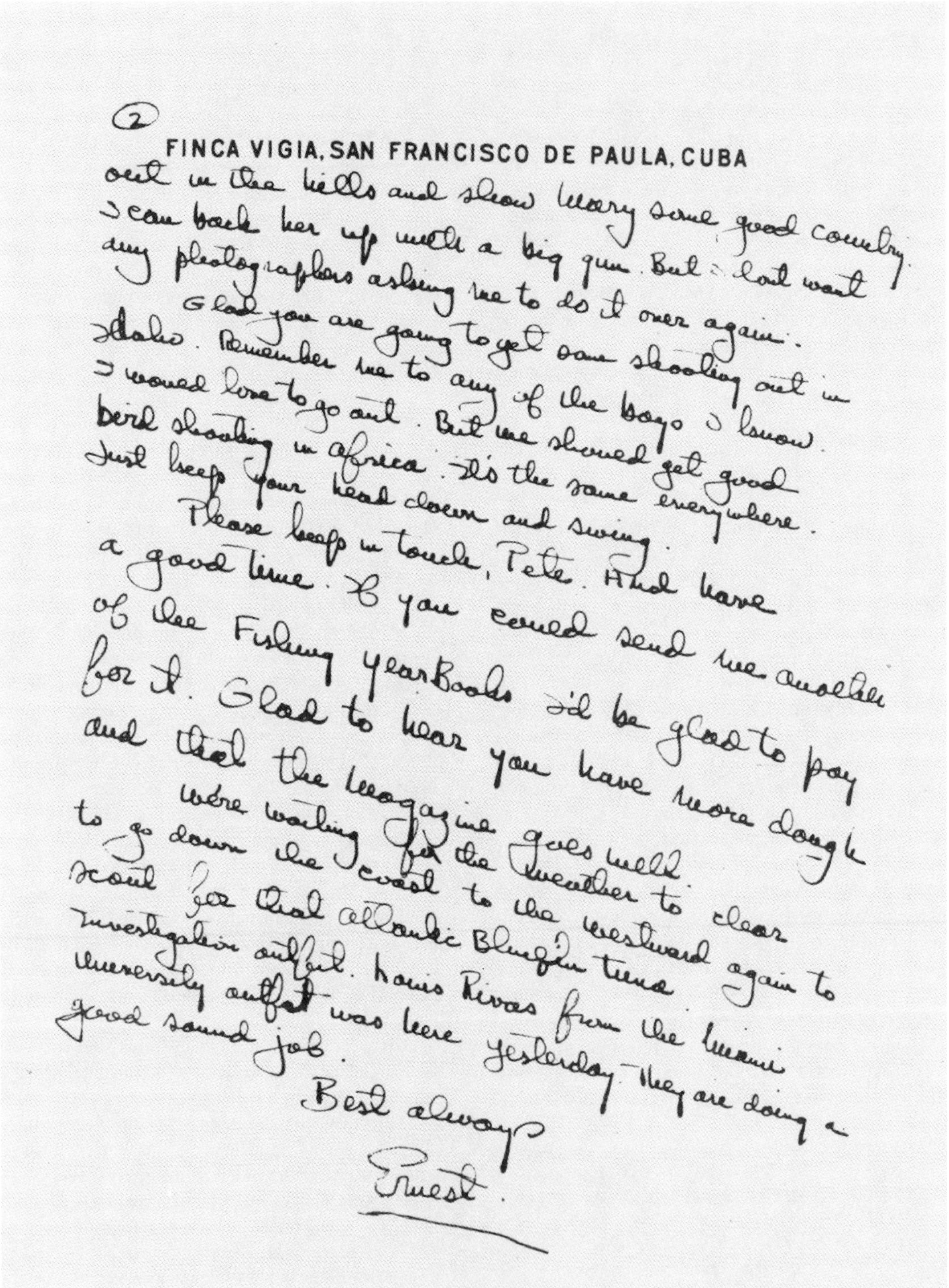

(2)

FINCA VIGIA, SAN FRANCISCO DE PAULA, CUBA

out in the hills and show Mary some good country.
I can back her up with a big gun. But I don't want
any photographers asking me to do it over again.
Glad you are going to get some shooting out in
Idaho. Remember me to any of the boys I know.
I would love to go out. But we should get good
bird shooting in Africa. It's the same everywhere.
Just keep your head down and swing.

Please keep in touch, Pete. And have
a good time. If you could send me another
of the Fishing Year Books I'd be glad to pay
for it. Glad to hear you have more dough
and that the magazine goes well.

We were waiting for the weather to clear
to go down the coast to the westward again to
scout for that atlantic Bluefin tuna. Louis Rivas from the Miami
investigation outfit. Louis Rivas from the Miami
University outfit was here yesterday — they are doing a
good sound job.

Best always

Ernest.

Last page of Hemingway's letter on hunting to Peter Barrett, author of works on hunting and fishing, 20 January 1961 (Charles Hamilton Auctions, Sale Number 78, Item 199, 13 June 1974)

Hemingway near the end of his life in Ketchum, Idaho (photograph by John Bryson, Ernest Hemingway Collection, John F. Kennedy Library)

Mark Twain as he was also a twentieth-century Byron, but he was unquestionably a great writer, a great artist in prose, the inventor of a style that has influenced other writers more than any other in our time.

LILLIAN HELLMAN, playwright—He was a wonderful writer. I read proof on his first book when I was a 20-year-old at Horace Liveright [the publishing house]. "In Our Time," his first collection of short stories, came in as a manuscript, and I remember the great joy of taking it home that first night. I still think it was his best book.

OLIVER LaFARGE, novelist—The use of English without elaboration, the directness of statement, the clarity of his prose liberated me of an attempt to write in a "literary" manner. I think his more recent writing fell off badly, but I think he will stand as one of the very great short-story writers, and one of the great novelists. His use of dialogue to tell a story was absolutely extraordinary.

TENNESSEE WILLIAMS, playwright—To begin with a somewhat obvious statement, twentieth-century literature began with Proust's "The Remembrance of Things Past" and with Hemingway's "The Sun Also Rises," since literary history has already established the fact that Joyce was not and never was meant to be an artist with a comparably wide audience. Hemingway never retired from his life into his workshop. He knew that an artist's work, the heart of it, is finally himself and his life, and he accomplished as few artists that have lived in our time, or any, the almost impossibly difficult achievement of becoming, as a man, in the sight of the world and time he lived in, the embodiment of what his work meant, on its highest and most honest level, and it would seem that he continued this achievement until his moment of death, which he would undoubtedly call his "moment of truth," in all truth.

J. B. PRIESTLEY, British novelist and playwright—Hemingway had a tremendous influence on writers all over the world, and on the whole it was a good influence. He was a subtle writer with the ability to put his message over in a simple way. Mind you, I didn't always agree with his work.

CYRIL CONNOLLY, British author and critic—I think Hemingway was one of the half-dozen greatest living writers, a Titan of the age we live in. I put him with Joyce, Eliot and Yeats among the real founders of what is called the modern movement in writing. I think he still had a great deal to say.

CARL SANDBURG, poet and biographer—He was a writer who profoundly influenced style in America in the novel and the short story. He got a style going among many fellows using short words. He had no stock heroes. He chose his own order of people to love. His was a peculiar wisdom, sometimes a little bit flagrant, but his own.

V. S. PRITCHETT, author and critic—The thing that strikes me most in looking back over his writings was that he revived the vernacular tradition and this was a most important contribution to Anglo-American literature. He reintroduced speech as a way of conveying stories. The only writer we had at all like him was Kipling. His influence on the short story was enormous, wherever you go, whether in India, the Middle East or elsewhere, you find that young writers have read his short stories and are trying to imitate him.

C. P. SNOW, British novelist—He was a great original artist whose influence has spread all over the world. No novelist in the world has produced such a direct effect on other people's writing.

HARVEY BREIT, critic and playwright—He once told me he was working in a new mathematics, and I was skeptical. I thought that even great and simple men delude themselves. But it turned out he was working in it. He had staked out a unique ter-

Hemingway's death was front-page news throughout the world (The New York Times, *3 July 1961*)

rain. Over and beyond the battle cries that meant so much to so many of us, over and beyond his categorical imperatives of "nada" and "courage" and the struggle to last, to hold out, to be just, to love a good friend, and put down a bad enemy, over and beyond all these consistent truths in his work, he had found a language. It was more than an ear that recorded; it was a marvelous medium, immutable, through which all his experience passed, and an essence of truth resulted. He was a poet, really a poet, through his prose.

WILLIAM FAULKNER, novelist and Nobel laureate—One of the bravest and best, the strictest in principles, the severest of craftsmen, undeviating in his dedication to his craft; which is to arrest for a believable moment the antics of human beings involved in the comedy and tragedy of being alive. To the few who knew him well he was almost as good a man as the books he wrote. He is not dead. Generations not yet born of young men and women who want to write will refute that word as applied to him.

JOHN O'HARA—I can't think of any other in history who directly influenced so many writers. Especially young writers.

ROBERT FROST, poet—Ernest Hemingway was rough and unsparing with life. He was rough and unsparing with himself. It is like his brave free ways that he should die by accident with a weapon. Fortunately for us, if it is a time to speak of fortune, he gave himself time to make his greatness. His style dominated our story-telling long and short. I remember that fascination that made me want to read aloud "The Killers" to everybody that came along. He was a friend I shall miss. The country is in mourning.

The Mark Twain Journal, *11 (Summer 1962), was dedicated to Hemingway and included these appraisals.*

Andre Maurois

Every young writer in France is an admirer of Ernest Hemingway. As a matter of fact he had a great influence on the young French generation. His style is unique and has been imitated all over the world.

Upton Sinclair

I am afraid that anything I would say about poor Hemingway would not please his readers. He was one more of those pitiful victims of "John Barleycorn"; and if you want to know what I think about that read *The Cup of Fury.*

Robert Graves

I repeat I cannot write anything about Hemingway. *De mortius nil nisi bonum,* and I have nothing good that I can honestly say about him. His ways were not mine.

Langston Hughes

Ernest Hemingway was a highly readable writer, one whose stories lost no time in communicating themselves from the printed page to the reader, from dialogue on paper to dialogue sounding in one's own ears and carrying his tales forward as if the characters were alive and *right there* in person. The immediacy of Hemingway's reality conveys itself with more than deliberate speed, and with an impact few other writers so quickly and so compactly achieve. Some commentators said years ago that Hemingway was a writer's writer. He turned out to he a reader's writer as well.

Archibald MacLeish published this tribute to Hemingway in Life, *51 (14 July 1961), pp. 70–71.*

HIS MIRROR WAS DANGER

I wrote a poem some years ago in which there was a question about Hemingway and an answer:

. . . the lad in the Rue de Notre Dame des Champs
In the carpenter's loft on the left-hand side going down—
The lad with the supple look like a sleepy panther—
And what became of him? Fame became of him.
Veteran out of the wars before he was twenty:
Famous at twenty-five: thirty a master—
Whittled a style for his time from a walnut stick
In a carpenter's loft in a street of that April city.

Now, with his death, the question asks itself again: what became of him?

How shall that question be answered now? By the fame still? I don't suppose any writer since Byron has been as famous as Hemingway was when he died, but fame is a young man's passion. It has little to say to the fact of death.

Or is the style the answer? The style remains as surely as the fame. It has been praised, imitated and derided for 30 years, but it endures: the one intrinsic style our century has produced. And yet Hemingway was the last man to wish to be remembered as a stylist, and none of his critics, however much he has admired the style or detested it, has been able or willing to leave his judgment at that.

To answer one must go further back. It is not Hemingway's death or even the manner of his death which poses the question now: it is his life—the fact that his life is over and demands to be looked at, to be measured. What makes the answer difficult is that Hemingway's life was a strange life for a writer, as we think of writers in our time. Writers with us are supposed to be watchers: "God's spies" as John Keats put it once. They are supposed to spend themselves observing the world, watching history and mankind and themselves—particularly themselves: their unsaid thoughts, their secret deeds and dreads. Hemingway was not a watcher: he was an actor in his life. He took part. What he took part in was not the private history of Ernest Hemingway or the social history of Oak Park, Ill. or the intellectual history of a generation of his fellow countrymen. What he took part in was a public—even a universal—history of wars and animals and gigantic fish. And he did take part. He could never go to a war—and he went to every war available to him—without engaging in it. He went to the First World War as an ambulance driver and got his knee smashed by a shell in a front-line trench where no one had sent him. He went to the war in Spain to write a scenario for a movie and learned how you washed the powder burns off your hands without water. He went to the last World War as a correspondent—and worried the high command by turning up with other tools than typewriters—mementos he called them. And between wars there were lions and elephants. And between elephants and lions there were marlin. Also bears.

Again, modern writers, if you can believe the novels, associate with other writers or with other writers' wives or with the people who hang around writers. Hemingway preferred boxers and bicycle racers in Paris, and Charlie Thompson, and Old Bra in Key West, and nightclub addicts in New York and matadors in Spain and commercial fishermen and game-cock fighters in Cuba. He had writer friends. Scott Fitzgerald was a good friend, and Dos Passos sometimes was and sometimes wasn't. But writers as writers—writers disguised as writers—he didn't fancy. He and I had lunch in the middle '20s with Wyndham Lewis, the painter who had set himself up briefly and locally as a literary dictator in London. When the two of us walked off home across the river, Hemingway astonished me by saying, "Did you notice? He ate with his gloves on." He had too—though there were no gloves.

Most modern writers are literary—more so than ever now that the critical mind has completed its conquest—but Hemingway wasn't literary. He read as much as most English professors and he remembered what he read, remembered it usefully, and in its relevance to himself—but he rarely talked about writing. Ezra Pound, the greatest and most successful teacher of writing in our time, gave him up. "The son of a bitch's *instincts* are right," said Pound. But you can't converse about instincts. Even Gide, the most articulate writer about writing in modern France, was defeated by that hulking body and artless air and charming smile. I had dragged Hemingway along to a French literary afternoon where Gide and Jules Romains and others of that generation sat on stiff-backed chairs around a bookshop wall talking as though they had rehearsed all morning, but Hemingway, whom all of them were watching, watched the floor. It was too much for Gide. He dropped the topic, whatever it was, and drew Hemingway aside to explain how he punished his cat. He punished his cat, he said, by lifting him up by the scruff of his neck and saying PHT! in his face. Whether Hemingway restrained a desire to hit him, I don't know. I was watching the back of his head.

A strange life for a writer and a difficult life to judge at the end. Indeed, a difficult life to judge before the end—which is perhaps why Hemingway attracted, alive, more critics of more schools and opinions than most writers who have been dead for centuries. Writers generally are judged by their work, but Hemingway's life kept threatening to get in the way of his work with the result that his critics never found themselves in agreement. Those who were drawn to him called him, as one of them actually did on the day of his death, "a man who lived it up to write it down." Those who were repelled—and most of the hostile critics seemed to have been repelled emotionally as well as intellectually—called him in one form of words or another a phony: a man who ran away from his real task to masquerade as a big game hunter or a hero or a tough guy. What they will say now I don't know—perhaps that he had run as far as he could and that the truth caught up with him at 7:30 on the morning of the second of July.

Both views are based on a misconception of the relation between a writer's task and a writer's life. Both conceive of life and writing as different and even contradictory things. The deploring critic thinks of Hemingway's life as a betrayal of his obligation: you don't fight marlin by the hour and watch the killing of 1,500 bulls if you are loyal to your craft. The admiring critic thinks of the obligation as incidental to the life: you shoot grizzlies and then you write about it. Neither understands the simple and primary fact that a writing—a true writing—is not the natural by-product of an isolated experience, nor the autonomous creation of an isolated man, but the consequence of a collision between the two. Neither realizes that the collision when it occurs, even when the experience is a lion in the gun sights or a German in a Normandy hedge, may provide, for the right writer, something more than a thrill and something very different from an escape. It may, indeed, provide a realization—precisely such a realization as the art of letters at its greatest is capable of providing: the realization of the meaning of a man. Danger is not the least revealing of the mirrors into which we look.

That this obvious fact was obvious to Hemingway is a matter of record. Long before he had money enough for a safari or time enough to compose a theory of esthetics, had he ever wished to compose one, he had learned that lesson. Of the time in his 20s when he was learning to write, he said, "I found the greatest difficulty, aside from knowing truly what you really felt, rather than what you were supposed to feel . . . was to put down what really happened in action; what the actual things were which produced the emotion that you experienced." The problem, that is to say, was to master the collision of man and event, writer and experience in *both* its terms: the perception of the event as it really was and the recognition of the emotion that the event really excited. A later remark of his added another dimension to the task. In a letter to a young man who had sent him some imitative work he said, ". . . see the things you write about not through my eyes and my ears but through your own with your language." To see "with language," to see "what really happened in action," and to recognize "what you really felt, rather than what you were supposed to feel," *with language* was a writer's task as Hemingway saw it. Most writers I think would agree that the task was well seen and that accomplishment of the task so defined would be anything but a betrayal of the obligation which every writer assumes. To put together what "really" happened and what you "really" felt as you faced it is not only to see the lion but to understand the man. The writer who can do this, as Hemingway demonstrated that he could, is no less a poet of the human experience—God's spy—than the writer who spies upon nearer and more familiar worlds.

What became of Hemingway? Fame became of him, yes, but something more, I think, than fame. Art became of him—became of him in the truest and the largest sense. Rilke once said of the writing of a verse: it is not enough merely to feel; one must also see and touch and know. But it is not enough, either, to see and touch and know: one must have memories of love and pain and death. But not even these memories are enough: the memories must be "turned to blood within us" so that they are no longer distinguishable from ourselves. Experience, Rilke was declaring, must turn into man before a poem can be written. Experience, that is to say, must reach such an intensity that it contains our own being. When that happens—when experience and man *so* meet—the poem may be written and when the poem is written we may discover who we are.

Hemingway brought himself to face experience of this intensity not once, but more than once. And what became of him was that great triumph.

Chapter Seven: 3 July 1961–1999

1964

5 May   Scribners publishes *A Moveable Feast*.

1967

8 May   *By Line: Ernest Hemingway*, a collection of nonfiction, is published by Scribners.

1969

13 August   *The Fifth Column and Four Stories of the Spanish Civil War* is published in New York City.

1970

6 October   Scribners publishes *Islands in the Stream*.

1972

17 April   *The Nick Adams Stories*, edited by Philip Young, is published by Scribners.

1980

18 July   The Hemingway Room is officially opened at the John F. Kennedy Library in Boston, Massachusetts.

1985

24 June   Scribners publishes *The Dangerous Summer*.

18 November *Dateline: Toronto*, a collection of Hemingway's articles for the *Toronto Star* and *Star Weekly*, is published by Scribners.

1986

28 May   *The Garden of Eden* is published by Scribners.

1987

2 December *The Complete Short Stories of Ernest Hemingway: The Finca Vigía Edition*, with an introduction by John, Patrick, and Gregory Hemingway, is published by Scribners.

1999

21 July   To mark the Hemingway Centenary, Scribners publishes Hemingway's book about his second African safari: *True at First Light,* edited by Patrick Hemingway.

After Hemingway's death President John F. Kennedy arranged for Mary Hemingway to travel to Cuba to retrieve her husband's papers. After Kennedy's assassination in 1963 she promised that the Hemingway papers would be housed in the Kennedy presidential library after it was completed. In 1980 the Ernest Hemingway collection was opened at the John F. Kennedy Library in Boston.

In 1963 Scribners announced that it would publish Hemingway's Paris memoir, which he had written in the late 1950s. On 5 May 1964 *A Moveable Feast* appeared, a series of sketches of Hemingway's friends and associates including Gertrude Stein, Ezra Pound, and F. Scott Fitzgerald in Paris. The book was well received, but some critics noted that the sketches were petty and cruel, especially the three portraits of Fitzgerald.

The next book with new Hemingway material was published on 6 October 1970. *Islands in the Stream* is the story of a painter, Thomas Hudson, and consists of three sections: "Bimini," about Hudson's relationship with his three sons; "Cuba," about Hudson and his former wife; and "At Sea," about his hunt for the crew of a German submarine. The book was the "land, sea and air novel" on which Hemingway had worked after World War II. While most critics were happy to have a new Hemingway novel, many judged the book to be uneven, with "Bimini" as the best section.

Hemingway's account of the Dominguín-Ordóñez bullfights of 1959 was published as *The Dangerous Summer* by Scribners on 24 June 1985. The book as published was closer to the *Life* article than to Hemingway's first draft. Again, reviewers were pleased to have a new Hemingway book but pointed out that it was weak compared to *Death in the Afternoon* and Hemingway's other works.

Less than a year later (28 May 1986) Scribners published *The Garden of Eden,* the novel Hemingway worked on during the late 1940s and mid 1950s. The book produced a mild sensation because of its depiction of Catherine Bourne's bisexuality and the role-switching in which she and her husband David engage. The plot treating painter Nick and Barbara had been eliminated. Most reviewers liked the book, but many Hemingway scholars criticized Scribners for the editing of the work: for them, eliminating material from Hemingway's manuscript misrepresented his intentions. *The Garden of Eden* was the worst violation of Hemingway's insistence

on textual control; but all of the books published from his work in progress were cut and edited after his death.

To celebrate the centenary of Hemingway's birth, on 21 July 1999 Scribners published *True at First Light,* the book he wrote about his 1953–1954 African safari; it was edited by Hemingway's son Patrick from a longer manuscript version. Excerpts from the so-called "African Journals" had appeared in three issues of *Sports Illustrated* (20 December 1971, 3 January 1972, and 10 January 1972).

This article appeared in The New York Times *on 29 July 1961, p. 21. It provoked a letter to the editor by novelist Glenway Wescott, the model for Robert Prentiss in* The Sun Also Rises. *Wescott's letter was published on 9 August.*

Mrs. Hemingway Is Cautious On Publication of Manuscripts

Says She Cannot Yet Tell if Any Will Reach Print— Burns Some Papers

HAVANA, July 28–There is no prospect that any new work by Ernest Hemingway will be published in the near future, according to his widow.

Mrs. Hemingway said she was unable to determine yet whether anything further would ever be published. She arrived here this week to go through her husband's papers and to discuss the possibility of setting up a Hemingway museum.

She said that, in accordance with her husband's instructions, she was reading the papers at their estate, twenty miles outside Havana, and burning all documents of a personal nature. These include a large number of letters the author had written over the last twenty years and never sent, as well as old bank books and check stubs.

In addition, she said, there were "hundreds of thousands of typewritten pages" of recent work.

"As his heir it is my duty to go carefully when it is a question of what to do about the disposal of any manuscripts," she said.

Mrs. Hemingway said she would have to see if he had left any instructions about the manuscript material, before deciding whether all or any part of it should be kept or destroyed.

Monument at Hemingway's grave, Ketchum, Idaho

What she is looking for, she said, besides any blanket instructions about the work, is "notes at the bottom of a page like 'burn this,' or 'this is pretty good.'"

Premier Fidel Castro has suggested to her that the home outside Havana be turned into a museum. Mrs. Hemingway said she felt "honored" by the proposal and recalled that "Ernest was very fond of the Cuban people."

Major Works Reported

On July 8, Mrs. Hemingway said her husband's unpublished works included some poetry and at least two novels including a major work in the vault of a Havana bank.

The writer, who was killed by an apparently self-inflicted gunshot wound on July 2 in Ketchum, Idaho, had earlier described one of the novels as "a big one all about the land, sea and the air."

In the current issue of *The Saturday Review,* Carlos Baker, an authority on Hemingway, writes that two completed manuscripts are in the hands of Charles Scrib-

ner's Sons. These are "The Dangerous Summer," an account of the 1959 bullfighting season in Spain, three excerpts from which appeared in Life magazine, and a collection of reminiscences of Paris in the Nineteen Twenties.

However, this was denied last night by Burroughs Mitchell, a vice president and editor of Scribner's. He said the final decision on what would be published was "up to Mrs. Hemingway."

Hemingway's Work

Novelist Urges That Unpublished Material Be Preserved

TO THE EDITOR OF THE NEW YORK TIMES:

Mrs. Hemingway having been reported as stating in your issue of July 29 that there are hundreds of thousands of typewritten pages of recent work by Ernest Hemingway, surely we are entitled to be hopeful of some further publication, unless she proceeds over-zealously to destroy it all. Evidently she admitted to The Times correspondent that she has not yet found instructions from Hemingway authorizing her to do so.

I feel impelled, almost honor-bound and duty-bound, to express my sadness and dismay at the possibility at any such waste and loss. In my opinion he was the most important and influential writer of his generation in the world. Any and every piece of his work, even unfinished work, is to be valued. Indeed, as he was a perfectionist, some things that he was not able to express to his satisfaction may prove to be of greater interest (to future biographers and students of literature if not to the general reading public) than certain of his second-best stories already published.

It is to be hoped that his publisher and his sons and close friends will not hesitate to call Mrs. Hemingway's attention to this before it is too late. Even Hemingway's own possible dissatisfaction with his unpublished texts ought not to weigh too heavily in the balance. He had been in ill health for some time.

In the course of literary history a good deal of immortal work has been preserved and published against the author's expressed wishes.

In the general world-wide lament for Hemingway's death there has been a constant note of gratitude to Mrs. Hemingway for her devotion and helpfulness which he so grandly acknowledged again and again, and at the compassion appropriate to the final fatal circumstance. I hope that I have not implied that her judgment of his literary art is less sure and less authoritative than anyone else's.

But the evaluation of posthumous literary material requires above all an objective mind or, better still, a number of objective minds. She ought not to expect objectivity of herself now. Let her not feel any anxiety about Hemingway's reputation.

All of his work may be confidently entrusted to the world for that general delight and edification which he intended and for which he labored, tiring himself to death.

GLENWAY WESCOTT.
Rosemont, N.J., Aug. 3, 1961.

Mary Hemingway published this article on the editing and publication of A Moveable Feast *in* The New York Times Book Review, *10 May 1964, pp. 26–27.*

The Making of the Book: A Chronicle and a Memoir

The conception and then the construction of "A Moveable Feast" went on for a long time in various places, but I think of it as beginning, prematurely, at San Lorenzo del Escorial, outside Madrid. Regretfully, as we always left every place, Ernest and I left our autumn home in the Felipe II hotel there on Nov. 17, 1956, and, with an Italian friend driving the overloaded Lancia, took the Guadarrama road towards Burgos and France. We had just squandered two gay and easy months watching the end-of-season bullfights in northern Spain, and between them had hunted partridge, walked, read and rested in the pine-spiced forests around the great monastery and its village.

Leaving, we followed back roads—enjoying the trees, bright golden poplars, sycamores turned daffodil-yellow or magenta, towering red oaks and rusty beeches; and we slowed down to prolong our last sight of the snow-capped Guadarrama ridges slashing the blue sky ahead of us like quick-frozen waves. We stopped a night at Biarritz, another night at Ernest's old hotel at Chartres, cheerful but drafty. When we reached the Ritz in Paris, we were assigned suite 56, which had a tiny sitting room and a large bedroom with a fireplace that smoked incurably.

By the time the Ritz baggage men in their blue smocks had relieved the Lancia of its high head-load of bags and scoured its insides of other bags, the sitting room was impassable and a narrow path led through the bedroom. (We seemed never to be able to go any-

Advertisement for the movie based on Hemingway's Nick Adams stories (20th Century-Fox, 1962). The script was written by A. E. Hotchner.

where with less than 30 pieces of luggage.) Ernest over-tipped the *bagagistes* as usual, but they glowered at him, cornered him and made a speech. Since 1936, when he had been on his way home from Spain, they had been making the same speech. They wanted him to know that this time it was *vraiment sérieux*. His trunks of the earlier days were falling apart in the hotel's basement. They could no longer be responsible for the contents. If Ernest would not reclaim them, the recourse *inévitable* would be to send the trunks to the Paris garbage-burning plant.

When we had unpacked and achieved our sort of order in our rooms, Ernest asked to have his old trunks brought upstairs. They were two small, fabric-covered, rectangular boxes, both opening at the seams, the sort of trunk, I imagined, which, neat and pristine, would have accompanied Henry James on his European journeys. The baggage men easily pried open the rusted locks, and Ernest was confronted with the blue-and-yellow-covered penciled notebooks and sheaves of typed papers, ancient newspaper cuttings, bad water colors done by old friends, a few cracked and faded books, some musty sweatshirts and withered sandals. Ernest had not seen the stuff since 1927, when he packed it and left it at the hotel before going to Key West. Tentatively, as a man would peer into the octopus tank in an aquarium, he looked at the remnants of his young manhood, picked up one notebook, then another and leafed through it, scanning.

"It's wonderful," he said, looking up from one. "It was just as hard for me to write then as it is now. Cheering." Even though Ernest was not writing anything but letters, our nine weeks in Paris that winter were more subdued than usual. Ernest was valiantly following a severely restricted diet which would reduce the cholesterol content of his blood, and we customarily dined in our room. While the racing lasted at Auteuil, we went there every day, lunching in the glassed-in box under the roof, undramatically making neither great losses nor big wins in our wagers. When the racing finished, we returned to our old habit of walking from the Ritz over to Ernest's favorite streets on the Left Bank, the Boulevard St.-Michel, the Rue de Seine where George Sand lived and Raymond Duncan ran his bizarre academy, the Rue Bonaparte where Edouard Manet was born, St.-Germain des Prés where Anatole France lived. At Christmas time when the Grands Boulevards bloomed with bright-colored stalls showing clothing, candy, geegaws and frivolities for sale, we prowled from one to another of the shooting galleries and blasted down the moving cardboard-duck targets. Consistently we won the best prizes, which were bottles of bad champagne, and delighted the proprietors by refusing to accept them.

Before we left Paris at the end of January, to sail to New York again in the Senlis suite of the Ile de France, Ernest went up the Champs Elysées to the luggage shop of Louis Vuitton and invested a month's income in bags. The valet on our floor and I helped him transfer the notebooks, papers and books from the ancient trunks into new ones, and the valet agreed to dispose of the clothing.

At sea on Jan. 26, 1957, I wrote in my diary: "The Ile goes from New York on a Caribbean cruise which touches at Matanzas [Cuba] and Papa has decided to stay aboard her, thus simplifying the transport homewards of our 33 pieces of luggage."

Except for a brief excursion to New York to loaf around Toots Shor's restaurant and see the middleweight championship between Sugar Ray Robinson and Carmen Basilio, we stayed home in Cuba for the rest of 1957. Our friend, Denis Zaphiro, had come from Kenya, where he was and is a game warden, to fish the Gulf Stream for marlin. We spent two or three days a week trailing marlin bait through that navy-blue river, but it was an unfruitful summer until August when Denis hooked and brought in two sizeable fish, one weighing more than 400 pounds, as I recall.

On nonfishing days Ernest went early to work at his typewriter on top of the bookcase in his room; I housekept and gardened, and we had a long swim together before lunch with or without guests. Afterwards we read, walked the *finca*'s three hills, had music and another swim at twilight. Now much of Ernest's afternoon reading was in his old notebooks. Soon after we returned from New York, he gave me a manuscript on which he had been working, a novel set in southern France in the twenties, to put into one of our safe deposit boxes in Havana.

He was going to do something about Paris in the early days, he said. Mostly on his typewriter, partly by pencil as he sat at our 10-foot-long library table, he began "A Moveable Feast." I retyped as usual, correcting spelling and punctuation and consulting him about phrases which I thought needed reorganization. By December he had written the opening chapter and the Gertrude Stein and Ford Madox Ford chapters.

"It's not much about you," I once objected. "I thought it was going to be an autobiography."

"It's biography by *remate*," Ernest said. *Remate* idiomatically is used to mean a two-wall shot in jai alai. "By reflection."

When we went to Idaho for the autumn bird shooting, he took the book with him, and when we went to Spain in the spring of 1959, he took some of the chapters with him. "Sketches," he called them, pretending to be sardonic. "In those days the editors always called them 'little sketches not short stories' and returned them."

In Spain Ernest was persuaded to do a book about the rivalry in the bull rings between the two great matadors, Antonio Ordoñez and his brother-in-law, Luis Miguel Dominguin, and he put the Paris book aside. But by the time he had finished the bullfight book, "The Dangerous Summer," and had read the abridgement of it published in Life, he put aside that book in turn. He was disgusted by the venality and injustices he had encountered in the bullfight business, and decided not to publish his work as a book. Instead he wrote more sketches about his first years in Paris and revised and polished his work.

He had planned, I guess, to do a second book about Paris, as he suggests in his preface to this one. One reason he would have preferred to do two small books rather than one large one is that he had found his longest book, "For Whom the Bell Tolls," too heavy to hold comfortably while reading in bed. "'The Bell' was too big," he said. "A man should never write anything too big to read in bed." We read in bed a great deal, to ourselves and aloud to each other.

④ and then go on from there. It was easy then because there was always one true sentence that you knew or had seen or had heard someone say. If I started to write elaborately or else like some one introducing or presenting something I found that I could cut that scroll work or ornament out and throw it away and start with the first true simple declarative sentence I had written. Up in that room I decided that I would write one story about each thing that I knew about. I was trying to do this all the time I was writing and it was very good and severe discipline. It was in that room too that I learned not to think about anything that I was writing from the time I stopped writing until I started again the next day. That way my subconscious would be working on it and at the same time I would be listening to other people, noticing everything, I hoped, learning, I hoped, and I would

Page from the manuscript for A Moveable Feast *(Ernest Hemingway Collection, John F. Kennedy Library)*

After Ernest died I found the typescript of "A Moveable Feast" in a blue box in his room in our house in Ketchum, Idaho, together with his dated draft of his preface and a list of titles, a check mark against this title as well as several others. Making a list of titles and choosing one were the final chores Ernest performed for a book. He must have considered the book finished except for the editing which even the most meticulous manuscripts require.

A year ago Ernest's longtime friend, Malcolm Cowley, the critic, read the typescript and urged me to publish it. When I could clear a space from other work waiting attention on my desk, I went over the book and gave it the same hard-headed editing I would have done if I had been copying from Ernest's original typing and hand script as I used to do in Cuba. Working toward lucidity I put in or removed commas, checked spelling, sometimes but rarely cut out repetitious words or phrases which I felt sure were accidental rather than intentional or for phonetic or poetic effect. With Harry Brague, Ernest's editor at Scribner's, I made a few further cuts when we went over the manuscript together, and we switched about a couple of the chapters for continuity's sake. No one added any word to the book.

A score of times Ernest and I walked the routes through Paris together which he describes having taken 40 years ago. They read accurately, but I was concerned that he might have put in a street where it did not belong. No matter if he left some out. A friend of mine on holiday in Paris followed the itineraries and reported they were correct. But I remained concerned. So I flew over and retraced all the steps Ernest wrote he took, first by myself and then with my friend, Gordon Parks, the photographer and writer. Ernest had made two mistakes in the spellings of street names. Otherwise his memory had been perfect.

Journalist Lewis Galantiére knew Hemingway in Paris. His review of Hemingway's memoir was published in The New York Times Book Review, *10 May 1964, pp. 1, 26.*

"There Is Never Any End to Paris"

'A Moveable Feast,' Vintage Hemingway, Is Full of Love, Loathing and Bitterness

When Ernest and Hadley Hemingway came to Paris in December, 1921, the dreary aftermath of World War I was receding and life on the Left Bank had begun to revive. Already, the beat had been marked out which young American aspirants in letters and the arts follow to this day. It ran and still runs, as everybody knows, the length of the Boulevard Montparnasse from the Closerie des Lilas at the Observatoire to the Restaurant du Petit Trianon opposite the dingy railway station, and by one route or another down to St.-Germain-des-Pres and the Seine.

There were detours and bypaths. Behind the boulevard, painters found studios and writers rooms in the direction of the Montparnasse Cemetery. Students drank beer at Balzar's in the Rue des Ecoles. Those who could afford it lunched in view of the Luxembourg Gardens at the Café de Médicis, where they drank the 1915 vintages of the Hospice de Beaune topped off by the Marquis d'Audiffred's *marc de Bourgogne.* John Dos Passos and the playwright John Howard Lawson had come upon the Rendezvous des Mariniers on the Ile Saint-Louis ("Monsieur Dos Passos!" Mme. Lecomte cried in 1920; "I used to darn his socks for him.") which 10 years later was taken over, like Sutton Place in New York, by—it must be agreed—a bearable species of "the rich and well-born."

Hemingway carried letters from Sherwood Anderson (doubtless from others, too), but in that small tranquil world there was no need of formal introduction. "Everybody" frequented the same half-dozen cafés, ate in one or another of the same score of restaurants. Acquaintance was easily made, talk was on matters of common interest; for this generation, still in the temper of "art for art's sake," ideological passions were as yet unknown. Artists and writers were a united family and nothing more than the conventional contempt for the bourgeoisie inherited from the romantics of 1830 divided them off from the rest of the world.

Along the route between Montparnasse and the St.-Germain quarter stood two rest camps in the Rue de l'Odéon. One was Adrienne Monnier's lending library, the Maison des Amis des Livres, where certain leading writers of the Nouvelle Revue Française forgathered every afternoon and one was privileged to hear their conversation. Gide, Valéry, Larbaud (translator and short-story writer), Léon-Paul Fargue (poet and night-wandering raconteur), Jules Romains and, when he was not absent *en poste,* the poet-ambassador Claudel. Here Larbaud, one evening, read his famous lecture that was the first evaluation of "Ulysses."

Across the way was the lending library of the Princeton parson's daughter with whom Mlle. Monnier shared a flat in the same street. Sylvia Beach's Shakespeare & Co. Miss Beach was to publish "Ulysses" in February 1922, and Joyce, not normally a man to circulate much, came in to pick up and return page-proofs, later to read reviews and hear reports of sales. Here also, one found and talked to every British and American author who turned up in Paris.

Adrienne was plump, beaming and voluble in the full-skirted Quaker-grey dress she wore in her shop. Sylvia, in a tailored suit, was bone-dry of body and laconic wit, receiving with a smile that verged at times on a sardonic leer, offering no conversation unless it was wanted. This straight-backed young woman, in whom every gesture displayed the old style of breeding, was endlessly tolerant of the most perverse human foibles. With Nelson Dean Jay of the Morgan bank, she was one of the two most civilized and authentic Americans in Paris.

There were, as yet, relatively few Americans about. Ezra Pound had settled in Paris; Gertrude Stein and Miss Toklas were in their *pavillon* in the Rue de Fleurus; Man Ray was there. Will Bradley was establishing the literary agency which Jenny, his widow, would manage so remarkably after his early death; Edna Millay, gay and sans make-up, had her own small circle. Janet Flanner and Virgil Thomson were already old Parisians; Hart Crane had come and gone. Harold Stearns, a Montmartre character, introduced one to his Harvard master, George Santayana, talked epistemology—and took to writing the racetrack column for *The Paris Herald,* under the by-line, Peter Pickem.

It was not until 1923 that Americans came in a flood, prompted by the European currency inflations or supported by Guggenheim fellowships. They arrived at a moment when the Right Bank had come to life, glittering with luxury and vibrant with new energy—the theaters of Dullin and Baty, a brilliant film world and, above all, the seasons of the Ballets Russes. It was here that Diaghileff, the most extraordinary animator of the arts since the Renaissance patrons, found employment for so many painters and composers—and without which Stravinsky's music might have gone long years unperformed.

On the Left Bank the light brightened, the cafés became more animated, and a general air of happiness spread from the homely fact that so many who frequented them were writers and artists actively at work. The miseries they may have known were of a private order; for them, at any rate, the time was not out of joint.

Such, in brief, was the Paris in which the Hemingways swam.

"A Moveable Feast" is composed of 20 sketches, rewritten from Hemingway's notebooks of the years 1921–1926. Though the volume has the air of a random compilation, it is in fact a calculated production, and this for two reasons: first, because embedded in its pages are messages to the few readers who will know for whom they are meant; and, secondly, because as an artist Hemingway never allowed himself to appear in undress.

"Emotions are the only facts," Havelock Ellis once wrote. This is a book of love, loathing and bitterness. Love of Paris is the matter of the parts in which Hemingway relates how he settled into a routine as a writer in the tranquil years before what he calls "the rich" arrived. Written with that controlled lyricism of which he was master, these pages are marvelously evocative.

Love of his young wife shines softly in his revelation of an adoring, undemanding nature, achieved through the extraordinary felicity and tenderness of the dialogue he lends Hadley—a true triumph of Hemingway's art. He loved Ezra Pound, and though he has little to tell about him—there is no portrayal, no record of his ideas or singularities—it is clear that this was a good and innocent man, able to disarm Hemingway's suspicion, which was the only path to his affection. Love again of Sylvia Beach, about whom he tells us little more, but who was the rock on which he could rest, the understanding soul to whom one need never tell more than one had a mind to reveal.

There were others Hemingway loved—Bill Bird, whom he does not write about and who printed Hemingway's first book (a pamphlet-length version of "In Our Time") at his Three Rivers Press; "Chink," his Anglo-Irish wartime comrade on the Italian front, referred to in passing; the poet Evan Shipman. But they were few, for Hemingway did not give himself easily; there was something wary, secretive, beneath his often boisterous gaiety.

Mostly, this is a book about people, and the choice he made among the many he knew remains perplexing, despite the prefatory note that it was made "for reasons sufficient to the writer." One asks at first why room was found for a brief moment with the painter Pascin that tells us nothing. Why, after 35 years, should Hemingway embalm an encounter with a flashy nonentity and another with an anonymous homosexual, both pieces savagely written and serving no literary purpose? Why, if he so disliked kindly and helpful old Ford Madox Ford, should he not tell us the reason, instead of printing a thin and stupid anecdote which concerns—but in this example unconvincingly—Ford's innocent mythomania (as the French call the telling of harmless fables)?

These and their like are quick pencil sketches; the portraits, "warts and all," are of Gertrude Stein and Scott Fitzgerald. Miss Stein was his first intimate friend in Paris. He had been sent to her by Sherwood Anderson, the author of the story, "I Want to Know Why," which Hemingway so brilliantly plagiarized in his own first successful story, "My Old Man." Hemingway is very good on Miss Stein–her egomania, her impatience of contradiction, her dislike of "the drudgery of revision and the obligation to make her writing unintelligible," her quaint preference for Ronald Firbank and Mrs. Belloc Lowndes to D. H. Lawrence and Aldous Huxley. He has a lot of sly and witty fun with her and her companion.

In one of their talks he received the impression that she was trying to persuade him of something more than simple toleration of homosexuality. Miss Stein had prepared at Johns Hopkins in psychology. This did not make her an authority, nor perhaps entirely objective, but it lent her a point of view. Hemingway, who always bristled at the mere sight of a deviate, writes, with the detachment appropriate to the occasion:

"Miss Stein thought that I was too uneducated about sex and I must admit that I had certain prejudices against homosexuality since I knew it in its more primitive aspects. I knew it was why you carried a knife. . . . Under questioning I tried to tell Miss Stein that when you were a boy in the company of men, you had to be prepared to kill a man, know how to do it, and really know that you would do it in order not to be interfered with. . . . If you knew you would kill, other people sensed it very quickly and you were let alone."

What is the significance of this reminiscence? Had that boy with a knife undergone a traumatic experience in the "company of men"–of tramps and on lake boats, as he specifies? Was this the proximate cause of the longing expressed in "Death in the Afternoon": "The only place where you could see life and death, i.e. violent death, now that the wars were over, was the bull ring and I wanted very much to go to Spain where I could study it"? Were war and blood sports a psychic need to which his prodigious talent responded by making of him the supreme poet of the age of violence in which he lived?

Finally, there is the much longer section–more than a quarter of the book–devoted to Scott Fitzgerald, from which Zelda Fitzgerald cannot be said to be left out. We are given first a highly comic episode describing a journey from Paris to Lyons and then back in a car left in Lyons by the Fitzgeralds. In this and in two shorter sketches which follow, Scott is dealt with clinically (one might say) but without petty malice, indeed, with an underlying affection; Zelda with cold hatred.

Then, in the final section, bearing the lyrical title, "There is Never Any End to Paris," the purport of the book is revealed. By a species of literary architectonics at which Flaubert would have cried

"Bravo!" this masterly artist arranges to give unity to his book, plead his case with the wife he left 30-odd years before, and at the same time curse from the grave (as it turns out) the small handful of readers who will know at whom his finger points–in particular two individuals: "the pilot fish" who led him to "the rich" and caused (he says) the corruption of his purity as artist and estrangement from his wife, and "another rich" to whom he felt he owed a grim legacy.

"Those who attract people by their happiness and their performance are usually inexperienced," he writes of himself. "They do not always learn about the good, the attractive, the charming, the soon-beloved, the generous, the understanding rich who have no bad qualities and who give each day the quality of a festival. . . . The rich come led by the pilot fish. . . . In those days I trusted the pilot fish. . . . Nothing ever catches him and it is only those who trust him who are caught and killed. . . . I wagged my tail with pleasure and plunged into the fiesta concept of life to see if I could not bring some fine attractive stick back, instead of thinking, 'If these bastards like it, what is wrong with it?'"

His second legacy is couched in this form: "We had already been infiltrated by another rich using the oldest trick there is. It is that an unmarried young woman . . . goes to live with the husband and wife and then unknowingly, innocently and unrelentingly sets out to marry the husband"–and in this case succeeds.

Par délicatesse, j'ai perdu ma vie; this, though in a raging tone, is Hemingway's last cry. Pathetic defense on the part of a man who sought to show– and, by an art in which credibility triumphs over verisimilitude, long persuaded us–that fortitude is the highest virtue, and that the savage is noble, is laconic, severe, animated by a sense of honor. And yet, in this baffling character there is something that goes deeper than pathos.

More than anything else, the book is a chant of love addressed to his first wife. He knew that in the invincible armor of her candor she possessed a strength greater than his own and forever denied him. Two natures struggled in the breast of this Faust–and they died in each other's grasp, so to say, the lower nature resisting with its last breath. Because there was this struggle, we must speak of tragedy, not of pathos.

Though this may seem at first blush a fragmentary book, it is not so. It should be read as a novel, belongs among the author's better works and is, as "mere writing," vintage Hemingway.

"This profile was one of a dozen small portraits, oils on wood panels, that I painted in Italy during the winter of 1922-23. The two of Hem and the one of Hadley, a beautiful redhead, were painted in their room at a Rapallo hotel. All of Hem's early manuscripts had just been lost; and he was writing and reworking the highly condensed one-page short stories that were later published as *in our time*, and which were the foundation of his literary style. For exercise, we used to box downstairs, our sole gallery an Italian taxi driver-timekeeper, who often was so appalled at our idea of fun that he forgot to signal the end of a round." —HENRY STRATER

Scribners
PUBLISHED BY CHARLES SCRIBNER'S SONS NEW YORK

HEMINGWAY
A Moveable Feast
SCRIBNERS

A Moveable Feast
SKETCHES OF THE AUTHOR'S LIFE IN PARIS IN THE TWENTIES

ERNEST HEMINGWAY

Dust jacket for Hemingway's posthumously published memoir of Paris in the 1920s

Canadian novelist Morley Callaghan published this review of A Moveable Feast *in* The Spectator, *212 (22 May 1964), p. 696. Callaghan had an advantage that most reviewers of the book lacked, since he had been in Paris in the 1920s and had been one of Hemingway's friends—until their boxing match in 1929.*

The Way It Was

The book opens with the young Hemingway sitting at a café on the Place St. Michel, and straightway the old familiar and terribly determined elegiac note is sounded. It is very disquieting. Is he going to try to recapture the rhythms of *A Farewell to Arms,* one wonders unhappily? But soon, and mainly because he is able to recapture some of the feeling he had had for his first wife, Hadley, and their small son in those Paris days between 1921 and 1926, the style gets straightened out; the sad, disturbing and often funny book gets going in its own right. Once again after all these years

we seem to see him sitting alone at the café, writing and hoping. It is very moving. We see him, too, as he watches the fishermen on the banks of the Seine, or goes into the Musée du Luxembourg to study the paintings of Cézanne, and wonders if he could get the same landscape effects in prose.

It was the time when he was writing those little stories that were something new in the language. Working in poverty, and in love with his wife, he was strangely happy. Having given up newspaper work, he was committed to writing and was turning out a kind of story that was so suggestive, so stripped, so objective, so effective in capturing pure sensation that it became a unique kind of poetry. Never again was he to be as original or as objective as he had been in those days. When the time came to write this book, maybe he knew what he had lost. And maybe this knowledge explains the book's bitter tone.

But in those days he wasn't as self-absorbed or as isolated as he makes out. In fact, long before he wrote *The Sun Also Rises,* he had had a peculiar underground fame. And the wonderful thing about him at the time was that he had a generous interest in the work of other unknown writers, was in touch with them, and would

337

go out of his way to try to get them published in the little Paris magazines. Did he forget about the young writers who adored him? Why is it that the main thing he wanted to remember, or get down on paper, was that he had found perfect happiness in isolation, work and love—till other people came into the picture? And the only wisdom he has to offer now, looking back on it, is that other people, any people, are always the enemies of two who are in love and the enemies of the artist also. They smell out happiness, they move in to destroy it. It is always people, never himself, who are to blame.

And so he manages to give the impression that two star-crossed lovers, himself and Hadley, the *Farewell to Arms* theme again, had their happiness destroyed by the great enemy—people. A man's fate is in the people who are interested in him, and if you are ski-ing in the Alps with your girl and people find you there, you can't prevail against them. This is, surely, a pretty childish view of life.

Some of the people to be looked down on are done in the book as set pieces, and not at all in the flow of memories. This faulty structure is the great weakness of the book. And what frightening sketches of people who at one time knew and liked him! There is Ford Madox Ford, who, as editor of the *Transatlantic Review*, had printed some of Hemingway's early work, and who, even before the triumphant appearance of *The Sun Also Rises*, had written a front-page article in the *Herald Tribune Books*, New York, calling him the best young writer in America; Ernest Walsh, the Irish poet, an editor of *This Quarter*, who had first printed "Big Two-Hearted River" and "The Undefeated"; Gertrude Stein, once his motherly friend, who had belittled him in print; Wyndham Lewis, who over the years had deplored Hemingway's love of violence; Pascin, the painter, and Scott Fitzgerald, who as he says had been a loyal friend for years—until they fell out.

The touch he uses in these portraits is controlled, expert, humorous and apparently exact; he is like a proud pool player, who lines up the balls with his cue, says, "That one in the corner pocket," and sinks it cleanly. But underneath the surface humour—it's really a gallows humour—there is a long-nourished savagery, or downright venom, and in his portraits there is the quick leap for the jugular vein.

What a relief it is to find him expressing tenderness and respect and loyalty to Ezra Pound—or affection for Sylvia Beach. And a relief, too, to discover there was a young poet named Evan Shipman whom he liked. Otherwise one could gather he had no capacity for friendship at all. In a prefatory note he says there were many good friends. There were indeed. It is unfortunate that he didn't get some of his old simple friendliness into the book. How much fairer he would

have been to himself in revealing what he was really like in those days. He was actually an attractive, interesting, fascinating companion, dark and brooding though he might be with strange shrewd hunches about people that turned into grudges. He was likeable and simple in manner, too. Savagery that was in him only broke out when he went berserk. What a pity that he withheld so much of himself that was so boyish and engaging. It was all here for him to tell. He isn't berserk in this book. He is a mockingly amusing, cold killer with a weapon he often controls so beautifully—his own prose.

In those days he would tell you he disliked Ford. He would openly scoff at him. But his brother, in his hero-worshipping book, tells how Ford had been sent to visit the Hemingway family home in Chicago. Yet in the sketch Hemingway does of Ford, the two of them sitting at a café, a very expert, very funny sketch, he pictures Ford as a liar and a clown who gave off a body odour that fouled up the air. Was this all there was to Ford? Of course not, and he knew it.

It is true, too, that Wyndham Lewis was a difficult man to meet. He was so self-conscious, so worried that his importance would not be recognised, that he was always ill at ease and without any grace of manner. Hemingway and Lewis met in Pound's studio when Hemingway was teaching Pound to box. Looking back on the meeting, he believed he hated Lewis on sight. He can hardly express his loathing for the meanest-looking man I ever met. And here again Hemingway overdoes it. And why? Only God knows! He had no more interest in trying to understand Lewis than he had in understanding Ford. And yet these highly prejudiced, personal reactions are interesting. In them may be found the keynote to the brilliance of much of his work. With him everything was personal, his work became the projection of his personality. He was not concerned with fairness or charity, or moral judgments, just with his own sensations.

But I, for one, don't care whether or not he was fair to Gertrude Stein. That domineering woman had talked her way into a reputation, and had taken her cracks at him. Now he goes to work on her. It's the literary life, I suppose.

The best and happiest writing in the book, and in some ways the fairest picture he gives of anyone, is of Scott Fitzgerald. The writing turns free and easy. He forgets the Biblical rhythms. He is at home and happy with his subject. The description of a trip to Lyon with Fitzgerald is simply hilarious; it is more than that; he gives a wonderfully vivid glimpse of Fitzgerald in all his changing moods, drunk and sober, and recognises his talent. Yet on end, aside from recognition of the talent, Fitzgerald is so cut down as a person—well, as Hemingway tells it, even the bartender at the Ritz, where

Fitzgerald spent so much time, can't even remember him, but promised to try to do so, if old Hem will write about him and make him memorable.

The terrible disorder in Fitzgerald's life Hemingway blames on Zelda. Poor crazy Zelda, who, he says, was jealous of Scott, and liked to see him get drunk, knowing he wouldn't be able to work. And what may be just as fantastic is Hemingway's explanation of why he began to shy away from Scott. He saw that Scott liked walking in on him to interrupt him, and saw that it was all a plan to make it impossible for him to work. This leaves us with Fitzgerald doing to Hemingway what Zelda was doing to Fitzgerald. It gets mixed up and very complicated. But you must remember they were two men who dramatised everything, simply everything, including each other.

As the book draws to an end there is a curious revelation which is almost shocking in its candour. The idyllic love between Hemingway and his wife had continued up to the writing of *The Sun Also Rises*. When they are ski-ing happily in the Alps, some rich people seek them out. A rich girl moves in with them, and in no time Hemingway has two women, and then finally he has only one and it isn't Hadley any more. "Then you have the rich and nothing is ever as it was again," he says, and his life took another turn, and with sourness he blames the rich for moving in on him and taking away his happiness. Was he so weak and helpless in the presence of the rich? It is such a surprising revelation one can't at first quite believe it, and then comes the thought, it must be true, for it is the first time Hemingway has ever deliberately put himself in a bad light.

John W. Aldridge, author of After the Lost Generation, *reviewed* Islands in the Stream *(New York: Scribners, 1970) for the* Saturday Review, *53 (10 October 1970), pp. 23–26, 39. Like most reviewers, Aldridge found the posthumous novel to be uneven and inferior to Hemingway's other novels.*

Hemingway Between Triumph and Disaster

At the time of his death in 1961 Hemingway is known to have had at least four book-length manuscripts in various stages of preparation. There were the two nonfiction books: *A Moveable Feast,* his collection of Paris sketches published posthumously in 1964, and *The Dangerous Summer,* of which three portions dealing with the Ordoñez-Dominguín bullfights of 1959 had appeared serially in *Life* in 1960. In addition, he had been working on a very long but presumably unfin-

ished novel called *The Garden of Eden* and a book often referred to as the "Land, Sea, and Air Novel" based on Hemingway's experiences during World War II.

In spite of the quantities of gossip that have accumulated around the Hemingway tragedy over the last nine years, very little has been said about his still unpublished works. According to Carlos Baker, his official biographer, the complete text of *The Dangerous Summer* is now "locked away" at Charles Scribner's Sons and seems a generally mediocre piece of writing. Judging by the quality of the *Life* instalments, one would suppose that as a book it would be best kept locked away. Since 1961 it has been impossible to obtain reliable information on either the status or the whereabouts of the two fiction manuscripts, *The Garden of Eden* and the "Land, Sea, and Air Novel," and reports circulated during Hemingway's lifetime were contradictory in the extreme. There is some evidence that he may have worked sporadically on both right up to his final illness and breakdown. But one does not know how far he had progressed or what disposition was later made of them. It may be that they were among the unfinished materials found on his work table after his suicide. It may also be that they were finished and placed in deposit—as his widow and others have said was sometimes his custom—in bank vaults, at his publishers, or with certain trusted bartenders.

In any case, information has been so meager that undoubtedly few people outside Hemingway's immediate circle of family and friends were even aware that such a work as *The Garden of Eden* existed until Baker referred to it in his biography. The description he gives there is far from complete, and it would appear that he saw only a draft of the work in progress. But if the book is as preposterously bad as he makes it seem, one can only hope that the novel's publication will be delayed until such time as it can safely be offered as a literary curiosity too ancient to be any longer embarrassing. Baker characterizes it as "an experimental compound of past and present, filled with astonishing ineptitudes . . . a long and emptily hedonistic novel of young lovers in the old days of Grau-du-Roi and the Costa Brava: page after page of their talk was filled with inconsequential commentary on the color and condition of their hair, the food and drink they were always consuming, and the current state of their suntanned skins."

This is all we have heard about *The Garden of Eden,* and it would seem to be more than enough. About the original manuscript of the "Land, Sea, and Air Novel," on the other hand, we have heard a great deal for years, but what we have heard has told us little. In fact, ever since 1949, when Malcolm Cowley writing in *Life* confirmed the many rumors that Hemingway was engaged on a big new book about the war, the

"Land, Sea, and Air Novel" has been the most widely publicized literary mystery of the past two decades. Scarcely any of the information released during Hemingway's lifetime contained more than an oblique reference to the book's theme or subject matter. One learned only that the action was supposed to be divided into three parts corresponding roughly to the different phases of Hemingway's experience of the war, first as captain of his cruiser, the *Pilar,* during its service as an improvised submarine-chaser in the waters around Cuba, then as a correspondent with the RAF over France and Germany and finally with the Fourth Infantry Division during the Allied drive across Europe. Most of the publicity took the form of reports concerning his rate of progress with the book, and these were so contradictory that they served only to deepen the air of mystery surrounding the whole enterprise. They even caused one to wonder whether the book actually existed.

Cowley said that Hemingway began writing it before Pearl Harbor and by 1949 had completed more than a thousand pages. But as early as 1946 Hemingway had announced that he had completed 1,200 pages—a report which, if true, would indicate that in the following three years he made no progress at all. The columnist Leonard Lyons has been quoted as saying in 1954 that "the long novel is finished and is in a safe-deposit box in a Havana bank." But Hemingway apparently had not heard the news, for in July of 1955 he was still apprising the public of his progress. In fact, he seemed actually to have lost ground. The number of pages he said he had completed had dropped mysteriously to 900. Then a year later in a *Look* article he wrote that he had reached the 850th manuscript page, evidently having lost another fifty pages in the interval. Finally, more than two years later, his rate of loss having sharply accelerated, he is reported to have told Earl Wilson that he had "finished page six-sixty-seven today."

These contradictions may or may not be important in themselves. They may indicate only that Hemingway was speaking on one occasion of rough-draft pages and on another of finished pages. But they may also indicate that there was some real ambiguity about his progress on the book and perhaps about his imaginative relation to his materials. Surely, there is some ground for suspicion on both counts. If, as Cowley claims, Hemingway actually began the book before Pearl Harbor, he appears to have been sufficiently cavalier in his attitude toward it to be able to interrupt the writing again and again to do other things and even to take on other and, one would think, much less important literary projects. Between Pearl Harbor and 1949, in addition to his Q-boat operations with the *Pilar,* he

had been extremely active as a war correspondent, had produced a large quantity of journalism about his experiences, written several introductions to books, and edited the *Men at War* anthology, and in 1949 had suspended all other operations to write *Across the River and Into the Trees.* By 1952 the only material remotely related to the "Land, Sea, and Air Novel" which he apparently had ready to publish was *The Old Man and the Sea,* and that book had nothing to do with the war at sea.

Hemingway's desultory progress on his big novel might not by itself have seemed especially disconcerting when one considered his temperamental restlessness and the wide range of his interests. But there were certain facts that made it deeply disconcerting. For one thing, it was not at all like him to suspend work on his important books for long intervals. In the past he had followed a carefully disciplined routine and rarely allowed himself to be distracted from the writing of a book until it was finished. Yet now he appeared to be almost frantically seeking distraction and taking advantage of any excuse, however trivial, to avoid full commitment to the big novel.

Second, contrary to the statements made by his intimates, it had also not been Hemingway's habit in the past to put finished manuscripts in the bank for extended periods before publishing them. (He evidently did not follow this practice in the case of any of his earlier books.) One does not know whether the big novel, as originally conceived, was ever finished. But if it was and Hemingway thought it successful, there is little likelihood that he would have postponed its publication, particularly at a time when he is known to have been acutely conscious of the need to bolster his reputation with an important new work. Hence, it may be that either he was unable to finish the book as he had planned it, or he did finish it and was dissatisfied with the result.

Hemingway might well have had his doubts, for there was good reason to suppose that he could no longer rely on the absolute rightness of his instincts or work with anything resembling his old energy and endurance. He had apparently been in failing health for quite some time, perhaps even as far back as the war. But the injuries he suffered in the two African plane crashes of 1954 apparently brought him in the next few years to a condition of virtually complete physical and mental breakdown. It seemed obvious also from the internal evidence of the work published in the Fifties that his physical deterioration had been accompanied by a decline in creative vitality. In 1950 he published *Across the River and Into the Trees,* surely the poorest of his novels, and even though *The Old Man and the Sea* represented for many people a triumphant recovery, it could also be seen to have a quality of specious attractiveness and efficiency that in fiction so often results from the avoidance of more problems than are confronted and overcome. It was, in short, a safe book in the sense that it was made up of the best of Hemingway's old market-tested materials, stylistic and dramatic effects which at one time had been arrived at with some real originality and risk through a vital engagement of life, but which were now merely postures and autographs of famous but dead emotions. The problem was not only that Hemingway was sounding like himself in a manner that seemed synthetic. It was also that the self he sounded like was not the self he any longer was. Writing for him had apparently ceased to be an act of self-discovery and had become an act of self-resuscitation.

At any rate, as various commentators have indicated, Hemingway originally planned *The Old Man and the Sea* as a coda or perhaps a fourth part to the sea section of the "Land, Sea, and Air Novel." But, significantly, he chose instead to publish it as a separate short novel. While continuing to work on the big book, he may slowly have revised his original plan to the extent of limiting the action to those experiences relating to the sea only. It may also be, as Carlos Baker suggests, that certain of the materials concerning the war in Europe were incorporated into *Across the River and Into the Trees* and presumably were either used up in that way or never completed as a separate section of the projected long work. In any case, Hemingway may have decided—or his widow may have decided after his death—that a publishable novel could be made out of the sea materials alone, and it is this section, or surviving version, of the big book and not the big book itself (the remainder of which, if it was ever written, is still not accounted for) that has now been published, with some emendations by Mrs. Hemingway, under the title *Islands in the Stream.*

In it Hemingway tells the story of a painter named Thomas Hudson—whose circumstances and experiences in some ways closely resemble his own—during three phases of his life: in the mid-Thirties on the island of Bimini, where Hudson is living alone after a divorce and is visited by his three sons; a number of years later in Cuba during the war, when Hudson is involved in secret antisubmarine activities using his cruiser as a Q-boat; and a short time afterward when Hudson and his crew set out in search of survivors from a destroyed German submarine, this episode culminating in a gun battle and Hudson's wounding.

Knowing that this may well be the last new Hemingway novel we will ever see, one approaches it with mixture of wariness, awe, and considerable anxiety, hoping that through some charity of the gods it will turn out to be very good, but knowing also the chances against the novel's being other than very bad. It would be nice homage to be able to pronounce it a masterpiece. There is diminishment for each of us in the possibility that the book might prove a disaster. But the worst diminishment of all: if honesty forces it upon us to be equivocal, finicky, and faint, to say, as unfortunately one must, that the book is neither very good nor very bad, but that it is both, in some places downright wonderful, in others as sad and embarrassingly self-indulgent as the work of any sophomore.

In this respect it resembles *For Whom the Bell Tolls* perhaps more closely than it does any of the earlier novels. There are other obvious similarities between the two books, but they are most strikingly similar in the way each brings together in a single narrative—at times within the space of a single page—some of the best and worst features of Hemingway's writing. The interesting thing, furthermore, is that these features relate in both books to the same kinds of material. Those sections that are devoted mainly to the description of physical action are almost invariably excellent. Those in which the physical action is interrupted to give Robert Jordan and Thomas Hudson an opportunity to *think,* to analyze their feelings or to find intellectual justification for doing what they are about to do, are as vapid and pretentious as such passages nearly always are in Hemingway. Luckily, the two kinds of material are not present in equal amounts in either book: the passages describing physical action far outnumber the passages of intellectual analysis in both. But the element that finally saves *For Whom the Bell Tolls* is missing from *Islands in the Stream.*

In the latter there is no coherently formed or sufficiently compressed narrative structure in which the action can take on the intensity or the meaning it would seem potentially capable of developing. There is also no thematic design strong enough to support the weight of Hudson's sagging cerebral muscles or to give his thoughts the kind of relevance to the action that Jordan's can finally be seen to have. Where *For Whom the Bell Tolls* is held together by the rigid economy of the form and the tightly interlocking relationship of events occurring over a period of a few days, the new novel is composed of episodes much more widely spaced in time and only vaguely connected by an evolving plot. The result is that such dramatic tension as may be generated in any one of the episodes tends to be dissipated in the lapse of time separating it from the next. The problem is not simply that the book is divided into three parts but that, as a novel, it *disintegrates* into three parts or long short stories, and these are related only by the fact that Hudson is the central if somewhat opaque character in all of them.

Yet taken separately, as, given the looseness of structure, they must be taken, many of the episodes contain the most exciting and effective writing Hemingway has ever done. There is a marvelous ocean-fishing sequence in Part I, the account of a protracted and agonizing struggle by one of Hudson's young sons to bring in a giant fish. The pathos of the boy's almost superhuman effort—which of course ends in last-minute failure—is brilliantly evoked, and one realizes that here is a dimension of Hemingway one has seen before but perhaps not often enough, that side of his nature which was capable of responding not merely to bluster and bravado but with admiration for bravery in the weak and with tenderness toward weakness in the brave. There are also some nicely comic scenes in a Havana bar that are reminiscent of the better moments of *To Have and Have Not,* and the best sustained piece of writing in the book, the long story of the search for the German submariners ending in the gun battle. This is one of the most impressive descriptions of physical action to be found in Hemingway, comparable to the finest of them all, the account of El Sordo's last stand on the hilltop in *For Whom the Bell Tolls.*

Yet in spite of the high quality of individual episodes, one still senses a deficiency in the whole, which another comparison with *For Whom the Bell Tolls* may help to clarify. When he wrote that book, Hemingway was still close enough to the values and emotional responses of his early career to be able to use them to give a plausible edge of tragedy to Robert Jordan's story. Jordan was the climactic Hemingway hero and the last of the heroes able to embody convincingly the old attitudes about life, love, courage, and death. Even so, one saw that the old attitudes were being stretched extremely thin in Jordan. Already the Hemingway style, which had once been not merely a certain choice and arrangement of words but the verbalization of a distinct metaphysical view of experience, showed signs of hardening into a stance. The conviction was beginning to drain out of it, and it was obvious that Jordan, in those rather maudlin moments of introspection, was struggling hard to keep his old attitudes intact.

But one also saw that this very feature of the novel, this element of ideological strain, helped to provide it with its considerable dramatic tension. There was the conflict, never finally resolved, between Jordan's World War I negativism, the rather effete *Weltschmerz* of Jake Barnes and Frederic Henry, and the requirement imposed by his situation that he be positive and idealistic in his beliefs. Jordan had continually to persuade himself that he believed in the Loyalist cause, just as he had to persuade himself that he believed in the war and, with less success, in "Life, Liberty, and the Pursuit of Happiness."

Then there were the other sources of dramatic tension: the conflict between the desires of love and the demands of duty; the difficulties Jordan encountered in

trying to persuade the guerrillas that they should help him perform a mission in which he himself could not entirely believe; the poignancy of all emotions in the face of danger and the threat of death. There was all that Jordan stood to lose by the action of blowing the bridge. There were Maria and his possible future with her. There were all the experiences of life he had always enjoyed and wished to be able to enjoy again. These elements helped to convert what was in some ways a too heavily melodramatic novel into a work that had some real artistic complexity and truth.

But the situation of Thomas Hudson is very different, and the difference helps to account for what is most wrong with the new novel. Hudson is primarily the product of his past losses, sorrows, and mistakes. He has already lived a long life, and he has been much damaged in the process. No longer positively committed to the early Hemingway values, he yet retains the early skepticism which in him is fast souring into hopelessness. The simple fact is that, unlike his predecessors, he no longer believes in life and no longer enjoys life. By the time he is faced with his own certain death, he is carrying nothing but grief over the death of his three sons, the failure of his marriages, and all the emotions he is no longer able to feel. Nothing motivates him to take action except a vague stubborn sense of duty. He does not believe in this war or in any wars, and the idea of Life, Liberty, and the Pursuit of Happiness has become for him a sad joke indeed. Consequently, Hudson confronts his death like an automaton. He has gone through the motions and put on a good show, but he has had nothing to lose from the start. Hence, his actions have had no meaning. When he dies, he will be ready to die, not for the cause, not in order to save the girl he loves, but because he is tired to death of life. There is sadness in this but no real tragedy, because there is no sense of missed possibility, no conceivable alternative to dying.

It is evident that as he grew older Hemingway came to identify himself more and more explicitly with his fictional heroes and to draw increasingly on his own emotions and experiences in the creation of his heroes. Jake Barnes and Frederic Henry were essentially fantasy projections of what in some secret part of himself Hemingway wished he might be like. But Thomas Hudson and Colonel Cantwell of *Across the River and Into the Trees* are realistic projections of the tired, ailing, and disillusioned man he had by then actually become. And as the distance narrowed between himself and his heroes, his writing lost a crucial dimension. He began to try to live out his fantasies instead of projecting them in his fiction. His fiction became devitalized because the real force of his creativity was being expended in living the experience he imagined. It is even conceivable that in the end Hemingway succumbed to the limitations of the philosophy he had for years been developing in his work and endeavoring more and more to practice in his life. But that philosophy was tenable only for a young and healthy man who could afford to be cynical since his hold on life was vigorous, and he could never really believe in the possibility of his own death. Thus, when because of age and failing health Hemingway could no longer do the things that made you feel good afterwards, when the eyesight began to go and the legs went bad, and the condition of the liver would not allow you to drink, and it was no longer fun to hunt or fish or make love, then the limitations of that philosophy became intolerable. By then, however, there was no turning back. There was no way of building another more durable or complex set of values. Hemingway had succeeded in becoming his heroes, and finally he was beginning to die with them.

But art, when everything else failed, was always there. In the past there had always been art, the one dependable source of new hope and self-renewal. The world could collapse and it would not matter so long as you wrote carefully and well and tried always to write an absolutely true book. When he went down into the basement of his house that summer morning and selected the weapon that would end his life, Hemingway evidently forgot about art. It is a pity, because if art had saved him in the past, there was still a chance it might save him once again. There was, in fact, an excellent chance. For, in spite of its defects, the best parts of *Islands in the Stream* make clear that he had in his last years enough talent left to serve art successfully. If he had been able to recognize this and believe in it, he might have put the shotgun away and gone back upstairs to bed. But all he could believe in was the black emptiness and the pain. Besides, in that moment Hemingway had arrived at the kind of despair he had spent his whole life in flight from, the kind he could no longer evade through the killing of big game in Africa or by writing about the death of his heroes in his books. All the heroes were dead now. There was only himself.

Novelist John Updike reviewed Islands in the Stream *for the* New Statesman, *80 (16 October 1970), p. 489.*

Papa's Sad Testament

This book consists of material that the author during his lifetime did not see fit to publish; therefore it should not be held against him. That parts of it are good is entirely to his credit; that other parts are puerile and, in a pained way, aimless testifies to the odds against which Hemingway, in the last two decades of his life, brought anything to completion. It is, I think, to the discredit of his publishers that no introduction (the American edition does carry a very terse, uninformative note by Mary Hemingway) offers to describe from what stage of Hemingway's tormented later career *Islands in the Stream* was salvaged, or to estimate what its completed design might have been, or to confess what editorial choices were exercised in the preparation of this manuscript. Rather, a gallant wreck of a novel is paraded as the real thing, as if the public are such fools as to imagine a great writer's ghost is handing down books intact from Heaven.

So we are left to perform the elementary scholarly decencies ourselves. . . .

What we have, then, is a trio of large fragments crudely unified by a Caribbean setting and the nominal presence of Thomas Hudson. "Bimini" is a collection of episodes that show only a groping acquaintance with one another; "Cuba" is a lively but meandering excursion in local colour that, when the painter's first wife materializes, weirdly veers into a dark and private region; and "At Sea" is an adventure story of almost slick intensity. Hudson, if taken sequentially, does not grow but dwindles, from an affectionate and baffled father and artist into a rather too expertly raffish waterfront character into a bleak manhunter, a comic-book super-human holding unlooked-for-bubbles of stoic meditation and personal sorrow. Some conscious attempt is made to interlock the characterisations—the manhunter remembers that he is a painter, and gives us some hard-edged seascapes to prove it: the bar clown intermittently recalls that he is drowning his grief at the death of a son—but the real congruence of these masks is involuntary: all fit the face of Ernest Hemingway.

Whereas an achieved novel, however autobiographical, dissolves the author and directs our attention beyond him, *Islands in the Stream,* even where most effective, inspires us with a worried concern for the celebrity who wrote it.

Hemingway of course did not invent the world, nor pain, mutilation, and death. In his earlier work his harsh obsessions seem honorable and necessary; an entire generation of American men learned to speak in the accents of Hemingway's stoicism. But here, the tension of art has been snapped and the line between sensitive vision and psychopathy has been crossed. The "sea-chase story" is in many ways brilliant, but it has the falsity of the episode in Hemingway's real life upon which it was based. . . . Everything in "At Sea" is true, except the encounter with Germans and the imperatives of the mission, which was not demanded from above but invented and propelled from within. Such bravery is not grace under pressure but pressure forced in the hope of inducing Grace.

And even love becomes a species of cruelty, which divides women into whores and bitches on the one hand and on the other a single icy-perfect adored.

Love and death: fused complements in Hemingway's universe. Yet he never formulated the laws that bind them, never achieved the step of irony away from himself. He tried: this book opens in a mood of tonic breadth and humour, and closed with a sharp beatific vision of himself, Hudson, dying and beloved:

"I think I understand, Willie," he said.

"Oh shit," Willie said, "You never understand anybody that loves you."

The new generations, my impression is, want to abolish both war and love, not love as a physical act but love as a religion, a creed to help us suffer better. The sacred necessity of suffering no longer seems sacred or necessary, and Hemingway speaks across the Sixties as strangely as a medieval saint; I suspect few readers younger than myself could believe, from this sad broken testament, how we *did* love Hemingway and, after pity feels merely impudent, love him still.

Novelist William Kennedy reviewed The Dangerous Summer *in* The New York Times Book Review, *9 June 1985, pp. 1, 32–33, 35.*

The Last Olé

Here we have a great writer who set out to write an epilogue that turned into a book-length manuscript that died of unwieldiness but was years later edited to its literary essence and became a book, truly, and is here with us now, and is good.

The epilogue was conceived by Ernest Hemingway in 1959 to conclude a new edition of his 1932 treatise on bullfighting as life and art, "Death in the Afternoon." Life magazine editors heard of his plan and asked him to expand the piece into an article of a few thousand words, which they hoped to publish as successfully as they had published his novella, "The Old Man and the Sea."

Hemingway's subject for the epilogue was the *mano a mano* (or hand-to-hand, a duel) between Spain's two leading matadors, Luis Miguel Dominguín and his brother-in-law, Antonio Ordóñez. Hemingway wrote to his close friend, A. E. Hotchner: "It looked like one or the other of the men might be killed and Life wanted

coverage of it. Instead, it turned out to be the gradual destruction of one person by another with all the things that led up to it and made it. I had to establish the personality and the art and the basic differences between the two great artists and then show what happened, and you can't do that in 4,000 words."

This was Hemingway's way of apologizing for having extended the epilogue to 688 typed pages covered with 108,746 words. What had happened was that he turned both the *mano a mano* and the epilogue into a quest for, and a statement about, his own youth, his own heroism, his own art, his own immortality; for he was dying, psychically and artistically, and he seems to have intuited that.

Hemingway had begun his writing career in journalism and though he denigrated it in later life ("Journalism, after a point has been reached, can be a daily self-destruction for a serious creative writer"), he never really left it. The last two books on which he worked so diligently before his death in 1961 were this one and his superb nonfiction sketches of Paris in the 1920's, "A Moveable Feast."

He lived all his life with his own *mano a mano* between nonfiction and fiction, primarily believing that fiction was supreme. He told George Plimpton that "you make something through your invention that is not a representation but a whole new thing truer than anything true and alive, and you make it alive, and if you make it well enough, you give it immortality."

In the author's note to his 1935 book on big-game hunting, "The Green Hills of Africa," he also wrote this: "The writer has attempted to write an absolutely true book to see whether the shape of a country and the pattern of a month's action can, if truly presented, compete with a work of the imagination."

His use of the novelist's tools—dialogue, scene construction, interior monologues—in "The Green Hills" was the style that such New Journalists as Gay Talese and Tom Wolfe would popularize so abundantly well in the 1960's. Hemingway's Ego Journalism, wherein the writer's point of view is more important to the reader than the subject matter, would be carried to splendid new heights in a later generation by writers like Hunter Thompson and Norman Mailer.

"The Green Hills" of Hemingway, however, was only a valiant failure. The book perished in the bush from overkill: too much hunting detail, too much bang-bang banality, insufficient story. By contrast, his two fictional stories of Africa, "The Snows of Kilimanjaro" and "The Short Happy Life of Francis Macomber," were both masterworks.

By 1959, when Hemingway was 60 years old, his plan to write the bullfight epilogue trapped him anew in journalism, and he went to Spain. He followed the *corri-*

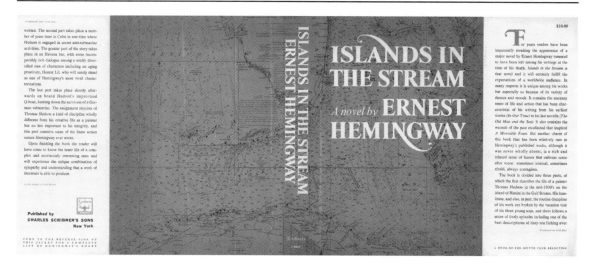

Dust jacket for Hemingway's "land, sea and air novel" published in 1970

das (afternoons of bullfighting) in which Dominguín and Ordóñez fought bulls. He worked manically at recording the small and large details of it all, wrote voluminously for five months and in September 1960 published three articles in Life.

I remember the articles. I looked forward to them but could not read them. I don't think I finished even one of the three. The great Hemingway had resuscitated all the boredom I'd felt in reading "The Green Hills." This was also the response of Life's other readers. The articles were a disaster. Nevertheless, plans continued at Hemingway's publishing house, Charles Scribner's Sons, to publish a book from the material. For many reasons, chief among them Hemingway's suicide in 1961, the book remained a manuscript of elephantiasis until now, 26 years after the writing.

"The Dangerous Summer" is a singular document, as studded with ironies as it is with taurine terminology. What it is also, because of the long hiatus between inception and publication, is the centerpiece of a much larger composite work that readers may put together for themselves. The basic books required for this composite are Hemingway's "Selected Letters"; the autobiography of his widow, Mary, "How It Was"; A. E. Hotchner's peculiar but valuable 1966 memoir, "Papa Hemingway"; Carlos Baker's biography, "Hemingway: A Life Story"; James A. Michener's nonfiction book on Spain, "Iberia"; and a long and sensitive memoir by a Spanish journalist, José Luis Castillo-Puche, called "Hemingway in Spain."

When they confront the subject of the aged Hemingway, from 1959 until his death and its aftermath, these books together offer a prismatic vision of the dying artist, a complex and profoundly dramatic story of a man's extraordinary effort to stay alive; so that when we come to Mr. Baker's succinct and powerful final sentence in the biography, we have a new comprehension not only of a writer's despair but of suicide as a not unreasonable conclusion to a blasted life. "He slipped in two shells," Mr. Baker writes, "lowered the gun butt carefully to the floor, leaned forward, pressed the twin barrels against his forehead just above the eyebrows and tripped both triggers."

"The Dangerous Summer," as centerpiece to Hemingway's final tragedy, does stand alone. It is novella-length, 45,000 words, with an introduction by James Michener that defines terms necessary for understanding the bullfight world as Hemingway describes it. Mr. Michener is reverential to the memory of Hemingway, but as an aficionado of the bulls himself he finds fault with Hemingway's conclusions.

Mr. Michener had access to the entire original manuscript and says it is so excessively detailed that most readers would not finish it. Hemingway knew it was far too long. Mr. Hotchner went to see him in Havana and reported that Hemingway, not trusting Life's editor to cut his work, had labored for 21 full days by himself and cut only 278 words.

Hemingway plaintively asked for Mr. Hotchner's help in the cutting but then strangely rejected all suggested cuts with explanations in writing to Mr. Hotchner, who was in the same room with him. Hemingway's mind was out of control and would get progressively worse. His vaunted ability to leave out what was irrelevant, his great talent for synthesis, were malfunctioning. Mr. Hotchner pressed on, but Hemingway continued to

First page of the manuscript for "The Summer People," a Nick Adams story written in the 1920s but not published until 1972 (Ernest Hemingway Collection, John F. Kennedy Library)

resist. "What I've written is Proustian in its cumulative effect, and if we eliminate detail we destroy that effect," he told Mr. Hotchner.

On the fourth day of talk Hemingway yielded, the cutting began, and 54,916 words were excised. These are Mr. Hotchner's figures, and they differ somewhat from Mr. Michener's; but then Mr. Hotchner did the cutting. The residual manuscript went to Life and formed the basis for the three articles. Charles A. Scribner Jr. said earlier this year that he tried to cut the script to publishable size in later years, eventually giving it to a Scribners editor named Michael Pietsch, who reduced it to its present size, "a wonderful job" by Mr. Scribner's lights.

And so here is Hemingway—who derided F. Scott Fitzgerald's "gigantic, preposterous" outline for "The Last Tycoon" and wrote that Fitzgerald would never have finished the book—unable to finish his own runaway journalism. Here is Hemingway—calling Thomas Wolfe the "over-bloated Lil Abner of literature" and saying that if Wolfe's editor (and his own), Maxwell Perkins of Scribners, "had not cut one-half million words out of Mr. Wolfe everybody would know how he was"—psychopathically viewing his own rampant verbosity as sacrosanct.

Nevertheless, I concur with Mr. Scribner that Mr. Pietsch has done a wonderful editing job. Hemingway was very cuttable, and the book is indeed wonderful; but the question remains: Whose wonderfulness is it? Is it half Hemingway? Hemingway by thirds? Should the byline read: "Words Put in by Hemingway, Words Taken Out by Hotchner and Pietsch"? When the same issue was raised with Thomas Wolfe about his reliance on Maxwell Perkins to produce a coherent book, Wolfe left Perkins, even left Scribners, to assert his independence.

The question is not easily answered, for there is another question: Does it really matter, in terms of what the finished book is? And just what is the book? When I began reading it, I felt instantly in the presence of the old Hemingway wit. At the Spanish border in 1953, his first return to Spain since the Spanish Civil War, he expects hostility because he fought against Franco. A border policeman asks: "Are you any relation of Hemingway the writer?" And Hemingway answers: "Of the same family." Instead of enmity he finds warm welcome, and the policeman has read all of his books.

He quickly takes us into the bullring and gives us a lesson on how to cheat at bullfighting. You shave the bull's horns so they are sensitive and he is not so deadly with them; or you use a young bull who does not yet know how to use his horns; or you drop a heavy sack of feed on the small of the bull's back so his hind legs are weakened and he is a diminished threat to the bull-

fighter. Hemingway accused the managers of the once-great Manolete of shaving horns, and when the articles appeared in Life, Hemingway was attacked by Spanish aficionados and idolaters of Manolete.

We soon meet Ordóñez, the son of Cayetano Ordóñez, who was Hemingway's friend in the 1920's and the model for the bullfighter Pedro Romero in "The Sun Also Rises." Hemingway tells Ordóñez he is better than his father. "I could see he had the three great requisites for a matador: courage, skill in his profession and grace in the presence of the danger of death." But in the same paragraph, after Ordóñez asks to see him, Hemingway tells himself: "Don't start being friends with bullfighters again and especially not with this one when you know how good he is and how much you will have to lose if anything happens to him." But Hemingway does not heed his own advice, could not heed it. He was in the grip of a compulsion to return to bullfighting, to revisit Pamplona, the setting of "The Sun Also Rises," where he had become a mythic figure and to re-create the past when he was living so well, writing so well.

He also meets the capable enemy, Dominguín, and describes him in a fine sentence: "Luis Miguel was a charmer, dark, tall, no hips, just a touch too long in the neck for a bullfighter, with a grave mocking face that went from professional disdain to easy laughter." There is a bronze life-size statue of Dominguín in his own home, and Hemingway finds this odd but uses it to define his qualified vision of Dominguín: "I thought Miguel looked better than his statue although his statue looked just a little bit nobler."

Hemingway returns to Spain in 1959 and very early on establishes the Dominguín-Ordóñez rivalry. Ordóñez emerges as a saintly fighter, who even when the bulls are stupid can work with them until they are brave. "His second bull was difficult too but he rebuilt him."

Dominguín alternates between being brave, noble and talented, and being a cheat: He "really loved to fight bulls and he forgot about being rich when he was in the ring. But he wanted the odds in his favor and the odds were the tampering with the horns."

Hemingway and his entourage traverse Spain by car, and he exults in victory like a great hunter: "We were like a happy tribe after a successful raid or a great killing." Along the way, as always in his best works, he celebrates food and wine and companionship and evokes a vivid sense of place in both present time and in memory.

These moments also serve as changes of pace from the tense reporting on the rivalry, the bulls, the wounds, the pain, the ascension toward the exalted climax. The competition peaks at Málaga on Aug. 14,

Chapter Seven: 3 July 1961–1999

The John F. Kennedy Library, the repository of the largest collection of Hemingway materials. In 1963 Mary Hemingway announced that her husband's papers would be donated to this library following its construction in Boston.

1959, with both matadors triumphing over their bulls. Hemingway even approves of Dominguín.

> He made two series of eight naturales [passes with a small red cloth] in beautiful style and then on a right-hand pass with the bull coming at him from the rear, the bull had him. . . . The horn seemed to go into his body and the bull tossed him a good six feet or more into the air. His arms and legs were spread wide, the sword and muleta were thrown clear and he fell on his head. The bull stepped on him trying to get the horn into him and missed him twice. . . . He was up in an instant. The horn had not gone in but had passed between his legs . . . and there was no wound. [He] paid no attention to what the bull had done to him and waving everyone away went on with his faena [work].

Dominguín goes on also to be overshadowed by Ordóñez in the fourth *mano a mano* at Ciudad Real, and Hemingway ends the chapter on a note of negative suspense: that Dominguín will now go on to Bilbao "to be destroyed."

The final chapter is a triumph—for Hemingway. He throws aside journalistic convention and as novelist enters into the heads of the matadors as they battle to the conclusion Hemingway knew was inevitable.

On Dominguín: "Too many things were piling up and he was running out of luck. It was one thing to live to be the number one in the world in his profession.

. . . It was another thing to be almost killed each time he went out to prove it."

On Ordóñez: "A bullfighter can never see the work of art that he is making. He has no chance to correct it as a painter or a writer has. . . . He can only fell it and hear the crowd's reaction to it. . . . The public belonged to him now. He looked up at them and let them know modestly but not humbly, that he knew it. [He] was happy that he owned them."

So that, in brief, is the book, and while I have lived remote from bullfighting all my life, have next to no personal interest in it and tend to identify with the bulls, I think nevertheless that "The Dangerous Summer" is one of the best sports books I have ever read. Not everyone could agree. Dominguín, who retired in 1961 and came back to the bulls in 1971, said in a 1972 book about him by Keith Botsford that Hemingway was "a commonplace bore . . . a crude and vulgar man" who "knew nothing about fighting bulls." He dismissed Ordóñez as a "cowardly fighter" with "feet of clay all the way up to his brain."

In "Iberia," Mr. Michener reports on the latter-day Ordóñez, the man Hemingway said could be one of the greatest matadors of all time. In a corrida at Pamplona the crowd dislikes his work and so Ordóñez spitefully kills the bull in a disgraceful way. "It was a shame-filled conclusion to a shameful performance,"

Mr. Michener says, and the crowd chants: "*Ordóñez, Ordóñez sinverguenza! Ordóñez, Ordóñez, paga la prensa*" ("Ordóñez, Ordóñez, shameless one! Ordóñez, Ordóñez, pays the newspapers"—to write well of him).

Mr. Castillo-Puche, who was close to Hemingway, argues in "Hemingway in Spain" that the *mano a mano* series was a publicity stunt, that Hemingway was suckered by the promoters and that Ordóñez used him to advance his career.

All of that may be true, and in the last judgment by the bulls of history, Hemingway may be gored in his journalistic femoral artery. But that is irrelevant to why this is an important and wonderful book. The value emerges from the subtext, which seems to have two principal elements: the drive to write this book and the behavior of the writer as he reports and writes it.

How does a man fight the dying of the light? Is it really with rage? Mr. Castillo-Puche writes: "I saw [Hemingway] get all confused, tear up whole sections of his manuscript, rip up photographs or fling them across the room in a fit of temper, swear at those present in the room and others everywhere, and swear at himself."

Also, while they are at the Pamplona fiesta, Hemingway, Ordóñez and other friends make "prisoners" of two young American women and keep them in thrall for a month. Hemingway writes that "turning up with a couple of prisoners is sometimes ill-received in martial circles." Mr. Castillo-Puche says that Hemingway's relations with all the young women in Spain that year were very chaste, but Hemingway's wife, Mary, was less than thrilled, especially when Hemingway took yet another "prisoner," a young Irish woman named Valery Danby-Smith, who, Mary says in her autobiography, "became Ernest's secretary-handmaiden." Miss Danby-Smith remained close to Hemingway until his death and eventually married his son Gregory.

Mary writes that in the new situation, a "nonstop circus," she became "inaudible" to Hemingway. Soon she "seemed also to be invisible, a worthless quality in a wife," and so returned to Cuba and wrote Hemingway that she was leaving him. He cabled his respect for her views but disagreed profoundly with her decision to leave. "Still love you" he added, and she stayed on until the end.

The pursuit of young women, the vicarious life as a matador, the preening before hordes of autograph-seekers in Pamplona, everything is monkey glandular to Hemingway: "The wine was as good as when you were twenty-one, and the food was as marvelous as always. There were the same songs and good new ones . . . The faces that were young once were old as mine but everyone remembered how we were."

The self-portrait and the portrait-in-the-round from the other books emerge with great clarity. The

mano a mano is also a story made to order for the dying man's need not to die. He creates Ordóñez as an immortal, for isn't that the status of all the very best dead people?

Hemingway went to Spain searching for youth and found mortality and madness. But what is clear is that this story, these sentences and paragraphs, however truncated from the original, are not the work of a lunatic, and could not have been written by anyone except Hemingway or his spirit. If this work had been publishable, or even conceivable, at this length and with this quality during his lifetime, he might not have shot himself. But that's not how it was.

It is only over Hemingway's dead body that this book could have come to be. And I think it very clever of Hemingway's spirit to relent about the editing and come back to Scribners to tell the folks there how to prepare the text.

Novelist E. L. Doctorow reviewed The Garden of Eden *(New York: Scribners, 1986) in* The New York Times Book Review, *18 May 1986, pp. 1, 44–45.*

Braver Than We Thought

Early in his career Ernest Hemingway devised the writing strategies he would follow for life: when composing a story he would withhold mention of its central problem; when writing a novel he would implant it in geography and, insofar as possible, he would know what time it was on every page; when writing anything he would construct the sentences so as to produce an emotion not by claiming it but by rendering precisely the experience to cause it. What he made of all this was a rigorous art of compressive power, if more suited to certain emotions than others. He was unquestionably a genius, but of the kind that advertises its limits. Critics were on to these from the very beginning, but in the forward-looking 1920's, they joined his readers to make him the writer for their time. His stuff was new. It moved. There was on every page of clear prose an implicit judgment of all other writing. The Hemingway voice hated pretense and cant and the rhetoric they rode in on.

The source of his material and spring to his imagination was his own life. Issues of intellect—history, myth, society—were beside the point. It was what his own eyes saw and heart felt that he cured into fiction. Accordingly he lived his life to see and feel as much as possible. There was no place on earth he was not at

Dust jacket for the 1985 publication of Hemingway's account of the 1959 bullfight season. The 45,000-word book was edited from Hemingway's 70,000-word draft.

home, except perhaps his birthplace. His parents' Middle Western provincialism made independence an easy passage for him. He married young and fathered a child–the traditional circumstances for settling down– and took his family with him to Europe in pursuit of excitements. He skied in the Austrian Alps, entrained to Paris for the bicycle races or prizefights, crossed the Pyrenees for the bullfights and made urgent side trips to mountain villages for the fishing or shooting. In America too, he drove back and forth from Idaho or Wyoming to Florida, never renting a place to live in for more than a season. He was divorced and remarried, with more children, before he bought a place of his own in Key West. But there was better fishing in Cuba, and a woman he secretly wooed there who was to become his third wife–and so on. It was Flaubert who said a writer has to sit quietly in one place, rooted in boredom, to get his work done. Hemingway lived in a kind of nomadic frenzy, but the *work* poured out of him. . . .

As his fame grew he was able in this or that remote paradise he had found to demolish his solitude by summoning friends or colleagues from other parts of the world. And they came, at whatever inconvenience to themselves, to fish or hunt or ride with him, but most importantly to drink with him. He had sporting friends, military friends, celebrity friends, literary friends and friends from the local saloon. . . . Most people are quiet in the world, and live in it tentatively, as if it is not theirs. Hemingway was its voracious consumer. People of every class were drawn to this behavior, and the boasting, charming or truculent boyishness of his ways, and to his ritual celebration of his appetites.

By and large he worked from life on a very short lead time. He wrote "The Sun Also Rises" while still seeing many of the people in Paris on whom he modeled its characters, and though it took him 10 years to use his World War I experiences for "A Farewell to Arms," by the time of the civil war in Spain he was making trips there knowing he was collecting the people, incidents and locales for "For Whom the Bell Tolls," a novel he completed in 1939, within months of the war's end. Only illness cut down his efficiency, or

His last novel.

The Garden of Eden
Ernest Hemingway

So provocative and sensual, it could only be published today.

- **Book-of-the-Month Club** Main Selection
- *Sports Illustrated* excerpt and cover feature
- *Life* magazine excerpt
- *New York Times Book Review*
  front-page excerpt
- 100,000-copy first printing
- Major national advertising, promotion and publicity
- National co-op advertising available
- Already making headlines coast-to-coast!

May $18.95 / 0-684-18693-4 / Shipping April 1986

Scribners 1846

Charles Scribner's Sons, 115 Fifth Avenue, New York, N.Y. 10003
For more information, contact your local sales representative, or phone toll-free 1-800-257-5755.
140 YEARS OF QUALITY PUBLISHING

Advertisement for Hemingway's novel about a writer, David Bourne, on the French Riviera in the 1920s (Publishers Weekly, 24 January 1986)

more often physical accidents, of which he had a great many; he ran cars into ditches and broke bones, or cut himself with knives, or scratched his eyes. But with the Second World War his ability to work quickly from life declined, and with it the justification of his techniques. Though he was prominently a correspondent in that war, the only novel he produced from it was the very weak "Across the River and Into the Trees," and that not published until 1950. People noted his decline and attributed it to the corruption of fame, but in the last decade of his life he wrote "A Moveable Feast," a memoir of his early days in Paris (published posthumously in 1964), and "The Old Man and the Sea," and seemed to have found again what he could do.

Hemingway talked of suicide all his life before he committed it. In 1954 his proneness to accident culminated in not one but two airplane crashes in East Africa where he had gone to hunt, and which left him with the concussion, crushed vertebrae, burns and internal injuries that turned him, in his 50's, into an old man. From a distance the physical punishment his body received during his lifetime seems to have been half of something, a boxing match with an invisible opponent, perhaps. His mind was never far from killing, neither in

actuality as he hunted or ran off to wars, nor in his work. He went after animals all his life. He shot lion and leopard and kudu in Africa, and grizzly bear in the Rockies; he shot grouse in Wyoming and pigeon in France; wherever he was he took what was available. And after he killed something it was not necessarily past his attention. His biographer, Carlos Baker, tells of the day, in Cuba, when Hemingway hooked and fought and landed a 512-pound marlin. He brought it to port in triumph, receiving the noisy congratulations of friends and acquaintances. But this was not, apparently, enough. After a night of drunken celebration, at 2 or 3 that morning, he was seen back at the dock, all alone under the moon; the great game fish hanging upside down on block and tackle, he was using it for a punching bag.

Since Hemingway's death in 1961, his estate and his publishers, Charles Scribner's Sons, have been catching up to him, issuing the work which, for one reason or another, he did not publish during his lifetime. He held back "A Moveable Feast" out of concern for the feelings of the people in it who might still be alive. But for the novel "Islands in the Stream" he seems to have had editorial misgivings. Even more deeply in this category is "The Garden of Eden," which he began in 1946 and worked on intermittently in the last 15 years of his life and left unfinished. It is a highly readable story, if not possibly the book he envisioned. As published it is composed of 30 short chapters running to about 70,000 words. A publisher's note advises that "some cuts" have been made in the manuscript, but according to Mr. Baker's biography, at one point a revised manuscript of the work ran to 48 chapters and 200,000 words, so the publisher's note is disingenuous. In an interview with The New York Times last December, a Scribners editor admitted to taking out a subplot in rough draft that he felt had not been integrated into the "main body" of the text, but this cut reduced the book's length by two-thirds. . . .

At first reading this is a surprising story to receive from the great outdoor athlete of American literature. He has not previously presented himself as a clinician of bedroom practices. Even more interesting is the passivity of his writer hero who, on the evidence, hates big-game hunting, and who is portrayed as totally subject to the powers of women, hapless before temptation and unable to take action in the face of adversity. The story is told from David Bourne's masculine point of view, in the intimate or pseudo-third person Hemingway preferred, but its major achievement is Catherine Bourne. There has not before been a female character who so dominates a Hemingway narrative. Catherine in fact may be the most impressive of any woman character in Hemingway's work, more substantive and dimensional than Pilar in "For Whom the Bell Tolls," or Brett Ashley in "The Sun Also Rises." Even though she is launched from the naïve premise that sexual fantasizing is a form of madness, she takes on the stature of the self-tortured Faustian, and is portrayed as a brilliant woman trapped into a vicarious participation in someone else's creativity. She represents the most informed and delicate reading Hemingway has given to any woman.

For Catherine Bourne alone this book will be read avidly. But there are additional things to make a reader happy. For considerable portions of the narrative, the dialogue is in tension, which cannot be said of "Across the River and Into the Trees," his late novel of the same period, and for which he looted some of the motifs of this work. And there are passages that show the old man writing to the same strength of his early work—a description of David Bourne catching a bass in the canal at Le Grau-du-Roi, for example, or swimming off the beach at La Napoule. In these cases the strategy of using landscape to portray moral states produces victory.

But to be able to list the discrete excellences of a book is to say also it falls short of realization. The other woman, and third main character, Marita, has not the weight to account for her willingness to move in on a marriage and lend herself to its disruption. She is colorless and largely unarticulated. David Bourne's passivity goes unexamined by the author, except as it may be a function of his profession. But the sad truth is that his writing, which we see in the elephant story, does not exonerate him. . . . The theme of a boy's initiation rites suggests to its own great disadvantage Faulkner's story on the same theme, "The Bear."

In David's character resides the ultimate deadness of the piece. His incapability in dealing with the crisis of his relationship does not mesh with his consummate self-assurance in handling the waiters, maids and hoteliers of Europe who, in this book as in Hemingway's others, come forward to supply the food and drink, the cork-screws and ice cubes and beds and fishing rods his young American colonists require. In fact so often does David Bourne perform his cultivated eating and drinking that a reader is depressed enough to wonder if Hemingway's real achievement in the early great novels was that of a travel writer who taught a provincial American audience what dishes to order, what drinks to prefer and how to deal with the European servant class. There are moments here when we feel we are not in France or Spain but in the provisional state of Yuppiedom. A reader is given to conclude that this shrewdest of

writers made an uncharacteristic mistake in not finding a war to destroy his lovers, or some action beside their own lovemaking to threaten their survival. The tone of solemn self-attention in this work rises to a portentousness that the 70,000 words of text cannot justify.

But here we are led back to the issue of editing a great writer's work after his death. As far as it is possible to tell from biography, and from the inventory of Hemingway manuscripts by Philip Young and Charles W. Mann, Hemingway intended "The Garden of Eden" as a major work. At one point he conceived of it as one of a trilogy of books in which the sea figured. Certainly its title suggests a governing theme of his creative life, the loss of paradise, the expulsion from the garden, which controls "The Sun Also Rises" and "A Farewell to Arms," among other books and stories. Apparently there is extant more than one manuscript version for scholars to chose from. Carlos Baker mentions the presence of another married couple in one of the versions, a painter named Nick, and his wife, Barbara. Of the same generation as David and Catherine Bourne, Nick (is Adams his last name?) and Barbara live in Paris. And there may be additional characters. Presumably the material involving them is in a less finished state and easily stripped away to find the spare, if skimpy, novel we have now in print. But the truth about editing the work of a dead writer in such circumstances is that you can only cut to affirm his strengths, to reiterate the strategies of style for which he is known; whereas he himself may have been writing to transcend them. This cannot have been the book Hemingway envisioned at the most ambitious moments of his struggle to realize it, a struggle that occupied him intensely for perhaps 45 years. And it should have been published for what it is, a piece of something, part of a design.

For there are clear signs here of something exciting going on, the enlargement of a writer's mind toward compassion, toward a less defensive construal of reality. The key is the character of Catherine Bourne. . . . But here she has grown to suggest in Hemingway the rudiments of feminist perspective. And as for David Bourne, he is unmistakably the younger literary brother of Jake Barnes, the newspaperman wounded to impotence in that first expatriate novel. But David's passivity is not physical and therefore more difficult to put across. He reminds us a bit, actually, of Robert Cohn, whom Jake Barnes despised for suffering quietly the belittling remarks of women in public. Perhaps Hemingway is learning to dispense his judgments more thoughtfully. Or per-

ERNEST HEMINGWAY

The Garden of Eden

A NOVEL

Dust jacket for the second Hemingway novel published from his work in progress after his death

not formally sufficient to the subject. I would like to think that as he began "The Garden of Eden," his very next novel after that war work, he realized this and wanted to retool, to remake himself. That he would fail is almost not the point—but that he would have tried, which is the true bravery of a writer, requiring more courage than facing down an elephant charge with a .303 Mannlicher.

This article from The New York Times, *24 August 1998, section E, pp. 1, 3, announces the publication of Hemingway's book recounting his 1953–1954 safari.*

A New Book By Hemingway

Blend of Life and Fiction Tells of African Bride
By RALPH BLUMENTHAL

In 1954, after surviving two African plane crashes, Mau Mau marauders and domestic life on safari with his fourth wife, Mary (and just maybe a mysterious tribal bride or two), Ernest Hemingway returned home to Cuba and began work on a long autobiographical novel.

Two years later, interrupted by the filming of "The Old Man and the Sea," he put aside the unfinished 200,000-word manuscript. With Fidel Castro's revolution, he abandoned Cuba and the book; in July 1961, just short of his 62d birthday, he took his life with a shotgun in Idaho.

Now, after a long repose in the limbo of restricted files in the John F. Kennedy Library in Boston, the book—edited down by half and described as the last unpublished full-length Hemingway work—is being prepared for publication in time for the centennial of the author's birth in Oak Park, Ill., next July 21.

"This is it; there are no more books," said Charles Scribner 3d, whose family imprint, now part of Simon & Schuster, is bringing out what it calls the fictional memoir, "True at First Light," as edited by Hemingway's 70-year-old middle son, Patrick.

A. E. Hotchner, who related anecdotes from the safari in his 1966 biography, "Papa Hemingway," called the release of the latest work "a big publishing event" but voiced surprise that Hemingway had never mentioned the book to him amid many discussions of other projects. "It's a mystery to me," he said.

The publishing plans were disclosed by Daily Variety this month, but the work was not unknown. Scholars inventoried the manuscript in 1969, and in

haps David Bourne was not designed as the hero of the piece at all.

With a large cast and perhaps multiple points of view, something else might have been intended than what we have, a revised view of the lost generation perhaps, some additional reading of a kind of American life *ex partia* with the larger context that would earn the tone of the book. There are enough clues here to suggest the unmistakable signs of a recycling of Hemingway's first materials toward less romance and less literary bigotry and greater truth. That is exciting because it gives evidence, despite his celebrity, despite his Nobel, despite the torments of his own physical self-punishment, of a writer still developing. Those same writing strategies Hemingway formulated to such triumph in his early work came to entrap him in the later. You can see this beginning to happen in his 1940 novel, "For Whom the Bell Tolls," where implanting the conception of the book in geography, and fixing all its action in time and relentlessly understating the sentences, were finally dramatic strategies

1971 and 1972 Sports Illustrated serialized a 50,000-word excerpt as Hemingway's "African Journal," part of which was included in a 1974 anthology, "The Enduring Hemingway."

Four other works that Hemingway left in varying stages of completion were previously published posthumously, to mixed reviews: "A Moveable Feast," "Islands in the Stream," "The Dangerous Summer" and "The Garden of Eden."

Few would rank these with quasi-autobiographical masterpieces like "A Farewell to Arms" and "The Sun Also Rises," and given the fanatical care Hemingway took with his writing there is some question of how happy he would be to have his reputation and last printed words entrusted solely to any editor, even a son. Patrick Hemingway said that he was aware of the responsibility and that aside from a few place names he had not changed any of his father's words, although he acknowledged that condensing the book inevitably reshaped it.

For the few who have read it, a mystique has long clung to the sprawling 850-page blend of autobiography and fiction, in part over the ambiguous character named Debba, an 18-year-old woman from the Wakamba tribe whom the narrator casually takes as a second wife.

The Hemingways both fed the intrigue by offering even richer versions of the story to biographers, although Patrick Hemingway, who took part in the safari, says the marriage to Debba is fictional.

"Did Ernest Hemingway have such an experience?" he said from his home in Bozeman, Mont. "I can tell you from all I know—and I don't know everything—he did not."

But because Hemingway's adventurous life and his fiction have been so intertwined, the new book is sure to raise questions about how much of the story is literally true. Hemingway was elliptical on the issue. All good books have something in common, he liked to say: "They are truer than if they had really happened."

"True at First Light," a title Patrick Hemingway chose from the text to suggest the deceptiveness of the senses, is based on Hemingway's second safari to East Africa, in 1953, just as "Green Hills of Africa" was based on his first, 20 years earlier. Some characters, notably the revered white hunter—in real life, Hemingway's friend Philip Percival, "the finest man that I know"—are the same.

But on that first safari Hemingway was accompanied by his second wife, Pauline Pfeiffer, Vogue's Paris correspondent, with whom he had two sons, Patrick and Gregory, and for whom he had divorced Hadley Richardson, who was the mother of his first son, John, called Bumby. By the second safari Hemingway had divorced Pauline, as well as his third wife, Martha Gell-

horn, also a writer, and had married Mary Welsh, a Time-Life correspondent whom he had met in wartime London.

The interplay of these relationships is a theme in the book, along with age and enlightenment, spirituality and the hypnotic spell of Africa.

A Lion's Roar, Not Like in Films

"You cannot describe a wild lion's roar," Hemingway writes. "You can only say that you listened and the lion roared. It is not at all like the noise the lion makes at the start of Metro-Goldwyn-Mayer pictures. When you hear it you first feel it in your scrotum and it runs all the way up through your body."

The book also tracks Mary Hemingway's obsessive quest to kill a cattle-thieving black lion as mythic and elusive as Melville's white whale. She gets her lion, but in a way that exposes painful fault lines in the marriage. Paris is in the book too, and Ezra Pound and baseball and prodigious drinking and meditations on the soul—"probably a spring of clear fresh water that never diminished in the drought and never froze in the winter."

Hemingway and Miss Mary, as she is called in the book, arrived in the Kenyan port of Mombasa in the summer of 1953 and set up camp at Percival's Kitanga Farm. The party included Denis Zaphiro, a game ranger nicknamed G. C., for "gin crazed," and Earl Theisen, a Look photographer. Hemingway had contracted to write a piece for the magazine to defray costs. Patrick, an art history major who had graduated magna cum laude from Harvard and become a licensed white hunter in Tanganyika, also joined them for a time, along with a safari staff of 22.

Hoping to counter the bad publicity from the terrorist uprising of the Kikuyu tribe against white landholders that became known as the Mau Mau emergency, and grateful for the tourists drawn by his books and movies, the Kenya authorities designated Hemingway honorary game warden for the region. For five months they hunted rogue lions that were poaching cattle, leopards, a wounded rhino, birds and other game.

Although Mary Hemingway kept a diary, Hemingway wrote no notes, as usual. "I just push the recall button and there it is," he told Mr. Hotchner.

In January 1954, the Hemingways were in a small plane over Murchison Falls when the bush pilot nicked a telephone line and crashed. The couple escaped with relatively minor injuries. Evacuated by a passing boat on the White Nile, they found a commercial pilot who offered to fly them to Entebbe in Uganda. On take-off

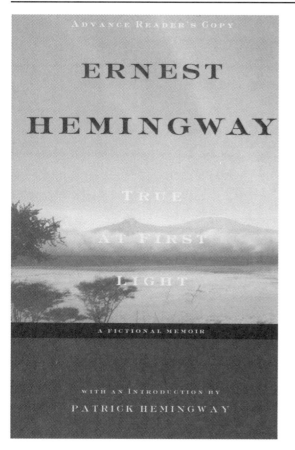

Cover for the advance copy of Hemingway's book based on his 1953–1954 safari

the plane burst into flames. This time they were more seriously hurt.

Back home safely that fall in his beloved Cuban refuge, Finca Vigía, or Lookout Farm, outside Havana, Hemingway grumbled his pleasure at having won the Nobel Prize for Literature and began work on the African book.

While the early 70's *Sports Illustrated* excerpts focus heavily on hunting, they also offer broader glimpses of a work that is now to be Hemingway's final testament, and perhaps a last introspective look into a famously complex and colorful literary colossus.

The narrator of "True at First Light" talks about a changed Africa and his boredom at reading so much about himself by fatuous people who pretend to know all about his inner life, and he quickly and playfully brings up "the matter of my fiancée"–Debba, "very beautiful and quite young and more than perfectly developed."

In the book, Miss Mary calls herself the jealous type, vowing to kill any woman who steals her husband's affections, but she says this doesn't apply to his African fiancée. Miss Mary says further, "Since when does a good loving husband not have a right to a fiancée if she only wishes to be a supplementary wife?"

Two biographies suggested that the account was not entirely fictional. In his authoritative 1969 biography, "Ernest Hemingway, A Life Story," Carlos Baker, drawing on Mary Hemingway's diaries, says that toward the end of the 1953 safari Hemingway showed signs of "wanting to go native," telling Mrs. Hemingway she was "depriving him of his new wife," the Wakamba girl Debba. Mrs. Hemingway, the account goes on, did not take offense, suggesting only that Debba "ought first to have a much needed bath."

Mary Hemingway left the camp for some pre-Christmas shopping in Nairobi, and she returned to find that Hemingway had taken up the spear and invited Debba and some of her friends into the camp, celebrating so energetically that they broke Mrs. Hemingway's bed. Warned of possible trouble from Debba's family, Hemingway returned her to her village, but she was among those invited back for Christmas celebrations, the Baker account concludes.

In "Papa Hemingway," Mr. Hotchner says that in Venice in 1954, Hemingway "told us of his startling nuptials," relating that when his wife was away in Nairobi, he had taken an 18-year-old Wakamba bride and "as local custom dictated, inherited her sister," a widow of 17.

"The three of them slept on a goatskin bed 14 feet wide, Ernest said, and when Mary returned she was very solicitous about the event and impressed with the lofty position Ernest had attained in the tribe by virtue of his matrimony," the Hotchner book recounts.

It goes on to report that shortly afterward, Hemingway counted on his fingers and said, "September I will have an African son."

"Lovely Wives" And 16,000 Words

Furthermore, Mr. Hotchner said that in a letter written to him on March 14, 1954, from aboard the ship Africa, Hemingway first recounted the native marriage, adding: "I'm very happy with my lovely wives with their impudence and solicitude and stacked better than M. Monroe but with good hard palms to their hands and smell wonderful."

In the same long letter Hemingway said he had dictated 16,000 words "and I hope I have kept it funny." It appears to be a reference to the Look article, which had already appeared as a photo-essay of hardly 2,000 words, so the rest probably become the kernel of "True at First Light." The letter is part of an exchange of correspondence with Hemingway that the Oxford University Press plans to bring out for the centennial, Mr. Hotchner said.

Still, he said, he was more than dubious of any actual marriage, given Hemingway's mischievous streak and love of practical jokes, as when he boasted of making love to the spy Mata Hari, although she was executed by the French the year before he arrived in Italy in 1918.

Moreover, the Look photographer, Mr. Theisen, in his letters home between August and October 1953 never mentioned Debba, according to a re-check of his correspondence by his daughter, Roxie Livingston, in Los Angeles.

Patrick Hemingway said furthermore that the manuscript made no mention of the sister-bride, a further sign the story was made up.

And no African son of Hemingway has ever emerged.

After Hemingway's suicide and despite the virtual state of war between Cuba and the United States after the 1961 Bay of Pigs invasion, President Kennedy helped arrange for Mrs. Hemingway to return to Finca Vigía, which President Castro planned to turn into a museum, to retrieve her husband's belongings, including the manuscript, left in a bank vault.

After Kennedy's assassination, in 1963, she placed the bulk of Hemingway's papers at the Kennedy Library. She died in 1986.

With the exception of "True at First Light" and the other uncompleted works, the papers were opened to the public at the library's temporary quarters in 1975.

The permanent Kennedy Library opened in 1980, and the collection is now centered in the Hemingway Room, where spread on the floor is the very real skin of the black lion Mary Hemingway shot in 1953.

Bibliography

BOOKS: *Three Stories and Ten Poems* (Paris: Contact, 1923; Bloomfield Hills, Mich.: Bruccoli Clark, 1977);

in our time (Paris: Three Mountains Press, 1924; London: Jackson, 1924; Bloomfield Hills, Mich.: Bruccoli Clark, 1977);

In Our Time (New York: Boni & Liveright, 1925; London: Cape, 1926; revised edition, New York: Scribners, 1930);

The Torrents of Spring (New York: Scribners, 1926; London: Cape, 1933);

Today Is Friday (Englewood, N.J.: As Stable, 1926);

The Sun Also Rises (New York: Scribners, 1926); republished as *Fiesta* (London: Cape, 1927);

Men Without Women (New York: Scribners, 1927; London: Cape, 1928);

A Farewell to Arms (New York: Scribners, 1929; London: Cape, 1929);

Death in the Afternoon (New York & London: Scribners, 1932; London: Cape, 1932);

God Rest You Merry Gentlemen (New York: House of Books, 1933);

Winner Take Nothing (New York & London: Scribners, 1933; London: Cape, 1934);

Green Hills of Africa (New York & London: Scribners, 1935; London: Cape, 1936);

To Have and Have Not (New York: Scribners, 1937; London: Cape, 1937);

The Spanish Earth (Cleveland: Savage, 1938);

The Fifth Column and the First Forty-nine Stories (New York: Scribners, 1938; London: Cape, 1939); republished as *The Short Stories of Ernest Hemingway* (New York: Scribners, 1954);

The Fifth Column: A Play in Three Acts (New York: Scribners, 1940; London: Cape, 1968);

For Whom the Bell Tolls (New York: Scribners, 1940; London: Cape, 1941);

Across the River and Into the Trees (London: Cape, 1950; New York: Scribners, 1950);

The Old Man and the Sea (New York: Scribners, 1952; London: Cape, 1952);

The Collected Poems, unauthorized edition (San Francisco, 1960);

Hemingway: The Wild Years, edited by Gene Z. Hanrahan (New York: Dell, 1962);

A Moveable Feast (New York: Scribners, 1964; London: Cape, 1964);

By-Line: Ernest Hemingway, edited by William White (New York: Scribners, 1967; London: Collins, 1968);

The Fifth Column and Four Stories of the Spanish Civil War (New York: Scribners, 1969);

Ernest Hemingway, Cub Reporter, edited by Matthew J. Bruccoli (Pittsburgh: University of Pittsburgh Press, 1970);

Islands in the Stream (New York: Scribners, 1970; London: Collins, 1970);

Ernest Hemingway's Apprenticeship, edited by Bruccoli (Washington, D.C.: Bruccoli Clark/NCR Microcard Books, 1971);

The Nick Adams Stories, edited by Philip Young (New York: Scribners, 1972);

Ernest Hemingway: 88 Poems, edited by Nicholas Gerogiannis (New York & London: Harcourt Brace Jovanovich/Bruccoli Clark, 1979); enlarged as *Complete Poems* (Lincoln & London: University of Nebraska Press, 1983);

Ernest Hemingway on Writing, edited by Larry W. Phillips (New York: Scribners, 1984; London: Granada, 1985);

The Dangerous Summer (New York: Scribners, 1985; London: Hamilton, 1985);

Ernest Hemingway: Dateline: Toronto, edited by White (New York: Scribners, 1985);

The Garden of Eden (New York: Scribners, 1986; London: Hamilton, 1987);

The Complete Short Stories of Ernest Hemingway (New York: Scribners, 1987);

The Sun Also Rises: A Facsimile Edition, 2 volumes, edited by Bruccoli (Detroit: Manly/Omnigraphics, 1990);

True at First Light, edited by Patrick Hemingway (New York: Scribner, 1999).

Collections:

The Viking Portable Library: Hemingway, edited with introduction by Malcolm Cowley (New York: Viking, 1944);

Bibliography

The Essential Hemingway (London: Cape, 1947);

The Hemingway Reader, foreword and prefaces by Charles Poore (New York: Scribners, 1953);

Three Novels of Ernest Hemingway: The Sun Also Rises, introduction by Malcolm Cowley; *A Farewell to Arms,* introduction by Robert Penn Warren; *The Old Man and the Sea,* introduction by Carlos Baker (New York: Scribners, 1962);

The Enduring Hemingway, edited with introduction by Charles Scribner Jr. (New York: Scribners, 1974).

Other:

"The Spanish War," *Fact,* no. 16 (15 July 1938): 7–72;

Men at War, edited with introduction by Ernest Hemingway (New York: Crown, 1942).

Letters:

Ernest Hemingway: Selected Letters, 1917–1961, edited by Carlos Baker (New York: Scribners, 1981);

Hemingway in Love and War: The Lost Diary of Agnes von Kurowsky, Her Letters and Correspondence of Ernest Hemingway, edited by Henry Serrano Villard and James Nagel (Boston: Northeastern University Press, 1989);

The Only Thing That Counts: The Ernest Hemingway/Maxwell Perkins Correspondence, 1925–1947, edited by Matthew J. Bruccoli, with the assistance of Robert W. Trogdon (New York: Scribners, 1996).

Interview:

Conversations with Ernest Hemingway, edited by Matthew J. Bruccoli (Jackson: University Press of Mississippi, 1986).

For Further Reading

BIBLIOGRAPHIES

Bruccoli, Matthew J., and C. E. Frazer Clark. *Hemingway at Auction 1930–1973*. Detroit: Gale Research, 1973.

Catalog of the Ernest Hemingway Collection at the John F. Kennedy Library. 2 volumes. Boston: G. K. Hall, 1982.

Hanneman, Audre. *Ernest Hemingway: A Comprehensive Bibliography*. Princeton, N.J.: Princeton University Press, 1967.

Hanneman. *Supplement to Ernest Hemingway: A Comprehensive Bibliography*. Princeton, N.J.: Princeton University Press, 1975.

Larson, Kelli. *Ernest Hemingway: A Reference Guide, 1974–1989*. Boston: G. K. Hall, 1990.

Wagner, Linda Welshimer. *Ernest Hemingway: A Reference Guide*. Boston: G. K. Hall, 1977.

Young, Philip, and Charles M. Mann. *The Hemingway Manuscripts: An Inventory*. University Park: Pennsylvania State University Press, 1969.

BIOGRAPHIES

Baker, Carlos. *Ernest Hemingway: A Life Story*. New York: Scribners, 1969.

Donaldson, Scott. *By Force of Will: The Life and Art of Ernest Hemingway*. New York: Viking, 1977.

Fuentes, Norberto. *Hemingway in Cuba*. Secaucus, N.J.: Lyle Stuart, 1984.

Griffin, Peter. *Along With Youth: Hemingway, The Early Years,* foreword by Jack Hemingway. New York: Oxford University Press, 1985.

Griffin. *Less Than a Treason: Hemingway in Paris*. New York: Oxford University Press, 1990.

Hemingway, Gregory. *Papa: A Personal Memoir,* preface by Norman Mailer. Boston: Houghton Mifflin, 1976.

Hemingway, Jack. *Misadventures of a Fly Fisherman: My Life With and Without Papa*. Dallas: Taylor, 1986.

Hemingway, Leicester. *My Brother, Ernest Hemingway*. Cleveland: World, 1962.

Hemingway, Mary. *How It Was*. New York: Knopf, 1976.

Kert, Bernice. *The Hemingway Women*. New York: Norton, 1983.

Miller, Madelaine Hemingway. *Ernie: Hemingway's Sister "Sunny" Remembers*. New York: Crown, 1975.

Reynolds, Michael. *Hemingway: The American Homecoming*. Cambridge, Mass.: Blackwell, 1992.

Reynolds. *Hemingway: An Annotated Chronology*. Detroit: Manly/Omnigraphics, 1991.

Reynolds. *Hemingway: The Final Years*. New York: Norton, 1999.

Reynolds. *Hemingway: The 1930s*. New York: Norton, 1997.

Reynolds. *Hemingway: The Paris Years*. Cambridge, Mass.: Blackwell, 1989.

Reynolds. *The Young Hemingway*. New York: Blackwell, 1986.

Sanford, Marcelline Hemingway. *At the Hemingways: A Family Portrait*. Boston: Little, Brown, 1962. Enlarged as *At the Hemingways: With Fifty Years of Correspondence Between Ernest and Marcelline Hemingway,* edited by John E. Sanford. Moscow: University of Idaho Press, 1999.

CRITICAL STUDIES

Astro, Richard, and Jackson J. Benson, eds. *Hemingway in Our Time*. Corvallis: Oregon State University Press, 1974.

For Further Reading

Baker, Carlos. *Hemingway: The Writer as Artist,* fourth edition. Princeton, N.J.: Princeton University Press, 1972.

Baker, ed. *Ernest Hemingway: Critiques of Four Major Novels.* New York: Scribners, 1962.

Baker, ed. *Hemingway and His Critics: An International Anthology.* New York: Hill & Wang, 1961.

Beegel, Susan F. *Hemingway's Craft of Omission: Four Manuscript Examples.* Ann Arbor, Mich.: UMI, 1988.

Beegel, ed. *Hemingway's Neglected Short Fiction: New Perspectives.* Ann Arbor, Mich.: UMI, 1989.

Benson, Jackson J. *Hemingway: The Writer's Art of Self-Defense.* Minneapolis: University of Minnesota Press, 1969.

Benson, ed. *New Critical Approaches to the Short Stories of Ernest Hemingway.* Durham, N.C.: Duke University Press, 1990.

Benson, ed. *The Short Stories of Ernest Hemingway: Critical Essays.* Durham, N.C.: Duke University Press, 1975.

Brasch, James D., and Joseph Sigman. *Hemingway's Library: A Composite Record.* New York: Garland, 1981.

Brenner, Gerry. *Concealments in Hemingway's Work.* Columbus: Ohio State University Press, 1983.

Brenner. The Old Man and the Sea: *Story of a Common Man.* New York: Twayne, 1991.

Burwell, Rose Marie. *Hemingway: The Postwar Years and the Posthumous Novels.* New York: Cambridge University Press, 1996.

Capellán, Angel. *Hemingway and the Hispanic World.* Ann Arbor, Mich.: UMI, 1985.

Cooper, Stephen. *The Politics of Ernest Hemingway.* Ann Arbor, Mich.: UMI, 1987.

DeFalco, Joseph. *The Hero in Hemingway's Short Stories.* Pittsburgh: University of Pittsburgh Press, 1963.

Donaldson, Scott, ed. *The Cambridge Companion to Hemingway.* New York: Cambridge University Press, 1996.

Fellner, Harriet. *Hemingway as Playwright:* The Fifth Column. Ann Arbor, Mich.: UMI, 1986.

Fenton, Charles A. *The Apprenticeship of Ernest Hemingway.* New York: Farrar, Straus & Young, 1954.

Flora, Joseph M. *Hemingway's Nick Adams.* Baton Rouge: Louisiana State University Press, 1982.

Gaggin, John. *Hemingway and Nineteenth-Century Aestheticism.* Ann Arbor, Mich.: UMI, 1988.

Grebstein, Sheldon Norman. *Hemingway's Craft.* Carbondale: Southern Illinois University Press, 1973.

Grimes, Larry E. *The Religious Design of Hemingway's Early Fiction.* Ann Arbor, Mich.: UMI, 1985.

Gurko, Leo. *Ernest Hemingway and the Pursuit of Heroism.* New York: Crowell, 1968.

Hovey, Richard B. *Hemingway: The Inward Terrain.* Seattle: University of Washington Press, 1968.

Howell, John M., ed. *Hemingway's African Stories: The Stories, Their Sources, The Critics.* New York: Scribners, 1969.

Lee, A. Robert, ed. *Ernest Hemingway: New Critical Essays.* Totowa, N.J.: Barnes & Noble, 1983.

Lewis, Robert W., Jr. *Hemingway on Love.* Austin: University of Texas Press, 1965.

Lewis, ed. *Hemingway in Italy and Other Essays.* New York: Praeger, 1990.

McCaffery, John K. M., ed. *Ernest Hemingway: The Man and His Work.* Cleveland: World, 1950.

Mandel, Miriam B. *Reading Hemingway: The Facts in the Fictions.* Metuchen, N.J.: Scarecrow Press, 1995.

Nagel, James, ed. *Ernest Hemingway: The Oak Park Legacy.* Tuscaloosa: University of Alabama Press, 1996.

Nagel, ed. *Ernest Hemingway: The Writer in Context.* Madison: University of Wisconsin Press, 1984.

Nahal, Chaman. *The Narrative Pattern in Ernest Hemingway's Fiction.* Rutherford, N.J.: Fairleigh Dickinson University Press, 1971.

Oldsey, Bernard. *Hemingway's Hidden Craft: The Writing of* A Farewell to Arms. University Park: Pennsylvania State University Press, 1979.

Oldsey, ed. *Ernest Hemingway: The Papers of a Writer.* New York: Garland, 1981.

Raeburn, John. *Fame Became of Him: Hemingway as Public Writer.* Bloomington: Indiana University Press, 1984.

Reynolds, Michael S. *Hemingway's First War: The Making of* A Farewell to Arms. Princeton, N.J.: Princeton University Press, 1976.

Reynolds. *Hemingway's Reading, 1910–1940: An Inventory*. Princeton, N.J.: Princeton University Press, 1981.

Reynolds. The Sun Also Rises: *A Novel of the Twenties*. Boston: Twayne, 1988.

Reynolds, ed. *Critical Essays on Ernest Hemingway's* In Our Time. Boston: G. K. Hall, 1983.

Rovit, Earl, and Gerry Brenner, *Ernest Hemingway*. Boston: Twayne, 1986.

Ryan, Frank L., ed. *The Immediate Critical Reception of Ernest Hemingway*. Washington, D.C.: University Press of America, 1980.

Sanderson, Rena, ed. *Blowing the Bridge: Essays on Hemingway and* For Whom the Bell Tolls. New York: Greenwood Press, 1992.

Sarason, Bertram D., ed. *Hemingway and The Sun Set*. Washington, D.C.: NCR/Microcard, 1972.

Scafella, Frank, ed. *Hemingway: Essays of Reassessment*. New York: Oxford University Press, 1991.

Smith, Paul. *A Reader's Guide to the Short Stories of Ernest Hemingway*. Boston: G. K. Hall, 1989.

Smith, ed. *New Essays on Hemingway's Short Fiction*. Cambridge & New York: Cambridge University Press, 1998.

Stephens, Robert O. *Hemingway's Nonfiction*. Chapel Hill: University of North Carolina Press, 1968.

Stephens, ed. *Ernest Hemingway: The Critical Reception*. N.p.: Franklin, 1977.

Svoboda, Frederic J. *Hemingway and* The Sun Also Rises: *The Crafting of a Style*. Lawrence: University Press of Kansas, 1983.

Svoboda and Joseph Waldmeir, eds. *Hemingway: Up in Michigan Perspectives*. East Lansing: Michigan State University Press, 1995.

Wagner, Linda Welshimer, ed. *Ernest Hemingway: Five Decades of Criticism*. East Lansing: Michigan State University Press, 1974.

Wagner, ed. *Ernest Hemingway: Six Decades of Criticism*. East Lansing: Michigan State University Press, 1987.

Wagner-Martin, Linda, ed. *Ernest Hemingway: Seven Decades of Criticism*. East Lansing: Michigan State University Press, 1998.

Waldhorn, Arthur. *A Reader's Guide to Ernest Hemingway*. New York: Farrar, Straus & Giroux, 1972.

Watts, Emily Stipes. *Ernest Hemingway and the Arts*. Urbana: University of Illinois Press, 1971.

Weber, Ronald. *Hemingway's Art of Non-Fiction*. New York: St. Martin's Press, 1990.

Whitlow, Roger. *Cassandra's Daughters: The Women in Hemingway*. Westport, Conn.: Greenwood Press, 1984.

Wylder, Delbert E. *Hemingway's Heroes*. Albuquerque: University of New Mexico Press, 1969.

Young, Philip. *Ernest Hemingway: A Reconsideration,* revised edition. University Park: Pennsylvania State University Press, 1966.

SPECIAL JOURNALS

Fitzgerald/Hemingway Annual 1969–1979. Washington: Microcard Editions, 1969–1976; Detroit: Bruccoli Clark/Gale, 1977–1979.

Hemingway Notes (1971–1974, 1979–1981).

Hemingway Review (1981–).

PAPERS

Ernest Hemingway's papers are at the John F. Kennedy Presidential Library in Boston. Other major collections of Hemingway material are at the Princeton University Library; the Harry Ransom Humanities Research Center, University of Texas at Austin; the University of Virginia Library; The Lilly Library, Indiana University; and the University of Delaware Library.

Index

Index

Index

Index

Index

Index

as character in *For Whom The Bell Tolls*, 231–232

Index

Index